W9-BBX-601

Revised Edition

Microprocessors
Theory and Applications
(Intel and Motorola)

M. Rafiquzzaman, Ph.D

Professor
California State Poly University
Pomona, California

Adjunct Professor
University of Southern California
Los Angeles, California

President
Rafi Technologies, Inc.
San Dimas, California

PRENTICE HALL, Englewood Cliffs, New Jersey 07632

Library of Congress Cataloging-in-Publication Data

Rafiquzzaman, Mohamed.
    Microprocessors : theory and applications (Intel and Motorola) /
M. Rafiquzzaman. -- Rev. ed.
        p.   cm.
    Rev. ed. of: Microcomputer theory and applications with the Intel
SDK-85. 2nd ed. c1987.
    Includes bibliographical references and index.
    ISBN 0-13-588146-3
    1. Microprocessors. 2. Intel 8086 (Microprocessor) 3. Motorola
68000 series microprocessors.   I. Rafiquzzaman, Mohamed.
Microcomputer theory and applications with Intel SDK-85. II. Title.
QA76.5.R2785 1992
004.16--dc20   91-34144
                                                        CIP

Acquisition Editor: Holly Hodder
Editor-in-Chief: Susan Willig
Production Editor: WordCrafters Editorial Services, Inc.
Copy Editor: Jean T. Peck
Cover Designer: Mary McCartney
Manufacturing Buyer: Ilene Levy
Prepress Buyer: Ed O'Dougherty
Supplements Editor: Judy Casillo

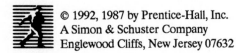 © 1992, 1987 by Prentice-Hall, Inc.
A Simon & Schuster Company
Englewood Cliffs, New Jersey 07632

All rights reserved. No part of this book may be
reproduced, in any form or by any means,
without permission in writing from the publisher.

Printed in the United States of America
10 9 8 7 6 5 4 3 2 1

ISBN 0-13-588146-3

Prentice-Hall International (UK) Limited, *London*
Prentice-Hall of Australia Pty. Limited, *Sydney*
Prentice-Hall Canada Inc., *Toronto*
Prentice-Hall Hispanoamericana, S.A., *Mexico*
Prentice-Hall of India Private Limited, *New Delhi*
Prentice-Hall of Japan, Inc., *Tokyo*
Simon & Schuster Asia Pte. Ltd., *Singapore*
Editora Prentice-Hall do Brasil, Ltda., *Rio de Janeiro*

To my parents,
my son Tito
and my brother Elan

This book is also dedicated to
the computer engineers and scientists
of the People's Republic of Bangladesh.
As Honorary Computer Advisor (State Minister) to the President,
I was able to enhance
computer education and training in Bangladesh.

Contents

Preface ix

1 INTRODUCTION TO
   MICROPROCESSORS AND
   MICROCOMPUTERS 1
1-1 Explanation of Terms, 1
1-2 Evolution of the Microprocessor, 3
1-3 Microcomputer Programming Languages, 3
     1-3-1 Machine Language, 4
     1-3-2 Assembly Language, 4
     1-3-3 High-Level Language, 5
1-4 Typical Practical Applications, 6
     1-4-1 Furnace Temperature Control, 6
     1-4-2 Personal Computers and Workstations, 7
     1-4-3 Real-Time Robotics Control, 8

2 MICROCOMPUTER ARCHITECTURE 9
2-1 Basic Blocks of a Microcomputer, 9
2-2 Typical Microcomputer Architecture, 9
     2-2-1 The Microcomputer Bus, 9
     2-2-2 Clock Signals, 10
2-3 The Single-Chip Microprocessor, 11
     2-3-1 Register Section, 12
     2-3-2 Control Unit, 21
     2-3-3 Arithmetic and Logic Unit (ALU), 22
     *2-3-4 Functional Representations of a Simple
            and a Typical Microprocessor, 22*
2-4 The Memory, 23
     2-4-1 Random-Access Memory (RAM), 26
     2-4-2 Read-Only Memory (ROM), 26
     2-4-3 READ and WRITE Operations, 27
     *2-4-4 Memory Array Design and Memory
            Interfacing, 29*

2-5 Input/Output (I/O), 31
     2-5-1 Some Basic Definitions, 33
     2-5-2 Programmed I/O, 34
     2-5-3 Interrupt I/O, 39
     2-5-4 Direct Memory Access (DMA), 43
     *2-5-5 Summary of Microcomputer I/O
            Methods, 45*
     2-5-6 Coprocessors, 45
Questions and Problems, 47

3 MICROCOMPUTER SOFTWARE
   CONCEPTS 49
3-1 Introduction, 49
3-2 Instruction Formats, 49
3-3 Addressing Modes, 50
3-4 Instruction Types, 54
     3-4-1 Data Transfer Instructions, 54
     3-4-2 Arithmetic Instructions, 54
     3-4-3 Logical Instructions, 54
     3-4-4 Program Control Instructions, 54
     3-4-5 Input/Output Instructions, 57
3-5 Introduction to Assembly Language
     Programming, 57
Questions and Problems, 59

4 INTEL 8085 61
4-1 Introduction, 61
4-2 Register Structure, 61
4-3 Memory Addressing, 62
4-4 8085 Addressing Modes, 63
4-5 8085 Instruction Set, 64
4-6 Timing Methods, 81
4-7 8085 CPU Pins and Associated Signals, 82

v

4-8   8085 Instruction Timing and Execution, 85
4-9   8085 Programmed I/O, 87
4-10   8085 Interrupt System, 94
4-11   8085 DMA, 101
4-12   8085 SID and SOD Lines, 102
4-13   8085-Based System Design, 102
Questions and Problems, 104

5   INTEL 8086   110

5-1   Introduction, 110
5-2   8086 Architecture, 111
5-3   8086 Addressing Modes, 115
5-4   8086 Instruction Set, 117
5-5   8086 Assembler-Dependent Instructions, 132
5-6   Typical 8086 Assembler Pseudoinstructions, 132
5-7   8086 Input/Output, 138
   5-7-1   Programmed I/O, 138
   5-7-2   8089 Input/Output Processor (IOP), 139
   5-7-3   8086 Interrupts, 140
   5-7-4   8086 DMA, 142
5-8   System Design Using 8086, 142
   5-8-1   Pins and Signals, 142
   5-8-2   8086 Basic System Concepts, 147
   5-8-3   Interfacing with Memories, 150
   5-8-4   I/O Ports, 151
   5-8-5   8086-Based Microcomputer, 152
Questions and Problems, 156

6   MOTOROLA MC68000   159

6-1   Introduction, 159
6-2   68000 Registers, 160
6-3   68000 Memory Addressing, 160
6-4   68000 Instruction Format, 161
6-5   68000 Addressing Modes, 162
6-6   68000 Instruction Set, 166
6-7   68000 STACK, 184
6-8   68000 Pins and Signals, 187
6-9   68000 READ and WRITE Cycle Timing
      Diagrams, 193
6-10   68000 Memory Interface, 193
6-11   68000 System Diagram, 196
6-12   Motorola 68000 I/O, 196
   6-12-1   68000 Programmed I/O, 196
   6-12-2   68000 Interrupt System, 201
   6-12-3   68000 DMA, 204
   6-12-4   68000 Exception Handling, 205
6-13   68000/2716/6116/6821-Based
      Microcomputer, 207
6-14   Multiprocessing with 68000 using TAS
      Instruction and AS Signal, 209
Questions and Problems, 209

7   TYPICAL 32-BIT MICROPROCESSORS   213

7-1   Introduction, 213
7-2   Intel 80386, 214
   7-2-1   Basic 80386 Programming Model, 217
   7-2-2   80386 Addressing Modes, 219
   7-2-3   80386 Instruction Set, 220
   7-2-4   80386 Memory, 226
   7-2-5   80386 I/O, 227
7-3   Motorola MC68020, 227
   7-3-1   MC68020 Functional Characteristics, 228
   7-3-2   MC68020 Programmer's Model, 231
   7-3-3   MC68020 Addressing Modes, 232
   7-3-4   MC68020 Instruction Set, 234
   7-3-5   MC68020 Hardware and I/O, 243
Questions and Problems, 246

8   PERIPHERAL INTERFACING   248

8-1   Parallel versus Serial Transmission, 248
8-2   Synchronous and Asynchronous Serial Data
      Transmission, 248
   8-2-1   Synchronous Serial Data
           Transmission, 248
   8-2-2   Asynchronous Serial Data
           Transmission, 249
   8-2-3   Universal Synchronous/Asynchronous
           Receivers/Transmitters (USARTs) and
           Universal Asynchronous Receivers/
           Transmitters (UARTs), 249
8-3   Interfacing of Hexadecimal Keyboard and
      Display Unit to a Microprocessor, 251
   8-3-1   Hexadecimal Keyboard, 251
   8-3-2   Hexadecimal Displays, 251
   8-3-3   Example of Hexadecimal Keyboard/
           Display Interface to the 8085, 252
8-4   Cassette Recorders, 255
   8-4-1   Kansas City Standard, 256
   8-4-2   Interfacing a Cassette Recorder to the
           Intel 8085, 259
8-5   CRT (Cathode Ray Tube) Terminal Interfacing to
      a Microprocessor, 263
   8-5-1   CRT Basics, 263
   8-5-2   The CRT Controller, 266
8-6   Printer Interface to a Microprocessor, 268
   8-6-1   LRC 7040 Printer, 268
   8-6-2   Interfacing the 8085 to the LRC 7040
           Using Direct Microprocessor Control, 269
   8-6-3   Printer Interface Using Printer Controller
           Chips, 269
8-7   Floppy Disk Interface to a Microprocessor, 272
8-8   DMA Controllers, 272
Questions and Problems, 276

9 INTERFACE STANDARDS 278

9-1 Parallel Interface, 278

    9-1-1 IEEE 488 Interface Bus, 278

    9-1-2 S-100 Bus Standard, 283

9-2 Serial Interface, 287

    9-2-1 RS232C, RS422, and RS423 Serial Interfaces, 287

    9-2-2 Current Loops, 292

Questions and Problems, 292

10 TYPICAL APPLICATIONS OF MICROPROCESSORS 293

10-1 SDK-85 as Two-Position Controller, 293

10-2 8085-Based RMS Meter, 295

    10-2-1 Introduction, 296

    10-2-2 Technical Discussion, 296

    10-2-3 Hewlett-Packard 64000 Development System, 296

    10-2-4 8085-Based Microcomputer, 298

    10-2-5 A/D Conversion Hardware, 300

    10-2-6 Software, 300

    10-2-7 Methodology, 303

    10-2-8 Results, 305

    10-2-9 Conclusion, 305

10-3 68000-Based System Design, 308

    10-3-1 Problem Statement, 308

    10-3-2 Solution Hardware, 308

    10-3-3 Software, 310

APPENDIX A DETAILED SDK-85 SCHEMATIC 314

APPENDIX B SDK-85 MONITOR 318

APPENDIX C SDK-85 TELETYPE OPERATION 353

APPENDIX D INTEL 8080/8085 ASSEMBLY LANGUAGE REFERENCE CARD 357

APPENDIX E NUMBER SYSTEMS, CODES, AND DIGITAL LOGIC 363

APPENDIX F SDK-85 — DETAILS 370

APPENDIX G INTEL 8085, 8086, AND SUPPORT CHIPS — DATA SHEETS 401

APPENDIX H MOTOROLA 68000 AND SUPPORT CHIPS — DATA SHEETS 420

APPENDIX I 8086 INSTRUCTION SET — DETAILS 433

GLOSSARY 455

BIBLIOGRAPHY 459

INDEX 461

Preface

The first and second editions of this book were based on the fundamental concepts associated with typical 8-bit and 16-bit microprocessors and microcomputers. These concepts were related to the Intel 8085 and the SDK-85 in detail. Some hardware and software aspects of typical 16-bit microprocessors, such as Intel 8086 and Motorola 68000, were also included.

However, with the growing popularity of various 16-bit microprocessors, it is now necessary to cover these processors at the undergraduate level. Therefore, treatment of typical 16-bit microprocessors, such as the Intel 8086 and the Motorola 68000, is provided in detail in this revised edition. Overviews of typical 32-bit microprocessors such as the Intel 80386/80486 and the Motorola 68020/68030/68040 are also included. Since the fundamental concept of 8-bit microprocessors, along with the Intel 8085/SDK-85, has proved its worth many times over in the intervening years, the SDK-85 has been retained as an appendix.

In this edition, the book is divided into ten chapters. Chapter 1 contains the basics of microprocessors, as in the first edition. Typical programming languages and practical applications, such as personal computers and robotics, are also included. Chapter 2 includes fundamentals of microcomputer architecture.

Chapter 3 covers software concepts of typical microprocessors. Included are addressing modes, typical instructions, and the concept of assemblers. Chapters 4 through 6 include details of architecture, instruction set, I/O, and system design associated with 8085, 8086, and 68000, respectively. Chapter 7 provides an overview of typical 32-bit microprocessors such as the Intel 80386/80486 and the Motorola 68020/68030/68040.

Chapter 8 provides the basics of peripheral interfacing. This chapter is the same as that in the second edition, except that DMA concepts relating to the 68000 are included. The materials covered in the second edition—such as interfacing of keyboard, CRT, printer, and floppy disk to a typical microprocessor—are retained. Chapter 9 contains a summary of interface standards such as IEEE 488, S-100, RS-232, and current loops. This chapter is the same as that in the second edition. Chapter 10 contains practical applications. Two system design examples using the 8085 and the 68000 are included in detail.

As with the second edition, the revised edition may be used as an undergraduate text in microprocessors. Students are expected to have some background in digital logic.

The author is indebted to Dr. W.C. Miller of Canada and to Dr. A.M. Patwari of Bangladesh for their support and inspiration throughout the writing effort. The author is also grateful to Mary MacDonald, Ann MacDonald, and Francisca Norton for typing all of the changes to the revised edition. Finally, the input of reviewers Gary G. Webster of Cincinnati Technical College and Herbert Hall, Jr. of Lakeland Community College is much appreciated.

1

Introduction to Microprocessors and Microcomputers

The basic blocks of a computer are the *Central Processing Unit (CPU)*, the *Input/Output (I/O)*, and the *Memory*. Due to advances in semiconductor technology, it is possible to fabricate the CPU on one or more chips. The result is the *microprocessor*. Both Metal-Oxide Semiconductor (MOS) and bipolar technologies can be used in this fabrication process. The CPU can be placed on a single chip when MOS technology is used. However, a number of chips are required with the bipolar technology. Along with the microprocessor chip, appropriate memory and I/O chips can be used to design a *microcomputer*. The pins on each one of these chips are then connected to the proper lines on the system bus, which consists of address, data, and control lines. Some manufacturers have designed a complete 8-bit microcomputer on a single chip with limited capabilities. Today, both single-chip microprocessors and single-chip microcomputers are being extensively used in a wide range of industrial and home applications.

This chapter first defines some basic terms associated with microprocessors. It then describes briefly the programming languages and evolution of the microprocessors. Finally, some typical practical applications are considered.

1–1 EXPLANATION OF TERMS*

Before we go on, it is necessary to understand some basic terms.

A *bit* is the abbreviation for the term *binary digit*. A binary digit can have only two values, represented by the symbols 0 and 1, whereas a decimal digit can have

*From *Microprocessors and Logic Design* by Krutz. Copyright © 1980 John Wiley & Sons, Inc. Reprinted by permission of John Wiley & Sons, Inc.

10 values, represented by the symbols 0 through 9. The bit values are easily implemented in electronic and magnetic media by two-state devices whose states portray either of the binary digits, 0 or 1. Examples of such two-state devices are a transistor that is conducting or not conducting, a capacitor that is charged or discharged, and a magnetic material that is magnetized north-to-south or south-to-north.

The *bit size* of a microprocessor refers to the number of bits that can be processed simultaneously by the basic arithmetic circuits of the microprocessor. A number of bits taken as a group in this manner is called a *word*. For example, the first commercial microprocessor, the Intel 4004, which was introduced in 1971, is a 4-bit machine and is said to process a 4-bit word or have a 4-bit word-length CPU. Because two particular word lengths are used, they are given specific names. An 8-bit word is referred to as a *byte*, and a 4-bit word is known as a *nibble*. It should be noted that a processor can perform calculations involving more than its bit size but must perform them sequentially, thus taking more time to complete the operation. In general, longer word lengths or bit sizes provide higher system capabilities, while shorter word lengths require fewer circuitry (commonly called *hardware*) and interconnections in the CPU.

An *Arithmetic and Logic Unit (ALU)* is a digital circuit that performs arithmetic and logic operations on two n-bit digital words. The value of n is normally 4, 8, 16, or 32. Typical operations performed by the ALU are addition, subtraction, ANDing, ORing, and comparison of two n-bit digit words.

The size of the ALU defines the size of the microprocessor. For example, the Motorola 68000 is a 16-bit microprocessor since its ALU is 16 bits wide. But, even though its data bus is 8 bits wide, the Motorola 68008

1

is also a 16-bit microprocessor since its ALU is 16 bits wide. The 32-bit microprocessors include multiple ALUs for parallel operations and thus achieve fast speed.

With these basic terms defined, the important distinction between a microprocessor and a microcomputer can be made. A *microprocessor* is the CPU of a microcomputer and normally must be augmented with peripheral support devices in order to function. In general, the CPU contains the ALU, control units and registers. The number of peripheral devices depends on the particular application involved and even varies within one application. As the microprocessor industry matures, more of these functions are being integrated onto large-scale integration (LSI) chips, which have a complexity greater than 100 gates in order to reduce the system package count. In general, a *microcomputer* consists of a microprocessor (CPU), input and output means, and a memory in which to store programs and data. The microcomputer can be implemented either on a single chip or on several chips containing a CPU, program and data memory, and I/O means.

An *address* is a pattern of 0's and 1's that represents a specific location in memory or a particular I/O device. Typical 8-bit microprocessors have 16 address lines, and, recalling that a bit can have a value of either 0 or 1, one sees that these 16 lines can produce 2^{16} unique 16-bit patterns from 0000000000000000 to 1111111111111111, representing 65,536 different address combinations.

Read-Only Memory (ROM) is a storage medium for the groups of bits called *words,* and its contents cannot normally be altered once programmed. A typical ROM is fabricated on an LSI chip and can store, for example, 2048 8-bit words, which can be individually accessed by presenting one of 2048 addresses to it. This ROM is referred to as a 2K-word by 8-bit ROM. 10110111 is an example of an 8-bit word that might be stored in one location in this memory. A ROM is a *nonvolatile* storage device, which means that its contents are retained in the event of a loss of power to the ROM chip. Because of this characteristic, ROMs are used to store instructions (programs) or data tables that must always be available to the microprocessor.

Random-Access Memory (RAM) is also a storage medium for groups of bits or words whose contents can not only be read but also dynamically altered at specific addresses. Furthermore, a RAM normally provides *volatile* storage, which means that its contents are lost in the event of a power failure. RAMs are fabricated on LSI chips and have typical densities from 4096 to 65,536 bits per chip. These bits can be organized in many ways, for example, as 4096-by-1-bit words or as 2048-by-8-bit words. RAMs are normally used as scratchpad memory for the storage of temporary data and intermediate results as well as programs that can be reloaded from a backup nonvolatile source.

A *register* can then be considered as volatile storage for a number of bits. These bits may be entered into the register simultaneously *(in parallel),* or sequentially *(serially)* from right to left or from left to right, 1 bit at a time. An 8-bit register storing the bits 11110000 is represented as follows:

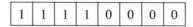

The term *bus* refers to a number of conductors organized to provide a means of communication among different elements in a microcomputer system. The conductors in the bus can be grouped in terms of their functions. A microprocessor normally has an address bus, a data bus, and a control bus. The address bits to memory or to an external device are sent out on the address bus. Instructions from memory and data to and from memory or external devices normally travel on the data bus. Control signals for the other buses and among system elements are transmitted on the control bus. Buses are sometimes bidirectional; that is, information can be transmitted in either direction on the bus but normally only in one direction at a time.

The *instruction set* of a microprocessor is the list of commands that the microprocessor is designed to execute. Typical instructions are ADD, SUBTRACT, and STORE. Individual instructions are coded as unique bit patterns that are recognized and executed by the microprocessor. If a microprocessor has 3 bits allocated to the representation of instructions, then the CPU will recognize a maximum of 2^3 or 8 different instructions. The microprocessor will then have 8 instructions in its instruction set. It is obvious that some instructions will be more suitable to a particular application than others.For example, if a microprocessor is to be used in a calculating mode, instructions such as ADD, SUBTRACT, MULTIPLY, and DIVIDE are desirable. In a control application, instructions inputting digitized signals into the processor and outputting digital control variables to external circuits are essential. The number of instructions necessary in an application will directly influence the amount of hardware in the chip set and the number and organization of the interconnecting bus lines.

A microcomputer requires synchronization among its components, and this is provided by the clock or timing circuits. The signals provided by the clock circuits are either single-phase or multiphase. A *single-phase clock* is a periodic signal and is distributed throughout the microcomputer on a single line. A *multiphase clock* consists of multiple periodic signals synchronized with one another but normally out of phase.

These terms will serve as a background for the remaining introductory discussions. A more detailed description is given in Chapters 2 and 3.

1–2 EVOLUTION OF THE MICROPROCESSOR

Intel Corporation is generally acknowledged as the company that introduced the microprocessor successfully into the marketplace. Its first microprocessor, the 4004, was introduced in 1971 and evolved from a development effort while making a calculator chip set. The 4004 microprocessor was the central component in the chip set, which was called the MCS-4. The other components in the set were a 4001 ROM, a 4002 RAM, and a 4003 shift register.

Shortly after the 4004 appeared in the commercial marketplace, three other general-purpose microprocessors were introduced. These devices were the Rockwell International 4-bit PPS-4, the Intel 8-bit 8008, and the National Semiconductor 16-bit IMP-16. Other companies such as General Electric, RCA, and Viatron had also made contributions to the development of the microprocessor prior to 1971.

The microprocessors introduced between 1971 and 1973 were the first-generation systems. They were designed using the PMOS (P-type MOS) technology. This technology provided low cost, slow speed, and low output currents and was not compatible with TTL (Transistor–Transistor Logic). After 1973, the second-generation microprocessors, such as the Motorola 6800 and 6809, Intel 8085, and Zilog Z80, evolved. These processors were fabricated using the NMOS (N-type MOS) technology. The NMOS process offered faster speed and higher density than PMOS and was TTL-compatible. After 1978, the third-generation microprocessors were introduced. These processors were 16 bits wide and included typical processors such as the Intel 8086/80186/80286 and the Motorola 68000/68010. These microprocessors were designed using the HMOS (High-density MOS) technology.

HMOS provides the following advantages over NMOS:

- Speed-Power-Product (SPP) of HMOS is 4 times better than that of NMOS. That is,

$$NMOS = 4 \quad \text{picojoules} \quad (PJ)$$
$$HMOS = 1 \quad \text{picojoule} \quad (PJ)$$

Note that

$$\begin{aligned}
\text{Speed-Power-Product} &= \text{speed} \quad \times \quad \text{power} \\
&= \text{nanosecond} \quad \times \quad \text{milliwatt} \\
&= \text{picojoules}
\end{aligned}$$

- Circuit densities provided by HMOS are approximately twice those of NMOS. That is,

$$NMOS = 4128 \quad \mu m^2/\text{gate}$$
$$HMOS = 1852.5 \quad \mu m^2/\text{gate}$$

where

$$1 \ \mu m \ (\text{micrometer}) = 10^{-6} \ \text{meter}$$

Recently, Intel utilized the HMOS technology to fabricate the 8085A. Thus, Intel offers a high-speed version of the 8085A called the 8085AH. The price of the 8085AH is higher than that of the 8085A.

In 1980, the fourth-generation microprocessors evolved. Intel introduced the first commercial 32-bit microprocessor, the problematic Intel 432. This processor was eventually discontinued by Intel. Since 1985, more 32-bit microprocessors have been introduced. These include the Motorola MC68020/68030/68040 and the Intel 80386/80486. These processors are fabricated using the low-power version of the HMOS technology called HCMOS, and they include an on-chip RAM called the *cache memory* to speed up program execution. The performance offered by a 32-bit microprocessor is more comparable to that of superminicomputers such as Digital Equipment Corporation's VAX11/750 and VAX11/780. Recently, Intel and Motorola introduced a 32-bit RISC (Reduced Instruction Set Computer) microprocessor (Intel 80960 and Motorola 88100) with a simplified instruction set.

Intel 80960 and Motorola 88100 are RISC microprocessors. The trend in microprocessors is not toward introduction of 64-bit microprocessors. Extensive research is being carried out for implementation of more on-chip functions and for improvement of the speeds of memory and I/O devices.

1–3 MICROCOMPUTER PROGRAMMING LANGUAGES

Programming varies from one microcomputer to another. Eight-bit microcomputers can be programmed using binary or hexadecimal numbers (machine language) and semi-English language statements (assembly language). On the other hand, the 16- and 32-bit microcomputers — in addition to machine and assembly language — use a more understandable human-oriented language called high-level language. Regardless of what type of language is used to write the programs, the microcomputers understand only binary numbers. Therefore, the programs must eventually be translated into their appropriate binary forms. The main methods of accomplishing this translation are discussed later.

Microcomputer programming languages can typically be divided into three main types:

1. Machine language
2. Assembly language
3. High-level language

A machine language program consists of either binary or hexadecimal OP (operation) codes. Programming a microcomputer with either one is relatively difficult since one must deal only with numbers. The architecture and microprograms of a microprocessor determine all its instructions. These instructions are called the microprocessor's *instruction set*. Programs in assembly and high-level languages are represented by instructions that use English-language-type statements. The programmer finds it relatively more convenient to write the programs in assembly or high-level language than in machine language. Since the microcomputers can only understand binary numbers, a translator must be used to convert the assembly or high-level programs into binary machine language so that the microprocessor can execute the programs. This is shown in Figure 1–1.

An assembler translates a program written in assembly language into a machine language program (object code). A compiler or interpreter, on the other hand, converts a high-level language program written in FORTRAN, BASIC, C, C++ and Pascal into a machine language program.

Assembly or high-level language programs are called *source codes*. Machine language programs are known as *object codes*. A translator converts source codes to object codes.

Next, we discuss the three main types of programming languages in more detail.

1–3–1 Machine Language

A microprocessor has a unique set of machine language instructions defined by its manufacturer. No two microprocessors have the same machine language instruction set. For example, the Intel 8085 microprocessor uses the code 10001110_2 for its addition instruction while the Motorola 6800 uses the code 10111001_2. Therefore, a machine language program for one microcomputer will not usually run on another microcomputer. A variation of this is the Zilog Z80 microprocessor, which duplicates the instruction set of the Intel 8080. In addition, the Z80 contains many more instructions.

At the most elementary level, a microprocessor program can be written using its instruction set in binary machine language. For example, a program written for adding two numbers uses the following Intel 8085 machine language:

$$00111110$$
$$00010000$$
$$11000110$$
$$00100000$$
$$00100001$$
$$00000000$$

$$00000010$$
$$01110111$$

Obviously, the program is very difficult to understand unless the programmer remembers all the 8085 codes, which is impractical. Since one finds it very inconvenient to work with 1's and 0's, it is almost impossible to write an error-free program at the first try. Also, it is very tiring for the programmer to enter a machine language program written in binary into the microcomputer's RAM. For example, the programmer needs a number of binary switches to enter the binary program. This is definitely subject to errors.

In order to increase the programmer's efficiency in writing a machine language program, hexadecimal numbers rather than binary numbers are used. The following is the same addition program in hexadecimal, using the Intel 8085 instruction set:

$$3E$$
$$10$$
$$C6$$
$$20$$
$$21$$
$$00$$
$$02$$
$$77$$

It is easier to detect an error in a hexadecimal program since each byte contains only two hexadecimal digits. One would enter a hexadecimal program using a hexadecimal keyboard. A keyboard monitor program in ROM, provided by the manufacturer, controls the hexadecimal keyboard. This program converts each key actuation into binary machine language in order for the microprocessor to understand the program.

1–3–2 Assembly Language

The next programming level is assembly language. Each instruction in an assembly language is composed of three or four fields as follows:

1. Label field
2. Instruction, mnemonic, or OP-code field
3. Operand field
4. Comment field

As an example, a typical program for adding two 8-bit numbers written in 8085 assembly language is given next (a number followed by H is a hexadecimal number):

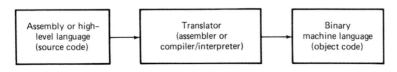

Figure 1–1 Translating assembly or high-level language into binary machine language. (Modified from *Introduction to Microprocessor System Design* by Garland. Copyright © 1979 McGraw-Hill, Inc.)

Label	Mnemonic	Operand		Comment
START	MVI	A, 10H	;	Move 10_{16} into accumulator
	ADI	20H	;	Add 20_{16} to contents of accumulator
	LXI	H, 0200H	;	Load register pair with 0200_{16}
	MOV	M, A	;	Move contents of accumulator into location 0200_{16}
	JMP	START	;	Jump to beginning of program

Obviously, programming in assembly language is more convenient than it is in machine language since each mnemonic gives an idea of the type of operation it is supposed to perform. Therefore, with the assembly language, the programmer does not have to find the numerical OP codes from a table of the instruction set. Thus, programming efficiency with assembly language is significantly improved.

There are two ways of converting an assembly language program into machine language, namely, via manual assembly or by using an assembler. With manual assembly, the programmer is the assembler. In other words, the programmer translates each OP code into its numerical machine language representation by looking up a table of the microprocessor's instruction set, which contains both assembly and machine language instructions. Manual assembly is acceptable for short programs but becomes very inconvenient for large programs. The Intel SDK-85 and most of the university kits are programmed using manual assembly.

The microcomputer can also perform the assembly function via a program called the *assembler*. The assembler program reads each assembly instruction of a program as ASCII (American Standard Code for Information Interchange) characters and translates them into the respective binary OP codes. As an example, consider the HLT instruction for the 8085. Its binary OP code is $0111\ 0110_2$. An assembler would convert HLT into $0111\ 0110_2$, as shown in Table 1–1.

An advantage of the assembler is address computation. Most programs use addresses within the program as data storage or as targets for jumps or calls. When programming in machine language, these addresses must be calculated by hand. Every time the program changes size, all the addresses must be recomputed. This is a time-consuming task. The assembler solves this problem by allowing the programmer to assign a symbol to an address. The programmer may then reference that address elsewhere by using the symbol. The assembler computes the actual address for the programmer and fills it in automatically.

Most assemblers use two passes to assemble a program. This means that they read the input program text twice. The first pass is used to compute the addresses of all labels in the program. In order to determine the address of a label, it is necessary to determine the total length of all the binary code preceding that label. Unfortunately, however, that address may be needed in that preceding code. Therefore, the first pass computes the addresses of all labels and stores them for the next pass, which generates the actual binary code.

Sometimes, the output of an assembler is not pure binary code but is a special binary code that requires further processing before the microprocessor can use it directly. This code, called *object code,* is processed by a program called a *linker*. The linker can combine several programs that were assembled separately into one large program. This is often useful when a large program is being written or when a library of often-used subroutines is stored in object codes.

In addition to the basic functions of instructions and address computation (labels), many assemblers provide additional "luxury" features. Commonly added features are conditionals and macros. Conditionals allow a program to be set up for multiple situations and then to be quickly assembled for the desired situation. Macros allow programmers to define their own instructions, permitting them to create their own specialized or more powerful instructions.

1–3–3 High-Level Language

As mentioned before, the programmer's efficiency with assembly language increases significantly compared to machine language. However, the programmer needs to be well acquainted with the microprocessor's architecture and its instruction set. Further, the programmer has to provide an OP code for each operation that the microprocessor has to carry out in order to execute a program. As an example, for adding two numbers, the programmer would instruct the microprocessor to load the first number into the accumulator, add the second number to the accumulator, and then store the result in memory. However, the programmer might find it tedious to write all the steps

TABLE 1–1
Conversion of HLT into Its Binary OP Code

Assembly Code	Binary Form of ASCII Codes as Seen by Assembler	Binary OP Code Created by Assembler
H	0100 1000	
L	0100 1100	0111 0110
T	0101 0100	

required for a large program. Also, in order to become a reasonably good machine and assembly language programmer, one needs to have a lot of experience.

High-level language programs composed of English-language-type statements rectify all the deficiencies of machine and assembly language programming just mentioned. The programmer does not need to be familiar with the internal microprocessor structure or its instruction set. Also, each statement in a high-level language corresponds to a number of assembly or machine language instructions. For example, consider the statement C = A + B written in the high-level language FORTRAN. This single statement adds the contents of A with B and stores the result in C. This is equivalent to a number of steps in machine or assembly language, as mentioned before. It should be pointed out that the letters A, B, and C here do not refer to particular registers within the microprocessor. They are memory addresses.

A number of high-level languages, such as FORTRAN, COBOL, BASIC, C, C++, and Pascal, are widely used these days. The 16- and 32-bit microprocessors, namely, the Intel 8086 and 80386/80486, Motorola 68000 and 68020/68030/68040, and others, can be programmed using most of these high-level languages. The 8-bit single-chip microprocessors and microcomputers are usually programmed using machine and assembly languages. The availability of the different types of high-level languages with each 16- and 32-bit microprocessor will vary. Pascal, named after the French mathematician, is one of the most popular high-level languages used for these microprocessors. Pascal is a very well-structured language used for both systems and applications programming. This structured format of Pascal makes it easier to develop and maintain programs.

High-level language is a problem-oriented language. The programmer does not have to know the details of the architecture of the microprocessor and its instruction set. Basically, the programmer follows the rules of the particular language being used to solve the problem at hand. A second advantage is that a program written in a particular high-level language can be executed by two different microcomputers, provided they both understand that language. For example, a program written in Pascal for an Intel 8086-based microcomputer will run on a Motorola 68000-based microcomputer because both microprocessors have a compiler to translate the Pascal language into their particular machine languages.

As mentioned before, like the assembly language program, a high-level language program requires a special program for converting the high-level statements into object codes. This program can be either an interpreter or a compiler. They are usually very large programs compared to assemblers.

An interpreter reads each high-level statement such as C = A + B and directs the microprocessor to perform the operations required to execute the statement.

The interpreter executes each statement separately but does not convert the entire program into machine language codes prior to execution. Hence, it does not generate an object program. Therefore, an interpreter is a program that executes a set of machine language instructions in response to each high-level statement in order to carry out the function. A compiler, however, converts each statement into a set of machine language instructions and also produces an object program that is stored in memory. This program must then be executed by the microprocessor to perform the required task in the high-level program. In summary, an interpreter executes each statement as it proceeds, without generating an object code, whereas a compiler converts a high-level program into an object program that is stored in memory. This program is then executed.

High-level language programs are slower and require more memory than assembly or machine language programs. Most microprocessor development systems have a number of high-level language compilers and interpreters for 16- and 32-bit microprocessors.

1–4 TYPICAL PRACTICAL APPLICATIONS

In order to put the microprocessor into perspective, it is important to explore its areas of application. The microprocessor, like any single processor, is a device that normally executes one instruction at a time in a sequential fashion, and typical instruction execution times are 500 nanoseconds (ns) to 2 microseconds (μs). If the time to execute the necessary instructions is greater than the minimum time allowed to handle the data, the microprocessor itself cannot meet the requirements of the application. Consider the example where binary data is being transmitted serially over a communication line to a microcomputer at a 2-MHz rate. This rate means that a new bit value is appearing at the input of the microcomputer every 500 ns. If the execution time for each instruction used to read in data from an input port is also 500 ns, but two such instructions are required to read in the data and store it in memory, the microcomputer will fall behind the incoming data. Thus, the microcomputer alone without some other means of reading the data into its memory at a higher rate would not be suitable for this application.

In the spectrum of applications, the microprocessor is well suited to dedicated controllers, personal computers, point-of-sale terminals, low-to-moderate-speed data communications systems, small dedicated processors (such as those in instruments and automobiles), and programmed logic replacement of random logic systems.

1–4–1 Furnace Temperature Control

In this section, a microprocessor-based dedicated controller will be considered. In Figure 1–2, it is desired to

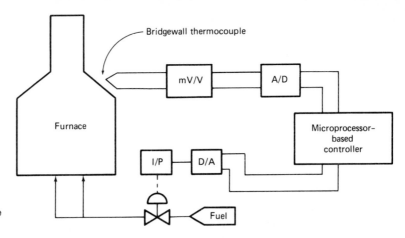

Figure 1-2 Furnace temperature control

control the temperature of the furnace by adjusting the fuel. This can be accomplished using a microprocessor as follows.

Basically, the temperature is sensed by the thermocouple, which is a millivolt signal. It is amplified by a mV/V amplifier to make the signal compatible for Analog-to-Digital (A/D) conversion. A microcomputer can be programmed to solve a Proportional-Integral-Derivative (PID) equation with the furnace bridge-wall temperature as input. The output of this equation is fed into a Digital-to-Analog (D/A) converter. The D/A output is then used to control the current/pneumatic (I/P) transducer for operating the control valve to adjust the fuel to the furnace. The desired temperature of the furnace can thus be achieved. This is called *Direct Digital Control (DDC)*. Using the DDC concept, manufacturers such as Honeywell have developed distributed microprocessor-based process control systems for controlling the analog processes.

1-4-2 Personal Computers and Workstations

A *personal computer (PC)* might be defined very broadly as the low-cost affordable computer used by an individual or a small group. This general definition usually includes low-cost, general-purpose computers. Microprocessors are extensively used these days to design them. Personal computers may be designed for specific market or application areas such as home computers and business personal computers. Typical examples include the IBM PC and the Apple Macintosh.

Typical applications of personal computers in the home include games, daily schedules, information directory, word processing, and recipes. Some business applications include the following:

- Computer-aided design and manufacturing
- Inventory and production control
- Spreadsheet applications
- Accounting

- Project management such as task scheduling and man-hour estimation
- Software development
- Statistical calculations

The interactive and user-friendly features of personal computers at low cost are making them very popular. Several personal computers can be interfaced with a central computer and then can be used as a distributed system. The software in the central computer can be accessed via the PC terminals.

Now let us discuss a specific application such as the use of LOTUS software on the IBM PC to perform circuit design and analysis. Circuit designers find spreadsheets, especially those with graphics, very useful. For example, the LOTUS software in an IBM PC can be used to simulate a typical logic component such as a NOT gate using the spreadsheet's built-in logical operations. By using such ability to simulate logic components with spreadsheet functions and operations in LOTUS, digital circuits can be designed. The power of the LOTUS spreadsheet program can also be used to draw digital circuits, analyze them, and plot the results.

A *workstation* is usually 16- or 32-bit microprocessor-based and can perform engineering-type functions such as 3-D graphics, IC layouts, and stress analysis.

The distinction between PCs and workstations is blurring. For example, Toshiba Corporation's PC can be used as an engineering workstation. Also, powerful RISC-based machines developed by IBM and Sun Microsystems have become available. Note that the basic idea behind RISC is for machines to cost less yet run faster by using a small set of simple instructions for their operations. Some of the features of RISC include few instructions and addressing modes, a fixed instruction format, instructions executed in one machine cycle, only call/return instructions accessing memory, and a control unit based on hardwired control rather than microprogramming. This allows a balance between hardware and software that makes a program run faster and more efficiently. An example of a RISC-based machine is the

IBM RISC computer which was introduced in February of 1990 and includes a family of four workstations.

In personal computers, Compaq's notebook computer, weighing 7.5 pounds, was introduced in October of 1990 and attracted much attention. It was based on a 20-MHz Intel 386SX microprocessor (32-bit microprocessor with 16-bit data bus). The 386SX is used in workstations.

In 1990, two main PC contenders, IBM and Apple, also tried to expand their marketplace by introducing redesigned computers and lower-priced machines. Examples include IBM's PS/1 family, which is aimed at the home computer market, and Apple's new Macintosh Classic, aimed at business, government, education, and the home. Also, in October of 1990, some graphics workstation vendors such as Silicon Graphics, Inc., introduced real-time 3-D graphics boards for PCs with an Intel microprocessor. The two-board set can be used with PCs using Intel 386- and 486-based microcomputers. Silicon Graphics, Inc., also offers advanced features such as real-time graphics manipulation.

The blurred line between PCs and workstations is due to utilization of the UNIX operating system. Note that the operating system is a program usually written by the manufacturer to manage the resources of the computer system. Two types of desktop computers will clearly distinguish the market in the future: (1) those that run with a DOS operating system and (2) those that run with a UNIX operating system. DOS machines will primarily be used as single-user systems for stand-alone applications. These machines, in the long run, will be in people's homes. UNIX is the only multitasking, multiuser, and multivendor operating system available today, which means that UNIX will be the *open* industry standard for years to come.

All future systems including those offered by IBM, Apple, and Sun Microsystems will either base themselves on UNIX or offer a form of it. UNIX is available on all PCs today in one form or another. Within five years, all high-end 386 and 486 PCs will be running UNIX with DOS emulation. This will eliminate dumb-terminal applications. Minicomputers and mainframes will become servers.

The other operating system in contention is OS/2. Although OS/2 offers the multitasking feature, it is still a single-user operating system. It will have some use because of the existing installed base of DOS applications. However, users are looking for open solutions and OS/2 is not open, especially not since IBM recently took back primary control over it.

1-4-3 Real-Time Robotics Control

Microcontrollers can be designed using microprocessors to efficiently perform real-time robotics control functions. The processing power of a microprocessor along with its real-time I/O features necessary for robotics control can be implemented on a single *integrated circuit (IC)* called the *microcontroller*.

Rather than interfacing a robot to a large computer, it is possible to distribute processing power by using several microcontrollers and then interfacing them with a small computer housed in the robot. This small computer can transmit the parameters to microcontrollers at the various points of required control.

Typical parameters necessary for robotics applications include position of a device; the number of events that occur; and various current, voltage, and temperature levels. The main advantage of the microcontroller is that it can take all these input parameters and compute the proper output with only a few external circuits. For applications requiring real-time I/O and using less than 4K bytes of memory, microcontrollers provide inexpensive and efficient solutions.

Typical examples of microcontrollers include Intel's MCS-96 and MCS-51 families. The MCS-96 family uses the Intel 8096 (16-bit single-chip microcomputer), whereas the MCS-51 family is designed using the Intel 8051 (8-bit single-chip microcomputer). Both microcomputers include on-chip RAM, optional ROM, timers, counters, and a serial port to provide a minimum chip-count system.

Distributed processing can be used in robotics control. By breaking down the complex task, hardware benefits that are similar to the software benefits of structured programming are gained. Since the small tasks seldom require large memory and frequently need real-time I/O, microcontrollers can be the most cost-effective component to use in the system.

Distributed processing works very well in robotics applications. With intelligence using microcontrollers at each axis, the master computer in the robot need only tell each axis how far to go, at what velocity to travel, and perhaps a few other parameters. The microcontroller at each axis will then handle details of moving the axis, thus freeing the master computer to coordinate the entire robot.

To provide communication between sections of a distributed processing network, it is desirable to have some form of serial-communication capability. Both the 8051 and 8096 have serial ports that can be used for this purpose.

2

Microcomputer Architecture

This chapter describes the fundamental material needed to understand the basic characteristics of microprocessors. It includes topics such as typical microcomputer architecture, timing signals, internal microprocessor structure, and Input/Output (I/O) techniques.

2–1 BASIC BLOCKS OF A MICROCOMPUTER

A microcomputer has three basic blocks: a Central Processing Unit, a Memory Unit, and an Input/Output Unit. The three elements are described in more detail in the following paragraphs.

Central Processing Unit (CPU)   The CPU executes all the instructions and performs arithmetic and logic operations on data. The CPU of the microcomputer is called the *microprocessor*. The MOS microprocessor is typically a single LSI chip that contains all of the control, arithmetic, and logic circuits of the microcomputer. The bipolar microprocessors (TTL, Schottky TTL, ECL) do not provide the high densities of MOS devices and therefore need more than one chip to implement a microprocessor.

Memory Unit   The Memory Unit stores both data and instructions. The memory section typically contains ROM and RAM chips. The ROM can only be read and is nonvolatile; that is, it retains its contents when the power is turned off. A ROM is used to store instructions and data that do not change. For example, it might store a table of codes for outputting data to a display external to the microcomputer for turning on a digit from 0 to 9.

One can read from and write into a RAM. The RAM is volatile; that is, it does not retain its contents when the power is turned off. A RAM is used to store programs and data that are temporary and might change during the course of executing a program.

Input/Output (I/O) Unit   An I/O unit transfers data between the microcomputer and the external devices. The transfer involves data, status, and control signals.

A single-chip microcomputer (such as the Intel 8048) has all three of the basic elements on one chip, whereas a single-chip microprocessor has separate chips for memory and I/O. Figure 2–1 shows the basic blocks of a microcomputer. These blocks are discussed in more detail in subsequent sections.

2–2 TYPICAL MICROCOMPUTER ARCHITECTURE

In this section, we describe the microcomputer structure in more detail. The various microcomputer architectures available today are basically the same in principle. The main variations are in the number of data and address bits and in the types of control signals they use.

In order to understand the basic principles of microcomputer architecture, it is necessary to investigate a typical microcomputer in detail. Once such a clear understanding is obtained, it will be easier to work with any specific microcomputer. Figure 2–2 illustrates the most simplified version of a typical microcomputer.

The figure shows the basic blocks of a microcomputer system. The various buses that connect these blocks are also shown. Although this figure looks very simple, it includes all the main elements of a typical microcomputer system.

2–2–1 The Microcomputer Bus

The microcomputer contains three buses, which carry all the address, data, and control information involved in

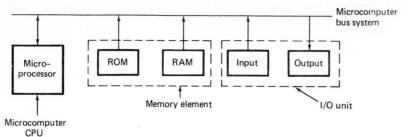

Figure 2-1 Basic blocks of microcomputer

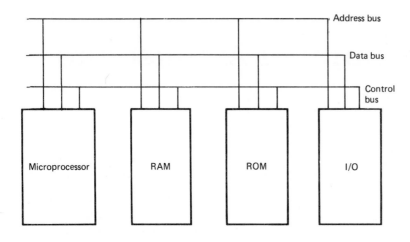

Figure 2-2 Simplified version of a typical microcomputer structure

program execution. These buses connect the microprocessor (CPU) to each of the ROM, RAM, and I/O elements so that information transfer between the microprocessor and any of the other elements can take place.

In the microcomputer, most information transfers are carried out with respect to the memory. When the memory is receiving data from another microcomputer element, it is called a *WRITE operation,* and data is written into a selected memory location. When the memory is sending data to another microcomputer element, it is called a *READ operation,* and data is being read from a selected memory location.

A more detailed description of the three buses involved in all the data transfers is given next.

Address Bus In this bus, information transfer takes place in only one direction, from the microprocessor to the memory or I/O elements. Therefore, this is called a *unidirectional* bus. For 8-bit microprocessors, this bus is typically 16 bits long. The CPU can generate $2^{16} = 65,536$ different possible addresses on this bus. A memory location or an I/O element can be represented by each one of these addresses. For example, an 8-bit data word can be stored in address 2000_{16}.

When the microprocessor wants to transfer information between itself and a certain memory location or I/O device, it generates the 16-bit address from an internal register on its 16 address pins A_0–A_{15}, which then appears on the address bus. These 16 address bits are decoded to determine the desired memory location or I/O device.

The decoding process normally requires hardware (decoders) not shown in Figure 2–2.

Data Bus In this bus, data can flow in both directions, to or from the microprocessor. Therefore, this is a *bidirectional* bus. In some microprocessors, the data pins are used to send other information such as address bits in addition to data. This means that the data pins are time-shared or multiplexed. The Intel 8085 microprocessor, used as the CPU in the Intel SDK-85 microcomputer, is an example where the lower 8 bits of the address are multiplexed on the data bus.

Control Bus This bus consists of a number of signals that are used to synchronize the operation of the individual microcomputer elements. The microprocessor sends some of these control signals to the other elements to indicate the type of operation being performed.

Each microcomputer has a unique set of control signals. However, there are some control signals that are common to most microprocessors. We describe some of these control signals later in this chapter.

2-2-2 Clock Signals

The system clock signals are contained in the control bus. These signals generate the appropriate clock periods during which instruction executions are carried out by the microprocessor. The clock signals vary from one microprocessor to another. Some microprocessors have an internal clock generator circuit to generate a clock signal.

Figure 2–3 Single- and two-phase clock systems

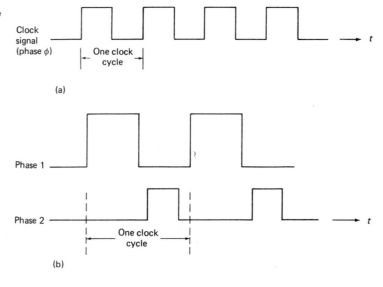

(a)

(b)

These microprocessors require an external crystal or an RC network to be connected at the appropriate microprocessor pins for setting the operating frequency. Other microprocessors do not have the internal clock generator circuit and require an external chip to generate the clock signals. For example, the Intel 8085 and 80186 do not require an external clock generator circuit. A crystal or an RC network connected to the appropriate microprocessor pins sets the operating frequency for the clock signals, which are generated on the microprocessor chip. Other microprocessors, such as the Intel 8086 and the Motorola 68000, require an external circuit to generate the clock signals. These manufacturers normally provide clock generator chips for use with their microprocessors. Many of the popular microprocessors (8085, 8086, 68000) operate from a single clock signal. Earlier microprocessors (8080, 6800, 6502) used a two-phase clock system with nonoverlapping pulses. Typical single-and two-phase clock signals are shown in Figure 2–3. Note that there are microprocessor clocks that are used for operations within the microprocessor and that there are memory clocks used to time the busy/idle states for memory. For example, the 6800 phase-one clock is a microprocessor clock and is not supposed to be used with memory. The 6800 uses a phase-two clock as the memory clock. On the other hand, the 8080 does not have any memory clock. The 8080 uses the read and write enable signals to encode the busy/idle states for memory.

2–3 THE SINGLE-CHIP MICROPROCESSOR

As mentioned before, the microprocessor is the CPU of the microcomputer. Therefore, the power of the microcomputer is determined by the capabilities of the microprocessor. Its clock frequency determines the speed of

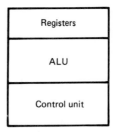

Figure 2–4 A microprocessor chip with the main functional elements

the microcomputer. The number of data and address pins on the microprocessor chip make up the microcomputer's word size and maximum memory size. The microcomputer's I/O and interfacing capabilities are determined by the control pins on the microprocessor chip.

The logic inside the microprocessor chip can be divided into three main areas: the register section, the control unit, and the Arithmetic and Logic Unit (ALU). A microprocessor chip with these three sections is shown in Figure 2–4.

The commercial microprocessor, fabricated using the MOS technology, is normally contained in a single chip. The microprocessor is comprised of a register section, one or more ALUs, and a control unit. Depending on the register section, the microprocessor can be classified as either an accumulator-based or a general-purpose register-based machine.

In an accumulator-based microprocessor, such as the Intel 8085 and the Motorola 6809, one of the operands is assumed to be held in a special register called the *accumulator*. All arithmetic and logic operations are performed using this register as one of the data sources. The result after the operation is stored in the accumulator. One-address instructions are very predominant in this organization. Eight-bit microprocessors are usually accumulator-based.

The general-purpose register-based microprocessor is usually popular with 16- and 32-bit microprocessors such as the Intel 8086/80386 and the Motorola 68000/68020. It is a general-purpose microprocessor since its registers can be used to hold data, memory addresses, or the results of arithmetic or logic operations. The number, size, and types of registers vary from one microprocessor to another. Some registers are general-purpose registers, while others are provided with dedicated functions. The general-purpose registers are used to store addresses or data for an indefinite period of time and then to retrieve data when needed. Two-address instructions are very predominant in this organization.

2–3–1 Register Section

While number, size, and types of registers vary from one microprocessor to another, the various registers in all microprocessors carry out similar operations. The register structures of microprocessors play a major role in designing the microprocessor architectures. Also, the register structures for a specific microprocessor determine how convenient and easy it is to program this microprocessor.

We first describe the most basic types of microprocessor registers, their functions, and how they are used. We then consider the other common types of registers.

Basic Microprocessor Registers There are four basic microprocessor registers: an instruction register, a program counter, a memory address register or data counter, and an accumulator.

Instruction Register (IR) The instruction register stores an instruction. The contents of an instruction register are always decoded by the microprocessor as an instruction. After fetching an instruction code from memory, the microprocessor stores it in the instruction register. The instruction is decoded internally by the microprocessor, which then performs the required operation.

Program Counter (PC) The program counter contains the address of the instruction or operation (OP) code. The program counter usually points to the next location; that is, it normally contains the address of the next instruction to be executed.

The PC is often called the IP (Instruction Pointer). Note the following features of the program counter:

1. Upon activating the microprocessor's RESET input, the address of the first instruction to be executed is loaded into the program counter.
2. In order to execute an instruction, the microprocessor typically places the contents of the program counter on the address bus and reads (fetches) the contents of this address, that is, instruction, from memory.

The program counter contents are automatically incremented by the microprocessor's internal logic. The microprocessor thus executes a program sequentially, unless the program contains an instruction such as a JUMP instruction, which changes the sequence.

3. The size of the program counter is determined by that of the address bus. The program counter is typically 32 bits wide for 32-bit microprocessors.
4. There are many instructions, such as JUMP and conditional JUMP, that change the contents of the program counter from its normal sequential address value. The program counter is loaded with the address specified in these instructions.

Memory Address Register (MAR) or Data Counter (DC) The memory address register or data counter contains the address of data. The microprocessor uses the address, which is stored in the memory address register, as a direct pointer to memory. The contents of the address is the actual data that is being transferred.

Accumulator (A) The 8-bit microprocessors are accumular-based machines and the accumulator is typically an 8-bit register. It is used to store the result after most ALU operations. Most microprocessors have instructions to shift or rotate the accumulator 1 bit to the right or left through the carry flag. The accumulator is typically used for inputting a byte from an external device into the accumulator or outputting a byte to an external device from the accumulator. Some microprocessors, such as the Motorola 6800, have more than one accumulator. In these microprocessors, the accumulator to be used by the instruction is specified in the OP code. The 16- and 32-bit microprocessors are general-purpose register-based machines and most registers (16- or 32-bit) can be used as accumulators.

Use of Basic Microprocessor Registers To provide a clear understanding of how the basic microprocessor registers are used, a binary addition program will be considered. The program logic will be explained by showing how each instruction changes the contents of the four registers.

Suppose that the contents of the memory location 2010_{16}, that is, [2010], are to be added with the contents of 2011_{16}, that is, [2011]. Note that [NNNN] indicates the contents of the memory location $NNNN_{16}$. Now assume that $[2010] = 02_{16}$ and $[2011] = 05_{16}$. The steps involved in accomplishing this addition can be summarized as follows:

1. Load the memory address register with the address of the first data to be added, that is, 2010_{16}.
2. Move the contents of this address to the accumulator.
3. Load the memory address register with the address of the second data to be added, that is, 2011_{16}.

4. Add the contents of this memory location to the data that was moved to the accumulator in step 2.

5. Store the sum in location 2011_{16}, destroying its original contents.

The following instructions for the Intel 8085 will be used to achieve this addition:

21_{16} Load the contents of the next two memory words into the low and high bytes, respectively, of the memory address register.

$7E_{16}$ Read the contents of the memory location addressed by the memory address register into the accumulator.

86_{16} Add the current contents of the accumulator to the contents of the memory location addressed by the memory address register.

77_{16} Store the contents of the accumulator into a memory location addressed by the memory address register.

The complete program in hexadecimal, starting at location 2000_{16}, is given in Figure 2–5. Assume that the microcomputer can be instructed that the starting address of the program is 2000_{16}. This means that the program counter initially contains 2000_{16}, the address of the first instruction to be executed. Note that the contents of the other three registers are not known at this point.

The microprocessor loads the contents of the memory location addressed by the program counter, that is, [2000], into the instruction register. The program counter contents are then incremented to 2001 by the microprocessor's internal logic. The register contents that result along with the program are given in Figure 2–6.

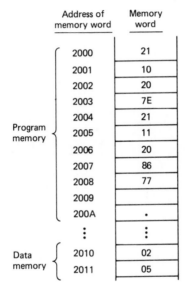

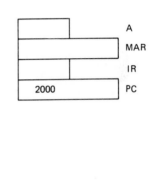

Figure 2–5   Microprocessor addition program

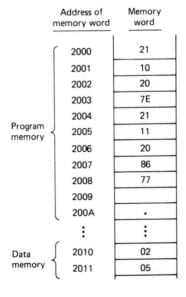

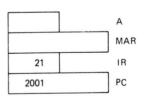

Figure 2–6   Microprocessor addition program

The OP code 21_{16} in the instruction register is executed by the microprocessor. The microprocessor then takes the appropriate action. Note that the instruction 21_{16} is performed in two steps. First, the contents of the memory location addressed by the program counter, that is, [2001], are loaded into the low-ordered byte of the memory address register; the high-order byte of the memory address register is assumed to contain zero. The contents of the program counter are then incremented to 2002. This is shown in Figure 2–7.

Next, the microprocessor loads the contents of the memory location addressed by the program counter into the high-order byte of the memory address register. The program counter contents are then incremented to 2003 by the microprocessor, as shown in Figure 2–8.

The contents of the memory location addressed by the program counter, that is, [2003], are then loaded into the instruction register. The contents of the program counter are incremented to 2004, as shown in Figure 2–9.

In response to the instruction $7E_{16}$ in the instruction register, the microprocessor loads the contents of the memory location addressed by the memory address register into the accumulator, as shown in Figure 2–10. Since 02 is not immediate data, the [program counter] is not incremented.

The next instruction (21) is the same as the first instruction. However, in this case, 2011_{16} instead of 2010_{16} is used. The microprocessor performs this instruction in three steps. First, instruction 21 is loaded into the instruction register and the program counter is incremented, as shown in Figure 2–11.

Next, [2005], that is, 11, is loaded into the low-order byte of the memory address register and the program counter is incremented, as shown in Figure 2–12.

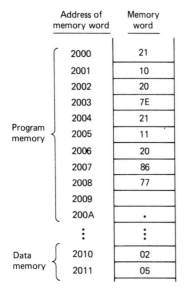

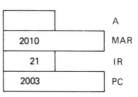

Figure 2–7 Microprocessor addition program

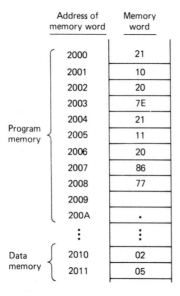

Figure 2–8 Microprocessor addition program

Address of memory word
Memory word
Program memory
2000 21
2001 10
2002 20
2003 7E
2004 21
2005 11
2006 20
2007 86
2008 77
2009
200A
Data memory
2010 02
2011 05
A
2010 MAR
7E IR
2004 PC

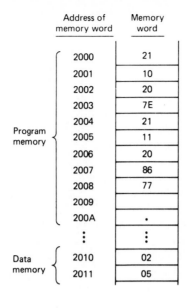

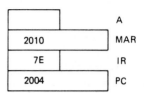

Figure 2–9 Microprocessor addition program

Address of memory word
Memory word
Program memory
2000 21
2001 10
2002 20
2003 7E
2004 21
2005 11
2006 20
2007 86
2008 77
2009
200A
Data memory
2010 02
2011 05
02 A
2010 MAR
7E IR
2004 PC

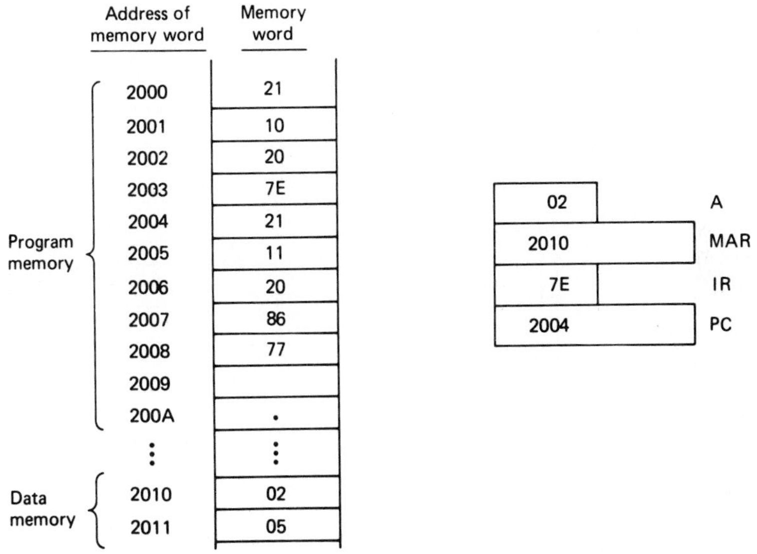

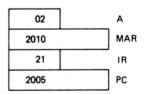

Figure 2–10 Microprocessor addition program

Address of memory word
Memory word
Program memory
2000 21
2001 10
2002 20
2003 7E
2004 21
2005 11
2006 20
2007 86
2008 77
2009
200A
Data memory
2010 02
2011 05
02 A
2010 MAR
21 IR
2005 PC

Figure 2–11 Microprocessor addition program

Finally, [2006], that is, 20, is loaded into the high-order byte of the memory address register. Note that the high-order byte of the memory address register was 20 from before. Hence, the high byte of the memory address register appears to be the same as before. The program counter is then incremented to 2007, as shown in Figure 2–13.

The microprocessor then loads [2007], that is, 86, into the instruction register and increments the program counter, as shown in Figure 2–14.

The microprocessor executes instruction 86. In response to this instruction, the microprocessor adds the contents of the memory location addressed by the memory address register, that is, [2011], to the contents of the accumulator. The result of addition 07 is then stored in the accumulator. Note that the program counter is not incremented since [2011], that is, 05, is not immediate data. This is shown in Figure 2–15.

The microprocessor loads the [2008], that is, 77, into the instruction register and increments the program counter, as shown in Figure 2–16.

The microprocessor executes instruction 77. This instruction causes the contents of the accumulator to be stored in the memory location addressed by the memory address register. Location 2011 contains 07, and its previous contents 05 are lost. The program counter is incremented. This is shown in Figure 2–17.

This completes the execution of the binary addition program.

Other Microprocessor Registers

General-Purpose Registers Although 8-bit microprocessors are accumulator based, they have a number of general-purpose registers for storing temporary data or for carrying out data transfers between various reg-

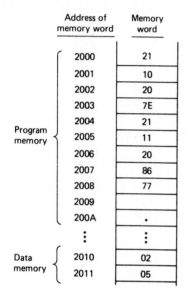

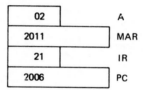

Figure 2–12 Microprocessor addition program

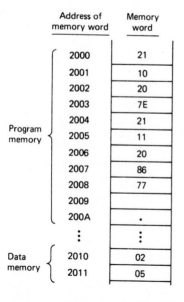

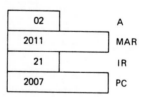

Figure 2–13 Microprocessor addition program

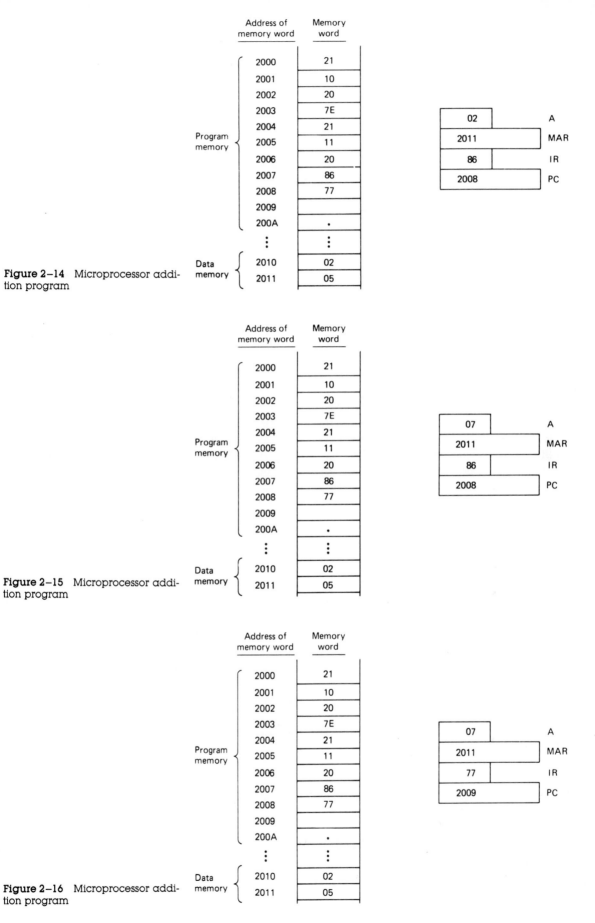

Figure 2–14 Microprocessor addition program

Figure 2–15 Microprocessor addition program

Figure 2–16 Microprocessor addition program

Address of memory word	Memory word
2000	21
2001	10
2002	20
2003	7E
2004	21
2005	11
2006	20
2007	86
2008	77
2009	
200A	•

| 2010 | 02 |
| 2011 | 07 |

Program memory = 2000–200A

Data memory = 2010–2011

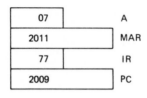

07	A
2011	MAR
77	IR
2009	PC

Figure 2–17 Microprocessor addition program

isters. The use of general-purpose registers speeds up the execution of a program since the microprocessor does not have to read data from external memory via the data bus if data is stored in one of its general-purpose registers. These registers are typically 8 bits long. However, sometimes two of these registers can be combined to form a 16-bit register, which can be used to hold an address during implied addressing. Note that implied addressing is a specific addressing mode used by some microprocessors. The address required by this mode is provided by a 16-bit register. The instructions using this mode are 1 byte long. The number of general-purpose registers will vary from one microprocessor to another. Some of the typical functions performed by instructions associated with the general-purpose registers are given next. We will use [REG] to indicate the contents of the general-purpose register and [M] to indicate the contents of a memory location.

1. Move [REG] to or from memory: [M] ← [REG] or [REG] ← [M].
2. Move the contents of one register to another: [REG1] ← [REG2].
3. Increment or decrement [REG] by 1: [REG] ← [REG] + 1 or [REG] ← [REG] − 1.
4. Load 16-bit data into a register pair (RP): [RP] ← 16-bit data.

As mentioned, 16- and 32-bit microprocessors are usually general-purpose-register based. Typical instructions for these processors include MOVE REG 1, REG 2 and ADD REG1, REG2. These processors have no accumulator; any general-purpose register can normally be used as the accumulator.

Index Register An index register is typically used as a counter, in address modification for an instruction, or

for general storage functions. The index register is particularly useful with instructions where tables or arrays of data are accessed. In this operation, the index register is used to modify the address portion of the instruction. Thus, the appropriate data in a table can be accessed. This is called *indexed addressing*. This addressing mode is available to the programmers of certain microprocessors. The effective address for an instruction using the indexed addressing mode is determined by adding the address portion of the instruction to the contents of the index register. Index registers are typically 8 to 16 bits long. Some microprocessors, such as the 8085, do not have any index registers. However, the capabilities of index registers can be obtained with the 8085 general-purpose registers by using proper instructions. In the 68000, all eight data registers can be used as index registers.

Barrel Shifter Typical 32-bit microprocessors such as the Intel 80386/80486 and the Motorola 68020/68030/68040 include a special type of shifter called a *barrel shifter* for performing fast shift operations. The barrel shifter is an on-chip component for 32-bit microprocessors and provides fast shift operations. For example, the 80386 barrel shifter can shift a number from 0 through 64 positions in one clock period (the clock rate is 16.67 MHz).

Status Register Also known as a *processor status word* or *condition code register,* the status register contains individual bits with each bit having special significance. The bits in the status register are called *flags.* The status of a specific microprocessor operation is indicated by each flag.

Each flag is set or reset by the microprocessor's internal logic to indicate the status of certain microprocessor operations such as arithmetic and logic operations.

The status flags are also used in conditional JUMP instructions. We will describe some of the common flags in the following paragraphs.

The *carry flag* is used to reflect the condition of whether or not the result generated by an arithmetic operation is greater than the microprocessor's word size. As an example, the addition of two 8-bit numbers might produce a carry. This carry is generated out of the eighth position, which results in setting the carry flag. However, the carry flag will be zero if no carry is generated from the addition. In multibyte arithmetic, any carry out of the low-byte addition must be added to the high-byte addition in order to obtain the correct result. This can be illustrated by the following example:

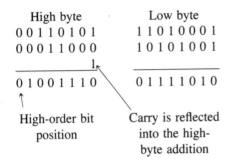

High byte	Low byte
0 0 1 1 0 1 0 1	1 1 0 1 0 0 0 1
0 0 0 1 1 0 0 0	1 0 1 0 1 0 0 1

High-order bit position

Carry is reflected into the high-byte addition

While performing BCD (Binary-Coded Decimal) arithmetic with 8-bit microprocessors, the carry out of the low nibble (4 bits) has a special significance. Since a BCD digit is represented by 4 bits, any carry out of the low 4 bits must be propagated into the high 4 bits for BCD arithmetic. This carry flag is known as the *auxiliary carry flag* (Intel 8085) and is set to 1 if the carry out of the low 4 bits is 1; otherwise, it is 0.

A *zero flag* is used to show whether the result of an operation is zero. It is set to 1 if the result is zero, and it is reset to 0 if the result is nonzero.

A *parity flag* is set to 1 to indicate whether the result of the last operation contains either an even number of 1's (even parity) or an odd number of 1's (odd parity), depending on the microprocessor. The type of parity flag used (even or odd) is determined by the microprocessor's internal structure and is not selectable.

The *sign flag*, also sometimes called the *negative flag*, is used to indicate whether the result of the last operation is positive or negative. If the most significant bit of the last operation is 1, then this flag is set to 1 to indicate that the result is negative. This flag is reset to 0 if the most significant bit of the result is zero, that is, if the result is positive.

The *overflow flag* arises from the representation of the sign flag by the most significant bit of a word in signed binary operation. The overflow flag is set to 1 if the result of an arithmetic operation is too big for the microprocessor's maximum word size; otherwise, it is reset to 0. In order to clearly understand the overflow flag, consider the following examples of 8-bit addition.

Let C_7 be the carry out of the most significant bit (sign bit) and C_6 be the carry out of the high-order data bit (seventh bit). We will show by means of numerical examples that as long as C_7 and C_6 are the same, the result is always correct. If, however, C_7 and C_6 are different, the result is incorrect and sets the overflow flag to 1.

Now consider the following cases.

- *Case 1:* C_7 and C_6 are the same.

$$
\begin{array}{llr}
 & 0\,0\,0\,0\,0\,1\,1\,0 & 06_{16} \\
 & 0\,0\,0\,1\,0\,1\,0\,0 & +14_{16} \\
\hline
C_7 = 0 \quad 0 & 0\,0\,0\,1\,1\,0\,1\,0 & 1A_{16} \\
 & \quad\quad C_6 = 0 &
\end{array}
$$

$$
\begin{array}{llr}
 & 0\,1\,1\,0\,1\,0\,0\,0 & 68_{16} \\
 & 1\,1\,1\,1\,1\,0\,1\,0 & -06_{16} \\
\hline
C_7 = 1 \quad 1 & 0\,1\,1\,0\,0\,0\,1\,0 & 62_{16} \\
 & \quad\quad C_6 = 1 &
\end{array}
$$

Therefore, when C_6 and C_7 are either both 0 or both 1, a correct answer is obtained.

- *Case 2:* C_6 and C_7 are different.

$$
\begin{array}{llr}
 & 0\,1\,0\,1\,1\,0\,0\,1 & 59_{16} \\
 & 0\,1\,0\,0\,0\,1\,0\,1 & +45_{16} \\
\hline
C_7 = 0 \quad 0 & 1\,0\,0\,1\,1\,1\,1\,0 & -62_{16} \\
 & \quad\quad C_6 = 1 &
\end{array}
$$

$C_6 = 1$ and $C_7 = 0$ give an incorrect answer because the result shows that the addition of two positive numbers is negative.

$$
\begin{array}{llr}
 & 1\,0\,1\,1\,0\,1\,1\,0 & -4A_{16} \\
 & 1\,0\,0\,0\,0\,0\,0\,1 & -7F_{16} \\
\hline
C_7 = 1 \quad 1 & 0\,0\,1\,1\,0\,1\,1\,1 & +37_{16} \\
 & \quad\quad C_6 = 0 &
\end{array}
$$

$C_6 = 0$ and $C_7 = 1$ provide an incorrect answer because the result indicates that the addition of two negative numbers is positive.

Hence, the overflow flag will be set to 0 if the carries C_6 and C_7 are the same, that is, if both C_7 and C_6 are either 0 or 1. On the other hand, the overflow flag will be set to 1 if the carries C_6 and C_7 are different. The answer is incorrect when the overflow flag is set to 1.

Therefore, the overflow flag is the EXCLUSIVE-OR of the carries C_6 and C_7:

$$\text{Overflow} = C_6 \oplus C_7$$

Stack Pointer Register (SP) A stack is a *Last-In-First-Out (LIFO)* memory in the sense that items that go in last will come out first. This occurs because the stack allows all read and write to be carried out through one end. The stack can be implemented in hardware or software. A hardware stack is often designed by using a set of high-speed registers in order to provide a fast response. The disadvantage of this approach is that the size of the stack is limited. A software stack can be implemented by using a number of RAM locations. The software stack provides an unlimited stack size but slow response. It is very popular with microprocessors. The stack is typically used by subroutines. Note that a subroutine is a program that performs operations frequently needed by the main or calling program.

The address of the stack is contained in a register called the *stack pointer*. Two instructions, PUSH and POP or PULL, are usually available with the stack. The PUSH operation is defined as writing to the top or bottom of the stack, whereas the POP or PULL operation means reading from the top or bottom of the stack. Some microprocessors access the stack from the top, while others access via the bottom. When the stack is accessed from the bottom, the stack pointer is incremented after a PUSH and decremented after a POP operation. On the other hand, when the stack is accessed from the top, the stack

pointer is decremented after a PUSH and incremented after a POP. Microprocessors (8-bit) either use the 8-bit accumulator or the 16-bit internal registers for performing the PUSH or POP operation. When the 8-bit accumulator is used, the stack pointer is incremented or decremented by 1, whereas the stack pointer is incremented or decremented by 2 when 16-bit registers are used. In 16- and 32-bit microprocessors, any general-purpose register can normally be used for PUSH or POP operation. This incrementing or decrementing of the stack pointer depends on whether the operation is a PUSH or a POP and also whether the stack is accessed from the top or the bottom.

We now illustrate the stack operations in more detail. We use 16-bit registers in Figures 2–18 and 2–19.

In Figure 2–18, the stack pointer is incremented by 2 to address location 20C7 after the PUSH. Now consider the POP operation of Figure 2–19. Note that, after the POP, the stack pointer is decremented by 2. [20C5] and [20C6] are assumed to be empty conceptually after the POP operation.

Consider the PUSH operation of Figure 2–20. The stack is accessed from the top. Note that the stack pointer is decremented by 2 after a PUSH. Next, consider the POP operation of Figure 2–21. The stack pointer is in-

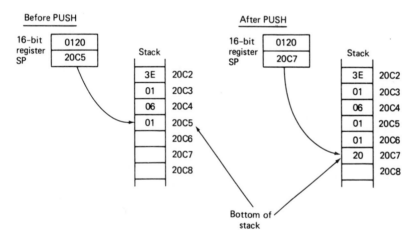

Figure 2–18 PUSH operation when accessing the stack from the bottom

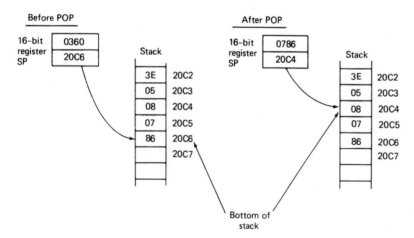

Figure 2–19 POP operation when accessing the stack from the bottom

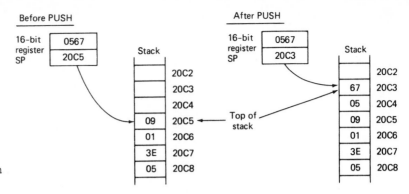

Figure 2–20 PUSH operation when accessing the stack from the top

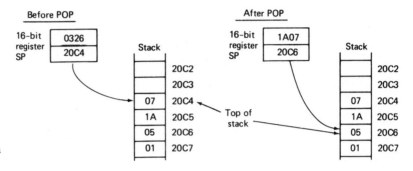

Figure 2–21 POP operation when accessing the stack from the top

cremented after the POP. [20C4] and [20C5] are assumed to be empty after the POP. Typical microprocessors such as the Intel 8085 and 8086/8088 and the Motorola 68000 access the system stack from the top.

2–3–2 Control Unit

The main purpose of this microprocessor section is to read and decode instructions from the program memory. In order to execute an instruction, the control unit steps through the appropriate blocks of the ALU based on the OP codes contained in the instruction register. The OP codes define the operations to be performed by the control unit in order to execute an instruction. The control unit interprets the contents of the instruction register and then responds to the instruction by generating a sequence of enable signals. These signals activate the appropriate ALU logic blocks to perform the required operation.

The control unit of the microprocessor performs instruction interpreting and sequencing. In the interpretation phase, the control unit reads instructions from memory using the program counter as a pointer. It then recognizes the instruction type, gets the necessary operands, and routes them to the appropriate functional units of the execution unit. Necessary signals are issued to the execution unit to perform the desired operations, and the results are routed to the specified destination. In the sequencing phase, the control unit determines the address of the next instruction to be executed and loads it into the program counter.

The control unit is typically designed using one of three techniques:

1. Hardwired control
2. Microprogramming
3. Nanoprogramming

The hardwired control unit is designed by physically connecting typical components such as gates and flip-flops. Zilog's 16-bit microprocessor Z8000 is designed using hardwired control. The microprogrammed control unit includes a control ROM for translating the instructions. The Intel 8086 is a microprogrammed microprocessor. Nanoprogramming includes two ROMs inside the control unit. The first ROM (microROM) stores all the addresses of the second ROM (nanoROM). If the microinstructions (which is the case with the 68000/68020/68030/68040) repeat many times in a microprogram, use of two-level ROMs provides tremendous memory savings. This is the reason that the control units of the 68000, 68020, 68030, and 68040 are nanoprogrammed.

Control Bus Signals The control unit generates the control signals that are outputted to the other microcomputer elements via the control bus. The control unit also takes appropriate actions in response to the control signals on the control bus provided by the other microcomputer elements.

The control signals vary from one microprocessor to another. For each specific microprocessor, these signals are described in detail in the manufacturer's manual. It is impossible to describe all the control signals for various manufacturers. However, we cover some of the common ones in the following paragraphs.

Reset This input is common to all microprocessors. When this input pin is driven HIGH or LOW (depending on the microprocessor), the program counter is reset to 0 in many microprocessors (such as the 8085). This means that the instruction stored at memory location 0000_{16} is executed first. In some other microprocessors, such as the MOS6502, the program counter is not cleared by activating the RESET input. In this case, the program counter is loaded from two locations (such as $FFFE_{16}$ and $FFFF_{16}$) predefined by the manufacturer. This means that these two locations contain the address of the first instruction to be executed. Some microprocessors, such as the Motorola 68020 32-bit microprocessor, initialize stack pointer and program counter after hardware reset. For example, upon activating the RESET input, the 68020 loads the 32-bit SP from location 0000 0000_{16} and the 32-bit PC from location 0000 0004_{16}.

Read/Write (R/$\overline{W}$) This output line is common to all microprocessors. The status of this line tells the other microcomputer elements whether the microprocessor is performing a READ or a WRITE operation. Microprocessors with a single clock signal use two separate control lines (two separate pins on the microprocessor chip), one for READ and one for WRITE. Microprocessors with a two-phase clock system use a single control line (one pin on the microprocessor chip) for both READ and WRITE operations. A HIGH signal on this line indicates a READ operation, and a LOW indicates a WRITE operation.

$\overline{READY}$ This is an input to the microprocessor. Slow devices (memory and I/O) use this signal to gain extra time to transfer data to or receive data from a microprocessor. The $\overline{READY}$ signal is usually a negative logic signal; that is, LOW means it is ready. Negative logic is extensively used in microprocessor control circuitry (because wire-ORing uses negative logic and most decoders output negative logic enable signals). Therefore, when the microprocessor selects a slow device, the device places a LOW on the $\overline{READY}$ pin. The microprocessor responds by suspending all its internal operations and enters a WAIT state. When the device is ready to send or receive data, it removes the $\overline{READY}$ signal. The microprocessor comes out of the WAIT state and performs the appropriate operation.

Interrupt Request (INT or IRQ) The external I/O devices can interrupt the microprocessor via this input pin on the microprocessor chip. When this signal is activated by the external devices, the microprocessor jumps to a special program called the *interrupt service routine*. This program is normally written by the user for performing tasks that the interrupting device wants the microprocessor to do. After executing the RETURN instruction at the end of this program, the microprocessor returns to the main program it was executing when the interrupt occurred.

2-3-3 Arithmetic and Logic Unit (ALU)

The ALU performs all the data manipulations, such as arithmetic and logic operations, inside the microprocessor. The size of the ALU conforms to the word length of the microcomputer. This means that a 16-bit microprocessor will have a 16-bit ALU. Typically, the ALU performs the following three functions:

1. Binary addition and logic operations
2. Finding 1's complement of data
3. Shifting or rotating the contents of the accumulator or some other register 1 bit to the left or right through carry

Some microprocessors have more than one ALU. The 68020 has three ALUs.

2-3-4 Functional Representations of a Simple and a Typical Microprocessor

Figure 2–22 shows the functional block diagram of a simple microprocessor. Note that the data bus shown is internal to the microprocessor chip and should not be confused with the system bus. The system bus is external to the microprocessor and is used to connect all the necessary chips to form a microcomputer. The buffer register in Figure 2–22 stores any data read from memory for further processing by the ALU. All other blocks of Figure 2–22 have been discussed in the previous sections.

Figure 2–23 shows the functional block diagram of a realistic microprocessor, the Intel 8085. The 8085's 8-bit data bus (AD_0–AD_7) is time multiplexed in order to transmit the 8 low-order address bits also. This low byte of the address, when combined with the high byte of the address (A_8–A_{15}), allows the 8085 to address a memory location using 16 bits. This provides the 8085 with a direct addressing capability of up to 64K bytes. The architecture of the 8085 can be divided into three main sections:

1. Register section
2. Arithmetic and logic unit (ALU)
3. Timing and control section (control unit)

The 8085 has a number of 8-bit and 16-bit registers. The 8-bit registers are the A, B, C, D, E, H, and L, processor status word (PSW) register (shown as flag flip-flops), and the instruction register. Register A is the accumulator; B, C, D, E, H, and L are general-purpose registers.

The 8-bit processor status word uses 5 of its bits as status flags in order to reflect the result of arithmetic or logical operations. The other 3 bits in this register are not used. Some of these 8-bit registers can be combined to form 16-bit registers. They are as follows:

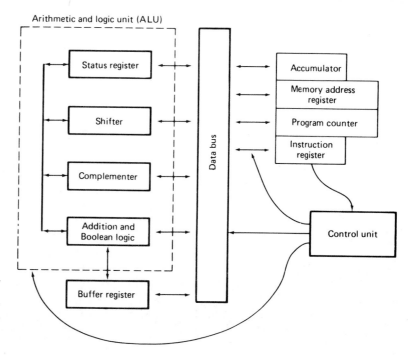

Arithmetic and logic unit (ALU)

Figure 2–22 Functional representation of a simple microprocessor (From *An Introduction to Microcomputers: Vol. 1, Basic Concepts,* 2nd Edition, by Osborne. Copyright © 1982 McGraw-Hill, Inc.)

High Byte	Low Byte
B	C
D	E
H	L
A	PSW

The H and L registers, when paired as a 16-bit register, can be used as a memory address register or data counter.

The 16-bit registers are the stack pointer and program counter. The ALU performs all the arithmetic, logic, and rotate operations for the 8085.

The control and timing section fetches and decodes instructions from memory and generates all the necessary control signals for the registers and ALU in order to execute them.

The 8085 also contains the functions of interrupt control and serial I/O control. These functions and others are described in more detail in the chapters that follow.

2–4 THE MEMORY

The main or external memory (or simply the memory) stores both instructions and data. For 8-bit microprocessors, the memory is divided into a number of 8-bit units called *memory words*. An 8-bit data is termed a *byte*. Therefore, for an 8-bit microprocessor, memory word and memory byte mean the same thing. A memory word is identified in the memory by an address. Eight-bit microprocessors use 16-bit addresses for accessing memory words. This provides a maximum of $2^{16} = 65,536$ memory addresses ranging from 0000_{16} to $FFFF_{16}$ in hexa-

decimal. A number of microprocessors, such as the Motorola 6800 and the MOS6502, divide the 65,536 memory locations or addresses into 256 blocks. Each of these blocks is called a *page* and contains 256 addresses. The Intel 8085 does not divide its memory into pages. As an example of paged memory, consider the memory shown in Figure 2–24.

The high byte of an address specifies the page number. As an example, consider address 0005_{16} of page 0. The high byte 00 of this address defines that this location is in page 0, and the low byte 05 specifies the address of the particular byte in page 0. The 8086, on the other hand, divides its memory into 64K segments with a total addressing capability of one megabyte.

An important characteristic of a memory is whether it is volatile or nonvolatile. The contents of a volatile memory are lost if the power is turned off. On the other hand, a nonvolatile memory retains its contents after the power is switched off. The best known nonvolatile memory is magnetic core.

In a broad sense, a microcomputer's memory system can be logically divided into three groups:

1. Processor memory
2. Primary or main memory
3. Secondary memory

Processor memory refers to a set of microprocessor registers. These registers hold temporary results when a computation is in progress. There is no speed disparity between these registers and the microprocessor because they are fabricated using the same technology. However,

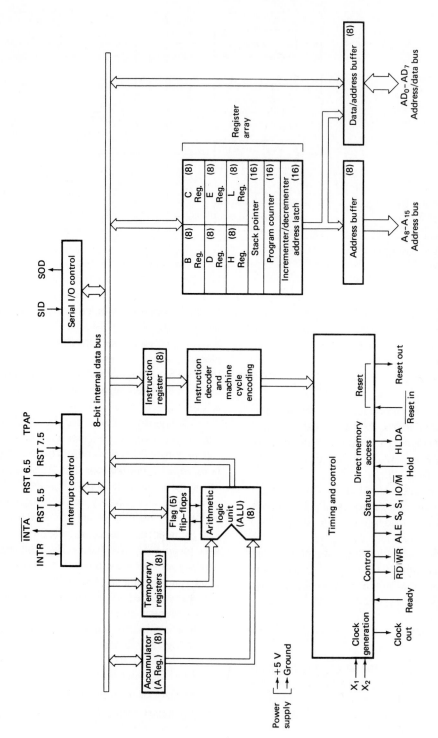

Figure 2–23 8085 microprocessor functional block diagram (Courtesy of Intel Corporation)

the cost involved in this approach forces a microcomputer architect to include only a few registers (usually 8 or 16) in the microprocessor.

Primary memory is the storage area in which all programs are executed. The microprocessor can directly access only those items that are stored in the primary memory. Therefore, all programs and data must be within the primary memory prior to execution. In earlier days, the primary memory was designed using magnetic cores. In modern computers, MOS technology is employed in the primary memory design. Usually, the size of the primary memory is much larger than that of the processor memory, and its operating speed is slower than the processor register's by a factor of 25 or 30.

Secondary memory refers to the storage medium comprising slow devices such as hard disks and floppies. These devices are used to hold large data files and huge programs such as compilers and database management systems that are not needed by the processor frequently. Sometimes, secondary memories are also referred to as *auxiliary* or *backup storage*.

Floppy disks are widely used as secondary memory in microcomputer systems. The floppy disk is a flat, round piece of plastic coated with a magnetically sensitive oxide material. It looks like a 45-RPM record and has a centering hole in its middle and an off-center index hole used by the disk drive for timing the revolution. The disk is provided with a protective jacket to prevent fingerprints or foreign matter from contaminating the disk's surface. Floppy disks are usually available in three dimensions: 8-, 5¼-, and 3½-inch diskettes. For a microprocessor-based system, the 5¼-inch and 3½-inch diskettes are typically used.

If each access is to a disk, then system throughput will be reduced to unacceptable levels. One way of solving this problem is to use a large and fast locally accessed semiconductor memory. Unfortunately, the storage cost per bit for this solution is very high. A combination of both off-board disk (secondary memory) and on-board semiconductor main memory must be designed into a system if the memory requirement for a specific application exceeds the microprocessor's direct addressing capability. This needs a device called the *Memory Management Unit (MMU)* to perform the following two tasks:

1. Manage the two-way flow of information between the primary (semiconductor) and secondary (disk) media.

2. Transfer blocks of data efficiently, keep track of block usage, and replace them in a nonarbitrary way. (The primary memory system must therefore be able to dynamically allocate memory space.)

An operating system software is required to support the MMU hardware to provide resource protection from cor-

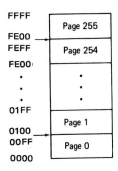

Figure 2-24 A memory divided into pages

ruption or abuse by users. Users must be able to protect areas of code from one another while maintaining their ability to communicate and share other areas of code. Typical 32-bit microprocessors such as the Motorola 68030/68040 and the Intel 80386/80486 include an on-chip MMU hardware.

Studies have shown that typical programs spend most of their execution times in a few main routines or tight loops. In this situation, the addresses generated by a microprocessor have the tendency to cluster around a small region in the main memory. This phenomenon is known as the *locality of reference*. Suppose that we insert a small but a fast memory (faster than the main memory by 5 or 6 times) to keep the most frequently needed information in this memory and that we instruct the microprocessor to access this fast memory (as opposed to the main memory). Then, the efficiency of program execution can be significantly improved. This newly added memory is known as the *cache memory*, a concept that was first implemented in the IBM 360/85 computer. Since this technique has proven to be very successful, it is included in minicomputer systems such as the PDP-11/70. With the rapid growth of IC technology, this idea is also gaining acceptance in the microprocessor world. For example, a small cache memory is implemented in typical 32-bit microprocessors such as the Motorola MC68030/68040 and the Intel 80386/80486.

The principal design goals of a memory system can be summarized as follows:

1. Adequate storage capacity must be provided.

2. Implementation cost must be minimized.

3. Processors must be allowed to operate at their maximum speed.

4. Programmers must be relieved from tedious memory management functions (such as dividing a large program into small segments or overlays so that each overlay can fit in the main memory).

5. All procedures that control information flow should guarantee that the memory space is utilized efficiently.

In order to design an efficient memory system, the computer engineer or scientist should be aware of the salient characteristics of different physical devices that are used to design a microcomputer's storage.

The most important factor of a memory system is its cost, usually expressed in dollars per bit. Suppose that a memory unit has B bits and it costs P dollars; then the cost per bit, C, will be P/B \$/bit. Therefore, a good design implies a very low cost per bit.

There are two parameters that will indicate the speed with which information can be transferred in and out of a memory:

1. Access time, or t_A
2. Cycle time, or t_c

The *access time* t_A is defined as the average time taken to read a unit of information from the memory. Sometimes, the access time t_A is also referred to as *read-access time*. Similarly, one can define write-access time. Usually, write-access time will be equal to read-access time. The *cycle time* t_c of a memory unit is defined as the average time lapse between two successive read operations.

The reciprocal of access time is called the *access rate* r_A, and it is written as

$$r_A = \frac{1}{t_A}$$

Usually, r_A is expressed in bits per second. Similarly, the reciprocal of cycle time t_c is often referred to as the *data transfer rate* or *bandwidth* r_c, and it can be written as

$$r_c = \frac{1}{t_c}$$

Again, r_c is expressed in bits per second. Note that bits per second is also the same as baud rate (1 baud is equivalent to 1 bit per second).

The third important characteristic of a memory unit is its access mode. The *access mode* refers to the manner in which information can be accessed from the memory. There are two major access modes. They are the *random-access* and *sequential-access* modes. In a random-access mode, any location of the memory can be accessed at random. In other words, in this mode, the access time t_A is independent of the location from which the data is read. In a sequential access, the memory is accessed only in a strictly sequential manner. For example, if we want to read the third record stored in a sequential-access memory, we have to skip the first two records. Therefore, in a sequential-access memory, the access time depends on the location in which data is stored. Sometimes, sequential-access memories are also referred to as *serial-access* memories. A bipolar memory and a magnetic tape are typical examples for random- and serial-access memories, respectively.

Random-access memory is much faster and more expensive than its sequential-access counterpart. In order to achieve a compromise, some memories combine both access modes discussed so far. These memories are called *semirandom* or *direct-access* memories. A typical example for a semirandom-access memory is a magnetic disk with one read/write head for each track. This arrangement permits any track to be accessed at random. However, access within a track must be made in a serial fashion.

Memories can be categorized into two main types: Read-Only Memory (ROM) and Random-Access Memory (RAM). As shown in Figure 2–25, ROMs and RAMs are then divided into a number of subcategories, which are discussed in the following paragraphs.

2-4-1 Random-Access Memory (RAM)

There are three types of RAM: dynamic RAM, static RAM, and pseudostatic RAM. Dynamic RAM stores data in capacitors; that is, it can hold data for a few milliseconds. Hence, dynamic RAMs are refreshed typically by using external refresh circuitry. Pseudostatic RAMs are dynamic RAMs with internal refresh. Finally, static RAM stores data in flip-flops. Therefore, this memory does not need to be refreshed. Most RAMs are volatile.

2-4-2 Read-Only Memory (ROM)

ROMs can only be read. This memory is nonvolatile. From the technology point of view, ROMs are divided into two main types: bipolar and MOS. As can be expected, bipolar ROMs are faster than MOS ROMs. Each type is further divided into two common types: mask ROM and programmable ROM (PROM). MOS ROMs contain one more type: erasable ROM (EPROM and EAROM).

Mask ROMs are programmed by a masking operation performed on the chip during the manufacturing process. The contents of mask ROMs are permanent and cannot be changed by the user. On the other hand, the programmable ROM (PROM) can be programmed by the user by means of proper equipment. However, once this type of memory is programmed, its contents cannot be changed. Erasable ROMs (EPROMs and EAROMs) can be programmed, and their contents can also be altered by using special equipment called the *PROM programmer*.

When a microcomputer is designed for a particular application, the permanent programs are stored in ROMs. Control memories are ROMs.

PROMs can be programmed by the user. Usually, the PROM chips are designed using diode matrices. These diodes can be selected by addressing via the pins on the chip. In order to program this memory, the selected

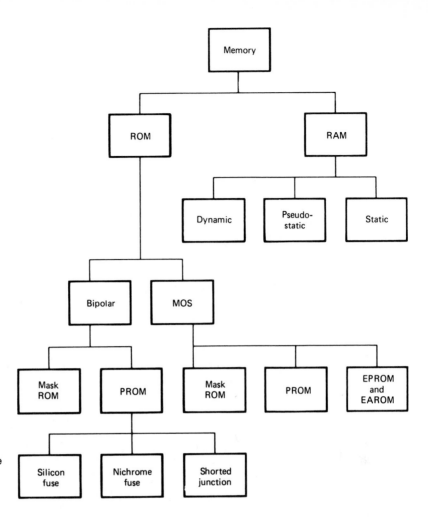

Figure 2–25 Summary of available semiconductor memories for microprocessor systems (Courtesy of Intel Corporation)

diodes are "blown" or "burned" by applying a voltage on the appropriate pins of the chip. This causes the memory to be permanently programmed.

Erasable PROMs (EPROMs) can be reprogrammed and erased. The chip must be removed from the microcomputer system for programming. This memory is erased by exposing the chip via a lid or window on the chip to ultraviolet light. Typical erase times vary between 10 and 30 minutes. The EPROM can be programmed by inserting the chip into a socket of the PROM programmer and providing proper addresses. The programming time typically varies from 1½ to 2 minutes. The EPROM is designed using the Floating Gate Avalanche Injection MOS (FAMOS) storage cells. FAMOS uses a floating gate that is isolated from the substrate. A metal gate is added above this floating gate, which provides an electrical means of erasure.

Electrically alterable ROMs (EAROMs) can be programmed without removing the memory from its sockets. These memories are also called *Read-Mostly Memories* (RMMs) since they have much slower write times than read times. Therefore, these memories are usually suited for operations where mostly reading rather than writing will be performed. The EAROMs are typically fabricated using the Metal-Nitride-Oxide Semiconductor (MNOS) technology or other technologies that use amorphous semiconductors such as tellurium. EAROMs are also commonly known as EEPROMs or E²PROMs.

2–4–3 READ and WRITE Operations

In order to execute an instruction, the microprocessor reads or fetches the OP code via the data bus from a memory location in the ROM/RAM external to the microprocessor. It then places the OP code (instruction) in the instruction register. Finally, the microprocessor executes the instruction. Therefore, the execution of an instruction consists of two portions: instruction fetch and instruction execute. We will consider the instruction fetch and the memory READ and memory WRITE timing diagrams in the following discussion, using a single clock (phase) signal. It is worth mentioning that microprocessors with a two-phase clock signal of the type shown in Figure 2–3 typically use a single pin on the chip for both READ and WRITE signals. A HIGH on this pin usually indicates a READ operation, and a LOW indicates a WRITE operation. On the other hand, microprocessors with a single clock signal use separate pins for READ and WRITE signals. Figure 2–26 shows a typical instruction fetch timing diagram.

In Figure 2–26, in order to fetch an instruction, when the clock signal (phase) goes to HIGH, the microprocessor places the contents of the program counter on the address bus via the address pins A_0–A_{15} on the chip. Note that, since each one of the lines A_0–A_{15} can be either HIGH or LOW, both transitions are shown for the address in Figure 2–26. The instruction fetch is basically a memory READ operation. Therefore, the microprocessor raises the signal on the READ pin to HIGH. As soon as the clock goes to LOW, the logic external to the microprocessor gets the contents of the memory location addressed by A_0–A_{15} and places them on the data bus D_0–D_7. The microprocessor then takes the data and stores it in the instruction register so that is gets interpreted as an instruction. This is called *instruction fetch*. The microprocessor performs this sequence of operations for every instruction.

We now describe the READ and WRITE timing diagrams. A typical READ timing diagram is shown in Figure 2–27. Memory READ is basically loading the contents of a memory location of the main ROM/RAM into the accumulator or some other internal register of the microprocessor. The address of the location is provided by the contents of the MAR. The READ timing diagram of Figure 2–27 can be explained as follows:

1. The microprocessor performs the instruction fetch cycle as before to READ the OP code.
2. The microprocessor interprets the OP code as a memory READ operation.
3. When the clock pin signal goes to HIGH, the microprocessor places the contents of the MAR on the address pins A_0–A_{15} of the chip.
4. At the same time, the microprocessor raises the READ pin signal to HIGH.
5. The logic external to the microprocessor gets the contents of the location in the main ROM/RAM addressed by the MAR and places them on the data bus D_0–D_7.
6. Finally, the microprocessor gets this data from the data bus via its pins D_0–D_7 and stores it in the accumulator or some other register.

Memory WRITE is basically storing the contents of the accumulator or some other register of the microprocessor into a memory location of the main RAM. The contents of the MAR provide the address of the location where data is to be stored. Figure 2–28 shows a typical WRITE timing diagram. It can be explained in the following way:

1. The microprocessor fetches the instruction code as before.
2. The microprocessor interprets the instruction code as a memory WRITE instruction and then proceeds to perform the DATA STORE cycle.
3. When the clock pin signal goes to HIGH, the microprocessor places the contents of the MAR on the address pins A_0–A_{15} of the chip.

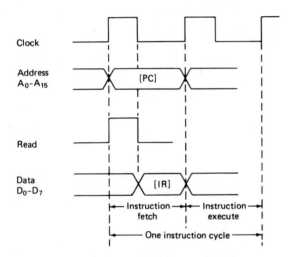

Figure 2–26 Typical instruction fetch timing diagram for an 8-bit microprocessor (From *An Introduction to Microcomputers: Vol. 1, Basic Concepts*, rev. ed., by Osborne. Copyright © 1980 McGraw-Hill, Inc.)

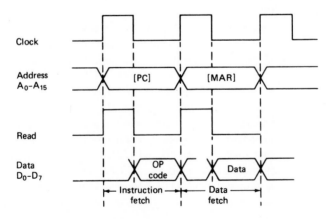

Figure 2–27 Typical memory READ timing diagram (From *An Introduction to Microcomputers: Vol. 1, Basic Concepts*, rev. ed., by Osborne. Copyright © 1980 McGraw-Hill, Inc.)

4. At the same time, the microprocessor raises the WRITE pin signal to HIGH.

5. The microprocessor places data to be stored from the contents of the accumulator or some other register onto the data pins D_0–D_7.

6. The logic external to the microprocessor stores the data from the accumulator or a register into a RAM location addressed by the MAR.

2–4–4 Memory Array Design and Memory Interfacing

From the previous discussions, we notice that the main memory of a microcomputer is realized using solid state technology. In this section, we show how to interface a memory system with a typical 8-bit microprocessor.

Now let us discuss how to design large ROM/RAM arrays. In particular, our discussion is focused on the design of memory arrays for a typical 8-bit microcomputer. The pertinent signals of a typical 8-bit microprocessor that are necessary for main memory interfacing are shown in Figure 2–29.

In Figure 2–29, there are 16 address lines, A_{15}–A_0, with A_0 being the least significant bit. This means that the microprocessor can directly address a maximum of $2^{16} = 65,536$ or 64K memory locations. The control line $IO/\overline{M}$ goes to LOW if a reference to a memory word is made, and it is held HIGH if the processor wants to communicate with an I/O port. Similarly, the control line $R/\overline{W}$ goes to HIGH in order to indicate that the operation

needed is READ, and it goes to LOW for a WRITE operation.

Note that all 16 address lines and the two control lines described so far are unidirectional in nature; that is, in these lines information always travels from the processor to external units. Also, in Figure 2–29, 8 bidirectional data lines, D_7–D_0 (with D_0 being the least significant bit), are shown. These lines are used to allow data transfer from the processor to external units and vice versa.

In a typical application, the total amount of main memory connected to a microprocessor is usually less than 64K and it is normally composed of a combination of both ROMs and RAMs. However, in the following discussion, we will illustrate for simplicity how to design a memory array using only the RAM chips.

The structure of a typical 1K × 8 RAM chip is shown in Figure 2–30. In this RAM chip, there are 10 address lines, A_9–A_0, so that we can access 1024 ($2^{10} = 1024$) different memory words. Also, in this chip, there are 8 bidirectional data lines, D_7–D_0, so that data can travel back and forth between the microprocessor and the memory unit. The three control lines $\overline{CS1}$, CS2, and $R/\overline{W}$ are used to control the RAM unit according to the truth table shown in Figure 2–31.

From the truth table of Figure 2–31, it can be concluded that the RAM unit is enabled only when $\overline{CS1} = 0$ and $CS2 = 1$. Under this condition, $R/\overline{W} = 0$ and $R/\overline{W} = 1$ imply that write and read operations, respectively, take place.

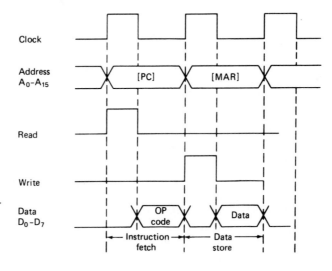

Figure 2–28 Typical memory WRITE timing diagram (From *An Introduction to Microcomputers: Vol. 1, Basic Concepts,* rev. ed., by Osborne. Copyright © 1980 McGraw-Hill, Inc.)

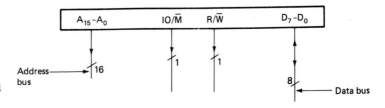

Figure 2–29 Pertinent signals of a typical 8-bit microprocessor required for main memory interfacing

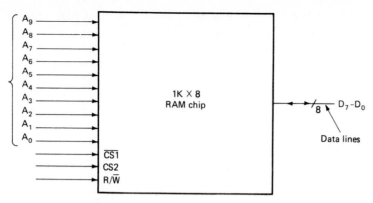

Figure 2-30 A typical 1K × 8 RAM chip

$\overline{CS1}$	CS2	R/$\overline{W}$	Function
0	1	0	Write operation
0	1	1	Read operation
1	X	X	The chip is not selected
X	0	X	The chip is not selected

Figure 2-31 Truth table for controlling RAM

In order to connect a microprocessor to ROM/ RAM chips, two address decoding techniques are usually used: the *linear decoding* and *fully decoding* techniques. Let us first discuss how to interconnect a microprocessor with a 4K RAM chip composed of four 1K RAM chips of Figure 2-30 using the linear decoding technique.

Figure 2-32 shows the linear decoding approach of accomplishing this. In this approach, the address lines A_9–A_0 of the microprocessor are connected to all RAM units. Similarly, the control lines IO/$\overline{M}$ and R/$\overline{W}$ of the microprocessor are connected to the control lines $\overline{CS1}$ and R/$\overline{W}$, respectively, of each RAM unit. The high-order address bits A_{10}–A_{13} directly act as chip selects. In particular, the address lines A_{10} and A_{11} select the RAM chips I and II, respectively. Similarly, the address lines A_{12} and A_{13} select the RAM chips III and IV, respectively. Figure 2-33 describes how the addresses are distributed among the four 1K RAM chips. This method is known as *linear select decoding,* and its primary advantage is that it does not require any decoding hardware. However, if both A_{10} and A_{11} are HIGH at the same time, both RAM chips I and II are selected and this causes a bus conflict. Because of this potential problem, the software must be designed in such a way that it never reads any address in which more than one of the bits A_{13}–A_{10} is HIGH. Another disadvantage of this method is that it wastes a large amount of address space. For example, whenever the address value is 8400 or 0400, the RAM

chip I is selected. In other words, the address 0400 is the mirror reflection of the address 8400; this situation is also called *memory foldback*. This technique is therefore limited to a small system. In particular, we can extend the system of Figure 2-32 up to a total capacity of 6K using A_{14} and A_{15} as chip selects for two more 1K RAM chips.

In order to resolve the problems with linear decoding, we use fully decoded memory addressing. In this technique, we use a decoder. The same 4K memory system designed using this technique is shown in Figure 2-34. Note that the decoder in the figure is very similar to a practical decoder such as the Intel 8205 with three chip enables.

In Figure 2-34, the decoder output selects one of the four 1K RAM chips depending on the values of A_{12}, A_{11}, and A_{10} as described here:

A_{12}	A_{11}	A_{10}	Selected RAM Chip
0	0	0	RAM chip I
0	0	1	RAM chip II
0	1	0	RAM chip III
0	1	1	RAM chip IV

Note that the decoder output will be enabled only when $\overline{E}_3 = \overline{E}_2 = 0$ and $E_1 = 1$. Therefore, in the organization of Figure 2-34, when any one of the high-order bits A_{15}, A_{14}, or A_{13} is 1, the decoder will be disabled and thus none of the RAM chips will be selected. In this arrange-

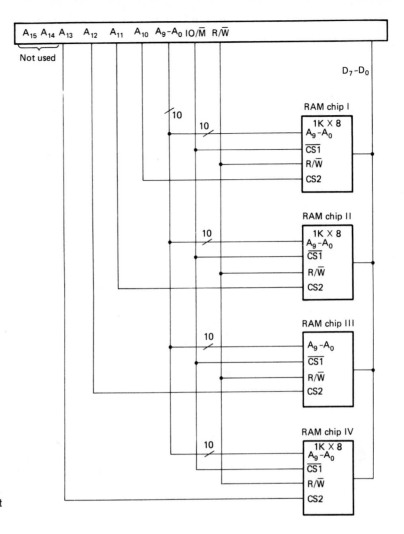

Figure 2–32 Microprocessor connected to 4K RAM using linear select decoding technique

ment, the memory addresses are assigned as shown in Figure 2–35.

From the address map of Figure 2–35, it is easy to see that this approach does not waste address space. In other words, this method does not result in memory foldback. Finally, although the 3-to-8 decoder of Figure 2–34 can select eight 1K RAM chips, its full capability is not used in this example.

2–5 INPUT/OUTPUT (I/O)

The *I/O operation* is defined as the transfer of data between the microcomputer system and the external world. The I/O logic is typically contained in the ROM or RAM chip; that is, the memory chips usually have the capabilities of performing all the I/O operations in addition to memory functions. There are typically three main ways of transferring data between the microcomputer system and the external devices: programmed I/O, interrupt I/O, and direct memory access (DMA).

Address Range in Hexadecimal	RAM Chip Number
0400–07FF	I
0800–0BFF	II
1000–13FF	III
2000–23FF	IV

Figure 2–33 Address map of the memory organization of Figure 2–32

Programmed I/O   Using this technique, the microprocessor executes a program to perform all data transfers between the microcomputer system and the external devices via one or more registers called *I/O ports*. The main characteristic of this type of I/O technique is that the external device carries out the functions as dictated by the program inside the microcomputer memory. In other words, the microprocessor completely controls all the transfers.

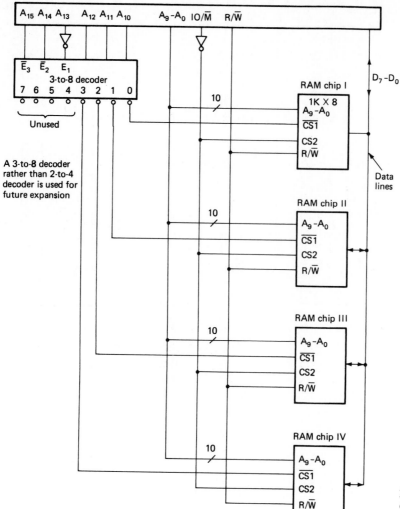

Figure 2–34 Interconnecting a microprocessor with a 4K RAM using fully decoded memory addressing

Address Range in Hexadecimal	RAM Chip Number
0000–03FF	I
0400–07FF	II
0800–0BFF	III
0C00–0FFF	IV

Figure 2–35 Address map of the memory organization of Figure 2–34

Interrupt I/O In this technique, an external device can force the microcomputer system to stop executing the current program temporarily so that it can execute another program known as the *interrupt service routine*. This routine satisfies the needs of the external device. After having completed this program, the microprocessor returns to the program that it was executing before the interrupt.

Direct Memory Access (DMA) In this type of I/O technique, data can be transferred between the microcomputer memory and external devices without any microprocessor involvement. DMA is typically used to transfer blocks of data between microcomputer memory and external devices. An interface chip called the *DMA controller chip* is used with the microprocessor for transferring data via DMA.

For a microcomputer with an operating system, the user works with virtual I/O devices. The user does not have to be familiar with the characteristics of the physical I/O devices. Instead, the user performs data transfers between the microcomputer and the physical I/O devices indirectly by calling the I/O routines provided by the operating system using virtual I/O instructions.

For 16-bit microprocessors (such as Intel 8086), a separate intelligent I/O processor (IOP) or *data channel* is sometimes provided to route all I/O transfers. However, for 8-bit microcomputers, in order to make the system inexpensive, a separate interface rather than a smart I/O processor is provided with each I/O device. Note that the I/O processors control the major I/O functions and relieve the microcomputer of these tasks.

The interfaces communicate with the microprocessor via the I/O bus. The I/O bus carries three types of signals: the device address, data, and command.

A typical I/O instruction has three fields: the OP-code, device-address, and command fields. When the microcomputer executes the I/O instruction, the control unit decodes the OP-code field and identifies it as an I/O instruction. The microprocessor then places the device address and the command from the respective fields of the I/O instruction on the I/O bus. The interfaces connected to the I/O bus decode this address, and the appropriate interface is thus selected. The identified interface then decodes the command lines and determines the function to be performed. Typical functions include inputting data from an input device into the microprocessor and outputting data to an output device from the microprocessor.

Some of the basic terms associated with I/O transfer are considered next. Then, the three I/O transfer techniques are discussed in detail.

2–5–1 Some Basic Definitions

During data transfer, the signals that flow between the microprocessor and an external device can be categorized as two types: control and data. The control signals typically include microprocessor outputs for initiating a data transfer and interrupt signals from external devices. Data is typically in binary, representing alphanumeric, BCD, or some other codes.

Handshaking The transfer of control information between the microprocessor and an external device is called *handshaking*.

Buffers A *buffer* is a circuit used to isolate one or more signal sources from the portion or portions of the microprocessor system using the signal. Buffers may provide current amplification or voltage-level translation and may be unidirectional or bidirectional.

One important use of a buffer is in a microprocessor input port. There, the buffer serves to isolate input data from the microprocessor data bus until input data is requested by the microprocessor.

Since the MOS chips produce small drive currents and can seldom handle more than a single TTL load directly, another important use of a buffer is in a MOS microprocessor output port for driving devices such as LEDs, which require large currents (typically 10 to 20 mA). A typical example of a buffer is a discrete transistor or an inverter.

Note that a commonly used buffer is a tristate buffer, which has three output states: logic 0 and 1 and a high-impedance state. The tristate buffer is typically enabled by a control signal to provide logic 0 or 1 outputs. This type of buffer can also be disabled by the control signal to place it in a high-impedance state and thus electrically disconnect it from any logic circuits to which it is physically connected.

Analog-to-Digital (A/D) Converter An A/D converter transforms an analog voltage into its digital equivalent. Therefore, for a microprocessor to process analog data, these signals must be brought into the microprocessor via an A/D converter. We now describe briefly the main signals on a typical tristate A/D converter chip, as shown in Figure 2–36.

The A/D converter converts an analog voltage V_x of a certain range (typically 0 to 10 V) into an 8-bit binary output at the D_7–D_0 pins. A pulse can be applied at the A/D converter's START pin in order to start the conversion. This will reset the DATA VALID signal of the converter to LOW. This signal stays LOW during the conversion process. As soon as the end of conversion occurs, the DATA VALID signal goes to HIGH. Since the output of the A/D converter is tristated, a LOW on the A/D $\overline{\text{OUTPUT ENABLE}}$ signal will transfer the A/D converter's output. On the other hand, a HIGH at

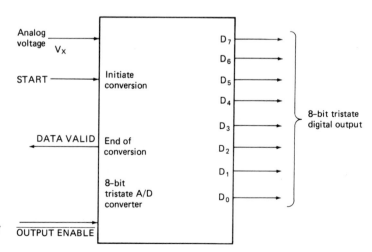

Figure 2–36 Typical 8-bit tristate A/D converter

the A/D ENABLE pin will place the A/D converter's 8-bit output in the high-impedance state.

Sample and Hold   Suppose that it is desired to convert an analog signal into its digital form by means of an A/D converter. If the amplitude of this signal varies quite fast with respect to time, the value of the analog signal might be changed during the conversion process. That is, the value of the analog signal might be different at the end of the conversion than it was at the start of the conversion. However, it is highly desirable that the analog input remains at a constant value during the conversion process. In order to achieve this, a *sample and hold* circuit at the input of the A/D converter is required. This circuit uses an electronic analog switch in order to sample the analog signal, which is then stored on the capacitor. The A/D converter then transforms this stored voltage into digital form. At the end of the conversion, a new sample of the analog signal is taken and stored in the capacitor for conversion. The sample and hold circuit thus keeps the analog signal fixed during the conversion process by storing it on the capacitor.

Acquisition time and aperture time are two typical terms associated with the sample and hold circuits. *Acquisition time* is defined as the time needed for turning on the switch and charging up the capacitor to the analog voltage. *Aperture time* is the time needed for the analog switch to be turned off after a sample is taken. In an ideal case, these two times should be zero in order to avoid any effect due to variation of the analog signal.

An example of a typical sample and hold circuit is shown in Figure 2–37. The CMOS analog switch 4066 has very low resistance when turned on. Hence, when the switch is closed, the RC time constant is very small and the capacitor is quickly charged to the input sample. When the switch is opened, it is in a high-impedance state. Therefore, the capacitor holds its charge for a very long time. The noninverting buffer 13741 presents this capacitor voltage into the input of the A/D converter. The inverter and transistor combination is used to convert the active HIGH logic of +5 V to +15 V logic level. This 15-V level is required to close the analog switch.

When a sample command signal is applied, the output of the 13741 buffer follows the time-varying voltage input. When the sample command is taken away, the output holds the last instantaneous voltage value sampled at the input.

We will use the sample and hold circuit of Figure 2–37 in some of the examples that are discussed later.

2–5–2 Programmed I/O

Using this method of I/O transfer, the microprocessor communicates with an external device via an I/O port buffer, commonly called an *I/O port*. These I/O ports are occasionally fabricated by the manufacturer in the same chip as the memory chip in order to achieve minimum chip count for small system applications. In other words, a single chip will usually have both ROM and I/O or RAM and I/O. For example, the Intel 8155 contains 256 bytes of RAM and three I/O ports, and the 8355/8755 has 2K of ROM/EPROM with two I/O ports.

Typically, there are two registers associated with each I/O port. These are a *data register* and a *data direction register*. The data register will contain the actual data being inputted into or outputted form the microprocessor. The data direction register is an output register, and its purpose is to configure each bit in the data register as input or output. That is to say, one can set up each bit in the data register as either input or output by writing a 1 or 0 in the corresponding bit of the data direction register. For example, consider the following:

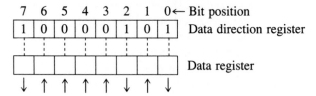

Typically, writing a 1 in a particular bit in the data direction register will configure the corresponding bit in the data register as an output. On the other hand, a 0 in a specific bit position in the data direction register will make the corresponding bit in the data register an input. In other words, if $1000\,0101_2$ or 85_{16} is outputted by the microprocessor into the data direction register, then bits 0, 2, and 7 in the data register are configured as outputs. Bits 1, 3, 4, 5, and 6 in the data register are set up as inputs. Therefore, the microprocessor can send outputs to external devices such as LEDs connected to bits 0, 2,

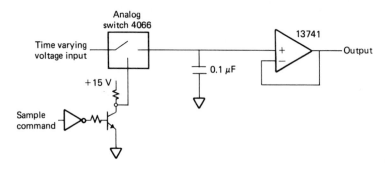

Figure 2–37 A typical sample and hold circuit

and 7 through a proper interface. Since the microprocessor has to send 1 byte in order to output to bits 0, 2, and 7, the outputs to other bits (1, 3, 4, 5, and 6) will not be affected since these are configured as inputs. Similarly, while inputting bits 1, 3, 4, 5, and 6 into the microprocessor, bits 0, 2, and 7, which are set up as outputs, will also be read. However, while receiving input data from an I/O port, the microcomputer places a value, probably 0, at the bits configured as outputs and the program must interpret them as don't cares. On the other hand, the microcomputer's outputs to bits configured as inputs are disabled.

In some I/O chips, there is only one data direction register, known as the *command* or *control register,* for configuring all I/O ports as either inputs or outputs. A particular bit in the control register will set up all 8 bits in an I/O port as either all input or all output. As an example, suppose that there are two I/O ports in an I/O chip and one control register, as shown in Figure 2–38.

Assume that bits 0 and 1 in the control register configure the I/O ports A and B, respectively. Normally, a 0 in one of these bit positions will configure the corresponding I/O port as an input port, whereas a 1 will configure the corresponding I/O port as an output port. For example, in Figure 2–38, a 0 at bit position 0 of the control register will set up all 8 bits of the I/O port A as inputs. A 1 at bit position 1 in the control register will configure all 8 bits of the I/O port B as outputs.

There are some I/O ports, called *handshake ports,* that have dual functions. These ports can be used by the microprocessor in the usual way for inputting data from or outputting data to external devices. These ports may also be used as a control register for transferring data via other ports using handshaking.

Standard I/O versus Memory-Mapped I/O
There are two ways of addressing an I/O port: standard I/O and memory-mapped I/O. The standard I/O typically utilizes a control pin on the microprocessor chip commonly called the $IO/\overline{M}$ control signal. A HIGH on this pin indicates an I/O operation, whereas a LOW indicates a memory operation. Note that execution of IN and OUT instructions sets $IO/\overline{M}$ to HIGH. If $IO/\overline{M}$ is output by the microprocessor in order to distinguish between I/O and memory operation, then the microprocessor is said to utilize standard I/O. On the other hand, if the microprocessor does not utilize the $IO/\overline{M}$, then the microprocessor does not differentiate between I/O and memory. In this case, the microprocessor uses RAM addresses to represent I/O ports, and this is called *memory-mapped I/O.*

Each technique has its advantages and disadvantages. One of the advantages of memory-mapped I/O is that, since the I/O port addresses are configured as memory addresses, one can use all the microprocessor's instructions that reference memory addresses for the I/O ports. This means that one can perform arithmetic and logic operations and many other functions on port data. On the other hand, using standard I/O, in order to perform any arithmetic or logic operations, one must move the port data into the accumulator.

With standard I/O, one typically uses 2-byte instructions, namely, IN and OUT, as follows:

IN
XX   Port number } 2-byte instruction for inputting data from specified port into accumulator

OUT
XX   Port number } 2-byte instruction for outputting data from accumulator into specified I/O port

With memory-mapped I/O, one uses 3-byte instructions, namely, LDA and STA, as follows:

LDA
XX } I/O port address
XX } mapped into memory } 3-byte instruction for inputting a byte into accumulator

STA
XX } I/O port address
XX } mapped into memory } 3-byte instruction for outputting data from accumulator into specified I/O port

Therefore, with memory-mapped I/O, 3-byte instructions, such as LDA and STA, are required for inputting or outputting data. With standard I/O, 2-byte instructions, such as IN and OUT, are used for inputting or outputting a byte; the I/O address space is smaller and hence requires a 1 byte address to specify the I/O address. This is typical in 8-bit microprocessors such as the 8085.

Another disadvantage of memory-mapped I/O is that it reduces the maximum size of the memory. This occurs because the most significant bit (A_{15}) of the address is typically used to distinguish between I/O and memory. If $A_{15} = 1$, an I/O port is selected; if $A_{15} = 0$, a memory location is selected. This means that memory locations $7FFF_{16}$ and below will access memory words, and mem-

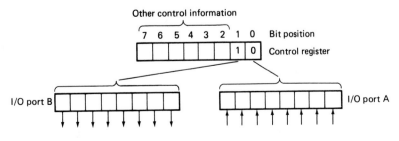

Figure 2–38 Configuring ports A and B by the control register

ory locations 8000_{16} and above will access I/O port buffers; that is, the maximum size of the microcomputer memory is reduced from 64K to 32K bytes. However, 16- and 32-bit microprocessors such as the Motorola 68000 and 68020 provide special control signals for performing memory-mapped I/O. Thus, these processors do not use the most significant bit of the address lines for memory-mapped I/O and, therefore, do not waste memory space.

Unconditional versus Conditional Programmed I/O Programmed I/O is basically a microprocessor-initiated I/O transfer technique. The microprocessor executes a program for performing data transfer between an internal register (usually the accumulator) and an external device. Programmed I/O can be either unconditional or conditional. In unconditional I/O, data transfer occurs at any time; that is, the external device must always be ready for data transfer. A typical example is that the microprocessor outputs a 7-bit code via an I/O port in order to drive a seven-segment LED display connected to this port. With conditional I/O, data transfer between the microprocessor and an external device occurs via handshaking; that is, the microprocessor executes a program in order to verify whether the external device is ready to transfer data. In this technique, the microprocessor inputs the status of the external device (DATA VALID signal for an A/D converter) and checks this status in order to determine whether the device is ready for data transfer. The microprocessor sends data to or receives data from the device when the device is ready. The flowchart in Figure 2–39 demonstrates the concept of conditional I/O.

At ①, the microprocessor inputs the status of the device via an I/O port. At ②, the microprocessor shifts this status bit to the carry in order to determine

whether the external device is ready. If the device is not ready, the microprocessor waits in a wait loop. However, if the device is ready, the program goes to ③ and performs the data transfer. The microprocessor then continues with the rest of the program. This type of programmed I/O requires the exchange of control signals or handshaking between the microprocessor and the external device.

We now describe how the concepts associated with conditional I/O can be used for interfacing an A/D converter to a microprocessor. Figure 2–40 shows such an example. In the following list, all the steps involved in converting the analog voltage to a digital signal in Figure 2–40 are described:

1. The microprocessor sends a pulse to the START pin of the A/D converter via bit 0 of port A.
2. The microprocessor then polls the DATA VALID signal via bit 1 of port A in order to see whether the conversion is complete (that is, whether DATA VALID is HIGH). If this is true, then the microprocessor sends a LOW to the $\overline{\text{OUTPUT ENABLE}}$ pin of the A/D converter. The microprocessor then inputs the A/D converter's output into the microprocessor via port B. If the conversion is not completed (that is, DATA VALID is LOW), then the microprocessor keeps polling the DATA VALID signal.

A flowchart for accomplishing this is shown in Figure 2–41.

A disadvantage of the conditional programmed I/O is that the microprocessor needs to poll the status bit (DATA VALID for the A/D converter just described) by waiting in a loop. For a slow device, this waiting may slow down the microprocessor's ability for processing other data. In such a situation, other I/O techniques that are described later must be used.

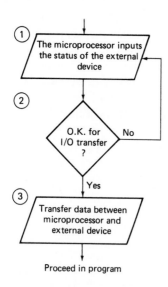

Figure 2-39 Conditional programmed I/O

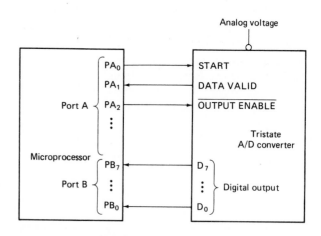

Figure 2-40 Interfacing a microprocessor to an A/D converter

Typical Microprocessor I/O Circuits

Microprocessor Input Circuit Figure 2–42 illustrates a typical microprocessor input circuit used to input a single bit into the microprocessor. Eight such circuits are required for an 8-bit input port. The main feature of the circuit is its MOS input transistor Q_1. A HIGH at the input will turn the MOS transistor Q_1 on, and a LOW will turn it off. These ON and OFF states of Q_1 make it a variable resistor. The voltages across this resistance at the two states are used to define the input logic levels. The MOS transistor Q_2 is used as a MOS resistance.

MOS microprocessor circuits are characterized by their extremely high input impedances. MOS transistors are charge-oriented devices and only draw gate or input current when they are changing their resistances (current is induced by a building of charge). The more often the input logic state is changed, the more power the input circuit will consume. Due to this charge-transfer characteristic, MOS-based microprocessor inputs are treated as capacitive loads.

Because MOS devices have high impedances, the microprocessor input circuits are highly susceptible to static electricity damage. Figure 2–42 shows a Zener diode on the MOS transistor input. If the voltage exceeds the maximum safe voltage, the Zener diode provides a low-impedance path to the ground to absorb the charge.

External devices are connected to a microprocessor input circuit via proper interface. As an example, a simple switch can be connected to the input of a typical microcomputer system via an input port for inputting 1 bit of information, as shown in Figure 2–43. R_1 is used for limiting the switch current, and R_2 is required for protection against static discharge.

Microprocessor Output Circuit MOS microprocessors draw much less power and work with much lower currents than TTL systems (when run at low frequencies), and their drivers use much less current. In principle, however, the MOS driver is very much like the TTL totem-pole driver. Instead of using bipolar transistors (*npn* in most cases), MOS transistors are used. Let us briefly review the TTL totem-pole driver circuit shown in Figure 2–44.

The circuit operates as follows. Suppose that the base of transistor Q_1 is at a logic 1 voltage level. Q_1 is ON, and its collector voltage is LOW, which in effect turns Q_3 OFF. The emitter of Q_1 is HIGH, which turns Q_2 ON, and its collector has a LOW output level. Hence, the current I_{sink} flows from the output circuits through Q_2 to its emitter ground. During circuit design, one should limit the current I_{sink} to avoid burning the Q_2 transistor. Now assume that the base of transistor Q_1 is at a logic 0 voltage

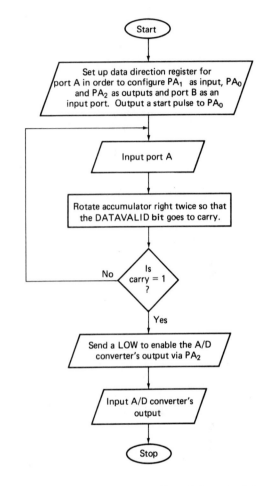

Figure 2–41 Flowchart for inputting A/D output into a microprocessor using programmed I/O

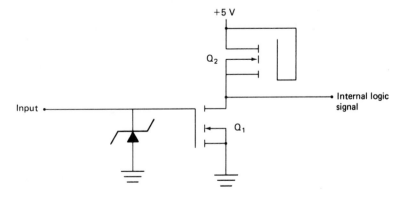

Figure 2–42 Microprocessor input circuit

level. Q_1 is OFF, and no current flows through the emitter of Q_1. This in effect turns Q_2 OFF. However, since Q_1 is OFF, current flows from the 5-V source through R_1 (1.6 kΩ) into the base of Q_3, turning Q_3 ON, and a current I_{source} flows from the 5-V source through R_3, Q_3, and D_1 into the output. This I_{source} can be amplified with output buffers to drive devices that require a large input current. As mentioned before, the MOS microprocessor output is very much like the TTL totem-pole output just described.

A typical NMOS microprocessor output is shown in Figure 2–45. Eight such circuits are required for an 8-bit output port. Early LSI NMOS circuits, such as the Intel 8080 microprocessor, used a V_{CC} of +5 V and a

V_{BB} bias supply of −5 V. They also used a V_{DD} supply of +12 V to improve the speed of internal circuits and to provide outputs that could supply TTL voltage levels and could sink enough current to pull a TTL input to a LOW state. Later NMOS circuits, such as the circuitry of Figure 2–45, used silicon-gate technology and a push–pull output structure to provide a sufficient drive for a single TTL load, while using only a single +5 V supply.

The most important characteristic of MOS drivers is their current drive capability. Most microprocessors use MOS drivers to generate TTL-compatible outputs, but, due to the low-power characteristics of MOS devices, these outputs are usually capable of driving only one standard TTL load. The current drive capability of a MOS driver is generally specified in a different way than that of a TTL driver. The MOS driver acts like a resistor.

Let us now explain the operation of the circuit of Figure 2–45. When Q_1 is ON, Q_2 is OFF, and I_{sink} will flow from the external device into Q_1. Also, when Q_2 is ON, Q_1 is OFF, and I_{source} will flow from Q_2 into the output device.

To illustrate the basic design concepts of how an NMOS microprocessor with an output circuit like that of

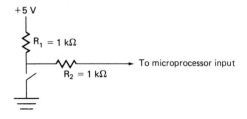

Figure 2–43 A switch input to a typical microcomputer

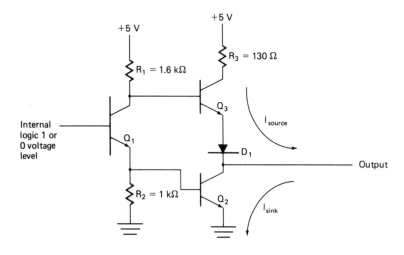

Figure 2–44 TTL totem-pole output

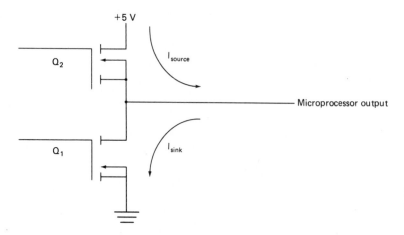

Figure 2–45 NMOS microprocessor's typical output circuit

Figure 2–45 can be used to drive external devices, consider the following example. Suppose that an NMOS microprocessor is required to drive an LED. A typical hardware interface is shown in Figure 2–46.

Assume that the current I_{source} is 400 μA (usually represented by a negative sign, such as $I_{OH} = -400$ μA, which indicates that the chip is losing current), with a minimum voltage V_A of 2.4 V at point A, and that the LED requires 10 mA at 1.7 V. Therefore, a buffer will be required at the microprocessor output to increase its current drive capability to drive the LED. We now design the interface; that is, we determine the values of R_1, R_2, and β for the transistor Q_3.

The operation of the circuit is as follows. Suppose that the microprocessor is programmed to send an output to turn Q_1 ON and Q_2 OFF. Point A, the drain of Q_1 in Figure 2–46, is LOW, which turns Q_3 OFF. I_{sink} is zero, and Q_3 essentially provides isolation in this case. Now, if the microprocessor is programmed to turn Q_2 ON and Q_1 OFF, I_{source} flows from the 5-V source through Q_2 into the base of Q_3, turning Q_3 ON:

$$R_1 = \frac{V_A - V_{BE}(Q_3)}{400 \ \mu A} = \frac{2.4 - 0.7}{400 \ \mu A} = 4.25 \ k\Omega$$

Since $I_{LED} = 10$ mA at 1.7 V and assuming that V_{CE} (saturation) $\simeq 0$ V,

$$R_2 = \frac{5 - 1.7 - V_{CE}(Q_3)}{10 \ mA} =$$

$$\frac{3.3}{10 \ mA} = 330 \ \Omega$$

Also, since $I_{source} = 400 \ \mu A = I_B(Q_3)$, β for transistor Q_3 is

$$\beta = \frac{I_C(Q_3)}{I_B(Q_3)} = \frac{10 \ mA}{400 \ \mu A} = \frac{10 \times 10^{-3}}{400 \times 10^{-6}} = 25$$

Therefore, the interface design is complete, and a transistor with a minimum of saturation, β = 25, $R_1 = 4.25$ kΩ, and $R_2 = 330 \ \Omega$ is required.

2–5–3 Interrupt I/O

Microcomputers can transfer data to or from an external device using the interrupt I/O. In order to accomplish this, the microcomputer uses a pin on the microprocessor chip called the *interrupt pin* (INT). The external I/O device is connected to this pin. When the device wants to communicate with the microcomputer, it makes the signal on the interrupt line HIGH or LOW, depending on the microcomputer. In response, the microcomputer completes the current instruction and pushes at least the contents of the current program counter and maybe some other internal registers onto the stack. It then automatically loads an address into the program counter in order to branch to a subroutine-like program written by the user. This program is called the *interrupt service routine*. It is a program that the external device wants the microprocessor to execute in order to transfer data. The last instruction of the service routine is a RETURN instruction, which is the same instruction typically used at the end of the subroutine. This instruction pops the address (which was pushed onto the stack before going to the service routine) from the stack into the program counter. The microcomputer then continues in the main program that it had been executing.

Interfacing an A/D Converter to a Typical Microcomputer via Interrupt I/O   Let us now illustrate the concept of interrupt I/O by using Figure 2–47. Suppose that in Figure 2–47 the microcomputer is required to read the output of the A/D converter (external device) via port 01, using interrupt I/O.

Assume that the microcomputer is executing the main

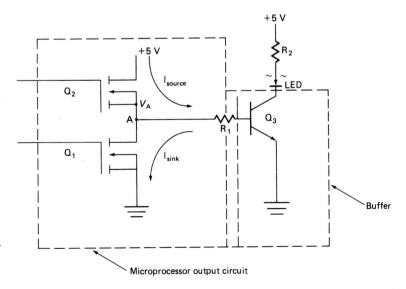

Figure 2–46 A microprocessor interface for driving an LED

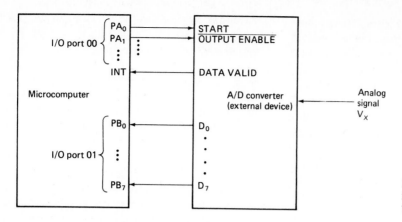

Figure 2–47 A/D converter interfaced to a microcomputer via an interrupt I/O

program (8085 instructions are used) as follows (the program is arbitrarily chosen):

	•	
	•	
	•	
2005	3E	MVI A, 03
2006	03	
2007	D3	OUT 00
2008	00	
2009	3E	MVI A, 02
200A	02	
200B	D3	OUT 00
200C	00	
200D	3A	LDA 2035
200E	35	
200F	20	
2010	E6	ANI 02
2011	02	

Assume that prior to location 2005 ports 00 and 01 are both configured as shown and the stack pointer is initialized. Instructions 2005–200C provide the START pulse and send a HIGH to the $\overline{\text{OUTPUT ENABLE}}$ for the A/D converter in Figure 2–47. Note that the $\overline{\text{OUTPUT ENABLE}}$ must be HIGH to disable any output at this point. The microcomputer then proceeds to execute LDA 2035 at 200D. Suppose that during execution of this instruction, the DATA VALID in Figure 2–47 goes to HIGH, indicating that the conversion is complete. This makes the interrupt signal INT HIGH.

Now assume that the microcomputer responds to a HIGH at the INT pin. Therefore, a HIGH at the DATA VALID will interrupt the processor. The microcomputer completes the current instruction, pushes the current contents of the program counter (2010 in this case) in the stack, and branches to a service routine. The microcomputer manufacturer typically defines the starting address where the user writes the service routine. Assume that it is 3015 in this case. Therefore, the microcomputer branches to 3015, where the user can write a service

routine as follows to input the A/D converter's output lines:

3015	3E	MVI A, 00	Enable A/D converter
3016	00		
3017	D3	OUT 00	
3018	00		
3019	DB	IN 01	Input A/D output
301A	01		
301B	FB	EI	Enable interrupt
301C	C9	RET	Return

In this interrupt service routine, the microcomputer inputs the A/D converter's output into the accumulator. EI at 301B enables the microcomputer's interrupt capability so that it can accept other interrupts. This is because some microprocessors, such as the 8080/8085, automatically disable their interrupt capability once they respond to an interrupt. We will elaborate on this later. Now RET at 301C pops 2010 from the stack and loads the program counter with it. The microcomputer thus continues in the main program.

Main Characteristics of Interrupt I/O   The previous discussion gives a very basic concept of interrupt I/O. We now highlight the main features of interrupt I/O in the following paragraphs.

Interrupt Types   There are typically two types of interrupts. These are external interrupts and internal interrupts.

External interrupts are usually initiated via the microcomputer's interrupt pins by external devices such as A/D converters. A simple example of an external interrupt was given in the previous section. External interrupts can further be divided into two types. These are maskable and nonmaskable. A *maskable* interrupt can be enabled or disabled by executing instructions such as EI or DI. If the microcomputer's interrupt is disabled, the microcomputer ignores a maskable interrupt. Some processors, such as the Intel 8086, have an interrupt flag bit in the processor status register. When the interrupt is disabled, the interrupt flag bit is set to 1 so that no maskable interrupts are recognized by the processor. On the other hand, the interrupt flag bit is reset to 0 when the interrupt is enabled.

The *nonmaskable* interrupt has the higher priority over the maskable interrupt and cannot be enabled or disabled by instructions. This means that if both maskable and nonmaskable interrupts are activated at the same time, then the processor will service the nonmaskable interrupt first. The nonmaskable interrupt is typically used as a power failure interrupt. Note that the processors normally use $+5$ V dc, which is derived from the normal 110 V ac. Now, assume that if the power falls below 90 V ac, the dc voltage of $+5$ V cannot be maintained. However, it takes a few milliseconds before the ac power drops so low (below 90 V ac) that $+5$ V cannot be maintained. In these few milliseconds, the power failure sensing circuitry can interrupt the processor and an interrupt service routine can be executed. This program can be written to store critical data in nonvolatile memory such as a battery backed-up CMOS RAM. Now, on return of power, the interrupted program can continue without any loss of data.

Some processors are also provided with a maskable handshake interrupt. This type of interrupt is usually implemented using two pins, namely, INTR and $\overline{\text{INTA}}$. When the INTR pin is activated by an external device, the microprocessor usually completes the current instruction, saves at least the current program counter onto the stack, and generates an Interrupt Acknowledge ($\overline{\text{INTA}}$) for the external device. In response to $\overline{\text{INTA}}$, the external device provides an instruction such as CALL using external hardware on the data bus of the microcomputer. This instruction is then read and executed by the microcomputer in order to branch to the desired service routine.

Internal interrupts are activated internally by exceptional conditions such as overflow, division by zero, and execution of an illegal OP code. Internal interrupts are handled in the same way as external interrupts. The user usually writes a service routine to take corrective measures and to provide an indication (such as a visual indication) in order to inform the user that an exceptional condition has occurred.

Internal interrupts can also be activated by execution of software interrupt instructions, or TRAPs. When one of these instructions is executed, the processor is interrupted and serviced in the same way as external interrupts. Software interrupt instructions are usually used to call the operating system. These instructions are shorter than subroutine calls, and they do not need the calling program to know the operating system's address in memory. The software interrupt instructions allow the user to switch from the user to the supervisor mode. For some processors, a software interrupt is usually the only way to call the operating system since a subroutine call to an address in the operating system is not allowed.

Interrupt Address Vector   In order to service an interrupt, the technique to find the starting address of the service routine (commonly known as the *interrupt address vector*) varies from one processor to another. With some processors, the manufacturers define the fixed starting address for each interrupt. For some other processors, the manufacturers use an indirect approach. They define fixed locations in which the interrupt address vector is stored.

Saving the Microprocessor Registers   When a processor is interrupted, it saves at least the program counter onto the stack so that the processor can return to the main program after executing the service routine. Some processors save only one or two registers, such as the program counter and status register, onto the stack before going to the service routine. Some other processors save all microprocessor registers before going to the service routine. The user should know the specific registers that the processor saves prior to executing the service routine. This will help the user to use the appropriate return instruction at the end of the service routine in order to restore the original conditions upon return to the main program.

Interrupt Priorities   A processor is usually provided with one or more interrupt pins on the chip. Therefore, a special mechanism is necessary to handle interrupts from several devices that share one of these interrupt lines. There are two main ways of servicing multiple interrupts. These are the polled and daisy chain techniques.

Polled Interrupts   Polled interrupts are handled using mostly software and are, therefore, slower compared to daisy chain interrupts. The processor responds to an interrupt by executing one general service routine for all devices. The priorities of devices are determined by the order in which the routine polls each device. In order to service an interrupt, the processor checks the status of each device in the general service routine starting with the highest priority device. Once the processor determines the source of the interrupt, it branches to the service routine for the device. Figure 2–48 shows a typical configuration of the polled interrupt system.

In Figure 2–48, several external devices (Device 1, Device 2, . . . , Device N) are connected to a single interrupt line (INT) of the processor. When one or more devices activate the INT line HIGH, the processor pushes the program counter and maybe some other registers. It then branches to an address defined by the manufacturer of the processor. The user can write a program at this address in order to poll each device starting with the highest priority device in order to find the source of the interrupt. Suppose that the devices in Figure 2–48 are A/D converters. Each converter, along with the associated logic for polling, is shown in Figure 2–49. Note

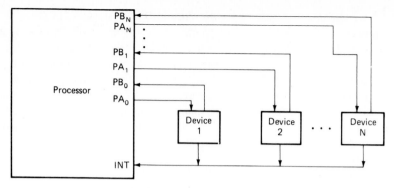

Figure 2–48 Polled interrupt

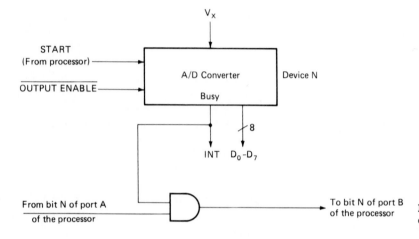

Figure 2–49 Device N and associated logic for polled interrupt

that in Figure 2–48 the device outputs connected to the INT line are ORed together (not shown in the figure) so that one or more active OR gate inputs will interrupt the processor.

Let us assume that in Figure 2–48 two A/D converters (Device 1 and Device 2) are provided with the START pulse by the processor at nearly the same time. Suppose that the user assigns Device 2 with the higher priority. The user sets up this priority mechanism in the general service routine. For example, when the BUSY signals from Device 1 and/or 2 become HIGH, indicating the end of conversion, the processor is interrupted. In response, the processor pushes at least the program counter onto the stack and loads the program counter with the interrupt address vector defined by the manufacturer. The general interrupt service routine written at this address by the user determines the source of the interrupt as follows. It sends a 1 to PA_1 for Device 2 because this device has the higher priority. If this device has generated the interrupt, then the output (PB_1) of the AND gate in Figure 2–49 becomes HIGH, indicating to the processor that Device 2 has generated this interrupt. On the other hand, if the output of the AND gate is 0, the processor sends a HIGH to PA_0 and checks the output (PB_0) for HIGH. Once the source of the interrupt is determined, the processor can be programmed to jump to the service routine for the particular device. The service routine con-

sists of enabling the A/D converter and inputting the converter's outputs into the processor.

Polled interrupts are very simple. But, for a large number of devices, the time required to poll each device may exceed the time to service the device. In such a case, a faster mechanism such as the daisy chain approach can be used.

Daisy Chain Interrupts   In this technique, the devices are connected in a daisy chain fashion, as shown in Figure 2–50, in order to set up the priority systems.

Suppose that one or more devices interrupt the processor. In response, the processor pushes at least the program counter and then generates an Interrupt Acknowledge ($\overline{INTA}$) signal to the highest priority device, which is Device 1 in this case. If this device has generated the interrupt, it will accept the $\overline{INTA}$; otherwise, it will pass the $\overline{INTA}$ onto the next device until the $\overline{INTA}$ is accepted by the interrupting device. Once accepted, the device provides a means to the processor for finding the interrupt address vector using external hardware. Let us assume that the devices in Figure 2–50 are A/D converters. Figure 2–51 provides a schematic for each device and the associated logic. Note that in Figure 2–50 the device outputs connected to the INT line are ORed together (not shown in the figure) and that the output of the OR gate is connected to the INT line.

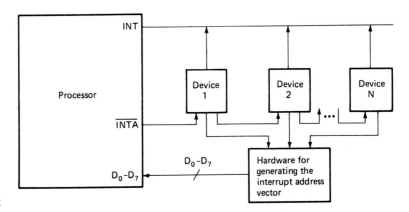

Figure 2–50 Daisy chain interrupt

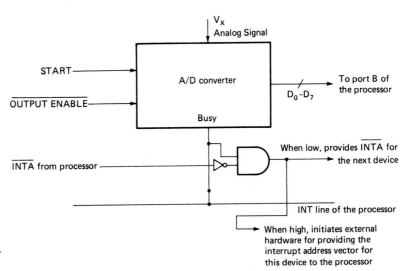

Figure 2–51 Each device and associated logic in daisy chain

Suppose that in Figure 2–50 the processor sends a pulse to start the conversions of A/D converter Devices 1 and 2 at nearly the same time. When the BUSY signal goes to HIGH, the processor is interrupted via the INT line. The processor pushes the program counter and maybe some other registers and then generates Interrupt Acknowledge LOW ($\overline{\text{INTA}}$) to the highest priority device (Device 1 in Figure 2–50). Device 1 has the highest priority because Device 1 is the first device in the daisy chain configuration receiving $\overline{\text{INTA}}$. If A/D converter 1 has generated the BUSY HIGH, then the output of the AND gate becomes HIGH. This signal can be used to enable external hardware to provide the interrupt address vector on the processor's data lines. The processor then branches to the service routine. This program consists of enabling the converter and inputting the A/D output into the processor via port B. However, if A/D converter 1 does not generate the BUSY HIGH, then the output of the AND gate in Figure 2–51 becomes LOW, which is an input to Device 2 logic, and the same sequence of operations takes place.

Note that in the daisy chain, each device has the same logic except the last device, which must accept the $\overline{\text{INTA}}$.

2-5-4 Direct Memory Access (DMA)

Programmed I/O and interrupt I/O provide data transfer between the microprocessor and external devices. However, there are various instances when data must be moved between memory and external devices. For example, with a mass storage device, such as a cassette recorder, one may want to input or output programs or data to or from the microcomputer RAM. This can typically be handled using two methods. The first method uses programmed I/O. The microcomputer can be programmed to input data from an I/O device into the RAM or output data from the RAM to an I/O device. Obviously, in this method the microprocessor is involved in the data transfer. For typical microprocessors, 1 byte of data can be transferred between the RAM and an I/O device in 5 to 10 μs using programmed I/O. The second method, called *direct memory access (DMA)*, transfers data directly between the RAM and an I/O device without involving the microprocessor. Using this technique, the transfer of 1 byte of data typically requires 1 μs. DMA is extensively used in transferring large blocks of data between a peripheral device and the microcomputer memory.

Since DMA performs data transfer between memory

and an external device without involving the microprocessor, the DMA interface or controller chip must be able to perform memory READ and WRITE operations in a similar way as the microprocessor. A DMA controller chip typically provides the following:

1. The DMA controller chip puts the microprocessor in a HOLD state by means of the HOLD control signal. The microprocessor then stops executing the program and disconnects the address, data, and memory control lines from its bus by placing them in a high-impedance state.

2. The DMA controller chip takes over the microcomputer bus as soon as it receives the DMA acknowledge signal from the microprocessor. It puts the RAM location on the address bus and the appropriate control signal on the control bus in order to transfer data between the RAM and an I/O device.

3. The DMA controller chip controls all data transfer. After completion of data transfer, it transfers control of the system bus to the microcomputer by removing the microprocessor from the HOLD state.

From the preceding description, it is obvious that the functions performed by the DMA controller chip are identical in many ways to those performed by the microprocessor. Many microprocessor manufacturers have designed DMA controller chips. These DMA controllers can be used to control the direct transfer of data between memory and several (typically four to eight) I/O devices. Two types of DMA are used with microprocessors: microprocessor-halt DMA and interleaved DMA.

Microprocessor-Halt DMA In this type of DMA, data transfer is performed between the memory and a peripheral device either by completely stopping the microprocessor until the transfer is completed or by a technique called *cycle stealing*. In either case, the microprocessor is stopped for DMA operation. The first method transfers a complete block of data and is therefore known as *block transfer DMA*. On the other hand, with cycle stealing DMA, data transfer occurs on a byte transfer basis until the transfer is completed. The decision of which type of DMA should be used depends on the length of the data block. If the data block is large, block transfer DMA is recommended. On the other hand, for small data blocks, cycle stealing DMA is used. Also, if the microprocessor cannot be kept inactive in a particular application for the time needed for the block transfer, cycle stealing DMA must be used. With either block transfer or cycle stealing, a DMA controller chip controls the DMA operation. This chip typically consists of an address register (containing the address of the data to be transferred to or from) and a counter (containing the length of the data to be transferred). The address register is incremented by 1 each time a byte is transferred. Thus,

data is transferred in a sequential order. The counter containing the length of data is decremented by 1 each time a byte is transferred. When this counter reaches zero, the DMA transfer is completed. The microprocessor then takes over the bus. The DMA controller is not independent of the microprocessor. The address register and the counter are normally loaded by the microprocessor.

We now describe block transfer DMA and cycle stealing DMA in more detail.

Block Transfer DMA This is the most common type of DMA used with microprocessors. As mentioned before, in this type of DMA, the peripheral device requests the DMA transfer via the DMA request line, which is connected directly or through a DMA controller chip to the microprocessor. The microprocessor completes the current instruction and sends a HOLD acknowledge to the DMA controller chip, which in turn sends a DMA ACK signal to the I/O device in order to indicate that the bus can be used for DMA operation. The DMA controller chip then completes the DMA transfer and transfers the control of the bus to the microprocessor.

Figure 2–52 shows a typical diagram of block transfer DMA. In Figure 2–52, the I/O device requests the DMA transfer via the DMA request line connected to the DMA controller chip. In response to this request, the DMA controller chip sends a HOLD signal to the microprocessor. The DMA controller chip then waits for the HOLD acknowledge (HLDA) signal from the microprocessor. On receipt of this HLDA, the DMA controller chip sends a DMA ACK signal to the I/O device. The DMA controller then takes over the bus and controls data transfer between the RAM and I/O device. On completion of data transfer, the controller chip returns the bus to the microprocessor by disabling the HOLD and DMA ACK signals.

The DMA controller chip usually has at least three registers that are normally selected by the controller's register select (RS) line. These three registers are an address register, a terminal count register, and a status register. Both address and terminal count registers are initialized by the CPU. The address register contains the starting address of data to be transferred, and the terminal count register contains the desired block of data to be transferred. The status register contains information such as completion of the DMA transfer.

Cycle Stealing DMA In this technique, the DMA controller transfers a byte of data between the memory and a peripheral device by stealing a clock cycle of the microprocessor. The DMA controller will complete the transfer by bypassing the microprocessor and generating proper signals to complete the transfer. Since the microprocessor is operated by an external clock, it is quite

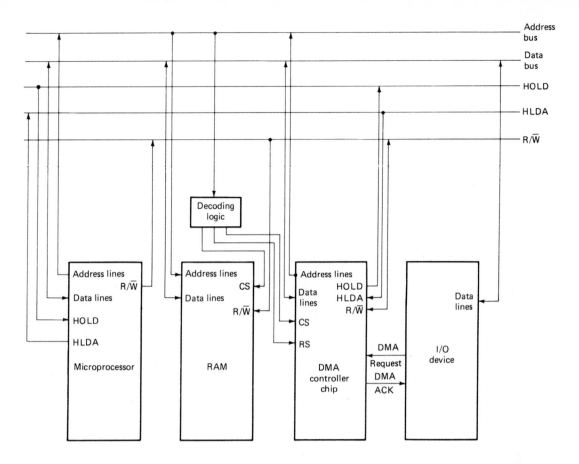

Figure 2–52 A typical DMA system

simple to stop the microprocessor momentarily. This is accomplished by not providing the clock signal to the microprocessor. An $\overline{\text{INHIBIT}}$ signal is used for this purpose. This $\overline{\text{INHIBIT}}$ is normally HIGH and is logically ANDed with the system clock to generate the microprocessor clock.

In order to perform a DMA transfer, the DMA controller stops the microprocessor by lowering the $\overline{\text{INHIBIT}}$ signal to LOW. The DMA controller then takes over the control of the microprocessor system bus for the time that the microprocessor is stopped. Using cycle stealing, data is transferred 1 byte at a time. The DMA controller requests the microprocessor for each byte to be transferred.

Interleaved DMA Interleaved DMA is a more complex type of DMA operation. Using this technique, the DMA controller takes over the system bus when the microprocessor is not using it. For example, the microprocessor does not use the bus when it performs internal operations, such as decoding an instruction, or ALU operations. The DMA controller takes advantage of those times in order to transfer data, and this is called *interleaved DMA*. One of the main characteristics of interleaved DMA is that data transfer occurs without stopping

the microprocessor. With interleaved DMA, each data transfer includes 1 byte per instruction cycle.

2–5–5 Summary of Microcomputer I/O Methods

Figure 2–53 summarizes the I/O structure (explained so far) of typical microcomputers.

2–5–6 Coprocessors

In typical 8-bit microprocessors such as the Intel 8085 and the Zilog Z80, technology places a limit on the chip area. In consequence, these microprocessors include no hardware or firmware for performing scientific computations such as floating-point arithmetic, matrix manipulation, and graphic-data processing. Therefore, users of these systems must write these programs. Unfortunately, this approach is unacceptable in high-speed applications since program execution takes a significant amount of time. To eliminate this problem, coprocessors are used.

In this approach, a single chip is built for performing scientific computations at high speed. However, the chip is regarded as a companion to the original or host microprocessor. Typically, each special operation is en-

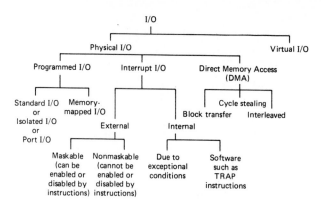

Figure 2-53 I/O Structure of typical microcomputers. (Reprinted with permission from Rafiquzzaman, M. *Microprocessors and Microcomputer-Based System Design*, copyright © 1990 CRC Press, Inc., Boca Raton, Florida.)

coded as an instruction that can be interpreted only by the companion processor. When the companion microprocessor encounters one of these special instructions, it assumes the processing functions independent of the host microprocessor. The companion microprocessor that operates in this manner is called the *coprocessor*. This concept not only extends the capabilities of the host microprocessor but also increases the processing rate of the system. The coprocessor concept is widely used with typical 32-bit microprocessors such as the Motorola 68020 and the Intel 80386.

Functionally, the coprocessor provides a logical extension of the programmer's model in the way of instructions, registers, and operand types. This extension is transparent to the programmer. It is important to make the distinction between standard peripheral hardware and a coprocessor.

A coprocessor is a device that has the capability of communicating with the main processor through the protocol defined as the *coprocessor interface*. As mentioned before, the coprocessor also adds additional instructions, registers, and data types that are not directly supported by the main processor. The coprocessor provides capabilities to the user without appearing to be hardware external to the main processor.

Standard peripheral hardware, on the other hand, is generally accessed through the use of interface registers mapped into the memory space of the main processor. The programmer uses standard processor instructions to access the peripheral interface registers and thus utilize the services provided by the peripheral. It should be pointed out that, even though a peripheral can provide capabilities equivalent to a coprocessor for many applications, the programmer must implement the communication protocol between the main processor and the peripheral necessary to use the peripheral hardware. Two main techniques may be used to pass commands to a coprocessor. These are the intelligent monitor interface and coprocessors using special signals.

In the intelligent monitor interface, the coprocessor monitors the instruction stream by obtaining commands directly from the bus at the same time as the main processor. The Intel 80387 (floating-point coprocessor) is of this type; it monitors the instruction stream simultaneously with a 32-bit main processor such as the Intel 80386. This has the obvious advantage of requiring no additional bus cycles to pass the content of the instruction word to the coprocessor. One of the main disadvantages of this approach is that each coprocessor in the system must duplicate the bus monitoring circuitry and instruction queue, tracking all branches, wait state, operand fetches, and instruction fetches.

In the second type, the coprocessor may be explicitly addressed by certain instructions, which initiate a special sequence of microinstructions in the main processor to effect command and operand transfer. In this approach, when the main processor executes a coprocessor instruction, it decodes the instruction and writes a command in the command register (one of the interface registers in the coprocessor) to specify the operation required by the coprocessor. In response, the coprocessor writes data back in the response register (one of the interface registers). The main processor can read these data, which tell it certain information such as whether additional information is required by the coprocessor to carry out the operation. If such information is required, the main processor provides this; otherwise, the coprocessor carries out the operation concurrently with the main processor and provides the result.

An advantage of this approach is that no special signals are required for the coprocessor interface. One of the main disadvantages of this method is that once the main processor detects a coprocessor instruction, the main processor has to use bus bandwidth and timing to transmit the command to the appropriate coprocessor. The Motorola 68881 (floating-point coprocessor) is of this type. This coprocessor is designed primarily for a 32-bit microprocessor such as the Motorola MC68020.

2–1. What is the difference between a single-chip microprocessor and a single-chip microcomputer?

2–2. A microprocessor uses eight address lines for accessing a memory. What is the maximum size of the memory that can be directly addressed by this microprocessor?

2–3. What is the difference between:
   (a) Program counter (PC) and memory address register (MAR)?
   (b) Accumulator (A) and instruction register (IR)?

2–4. Assume that a microprocessor is currently executing an instruction addressed by 2000_{16}. What are the current contents of the program counter?

2–5. Find the sign, carry, zero, and overflow flags of the following:
   (a) $09_{16} + 17_{16}$
   (b) $A5_{16} - A5_{16}$
   (c) $71_{16} - A9_{16}$
   (d) $6E_{16} + 3A_{16}$
   (e) $7E_{16} + 7E_{16}$

2–6. What is meant by PUSH and POP operations in the stack?

2–7. Supose that an 8-bit microprocessor has a 16-bit stack pointer and uses a 16-bit register in order to access the stack from the top. Assume that initially the stack pointer and the 16-bit register contain $20C0_{16}$ and 0205_{16}, respectively. After a PUSH operation:
   (a) What are the contents of the stack pointer?
   (b) What are the contents of memory locations $20BE_{16}$ and $20BF_{16}$?

2–8. What is meant by a multiplexed address and data bus?

2–9. How many 16-bit registers does the 8085 have? Name them.

2–10. Which register pair is the memory address register of the 8085?

2–11. An 8-bit microprocessor has a memory of 8K words that are divided into 256 pages. What is the size of each page?

2–12. What is the difference between EPROM and PROM? Are both types available with bipolar and also MOS technologies?

2–13. Assuming a single clock signal and four registers (PC, MAR, A, and IR) for a microprocessor, draw a timing diagram for loading the memory address register. Explain the sequence of events relating them to the four registers.

2–14. Given a memory with a 14-bit address and 8-bit word size:
   (a) How many bytes can be stored in this memory?

(b) If this memory were constructed from 1K × 1-bit RAMs, how many memory chips would be required?
(c) How many bits would be used for chip select?

2–15. Define the three types of I/O. Identify each one as either "microprocessor initiated" or "device initiated."

2–16. Explain the following terms:
   (a) Volatility
   (b) Dynamic memory

2–17. Describe the advantages of an EAROM over the EPROM.

2–18. The block diagram of a 256 × 4 RAM chip is shown in Figure P2–18. In this arrangement, the memory chip is enabled only when $\overline{CS1} = L$ and $CS2 = H$. Realize a 2K × 8 RAM system using this chip as the building block. Draw a neat logic diagram of your implementation.

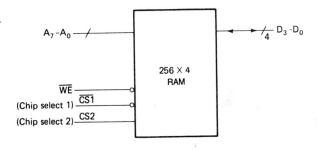

Figure P2–18

2–19. Derive the logic equations for $\overline{MEMR}$, and $\overline{MEMW}$ from the control signals $IO/\overline{M}$, $\overline{RD}$, and $\overline{WR}$.

2–20. Explain why it is necessary to buffer an 8-bit microprocessor using the 74LS244 and 74LS245 IC chips.

2–21. Mention the advantages and disadvantages of the linear select decoding technique.

2–22. Consider the hardware schematic shown in Figure P2–22.
   (a) Determine the address map of this system.
   (b) Is there any memory foldback in this organization? Clearly justify your answer.

2–23. Interface an 8-bit microprocessor with a 2K × 8 ROM chip and two 1K × 8 chips such that the following address map is realized:

Device	Size	Address Assignment
ROM chip	2K × 8	0800–0FFF
RAM chip 0	1K × 8	1000–13FF
RAM chip 1	1K × 8	4000–43FF

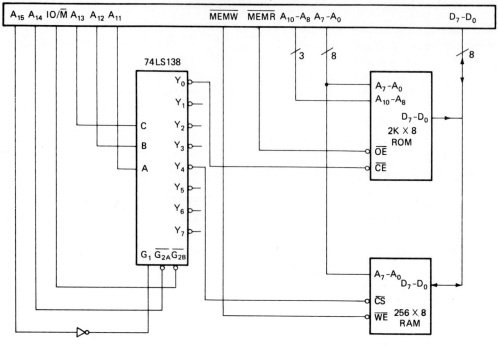

8-bit Buffered Microprocessor

Figure P2–22

2–24. Repeat Problem 2–23, but this time realize the following address map:

Device	Size	Address Assignment
ROM chip	2K × 8	0000–07FF
RAM chip 0	1K × 8	0800–08FF
RAM chip 1	1K × 8	0000–0FFF

2–25. What is meant by:
   (a) Handshaking?
   (b) Buffers?

2–26. Describe briefly the reasons for using a sample and hold circuit in a microprocessor application for inputting an analog voltage.

2–27. Define the basic types of I/O transfers.

2–28. How many different types of I/O ports are available in a typical microprocessor? Discuss them.

2–29. A microprocessor is required to drive an LED that takes 20 mA at 2 V. Assume that the microprocessor can source up to 500 μA of current at a minimum voltage of 2V.
   (a) Design an interface using a discrete transistor.
   (b) Design an interface using a 7406 buffer.

2–30. What is the difference between a maskable and a nonmaskable interrupt? What do you mean by handshake interrupt?

2–31. What is the difference between polled versus vec-tored interrupts? How are they used to handle multiple interrupts?

2–32. Suppose that a microprocessor has two I/O ports (port A and B). Each I/O port has a data direction register whereby each bit in the I/O port can individually be configured as either input or output. Suppose that the microprocessor is required to compare two voltages V_1 and V_2 with a reference voltage V_{ref}. If $V_{ref} > V_1$, the microprocessor will turn two LEDs connected to bits 0 and 1 of port A on and off, respectively. On the other hand, if $V_2 > V_{ref}$, the microprocessor will turn the LEDs connected to bits 0 and 1 of port A off and on, respectively. Assume that in the circuit only one of the conditions will occur at one time; that is, either $V_{ref} > V_1$ or $V_2 > V_{ref}$. Design the interface hardware by means of a block diagram and then:
   (a) Explain the circuit using programmed I/O.
   (b) Explain the circuit using interrupt I/O.

2–33. What is the difference between cycle stealing DMA and interleaved DMA? What is meant by block transfer DMA?

2–34. What is the difference between the return from interrupt (RTI) and return from subroutine (RTS) instructions? Do these instructions perform the same functions for all microprocessors?

2–35. Discuss the main features of typical coprocessors.

3

Microcomputer Software Concepts

This chapter discusses some important characteristics of microcomputer software concepts. Topics include microcomputer addressing modes, instruction types, and assembly language programming.

3-1 INTRODUCTION

We know that an instruction manipulates stored data and a sequence of instructions constitutes a program. In general, an instruction has two components:

1. Operation-code (OP-code) field
2. Address field

The *OP-code field* specifies how data is to be manipulated. A data item may reside within a microprocessor register or in the main memory. Thus, the purpose of the *address field* is to indicate the address of a data item. Also, there are operations that require data to be stored in two or more addresses. This means that the address field may contain more than one address. For example, consider the following instruction:

$$\underbrace{\text{ADD}}_{\text{OP-code field}} \qquad \underbrace{\text{R1,R0}}_{\text{Address field}}$$

Assume that this microcomputer uses R1 as the source register and R0 as the destination register. The instruction then adds the contents of microprocessor registers R0 and R1 and saves the sum in register R0.

The number and types of instructions supported by a microprocessor may vary from one microprocessor to another and primarily depend on the architecture of a particular machine.

3-2 INSTRUCTION FORMATS

Depending on the number of addresses specified, we have the following instruction formats:

- Three-address format
- Two-address format
- One-address format
- Zero-address format

The three-address format takes the following general form:

⟨OP code⟩ Addr1, Addr2, Addr3

Some typical *three-address instructions* are specified next:

MUL	A, B, C	;	C ← A * B
ADD	A, B, C	;	C ← A + B
SUB	R1, R2, R3	;	R3 ← R1 − R2;

In this specification, all alpha characters are assumed to represent memory addresses and the string that begins with the letter R indicates a register. The third address of this type of instruction is usually referred to as the *destination address*. The result of an operation is always assumed to be saved in the destination address. The three-address format is available with 32-bit microprocessors such as the Intel 80386.

If we drop the third address from the three-address format, we obtain the two-address format. Its general form is as follows:

⟨OP code⟩ Addr1, Addr2

Some typical *two-address instructions* are listed next:

MOV	A, R1	;	R1 ← A
ADD	C, R2	;	R2 ← R2 + C
SUB	R1, R2	;	R2 ← R2 − R1

In this format, the addresses Addr1 and Addr2, respectively represent source and destination addresses. Some typical *one-address instructions* are listed next:

LDA	B	;	Acc ← B
ADD	C	;	Acc ← Acc + C

```
MUL    D      ;    Acc ← Acc * D
STA    E      ;    E   ← Acc
```

Instructions that do not require any addresses are called *zero-address instructions*. All microprocessors include some zero-address instructions in the instruction set. Typical examples of zero-address instructions are STC (set carry) and NOP.

3-3 ADDRESSING MODES

The sequence of operations that a microprocessor has to carry out while executing an instruction is called its *instruction cycle*. The most important activity in an instruction cycle is the determination of the operand and destination addresses. The manner in which a microprocessor accomplishes this task is called the *addressing mode*.

Now, let us present the typical microprocessor addressing modes and relate them to the instruction sets of popular processors such as the Intel 8085, Zilog Z80, and the Motorola 68000.

An instruction is said to have an *inherent addressing mode* if its OP code indicates the address of the operand, which is usually the contents of a microprocessor register. For example, consider the following instruction:

```
CMA    ;    Complement accumulator register
```

Since the OP code implies the address of the operand, the processor does not have to compute the operand address. This mode is very common with 8-bit microprocessors such as the I8085, Z80, and MC6809. This mode is also known as implied addressing.

Whenever an instruction contains the operand value, it is called an *immediate mode instruction*. For example, consider the following instruction:

```
ADD #16, R0    ;    (R0) ← (R0) + 16
```

In this instruction, the symbol # indicates that it is an immediate mode instruction. This convention is adopted in microprocessors such as the MC68000. In these systems, the machine representation of this instruction occupies two consecutive memory words: The first word will hold the OP code while the next word will hold the data value (in this case, it is 16). This means that in order to execute this instruction, the microprocessor has to access the memory twice.

An instruction is said to have an *absolute addressing mode* if it contains the address of the operand. For example, consider the following instruction:

```
MOVE 2000, R0    ;    R0 ← M(2000)
```

This instruction copies the contents of the memory location 2000 in the microprocessor register R0. Note that in this move instruction the source operand is in the absolute mode. This mode is also called the *direct mode*.

Sometimes, it is possible that an instruction may contain the address of an address of an operand. In such a case, the addressing mode is referred to as a *memory indirect addressing mode*. For example, consider the following instruction:

```
MOVE (2000), R0    ;    R0 ← M(M(2000))
```

The pictorial representation of this instruction is shown in Figure 3-1. From this figure, we notice that the machine code of this instruction contains the indirect address 2000 as its second word. So, the processor interprets the contents of the memory location 2000 as the address of the operand. Thus, the contents of the memory location 2400, that is, the value 1600, will be copied into the microprocessor register R0. It is easy to see that, in order to execute a memory indirect MOVE instruction, the system needs to access the memory 4 times. Since a memory access is a slow process, this mode significantly delays the instruction execution.

An instruction is said to have a *register mode* if it contains a register address as opposed to a memory address. This means that in this mode the operand values are held in the microprocessor registers. For example, consider the following register mode add instruction:

```
ADD R1, R0    ;    (R0) ← (R1) + (R0)
```

In the register addressing mode, the *effective address (EA)* of an operand is a microprocessor register. Since many contemporary microprocessors have only a small number of registers, the machine representation of a register mode instruction requires only a few bits. Thus, we can conserve memory space by utilizing register mode instructions. Also, notice that in this mode the processor does not require any memory reference for data retrieval,

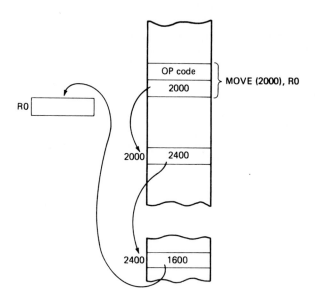

Figure 3-1 Representation of memory indirect move instruction

and hence the instruction execution rate can be considerably increased. However, since there is always a limit on the number of microprocessor registers, it is not possible to handle a large number of operands by the exclusive use of the register addressing mode.

Whenever an instruction specifies a microprocessor register that holds the address of an operand, the resulting addressing mode is known as the *register indirect mode*. From this definition, it follows that the EA of an operand in the register indirect mode is the contents of a microprocessor register R. More formally, we write this result as follows:

$$EA = (R)$$

In order to illustrate this idea clearly, consider the following instruction:

MOVE (R1),(R0)   ;   M((R0)) ← M((R1))

Here, both operands of the MOVE instruction are in the indirect mode. Assume that the following configuration exists:

$$(R1) = 2000$$
$$(R0) = 3000$$
$$M(2000) = 0634$$
$$M(3000) = 1437$$

This instruction copies the contents of the memory location whose address is specified in the microprocessor register R1 into that location whose address is specified in the microprocessor register R0. Thus, after the execution of this instruction, the memory location 3000 will contain the value 0634. Note that, whenever a microprocessor register is used as a data pointer, the assembler convention is to enclose that register using a set of parentheses.

An important concept used in the context of addressing modes is the idea of *address modification*. In this approach, the EA of an operand is expressed as the sum of two parameters: *reference address (RA)* and *modifier (M)*. More formally,

$$EA = RA + M$$

The modifier M is also called the *offset* or *displacement*. Such an address modification principle is the basic concept associated with the following addressing modes:

- Indexed mode
- Base register mode
- Relative mode

In the *indexed mode,* the value of RA is included in the instruction and the register contains the value M. In particular, the register X is called the *index register.* This mode is very useful for accessing arrays. For example, consider the following Pascal integer array Y:

var y : array [0..9] of integer;

Assume that each element of this array requires 1 byte and that the entire array is configured in the memory as shown in Figure 3–2. From this figure, we notice that the array starts at the memory address 0100. We assume that the index register X contains the value 0002 and that we want to execute the following indexed mode load instruction:

LDA 0100 (X)

This instruction indicates that the register X is used as the index register. Its machine representation includes the reference address 0100, which is the starting address of the array Y (see Figure 3–2). Under this situation, the EA of the operand is as follows:

$$
\begin{aligned}
EA &= RA + (X) \\
&= 0100 + 2 \\
&= 0102
\end{aligned}
$$

Therefore, when this instruction is executed, the contents of the memory location 0102 will be transferred to the A register. Note that this memory address actually holds the array element Y[2]. Also, since the register X contains the required index value of the array element, it is referred to as the index register. Now, in order to access the third element of the array Y, we only need to increment the register X by 1, and this operation can be performed quickly. Thus, the indexed mode allows a programmer to carry out array manipulations in an efficient manner.

In *base register addressing,* the parameter RA is held in a separate register called the *base register,* and the modifier M is included in the instruction. This mode is very significant in a system that provides a virtual memory support. In particular, the base register mode finds application in segmented memory systems. In these systems, the base register holds the base address (or the starting address) of a segment.

In general, the size of the indexed mode modifier M will be the same as the number of bits required to specify a memory address. On the other hand, in the base register mode, the number of bits in the modifier field M may be less than the number of bits required for a direct memory reference.

The contents of the M field are often interpreted as a 2's complement number. Whenever the sizes of the modifier and the memory address fields are unequal, the sign-extended form of M is used in the effective address calculation.

If we configure the PC as the base register, then the *relative addressing mode* results. This mode is particularly useful in order to design a short branch instruction. For example, consider the Z80 branch instruction JP 0248H, where H indicates 0248 as a hexadecimal number. This instruction is equivalent to the high-level language statement GOTO 0248. The machine representation of this instruction requires 3 bytes: 1 byte for the OP code (C3) and 2 bytes for the branch address (0248).

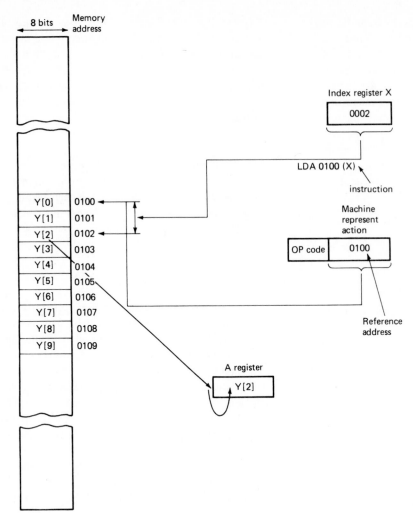

Figure 3-2 Use of the indexed addressing mode in accessing arrays

Assume that this instruction is stored as shown in Figure 3–3(a). Since the PC always holds the address of the next instruction to be executed, implementation of a branch instruction implies loading the PC with the branch address.

Alternatively, consider the Z80 relative branch instruction JR 02, where the numerical value 02 represents the value of the modifier or offset. The machine representation of this instruction requires only 2 bytes: 1 byte for the OP code (18) and 1 more byte to hold the offset value 02. If we assume that this instruction is stored as shown in Figure 3–3(b), then the execution of this instruction can be explained as follows:

1. The entire instruction is fetched.
2. Since this is a 2-byte instruction, after the instruction fetch, the PC will contain 0246 (0244 + 2).
3. The branch address is computed as follows:

Branch = Current contents + Offset value of the PC
  = 0246 + 02
  = 0248

4. Finally, the PC is loaded with this branch address, and thus the next instruction to be executed is the one that is located in the memory location 0248H, where H indicates that 0248 is a hexadecimal number.

It should be pointed out that when the offset is a negative number, reverse branching takes place. For example, consider JR −06 with all other data (in hex) as in Figure 3–3(b). In this case, 06 will be subtracted from 0246. Since this is a subtraction of an 8-bit signed number from a 16-bit signed number, the correct result is obtained if the 8-bit number (−06) is sign extended and then subtracted from 0246 using its 2's complement, ignoring the final carry as follows:

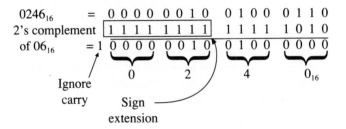

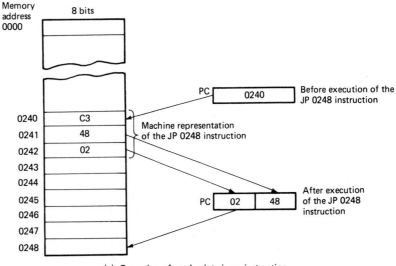

(a) Operation of an absolute jump instruction

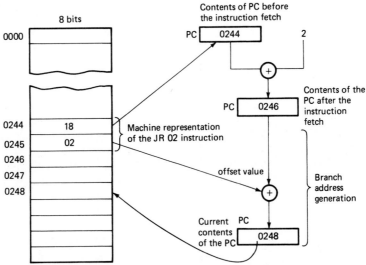

(b) Operation of a relative branch instruction

Figure 3–3 Mechanics of absolute and relative branch instructions (all numbers are in hexadecimal form)

Note that, since the offset value is normally an 8-bit quantity, we can only branch -128 to $+127$ bytes relative to the current contents of the PC (0 is considered positive). In most microcomputers, conditional branching instructions utilize the relative mode. These microcomputers typically have an absolute unconditional branching. If one needs to go beyond the -128_{10} to $+127_{10}$ range with conditional branching, then one can use the unconditional branching instruction anywhere in this range to branch to any location within the microcomputer's directly addressable memory.

Another important aspect of the relative addressing mode is its ability to produce a relocatable program. For example, consider the situation shown in Figure 3–3(b). In this configuration, we assume only that the branch address is 2 bytes away from the current contents of the PC. This means that, when we relocate this program, the JR 02 instruction will be placed in a different location

and we will thus obtain a different value for the current contents of the PC. Nevertheless, the program execution will produce the same result because the system identifies the branch address as the one that is located 2 bytes away from the current contents of the PC.

Now, let us discuss the usefulness of the various addressing modes. Note that the implementation of a particular addressing mode is largely dependent on the processor organization. In a processor with many general registers, the indexed and indirect addressing modes are easy to realize. If a microcomputer supports powerful addressing modes, the task of designing language translators, operating systems, and efficient application programs can be greatly simplified.

The absolute and relative modes allow one to write position-independent programs. A program is said to be *position independent* if it can be placed anywhere in memory. This is a desirable feature for operating system designers because it allows the operating system to relocate programs in a dynamic manner. In a multiuser system, many different users may need the same library program provided by the operating system. If this library routine is position independent, then the operating system can load the machine code of this routine into any available portion of the main memory.

3-4 INSTRUCTION TYPES

The purpose of an instruction set is to facilitate the quick development of efficient programs by users. An ideal instruction set should also reflect the power of the underlying architecture so that a user can take advantage of it while developing programs. In general, instructions available in a processor may be broadly classified into five groups:

1. Data transfer
2. Arithmetic
3. Logical
4. Program control
5. Input/Output

3-4-1 Data Transfer Instructions

These instructions are primarily concerned with the data transfer between the processor and main memory. Typically, an ideal instruction set must be able to handle the following transfers:

- Register to register
- Register to memory
- Memory to register
- Memory to memory

A typical example of a data transfer instruction is MOV B,C with the Intel 8085. This instruction moves the contents of register C to register B. Note that the Intel 8085 uses the first operand (B in this case) as the destination and the second operand (C in this case) as the source.

3-4-2 Arithmetic Instructions

All instruction sets include ADD and SUBTRACT instructions. The instruction sets of 16- and 32-bit microprocessors such as the Intel 8086 and the Motorola MC68000/68020 include multiplication and division. This means that these microprocessors include hardware elements for performing multiplication and division. Also, many data processing applications require the system to manipulate decimal data quickly. For this purpose, the instruction set of modern microprocessors includes instructions that can exclusively process BCD numbers. For example, the ABCD instruction of the MC68000 processor is capable of adding two BCD numbers stored in the main memory. Similarly, floating-point number

manipulation is a distinguishing feature with scientific programming. In order to facilitate this manipulation, some large processors include floating-point instructions in their instruction sets. For example, the extended instruction set of the PDP-11/70 computer includes instructions such as MULF and DIVF in order to multiply and divide floating-point numbers. It is important to emphasize that, in order to speed up the floating-point arithmetic operations, the PDP-11/70 CPU includes six additional 32-bit general-purpose floating-point registers, F0 through F5, and the floating-point coprocessor FP-11. With the advent of VLSI technology, it is possible to realize numerous coprocessors that are compatible with microprocessors. For example, the I8087, AM9511, and MC68881 coprocessor chips are compatible with the I8086, I8085, and MC68020 microprocessors, respectively. Likewise, Motorola's floating-point ROM chip, the MC6839, can be interfaced with the MC6800 microprocessor in order to allow it to handle floating-point computations.

3-4-3 Logical Instructions

Invariably, the instruction sets of typical microprocessors include instructions in order to perform the Boolean AND, OR, NOT, and EXCLUSIVE-OR operations on a bit-by-bit basis. These instruction sets also include the following SHIFT instructions:

- Arithmetic shift (left or right)
- Logical shift (left or right)
- Rotate (left or right) through or without the carry flag

In fact, the MC68000 instruction sets include elegant SHIFT instructions. For example, consider the following SHIFT instruction:

$$LSR.W \ \#6,D2$$

This instruction performs a left logical shift of the low-order 16 bits of the data register D2 by six places. Note that in the 68000, register D2 is a 32-bit register.

Two other important logical instructions are the COMPARE and TEST instructions. The COMPARE instruction subtracts the two operands and affects only the status flags without providing any result of subtraction. The MC68000 instruction set allows a programmer to perform memory-to-memory compare operations. The TEST instruction simply tests the specified operand with zero and sets the Z flag depending on the status of the tested operand.

3-4-4 Program Control Instructions

In a conventional microcomputer, instructions are always executed in the same order in which they are presented. In many real-life programs, the flow of control depends on the result of computation. In this situation, a program can select a particular sequence of instructions to execute, based on the results of computation. Instructions that realize this idea are called *program control instructions*. In general, some of these instructions may be classified into the following groups:

- Unconditional branch instructions
- Conditional branch instructions
- Subroutine call instructions

As seen earlier, an *unconditional branch instruction* transfers the control to the specified address regardless of the status of the computation. Some processors, such as the MC68000, include both the absolute and relative branch instructions in their instruction sets. On the other hand, the 8085 contains only an absolute branch instruction.

A *conditional branch instruction* works as follows:

If ⟨condition⟩ *then* branch to execute a new instruction
else execute the following instruction

In this situation, we assume that the condition flags are already set by some instruction that immediately precedes the conditional branch instruction. Typically, the instruction may be an arithmetic (such as ADD, SUBTRACT, INCREMENT, or DECREMENT instructions) or a logical instruction (such as TEST or COMPARE instructions). Using the conditional flag settings, we can realize traditional relational operators such as equal to, not equal to, greater than, greater than or equal to, less than, or less than or equal to.

For example, consider the following 8085 instruction sequence:

```
        LDA   BEGIN    ;   Load 'A' with [BEGIN]
        MVI   C, 03    ;   C ← 03
        SUB   C        ;   [A] ← [A] − [C]
        JZ    START    ;   Jump to START if Z = 1
        MOV   A, C      ;   If Z = 0, do this
        —     —
        —     —
        —     —
START   HLT            ;   Halt
```

In this example, if the result of the subtraction is zero (i.e., Z = 1), then the program will jump to START; otherwise, MOV A, C is executed.

A *subroutine* is a special program for performing repeatedly needed tasks such as searching, sorting, and binary-to-ASCII code conversion. Typically, a subroutine may be written, assembled, and tested separately. Since each subroutine CALL replaces several lines of code, the size of the calling program can be optimized. In principle, a large program can be thought of as a collection of independent program modules, where each module may be a subroutine or a set of subroutines. This

is the key feature of the modern software approach called *modular programming*. In this method, a programmer has a global view of all components of a large program, and thus efficient programs can be developed within a short period of time. Also, since each subroutine can be independently tested, it follows that the modular programming approach considerably improves the overall software reliability. The subroutine concept strongly encourages the idea of program sharing. For example, in a multiuser system, several user programs may share the same I/O subroutine provided by the operating system. In this way, a user does not have to spend time developing I/O routines.

Subroutine calls and returns from subroutines are usually handled by two special instructions, namely, CALL and RET, respectively. The CALL instruction is of the form CALL ⟨addr⟩, where the parameter ⟨addr⟩ refers to the address of the first instruction of the subroutine. When this instruction is executed, the current contents of the PC are saved in the stack and the PC is loaded with ⟨addr⟩. Note that the current contents of the PC provide the address of the instruction that immediately follows the CALL instruction. This address is also called the return address because this is the point where execution of the calling program will take place after exiting from the subroutine. Thus, the CALL instruction is functionally equivalent to the following instruction sequence:

```
PUSH   PC      ;   Save return address in stack
JMP    addr    ;   Branch to subroutine
```

The RET instruction is usually the last instruction of the subroutine. When this instruction is executed, the return address previously saved in the stack is retrieved and is loaded into the PC. Thus, the control is transferred to the calling program. In concept, a RET instruction is functionally equivalent to POP PC.

At this point, one may be wondering why the return address is not saved in a microprocessor register rather than in the stack. Some computers such as the PDP-11/70 use this approach. That is, the PDD11/70 uses one of its CPU registers to save the return address. However, this arrangement fails to work if we need to implement nested subroutine calls. *Subroutine nesting* refers to the situation in which one subroutine calls another.

For example, consider a main program M and two subroutines P and Q as shown in Figure 3–4(a). In this arrangement, the main program calls subroutine P and this subroutine in turn calls subroutine Q. In this situation, the expected control flow sequence is shown in Figure 3–4(b). Note that parameters MR and PR refer to the return addresses of the main program M and the subroutine P, respectively.

When the main program calls the subroutine P, the return address MR is pushed into the stack (see Figure 3–4c) and the control is transferred to the subroutine P. Similarly, when the subroutine P calls the subroutine Q,

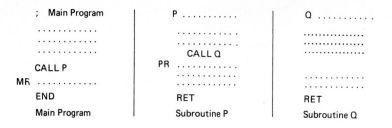

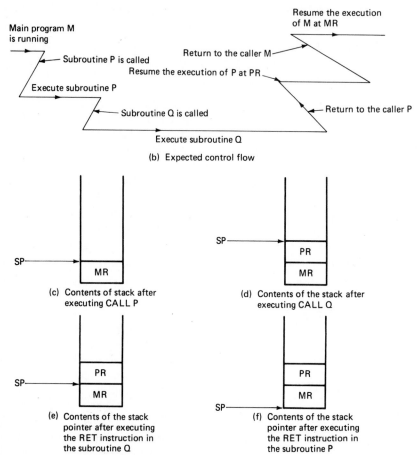

(a) A typical two level subroutine nesting

(b) Expected control flow

(c) Contents of stack after executing CALL P

(d) Contents of the stack after executing CALL Q

(e) Contents of the stack pointer after executing the RET instruction in the subroutine Q

(f) Contents of the stack pointer after executing the RET instruction in the subroutine P

Figure 3–4 Implementation of a two-level subroutine nesting

the return address PR is pushed into the stack (see Figure 3–4d) and the control is transferred to the subroutine Q. When the subroutine Q completes its execution, the return address is retrieved from the stack and loaded into the PC. Since the return address is PR, the execution of the subroutine P is resumed. Similarly, when the subroutine P terminates, the return address MR (see Figure 3–4e) is retrieved from the stack and loaded into the PC. Thus, the execution of the main program is resumed. It is important to realize that, in order to implement subroutine nesting, we need to retrieve the return addresses exactly in the reverse order in which they are saved. Since a stack is a LIFO (Last In, First Out) data structure, its use is a natural solution to this problem. Suppose that we use a microprocessor register to save the return address. Then, the return address PR will write over the

return address MR, and, therefore, control will not be transferred to the main program at all.

Solutions to some problems such as traversing a binary tree are naturally recursive, and thus they are precisely solved by writing recursive subroutines. A subroutine is said to be *recursive* if it calls itself. Since a recursive evaluation involves a descent process all the way to the basic part of the recursive definition and then an ascent process all the way up exactly in the reverse order, the use of a stack offers a natural solution for implementing recursive subroutines.

The registers involved in implementing a subroutine call are called *linkage registers,* and the entire process is known as the *subroutine linkage convention.* In all microprocessors, the PC is used as the linkage register. On the other hand, in the PDP-11/70 computer, any CPU register can be configured as a linkage register under program control. Also, in the majority of the processors, the system hardware automatically uses the SP in response to CALL and RET instructions. A notable exception to this is Motorola's 8-bit microprocessor, the MC6809. The microprocessor entails two dedicated 16-bit registers: U (user stack pointer) and S (hardware stack pointer). In this microprocessor, the system hardware automatically uses the stack pointer S for handling subroutine calls and returns. A user can utilize the stack pointer U in order to configure a temporary data storage area in a different portion of the stack. Thus, the user stack area does not cause any interference to the subroutine linkage.

As mentioned before, subroutines are written to handle a specific task. The effective use of subroutine calls is a method for transferring data from the caller to the subroutine and vice versa. This aspect is often referred to as the *parameter* or *argument passing convention*. High-level languages such as Pascal and Ada adopt typical parameter passing conventions such as call by value and call by reference.

In the call-by-value approach, the main program transfers a parameter to a subroutine by simply copying the parameter value in the local variable created at the time when the subroutine becomes active. This means that when the subroutine changes the value of this local variable, the actual parameter of the main program does not receive this change. This is a desirable property for function subprograms because we do not want a function to alter the value of its argument. Rather, we expect a function to return a unique value to the caller.

On the other hand, in the call-by-reference approach, the main program transfers the address of a parameter to a subroutine. Thus, a subroutine can alter the value of the parameter that belongs to a caller. Note that this approach allows a subroutine to transmit the results to the caller. The ability of a subroutine to alter the variables of the calling program is known as the *side effect*. It follows that there is no side effect with the call-by-value approach. However, the call-by-reference approach utilizes the side effect for passing the results to the caller.

3-4-5 Input/Output Instructions

These instructions allow a processor to perform input and output operations. Typically, an input instruction allows a peripheral to transfer a word to either a register or the main memory. Similarly, an output instruction enables a processor to transfer a word into the buffer register of the peripheral device. It is interesting to note that some instruction sets include instructions that can transfer a block of words. For example, the INIR and OTIR instructions of the Z80 microprocessor allow a programmer to transfer a block of words from an input device to the

main memory and from the main memory to an output device, respectively.

3-5 INTRODUCTION TO ASSEMBLY LANGUAGE PROGRAMMING

As mentioned in Chapter 1, programs in assembly language are represented by instructions that use English-language-type commands. The programmer finds it relatively more convenient to write the programs in assembly than in machine language. However, a translator (assembler) must be used to convert the assembly language programs into binary machine language programs (object codes) so that the processor can execute them.

There are various types of assemblers available today. We define some of them in the following paragraphs.

One-Pass Assembler This assembler goes through the assembly language program once and translates the assembly language program into a machine language program. This assembler has the problem of defining forward references. This means that a JUMP instruction using an address that appears later in the program must be defined by the programmer after the program is assembled.

Two-Pass Assembler This assembler scans the assembly language program twice. In the first pass, this assembler creates a symbol table. A *symbol table* consists of labels with addresses assigned to them. This way labels can be used for JUMP statements, and no address calculation has to be done by the user. On the second pass, the assumbler translates the assembly language program into the machine code. The two-pass assembler is more desirable and much easier to use.

Macroassembler This type of assembler translates a program written in macrolanguage into the machine language. This assembler lets the programmer define all instruction sequences using macros. Note that, by using macros, the programmer can assign a name to an instruction sequence that appears repeatedly in a program. The programmer can thus avoid writing an instruction sequence that is required many times in a program by using macros. The macroassembler replaces a macroname with the appropriate instruction sequence each time it encounters a macroname.

It is interesting to see the difference between a subroutine and a macroprogram. A specific subroutine occurs once in a program. A subroutine is executed by CALLing it from a main program. The program execution jumps out of the main program and then executes the subroutine. At the end of the subroutine, a RET instruction is used to resume program execution following the CALL SUBROUTINE instruction in the main program. A macro, on the other hand, does not cause the program execution to branch out of the main program. Each time a macro occurs, it is replaced with the appropriate instruction sequence in the main program. Typical advantages of using macros are shorter source programs and better program documentation. A typical disadvantage is that effects on registers and flags may not be obvious.

Conditional macroassembly is very useful in determining whether or not an instruction sequence shall be included in the assembly depending on a condition that is true or false. If two different programs are to be executed repeatedly based on a condition that can be either true or false, it is convenient to use conditional macros. Based on each condition, a particular program is assembled. Each condition and the appropriate program are included typically within IF and ENDIF pseudoinstructions.

Cross Assembler   This type of assembler is typically resident on the processor and assembles programs for another for which it is written. The cross assembler program is written in a high-level language so that it can run on different types of processors that understand the same high-level language.

Resident Assembler   This type of assembler assembles programs for a processor in which it is resident. The resident assembler may slow down the operation of the processor on which it runs.

Meta-assembler   This type of assembler can assemble programs for many different types of processors. The programmer usually defines the particular processor being used.

As mentioned before, each line of an assembly language program consists of four fields. These are the label field, mnemonic or OP-code field, operand field, and comment field. The assembler ignores the comment field but translates the other three fields. The label field must start with an uppercase alpha character. The assembler must know where one field starts and another ends. Most assemblers allow the programmer to use a special symbol or delimiter to indicate the beginning or end of each field. Typical delimiters used are spaces, commas, semicolons, and colons:

space	between each field
,	between addresses in an operand field
;	before a comment
: or none	after a label

In order to handle numbers, most assemblers consider all numbers as decimal numbers unless specified. Most assemblers will also allow binary, octal, or hexadecimal numbers. The user must define the type of number system used in some ways. This is usually done by using a letter following the number. Typical letters used are:

B	for	binary
Q	for	octal
H	for	hexadecimal

Assemblers generally require hexadecimal numbers to start with a digit. A 0 is typically used if the first digit of the hexadecimal number is a letter. This is done in order to distinguish between numbers and labels. For example, most assemblers will require the number A5H to be represented as 0A5H. Therefore, the 8085 assembler will not accept the 8085 instruction MVI A, FFH and will give an error. The correct format for this instruction is MVI A, 0FFH.

Assemblers use pseudo-instructions or directives to make the formatting of the edited text easier. These pseudo-instructions are not directly translated into machine language instructions. They equate labels to addresses, assign the program in certain areas of memory, or insert titles, page numbers, etc. In order to use the assembler directives or pseudo-instructions, the programmer puts them in the OP-code field, and, if the pseudo-instructions require an address or data, the programmer places them in the label or data field. Typical pseudo-instructions are ORIGIN (ORG), EQUATE (EQU), DEFINE BYTE (DB), and DEFINE WORD (DW).

Origin (ORG)   The pseudo-instruction ORG lets the programmer place the programs anywhere in memory. Internally, the assembler maintains a program-counter-type register called the *address counter*. This counter maintains the address of the next instruction or data to be processed.

An ORG pseudo-instruction is similar in concept to the JUMP instruction. Recall that the JUMP instruction causes the processor to place a new address in the program counter. Similarly, the ORG pseudo-instruction causes the assembler to place a new value in the address counter.

Typical ORG statements are:

ORG	7000H
MVI	A, 02H

The 8085 assembler will generate the following code for these statements:

7000	3E
7001	02

Therefore, the ORG will assign the address in its operand field to the next instruction. Note that 3E is the hexadecimal code for the instruction MVI A, data for the 8085.

Most assemblers assign a value of zero to the starting address of a program if the programmer does not define this by means of an ORG.

Equate (EQU)   The pseudo-instruction EQU assigns a value in its operand field to an address in its label field.

This allows the user to assign a numeric value to a symbolic name. The user can then use the symbolic name in the program instead of its numeric value. This reduces errors.

A typical example of EQU is START EQU 0200H, which assigns the value 0200 in hexadecimal to the label START. Another example is:

```
PORTA    EQU    40H
         MVI    A, 0FFH
         OUT    PORTA
```

In this example, the EQU gives PORTA the value 40 hex, and 0FF hex is the data to be written into the accumulator by MVI A, 0FFH. OUT PORTA then outputs this data 0FF hex to port 40, which has already been equated to PORTA before.

Note that, if a label in the operand field is equated to another label in the label field, then the label in the operand field must be previously defined. For example, the EQU statement

```
BEGIN    EQU    START
```

will generate an error unless START is defined previously with a numeric value.

Define Byte (DB) The pseudo-instruction DB is usually used to set a memory location to a certain byte value. For example,

```
START    DB    45H
```

will assign the data 45 hex to the label START.

With some assemblers, the DB pseudo-instruction can be used to generate a table of data as follows:

```
         ORG    7000H
TABLE    DB     20H, 30H, 40H, 50H
```

In this case, 20 hex is the first data of the memory location 7000; 30 hex, 40 hex, and 50 hex occupy the next three memory locations. Therefore, the data in memory will look like this:

```
7000    20
7001    30
7002    40
7003    50
```

Define Word (DW) The pseudo-instruction DW is typically used to assign a 16-bit value to two memory locations. For example,

```
         ORG    7000H
START    DW     4AC2H
```

will assign C2 to location 7000 and 4A to location 7001. It is assumed that the assembler will assign the low byte first (C2) and then the high byte (4A).

With some assemblers, the DW pseudo-instruction can be used to generate a table of 16-bit data as follows:

```
           ORG    8000H
POINTER    DW     5000H, 6000H, 7000H
```

In this case, the three 16-bit values 5000H, 6000H, and 7000H are assigned to memory locations starting at the address 8000H. That is, the array would look like this:

```
8000    00
8001    50
8002    00
8003    60
8004    00
8005    70
```

Assemblers also use a number of housekeeping pseudo-instructions. Typical housekeeping pseudo-instructions are TITLE, PAGE, END, and LIST. The following are the housekeeping pseudo-instructions that control the assembler operation and its program listing.

Title This pseudo-instruction prints the specified heading at the top of each page of the program listing. For example,

```
TITLE    "SQUARE ROOT ALGORITHM"
```

will print the name "SQUARE ROOT ALGORITHM" on top of each page.

Page This pseudo-instruction skips to the next line.

End This pseudo-instruction indicates the end of the assembly language source program.

List This pseudo-instruction directs the assembler to print the assembler source program.

QUESTIONS AND PROBLEMS

3-1. What are the characteristics of a good instruction format?

3-2. Using a minimum number of zero-address instructions, write a program equivalent to each of the following Pascal statements:
(a) Z: = A + B * C + D
(b) Z: = A * (B + C) * (D + E)
(c) Z: = A + B * C + B * D * E + B * D * F

3-3. Write a program equivalent to the following Pascal assignment statement:

Z: = (A + (B * C) + (D * E) − (F/G) − (H * I))

Use only the following:
(a) Three-address instructions
(b) Two-address instructions

(c) One-address instructions

(d) Zero-address instructions

3-4. What is the essential difference between the base register and the index register addressing modes?

3-5. Describe some important uses of each of the following addressing modes:

(a) Immediate

(b) Indexed

(c) Base register

(d) Relative

3-6. In hypothetical microcomputer, the system can directly address 16M bytes. The microprocessor has 16 base registers. Determine the size of the displacement field so that we can address 6.25% of the total memory addresses (without changing the contents of the base registers).

3-7. A microcomputer's instruction set supports the following Boolean instructions:

$$\text{XOR} \quad \text{X, Y} \quad ; \quad Y \leftarrow X \oplus Y$$
$$\text{AND} \quad \text{X, Y} \quad ; \quad Y \leftarrow X \wedge Y$$

Explain how you will perform the Boolean OR operation $Y \leftarrow X \vee Y$ using these two instructions.

3-8. Assume that a microprocessor has only the two registers R_1 and R_2 and that only the following instruction is available:

$$\text{XOR} \quad R_i, R_j \quad ; \quad R_j \leftarrow R_i \oplus R_j$$
$$\qquad\qquad\qquad ; \quad i,j = 1,2$$

Using this XOR instruction, find an instruction sequence in order to exchange the contents of the registers R_1 and R_2.

3-9. What are the merits and demerits of a relative branch instruction?

3-10. Consider the following SABN (subtract and branch if the result is negative) instruction:

$$\text{SABN} \quad \text{X, Y, Z} \quad ; \quad M(Y) \leftarrow M(Y) - M(X)$$
$$\qquad\qquad\qquad\qquad ; \quad \text{if } M(Y) < 0$$
$$\qquad\qquad\qquad\qquad ; \quad \text{then branch to Z}$$

Using only the SABN instruction, find a sequence in order to perform the following operation:

$$M(101) \leftarrow M(100) + M(101)$$

Assume that the SABN instruction typically occupies one memory word.

3-11. What are the significant advantages of subroutines?

3-12. Explain the use of a stack in implementing subroutine calls.

3-13. Assume an 8-bit microprocessor. Find the effective address and the contents of the affected registers after execution of the following instructions (assume that all numbers are in hexadecimal):

(a) Assume that register R0 contains 05_{16} before execution of the ADD instruction ADD #5, R0.

(b) Assume that index register X contains 02_{16} and memory location 2002_{16} contains 07_{16} before execution of the LDA instruction LDA 2000H (X).

3-14. Suppose that an 8-bit microprocessor uses relative addressing for conditional branch instructions. All numbers are in hexadecimal and negative offsets are represented by 2's complement arithmetic. If the condition is true, find the address of the next instruction to be executed and the contents of the program counter after execution of each of the following instructions:

(a) 2000   25   Jump relative if carry is 1
    2001   07   Offset

(b) 2000   25   Jump relative if carry is 1
    2001   F5   Offset

3-15. What are the contents of the program counter after execution of the following instruction:

2000	1A	Jump 2000
2001	00	Address low byte
2002	20	Address high byte

4

Intel 8085

This chapter contains hardware, software, and interfacing features of the Intel 8085. Topics include the 8085's registers, addressing modes, instruction set, and system design.

4-1 INTRODUCTION

The 8085 is an 8-bit NMOS microprocessor. It is packaged in a 40-pin dual in-line package (DIP). The 8085 requires a $+5$ V supply and has integrated the clock generation, system control, and interrupt circuitry in the same chip. The 8085 can be operated from an internal clock frequency of either 3.03 MHz maximum (8085A) or 5 MHz maximum (8085A-2).

The 8085 has three enhanced versions, namely, the 8085AH, 8085AH-2, and 8085AH-1. These processors are designed using the HMOS (High-density MOS) technology. Each is packaged in a 40-pin DIP like the 8085. These enhanced microprocessors consume 20% lower power than the 8085A. The internal clock frequencies of the 8085AH, 8085AH-2, and 8085AH-1 are 3, 5, and 6 MHz, respectively. These HMOS 8-bit microprocessors are expensive compared to the NMOS 8-bit 8085A.

4-2 REGISTER STRUCTURE

The 8085's registers and status flags are shown in Figure 4-1. The accumulator (A) is an 8-bit register and has its usual meaning. Most arithmetic and logic operations are performed using the accumulator. All I/O data transfers between the 8085 and the I/O devices are performed via the accumulator. Also, there are a number of instructions that move data between the accumulator and memory.

The B, C, D, E, H, and L registers are each 8 bits long. Registers H and L are the memory address register

or data counter. This means that these two registers are used to store the 16-bit address of an 8-bit data being accessed from memory. This is the implied or register indirect addressing mode. There are a number of instructions, such as MOV reg, M and MOV M, reg, that move data between any register and memory location addressed by H and L. However, using any other memory reference instruction, data transfer takes place between a memory location and the only microprocessor register, the accumulator. The instruction LDAX B, for loading the accumulator with the contents of a memory location addressed by BC, is a typical example.

Registers B, C, D, and E are secondary accumulators or data counters. There are a number of instructions to move data between any two registers. There are also a few instructions that combine registers B and C or D and E as a 16-bit data counter with the high byte of a pair contained in the first register and the low byte in the second. These instructions typically include LDAX B, LDAX D, STAX B, and STAX D, which transfer data between memory and the accumulator.

Each of these 8-bit registers can be incremented and decremented by a single-byte instruction. There are a number of instructions that combine two of these 8-bit registers to form 16-bit register pairs as follows:

PSW	and	A
B	and	C
D	and	E
H	and	L
High-order byte		Low-order byte

The 16-bit register pair obtained by combining the accumulator and the program status word (PSW) is used only for stack operations. Arithmetic operations use B and C, or D and E, or H and L as 16-bit data registers.

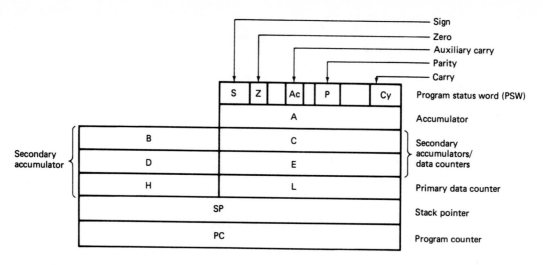

Figure 4–1 8085 microprocessor registers and status flags (From *8080A/8085 Assembly Language Programming* by Leventhal. Copyright © 1978 McGraw-Hill, Inc.)

The *program status word* consists of five status flags. These are described next.

The *carry flag (Cy)* reflects the final carry out of the most significant bit of any arithmetic operation. Any logic instruction resets or clears the carry flag. This flag is also used by the shift and rotate instructions. The 8085 does not have any CLEAR CARRY instruction. One way of clearing the carry will be by ORing or ANDing the accumulator with itself.

The *parity status flag (P)* is set to 1 if an arithmetic or logic instruction generates an answer with even parity, that is, containing an even number of 1 bits. This flag is 0 if the arithmetic or logic instruction generates an answer with odd parity, that is, containing an odd number of 1's.

The *auxiliary carry flag (Ac)* reflects any carry from bit 3 to bit 4 (assuming an 8-bit data with bit 0 as the least significant bit and bit 7 as the most significant bit) due to an arithmetic operation. This flag is useful for BCD operations.

The *zero flag (Z)* is set to 1 whenever an arithmetic or logic operation produces a result of zero. The zero flag is cleared to 0 for a nonzero result due to an arithmetic or a logic operation.

The *sign status flag (S)* is set to the value of the most significant bit of the result in the accumulator after an arithmetic or logic operation. This provides a range of -128_{10} to $+127_{10}$ (with 0 being considered positive) as the 8085's data-handling capacity.

The 8085 does not have any overflow flag. Note that the execution of arithmetic or logic instructions in the 8085 affects the flags. All conditional instructions in the 8085 instruction set use one of the status flags as the required condition.

The *stack pointer (SP)* is 16 bits long. All stack operations with the 8085 use 16-bit register pairs. The stack pointer contains the address of the last data byte written into the stack. It is decremented by 2 each time 2 bytes of data are written or pushed onto the stack and is incremented by 2 each time 2 bytes of data are read from or pulled off the stack; that is, the top of the stack has the lowest address in the stack that grows downward.

The *program counter (PC)* is 16 bits long to address up to 64K of memory. It usually addresses the next instruction to be executed.

4–3 MEMORY ADDRESSING

When addressing a memory location, the 8085 uses either register indirect or direct memory addressing. With register indirect addressing, the H and L registers perform the function of the memory address register or data counter; that is, the H,L pair holds the address of data. With this mode, data transfer may occur between the addressed memory location and any one of the registers A, B, C, D, E, H, or L. This is shown in Figure 4–2.

Also, some instructions, such as LDAX B, LDAX D, STAX B, and STAX D, use registers B and C or D and E to hold the address of data. These instructions transfer data between the accumulator and the memory location addressed by registers B and C or D and E using the register indirect mode.

There are also a few instructions, such as the STA ppqq, that use the direct memory addressing mode to move data between the accumulator and the memory. These instructions use 3 bytes, with the first byte as the OP code followed by 2 bytes of address. The meaning of these instructions is demonstrated in Figure 4–3.

As mentioned before, the stack is basically a part of the RAM. Therefore, PUSH and POP instructions are memory reference instructions.

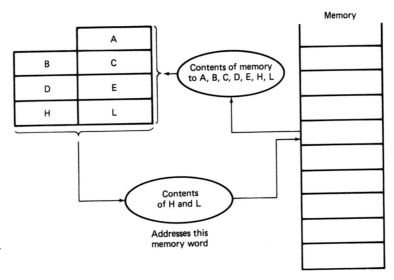

Figure 4–2 8085 register indirect memory addressing (From *8080A/ 8085 Assembly Language Programming* by Leventhal. Copyright © 1978 McGraw-Hill, Inc.)

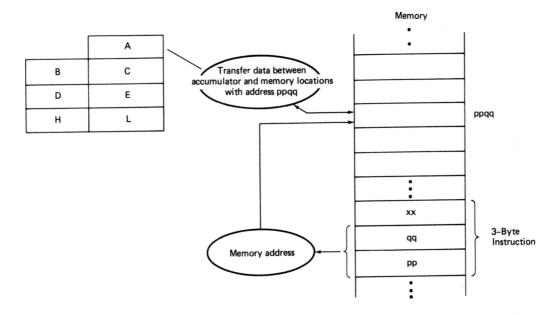

Figure 4–3 8085 direct memory addressing (From *8080A/8085 Assembly Language Programming* by Leventhal. Copyright © 1978 McGraw-Hill, Inc.)

All 8085 JUMP instructions use direct or absolute addressing and are 3 bytes long, with the first byte as the OP code followed by 2 bytes of address. This address specifies the memory location to which the program would branch.

A JUMP instruction interprets the address that it would branch to in the following ways:

1. *Direct* — The JUMP instructions use direct addressing and contain 3 bytes. The first byte is the OP code, followed by 2 bytes of the 16-bit address where it would branch to unconditionally or based on a condition if satisfied. For example, JMP 2020 unconditionally branches to location 2020. On the other hand, JZ504FH branches to 504_{16} if the Z-flag is one.

2. *Implied or Inherent* — The JUMP instructions using this addressing mode are 1 byte long. A 16-bit register pair contains the address of the next instruction to be executed. For example, the instruction PCHL unconditionally branches to a location addressed by the H,L pair.

4–4   8085 ADDRESSING MODES

The 8085 has five addressing modes:

Direct   Instructions using this mode specify the effective address as part of the instruction. Instructions using this mode contain 3 bytes, with the first byte as the OP code followed by 2 bytes of address of data (the low-order byte of the address in byte 2, the high-order byte of the address in byte 3). As an example, consider LDA 2035H. This instruction loads the accumulator with the contents of memory location 2035_{16}. This mode is also called the *absolute* mode.

Register   This mode specifies the register or register pair that contains data. For example, MOV B, C moves the contents of register C to register B.

Register Indirect   This mode contains a register pair that stores the address of data (the high-order byte of the address in the first register of the pair, the low-order byte in the second). As an example, LDAX B loads the accumulator with the contents of a memory location addressed by the B,C register pair.

Implied or Inherent   The instructions using this mode have no operands. Examples include STC (set the carry flag).

Immediate   For an 8-bit data, this mode uses 2 bytes, with the first byte as the OP code followed by 1 byte of data. On the other hand, for 16-bit data, this instruction contains 3 bytes, with the first byte as the OP code fol-

lowed by 2 bytes of data. For example, MVI B, 05 loads register B with 5, while LXI H, 7A21H loads register H with $7A_{16}$ and register L with 21_{16}.

4–5   8085 INSTRUCTION SET

As mentioned before, the 8085 uses 16-bit addresses. Since the 8085 is byte-addressable machine, it follows that it can directly address 65,536 (2^{16}) distinct memory locations. The addressing structure of the 8085 processor is shown in Figure 4–4.

From this figure, we notice that two consecutive memory locations may be used to represent a 16-bit data item. However, according to the Intel convention, the high-order byte of a 16-bit quantity is always assigned to the high memory address.

The 8085 instructions are 1 to 3 bytes long. These formats are shown in Figure 4–5.

Table 4–1 lists the 8085 instructions in alphabetical order. The object codes and instruction cycles are also included. When two instruction cycles are shown, the first is for "condition not met" whereas the second is for

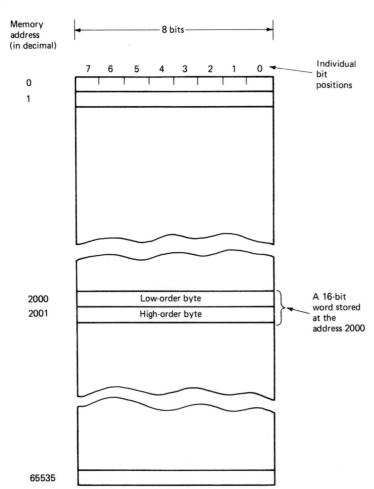

Figure 4–4   8085 addressing structure

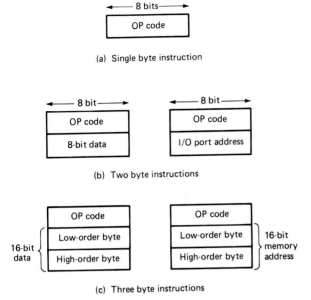

(a) Single byte instruction

(b) Two byte instructions

16-bit data

16-bit memory address

(c) Three byte instructions

Figure 4–5 8085 instruction formats

"condition met." Tables 4–2 and 4–3 provide the 8085 instructions in OP-code sequence and those affecting the status flags. Note that not all 8085 instructions affect the status flags.

The 8085 instruction set contains 74 basic instructions, and they support conventional addressing modes such as the immediate, register, absolute, and register indirect addressing modes. In describing the 8085 instruction set, we will use the symbols in Figure 4–6.

The 8085 MOVE instructions transfer 8-bit data from one register to another, register to memory, and vice versa. A complete summary of these instructions is presented in Figure 4–7.

The 8085 instruction set also accomplishes the 8-bit and 16-bit data transfers using the load and store instructions. These instructions are summarized in Figure 4–8.

From Figure 4–8, we notice that we adopt the following convention when we specify a register pair in the instruction.

TABLE 4–1
Summary of 8085 Instruction Set

Instruction	OP Code	Bytes	Cycles	Operations Performed
ACI DATA	CE	2	7	$[A] \leftarrow [A]$ + second instruction byte + [Cy]
ADC A	8F	1	4	$[A] \leftarrow [A] + [A] + [Cy]$
ADC B	88	1	4	$[A] \leftarrow [A] + [B] + [Cy]$
ADC C	89	1	4	$[A] \leftarrow [A] + [C] + [Cy]$
ADC D	8A	1	4	$[A] \leftarrow [A] + [D] + [Cy]$
ADC E	8B	1	4	$[A] \leftarrow [A] + [E] + [Cy]$
ADC H	8C	1	4	$[A] \leftarrow [A] + [H] + [Cy]$
ADC L	8D	1	4	$[A] \leftarrow [A] + [L] + [Cy]$
ADC M	8E	1	7	$[A] \leftarrow [A] + [[H\ L]] + [Cy]$
ADD A	87	1	4	$[A] \leftarrow [A] + [A]$
ADD B	80	1	4	$[A] \leftarrow [A] + [B]$
ADD C	81	1	4	$[A] \leftarrow [A] + [C]$
ADD D	82	1	4	$[A] \leftarrow [A] + [D]$
ADD E	83	1	4	$[A] \leftarrow [A] + [E]$
ADD H	84	1	4	$[A] \leftarrow [A] + [H]$
ADD L	85	1	4	$[A] \leftarrow [A] + [L]$
ADD M	86	1	7	$[A] \leftarrow [A] + [[H\ L]]$
ADI DATA	C6	2	7	$[A] \leftarrow [A]$ + second instruction byte
ANA A	A7	1	4	$[A] \leftarrow [A] \wedge [A]$
ANA B	A0	1	4	$[A] \leftarrow [A] \wedge [B]$
ANA C	A1	1	4	$[A] \leftarrow [A] \wedge [C]$
ANA D	A2	1	4	$[A] \leftarrow [A] \wedge [D]$
ANA E	A3	1	4	$[A] \leftarrow [A] \wedge [E]$
ANA H	A4	1	4	$[A] \leftarrow [A] \wedge [H]$
ANA L	A5	1	4	$[A] \leftarrow [A] \wedge [L]$
ANA M	A6	1	4	$[A] \leftarrow [A] \wedge [[H\ L]]$
ANI DATA	E6	2	7	$[A] \leftarrow [A] \wedge$ second instruction byte
CALL ppqq	CD	3	18	Call A subroutine addressed by ppqq
CC ppqq	DC	3	9/18	Call a subroutine addressed by ppqq if Cy = 1

All mnemonics copyright Intel Corporation 1976.

(continued)

TABLE 4–1
Summary of 8085 Instruction Set (cont.)

Instruction	OP Code	Bytes	Cycles	Operations Performed
CM ppqq	FC	3	9/18	Call a subroutine addressed by ppqq if S = 1
CMA	2F	1	4	[A] ← 1's complement of [A]
CMC	3F	1	4	[Cy] ← 1's complement of [Cy]
CMP A	BF	1	4	[A] − [A]
CMP B	B8	1	4	[A] − [B]
CMP C	B9	1	4	[A] − [C]
CMP D	BA	1	4	[A] − [D]
CMP E	BB	1	4	[A] − [E]
CMP H	BC	1	4	[A] − [H]
CMP L	BD	1	4	[A] − [L]
CMP M	BE	1	7	[A] − [[H L]]
CNC ppqq	D4	3	9/18	Call a subroutine addressed by ppqq if Cy = 0
CNZ ppqq	C4	3	9/18	Call a subroutine addressed by ppqq if Z = 0
CP ppqq	F4	3	9/18	Call a subroutine addressed by ppqq if S = 0
CPE ppqq	EC	3	9/18	Call a subroutine addressed by ppqq if P = 1
CPI DATA	FE	2	7	[A] − second instruction byte
CPO ppqq	E4	3	9/18	Call a subroutine addressed by ppqq if P = 0
CZ ppqq	CC	3	9/18	Call a subroutine addressed by ppqq if Z = 1
DAA	27	1	4	Decimal adjust accumulator
DAD B	09	1	10	[HL] ← [HL] + [BC]
DAD D	19	1	10	[HL] ← [HL] + [DE]
DAD H	29	1	10	[HL] ← [HL] + [HL]
DAD SP	39	1	10	[HL] ← [HL] + [SP]
DCR A	3D	1	4	[A] ← [A] − 1
DCR B	05	1	4	[B] ← [B] − 1
DCR C	0D	1	4	[C] ← [C] − 1
DCR D	15	1	4	[D] ← [D] − 1
DCR E	1D	1	4	[E] ← [E] − 1
DCR H	25	1	4	[H] ← [H] − 1
DCR L	2D	1	4	[L] ← [L] − 1
DCR M	35	1	4	[[HL]] ← [[HL]] − 1
DCX B	0B	1	6	[BC] ← [BC] − 1
DCX D	1B	1	6	[DE] ← [DE] − 1
DCX H	2B	1	6	[HL] ← [HL] − 1
DCX SP	3B	1	6	[SP] ← [SP] − 1
DI	F3	1	4	Disable interrupts
EI	FB	1	4	Enable interrupts
HLT	76	1	5	Halt
IN PORT	DB	2	10	[A] ← [specified port]
INR A	3C	1	4	[A] ← [A] + 1
INR B	04	1	4	[B] ← [B] + 1
INR C	0C	1	4	[C] ← [C] + 1
INR D	14	1	4	[D] ← [D] + 1
INR E	1C	1	4	[E] ← [E] + 1
INR H	24	1	4	[H] ← [H] + 1
INR L	2C	1	4	[L] ← [L] + 1
INR M	34	1	4	[[HL]] ← [[HL]] + 1
INX B	03	1	6	[BC] ← [BC] + 1
INX D	13	1	6	[DE] ← [DE] + 1
INX H	23	1	6	[HL] ← [HL] + 1
INX SP	33	1	6	[SP] ← [SP] + 1
JC ppqq	DA	3	7/10	Jump to ppqq if Cy = 1
JM ppqq	FA	3	7/10	Jump to ppqq if S = 1
JMP ppqq	C3	3	10	Jump to ppqq
JNC ppqq	D2	3	7/10	Jump to ppqq if Cy = 0
JNZ ppqq	C2	3	7/10	Jump to ppqq if Z = 0
JP ppqq	F2	3	7/10	Jump to ppqq if S = 0
JPE ppqq	EA	3	7/10	Jump to ppqq if P = 1
JPO ppqq	E2	3	7/10	Jump to ppqq if P = 0
JZ ppqq	CA	3	7/10	Jump to ppqq if Z = 1

All mnemonics copyright Intel Corporation 1976.

TABLE 4-1
Summary of 8085 Instruction Set (cont.)

Instruction	OP Code	Bytes	Cycles	Operations Performed
LDA ppqq	3A	3	13	[A] ← [ppqq]
LDAX B	0A	1	7	[A] ← [[BC]]
LDAX D	1A	1	7	[A] ← [[DE]]
LHLD ppqq	2A	3	16	[L] ← [ppqq], [H] ← [ppqq + 1]
LXI B	01	3	10	[BC] ← second and third instruction bytes
LXI D	11	3	10	[DE] ← second and third instruction bytes
LXI H	21	3	10	[HL] ← second and third instruction bytes
LXI SP	31	3	10	[SP] ← second and third instruction bytes
MOV A,A	7F	1	4	[A] ← [A]
MOV A,B	78	1	4	[A] ← [B]
MOV A,C	79	1	4	[A] ← [C]
MOV A,D	7A	1	4	[A] ← [D]
MOV A,E	7B	1	4	[A] ← [E]
MOV A,H	7C	1	4	[A] ← [H]
MOV A,L	7D	1	4	[A] ← [L]
MOV A,M	7E	1	7	[A] ← [[HL]]
MOV B,A	47	1	4	[B] ← [A]
MOV B,B	40	1	4	[B] ← [B]
MOV B,C	41	1	4	[B] ← [C]
MOV B,D	42	1	4	[B] ← [D]
MOV B,E	43	1	4	[B] ← [E]
MOV B,H	44	1	4	[B] ← [H]
MOV B,L	45	1	4	[B] ← [L]
MOV B,M	46	1	7	[B] ← [[HL]]
MOV C,A	4F	1	4	[C] ← [A]
MOV C,B	48	1	4	[C] ← [B]
MOV C,C	49	1	4	[C] ← [C]
MOV C,D	4A	1	4	[C] ← [D]
MOV C,E	4B	1	4	[C] ← [E]
MOV C,H	4C	1	4	[C] ← [H]
MOV C,L	4D	1	4	[C] ← [L]
MOV C,M	4E	1	7	[C] ← [[HL]]
MOV D,A	57	1	4	[D] ← [A]
MOV D,B	50	1	4	[D] ← [B]
MOV D,C	51	1	4	[D] ← [C]
MOV D,D	52	1	4	[D] ← [D]
MOV D,E	53	1	4	[D] ← [E]
MOV D,H	54	1	4	[D] ← [H]
MOV D,L	55	1	4	[D] ← [L]
MOV D,M	56	1	7	[D] ← [[HL]]
MOV E,A	5F	1	4	[E] ← [A]
MOV E,B	58	1	5	[E] ← [B]
MOV E,C	59	1	4	[E] ← [C]
MOV E,D	5A	1	4	[E] ← [D]
MOV E,E	5B	1	4	[E] ← [E]
MOV E,H	5C	1	4	[E] ← [H]
MOV E,L	5D	1	4	[E] ← [L]
MOV E,M	5E	1	7	[E] ← [[HL]]
MOV H,A	67	1	4	[H] ← [A]
MOV H,B	60	1	4	[H] ← [B]
MOV H,C	61	1	4	[H] ← [C]
MOV H,D	62	1	4	[H] ← [D]
MOV H,E	63	1	4	[H] ← [E]
MOV H,H	64	1	4	[H] ← [H]
MOV H,L	65	1	4	[H] ← [L]
MOV H,M	66	1	7	[H] ← [[HL]]
MOV L,A	6F	1	4	[L] ← [A]
MOV L,B	68	1	4	[L] ← [B]
MOV L,C	69	1	4	[L] ← [C]
MOV L,D	6A	1	4	[L] ← [D]
MOV L,E	6B	1	4	[L] ← [E]

All mnemonics copyright Intel Corporation 1976.

(continued)

TABLE 4-1
Summary of 8085 Instruction Set (cont.)

Instruction	OP Code	Bytes	Cycles	Operations Performed
MOV L,H	6C	1	4	$[L] \leftarrow [H]$
MOV L,L	6D	1	4	$[L] \leftarrow [L]$
MOV L,M	6E	1	7	$[L] \leftarrow [[HL]]$
MOV M,A	77	1	7	$[[HL]] \leftarrow [A]$
MOV M,B	70	1	7	$[[HL]] \leftarrow [B]$
MOV M,C	71	1	7	$[[HL]] \leftarrow [C]$
MOV M,D	72	1	7	$[[HL]] \leftarrow [D]$
MOV M,E	73	1	7	$[[HL]] \leftarrow [E]$
MOV M,H	74	1	7	$[[HL]] \leftarrow [H]$
MOV M,L	75	1	7	$[[HL]] \leftarrow [L]$
MVI A, DATA	3E	2	7	$[A] \leftarrow$ second instruction byte
MVI B, DATA	06	2	7	$[B] \leftarrow$ second instruction byte
MVI C, DATA	0E	2	7	$[C] \leftarrow$ second instruction byte
MVI D, DATA	16	2	7	$[D] \leftarrow$ second instruction byte
MVI E, DATA	1E	2	7	$[E] \leftarrow$ second instruction byte
MVI H, DATA	26	2	7	$[H] \leftarrow$ second instruction byte
MVI L, DATA	2E	2	7	$[L] \leftarrow$ second instruction byte
MVI M, DATA	36	2	10	$[[HL]] \leftarrow$ second instruction byte
NOP	00	1	4	No operation
ORA A	B7	1	4	$[A] \leftarrow [A] \vee [A]$
ORA B	B0	1	4	$[A] \leftarrow [A] \vee [B]$
ORA C	B1	1	4	$[A] \leftarrow [A] \vee [C]$
ORA D	B2	1	4	$[A] \leftarrow [A] \vee [D]$
ORA E	B3	1	4	$[A] \leftarrow [A] \vee [E]$
ORA H	B4	1	4	$[A] \leftarrow [A] \vee [H]$
ORA L	B5	1	4	$[A] \leftarrow [A] \vee [L]$
ORA M	B6	1	7	$[A] \leftarrow [A] \vee [[HL]]$
ORI DATA	F6	2	7	$[A] \leftarrow [A] \vee$ second instruction byte
OUT PORT	D3	2	10	[specified port] $\leftarrow [A]$
PCHL	E9	1	6	$[PCH]^a \leftarrow [H], [PCL]^a \leftarrow [L]$
POP B	C1	1	10	$[C] \leftarrow [[SP]], [SP] \leftarrow [SP] + 2$ $[B] \leftarrow [[SP] + 1]$
POP D	D1	1	10	$[E] \leftarrow [[SP]], [SP] \leftarrow [SP] + 2$ $[D] \leftarrow [[SP] + 1]$
POP H	E1	1	10	$[L] \leftarrow [[SP]], [SP] \leftarrow [SP] + 2$ $[H] \leftarrow [[SP] + 1]$
POP PSW	F1	1	10	$[A] \leftarrow [[SP] + 1], [PSW] \leftarrow [[SP]],$ $[SP] \leftarrow [SP] + 2$
PUSH B	C5	1	12	$[[SP] - 1] \leftarrow [B], [SP] \leftarrow [SP] - 2$ $[[SP] - 2] \leftarrow [C]$
PUSH D	D5	1	12	$[[SP] - 1] \leftarrow [D], [[SP] - 2] \leftarrow [E]$ $[SP] \leftarrow [SP] - 2$
PUSH H	E5	1	12	$[[SP] - 1] \leftarrow [H], [SP] \leftarrow [SP] - 2$ $[[SP] - 2] \leftarrow [L]$
PUSH PSW	F5	1	12	$[[SP] - 1] \leftarrow [A], [SP] \leftarrow [SP] - 2$ $[[SP] - 2] \leftarrow [PSW]$
RAL	17	1	4	A ← (rotate left through carry) ← Cy
RAR	1F	1	4	A → (rotate right through carry) → Cy
RC	D8	1	6/12	Return if carry. $[PC] \leftarrow [[SP]]$
RET	C9	1	10	$[PCL]^a \leftarrow [[SP]], [SP] \leftarrow [SP] + 2$ $[PCH]^a \leftarrow [[SP] + 1]$
RIM	20	1	4	Read interrupt mask.
RLC	07	1	4	Cy ← (rotate left) ← A
RM	F8	1	6/12	Return if minus. $[PC] \leftarrow [[SP]]$

All mnemonics copyright Intel Corporation 1976.
^{a} PCL–Program Counter Low byte; PCH–Program Counter High byte.

TABLE 4-1
Summary of 8085 Instruction Set (cont.)

Instruction	OP Code	Bytes	Cycles	Operations Performed
RNC	D0	1	6/12	Return if no carry. $[PC] \leftarrow [[SP]]$
RNZ	C0	1	6/12	Return if result not zero. $[PC] \leftarrow [[SP]]$
RP	F0	1	6/12	Return if positive. $[PC] \leftarrow [[SP]], [SP] \leftarrow [SP] + 2$
RPE	E8	1	6/12	Return if parity even. $[PC] \leftarrow [[SP]], [SP] \leftarrow [SP] + 2$
RPO	E0	1	6/12	Return if parity odd. $[PC] \leftarrow [[SP]], [SP] \leftarrow [SP] + 2$
RRC	0F	1	4	A → [rotate right through] → Cy
RST0	C7	1	12	Restart
RST1	CF	1	12	Restart
RST2	D7	1	12	Restart
RST3	DF	1	12	Restart
RST4	E7	1	12	Restart
RST5	EF	1	12	Restart
RST6	F7	1	12	Restart
RST7	FF	1	12	Restart
RZ	C8	1	6/12	Return if zero. $[PC] \leftarrow [[SP]]$
SBB A	9F	1	4	$[A] \leftarrow [A] - [A] - [Cy]$
SBB B	98	1	4	$[A] \leftarrow [A] - [B] - [Cy]$
SBB C	99	1	4	$[A] \leftarrow [A] - [C] - [Cy]$
SBB D	9A	1	4	$[A] \leftarrow [A] - [D] - [Cy]$
SBB E	9B	1	4	$[A] \leftarrow [A] - [E] - [Cy]$
SBB H	9C	1	4	$[A] \leftarrow [A] - [H] - [Cy]$
SBB L	9D	1	4	$[A] \leftarrow [A] - [L] - [Cy]$
SBB M	9E	1	7	$[A] \leftarrow [A] - [[HL]] - [Cy]$
SBI DATA	DE	2	7	$[A] \leftarrow [A] -$ second instruction byte $- [Cy]$
SHLD ppqq	22	3	16	$[ppqq] \leftarrow [L], [ppqq + 1] \leftarrow [H]$
SIM	30	1	4	Set interrupt mask
SPHL	F9	1	6	$[SP] \leftarrow [HL]$
STA ppqq	32	3	13	$[ppqq] \leftarrow [A]$
STAX B	02	1	7	$[[BC]] \leftarrow [A]$
STAX D	12	1	7	$[[DE]] \leftarrow [A]$
STC	37	1	4	$[Cy] \leftarrow 1$
SUB A	97	1	4	$[A] \leftarrow [A] - [A]$
SUB B	90	1	4	$[A] \leftarrow [A] - [B]$
SUB C	91	1	4	$[A] \leftarrow [A] - [C]$
SUB D	92	1	4	$[A] \leftarrow [A] - [D]$
SUB E	93	1	4	$[A] \leftarrow [A] - [E]$
SUB H	94	1	4	$[A] \leftarrow [A] - [H]$
SUB L	95	1	4	$[A] \leftarrow [A] - [L]$
SUB M	96	1	7	$[A] \leftarrow [A] - [[HL]]$
SUI DATA	D6	2	7	$[A] \leftarrow [A] -$ second instruction byte
XCHG	EB	1	4	$[D] \leftrightarrow [H], [E] \leftrightarrow [L]$
XRA A	AF	1	4	$[A] \leftarrow [A] \veebar [A]$
XRA B	A8	1	4	$[A] \leftarrow [A] \veebar [B]$
XRA C	A9	1	4	$[A] \leftarrow [A] \veebar [C]$
XRA D	AA	1	4	$[A] \leftarrow [A] \veebar [D]$
XRA E	AB	1	4	$[A] \leftarrow [A] \veebar [E]$
XRA H	AC	1	4	$[A] \leftarrow [A] \veebar [H]$
XRA L	AD	1	4	$[A] \leftarrow [A] \veebar [L]$
XRA M	AE	1	7	$[A] \leftarrow [A] \veebar [[HL]]$
XRI DATA	EE	2	7	$[A] \leftarrow [A] \veebar$ second instruction byte
XTHL	E3	1	16	$[[SP]] \leftrightarrow [L], [[SP] + 1] \leftrightarrow [H]$

[a]PCL—program counter low byte; PCH—program counter high byte.

$\veebar$ or $\oplus$ may be used to represent Exclusive-OR operation.

All mnemonics copyright Intel Corporation 1976.

TABLE 4–2
8085 Instructions in OP-Code Sequence

OP Code	Mnemonic	OP Code	Mnemonic	OP Code	Mnemonic	OP Code	Mnemonic	OP Code	Mnemonic	OP Code	Mnemonic
00	NOP	2B	DCX H	56	MOV D,M	81	ADD C	AC	XRA H	D7	RST 2
01	LXI B,D16	2C	INR L	57	MOV D,A	82	ADD D	AD	XRA L	D8	RC
02	STAX B	2D	DCR L	58	MOV E,B	83	ADD E	AE	XRA M	D9	—
03	INX B	2E	MVI L,D8	59	MOV E,C	84	ADD H	AF	XRA A	DA	JC Adr
04	INR B	2F	CMA	5A	MOV E,D	85	ADD L	B0	ORA B	DB	IN D8
05	DCR B	30	SIM	5B	MOV E,E	86	ADD M	B1	ORA C	DC	CC Adr
06	MVI B,D8	31	LXI SP,D16	5C	MOV E,H	87	ADD A	B2	ORA D	DD	—
07	RLC	32	STA Adr	5D	MOV E,L	88	ADC B	B3	ORA E	DE	SBI D8
08	—	33	INX SP	5E	MOV E,M	89	ADC C	B4	ORA H	DF	RST 3
09	DAD B	34	INR M	5F	MOV E,A	8A	ADC D	B5	ORA L	E0	RPO
0A	LDAX B	35	DCR M	60	MOV H,B	8B	ADC E	B6	ORA M	E1	POP H
0B	DCX B	36	MVI M,D8	61	MOV H,C	8C	ADC H	B7	ORA A	E2	JPO Adr
0C	INR C	37	STC	62	MOV H,D	8D	ADC L	B8	CMP B	E3	XTHL
0D	DCR C	38	—	63	MOV H,E	8E	ADC M	B9	CMP C	E4	CPO Adr
0E	MVI C,D8	39	DAD SP	64	MOV H,H	8F	ADC A	BA	CMP D	E5	PUSH H
0F	RRC	3A	LDA Adr	65	MOV H,L	90	SUB B	BB	CMP E	E6	ANI D8
10	—	3B	DCX SP	66	MOV H,M	91	SUB C	BC	CMP H	E7	RST 4
11	LXI D,D16	3C	INR A	67	MOV H,A	92	SUB D	BD	CMP L	E8	RPE
12	STAX D	3D	DCR A	68	MOV L,B	93	SUB E	BE	CMP M	E9	PCHL
13	INX D	3E	MVI A,D8	69	MOV L,C	94	SUB H	BF	CMP A	EA	JPE Adr
14	INR D	3F	CMC	6A	MOV L,D	95	SUB L	C0	RNZ	EB	XCHG
15	DCR D	40	MOV B,B	6B	MOV L,E	96	SUB M	C1	POP B	EC	CPE Adr
16	MVI D,D8	41	MOV B,C	6C	MOV L,H	97	SUB A	C2	JNZ Adr	ED	—
17	RAL	42	MOV B,D	6D	MOV L,L	98	SBB B	C3	JMP Adr	EE	XRI D8
18	—	43	MOV B,E	6E	MOV L,M	99	SBB C	C4	CNZ Adr	EF	RST 5
19	DAD D	44	MOV B,H	6F	MOV L,A	9A	SBB D	C5	PUSH B	F0	RP
1A	LDAX D	45	MOV B,L	70	MOV M,B	9B	SBB E	C6	ADI D8	F1	POP PSW
1B	DCX D	46	MOV B,M	71	MOV M,C	9C	SBB H	C7	RST 0	F2	JP Adr
1C	INR E	47	MOV B,A	72	MOV M,D	9D	SBB L	C8	RZ	F3	DI
1D	DCR E	48	MOV C,B	73	MOV M,E	9E	SBB M	C9	RET	F4	CP Adr
1E	MVI E,D8	49	MOV C,C	74	MOV M,H	9F	SBB A	CA	JZ Adr	F5	PUSH PSW
1F	RAR	4A	MOV C,D	75	MOV M,L	A0	ANA B	CB	—	F6	ORI D8
20	RIM	4B	MOV C,E	76	HLT	A1	ANA C	CC	CZ Adr	F7	RST 6
21	LXI H,D16	4C	MOV C,H	77	MOV M,A	A2	ANA D	CD	CALL Adr	F8	RM
22	SHLD Adr	4D	MOV C,L	78	MOV A,B	A3	ANA E	CE	ACI D8	F9	SPHL
23	INX H	4E	MOV C,M	79	MOV A,C	A4	ANA H	CF	RST 1	FA	JM Adr
24	INR H	4F	MOV C,A	7A	MOV A,D	A5	ANA L	D0	RNC	FB	EI
25	DCR H	50	MOV D,B	7B	MOV A,E	A6	ANA M	D1	POP D	FC	CM Adr
26	MVI H,D8	51	MOV D,C	7C	MOV A,H	A7	ANA A	D2	JNC Adr	FD	—
27	DAA	52	MOV D,D	7D	MOV A,L	A8	XRA B	D3	OUT D8	FE	CPI D8
28	—	53	MOV D,E	7E	MOV A,M	A9	XRA C	D4	CNC Adr	FF	RST 7
29	DAD H	54	MOV D,H	7F	MOV A,A	AA	XRA D	D5	PUSH D		
2A	LHLD Adr	55	MOV D,L	80	ADD B	AB	XRA E	D6	SUI D8		

Courtesy of Intel Corporation.

D8—constant, or logical/arithmetic expression that evaluates to an 8-bit data quantity; D16—constant, or logical/arithmetic expression that evaluates to a 16-bit data quantity; Adr—16-bit address.

All mnemonics copyright Intel Corporation 1976.

Symbol	Register Pair Used
B	B,C
D	D,E
H	H,L

Also, observe that in Figure 4–8 the 8085 processor does not provide LDAX H instruction. This is because the same result can be obtained by using the MOV A, M instruction. The 8085 includes a 1-byte exchange instruction called XCHG. The XCHG exchanges the 16-bit contents of D,E with H,L as follows:

$$[D] \leftrightarrow [H]$$
$$[E] \leftrightarrow [L]$$

The arithmetic instructions provided by the 8085 processor allow one to add (or subtract) two 8-bit data with or without carry (or borrow). The subtraction operation is realized by adding the 2's complement of the subtrahend to the minuend. During the subtraction operation, the carry flag will be treated as the borrow flag. In addition, the 8085 instruction set includes instructions to perform typical operations such as 16-bit addition, increment, and decrement. These instructions are summarized in Figure 4–9. For some instructions, such as ADD M in Figure 4–9, examples and comments are not included. This is due to limited space in the figure.

As far as logical operations are concerned, the 8085 includes some instructions to perform traditional Boolean operations such as AND, OR, and EXCLUSIVE-OR. In addition, instructions are available to complement the accumulator and to set the carry flag. The 8085 COMPARE instructions subtract the specified destination from the contents of the accumulator and affect the status flags according to the result. However, in this case, the result of the subtraction is not provided in the accumulator. All 8085 logical instructions are specified in Figure 4–10. For some instructions in this figure, examples and comments are not provided. This is due to limited space in the figure.

The AND instruction can be used to perform a masking operation. If the bit value in a particular bit position is desired in a word, the word can be logically ANDed

TABLE 4-3
8085 Instructions Affecting the Status Flags

Instructions[a]	Status Flags[b]				
	Cy	Ac	Z	S	P
ACI DATA	√	√	√	√	√
ADC reg	√	√	√	√	√
ADC M	√	√	√	√	√
ADD reg	√	√	√	√	√
ADD M	√	√	√	√	√
ADI DATA	√	√	√	√	√
ANA reg	0	1	√	√	√
ANA M	0	1	√	√	√
ANI DATA	0	1	√	√	√
CMC	√				
CMP reg	√	√	√	√	√
CMP M	√	√	√	√	√
CPI DATA	√	√	√	√	√
DAA	√	√	√	√	√
DAD rp	√				
DCR reg		√	√	√	√
DCR M		√	√	√	√
INR reg		√	√	√	√
INR M		√	√	√	√
ORA reg	0	0	√	√	√
ORA M	0	0	√	√	√
ORI DATA	0	0	√	√	√
RAL	√				
RAR	√				
RLC	√				
RRC	√				
SBB reg	√	√	√	√	√
SBB M	√	√	√	√	√
SBI DATA	√	√	√	√	√
STC	√				
SUB reg	√	√	√	√	√
SUB M	√	√	√	√	√
SUI DATA	√	√	√	√	√
XRA reg	0	0	√	√	√
XRA M	0	0	√	√	√
XRI DATA	0	0	√	√	√

[a] reg—8-bit register; M—memory; rp—16-bit register pair.

[b] Note that instructions which are not shown in the table do not affect the flags. √ indicates that the particular flag is affected; 0 or 1 indicates that these flags are always 0 or 1 after the corresponding instructions are executed.

All mnemonics copyright Intel Corporation 1976.

Symbol	Interpretation
r_1, r_2	8-bit register
rp	Register pair
data8	8-bit data
data16	16-bit data
M	Memory location indirectly addressed through the register pair H,L
addr16	16-bit memory address

Figure 4-6 Symbols to be used in 8085 instruction set

with appropriate masking data to accomplish this. For example, the bit value at bit 3 of the word 1011 X011 can be determined as follows:

$$\begin{array}{r}1011 \quad X011 \leftarrow \text{Word} \\ \text{AND} \quad 0000 \quad 1000 \leftarrow \text{Masking data} \\ \hline 0000 \quad X000 \leftarrow \text{Result} \end{array}$$

If the bit value X at bit 3 is 1, then the result is nonzero (Z = 0); otherwise, the result is zero (Z = 1). The Z flag can be tested using JZ (jump if Z = 1) or JNZ (jump if Z = 0) to determine whether X = 0 or 1.

The AND instruction can also be used to determine whether a binary number is odd or even by checking the least significant bit (LSB) of the number (LSB = 0 for even and LSB = 1 for odd). The XRA instruction can be used to find the 1's complement of a binary number by EXCLUSIVE-ORing the number with all 1's as follows:

$$\begin{array}{r}1010 \quad 1001 \leftarrow \text{Original number} \\ \text{XOR} \quad 1111 \quad 1111 \\ \hline 0101 \quad 0110 \leftarrow \text{1's complement of} \\ \text{original number} \end{array}$$

The 8085 instruction set includes instructions to rotate the contents of the A register to the left or right without or through the carry flag. They are summarized in Figure 4-11.

In the 8085 processor, only absolute mode branch instructions are available. For example, the unconditional branch instruction is of the form

JMP   addr16

There is also a 1-byte implied unconditional jump instruction, namely, PCHL. The PCHL loads [H] into the PC high byte and [L] into the PC low byte. That is, the PCHL performs an unconditional jump to a location addressed by the contents of H and L.

The general format of an 8085 conditional branch instruction is as follows:

J ⟨condition code⟩   addr16

where the condition code may represent one of the following conditions:

Conditional Jump	Condition	Comment
JZ	Z = 1	Z flag is set (result equal to zero)
JNZ	Z = 0	Z flag is reset (result not equal to zero)
JC	Cy = 1	Cy flag is set
JNC	Cy = 0	Cy flag is reset
JPO	P = 0	Parity is odd
JPE	P = 1	Parity is even

Instruction	Symbolic Description	Addressing Mode		Illustration	
		Source	Destination	Example	Comments
MOV r_1, r_2	$(r_1) \leftarrow (r_2)$	Register	Register	MOV A, B	Copy the contents of the register B into the register A
MOV r, M	$(r) \leftarrow M((HL))$	Register Indirect	Register	MOV A, M	Copy the contents of the memory location whose address is specified in the register pair H,L into the A register
MVI r, data8	$(r) \leftarrow data8$	Immediate	Register	MVI A, 08	Initialize the A register with the value 08
MOV M, r	$M((HL)) \leftarrow (r)$	Register	Register Indirect	MOV M, B	Copy the contents of the B register into the memory location addressed by H,L pair
MVI M, data8	$M((HL)) \leftarrow data8$	Immediate	Register Indirect	MVI M, 07	Initialize the memory location whose address is specified in the register pair H,L with the value 07

Figure 4–7 8085 move instructions

Conditional Jump	Condition	Comment
JP	S = 0	S flag is reset (or the number is positive)
JM	S = 1	S flag is set (or the number is negative)

For example, the following instruction sequence causes a branch to the memory address 2000_{16} only if the contents of the A and B registers are equal:

       CMP   B
       JZ   2000H

In the 8085, the subroutine call instruction is of the form

       CALL   addr16

The instruction RET transfers the control to the caller, and it should be the last instruction of the subroutine. Both instructions use the PC and SP for subroutine linkage.

For example, consider the following:

	Main Program	Subroutine
	—	SUB—
	—	—
	—	—
	CALL SUB	—
START	—	—
	—	—
	—	RET

The CALL SUB instruction pushes or saves the current PC contents (START, which is the address of the next instruction) onto the stack and loads the PC with the starting address of the subroutine (SUB) specified with the CALL instruction. The RET instruction at the end of the subroutine pops or reads the address START (saved onto the stack by the CALL instruction) into the PC and transfers control to the right place in the main program.

There are a number of conditional CALL instructions. These include the following:

CC	addr	;	Call if Cy = 1
CNC	addr	;	Call if Cy = 0
CZ	addr	;	Call if Z = 1
CNZ	addr	;	Call if Z = 0
CM	addr	;	Call if S = 1
CP	addr	;	Call if S = 0
CPE	addr	;	Call if P = 1
CPO	addr	;	Call if P = 0

Also, there are a number of conditional RETURN instructions. These are as follows:

RC	;	Return if Cy = 1
RNC	;	Return if Cy = 0
RZ	;	Return if Z = 1
RNZ	;	Return if Z = 0
RPE	;	Return if P = 1
RPO	;	Return if P = 0
RM	;	Return if S = 1
RP	;	Return if S = 0

There are eight 1-byte call instructions (RST 0 to 7), which have predefined addresses. The format for each of these instructions is as follows:

| Instruction | Symbolic Description | Restriction | Addressing Mode | | Illustration | |
			Source	Destination	Example	Comments
LDA addr16	$(A) \leftarrow M(addr16)$	The destination is always the accumulator register	Absolute	Register	LDA 2000	Load the accumulator with the contents of the memory location whose address is 2000
LHLD addr16	$(L) \leftarrow M(addr16)$ $(H) \leftarrow M(addr16 +1)$	The destination is always the register pair H,L	Absolute	Register	LHLD 2000	Load the H and L registers with contents of the memory locations 2001 and 2000 respectively
LXI rp, data16	$(rp) \leftarrow data16$	rp may be HL, DE, BC or SP	Immediate	Register	LXI H, 2024	$H \leftarrow 20_{16}$ $L \leftarrow 24_{16}$
LDAX rp	$(A) \leftarrow M((rp))$	Destination is always the accumulator; also rp may be either B,C or D,E	Register Indirect	Register	LDAX B	Load the accumulator with the contents of the memory location whose address is specified with the register pair B,C
STA addr16	$M(addr16) \leftarrow (A)$	Source is always the accumulator register	Register	Absolute	STA 2001	Save the contents of the accumulator into the memory location whose address is 2001
SHLD addr16	$M(addr16) \leftarrow (L)$ $M(addr16+1) \leftarrow (H)$	The source is always the register pair H,L	Register	Absolute	SHLD 2000	$M(2000) \leftarrow (L)$ $M(2001) \leftarrow (H)$
STAX rp	$M((rp)) \leftarrow (A)$	The source is always the accumulator register and the register pair may be B,C or D,E	Register	Register Indirect	STAX D	Save the contents of the accumulator register into the memory location whose address is specified with the register pair D,E

Figure 4-8 8085 load and store instructions

11 XXX 111

where XXX is

000	for RST0	100	for RST4
001	for RST1	101	for RST5
010	for RST2	110	for RST6
011	for RST3	111	for RST7

RSTs are 1-byte call instructions used mainly with interrupts. Each RST has a predefined address. However,

Operation	Instruction	Interpretation	Addressing Mode	Illustration	
				Example	Comments
8-bit addition	ADD r	(A) ← (A) + (r)	Register	ADD B	(A) ← (A) + (B)
	ADI data8	(A) ← (A) + data8	Immediate	ADI 05	(A) ← (A) + 05
	ADD M	(A) ← (A) + M((HL))	Register Indirect	—	—
8-bit addition with a carry	ADC r	(A) ← (A) + (r) + Cy	Register	ADC C	(A) ← (A) + (C) + Cy
	ACI data8	(A) ← (A) + data8 + Cy	Immediate	ACI 07	(A) ← (A) + 07 + Cy
	ADC M	(A) ← (A) + M((HL)) + Cy	Register Indirect	—	—
8-bit subtraction	SUB r	(A) ← (A) − (r)	Register	SUB C	(A) ← (A) − (C)
	SUI data8	(A) ← (A) − data8	Immediate	SUI 03	(A) ← (A) − 03
	SUB M	(A) ← (A) − M((HL))	Register Indirect	—	—
8-bit subtraction with a borrow	SBB r	(A) ← (A) − (r) − Cy	Register	SBB D	(A) ← (A) − (D) − Cy
	SBI data8	(A) ← (A) − data8 − Cy	Immediate	SBI 04	(A) ← (A) − 04 − Cy
	SBB M	(A) ← (A) − M((HL)) − Cy	Register Indirect	—	—
16-bit addition	DAD rp	(HL) ← (HL) + (rp)	Register	DAD B	(HL) ← (HL) + (BC)
Decimal adjust	DAA	Convert the 8-bit number stored in the accumulator into BCD	Inherent	—	—
8-bit increment	INR r	(r) ← (r) + 1	Register	INR B	(B) ← (B) + 1
	INR M	M((HL)) ← M((HL)) +1	Register Indirect	—	—
*16-bit increment	INX rp	(rp) ← (rp) + 1	Register	INX D	(DE) ← (DE) + 1
8-bit decrement	DCR r	(r) ← (r) − 1	Register	DCR B	(B) ← (B) − 1
	DCR M	M((HL) ← M((HL)) − 1	Register Indirect	—	—
*16-bit decrement	DCX rp	(rp) ← (rp) − 1	Register	—	—

*rp = BC, DE, HL, or SP

Figure 4-9 8085 arithmetic instructions

RST0 and the hardware reset vector have the same address, 0000. Therefore, use of RST0 is not usually recommended. The RSTs cause the 8085 to push the PC onto the stack. The 8085 then loads the PC with a predefined address based on the particular RST being used.

A 3-bit code in the OP code for a particular RST determines the address to which the program would branch:

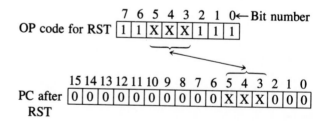

Operation	Instruction	Interpretation	Addressing Mode	Illustration	
				Example	*Comments*
Boolean AND	ANA r	$(A) \leftarrow (A) \wedge (r)$	Register	ANA B	$(A) \leftarrow (A) \wedge (B)$
	ANI data8	$(A) \leftarrow (A) \wedge$ data8	Immediate	ANI 0F	$(A) \leftarrow (A) \wedge 00001111$
	ANA M	$(A) \leftarrow (A) \wedge M((HL))$	Register Indirect	—	—
Boolean OR	ORA r	$(A) \leftarrow (A) \vee (r)$	Register	ORA C	$(A) \leftarrow (A) \vee (C)$
	ORI data8	$(A) \leftarrow (A) \vee$ data8	Immediate	ORI 08	$(A) \leftarrow (A) \vee 00001000$
	ORA M	$(A) \leftarrow (A) \vee M((HL))$	Register Indirect	—	—
Boolean EXCLUSIVE-OR	XRA r	$(A) \leftarrow (A) \oplus (r)$	Register	XRA A	$(A) \leftarrow (A) \oplus (A)$
	XRI data8	$(A) \leftarrow (A) \oplus$ data8	Immediate	XRI 03	$(A) \leftarrow (A) \oplus 00000011$
	XRA M	$(A) \leftarrow (A) \oplus M((HL))$	Register Indirect	—	—
Compare	CMP r	$(A) - (r)$ and affect flags	Register	CMP D	Compare (A) register with (D) register
	CPI data8	$(A) -$ data8 and affect flags	Immediate	CPI 05	Compare (A) with 05
	CMP M	$(A) - M((HL))$ and affect flags	Register Indirect	—	—
Complement	CMA	$(A) \leftarrow (A)'$	Inherent	—	—
Bit manipulation	STC	$Cy \leftarrow 1$ (set carry to 1)	Inherent	—	—
	CMC	$Cy \leftarrow Cy'$ (complement carry flag)	Inherent		

The symbols $\vee\!\!\!\!- $ or $\oplus$ may be used to represent Exclusive-OR operation.

Figure 4–10 8085 logical instructions

The vector addresses for the RSTs are listed in Table 4–4. Note that a limited number of locations are available for each RST instruction. This may not provide enough locations for writing a complete subroutine. Therefore, one may place an unconditional jump at the vector address to jump to an address in RAM where the actual subroutine is written.

The 8085 stack manipulation instructions allow one to save and retrieve the contents of the register pairs into and from the stack, respectively. For example, the following instruction saves the register pair B,C into the stack:

```
PUSH  B    ; (SP)  ← (SP)  − 1
           ; (M((SP))  ← (B)
           ; (SP)  ← (SP)  − 1
           ; M((SP))  ← (C)
```

Similarly, the instruction POP D retrieves the top two words of the stack and places them into the registers E and D in that order:

TABLE 4–4
RST0–RST7 Vector Addresses

Instruction	*OP Code (Hexadecimal)*	*Vector Address (Hexadecimal)*
RST0	C7	0000
RST1	CF	0008
RST2	D7	0010
RST3	DF	0018
RST4	E7	0020
RST5	EF	0028
RST6	F7	0030
RST7	FF	0038

```
POP  D    ; (E)  ← M((SP))
          ; (SP)  ← (SP)  + 1
          ; (D)  ← M((SP))
          ; (SP)  ← (SP)  + 1
```

Instruction	Interpretation	Illustration
RLC	Rotate left accumulator by one position without the carry flag Cy	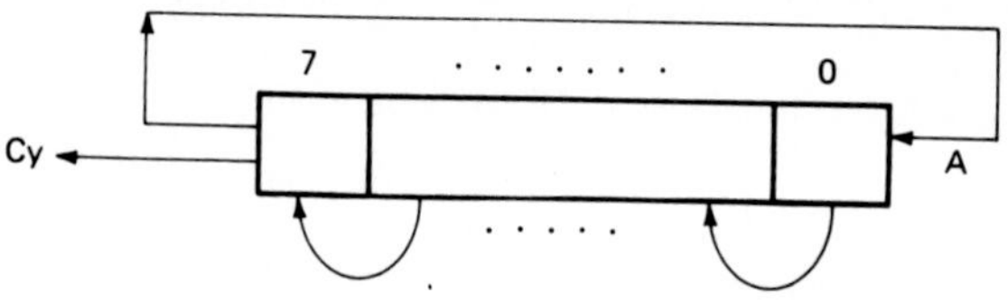
RRC	Rotate right accumulator by one position without the carry flag Cy	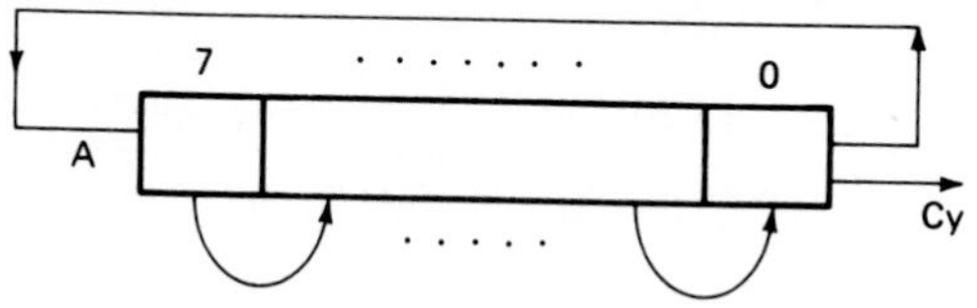
RAR	Rotate right accumulator by one position through the carry flag	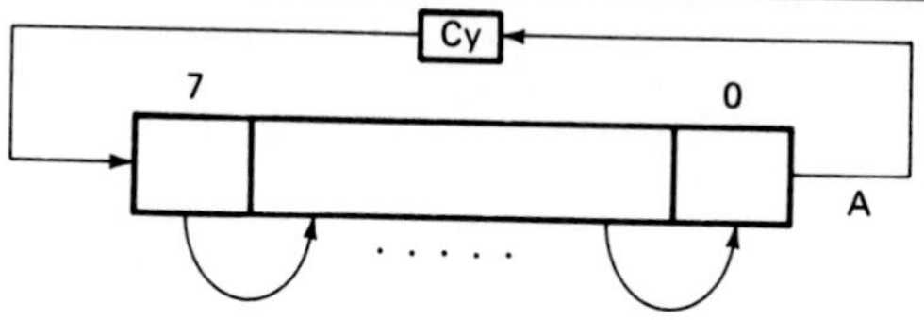
RAL	Rotate left accumulator by one position through the carry flag	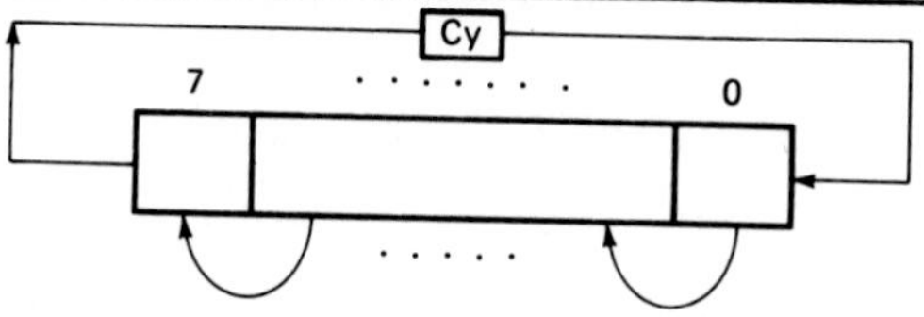

Figure 4-11   8085 rotate instructions

This means that all microprocessor registers can be saved onto the stack using the following instruction sequence:

PUSH PSW	;	Save flags and A register
PUSH B	;	Save B,C pair
PUSH D	;	Save D,E pair
PUSH H	;	Save H,L pair

Similarly, the saved status can be restored by using the following sequence of POP instructions in reverse order:

POP H	;	Restore H,L pair
POP D	;	Restore D,E pair
POP B	;	Restore B,C pair
POP PSW	;	Restore flags and A register

There are two other stack instructions: SPHL and XTHL. SPHL is a 1-byte instruction. It moves [L] to the SP high byte and [H] to the SP low byte. XTHL is also a 1-byte instruction. It exchanges [L] with the top of the stack addressed by SP and [H] with the next stack addressed by SP + 1. That is, XTHL performs the following:

$$[[SP]] \leftrightarrow [L]$$
$$[[SP + 1]] \leftrightarrow [H]$$

The 8085 can use either standard or memory-mapped I/O. Using standard I/O, the input and output instructions have the following format:

IN ⟨8-bit port address⟩ ; Input instruction
OUT ⟨8-bit port address⟩ ; Output instruction

For example, the instruction IN 52H transfers the contents of the input port with address 52_{16} into the accumulator. Similarly, the instruction OUT 41H transfers the contents of the accumulator to the output port with address 41_{16}. Using memory-mapped I/O, LDA addr and STA addr can be used as input and output instructions, respectively.

The 8085 HLT instruction forces the microprocessor to enter into the halt state. Similarly, the dummy instruction NOP neither achieves any result nor affects any microprocessor registers. This is a very useful instruction for producing accurate software delay routines and inserting diagnostic messages.

The 8085 8-bit increment (INR) and decrement (DCR) instructions affect the status flags. However, the

16-bit increment (INX) and decrement (DCX) instructions do not affect the flags. Therefore, while using these instructions in a loop counter value greater than 256_{10}, some other instructions must be used with DCX or INX to affect the flags after their execution. For example, the following instruction sequence will affect the flags for DCX:

	LXI	B, 16-BIT DATA	; Load initial 16-bit loop count to B,C
	—		
	—		
	—		
LOOP	DCX	B	; Decrement counter
	MOV	A, B	; Move B to A to test zero
	ORA	C	; Logically OR with A
	JNZ	LOOP	; Jump if not zero
	—		
	—		
	—		

There are four 1-byte 8085 interrupt instructions. These are DI, EI, RIM, and SIM. DI disables the 8085's maskable interrupt capability. EI, on the other hand, enables the 8085's maskable interrupt capability.

RIM is a 1-byte instruction. It loads the accumulator with 8 bits of data as shown in Figure 4–12(a). Bits 0, 1, and 2 provide the values of the RST5.5, RST6.5, and RST7.5 mask bits, respectively. If the mask bit corresponding to a particular RST is one, the RST is disabled; a zero in a specific RST (bits 0, 1, and 2) means that the RST is enabled. If the interrupt enable bit (bit 3) is zero, the 8085's maskable interrupt capability is disabled; the interrupt is enabled if this bit is one. A "one" in a particular interrupt pending bit indicates that an interrupt is being requested on the identified RST line; if this bit is zero, no interrupt is waiting to serviced. The serial input data (bit 7) indicates the value of the SID pin.

The SIM instruction outputs the contents of the accumulator to define interrupt mask bits and the serial output data line. The bits in the accumulator before execution of the SIM are defined as shown in Figure 4–12(b). If the mask set enable bit is set to one, interrupt mask bits for RST7.5, RST 6.5, and RST5.5 are sent out; a zero value at the mask set enable does not affect the interrupt mask bits. A one at a particular interrupt mask disables that interrupt, and a zero enables it. The Reset RST7.5, if set to one, resets an internal flip-flop to zero in order to disable the 7.5 interrupt. If the serial output enable is one, the serial output data is sent to the SOD pin (bit 7).

The interrupt instructions will be covered in detail during discussion of the 8085 interrupts.

Basically, an 8085 program is a sequence of assembly language instructions. As discussed before, each in-

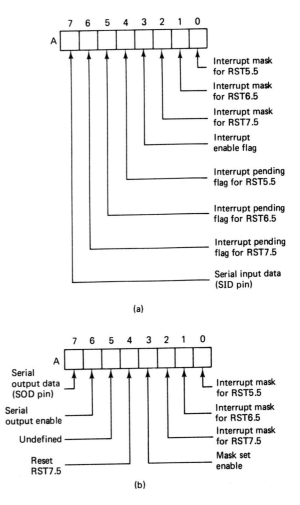

(a)

(b)

Figure 4–12 Accumulator data format
(a) Accumulator data format after execution of the RIM
(b) Accumulator data format before execution of the SIM

struction in an assembly language program is specified according to the following format:

⟨Label field⟩ ⟨OP-code field⟩ ⟨Operand field⟩
⟨Comments⟩

The OP-code field specifies the OP-code or mnemonic, and the operand address field indicates the operands involved. These two fields must be separated from each other by at least a single blank space. Also, if the operand field contains more than one operand, then they must be separated from one another by a comma. The comment field is useful only to users, and it is ignored by the assembler. The beginning of a comment field is indicated by a semicolon. The label field is an optional field, and it allows a user to assign a symbolic name to a memory address.

The use of labels significantly increases the program readability. For example, consider the Pascal assignment statement

$$Z: = X + 10$$

In this example, we assume that X and Z are addresses of 8-bit integer variables. The 8085 assembly language of this Pascal statement is as follows:

```
        ORG   1000H
TEN     EQU   10
START   LDA   X        ;  Load accumulator with (X)
        ADI   TEN      ;  Add 10 to A
        STA   Z        ;  Store result in Z
        HLT
X       DB    05
Z       DS    1        ;  Reserve a byte for variable Z
        END
```

In this program, besides the regular OP-code mnemonics, we also see some other mnemonics such as ORG, DB, DS, and END. These OP codes are called *pseudo-OPs*. As mentioned before, a pseudo-OP instruction does not produce a machine code; rather it serves as an assembler directive. For example, the pseudo-OP ORG 1000H instructs the assembler to load the object code of this program starting at memory location 1000_{16}. Note that the suffix H indicates that the number is an hexadecimal number. On the other hand, if there is no such suffix, then the assembler interprets the number as a decimal number. The END directive informs the assembler that the end of the program is reached, and thus the assembly process terminates. The EQU directive assigns the decimal value 10 to the label TEN. The DB directive allows a user to define a data byte. In particular, in this program, the assembler processes the DB directive as follows:

- The address of the memory byte next to the byte containing the HLT instruction is assigned to the symbol X.
- Also, the assembler initializes this address (assigned to the symbol X) with the value 05. This is the value held by the variable X.

In a similar manner, a programmer can define a 16-bit data by employing the DW (define word) directive. The purpose of the DS (define storage) directive is to reserve storage space for a variable or an array.

Example 4–1

Write an 8085 assembly language program to implement the following Pascal assignment statement:

$$X: = X + Y$$

Assume that X and Y hold 32-bit integers.

Solution

```
        ORG   1000H
SIZE    EQU   04       ;  Numbers are 4 bytes long
        MVI   B, SIZE  ;  Initialize B register with the
                       ;  size
                       ;  of the number
        LXI   H, Y     ;  Point register pair H,L to Y
```

```
        LXI   D, X     ;  Point register pair D,E to X
        XRA   A        ;  Clear carry flag
LOOP    LDAX  D        ;  Move 1 byte of X into A
        ADC   M        ;  Add with corresponding byte
                       ;  of Y
        STAX  D        ;  Save result in X
        INX   H        ;  Advance data
        INX   D        ;  Pointers
        DCR   B        ;  Decrement loop index
        JNZ   LOOP     ;  If not zero then loop
        HLT
X       DB    02H      ;  Low-order byte of X
        DB    13H
        DB    14H
        DB    20H      ;  High-order byte of X
Y       DB    05H      ;  Low-order byte of Y
        DB    04H
        DB    08H
        DB    11H      ;  High-order byte of Y
        END
```

When this program is executed, we obtain the following result:

$$X = 20 \ 14 \ 13 \ 02$$
$$+$$
$$Y = \underline{11 \ 08 \ 04 \ 05}$$
$$X = \underline{31 \ 1C \ 17 \ 07}$$

Also observe the usage of the addition with the carry instruction ADC in this multiprecision arithmetic operation.

Example 4–2

In the following instruction sequence, find the carry flag. What are the contents of the accumulator?

2000	37	STC	Set carry flag
2001	3E	MVI A, 01	[A] ← 01
2002	01		
2003	1F	RAR	
		•	
		•	
		•	

Solution

The STC instruction sets the carry flag to 1. The MVI instruction loads 01_{16} into the accumulator. The RAR instruction rotates the accumulator 1 bit to the right. This is illustrated in Figure E4–2.

Example 4–3

Find the contents of the program counter after the execution of the PCHL instruction in the following program. Assume that the stack pointer is initialized to $20C2_{16}$.

| 2000 | 11 | LXI D, 204AH [D,E] ← 204A |
| 2001 | 4A | |

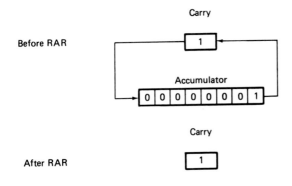

Before RAR

Carry

Accumulator

After RAR

Carry

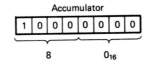

Accumulator

$$8 \qquad 0_{16}$$

Figure E4-2

2002	20		
2003	3E	MVI A, 05	[A] ← 05
2004	05		
2005	12	STAX D	[204AH] ← 05
2006	21	LXI H, 2048	[H,L] ← 2048
2007	48		
2008	20		
2009	EB	XCHG	[D,E] ↔ [H,L]
200A	E9	PCHL	[PC] ← 204AH
200B	C3	JMP 200BH	
200C	0B		
200D	20		

Solution

The LXI D instruction loads register pair D,E with 204A. MVI loads 05 into the accumulator. The STAX instruction stores the contents of the accumulator (05) into the memory location addressed by 204A (contents of register pair D,E).

LXI H loads 2048 into register pair H,L. The XCHG instruction swaps the D,E register contents 204A with the H,L register contents 2048; that is, after execution of the XCHG instruction, register pair H,L contains 204A and register pair D,E contains 2048. Hence, after the execution of the PCHL instruction, the program counter is loaded with 204A (contents of register pair H,L).

Example 4-4

Assume that the accumulator is loaded with the data word 01101101 and that the contents of memory address 0120 are 01001001. For the following, determine the values of the carry and zero flags after execution of each of the CMP instructions. All values are in hexadecimal.

2000	21	LXI H, 0120	[H,L] ← 0120
2001	20		
2002	01		
2003	BE	CMP M	[A] − [[H] [L]]
2004	FE	CPI 6FH	[A] − 6F
2005	6F		
2006	FE	CPI 6DH	[A] − 6D
2007	6D		
2008	C3	JMP 2008	
2009	08		
200A	20		

Solution

CMP compares the specified byte with the contents of the accumulator and indicates the result by adjusting the carry and zero flags. The zero flag indicates equality. No carry indicates that the accumulator is greater than the specified byte; a carry indicates that the accumulator is less than the byte. In this example, the CMP instruction compares the contents of memory location 0120_{16} with that of the accumulator. Since the accumulator contents 01101101 are greater than the contents of 0120_{16} (01001001), the carry flag is set to 0 and the zero flag is 0.

After execution of the CPI instruction in memory location 2004_{16}, the contents of the accumulator are compared with the data word $6F_{16} = 01101111_2$ using immediate addressing. Since the content of the accumulator is equal to $6D_{16}$, which is less than $6F_{16}$, the carry flag will be 1 and the zero flag will be 0. Finally, after execution of the CPI instruction in location 2006_{16}, the contents of the accumulator are compared with the data word $6D_{16}$ using immediate addressing. Since they are equal, the carry flag will be 0 and the zero flag will be 1.

Example 4-5

A calling program starting at location 2002 calls a subroutine starting at 200A. The subroutine is required to shift a 16-bit number located at 2000 (low byte) and 2001 (high byte) 1 bit to the left. The calling program will then store this result in register pair D,E. Write the calling program and the subroutine in the 8085 assembly language.

Solution

The calling program and the subroutine are as follows:

Calling Program

```
ORG   2002H
LXI   SP, 2050H    ; Initialize SP
LHLD  START        ; Load data
CALL  SUBR         ; Call subroutine
```

```
         XCHG                    ;  [D,E] ↔ [H,L]
         HLT
         ORG    2000H
START    DB     DATAₗ, DATAₕ
         END
```

Subroutine

```
         ORG    200AH
SUBR     DAD H                   ;  Shift 16-bit data left once
         RET                     ;  Return
```

These programs are useful if a string of 16-bit numbers is loaded into locations 2000 and 2001 one after another and then shifted 1 bit to the left. The programs are written to shift one such 16-bit number.

We now explain the logic in the program. Locations 2000 and 2001 contain the low and high bytes of the data, respectively. LHLD START loads the contents of 2000 (data low byte) into register L and the contents of 2001 (data high byte) into register H. CALL SUBR pushes the contents of the program counter onto the stack and branches to 200A. DAD H at 200A adds the contents of the 16-bit register with itself; that is, it performs a 16-bit left shift. RET at 200B pops the return address from the stack and places it in the program counter so that the program resumes execution at XCHG. XCHG exchanges [D,E] with [H,L]. In other words, the result of the 16-bit left shift is transferred to the D,E register as required in the program. HLT stops the program.

Example 4–6

Write an 8085 assembly language program to subtract a 16-bit number in locations 3000H (high byte) and 3001H (low byte) from another 16-bit number stored in locations 3002H (high byte) and 3003H (low byte). Store the result in register pair D,E.

Solution

```
         ORG  500H
         LDA  MEM2      ;  Load low byte of Number 2
         LXI  H, 3001H  ;  Subtract from
         SUB  M         ;  low byte of Number 1
         MOV  E, A      ;  Store result in E
         LDA  MEM1      ;  Load high byte of Number 1
         DCX  H
         SBB  M         ;  Subtract with borrow
         MOV  D, A      ;  Store result in D
         HLT
         ORG  3000H
         DB   DATA1
         DB   DATA2
MEM1     DB   DATA3
```

```
MEM2     DB   DATA4
         END
```

Example 4–7

Write an 8085 assembly language program to perform a parity check on an 8-bit word in location 4000_{16}. If the parity is odd, store DD_{16} in location 4000_{16}. However, if the parity is even, store EE_{16} in location 4000_{16}.

Solution

```
         ORG  2000H
         LDA  PARITY    ;  Load 8-bit
                        ;  data into A
         ADI  00H       ;  Add with
                        ;  00H to affect
                        ;  flags
         JPO  ODD       ;  Check for
                        ;  odd parity
         MVI  A, 0EEH   ;  If parity
                        ;  even, store
                        ;  EEH
         STA  PARITY    ;  in 4000H
         HLT            ;  Stop
ODD      MVI  A, 0DDH   ;  If parity
                        ;  odd, store
         STA  PARITY    ;  DDH in 4000H
         HLT            ;  Stop
         ORG  4000H
PARITY   DB   DATA
         END
```

Note that address 2000H at ORG 2000H is arbitrarily chosen.

Example 4–8

Write an 8085 subroutine to compute $Y = 4X^2$. Assume that X is an 8-bit unsigned number. Also assume that the result $Y = 4X^2$ can be accommodated in 16 bits. Store the result in register pair H,L.

Solution

```
SQRE    PUSH  B         ;  Save B,C pair
        PUSH  D         ;  Save D,E pair
        LXI   H, 0      ;  Initialize product to zero
        MOV   A, MULT   ;  Move multiplicand to A
        MOV   E, MULT   ;  Move multiplier to E
        MVI   D, 0      ;  Convert multiplier to
                        ;  unsigned 16 bits in D,E
START   DAD   D         ;  Compute
        DCR   A         ;  Xi² in H,L
```

```
        JNZ    START
        DAD    H              ; Compute 2X²
        DAD    H              ; Compute 4X²
        POP    D              ; Restore
        POP    B              ; registers
        RET
```

Example 4-9

Write a subroutine in 8085 assembly language to check whether a 16-bit number in locations 3000_{16} (low byte) and 3001_{16} (high byte) is odd or even. If the number is odd, store DD_{16} in location 3000_{16}; if the number is even, store EE_{16} in location 3000_{16}. Also write the main program to initialize the stack pointer to 5020_{16}, load the 8-bit number to be checked for odd or even in A, store DD_{16} or EE_{16} depending on the result, and stop.

Solution

We have to write a program to check only the least significant bit of the low byte at 3000_{16}.

Main Program

```
            ORG    4000H
            LXI    SP, 5020H    ; Initialize SP
            LDA    START        ; Load number
            CALL   CHECK        ; Call subroutine
            STA    START        ; Store DD₁₆ or EE₁₆
            HLT                 ; Stop
            ORG    3000H
START       DB     DATA
            END
```

Subroutine

```
            ORG    7000H
CHECK       RAR                 ; Rotate 'A' for
                                ; checking
            JNC    EVEN         ; Jump if even
            MVI    A, 0DDH      ; Store DD₁₆
            JMP    RETURN       ; if odd and return
EVEN        MVI    A, 0EEH      ; Store EE₁₆
RETURN      RET                 ; if even and return
```

Example 4-10

Write an 8085 assembly language program to clear 85_{16} consecutive bytes starting at 3000_{16}.

Solution

```
            ORG    2000H
            MVI    A, 85H       ; Load 'A' with number
                                ; of bytes to be cleared
            LXI    H, 3000H     ; Load H,L with 3000H
LOOP        MVI    M, 00H       ; Clear memory location
            INX    H            ; Increment address
```

```
            DCR    A            ; Decrement loop counter
            JNZ    LOOP         ; Jump to loop if
                                ; loop counter zero
            HLT                 ; Stop
```

4-6 TIMING METHODS

Timing concepts are very important in microprocessor applications. Typically, in sequential process control, the microprocessor is required to provide time delays for on–off devices such as pumps or motor-operated valves. DELAY routines are used to provide such time delays. Time delay programs reside in microcomputer memory and are not capable of handling complicated timing requirements. To keep things simple, however, we only consider delay routines in this section.

A delay program typically has an input register that contains the initial count. The register pair D,E can be used for this purpose. A typical DELAY routine is given next:

```
DELAY  DCX  D       ; Decrement the D,E con-
                    ; tents
       MOV  A, D
       ORA  E       ; Are the contents zero?
       JNZ  DELAY
       RET
```

We now calculate the total time required by the DELAY routine using the following data:

Instruction	Number of Cycles
CALL	18
DCX D	6
MOV A, D	4
ORA E	4
JNZ	7/10
RET	10

Note here that, if the JNZ condition is met (Z = 0), then ten cycles are required and the program branches back to the DCX D instruction. However, if the JNZ condition is not met (Z = 1), then seven cycles are required and the program executes the next instruction, that is, the RET instruction. Also note that the CALL instruction is used in the main program written by the user and that the 3-byte instruction CALL DELAY is used.

For each iteration in which the JNZ condition is met (Z = 0), the number of cycles is equal to

cycles for DCX D + cycles for MOV A, D + cycles for ORA E + cycles for JNZ
$$= 6 + 4 + 4 + 10 = 24 \text{ cycles}$$

These 24 cycles will be performed $(y - 1)$ times, where y is the initial contents of D,E. For the final iteration in which no jump is performed and the JNZ condition is not satisfied ($Z \neq 0$), the number of cycles is equal to

cycles for DCX D + cycles for MOV A, D + cycles for ORA E + cycles for JNZ + cycles for RET
$$= 6 + 4 + 4 + 7 + 10 = 31 \text{ cycles}$$

Therefore, the time used, including a CALL instruction, is

$$18 + 31 + 24(y - 1) = 49 + 24(y - 1) \text{ clock cycles}$$

Suppose that in a program a delay time of $\frac{1}{3}$ ms is desired. The DELAY routine can be used to accomplish this in the following way. Each cycle of the 8085 clock is $\frac{1}{3}$ μs (3 MHz). The number of cycles required in the DELAY routine is

$$\frac{\frac{1}{3} \text{ ms}}{\frac{1}{3} \text{ } \mu\text{s}} = \frac{10^{-3}}{10^{-6}} = 1000 \text{ cycles}$$

Therefore, the initial counter value y of the D,E register pair can be calculated as follows:

$$49 + 24(y - 1) = 1000$$
$$24(y - 1) = 951$$
$$y = \frac{951}{24} + 1 \simeq 40_{10} = 28_{16}$$

Therefore, in the program the D,E register pair can be loaded with 0028_{16} and the DELAY routine can be called to obtain $\frac{1}{3}$ ms of time delay. Table 4–5 contains some typical delays that can be obtained.

The following program produces a delay of 10 ms:

LXI   SP, 20C2H   ; Set stack pointer
LXI   D, 04E1H   ; Load D,E with initial count value of 04E1 to provide 10 ms of delay
CALL DELAY   ; Call DELAY routine
HLT   ; Stop

The delay times can be increased by using a counter. Suppose that a delay of 5 s is desired in a program. From Table 4–5, an initial count of $30D3_{16}$ produces a 100-ms delay. We can use a counter along with the 100-ms delay to obtain a 10-s delay as follows:

$$(100 \text{ ms})X = 10 \text{ s}$$

TABLE 4–5
Time Intervals with Corresponding Counts

Time Interval, 3-MHz Clock (Milliseconds)	Initial Count (Hexadecimal)
$\frac{1}{3}$	0028
1	007C
2	00F9
100	30D3

$$= \frac{10}{(100)(10^{-3})} = 100$$

Therefore, a counter of 100_{10} or 64_{16} is required. Now, the program for a 10-s delay can be written as follows:

	LXI	SP, 3000H	; Initialize SP
	MVI	C, 100	; Do delay loop 100 times
START	LXI	D, 30D3H	; Load counter
	CALL	DELAY	; Call delay
	DCR	C	; Decrement C
	JNZ	START	; Check if zero
	HLT		

In this program, the execution times of DCR C and JNZ START are very small compared to 10 s. Therefore, they are not considered in computing the delay.

4–7   8085 CPU PINS AND ASSOCIATED SIGNALS

The 8085 is a 40-pin dual in-line package (DIP). Figure 4–13 shows the 8085 pins and signals. The pin names, along with their description and type, are summarized as follows:

Pin Name	Description	Type
AD_0–AD_7	Address/data bus	Bidirectional, tristate
A_8–A_{15}	Address bus	Output, tristate
ALE	Address latch enable	Output, tristate
$\overline{RD}$	Read control	Output, tristate
$\overline{WR}$	Write control	Output, tristate
$IO/\overline{M}$	I/O or memory indicator	Output, tristate
S_0, S_1	Bus-state indicators	Output
READY	Wait-state request	Input
SID	Serial input data	Input
SOD	Serial output data	Output
HOLD	Hold request	Input
HLDA	Hold acknowledge	Output
INTR	Interrupt request	Input
TRAP	Nonmaskable interrupt request	Input
RST5.5	Hardware vectored	Input
RST6.5	Hardware vectored interrupt request	Input
RST7.5	Hardware vectored	Input
$\overline{INTA}$	Interrupt acknowledge	Output
RESET IN	System reset	Input
RESET OUT	Peripherals reset	Output
X_1, X_2	Crystal or RC connection	Input
CLK (OUT)	Clock signal	Output
V_{cc}, V_{ss}	Power, ground	

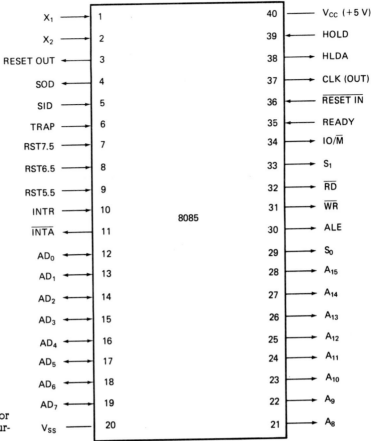

Figure 4–13 8085 microprocessor signals and pin assignments (Courtesy of Intel Corporation)

The low-order address byte and data lines AD_0–AD_7 are multiplexed. Therefore, these lines are bidirectional. The beginning of an instruction is indicated by the rising edge of the ALE signal. At the falling edge of ALE, the low byte of the address is automatically latched by some of the 8085 support chips such as the 8155 and 8355: AD_7–AD_0 lines can then be used as data lines. Note that ALE is an input to these support chips. However, if the support chips do not latch AD_0–AD_7, then external latches are required to generate the eight separate address lines A_7–A_0 at the falling edge of ALE.

Pins A_8–A_{15} are unidirectional and contain the high byte of the address.

The $\overline{RD}$ pin signal is outputted LOW by the 8085 during a memory or I/O READ operation. Similarly, the $\overline{WR}$ pin signal is outputted LOW during a memory or I/O WRITE.

Next, we explain the purpose of the $IO/\overline{M}$, S_0, and S_1 signals. The $IO/\overline{M}$ signal is outputted HIGH by the 8085 to indicate execution of an I/O instruction such as IN or OUT. This pin is outputted LOW during execution of a memory instruction such as LDA 2050H.

The $IO/\overline{M}$, S_0, and S_1 are outputted by the 8085 during its internal operations, which can be interpreted as follows:

$\overline{IO/M}$	S_1	S_0	*Operation Performed by the 8085*
0	0	1	Memory WRITE
0	1	0	Memory READ
1	0	1	I/O WRITE
1	1	0	I/O READ
0	1	1	OP code fetch
1	1	1	Interrupt acknowledge

Figure 4–14 illustrates the utilization of the ALE and AD_0–AD_7 signals for interfacing an EPROM and a RAM. The 2716 is a 2K $\times$ 8 EPROM with separate address and data lines without any built-in latches. This means that a separate latch such as the 74LS373 must be used to isolate the 8085 low-byte address and D_0–D_7 data lines at the falling edge of ALE, as shown in Figure 4–14(a). The 8155 contains a 256-byte static RAM, three user ports, and a 14-bit timer. The 8155 is designed for the 8085 in the sense that it has built-in latches with ALE as input along with multiplexed address (low byte) and data lines, AD_0–AD_7. Therefore, as shown in Figure 4–14(b), external latches are not required.

The READY input can be used by the slower external devices for obtaining extra time in order to communicate with the 8085. The READY signal (when LOW) can be utilized to provide wait-state clock periods in the 8085

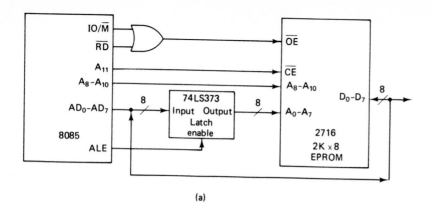

(a)

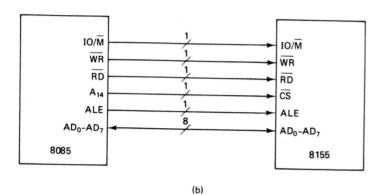

(b)

Figure 4–14 8085's interface to external device using ALE and multiplexed AD_0–AD_7 pins

machine cycle. If READY is HIGH during a read or write cycle, it indicates that the memory or peripheral is ready to send or receive data.

The serial input data (SID) and serial output data (SOD) lines are associated with the 8085 serial I/O transfer. The SOD line can be used to output the most significant bit of the accumulator. The SID signal can be used to input the SID pin to the most significant bit of the accumulator.

The HOLD and HLDA signals are used for the direct memory access (DMA) type of data transfer. The external devices place a HIGH on this line in order to take control of the system bus. The HOLD function is acknowledged by the 8085 by placing a HIGH output on the HLDA pin.

The signals on the TRAP, RST7.5, RST6.5, RST5.5, INTR, and INTA are related to the 8085 interrupt signals. TRAP is a nonmaskable interrupt; that is, it cannot be disabled. The TRAP has the highest priority. RST7.5, RST6.5, and RST5.5 are maskable interrupts used by the external devices whose vector addresses are generated automatically. INTA is an interrupt acknowledge signal that is pulsed LOW by the 8085 in response to the interrupt INTR request. In order to service INTR, one of the eight OP codes (RST_0–RST_7) has to be provided on the 8085 AD_0–AD_7 bus by external logic. The 8085 then executes this instruction and vectors to the appropriate address to service the interrupt.

Since the 8085 has the clock generation circuit on the chip, the clock signal is generated by connecting a circuit to the X_1 and X_2 pins. The 8085A can operate with a maximum clock frequency of 3.03 MHz, and the 8085A-2 can be driven with a maximum 5-MHz clock. The 8085 clock frequency can be generated by a crystal, an LC tuned circuit, or an external clock circuit. The frequency at X_1X_2 is divided by 2 internally. This means that, in order to obtain 3.03 MHz, a clock source of 6.06 MHz must be connected to X_1X_2. For crystals with less than 4 MHz, a capacitor of 20 pF should be connected between X_2 and a ground to ensure the starting up of the crystal at the right frequency (Figure 4–15).

A *parallel-resonant LC circuit,* shown in Figure 4–16, can also be used as the frequency source for the 8085. The values of L_{ext} and C_{ext} can be chosen using the following formula:

$$f = \frac{1}{2\pi L_{ext}(C_{ext} + C_{int})}$$

To minimize variations in frequency, it is recommended that a value for C_{ext} should be chosen as twice that of C_{int}, or 30 pf. The use of an LC circuit is not recommended for external frequencies higher than approximately 5 MHz.

An RC circuit may also be used as the clock source for the 8085A if an accurate clock frequency is of no concern. Its advantage is the low component cost. Figure

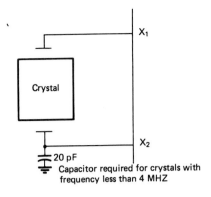

Figure 4-15 Crystal connection to X_1 and X_2 pins (Courtesy of Intel Corporation)

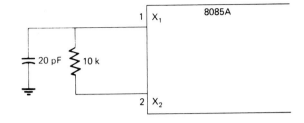

Figure 4-17 RC circuit clock source (Courtesy of Intel Corporation)

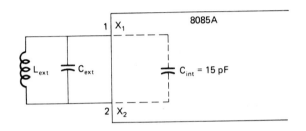

Figure 4-16 LC tuned circuit clock driver (Courtesy of Intel Corporation)

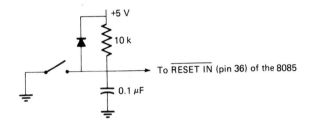

Figure 4-18 8085 reset circuit (Courtesy of Intel Corporation)

4-17 shows a clock circuit for generating an approximate external frequency of 3 MHz. Note that frequencies greatly higher or lower than 3 MHz should not be attempted on this circuit.

There is a TTL signal that is output on pin 37, called the CLK (OUT) signal. This signal can be used by other external microprocessors or by the microcomputer's peripheral chips.

The $\overline{\text{RESET IN}}$ signal, when pulsed LOW, causes the 8085 to execute the first instruction at the 0000_{16} location. In addition, the 8085 resets the instruction register, interrupt mask (RST5.5, RST6.5, and RST7.5) bits, and other registers. The $\overline{\text{RESET IN}}$ must be held LOW for at least three clock periods. A typical 8085 reset circuit is shown in Figure 4-18. In this circuit, when the switch is activated, $\overline{\text{RESET IN}}$ is driven to LOW with a large time constant providing adequate time to reset the system.

The 8085 requires a minimum operating voltage of 4.75 V. Upon power-on, the 8085 achieves this voltage after 500 ms. The reset circuit of Figure 4-18 resets the 8085 upon activation of the switch. The voltage across the 0.1 μF capacitor is zero on power-up. The capacitor then charges to V_{CC} after a definite time determined by the time constant RC. The chosen values of RC in the figure will drive the $\overline{\text{RESET IN}}$ pin to LOW for at least three clock periods. In this case, after activating the switch, the $\overline{\text{RESET IN}}$ will be LOW (assuming the ca-

pacitor charge time is equal to the discharge time) for 10 K × 0.1 μF = 1 ms, which is greater than three clock periods (3 × ⅓ μs = 1 μs) of the 3-MHz 8085.

During normal operation of the 8085, activation of the switch will short the capacitor to ground and will discharge it. When the switch is opened, the capacitor charges and the $\overline{\text{RESET IN}}$ pin becomes HIGH. Upon hardware reset, the 8085 clears the PC, IR, HALT flip-flop, and some other registers; the 8085 registers PSW, A, B, C, D, E, H, and L are unaffected.

The RESET OUT, when driven to HIGH by the 8085, resets the other chips connected to this line. It should be pointed out that, if certain lines such as the HOLD and interrupt pins are unused, then they must be connected to a ground.

4-8 8085 INSTRUCTION TIMING AND EXECUTION

An 8085 instruction's execution consists of a number of machine cycles. These cycles vary from one to five (MC₁–MC₅) depending on the instruction. Each machine cycle contains a number of 320-ns clock periods. The first machine cycle will be executed by either four or six clock periods, and the machine cycles that follow will have three clock periods. This is shown in Figure 4-19.

The shaded MCs indicate that these machine cycles are required by certain instructions. Similarly, the shaded clock periods (T_5 and T_6) mean that they are needed in MC₁ by some instructions.

The clock periods within a machine cycle can be illustrated as shown in Figure 4-20. Note that the be-

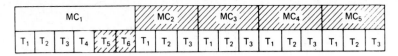

Figure 4-19 8085 machine cycles

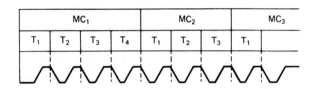

Figure 4-20 Clock periods within a machine cycle

ginning of a new machine cycle is indicated on the 8085 by outputting the address latch enable (ALE) signal HIGH. During this time, lines AD_0–AD_7 are used for placing the low byte of the address.

When the ALE signal goes LOW, the low byte of the address should be latched so that the AD_0–AD_7 lines can be used for transferring data.

We now discuss the timing diagrams for instruction fetch, memory READ, and memory WRITE.

8085 Instruction Fetch Timing Diagram Figure 4–21 shows the 8085 instruction fetch timing diagram. The instruction fetch cycle requires either four or six clock periods. The machine cycles that follow will need three clock periods.

The purpose of an instruction fetch is to read the contents of a memory location containing an instruction addressed by the program counter and to place it in the instruction register. The 8085 instruction fetch timing diagram shown in Figure 4–21 can be explained in the following way:

1. The 8085 puts a LOW on the IO/$\overline{M}$ line of the system bus, indicating a memory operation.
2. The 8085 sets $S_0 = 1$ and $S_1 = 1$ on the system bus, indicating the memory fetch operation.
3. The 8085 places the program counter high byte on the A_8–A_{15} lines and the program counter low byte on the AD_0–AD_7 lines of the system bus. The 8085 also sets the ALE signal to HIGH. As soon as the ALE signal goes to LOW, the program counter low byte on the AD_0–AD_7 is latched automatically by some 8085 support chips such as the 8155 (if 8085 support chips are not used, these lines must be latched using external latches) since these lines will be used as data lines for reading the OP code.
4. At the beginning of T_2 in MC_1, the 8085 puts the $\overline{RD}$ line to LOW, indicating a READ operation. After some time, the 8085 loads the OP code (the contents of the memory location addressed by the program counter) into the instruction register.

5. During the T_4 clock period in MC_1, the 8085 decodes the instruction.

8085 Memory READ Timing Diagram Figure 4–22 shows a memory READ timing diagram. As seen by the external logic, the status of the S_0 and S_1 signals indicates whether the operation is instruction fetch or memory READ; for example, $S_0 = 1$, $S_1 = 1$ during instruction fetch and $S_0 = 0$, $S_1 = 1$ during memory READ.

The purpose of a memory READ is to read the contents of a memory location addressed by a register pair, such as the H,L pair, and place the data in a microprocessor register such as the accumulator. Let us explain the 8085 memory READ timing diagram of Figure 4–22 in more detail:

1. The 8085 uses machine cycle MC_1 to fetch and decode the instruction. It then performs the memory READ operation in MC_2.
2. The 8085 continues to maintain IO/$\overline{M}$ at LOW in MC_2, indicating a memory READ operation.
3. The 8085 puts $S_0 = 0$, $S_1 = 1$, indicating a memory READ operation.
4. The 8085 places the contents of the high byte of the memory address register, such as the contents of the H register, on lines A_8–A_{15}.
5. The 8085 places the contents of the low byte of the memory address register, such as the contents of the L register, in lines AD_0–AD_7.
6. The 8085 sets ALE to HIGH, indicating the beginning of MC_2. As soon as ALE goes to LOW, the memory chip must latch the low byte of the address lines since the same lines are going to be used as data lines.
7. The 8085 puts the $\overline{RD}$ signal to LOW, indicating a memory READ operation.
8. The external logic gets the data from the memory location addressed by the memory address register, such as the H,L pair, and places the data into a register such as the accumulator.

8085 Memory WRITE Timing Diagram Figure 4–23 shows a memory WRITE timing diagram. As seen by the external logic, the signals $S_0 = 1$, $S_1 = 0$, and $\overline{WR} = 0$ indicate a memory WRITE operation.

The purpose of a memory WRITE is to store the contents of the 8085 register, such as the accumulator, into a memory location addressed by a register pair, such as the H,L pair. The memory WRITE timing diagram of Figure 4–23 is explained in the following way:

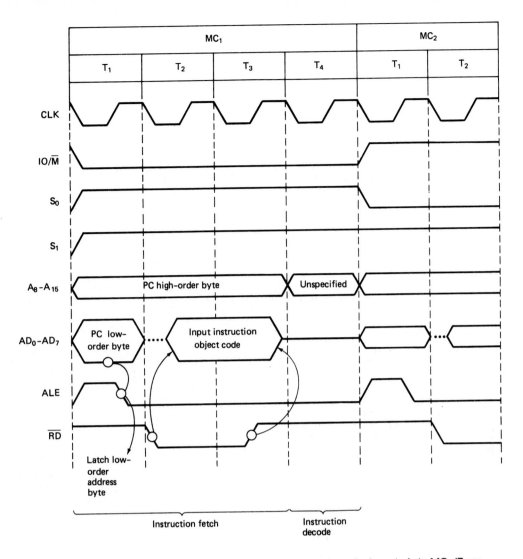

Figure 4-21 8085 instruction fetch timing diagram using four clock periods in MC_1 (From *The Osborne Four- and Eight-Bit Microprocessor Handbook* by Osborne and Kane. Copyright © 1980 McGraw-Hill, Inc.)

1. The 8085 uses machine cycle MC_1 to fetch and decode the instruction. It then executes the memory WRITE instruction in MC_2.

2. The 8085 continues to maintain IO/$\overline{M}$ at LOW, indicating a memory operation.

3. The 8085 puts $S_0 = 1$, $S_1 = 0$, indicating a memory WRITE operation.

4. The 8085 places the memory address register high byte, such as the contents of the H register, on lines A_8–A_{15}.

5. The 8085 places the memory address register low byte, such as the contents of the L register, on lines AD_0–AD_7.

6. The 8085 sets ALE to HIGH, indicating the beginning of MC_2. As soon as ALE goes to LOW, the memory chip must latch the low byte of the address lines since the same lines are going to be used as data lines.

7. The 8085 puts the $\overline{WR}$ signal to LOW, indicating a memory WRITE operation.

8. It also places the contents of the register, say, the accumulator, on data lines AD_0–AD_7.

9. The external logic gets the data from the lines AD_0–AD_7 and stores the data in the memory location addressed by the memory address register, such as the H,L pair.

4-9 8085 PROGRAMMED I/O

There are two I/O instructions in the 8085, namely, IN and OUT. These instructions are 2 bytes long. The first byte defines the OP code of the instruction, and the second byte specifies the I/O port number. Execution of the IN PORT instruction causes the 8085 to receive 1 byte of data into the accumulator from a specified I/O port. On the other hand, the OUT PORT instruction, when exe-

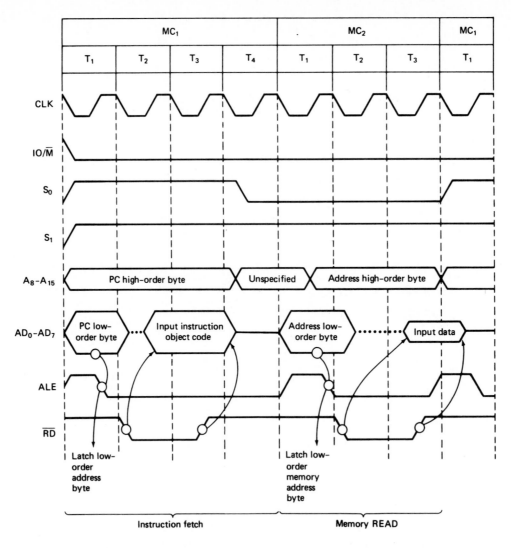

Figure 4-22 8085 memory READ timing diagram with instruction fetch cycle (From *The Osborne Four- and Eight-Bit Microprocessor Handbook* by Osborne and Kane. Copyright © 1980 McGraw-Hill, Inc.)

cuted, causes the 8085 to send 1 byte of data from the accumulator into a specified I/O port.

The 8085 can access I/O ports using either standard I/O or memory-mapped I/O.

In standard I/O, the 8085 inputs or outputs data using IN or OUT instructions. Each of these instructions requires 2 bytes. The first byte contains the OP code followed by the second byte defining the I/O port number. The IN PORT instruction loads a byte into the accumulator from an I/O port defined in the instruction. The OUT PORT outputs a byte from the accumulator into an I/O port specified in the instruction.

In memory-mapped I/O, the 8085 maps I/O ports as memory addresses. Hence, LDA addr or STA addr instructions are used to input or output data to or from the 8085. The 8085's programmed I/O capabilities are obtained via the support chips, namely, the 8355/8755 and 8155/8156. As mentioned before, the 8355/8755 contains

a 2K byte ROM/EPROM and two 8-bit I/O ports (ports A and B).

The 8155/8156 contains a 256-byte RAM, two 8-bit and one 6-bit I/O ports, and a 16-bit programmable timer. The only difference between the 8155 and 8156 is that chip enable is LOW on the 8155 and it is HIGH on the 8156. We now describe the I/O ports associated with 8355/8755 and 8155/8156 in the following paragraphs.

8355/8755 I/O Ports Two 8-bit ports are included in the 8355/8755. These are ports A and B. Another 8-bit port, called the *data direction register,* is associated with each one of these ports. These direction registers (DDRA and DDRB) can be used to configure each bit in ports A or B as either input or output. For example, a "0" written into a bit position of the data direction register sets up the corresponding bit in the I/O port as

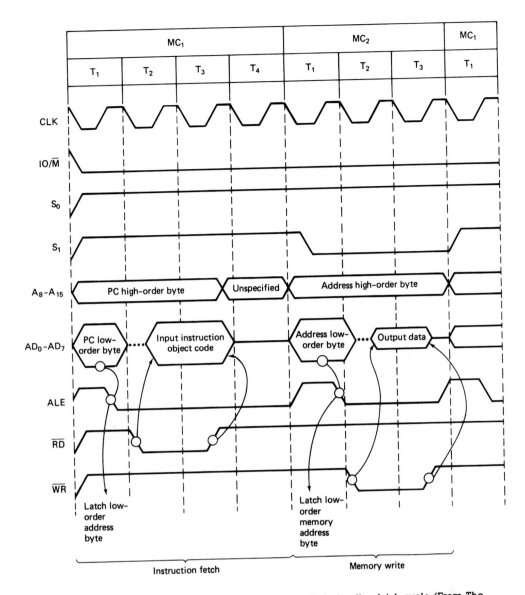

Figure 4–23 8085 memory WRITE timing diagram with instruction fetch cycle (From *The Osborne Four- and Eight-Bit Microprocessor Handbook* by Osborne and Kane. Copyright © 1980 McGraw-Hill, Inc.)

input. On the other hand, a "1" written in a particular bit position in the data direction register sets up the corresponding bit in the I/O port as output. For example, consider the following instruction sequence:

        MVI   A, 05H
        OUT   DDRA

This instruction sequence assumes DDRA as the data direction register for port A. The bits of port A are configured as follows:

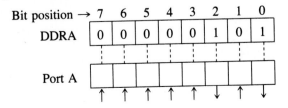

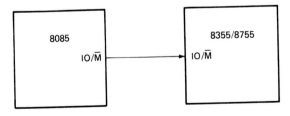

Figure 4–24 Interfacing the 8085 with 8355/8755 via the IO/$\overline{\text{M}}$ pin

The 8355/8755 uses the IO/$\overline{\text{M}}$ pin on the chip in order to distinguish between standard and memory-mapped I/O. This pin is controlled by the 8085 as shown in Figure 4–24.

The 8085 outputs a HIGH on the IO/$\overline{\text{M}}$ pin when it executes either an IN or OUT instruction. This means that IO/$\overline{\text{M}}$ in the 8355/8755 becomes HIGH after execution of IN or OUT. This, in turn, tells the 8355/8755 to decode the AD_1 and AD_0 lines in order to obtain the 8-bit address of various ports in the chip as follows:

AD_1	AD_0	Port Name
0	0	Port A
0	1	Port B
1	0	DDRA
1	1	DDRB

The other 6 bits of each 8-bit port address are don't cares. This means that these bits can be either 1's or 0's. The 8355/8755 standard I/O is illustrated in Figure 4–25.

Since the 8355/8755 is provided with 2K bytes of memory, the 11 address lines A_0–A_{10} are required for memory addressing. Since the 8085 has 16 address pins, A_0–A_{15}, pins A_{11}–A_{15} will not be used for memory addressing. Note that the 8355/8755 includes two chip enables, CE and $\overline{\text{CE}}$. In Figure 4–25, these two chip enables are connected to V_{CC} and A_{11}, respectively. It should be pointed out that the 8085 duplicates the low and high bytes of the 16-bit address lines with the port address when it executes an IN or OUT instruction. This means that if the 8085 executes an IN 01 instruction, it places 0101_{16} on the 16 address lines. Note that in Figure 4–25 $A_{11} = 0$ for both memory and port addressing. This is because $A_{11} = 0$ enables this chip. When the 8085 executes an LDA addr or STA addr instruction, IO/$\overline{\text{M}}$ becomes LOW. This tells the 8355/8755 to interpret A_0–A_{10} as memory addresses. On the other hand, when the 8085 executes an IN PORT or OUT PORT instruction, the 8085 drives IO/$\overline{\text{M}}$ to HIGH. This tells the 8355/8755 to decode AD_1 and AD_0 for I/O port addresses. The port addresses are as follows:

	A_{15} AD_7	A_{14} AD_6	A_{13} AD_5	A_{12} AD_4	A_{11} AD_3	A_{10} AD_2	A_9 AD_1	A_8 AD_0	Port Address (Hex)
Port A	X	X	X	X	0	X	0	0	00
Port B	X	X	X	X	0	X	0	1	01
DDRA	X	X	X	X	0	X	1	0	02
DDRB	X	X	X	X	0	X	1	1	03

X is a don't care. Assume X is 0 in the preceding list.

Let us now discuss 8355/8755 memory-mapped I/O. Figure 4–26 provides such an example. In Figure 4–26, A_{11} must be 0 for selecting the 8355/8755 and A_{15} is connected to IO/$\overline{\text{M}}$ of the 8355/8755. When $A_{15} = 1$, IO/$\overline{\text{M}}$ becomes HIGH. This tells the 8355/8755 chip to decode AD_1 and AD_0 for obtaining I/O port addresses. For example, if we assume that all don't cares in the I/O port address are 1's then the I/O port addresses will be mapped into memory locations as follows:

Port Name	16-Bit Memory Address
I/O port A	$F7FC_{16}$
I/O port B	$F7FD_{16}$
DDRA	$F7FE_{16}$
DDRB	$F7FF_{16}$

Note that in Figure 4–26 memory addresses are mapped as 7000_{16} through $77FF_{16}$ assuming all don't cares to be 1's.

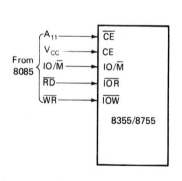

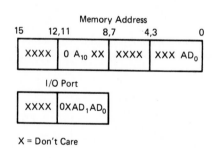

X = Don't Care

Figure 4–25 8355/8755 standard I/O

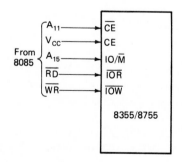

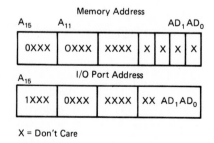

X = Don't Care

Figure 4–26 8355/8755 memory-mapped I/O

Note that the port addresses just listed may not physically exist in memory. However, input or output operations with these ports can be accomplished by generating the necessary signals by executing LDA or STA instructions with these addresses. For example, outputting to DDRA or DDRB can be accomplished via storing to locations F7FE$_{16}$ or F7FF$_{16}$, respectively.

The instructions STA F7FEH or STA F7FFH will generate all of the required signals for OUT DDRA or OUT DDRB, respectively. For example, upon execution of the STA F7FEH, the 8085 sends a LOW to the $\overline{WR}$ pin and places F7FE$_{16}$ on the address bus. This will make $A_{15} = 1$, $A_{11} = 0$, $AD_1 = 1$, and $AD_0 = 0$ and thus will make $IO/\overline{M} = 1$, $\overline{CE} = 0$, and $\overline{IOW} = 0$ on the 8355/8755 in Figure 4–26. When ALE goes to LOW, the 8085 places the contents of the accumulator on the AD_7–AD_0 pins. The 8355/8755 then takes this data and writes into DDRA. Therefore, STA F7FEH is equivalent to the OUT DDRA instruction, although the location F7FEH is nonexistent in an 8085-based microcomputer memory map.

8155/8156 I/O Ports
The 8155 or 8156 includes 256 bytes of static RAM and three parallel I/O ports. These ports are port A (8-bit), port B (8-bit), and port C (6-bit). By "parallel," it is meant that all bits of the port are configured as either all input or all output. Bit-by-bit configurations like the 8355/8755 are not permitted. The only difference between the 8155 and 8156 is that the 8155 has a LOW chip enable ($\overline{CE}$) while the 8156 includes a HIGH chip enable (CE).

The 8155/8156 ports are configured by another port called the *command status register* (CSR). When data are outputted to the CSR via the accumulator, each bit is interpreted as a command bit to set up ports and a control timer as shown in Figure 4–27. Port C can be used as a 6-bit parallel port or as a control port to support data transfer between the 8085 and an external device via ports A and B using handshaking. Note that handshaking means data transfer via exchange of control signals. Two bits (bits 2 and 3) are required in the CSR to configure port C. Note that port A interrupt and port B interrupt are associated with handshaking and are different from the 8085 interrupts. For example, port A interrupt is HIGH when data are ready to be transferred using handshaking signals such as port A buffer full and port A strobe. The port A interrupt (PC0 in ALT3) can be connected to an 8085 interrupt pin, and data can be transferred to or from the 8085 via port A by executing appropriate instructions in the interrupt service routine.

When the 8085 reads the CSR, it accesses the status register, and information such as the status of handshaking signals and the timer interrupt is obtained. Three bits are used to decode the 8155 six ports (CSR, port A, port B, port C, timer-high port, timer-low port) as follows:

AD_2	AD_1	AD_0	Port Selected
0	0	0	CSR
0	0	1	Port A
0	1	0	Port B
0	1	1	Port C
1	0	0	Timer-low port
1	0	1	Timer-high port

A typical interface between the 8085 and 8155 is shown in Figure 4–28. Consider Figure 4–28(a). Since

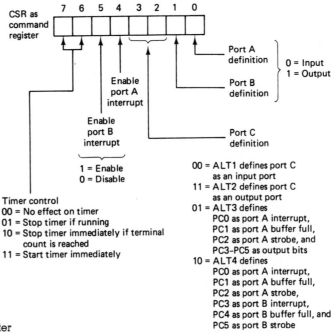

Figure 4–27 CSR format as command register

the 8085 duplicates the low-byte address bus with the high-byte address (i.e., AD_7–AD_0 same as A_{15}–A_8 for 8085 standard I/O), the address pins AD_2–AD_0 will be the same as A_{10}–A_8. This means that the pins A_{10}–A_8 must not be used as chip enables since they will be used for decoding of port addresses. Therefore, A_{14} is used as the chip enable in the figure. The unused address lines A_{11}–A_{13} and A_{15} are don't cares and are assumed to be 1's in the following list. Therefore, the port addresses are as follows:

	A_{15} AD_7	A_{14} AD_6	A_{13} AD_5	A_{12} AD_4	A_{11} AD_3	A_{10} AD_2	A_9 AD_1	A_8 AD_0	Port Address
CSR	1	0	1	1	1	0	0	0	B8H
Port A	1	0	1	1	1	0	0	1	B9H
Port B	1	0	1	1	1	0	1	0	BAH
Port C	1	0	1	1	1	0	1	1	BBH

For memory-mapped I/O, consider Figure 4–28(b). In this case, the 8085 low-byte and high-byte address bus are not duplicated. The port addresses will have 16-bit addresses as follows (assume the unused address pins A_8–A_{13} to be 0's:

	A_{15}	A_{14}	A_{13}	A_{12}	A_{11}	A_{10}	A_9	A_8	AD_7	AD_6	AD_5	AD_4	AD_3	AD_2	AD_1	AD_0	Port Address
CSR	*1*	*0*	*0*	*0*	*0*	*0*	*0*	*0*	*0*	*0*	*0*	*0*	*0*	*0*	*0*	*0*	8000_{16}
Port A	*1*	*0*	*0*	*0*	*0*	*0*	*0*	*0*	*0*	*0*	*0*	*0*	*0*	*0*	*0*	*1*	8001_{16}
Port B	*1*	*0*	*0*	*0*	*0*	*0*	*0*	*0*	*0*	*0*	*0*	*0*	*0*	*0*	*1*	*0*	8002_{16}
Port C	*1*	*0*	*0*	*0*	*0*	*0*	*0*	*0*	*0*	*0*	*0*	*0*	*0*	*0*	*1*	*1*	8003_{16}

Like the 8355/8755 memory-mapped I/O, the port addresses just listed may not physically exist in the microcomputer's main memory map. However, read or write operations with them will generate the necessary signals for input or output transfer with the ports. Assuming all don't cares to be 0's, the memory map of either configuration in Figure 4–28(a) or 4–28(b) includes addresses 0000H through 00FFH.

Example 4–11

An 8085–8355-based microcomputer is required to drive an LED connected to bit 0 of port A based on the input conditions set by a switch on bit 1 of port A. The input/output conditions are as follows: If the input to bit 1 of port A is HIGH, then the LED will be turned ON; otherwise, the LED will be turned OFF. Assume that a HIGH will turn the LED ON and that a LOW will turn it OFF. Write an 8085 assembly language program to accomplish this.

Solution

```
        ORG   5000H
PORT A  EQU   00H
DDRA    EQU   02H
        MVI   A, 01H    ; Configure port A
        OUT   DDRA
START   IN    PORT A    ; Input port A
        RAR             ; Rotate switch to LED
                          position
        OUT   PORT A    ; Output to LED
        JMP   START     ; Stop
```

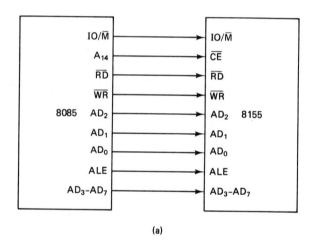

(a)

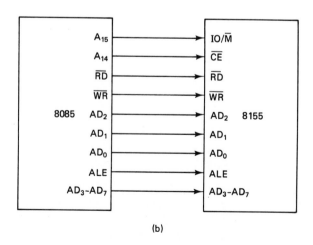

(b)

Figure 4–28 8085–8155 interface for I/O ports

Example 4–12

An 8085–8155-based microcomputer is required to drive an LED connected to bit 0 of port A based on two switch inputs connected to bits 6 and 7 of port A. If both switches are either HIGH or LOW, turn the LED ON; otherwise, turn if OFF. Assume that a HIGH will turn the LED ON and that a LOW will turn it OFF. Use port addresses of CSR and port A as 20_{16} and 21_{16}, respectively. Write an 8085 assembly language program to accomplish this.

Solution

```
        ORG  300H
CSR     EQU  20H
PORT A  EQU  21H
START   MVI  A, 00H    ; Configure port A
        OUT  CSR       ; as input
        IN   PORT A    ; Input port A
        ANI  0C0H      ; Retain bits 6 and 7
        JPE  LEDON     ; If both switches HIGH,
                       ; turn LED ON
        MVI  A, 01H    ; Otherwise, configure
        OUT  CSR       ; port A as output
        MVI  A, 00H    ; and turn LED OFF
        OUT  PORT A    ;
        JMP  START     ; Jump to START
LEDON   MVI  A, 01H    ; Configure port A
        OUT  CSR       ; as output
        OUT  PORT A    ; Turn LED ON
        JMP  START     ; Jump to START
```

Example 4–13

Write an 8085 assembly language program to turn ON an LED connected to bit 4 of the 8155 I/O port B. Use address of port B as 22_{16}.

Solution

```
        ORG  5000H
PORT B  EQU  22H
        MVI  A, 02H    ; Configure
        OUT  CSR       ; port B as output
        MVI  A, 10H    ; Output HIGH
        OUT  PORT B    ; to LED
        HLT
```

Example 4–14

An 8085–8355-based microcomputer is required to drive a common anode seven-segment display connected to port A as shown in Figure E4–14. Write an 8085 assembly language program to display a single hexadecimal digit (0 to F) from location 4000_{16}. Use a lookup table. Note

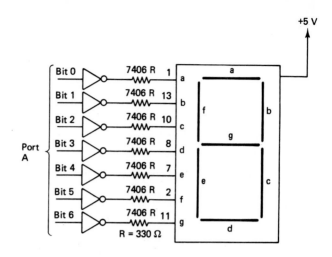

Figure E4–14

that the 7406 shown in the figure contains six inverting buffers on one 7406. Therefore, two 7406's or one 7406 and one transistor are required for the seven segments. Use port addresses of DDRA and port A as 42H and 40H, respectively.

Solution

The decode table can be obtained as follows:

Hex Digit	Bits								Decode Byte (HEX)
	7	6	5	4	3	2	1	0	
		g	f	e	d	c	b	a	
0	0	0	1	1	1	1	1	1	3F
1	0	0	0	0	0	1	1	0	06
2	0	1	0	1	1	0	1	1	5B
3	0	1	0	0	1	1	1	1	4F
4	0	1	1	0	0	1	1	0	66
5	0	1	1	0	1	1	0	1	6D
6	0	1	1	1	1	1	0	1	7D
7	0	0	0	0	0	1	1	1	07
8	0	1	1	1	1	1	1	1	7F
9	0	1	1	0	0	1	1	1	67
A	0	1	1	1	0	1	1	1	77
B	0	1	1	1	1	1	0	0	7C
C	0	0	1	1	1	0	0	1	39
D	0	1	0	1	1	1	1	0	5E
E	0	1	1	1	1	0	0	1	79
F	0	1	1	1	0	0	0	1	71

```
        ORG  5000H
DDRA    EQU  42H
PORT A  EQU  40H
        MVI  A, 7FH
        OUT  DDRA      ; Port A
        LXI  H, 4015H  ; Load H,L with
                       ; starting address of
                       ; table
```

```
        LXI     D, 0000H   ;  Load 0000H to D,E
        LDA     DIGIT      ;  Load digit to be
                           ;  ON into A
        MOV     E, A       ;  Move digit to E
        DAD     D          ;  Determine digit
                           ;  address
        MOVE    A, M       ;  Load decode byte to A
        OUT     PORT A     ;  Outport decode byte
        HLT                ;  to display

        ORG     4015H
TABLE   DB      3FH, 06H, 5BH, 4FH
        DB      66H, 6DH, 7DH, 07H
        DB      7FH, 67H, 77H, 7CH
        DB      39H, 5EH, 79H, 71H
        ORG     4000H
DIGIT   DB      DATA
        END
```

4–10 8085 INTERRUPT SYSTEM

There are five interrupt inputs on the 8085: TRAP, RST7.5, RST6.5, RST5.5, and INTR. If all the five interrupts are HIGH, requesting service, the TRAP has the highest priority, followed by RST7.5, RST6.5, RST5.5, and INTR.

TRAP is a nonmaskable interrupt; that is, it cannot be disabled by an instruction. RST7.5, RST6.5, RST5.5, and INTR are maskable interrupts; that is, they can be enabled or disabled by instructions such as EI or DI, respectively. INTR is a maskable interrupt but uses handshaking. In order for a maskable interrupt to be serviced by the 8085, the following conditions must be satisfied:

1. The 8085 interrupt system must be enabled.
2. The interrupt input on the chip must have the proper signal.
3. The 8085 must complete execution of the current instruction.

The following discussion will provide the main features of the various interrupt inputs of the 8085.

TRAP TRAP is a nonmaskable interrupt and has the highest priority. It cannot be disabled by an instruction. TRAP requires both a leading edge and a HIGH level in order for the 8085 to respond to this interrupt. This means that, if the signal on the TRAP pin has a leading edge and a sustained HIGH level, the microprocessor completes the current instruction, pushes the program counter in the stack, and branches to location 0024_{16}. In order to accept another interrupt (leading edge and HIGH level) on the TRAP line, the previous TRAP interrupt can be disabled by the falling edge. This avoids multiple interrupts from the same device.

RST7.5 RST7.5 is a maskable interrupt. This means that it can be enabled or disabled using an instruction such as SIM. This interrupt is leading-edge sensitive. This leading edge, when it appears at the RST7.5 pin, causes the 8085 to complete execution of the current instruction, push the current program counter contents in the stack, and branch to $003C_{16}$. The leading edge also sets an internal D flip-flop so that it remembers the RST7.5 interrupt. Note that recognition of the RST7.5 automatically disables the 8085 system interrupt.

RST6.5 RST6.5 is a maskable interrupt. It can be enabled or disabled using the SIM instruction. RST6.5 responds to a HIGH level on its interrupt pin. In other words, a HIGH at the RST6.5 causes the 8085 to complete execution of the current instruction, push the current program counter contents in the stack, and branch to location 0034_{16}. Recognition of the RST6.5 automatically disables the 8085 system interrupt.

RST5.5 RST5.5 is a maskable interrupt. It can be enabled or disabled by the SIM instruction. RST5.5 responds to a HIGH level on its interrupt pin. This HIGH level causes the 8085 to complete execution of the current instruction, push the current contents of the program counter in the stack, and branch to location $002C_{16}$. Note that, as with RST7.5 and RST6.5, recognition of the RST5.5 disables the 8085 system interrupt.

INTR INTR is a maskable interrupt. It uses handshaking. A HIGH level on this pin causes the 8085 to complete execution of the current instruction, push the current program counter contents in the stack, and generate an interrupt acknowledge ($\overline{INTA}$) LOW pulse on the control bus. The 8085 then expects either a 1-byte CALL (RST0–RST7) or a 3-byte CALL. This instruction must be provided by external hardware. In other words, the $\overline{INTA}$ can be used to enable a tristate buffer. The output of this buffer can be connected to the 8085 data lines. The buffer can be designed to provide the appropriate OP code on the data lines. Note that the occurrence of $\overline{INTA}$ turns off the 8085 interrupt system in order to avoid multiple interrupts from a single device. Also note that there are eight RST instructions (RST0–RST7). Each of these RST instructions has a vector address. These were shown earlier in Table 4–4.

Let us now identify the characteristics of an $\overline{INTA}$ machine cycle. The $\overline{INTA}$ machine cycle is the same as the instruction fetch cycle with the following differences:

1. The 8085 generates an $\overline{INTA}$ pulse rather than a $\overline{MEMR}$ pulse. An RST instruction is then fetched and executed.
2. The 8085 does not increment the program counter contents in order to return to the proper location after servicing the interrupt.

3. The generation of $\overline{\text{INTA}}$ disables the 8085 interrupt capability in order to avoid multiple interrupts.

The interrupt acknowledge timing diagram is given in Figure 4–29. In response to a HIGH on the INTR, the 8085 proceeds with the sequence of events shown in the figure if the 8085 system interrupt is enabled by the EI instruction. Before the MC_i T_1 cycle, the 8085 checks all the interrupts. If INTR is the only interrupt and if the 8085 system interrupt is enabled, the 8085 will turn off the system interrupt and then make the $\overline{\text{INTA}}$ LOW for about two T states (T_2 and T_3 cycles of MC_1 in Figure 4–29). This $\overline{\text{INTA}}$ signal can be used to enable an external hardware to provide an OP code on the data bus. The 8085 can then read this OP code. Typically, the 1-byte RST or 3-byte CALL instruction can be used as the OP code. If the 3-byte CALL is used, then the 8085 will generate two additional $\overline{\text{INTA}}$ cycles in order to fetch all 3 bytes of the instruction. However, on the other hand, if RST is used, then no additional $\overline{\text{INTA}}$ is required. Figure 4–29 shows that, in response to $\overline{\text{INTA}}$, a CALL OP code is generated on the data bus during MC_1. The CALL OP code could have been placed there by a device like the Intel 8259 programmable interrupt controller. At this point, only the OP code for the CALL (CD_{16}) is

fetched by the 8085. The 8085 executes this instruction and determines that it needs 2 more bytes (the address portion of the 3-byte instruction). The 8085 then generates a second $\overline{\text{INTA}}$ cycle in MC_2 followed by a third $\overline{\text{INTA}}$ cycle in MC_3 in order to fetch the address portion of the CALL instruction from the 8259. The 8085 executes the CALL instruction and branches to the interrupt service routine located at an address specified in the CALL instruction. Note that the 8085 does not increment the program counter contents during the three $\overline{\text{INTA}}$ cycles so that the appropriate program counter value is pushed in the stack during MC_4 and MC_5.

Also note that the recognition of any maskable interrupt (RST7.5, RST6.5, RST5.5, and INTR) disables all interrupts. Therefore, in order for the 8085 to accept another interrupt, the last two instructions of the interrupt service routine will be EI followed by RET.

One can produce a single RST instruction, say, RST7 (OP code FF in hexadecimal) using a 74LS244 octal buffer. The inputs I_0–I_7 of the 74LS244 are connected to HIGH, and its output enable line $\overline{\text{OE}}$ is tied to $\overline{\text{INTA}}$. In response to $\overline{\text{INTA}}$ LOW, the 74LS244 places FF in hexadecimal (RST7) on the data bus. Figure 4–30 shows a typical circuit.

An 8-to-3 encoder, such as the 74LS148, can be

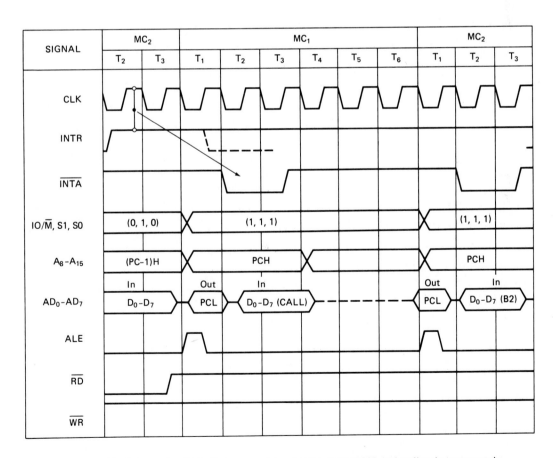

Figure 4–29 Interrupt acknowledge machine cycles (with CALL instruction in response to INTR) (Courtesy of Intel Corporation)

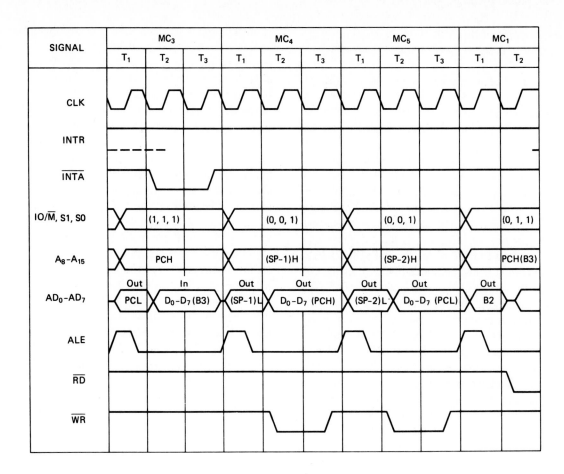

Figure 4–29 Interrupt acknowledge machine cycles (cont.)

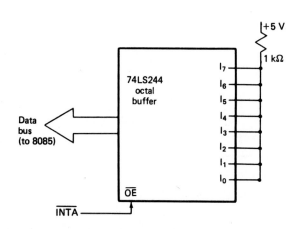

Figure 4–30 Using the 74LS244 octal buffer to provide the RST7 instruction

used along with the 74LS244 in order to generate all eight RST instructions. This is shown in Figure 4–31. The encoder generates active LOW outputs. This means that, if the input $\overline{R_4}$ is connected to the 74LS148, the encoder inverts the 3-bit binary code 100_2 of 4_{10} into 011_2. Note that 011_2 is the active LOW representation of 4. The number 4 corresponds to the fourth input $\overline{R_4}$ applied to the encoder.

In Figure 4–31, the encoder provides three active LOW otuput bits to the 74LS244. The purpose is to place one of the eight RST instructions on the data bus of the 8085 in response to the $\overline{INTA}$ signal. Remember that the inputs and outputs of a 74LS148 encoder are active LOW. As a result, a LOW level on input $\overline{R_0}$ produces the RST7 instruction (OP code FF_{16}) and input $\overline{R_7}$ produces the RST0 instruction (OP code $C7_{16}$), which has the same address as RESET.

As mentioned before in this chapter, the OP code for each RST instruction is

$$11\ CCC\ 111$$

where CCC is

000	for RST0
001	for RST1
010	for RST2
011	for RST3
100	for RST4
101	for RST5
110	for RST6
111	for RST7

In Figure 4–31, the output of the encoder $\overline{Q_2}, \overline{Q_1}, \overline{Q_0}$ provides CCC for the RST instruction. For example, if

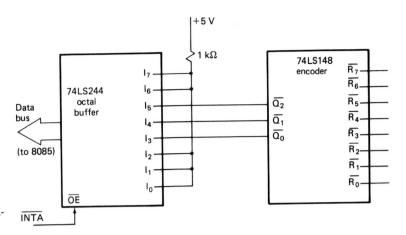

Figure 4–31 Forming eight RST instructions with a priority encoder

one places $\overline{R_0}$ to LOW, $\overline{Q_2}$, $\overline{Q_1}$, $\overline{Q_0}$ will be 111; that is, I_5, I_4, I_3 of the 74LS244 will be set to 111. Since the other lines, I_0, I_1, I_2, I_6, I_7, are all tied HIGH, the 74LS244 will provide FF_{16} (OP code for the RST7) on the 8085 data bus as soon as the $\overline{INTA}$ is driven to LOW by the 8085 in response to INTR.

Similarly, by activating the other inputs $\overline{R_1}$–$\overline{R_7}$ of the encoder to LOW, the other 1-byte CALL instructions RST0–RST6 can be generated on the 8085 data bus. The encoder only differentiates between simultaneous active inputs and provides an output that corresponds to the highest priority input (RST7, highest; RST0, lowest).

Table 4–6 provides a summary of the 8085 interrupts and the regular RST instructions. Figure 4–32 shows the 8085 interrupt structure.

Let us elaborate on Figure 4–32. Execution of the EI instruction sets the RS flip-flop and makes one of the inputs to the AND gates 1–4 HIGH. Hence, in order for all the interrupts (except TRAP) to work, the interrupt system must be enabled. Execution of DI clears the RS flip-flop and disables all interrupts except TRAP. As mentioned before, the SIM instruction outputs the contents of the accumulator, which can be interpreted as shown in Figure 4–33.

The interrupt mask function is executed only if the mask set enable bit is 1. Suppose that, if $0E_{16}$ is stored in the accumulator and the SIM instruction is executed, 1 will be sent to the interrupt mask for RST7.5 and RST6.5, and 0 will be sent to RST5.5. That is, in Figure 4–32, 1 will be sent to one of the inputs of the AND gates 1 and 2, and 0 will be sent to one of the inputs of the AND gate 3. These signals are inverted at the AND gate inputs (shown by circles), providing LOW outputs for AND gates 1 and 2, and a HIGH input to AND gate 3. Therefore, in order to enable RST7.5, RST6.5, or RST5.5, the interrupt system must be enabled, the appropriate interrupt signal (leading edge or HIGH level) at the respective pins must be available.

For example, consider the RST7.5 interrupt. Executing the EI and SIM instructions, the interrupt system can be enabled, and also the interrupt mask bit for RST7.5

TABLE 4–6
Restart Instructions and Interrupt Inputs (Courtesy of Intel Corporation)

Instruction or Input	Code (Hexadecimal)	Vector Address (Hexadecimal)
RST0	C7	0000
RST1	CF	0008
RST2	D7	0010
RST3	DF	0018
RST4	E7	0020
TRAP	Hardware interrupt	0024
RST5	EF	0028
RST5.5	Hardware interrupt	002C
RST6	F7	0030
RST6.5	Hardware interrupt	0034
RST7	FF	0038
RST7.5	Hardware interrupt	003C

can be set to LOW, making the two inputs to AND gate 1 HIGH. The third input to this AND gate can be set to HIGH by a leading edge at the RST7.5 pin. This sets the D flip-flop, thus making the output of AND gate 1 HIGH and enabling RST7.5. The 8085 branches to location $003C_{16}$, where a 3-byte JMP instruction takes the program to the service routine. RST5.5 and RST6.5 can similarly be explained from Figure 4–32. Notice that the RST7.5 can be disabled in two ways:

1. Setting the mask bit for RST7.5 to 1 by executing the SIM instruction.

2. Setting the Reset RST7.5 bit to 1 by executing the SIM instruction. This makes one of the inputs to the NOR gate HIGH, which is connected to the clear line (CLR) of the D flip-flop, making its output LOW (Q = 0). This puts the output of AND gate 1 to a LOW, disabling RST7.5.

From Figure 4–32, it can also be seen that a leading edge and a HIGH level at the TRAP interrupt pin takes the 8085 to location 0024_{16}, where a 3-byte CALL can be executed to go to the service routine. Note that

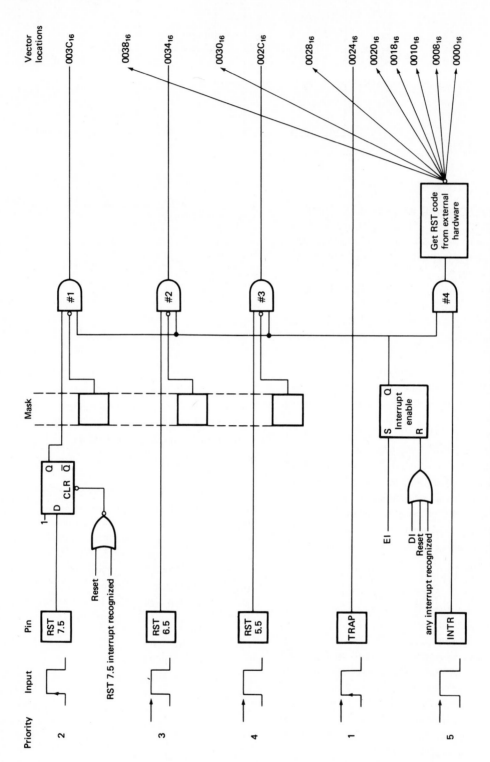

Figure 4–32 8085 interrupt structure (Courtesy of Intel Corporation)

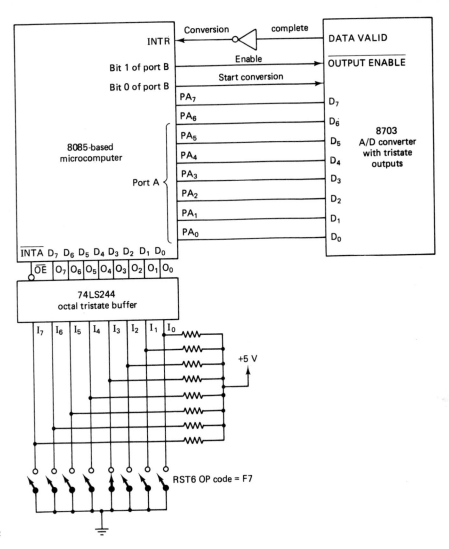

Figure 4–37 8085–8703 schematic

service routine. The interrupt service routine can be written to send a LOW output through bit 1 of port B to enable the $\overline{\text{OUTPUT ENABLE}}$ and then input the 8-bit A/D output through the I/O port A. Note that, as in the RST6.5, the duration between the occurrence of the INTR and the inputting of the A/D output into the 8085 is much more than 5 μs. This means that the A/D output is input into the 8085 after the 8703 latches the data.

4–11 8085 DMA

The Intel 8257 DMA controller chip is a 40-pin DIP and is programmable. It is compatible with the 8085 microprocessor. The 8257 is a four-channel DMA controller with priority logic built into the chip. This means that the 8257 provides for DMA transfers for a maximum of up to four devices via the DMA request lines DRQ_0–DRQ_3 (DRQ_0 has the highest priority and DRQ_3 the lowest). Associated with each DRQ is a DMA acknowledge line ($\overline{DACK_0}$–$\overline{DACK_3}$ for the four DMA requests DRQ_0–

DRQ_3). Note that the $\overline{DACK}$ signals are active LOW. The 8257 uses the 8085 HOLD pin in order to take over the system bus. After initializing the 8257 by the 8085, the 8257 performs the DMA operation in order to transfer a block of data of up to 16,384 bytes between the memory and a peripheral without involving the microprocessor. A typical 8085–8257 interface is shown in Figure 4–38.

An I/O device can request for a DMA transfer by raising the DMA request (DRQ) line of one of the channels of the 8257. In response, the 8257 will send a HOLD request (HRQ) to the 8085. The 8257 waits for the HOLD acknowledge (HLDA) from the 8085. On receipt of the HLDA from the 8085, the 8257 generates a LOW on the $\overline{DACK}$ lines for the I/O device. Note that the $\overline{DACK}$ is used as a chip select bit for the I/O device. The 8257 sends the READ or WRITE control signals, and an 8-bit data is transferred between the I/O and memory. On completion of the data transfer, the $\overline{DACK}$ is set to HIGH, and the HRQ line is reset to LOW in order to transfer control of the bus to the 8085. The 8257 utilizes four clock cycles in order to transfer 8 bits of data.

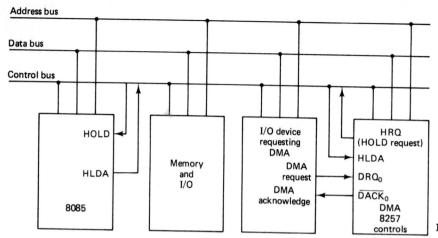

Figure 4-38 An 8085-8257 interface

The 8257 has three main registers. These are a 16-bit DMA address register, a terminal count register, and a status register. Both address and terminal count registers must be initialized before a DMA operation. The DMA address register is initialized with the starting address of the memory to be written into or read from. The low-order 14 bits of the terminal count register are initialized with the value $(n - 1)$, where n is the desired number of DMA cycles. A terminal count (TC) pin on the 8257 is set to HIGH in order to indicate to the peripheral device that the present DMA cycle is the last cycle. An 8-bit status register in the 8257 is used to indicate which channels have attained a terminal count.

4-12 8085 SID AND SOD LINES

Serial I/O is extensively used for data transfer between a peripheral device and the microprocessor. Since microprocessors perform internal operations in parallel, conversion of data from parallel to serial and vice versa is required to provide communication between the microprocessor and the serial I/O. The 8085 provides serial I/O capabilities via SID (serial input data) and SOD (serial output data) lines.

One can transfer data to or from the SID or SOD lines using the instructions RIM (20_{16}) and SIM (30_{16}). After executing the RIM instruction, the bits in the accumulator are interpreted as follows:

1. Serial input bit is bit 7 of the accumulator.
2. Bits 0–6 are interrupt masks, the interrupt enable bit, and pending interrupts.

The SIM instruction sends the contents of the accumulator to the interrupt mask register and serial output line. Therefore, before executing the SIM, the accumulator must be loaded with proper data. The contents of the accumulator are interpreted as follows:

1. Bit 7 of the accumulator is the serial output bit.

2. The SOD enable bit is bit 6 of the accumulator. This bit must be 1 in order to output bit 7 of the accumulator to the SOD line.
3. Bits 0–5 are interrupt masks, enables, and resets.

Example 4-16

An 8085–8155-based microcomputer is required to input a switch via the SID line and output the switch status to an LED connected to the SOD line. Write an 8085 assembly language program to accomplish this.

Solution

```
        ORG  5000H
START   RIM            ; Bit 7 of 'A' is SID
        ORI  40H       ; Set SOD enable to 1
        SIM            ; Output to LED
        JMP  START     ; Repeat
```

4-13 8085-BASED SYSTEM DESIGN*

In order to illustrate the concepts associated with 8085-based system design, a microcomputer with a 2K EPROM (2716), a 256-byte RAM, and three ports (8155) is designed. A hardware schematic is included. Also, an 8085 assembly language program is provided to multiply 4-bit numbers entered via DIP switches connected to port A. The 8-bit product is displayed on two seven-segment displays interfaced via port B. Repeated addition will be used for multiplication. Figure 4–39 shows a schematic of the hardware design. Full decoding using the 74LS138 decoder is utilized. Texas Instruments TIL 311's displays with on-chip decoder are used. The memory and I/O maps are as follows:

*Reprinted with permission from *Microprocessors and Microcomputer-Based System Design* by M. Rafiquzzaman, Copyright © CRC Press, Inc., Boca Raton, FL, 1990.

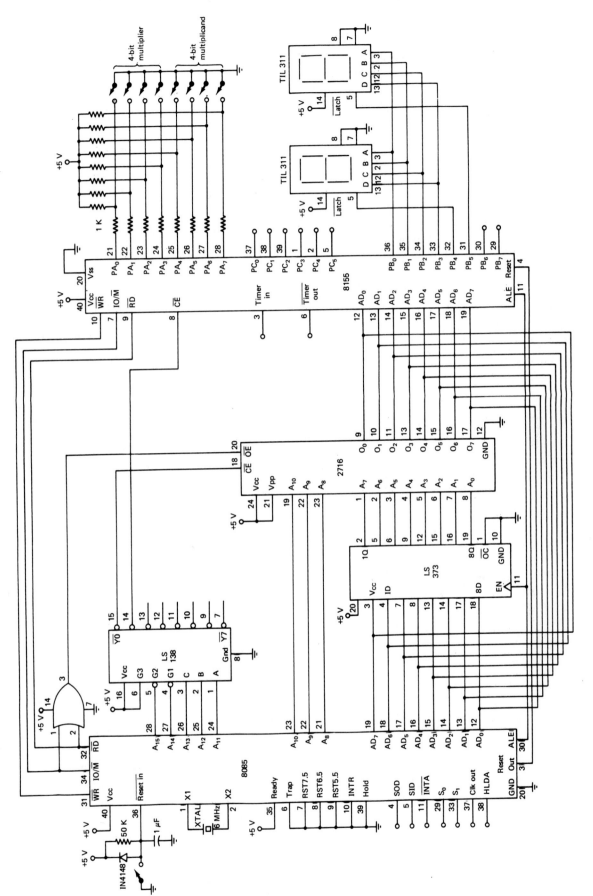

Figure 4-39 8085-based system design

- *Memory map:*

2716

A_{15} A_{14} A_{13} A_{12} A_{11} A_{10} A_9 A_8 AD_7 AD_6 AD_5 AD_4AD_3 $AD_2AD_1AD_0$

0   0   0   0 { ←————————— all 1's or 0's —————————→ }

Result 0000H–07FFH

8155

A_{15} A_{14} A_{13} A_{12} A_{11} A_{10} A_9A_8 AD_7 AD_6 AD_5 AD_4AD_3 $AD_2AD_1AD_0$

0   0   0   0   1   0   0   0 { ←———— all 1's or 0's ————→ }

Result 0800H–08FFH

- *I/O map using standard I/O:*

	A_{15} AD_7	A_{14} AD_6	A_{13} AD_5	A_{12} AD_4	A_{11} AD_3	A_{10} AD_2	A_9 AD_1	A_8 AD_0	Port Address
CSR	0	0	0	0	1	0	0	0	08H
Port A	0	0	0	0	1	0	0	1	09H
Port B	0	0	0	0	1	0	1	0	0AH
Port C	0	0	0	0	1	0	1	1	0BH

The 8085 assembly language program for performing 4-bit × 4-bit multiplication is provided as follows:

```
CSR     EQU   08H
PORT A  EQU   09H
PORT B  EQU   0AH
REPEAT  MVI   A, 02H    ; Configure port A as in-
                          put
        OUT   CSR       ; and port B as output
        MVI   L, 00H    ; Initialize product to zero
        IN    PORT A    ; Input multiplier and
                          multiplicand
        MOV   B, A      ; Save multiplicand and
                          multiplier in B
        ANI   0FH       ; Mask multiplicand and
                          retain multiplier
        MOV   C, A      ; Save 4-bit multiplier in
                          C
        MOV   A, B      ; Move multiplicand and
                          multiplier to A
        RAR             ; Move 4-bit multiplicand
        RAR             ; (upper nibble of A)
        RAR             ; into LOW nibble
        RAR             ; of
                        ; accumulator
        ANI   0FH       ; Mask HIGH nibble and
                          retain multiplicand
START   ADD   L         ; Perform repeated addi-
                          tion
```

```
        DCR   C         ; Decrement multiplier
                          value
        JNZ   START     ; If Z = 0, repeat addi-
                          tion
                        ; else product in L
        MOV   A, L      ; Move product to A
        ANI   0FH       ; Retain product LOW
                          nibble and
        MOV   H, A      ; Save in H
        MOV   A, L      ; Move product to A
        RAR             ; Move
        RAR             ; HIGH nibble
        RAR             ; of product
        RAR             ; to LOW nibble
                        ; of A
        ANI   2FH       ; Retain HIGH nibble of
                          product and enable latch
        OUT   PORT B    ; of HIGH hex display
                          and disable LOW latch
                        ; Display HIGH nibble of
                          product
        MOV   A, H      ; Move LOW product nib-
                          ble to A
        ANI   1FH       ; Enable LOW latch and
                          disable HIGH latch
        OUT   PORT B    ; Display LOW nibble of
                          product
        JMP   REPEAT    ; on LOW display and
                          continue
```

This program can be assembled. The 2716 can then be programmed by using an EPROM programmer with the machine code of the preceding program starting at location 0000H. Then, upon activation of the switch at the 8085 reset input, the dip switch LOW and HIGH nibbles will be multiplied and the result of the multiplication will be displayed on the two TIL 311s. By changing DIP switch inputs at port A, new results can be displayed.

QUESTIONS AND PROBLEMS

4–1. (a) What is the difference between the SUB-TRACT and COMPARE instructions?
(b) If [H,L] = 2005_{16} and [A] = 03_{16}, then what are the contents of location 2005 after exe-cution of MOV M, A and STA 2005 instruc-tions?

4–2. What does each of the following 8085 instructions do?

(a) DAD H

(b) ANA A

(c) MOV E, E

(d) STC
 CMC

4-3. What does the following 8085 instruction sequence do after execution?

.

.

XTHL
XTHL
XTHL
XTHL

4-4. Assume $[2006_{16}] = 06_{16}$ and $[2007_{16}] = 07_{16}$. What are the contents of the H and L registers after execution of LHLD 2006H?

4-5. In the following, after POP PSW is executed, what are the contents of the 8085 processor status word (PSW) and accumulator (A)? Assume that [20C2] = 01 and [20C3] = 05.

LXI SP, 20C2H

POP PSW

4-6. Write an instruction sequence using the LXI and PCHL instructions in order to jump unconditionally to 2010H.

4-7. In the following instruction sequence, find the contents of the H,L register pair after execution of the instruction DAD B. Assume [2000H] = 01H and [2001H] = 00H.

LXI B, 2000H

LHLD 2000H

DAD B

HLT

4-8. In the following 8085 instruction sequence, after execution of the instruction RLC, find the carry flag, zero flag, and the contents of the accumulator. Also, determine the address of the next instruction to be executed after executing the JNC at 2000.

2000	37	STC
2001	3E	MVI A, 80
2002	80	
2003	07	RLC
2004	D2	JNC 2000
2005	00	
2006	20	
2007	3D	DCR A

.

.

.

4-9. Write a program in 8085 assembly language for shifting a 16-bit binary number 1 bit to the right.

4-10. It is desired to subtract a 16-bit number at locations 2000 (high byte) and 2001 (low byte) from another 16-bit number at 2002 (low byte) and 2003 (high byte). If the result of the subtraction is positive, store 11_{16} at 2004_{16}. On the other hand, if the result of the subtraction is negative, store FF_{16} at location 2004_{16}. Finally, if the result is zero, store 01_{16} at location 2004_{16}. Write a program in 8085 assembly language for performing this.

4-11. What function is performed when each of the following 8085 instructions is separately executed? Find another 8085 single instruction for each.

(a) ADI 0FFH

(b) XRI 0FFH

(c) ORI 0FFH

(d) ANI 00H

4-12. Write an 8085 program segment that will simulate the indexed addressing mode. Typically, your program must load the accumulator with the contents of the memory location whose address is [H,L] + some 16-bit displacement X.

4-13. The following 8085 program is supposed to clear a block of 100 memory bytes starting at address 2000H:

	ORG	1000H
BSIZE	EQU	100
	LXI	B, BSIZE
	LXI	H, START
	XRA	A
LOOP	MOV	M, A
	INX	H
	DCX	B
	JNZ	LOOP
	HLT	
START	DS	2000H
	END	

Determine whether this program will work. Modify as necessary. *Hint:* The XRA A instruction sets the Z flag, but the LXI, INX, and DCX instructions do not affect the Z flag.

4-14. Write an 8085 assembly language program for each of the following cases:

(a) Divide the 32-bit 2's complement number stored starting at address 2000H (LSB first) by 32.

(b) Negate the number of part (a).

4-15. Write an 8085 assembly language program to add two 24-bit numbers.

4-16. Using the 8085 programming language, write the assembly program for the following:

(a) Add the 16-bit number in memory locations 2000_{16} and 2001_{16} to the 16-bit number in memory locations 2002_{16} and 2003_{16}. The most significant 8 bits of the two numbers to be added are in memory locations 2001_{16} and 2003_{16}. Store result in DE.

(b) Store the larger of the contents of memory locations 2000_{16} and 2001_{16} in location 2000_{16}. Assume that the memory locations 2000_{16} and 2001_{16} contain unsigned binary numbers.

(c) Move into the accumulator the square of the contents of memory location 2000_{16} from a lookup table containing the squares of the numbers from 0 to 9. Assume that the memory location 2000_{16} contains a number between 0 and 9 inclusive.

4–17. Write a program to move into the accumulator the number of negative elements (most significant bit 1) in a data set. The length of the set is 10_{10} ($0A_{16}$), and it is stored in memory location 2000_{16}. The data starts in memory location 2001_{16}.

4–18. (a) Draw a flowchart to find the maximum data in a data set. The size of the data set is 10_{10} ($0A_{16}$) and is stored in memory location 2000_{16}. The first data is contained in memory location 2001_{16}. Assume that the numbers in the data set are all 8-bit unsigned binary numbers.

(b) Convert the flowchart to an 8085 assembly language program to store the result in the accumulator.

4–19. Write an 8085 assembly language program to add two BCD numbers stored in locations 2000_{16} and 2001_{16}.

4–20. Repeat Example 4–7 without using the instructions involving the parity flag.

4–21. It is desired to add a 16-bit number contained in the B,C register pair with another 16-bit number in the H,L pair. If the result of addition is even, store EE_{16} in the accumulator. If the result of addition is odd, store DD_{16} in the accumulator.

(a) Flowchart the problem.

(b) Convert the flowchart to an 8085 assembly language program.

4–22. Write an 8085 assembly language program to divide a number at location 2000_{16} by 128_{10} at location 2001_{16}. Neglect the remainder. Store the quotient in the accumulator.

4–23. Write a subroutine in 8085 assembly language to compute $Y = X_1^2 + X_2^2$. Assume X_1 and X_2 are 8-bit unsigned numbers stored in locations 3000_{16} and 3001_{16}, respectively. Also, write the main program to call this subroutine to compute $Z = (X_1^2 + X_2^2)/4$. Discard the remainder of the division. Store the quotient in the H,L pair.

4–24. An 8085–8355-based microcomputer is required to perform the following functions:

1. Ports A and B have two switch inputs (con-

nected to bits 1 and 2) and one LED output (connected to bit 0) each.

2. The LED at port A is to be turned ON and the LED at port B is to be turned OFF if port A has more HIGH inputs than port B.

3. The port A LED is to be OFF and the port B LED ON if port B has more HIGH inputs than port A.

4. If the number of HIGH inputs for each port are equal, both LEDs are to be turned ON.

(a) Flowchart the problem.

(b) Convert the flowchart to an 8085 assembly language program.

4–25. Using an 8085–8156-based microcomputer, the following functions are to be performed:

1. Port A has three input switches (bits 1, 2, and 3), and one output LED is connected to bit 0.

2. Port B has one output LED connected to bit 2.

3. The port A LED is to be ON and the port B LED is to be OFF if port A has an even number of HIGH inputs.

4. The port B LED is to be ON and the port A LED is to be OFF if port A has an odd number of HIGH inputs.

(a) Flowchart the problem.

(b) Convert the flowchart to an 8085 assembly language program.

4–26. Flowchart and write an 8085 assembly language program for using an 8085–8155-based microcomputer as an integrated circuit tester. Figure P4–26 shows the I/O hardware needed to test a NAND gate. The microcomputer is to be programmed to generate the various logic conditions for the NAND inputs, monitor the NAND output, and activate the LED connected to bit 3 of port A if the chip is found to be faulty. Otherwise, turn ON the LED connected to bit 4 of port A. The test sequence will consist of all four different combinations of the inputs.

4–27. Write a program in 8085 assembly language to turn ON an LED connected to bit 0 of port A of an 8085–8355-based microcomputer after 20 seconds.

4–28. Will the circuit shown in Figure P4–28 work? If so, determine the memory and I/O maps in hexadecimal. If not, justify briefly, modify the circuit to work, and then determine memory and I/O maps in hexadecimal. Use only the pins and signals shown. Assume all don't cares to be 1's.

4–29. Interface the 8155 RAM chip shown in Figure P4–29 to obtain the memory map FE00H–FEFFH. Show only the connections for the pins shown. Assume all unused address lines to be 1's.

4–30. Identify the maskable and nonmaskable interrupts on the 8085.

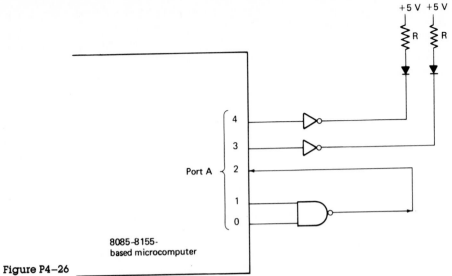

Figure P4-26

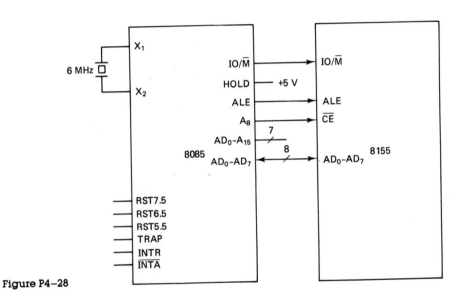

Figure P4-28

Figure P4-29

4-31. In the circuit of Figure P4–31, the 8085/8755 microcomputer is required to turn ON an LED through bit 0 of port A if the voltage measurement at the comparator input is greater than 3 V. Use the RST6 instruction to obtain the following:

(a) Design the interface hardware.

(b) Flowchart the problem.

(c) Convert the flowchart to an 8085 assembly language program.

4-32. Repeat Example 4–15 using programmed I/O in the following way:

1. The microcomputer will send an output through an I/O port to start the A/D conversion.

2. The microcomputer will wait in a loop and poll the DATA VALID signal until the conversion is completed.

3. The microcomputer will then input the A/D converter's output.

Write a program in 8085 assembly language to output the A/D converter's output eight LEDs connected to a port.

4-33. Software Successive Approximation Conversion Using a Microcomputer*

Introduction The hardware required for D/A conversion is much less expensive than that required for A/D conversion. A microprocessor executing a successive approximation algorithm can be used in conjunction with a low-cost D/A converter to perform the more expensive function of A/D conversion. The scheme for doing this is shown in Figure P4–33.

In this successive approximation scheme, the microcomputer executes a program designed to search

*From *Introduction to Microprocessor System Design* by Garland. Copyright © 1979 McGraw-Hill, Inc.

for the digital representation of the analog input voltage V_X. The output of the analog comparator signifies to the microcomputer whether the current guess G_N is too high ($D_N = 0$) or too low ($D_N = 1$). Note that there must be no significant change in the analog input voltage during this search (or conversion) process.

Algorithm Given that all analog input voltages are equally likely, the most efficient search algorithm for the successive approximation converter is the so-called binary search. The binary search algorithm is designed so that each guess of the microprocessor yields maximum information about the value of the analog input voltage. The first guess G_1 is the number 10000000, for it is equally likely that the analog voltage will be above or below this value. If the first guess is too low ($D_1 = 1$), the next guess is 11000000. If the first guess is too high ($D_1 = 0$), the next guess is 01000000. In this way, just nine such guesses are required to arrive at the answer.

Mathematically, the binary search can be described as follows: Let G_N be the Nth guess of the microcomputer; let D_N be the output of the analog comparator immediately following the Nth guess; and let V_X be the analog input voltage. $D_N = 0$ if $G_N > V_X$ and $D_N = 1$ if $G_N < V_X$. Then the values of the guesses are:

$$G_1 = 1000\ 0000$$
$$G_2 = D_1\ 100\ 0000$$
$$G_3 = D_1\ D_2\ 10\ 0000$$
$$\bullet$$
$$\bullet$$
$$\bullet$$
$$G_8 = D_1\ D_2\ D_3\ D_4\ D_5\ D_6\ D_7\ 1$$
$$G_9 = D_1\ D_2\ D_3\ D_4\ D_5\ D_6\ D_7\ D_8$$

Using the concepts just described, design an 8085-based microcomputer system and write a program in 8085 assembly language to perform the software successive-approximation A/D conversion.

4-34. Repeat Example 4–15 for both INTR and RST6.5 interrupts using the 8703 tristate A/D converter and do the following:

(a) Design and implement the necessary hardware interface.

(b) Write a program in 8085 assembly language to read and display the output of the 8703 for an analog voltage signal applied to the 8703 input.

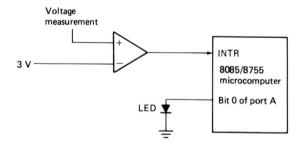

Figure P4–31

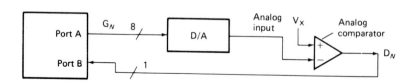

Figure P4–33

(c) Convert the flowchart to an 8085 assembly language program. Store the result in A.

4–35. It is desired to interface a pump to an 8085–8155-based microcomputer. The pump can be started by the microcomputer at the trailing edge of a START pulse via bit 2 of port A. When the pump runs, a status signal from the pump called 'PUMP RUNNING' goes to HIGH. The microcomputer polls this status via bit 0 of port A. If the pump runs, the microcomputer turns an LED ON connected to bit 4 of port A; otherwise, the LED is turned OFF. Write an 8085 assembly language program to accomplish this.

4–36. Repeat Problem 4–35 using both RST6.5 and INTR interrupts.

4–37. Discuss 8085 DMA.

4–38. Write an 8085 assembly language program to shift the contents of the D,E register pair twice to the left without using any ROTATE instructions. After shifting, if the contents of D,E are nonzero, then turn OFF an LED connected at bit 3 of port A, and store FF_{16} in the accumulator. On the other hand, if the contents of D,E are 0000_{16}, then turn the LED ON. Assume an 8085/8355 microcomputer.

4–39. In Figure P4–39, if the A/D is being serviced currently by the 8085 and the interrupt from the pump occurs, explain briefly what the user needs to do in the service routine of the A/D in order that the pump will be serviced before the A/D.

4–40. Assume an 8085–8156-based microcomputer.

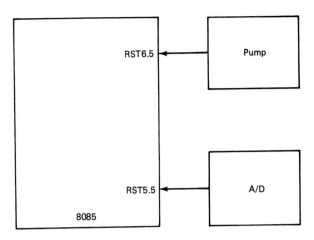

Figure P4–39

Suppose that three switches are connected to bits 0 and 1 of port C and the SID pin. Also, an LED is connected to the SOD pin. Write an 8085 assembly language program to turn the LED ON if all switches are HIGH; otherwise, turn the LED OFF.

4–41. Interface an 8085 to one 2716 and one 8155 using the following:
(a) Standard I/O and linear decoding
(b) Standard I/O and fully decoding
(c) Memory-mapped I/O and linear decoding
(d) Memory-mapped I/O and fully decoding
Draw neat schematics of your design and determine memory and I/O maps in each case.

5

Intel 8086

This chapter contains the basic features of the Intel 8086 microprocessor. Topics such as 8086 architecture, assembly language programming, memory and I/O interfacing, and 8086-based system design are included.

5-1 INTRODUCTION

The 8086 was Intel's first 16-bit microprocessor. Its design is based on the 8080 but is not directly compatible with the 8080. The 8086 can directly address 1 megabyte of memory. It uses a segmented memory. An interesting feature of 8086 is that it prefetches up to 6 instruction bytes from memory and queues them in order to speed up instruction execution.

The memory in the 8086-based microcomputer is organized as bytes. Each byte can be uniquely addressed with 20-bit addresses of 00000_{16}, 00001_{16}, . . . , $FFFFF_{16}$. An 8086 word in memory consists of any two consecutive bytes; the smaller address containing the high byte specifies the word, while the higher address contains the low byte. The 8086 always accesses a 16-bit word to or from memory. This means that a word instruction accessing a word starting at an even address can perform its function with one memory access. A word instruction starting at an odd address, however, must perform two memory accesses to two consecutive memory even addresses, discarding the unwanted bytes of each. For byte access starting at odd address N, the byte at the previous even address $N - 1$ is also accessed but discarded. Similarly, for byte access starting at even address N, the byte with odd address $N + 1$ is also accessed but discarded.

The 8086 register names followed by the letters X, H, or L in an instruction for data transfer between register and memory specify whether the transfer is 16-bit or 8-bit. For example, consider MOV AX, START. If the 20-bit address START is an even number such as 02212_{16}, then this instruction loads the low (AL) and high (AH) bytes of the 8086 16-bit register AX with the contents of memory locations 02212_{16} and 02213_{16}, respectively, in a single access. Now, if START is an odd number such as 02213_{16}, then the MOV AX, START instruction loads AL and AH with the contents of memory locations 02213_{16} and 02214_{16}, respectively, in two accesses. The 8086 also accesses memory locations 02212_{16} and 02215_{16} but ignores their contents.

Next, consider MOV AL, START. If START is an even number such as 30156_{16}, then this instruction accesses both addresses 30156_{16} and 30157_{16} but loads AL with the contents of 30156_{16} and ignores the contents of 30157_{16}. However, if START is an odd number such as 30157_{16}, then MOV AL, START loads AL with the contents of 30157_{16}. The 8086, in this case, also reads the contents of 30156_{16} but discards it.

The 8086 is packaged in a 40-pin DIP. A single $+5$ V power supply is required. The clock input signal is generated by the 8284 clock generator/driver chip. Instruction execution times vary between 2 clock cycles and 30 clock cycles.

There are three versions of the 8086. These are the 8086, 8086-2, and 8086-4. There is no difference between the three versions other than the maximum allowed clock speeds. The 8086 can be operated from a maximum clock frequency of 5 MHz. The maximum clock frequencies of the 8086-2 and 8086-4 are 8 MHz and 4 MHz, respectively.

The 8086 family consists of two types of 16-bit microprocessors, the 8086 and 8088. The main difference is how the processors communicate with the outside world. The 8088 has an 8-bit external data path to memory and I/O, while the 8086 has a 16-bit external data path. This means that the 8088 will have to do two READ operations to read a 16-bit word into memory. In most other respects, the processors are identical. Note that the 8088 accesses memory in bytes. No alterations are needed to run software written for one microprocessor on the other. Because of similarities, only the 8086 will be considered here. The 8088 is used in designing the IBM personal computer.

An 8086 can be configured as a small uniprocessor system (minimum mode when the MN/$\overline{\text{MX}}$ pin is tied to HIGH) or as a multiprocessor system (maximum mode when the MN/$\overline{\text{MX}}$ pin is tied to LOW). In a given system, the MN/$\overline{\text{MX}}$ pin is permanently tied to either HIGH or LOW. Some of the 8086 pins have dual functions depending on the selection of the MN/$\overline{\text{MX}}$ pin level. In the minimum mode (MN/$\overline{\text{MX}}$ pin HIGH), these pins transfer control signals directly to memory and I/O devices. In the maximum mode (MN/$\overline{\text{MX}}$ pin LOW), these same pins have different functions that facilitate multiprocessor systems. In the maximum mode, the control functions normally present in minimum mode are assumed by a support chip, the 8288 bus controller.

Due to technological advances, Intel introduced the high-performance 80186 and 80188, which are enhanced versions of the 8086 and 8088, respectively. The 8-MHz 80186/80188 provides 2 times greater throughput than the standard 5-MHz 8086/8088. Both have integrated several new peripheral functional units, such as a DMA controller, a 16-bit timer unit, and an interrupt controller unit, into a single chip. Just like the 8086 and 8088, the 80186 has a 16-bit data bus and the 80188 has an 8-bit data bus; otherwise, the architecture and instruction set of the 80186 and 80188 are identical. The 80186/80188 has an on-chip clock generator so that only an external crystal is required to generate the clock. The 80186/80188 can operate at either a 6- or an 8-MHz internal clock frequency. Like the 8085, the crystal frequency is divided by 2 internally. In other words, external crystals of 12 or 16 MHz must be connected to generate the 6- or 8-MHz internal clock frequency. The 80186/80188 is fabricated in a 68-pin package. Both processors have on-chip priority interrupt controller circuits to provide five interrupt pins. Like the 8086/8088, the 80186/80188 can directly address 1 megabyte of memory. The 80186/80188 is provided with 10 new instructions beyond the 8086/8088 instruction set. Examples of these instructions include INS and OUTS for inputting and outputting a string byte or string word.

The 80286, on the other hand, has added memory protection and management capabilities to the basic 8086 architecture. An 8-MHz 80286 provides up to 6 times greater throughput than the 5-MHz 8086. The 80286 is fabricated in a 68-pin package. The 80286 can be operated at a clock frequency of 4, 6, or 8 MHz. An external 82284 clock generator chip is required to generate the clock. The 80286 divides the external clock by 2 to generate the internal clock. The 80286 can be operated

in two modes, real address and protected virtual address. The real address mode emulates a very high-performance 8086. In this mode, the 80286 can directly address 1 megabyte of memory. The 80286, in the virtual address mode, can directly address 16 megabytes of memory. The virtual address mode provides (in addition to the real address mode capabilities) virtual memory management as well as task management and protection. The programmer can select one of these modes by loading appropriate data in the 16-bit machine status word (MSW) register by using load and store instructions. Two examples of these instructions are LMSW (load MSW register) and SMSW (store MSW register).

The 80286 is used as the microprocessor of the IBM PC/AT personal computer. An enhanced version of the 80286 is the 32-bit 80386 microprocessor, which will be covered later. The 80386 is used as the microprocessor in the IBM 386PC. The 80486 is Intel's newest 32-bit microprocessor. It is based on the Intel 386 and includes on-chip floating-point circuitry. IBM's newest 486 PC contains the 80486 chip.

5–2 8086 ARCHITECTURE

Figure 5–1 shows the block diagram of the 8086 microprocessor. As shown in the figure, the 8086 microprocessor is divided internally into two separate units. These are the Bus Interface Unit (BIU) and the Execution Unit (EU). The two units function independently. The BIU fetches instructions, reads operands, and writes results. The EU executes instructions that have already been fetched by the BIU so that the instruction fetch overlaps with execution.

A 16-bit Arithmetic and Logic Unit (ALU) in the EU maintains the microprocessor status and control flags and manipulates the general registers and instruction operands. The BIU provides all external bus operations. The BIU contains segment registers and instruction pointer, instruction queue, and address generation/bus control circuitry to provide functions such as the fetching and queueing of instructions and bus control.

Bus Interface Unit The BIU's instruction queue is a First-In-First-Out (FIFO) group of registers in which up to 6 bytes of instruction code are prefetched from memory ahead of time. This is done in order to speed up program execution by overlapping instruction fetch with execution. This mechanism is known as *pipelining*. If the queue is full and the EU does not request BIU to access memory, the BIU does not perform any bus cycle. On the other hand, if the BIU is not full and if it can store at least 2 bytes and the EU does not request it to access memory, the BIU may prefetch instructions. However, if the BIU is interrupted by the EU for memory access while the BIU is in the process of fetching an instruction, the BIU first completes fetching and then

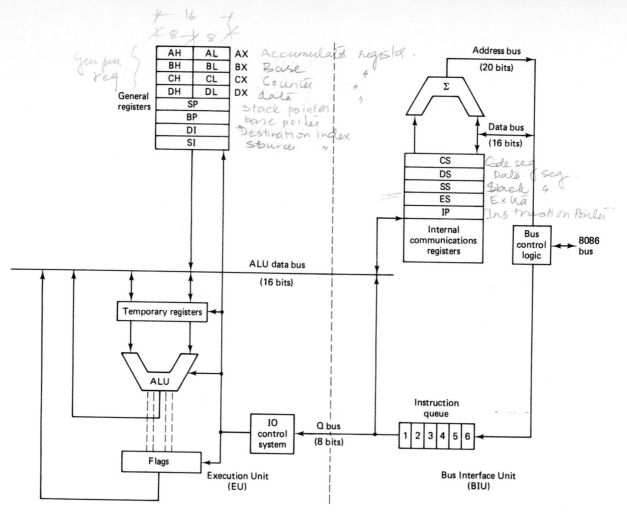

Figure 5-1 Internal architecture of the 8086. (Courtesy of Intel)

services the EU: The queue allows the BIU to keep the EU supplied with prefetched instructions without tying up the system bus. If an instruction such as a JUMP or CALL SUBROUTINE is encountered, the BIU will reset the queue and begin refilling after passing the new instruction to the EU.

The BIU contains a dedicated adder, which is used to produce the 20-bit address. The bus control logic of the BIU generates all the bus control signals, such as the READ and WRITE signals, for memory and I/O.

The BIU also has four 16-bit segment registers. These are the *code segment* (CS), *data segment* (DS), *stack segment* (SS), and *extra segment* (ES) registers. The 8086's 1-megabyte memory is divided into segments of up to 64K bytes each. The 8086 can directly address four segments (256K bytes within the 1 megabyte of memory) at a particular time. Programs obtain access to code and data in the segments by changing the segment register contents to point to the desired segments.

- All program instructions must be located in main memory pointed to by the 16-bit *CS register* with a 16-bit offset in the segment contained in the 16-bit *instruction pointer (IP)*. The BIU computes the 20-

bit physical address internally using the programmer-provided logical address (16-bit contents of CS and IP) by logically shifting the contents of CS 4 bits to the left and then adding the 16-bit contents of IP. That is, the CS is multiplied by 16_{10} by the BIU for computing the 20-bit physical address. This means that all instructions of a program are relative to the contents of the CS register multiplied by 16 and then offset is added provided by the 16-bit contents of IP. The BIU always inserts four zeros for the lowest 4 bits of the 20-bit starting address (physical) of a segment. In other words, the CS contains the base or start of the current code segment, and the IP contains the distance or offset from this address to the next instruction byte to be fetched. Note that immediate data are considered as part of the code segment.

- The *SS register* points to the current stack. The 20-bit physical stack address is calculated from the SS and SP (stack pointer) for stack instructions such as PUSH and POP. The programmer can use the BP (base pointer) instead of the SP for accessing the stack using the based addressing mode. In this case,

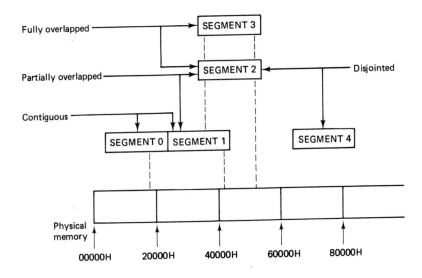

the 20-bit physical stack address is calculated from the BP and SS.

- The *DS register* points to the current data segment; operands for most instructions are fetched from this segment. The 16-bit contents of the SI (source index) or DI (destination index) or a 16-bit displacement are used as offset for computing the 20-bit physical address.

- The *ES register* points to the extra segment in which data (in excess of 64K pointed to by the DS) is stored. String instructions always use the ES and DI to determine the 20-bit physical address for the destination.

The segments can be contiguous, partially overlapped, fully overlapped, or disjointed. An example of how five segments (SEGMENT 0 through SEGMENT 4) may be stored in physical memory is shown at the top of this page. In this example, SEGMENTs 0 and 1 are contiguous (adjacent), SEGMENTs 1 and 2 are partially overlapped, SEGMENTs 2 and 3 are fully overlapped, and SEGMENTs 2 and 4 are disjointed.

Every segment must start on 16-byte memory boundaries. Typical examples of values of segments should then be selected based on physical addresses starting at 00000_{16}, 00010_{16}, 00020_{16}, 00030_{16}, . . . , $FFFF0_{16}$,. A physical memory location may be mapped into (contained in) one or more logical segments. Many applications can be written to simply initialize the segment registers and then forget them.

A segment can be pointed to by more than one segment register. For example, the DS and ES may point to the same segment in memory if a string located in that segment is used as a source segment in one string instruction and a destination segment in another string instruction. Note that, for string instructions, a destination segment must be pointed to by the ES.

It should be pointed out that codes should not be written within 6 bytes of the end of physical memory. Failure to comply with this guideline may result in an attempted OP-code fetch from nonexistent memory, hanging the microprocessor if READY is not returned. One example of four currently addressable segments is shown next:

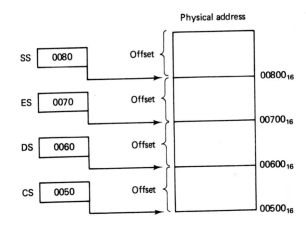

Execution Unit The EU decodes and executes instructions. A decoder in the EU control system translates instructions. The EU has a 16-bit ALU for performing arithmetic and logic operations.

The EU has nine 16-bit registers. These are the AX, BX, CX, DX, SP, BP, SI, and DI, and flag register. The 16-bit general registers AX, BX, CX, and DX can be used as two 8-bit registers (AH, AL; BH, BL; CH, CL; DH, DL). For example, the 16-bit register DX can be considered as two 8-bit registers DH (high byte of DX) and DL (low byte of DX). The general-purpose registers AX, BX, CX, and DX are named after special functions carried out by each one of them.

- The *AX register*, for example, is called the 16-bit *accumulator* while the AL is the 8-bit accumulator.

The use of accumulator registers is assumed by some instructions. The I/O (IN or OUT) instructions always use the AX or AL for inputting/outputting 16- or 8-bit data to or from an I/O port. Multiplication and division instructions also use the AX or AL. The AL register is the same as the 8085 A register.

- The *BX register* is called the *base* register. This is the only general-purpose register whose contents can be used for addressing 8086 memory. All memory references utilizing this register content for addressing use the DS as the default segment register. The BX register is similar to the 8085 H,L register. In other words, the 8086 BH and BL are equivalent to the 8085 H and L registers, respectively.

- The *CX register* is known as the *counter* register because some instructions, such as SHIFT, ROTATE, and LOOP, use the contents of CX as a counter. For example, the instruction LOOP START will automatically decrement CX by 1 without affecting flags and will check if [CX] = 0. If it is zero, the 8086 executes the next instruction; otherwise, the 8086 branches to the label START.

- The *DX register,* or *data* register, is used to hold the high 16-bit result (data) in 16 × 16 multiplication or the high 16-bit dividend (data) before a 32 ÷ 16 division and the 16-bit remainder after the division.

- The two *pointer registers*, SP (stack pointer) and BP (base pointer), are used to access data in the stack segment. The SP is used as an offset from the current SS during execution of instructions that involve the stack segment in external memory. The SP contents are automatically updated (incremented or decremented) due to execution of a POP or PUSH instruction. The BP contains an offset address in the

current SS. This offset is used by instructions utilizing the based addressing mode.

- The two *index registers,* SI (source index) and DI (destination index), are used in indexed addressing. Note that instructions that process data strings use the SI and DI index registers together with the DS and ES, respectively, in order to distinguish between the source and destination addresses.

- The *flag register* in the EU holds the status flags, typically after an ALU operation. The EU sets or resets these flags to reflect certain properties of the results of arithmetic and logic operations.

Figure 5–2 summarizes the 8086 registers. It shows the nine 16-bit registers in the EU. As described earlier, each one of the AX, BX, CX, and DX registers can be used as two 8-bit registers or as one 16-bit register. The other registers can be accessed as 16-bit registers. Also shown are the four 16-bit segment registers and the 16-bit IP in the BIU. The IP is similar to the 8085 PC. The CS register points to the current code segment from which instructions are fetched. The effective address is derived from the CS and IP. The SS register points to the current stack. The effective address is obtained from the SS and SP. The DS register points to the current data segment. The ES register points to the current extra segment where data is usually stored.

Figure 5–3 shows the 8086 flag register. The 8086 has six 1-bit status flags. Let us now explain these flags.

1. AF (auxiliary carry flag) is set if there is a carry from the low nibble into the high nibble or a borrow from the high nibble into the low nibble of the low-order 8 bits of a 16-bit number. This flag is used by BCD arithmetic instructions; otherwise, AF is zero.

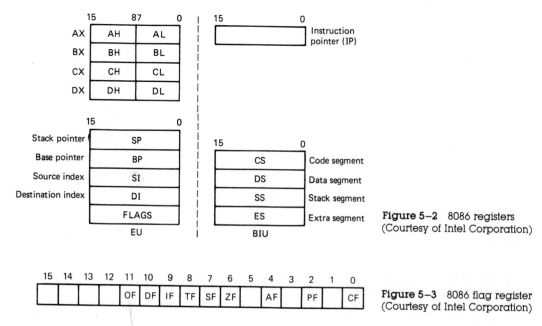

Figure 5–2 8086 registers (Courtesy of Intel Corporation)

Figure 5–3 8086 flag register (Courtesy of Intel Corporation)

2. CF (carry flag) is set if there is a carry from addition or a borrow from subtraction.

3. OF (overflow flag) is set if there is an arithmetic overflow, i.e., if the size of the result exceeds the capacity of the destination location. An interrupt on overflow instruction is available to generate an interrupt in this situation; otherwise, it is zero.

4. SF (sign flag) is set if the most significant bit of the result is one; otherwise, it is zero.

5. PF (parity flag) is set if the result has even parity; PF is zero for odd parity of the result.

6. ZF (zero flag) is set if the result is zero; ZF is zero for a nonzero result.

The 8086 has three control bits in the flag register that can be set or cleared by the programmer:

1. Setting DF (direction flag) causes string instructions to auto-decrement; clearing DF causes string instructions to auto-increment.

2. Setting IF (interrupt flag) causes the 8086 to recognize external maskable interrupts; clearing IF disables these interrupts.

3. Setting TF (trap flag) puts the 8086 in the single-step mode. In this mode, the 8086 generates an internal interrupt after execution of each instruction. The user can write a service routine at the interrupt address vector to display the desired registers and memory locations. The user can thus debug a program.

5–3 8086 ADDRESSING MODES

The 8086 provides various addressing modes to access instruction operands. Operands may be contained in registers, within the instruction OP code, in memory, or in I/O ports.

The 8086 has 12 addressing modes. These modes can be classified into five groups:

1. Register and immediate modes
2. Memory addressing modes
3. Port addressing mode
4. Relative addressing mode
5. Implied addressing mode

Register and Immediate Modes In register mode, source operands, destination operands, or both may be contained in registers. For example, MOV AX, BX moves the 16-bit contents of BX into AX. On the other hand, MOV AL, BL moves the 8-bit contents of BL into AL.

In immediate mode, 8- or 16-bit data can be specified as part of the instruction. For example, MOV CX, 5062H moves the 16-bit data 5062_{16} into register CX.

Memory Addressing Modes The EU has direct access to all registers and data for register and immediate modes. However, the EU cannot directly access the memory operands. It must use the BIU in order to access memory operands. For example, when the EU needs a memory operand, it sends an offset value to the BIU. This offset is added to the contents of a segment register after shifting it 4 times to the left, generating a 20-bit physical address. For example, suppose that the contents of a segment register is 2052_{16} and the offset is 0020_{16}. Now, in order to generate the 20-bit physical address, the EU passes this offset to the BIU. The BIU then shifts the segment register 4 times to the left, obtains 20520_{16} and then adds the 0020_{16} offset to provide the 20-bit physical address 20540_{16}. Note that the 8086 must use a segment register whenever it accesses the memory. Also, every memory addressing mode has a standard default segment register. However, a segment override instruction can be placed before most of the memory operand instructions whose default segment register is to be overridden. For example, INC BYTE PTR [START] will increment the 8-bit contents of a memory location in DS with offset START by 1. However, segment DS can be overridden by ES as follows: INC ES: BYTE PTR [START]. Segments cannot be overridden for stack reference instructions (such as PUSH and POP). The destination segment of a string segment, which must be ES (if a prefix is used with a string instruction, only the source segment DS can be overridden) cannot be overridden. The code segment (CS) register used in program memory addressing cannot be overridden.

The EU calculates an offset from the instruction for a memory operand. This offset is called the operand's *effective address*, or EA. It is a 16-bit number that represents the operand's distance in bytes from the start of the segment in which it resides.

The various memory addressing modes will now be described.

Memory Direct Addressing In this mode, the effective address is taken directly from the displacement field of the instruction. No registers are involved. For example, MOV BX, START moves the contents of the 20-bit address computed from DS and START to BX. Some assemblers use square brackets around START to indicate that the contents of the memory location(s) are at a displacement START from the segment DS. If square brackets are not used, then the programmer must define START as a 16-bit offset by using the assembler pseudo-instruction DW.

Register Indirect Addressing The effective address of a memory operand may be taken directly from one of the base or index registers (BX, BP, SI, DI). For example, consider MOV CX, [BX]. If [DS] = 2000_{16}, [BX] =

0004_{16}, and $[20004_{16}] = 0224_{16}$, then, after MOV CX, [BX], the contents of CX is 0224_{16}. Note that the segment register used in MOV CX, [BX] can be overridden, such as MOV CX,ES: [BX]. Now, the MOV instruction will use ES instead of DS. If $[ES] = 1000_{16}$ and $[10004_{16}] = 0002_{16}$, then, after MOV CX,ES: [BX], the register CX will contain 0002_{16}.

Based Addressing   In this mode, the effective address is the sum of a displacement value (signed 8-bit or unsigned 16-bit) and the contents of register BX or BP. For example, MOV AX, 4[BX] moves the contents of the 20-bit address computed from a segment register and [BX + 4] into AX. The segment register is DS or SS. The displacement (4 in this case) can be 16-bit or sign-extended 8-bit. This means that if the displacement is 8-bit, then the 8086 sign extends this to 16-bit. Segment register SS is used when the stack is accessed; otherwise, this mode uses segment register DS. When memory is accessed, the 20-bit physical address is computed from BX and DS. On the other hand, when the stack is accessed, the 20-bit physical address is computed from BP and SS. Note that BP may be considered as the user stack pointer while SP is the system stack pointer. This is because SP is used by some 8086 instructions (such as CALL subroutine) automatically.

The based addressing mode with BP is a very convenient way to access stack data. BP can be used as a stack pointer in SS to access local variables. Consider the following instruction sequence (arbitrarily chosen to illustrate the use of BP for stack):

PUSH BP	;	Save BP
MOV BP, SP	;	Establish BP
PUSH CX	;	Save CX
SUB SP, 6	;	Allocate 3 words of
	;	stack for local variables
MOV −4 [BP], BX	;	Push BX onto stack using BP
MOV −6 [BP], AX	;	Push AX onto stack using BP
MOV −8 [BP], DX	;	Push DX onto stack using BP
ADD SP, 6	;	Deallocate stack
POP CX	;	Restore CX
POP BP	;	Restore BP

This instruction sequence can be be depicted as follows:

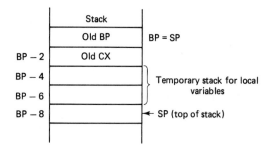

Indexed Addressing   In this mode, the effective address is calculated from the sum of a displacement value and the contents of register SI or DI. For example, MOV AX, VALUE [SI] moves the contents of the 20-bit address computed from VALUE, SI and the segment register into AX. The segment register is DS. The displacement (VALUE in this case) can be unsigned 16-bit or sign-extended 8-bit.

Based Indexed Addressing   In this mode, the effective address is computed from the sum of a base register (BX or BP), an index register (SI or DI), and a displacement. For example, MOV AX, 4[BX][SI] moves the contents of the 20-bit address computed from the segment register and [BX] + [SI] + 4 into AX. The segment register is DS. The displacement can be unsigned 16-bit or sign-extended 8-bit.

String Addressing   This mode uses index registers. SI is assumed to point to the first byte or word of the source string, and DI is assumed to point to the first byte or word of the destination when a string instruction is executed. The SI or DI is automatically incremented or decremented to point to the next byte or word depending on DF. The default segment register for source is DS, and it may be overridden; the segment register for destination must be ES. An example is MOVS WORD. If $[DF] = 0$, $[DS] = 3000_{16}$, $[SI] = 0020_{16}$, $[ES] = 5000_{16}$, $[DI] = 0040_{16}$, $[30020] = 30_{16}$, $[30021] = 05_{16}$, $[50040] = 06_{16}$, and $[50041] = 20_{16}$, then, after this MOVS, $[50040] = 30_{16}$, $[50041] = 05_{16}$, $[SI] = 0022_{16}$, and $[DI] = 0042_{16}$.

Port Addressing   Two I/O port addressing modes can be used: the direct port and indirect port modes. In either case, 8- or 16-bit I/O transfers must take place via AL or AX, respectively.

In direct port mode, the port number is an 8-bit immediate operand to access 256 ports. For example, IN AL, 02 moves the contents of port 02 to AL.

In indirect port mode, the port number is taken from DX allowing 64K bytes or 32K words of ports. For example, suppose $[DX] = 0020$, $[port\ 0020] = 02_{16}$, and $[port\ 0021] = 03_{16}$, then, after IN AX, DX, register AX contains 0302_{16}. On the other hand, after IN AL, DX, register AL contains 02_{16}.

Relative Addressing Mode   Instructions using this mode specify the operand as a signed 8-bit displacement relative to PC. An example is JNC START. This instruction means that if carry = 0, then PC is loaded with current PC contents plus the 8-bit signed value of START; otherwise, the next instruction is executed.

Implied Addressing Mode   Instructions using this mode have no operands. An example is CLC, which clears the carry flag to zero.

5-4 8086 INSTRUCTION SET

The 8086 instruction set contains equivalents to the instructions typically found in the 8085 plus many new instructions. Some of the new operations include multiplication and division (both signed and unsigned), string operations, bit manipulation instructions, and interrupt instructions.

The 8086 has approximately 117 different instructions with about 300 OP codes. The 8086 instruction set contains no-operand, single-operand, and two-operand instructions. Except for string instructions that involve array operation, 8086 instructions do not permit memory-to-memory operations.

Table 5-1 is a summary of 8086 instructions in alphabetical order. A detailed description of 8086 instructions is included in Appendix I.

TABLE 5-1
Summary of 8086 Instruction Set

Instruction	Interpretation	Comments
AAA	ASCII adjust [AL] after addition	Instruction has implied addressing mode; is used to adjust [AL] after addition of two ASCII characters
AAD	ASCII adjust for division	Instruction has implied addressing mode; converts two unpacked BCD digits in AX into equivalent binary numbers in AL; must be used before dividing two unpacked BCD digits by an unpacked BCD byte
AAM	ASCII adjust after multiplication	Instruction has implied addressing mode; after multiplying two unpacked BCD numbers, adjust product in AX to become an unpacked BCD result; ZF, SF, and PF affected
AAS	ASCII adjust [AL] after subtraction	Instruction has implied addressing mode; is used to adjust [AL] after subtraction of two ASCII characters
ADC mem/reg 1, mem/reg 2	[mem/reg 1] ← [mem/reg 1] + [mem/reg 2] + CY	Memory or register can be 8- or 16-bit; all flags affected; no segment registers allowed; no memory-to-memory ADC permitted
ADC mem, data	[mem] ← [mem] + data + CY	Data can be 8- or 16-bit; mem uses DS as segment register; all flags affected
ADC reg, data	[reg] ← [reg] + data + CY	Data can be 8- or 16-bit; register cannot be segment register; all flags affected
ADD mem/reg 1, mem/reg 2	[mem/reg 1] ← [mem/reg 2] + [mem/reg 1]	Add two 8- or 16-bit data; no memory-to-memory ADD permitted; all flags affected; mem uses DS as segment register; reg 1 or reg 2 cannot be segment register
ADD mem, data	[mem] ← [mem] + data	Mem uses DS as segment register; data can be 8- or 16-bit; all flags affected
ADD reg, data	[reg] ← [reg] + data	Data can be 8- or 16-bit; no segment registers allowed; all flags affected
AND mem/reg 1, mem/reg 2	[mem/reg 1] ← [mem/reg 1] ∧ [mem/reg 2]	Instruction logically ANDs 8- or 16-bit data in [mem/reg 2]; all flags affected; OF and CF cleared to zero; no segment registers allowed; no memory-to-memory operation allowed; mem uses DS as segment register
AND mem, data	[mem] ← [mem] ∧ data	Data can be 8- or 16-bit; mem uses DS as segment register; all flags affected; OF and CF cleared to zero
AND reg, data	[reg] ← [reg] ∧ data	Data can be 8- or 16-bit; reg cannot be segment register; all flags affected; OF and CF cleared to zero
CALL PROC (NEAR)	Call a subroutine in same segment with signed 16-bit displacement (to call a subroutine in ± 32K)	NEAR in the statement BEGIN PROC NEAR indicates subroutine "BEGIN" is in same segment and is 16-bit signed; CALL BEGIN instruction decrements SP by 2, pushes IP onto stack, then adds signed 16-bit value of BEGIN to IP; CS is unchanged; thus a subroutine is called in same segment (intrasegment direct)
CALL reg16	Call a subroutine in same segment addressed by contents of a 16-bit general register	8086 decrements SP by 2 and pushes IP onto stack; then specified 16-bit register contents (such as BX, SI, DI) provide new value for IP; CS is unchanged (intrasegment indirect)
CALL mem16	Call a subroutine by contents of a memory location	8086 decrements SP by 2 and pushes IP onto stack; 8086 then loads contents of a memory location addressed by contents of a 16-bit reg-

Reprinted with permission from *Microprocessors and Microcomputer-Based System Design* by M. Rafiquzzaman, Copyright 1990 by CRC Press, Inc., Boca Raton, FL.

Continued.

TABLE 5-1
Summary of 8086 Instruction Set — cont'd

Instruction	Interpretation	Comments
	pointed to by 8086 16-bit register such as BX, SI, and DI	ister such as BX, SI, DI into IP; [CS] is unchanged (intrasegment indirect)
CALL PROC (FAR)	Call a subroutine in another segment	FAR in statement BEGIN PROC FAR indicates subroutine "BEGIN" is in another segment and value of BEGIN is 32 bits wide; 8086 decrements SP by 2, pushes CS onto stack, and moves low 16-bit value of specified 32-bit number such as "BEGIN" in CALL BEGIN into CS; SP is again decremented by 2; IP is pushed onto stack; IP is then loaded with high 16-bit value of BEGIN; thus subroutine is called in another code segment (intersegment direct)
CALL DWORD PTR [reg16]	Call a subroutine in another segment	Instruction decrements SP by 2 and pushes CS onto stack; CS is then loaded with contents of memory locations addressed by [reg16 + 2] and [reg16 + 3] in DS; SP is again decremented by 2; IP is pushed onto stack; IP is then loaded with contents of memory locations addressed by [reg16] and [reg16 + 1] in DS; typical 8086 registers used for reg16 are BX, SI, DI (intersegment indirect)
CBW	Convert a byte to a word	Extend sign bit (bit 7) of AL into AH
CLC	CF ← 0	Clear carry flag to zero
CLD	DF ← 0	Clear direction flag to zero
CLI	IF ← 0	Clear interrupt enable flag to zero to disable maskable interrupts
CMC	CF ← CF'	1's complement carry
CMP mem/reg 1, mem/reg 2	[mem/reg 1] − [mem/reg 2], flags affected	mem/reg can be 8- or 16-bit; no memory-to-memory comparison allowed; result of subtraction not provided; all flags affected
CMP mem/reg, data	[mem/reg] − data, flags affected	Subtracts 8- or 16-bit data from [mem/reg] and affects flags; no result provided
CMPS BYTE or CMPSB	FOR BYTE [[SI]] − [[DI]], flags affected [SI] ← [SI] ± 1 [DI] ← [DI] ± 1	8- or 16-bit data addressed by [DI] in ES is subtracted from 8- or 16-bit data addressed by SI in DS; flags affected without providing any result; if DF = 0, then SI and DI are decremented by 1 for byte or 2 for word; segment register ES in destination cannot be overridden
COMPS WORD or CMPSW	FOR WORD [[SI]] − [[DI]], flags affected [SI] ← [SI] ± 2 [DI] ← [DI] ± 2	
CWD	Convert a word to 32 bits	Extend sign bit (bit 15) of AX into DX
DAA	Decimal adjust [AL] after addition	Instruction uses implied addressing mode; converts [AL] into BCD; should be used after BCD addition
DAS	Decimal adjust [AL] after subtraction	Instruction uses implied addressing mode; converts [AL] into BCD; should be used after BCD subtraction
DEC reg16	[reg16] ← [reg16] − 1	1-byte instruction used to decrement a 16-bit register except segment register; carry flag not affected
DEC mem/reg8	[mem] ← [mem] − 1 or [reg8] ← [reg8] − 1	Used to decrement a byte or word in memory or an 8-bit register content; segment register cannot be decremented; carry flag not affected
DIV mem/reg	16 ÷ 8 division: $\dfrac{[AX]}{[mem8/reg8]}$ [AH] ← remainder [AL] ← quotient 32 ÷ 16 division: $\dfrac{[DX]\ [AX]}{[mem16/reg16]}$ [DX] ← remainder [AX] ← quotient	Mem/reg is 8-bit for 16-bit by 8-bit division and 16-bit for 32-bit by 16-bit division; unsigned division; no flags affected; division by zero automatically generates internal interrupt

TABLE 5-1
Summary of 8086 Instruction Set — cont'd

Instruction	Interpretation	Comments
ESC external OP code, source	ESCAPE to external processes	Instruction used to pass instructions to coprocessor such as 8087 floating-point coprocessor, which simultaneously monitors system bus with 8086; coprocessor OP codes are 6 bits wide; coprocessor treats normal 8086 instructions as NOPs; 8086 fetches all instructions from memory; when 8086 encounters an ESC, usually treats it as NOP; coprocessor decodes this instruction and carries out operation using 6-bit OP code independent of 8086; for ESC OP code, memory, 8086 accesses data in memory for coprocessor; for ESC data, register, coprocessor operates on 8086 registers; 8086 treats this as NOP
HLT	HALT	Halt
IDIV mem/reg	Same as DIV mem/reg	Same as DIV mem/reg except this is signed division.
IMUL mem/reg	8×8 multiplication: $[AX] \leftarrow [AL]*[mem8/reg8]$ 16×16 multiplication: $[DX][AX] \leftarrow [AX]*[mem16/mem16]$	Mem/reg can be 8- or 16-bit; only CF and OF affected; signed multiplication
IN AL, DX	$[AL] \leftarrow [PORT\ DX]$	Input AL with 8-bit contents of port addressed by DX; 1-byte instruction
IN AX, DX	$[AX] \leftarrow [PORT\ DX]$	Input AX with 16-bit contents of port addressed by DX and DX + 1; 1-byte instruction
IN AL, PORT	$[AL] \leftarrow [PORT]$	Input AL with 8-bit contents of port addressed by second byte of instruction
IN AX, PORT	$[AX] \leftarrow [PORT]$	Input AX with 16-bit contents of port addressed by 8-bit address in second byte of instruction
INC reg16	$[reg16] \leftarrow [reg16] + 1$	1-byte instruction used to increment a 16-bit register except segment register; carry flag not affected
INC mem/reg8	$[mem] \leftarrow [mem] + 1$ *or* $[reg8] \leftarrow [reg8] + 1$	2-byte instruction used to increment a byte or word in memory *or* an 8-bit register content; segment register cannot be incremented; carry flag not affected
INT n (n can be 0–255)	$[SP] \leftarrow [SP] - 2$ $[[SP]] \leftarrow$ flags $IF \leftarrow 0$ $TF \leftarrow 0$ $[SP] \leftarrow [SP] - 2$ $[[SP]] \leftarrow [CS]$ $[CS] \leftarrow 4n + 2$ $[SP] \leftarrow [SP] - 2$ $[[SP]] \leftarrow [IP]$ $[IP] \leftarrow 4n$	Software interrupts can be used as supervisor calls, i.e., request for service from an operating system; different interrupt type can be used for each type of service that operating system could supply for an application or program; software interrupts can also be used for checking interrupt service routines written for hardware-initiated interrupts
INTO	Interrupt on overflow	Generates internal interrupt if OF = 1; executes INT4; can be used after arithmetic operation to activate service routine if OF = 1; when INTO is executed and if OF = 1, operations similar to INTn take place
IRET	Interrupt return	POPs IP, CS, and flags from stack; used as return instruction at end of service routine for both hardware and software interrupts
JA/JNBE disp8	Jump if above/jump if not below equal	Jump if above/jump if not below or equal with 8-bit signed displacement; i.e., displacement can be from -128_{10} to $+127_{10}$, 0 being positive; JA and JNBE are mnemonics representing same instruction; jump if both CF and ZF = 0; used for unsigned comparison
JAE/JNB/JNC disp8	Jump if above or equal/jump if not below/jump if no carry	Same as JA/JNBE except that 8086 jumps if CF = 0; used for unsigned comparison

Continued.

TABLE 5–1
Summary of 8086 Instruction Set — cont'd

Instruction	Interpretation	Comments
JB/JC/JNAE disp8	Jump if below/jump if carry/ jump if not above or equal	Same as JA/JNBE except that jump is taken if CF = 1; used for unsigned comparison
JCXZ disp8	Jump if CX equal to zero	Jump if CX = 0; useful at beginning of a loop to bypass loop if CX = 0
JE/JZ disp8	Jump if equal/jump if zero	Same as JA/JNBE except that jump is taken if ZF = 1; used for both signed and unsigned comparison
JG/JNLE disp8	Jump if greater/jump if not less or equal	Same as JA/JNBE except that jump is taken if $((SF \oplus OF)$ or ZF) = 0; used for signed comparison
JGE/JNL disp8	Jump if greater or equal/jump if not less	Same as JA/JNBE except that jump is taken if $(SF \oplus OF)$ = 0; used for signed comparison
JL/JNGE disp8	Jump if less/jump if not greater or equal	Same as JA/JNBE except that jump is taken if $(SF \oplus OF)$ = 1; used for signed comparison
JLE/JNG disp8	Jump if less or equal/jump if not greater	Same as JA/JNBE except that jump is taken if $((SF \oplus OF)$ or ZF) = 1; used for signed comparison
JMP label	Unconditional jump with a signed 8-bit (SHORT) or signed 16-bit (NEAR) displacement in same segment	Label START can be signed 8-bit (called SHORT jump) or signed 16-bit (called NEAR jump) displacement; assembler usually determines displacement value; if assembler finds displacement value to be signed 8-bit (−128 to +127, 0 being positive), then it uses 2 bytes for instruction, 1 byte for OP code followed by a byte for displacement; assembler sign-extends 8-bit displacement and then adds it to IP; [CS] is unchanged; on the other hand, if assembler finds displacement to be signed 16-bit (±32K), then it uses 3 bytes for instruction, 1 byte for OP code followed by 2 bytes for displacement; assembler adds signed 16-bit displacement to IP; [CS] is unchanged; thus JMP provides jump in same segment (intrasegment direct jump)
JMP reg16	[IP] ← [reg16], [CS] is unchanged	Jump to address specified by contents of a 16-bit register such as BX, SI, DI in same code segment; in JMP BX, [BX] is loaded into IP and [CS] is unchanged (intrasegment memory indirect jump)
JMP mem16	[IP] ← [mem], [CS] is unchanged	Jump to address specified by contents of a 16-bit memory location addressed by 16-bit register such as BX, SI, DI; in JMP [BX], it copies contents of a memory location addressed by BX in DS into IP; CS is unchanged (intrasegment memory indirect jump)
JMP label (FAR)	Unconditionally jump to another segment	5-byte instruction; first byte is OP code followed by 4 bytes of 32-bit immediate data; bytes 2 and 3 are loaded into CS to jump unconditionally to another segment (intersegment direct)
JMP DWORD PTR [reg16]	Unconditionally jump to another segment	Instruction loads contents of memory locations addressed by [reg16] and [reg16 + 1] in DS into IP; then loads contents of memory locations addressed by [reg16 + 2] and [reg16 + 3] in DS into CS; typical 8086 registers used for reg16 are BX, SI, DI (intersegment indirect)
JNE/JNZ disp8	Jump if not equal/jump if not zero	Same as JA/JNBE except that jump is taken if ZF = 0; used for both signed and unsigned comparison
JNO disp8	Jump if not overflow	Same as JA/JNBE except that jump is taken if OF = 0
JNP/JPO disp8	Jump if no parity/jump if partly odd	Same as JA/JNBE except that jump is taken if PF = 0
JNS disp8	Jump if not sign	Same as JA/JNBE except that jump is taken if SF = 0
JO disp8	Jump if overflow	Same as JA/JNBE except that jump is taken if OF = 1
JP/JPE disp8	Jump if parity/jump even	Same as JA/JNBE except that jump is taken if PF = 1
JS disp8	Jump if sign	Same as JA/JNBE except that jump is taken if SF = 1
LAHF	[AH] ← [flags, low byte]	Instruction has implied addressing mode; loads AH with low byte of flag register; no flags affected
LDS reg, mem	[reg] ← [mem] [DS] ← [mem + 2]	Load a 16-bit register (AX, BX, CX, DX, SP, BP, SI, DI) with contents of specified memory and load DS with contents of location that follows; no flags affected; DS used as segment register for mem

TABLE 5-1
Summary of 8086 Instruction Set — cont'd

Instruction	Interpretation	Comments
LEA reg, offset	[reg] ← [offset portion of address]	LEA (load effective address) loads value of source operand rather than its contents to register (such as SI, DI, BX), which are allowed to contain offset for accessing memory; no flags affected
LES reg, mem	[reg] ← [mem] [ES] ← [mem + 2]	DS used as segment register for mem; in LES DX, [BX], DX is loaded with 16-bit value from a memory location addressed by 20-bit physical address computed from DS and BX; 16-bit contents of next memory are loaded into ES; no flags affected
LOCK	Lock bus during next instruction	1-byte prefix causes 8086 (in maximum mode) to assert its bus LOCK signal while following instruction is executed; signal is used in multiprocessing; LOCK pin of 8086 can be used to LOCK other processors off system bus during execution of an instruction; thus 8086 can be assured of uninterrupted access to common system resources such as shared RAM
LODS BYTE *or* LODSB	FOR BYTE [AL] ← [[SI]] [SI] ← [SI] ± 1	Load 8-bit data into AL or 16-bit data into AX from memory location addressed by SI in segment DS; if DF = 0, then SI is incremented by 1 for byte or 2 for word after the load; if DF = 1, then SI is decremented by 1 for byte or 2 for word; no flags affected
LODS WORD *or* LODSW	FOR WORD [AX] ← [[SI]] [SI] ← [SI] ± 2	
LOOP disp8	Loop if CX not equal to zero	Decrement CX by 1 without affecting flags and loop with signed 8-bit displacement (from −128 to +127, 0 being positive) if CX ≠ 0
LOOPE/LOOPZ disp8	Loop while equal/loop while zero	Decrement CX by 1 without affecting flags and loop with signed 8-bit displacement if CX = 0 and ZF = 1, which results from execution of previous instruction
LOOPNE/ LOOPNZ disp8	Loop while not equal/loop while not zero	Decrement CX by 1 without affecting flags and loop with signed 8-bit displacement if CX ≠ 0 and ZF = 0, which results from execution of previous instruction
MOV mem/reg 2, mem/reg 1	[mem/reg 2] ← [mem/reg 1]	Mem uses DS as segment register; no memory-to-memory operation allowed; i.e., MOV mem, mem not permitted; segment register cannot be specified as reg 1 or reg 2; no flags affected
MOV mem, data	[mem] ← data	Mem uses DS as segment register; no flags affected
MOV reg, data	[reg] ← data	Segment register cannot be specified as reg; data can be 8- or 16-bit; no flags affected
MOV segreg, mem/reg	[segreg] ← [mem/reg]	Mem uses DS as segment register; used for initializing CS, DS, ES, SS; no flags affected
MOV mem/reg, segreg	[mem/reg] ← [segreg]	Mem uses DS as segment register; no flags affected
MOVS BYTE *or* MOVSB MOVS WORD *or* MOVSW	FOR BYTE [[DI]] ← [[SI]] [SI] ← [SI] ± 1 FOR WORD [[DI]] ← [[SI]] [SI] ← [SI] ± 2	Move 8- or 16-bit data from memory location addressed by SI in segment DS location addressed by DI in ES; segment DS can be overridden by a prefix but destination segment must be ES and cannot be overridden; if DF = 0, then SI is incremented by 1 for byte or 2 for word; if DF = 1, then SI is decremented by 1 for byte or 2 for word
MUL mem/reg	8 × 8 multiplication: [AX] ← [AL]* [mem8/reg8] 16 × 16 multiplication: [DX] [AX] ← [AX]* [mem16/reg16]	Mem/reg can be 8- or 16-bit; only CF and OF affected; unsigned multiplication
NEG mem/reg	[mem/reg] ← [mem/reg]' + 1	Mem/reg can be 8- or 16-bit; performs 2's complement subtraction of specified operand from zero; i.e., 2's complement of a number is formed; all flags affected except CF = 0 if [mem/reg] is zero; otherwise CF = 1
NOP	No operation	8086 does nothing

Continued.

TABLE 5–1
Summary of 8086 Instruction Set — cont'd

Instruction	Interpretation	Comments
NOT reg	[reg] ← [reg]'	reg can be 8- or 16-bit; segment registers not allowed; no flags affected; 1's complement reg
NOT mem	[mem] ← [mem]'	Mem uses DS as segment register; no flags affected; 1's complement mem
OR mem/reg 1, mem/reg 2	[mem/reg 1] ← [mem/reg 1] ∨ [mem/reg 2]	No memory-to-memory operation allowed; [mem] or [reg 1] or [reg 2] can be 8- or 16- bit; all flags affected with OF and CF cleared to zero; no segment registers allowed; mem uses DS as segment register
OR mem, data	[mem[← [mem] ∨ data	Mem and data can be 8- or 16-bit; mem uses DS as segment register; all flags affected with CF and OF cleared to zero
OR reg, data	[reg] ← [reg] ∨ data	Reg and data can be 8- or 16-bit; no segment registers allowed; all flags affected with CF and OF cleared to zero
OUT DX, AL	[PORT DX] ← [AL]	Output 8-bit contents of AL into an I/O port addressed by 16-bit contents of DX; 1-byte instruction
OUT DX, AX	[PORT DX] ← [AX]	Output 16-bit contents of AX into an I/O port addressed by 16-bit contents of DX; 1-byte instruction
OUT PORT, AL	[PORT] ← [AL]	Output 8-bit contents of AL into port specified in second byte of instruction
OUT PORT, AX	[PORT] ← [AX]	Output 16-bit contents of AX into port specified in second byte of instruction
POP mem	[mem] ← [[SP]] [SP] ← [SP] + 2	Mem uses DS as segment register; no flags affected
POP reg	[reg] ← [[SP]] [SP] ← [SP] + 2	Cannot be used to POP segment registers or flag register
POP segreg	[segreg] ← [[SP]] [SP] ← [SP] + 2	POP CS is illegal
POPF	[flags] ← [[SP]] [SP] ← [SP] + 2	Instruction pops top two stack bytes in 16-bit flag register
PUSH mem	[SP] ← [SP] − 2 [[SP]] ← [mem]	Mem uses DS as segment register; no flags affected; pushes 16-bit memory contents
PUSH reg	[SP] ← [SP] − 2 [[SP]] ← [reg]	Reg must be a 16-bit register; cannot be used to PUSH segment register or flag register
PUSH segreg	[SP] ← [SP] − 2 [[SP]] ← [segreg]	PUSH CS is illegal
PUSHF	[SP] ← [SP] − 2 [[SP]] ← [flags]	Instruction pushes 16-bit flag register onto stack
RCL mem/reg, 1	Rotate through carry left once byte or word in mem/reg	FOR BYTE FOR WORD
RCL mem/reg, CL	Rotate through carry left byte or word in mem/reg by [CL]	Operation same as RCL mem/reg, 1 except number of rotates is specified in CL for rotates up to 255; zero or negative rotates illegal FOR BYTE
RCR mem/reg, 1	Rotate through carry right once byte or word in mem/reg	FOR WORD

TABLE 5-1
Summary of 8086 Instruction Set — cont'd

Instruction	Interpretation	Comments
RCR mem/reg, CL	Rotate through carry right byte or word in mem/reg by [CL]	Operation same as RCR mem/reg, 1 except number of rotates is specified in CL for rotates up to 255; zero or negative rotates illegal
RET	• POPs IP for intrasegment CALLs • POPs IP and CS for inter-segment CALLs	Assembler generates intrasegment return if programmer has defined subroutine as NEAR; for intrasegment return, following operations take place: [IP] ← [[SP]], [SP] ← [SP] + 2; on the other hand, assembler generates intersegment return if subroutine has been defined as FAR; in this case, following operations take place: [IP] ← [[SP]], [SP] ← [SP] + 2, [CS] ← [[SP]], [SP] ← [SP] + 2; an optional 16-bit displacement "START" can be specified with inter-segment return such as RET START; in this case, 16-bit displacement is added to SP value; this feature may be used to discard parameter pushed onto stack before execution of CALL instruction
ROL mem/reg, 1	Rotate left once byte or word in mem/reg	FOR BYTE FOR WORD
ROL mem/reg, CL	Rotate left byte or word by contents of CL	[CL] contains rotate count up to 255; zero and negative shifts illegal; CL used to rotate count when rotate is greater than once; mem uses DS as segment register
ROR mem/reg, 1	Rotate right once byte or word in mem/reg	FOR BYTE FOR WORD
ROR mem/reg,CL	Rotate right byte or word in mem/reg by [CL]	Operation same as ROR mem/reg, 1; [CL] specifies number of rotates up to 255; zero and negative rotates illegal; mem uses DS as segment register
SAHF	[flags, low byte] ← [AH]	Instruction has implied addressing mode; contents of AH are stored into low byte of flag register; all flags affected
SAL mem/reg, 1	Shift arithmetic left once byte or word in mem/reg	Mem uses DS as segment register; reg cannot be segment registers; OF and CF affected; if sign bit is changed during or after shifting, OF is set to 1 FOR BYTE FOR WORD
SAL mem/reg, CL	Shift arithmetic left byte or word by shift count on CL	Operation same as SAL mem/reg, 1; CL contains shift count up to 255; zero and negative shifts illegal; [CL] used as shift count when

Continued.

TABLE 5-1
Summary of 8086 Instruction Set — cont'd

Instruction	Interpretation	Comments
		shift is greater than 1; OF and SF affected; if sign bit of [mem/reg] is changed during or after shifting, OF is set to 1; mem uses DS as segment register
SAR mem/reg, 1	Shift arithmetic right once byte or word in mem/reg	FOR BYTE
		FOR WORD
SAR mem/reg, CL	Shift arithmetic right byte or word in mem/reg by [CL]	Operation same as SAR mem/reg, 1; but shift count is specified in CL for shifts up to 255; zero and negative shifts illegal
SBB mem/reg 1, mem/reg 2	[mem/reg 1] ← [mem/reg 1] − [mem/reg 2] − CY	Same as SUB mem/reg 1, mem/reg 2 except this is a subtraction with borrow
SBB mem, data	[mem] ← [mem] − data − CY	Same as SUB mem, data except this is a subtraction with borrow
SBB reg, data	[reg] ← [reg] − data − CY	Same as SUB reg, data except this is a subtraction with borrow
SCAS BYTE or SCASB	FOR BYTE [AL] − [[DI]], flags affected, [DI] ← [DI] ± 1 FOR WORD	8- or 16-bit data addressed by [DI] in ES is subtracted from 8- or 16-bit data in AL or AX; flags affected without affecting [AL] or [AX] or string data; ES cannot be overridden; if DF = 0, then DI is incremented by 1 for byte or 2 for word; if DF = 1, then DI is decremented by 1 for byte or 2 for word
SCAS WORD or SCASW	[AX] − [[DI]], flags affected, [DI] ← [DI] ± 2	
SHL mem/reg, 1	Shift logical left once byte or word in mem/reg	Same as SAL mem/reg, 1
SHL mem/reg, CL	Shift logical left byte or word in mem/reg by shift count in CL	Same as SAL mem/reg, CL except OF is cleared to zero FOR BYTE
SHR mem/reg, 1	Shift right logical once byte or word in mem/reg	FOR WORD
SHR mem/reg, CL	Shift right logical byte or word in mem/reg by [CL]	Operation same as SHR mem/reg, 1; but shift count is specified in CL for shifts up to 255; zero and negative shifts illegal
STC	CF ← 1	Set carry flag to 1
STD	DF ← 1	Set direction flag to 1
STI	IF ← 1	Set interrupt enable flag to 1 to enable maskable interrupts
STOS BYTE or STOSB	FOR BYTE [[DI]] ← [AL] [DI] ← [DI] ± 1	Store 8-bit data from AL or 16-bit data from AX into memory location addressed by DI in segment ES; segment register ES cannot be overridden; if DF = 0, then DI is incremented by 1 for byte or 2 for word after the store
STOS WORD or STOSW	FOR WORD [[DI]] ← [AX] [DI] ← [DI] ± 2	
SUB mem/reg 1, mem/reg 2	[mem/reg 1] ← [mem/reg 1] − [mem/reg 2]	No memory-to-memory SUB permitted; all flags affected; mem uses DS as segment register
SUB mem, data	[mem] ← [mem] − data	Data can be 8- or 16-bit; mem uses DS as segment register; all flags affected
SUB reg, data	[reg] ← [reg] − data	Data can be 8- or 16-bit; all flags affected
TEST mem/reg 1, mem/reg 2	[mem/reg 1] − [mem/reg 2], no result, flags affected	No memory-to-memory TEST allowed; no result provided; all flags affected with CF and OF cleared to zero; [mem], [reg 1] or [reg 2]

TABLE 5–1
Summary of 8086 Instruction Set — cont'd

Instruction	Interpretation	Comments
		can be 8- or 16-bit; no segment registers allowed; mem uses DS as segment register
TEST mem, data	[mem] − data, no result, flags affected	mem and data can be 8- or 16-bit; no result provided; all flags affected with CF and OF cleared to zero; mem uses DS as segment register
TEST reg, data	[reg] − data, no result, flags affected	reg and data can be 8- or 16-bit; no result provided; all flags affected with CF and OF cleared to zero; reg cannot be segment register
WAIT	8086 enters wait state	Causes microprocessor to enter wait state if 8086 TEST pin is high; while in wait state, 8086 continues to check TEST pin for low; if TEST pin goes back to zero, 8086 executes next instruction; this feature can be used to synchronize operation of 8086 to an event in external hardware.
XCHG mem, reg	[mem] ↔ [reg]	reg and mem can be both 8- or 16-bit; mem uses DS as segment register; reg cannot be segment register; no flags affected
XCHG reg, reg	[reg] ↔ [reg]	reg can be 8- or 16-bit; reg cannot be segment register; no flags affected
XLAT	[AL] → [AL] + [BX]	Instruction is useful for translating characters from one code such as ASCII to another such as EBCDIC; no-operand instruction; called an instruction with implied addressing mode; loads AL with contents of a 20-bit physical address computed from DS, BX, and AL; can be used to read elements in a table where BX can be loaded with a 16-bit value to point to starting address (offset from DS) and AL can be loaded with element number (0 being first element number); no flags affected; XLAT is equivalent to MOV AL, [AL] [BX]
XOR mem/reg 1, mem/reg 2	[mem/reg 1] ← [mem/reg 1] ⊕ [mem/reg 2]	No memory-to-memory operation allowed; [mem] or [reg 1] can be 8- or 16-bit; all flags affected with CF and OF cleared to zero; mem uses DS as segment register
XOR mem, data	[mem] ← [mem] ⊕ data	Data and mem can be 8- or 16-bit; mem uses DS as segment register; mem cannot be segment register; all flags affected with CF and OF cleared to zero
XOR reg, data	[reg] ← [reg] ⊕ data	Same as XOR mem, data

Data Transfer Instructions Table 5–2 lists the 14 data transfer instructions. These instructions move single bytes and words between a register and I/O ports.

Let us explain some of the instructions in Table 5–2.

- MOV CX, DX copies the 16-bit contents of DX into CX. MOV AX, 2025H moves immediate data 2025H into the 16-bit register AX. MOV CH, [BX] moves the 8-bit contents of a memory location addressed by BX in segment register DS into CH. If [BX] = 0050H, [DS] = 2000H, and [20050H] = 08H, then, after MOV CH, [BX], the contents of CH will be 08H. MOV START [BP], CX moves the 16-bit (CL to first location and then CH) contents of CX into two memory locations addressed by the sum of the displacement START and BP in segment register SS. For example, if [CX] = 5009H, [BP] = 0030H, [SS] = 3000H, and START = 06H, then, after MOV START [BP], CX, physical memory location [30036H] = 09H and

[30037H] = 50H. Note that the segment register SS can be overridden by CS using MOV CS: START [BP], CX.

- LDS SI, [10H] loads register and DS from memory. For example, if [DS] = 2000H, [20010] = 0200H, and [20012] = 0100H, then, after LDS SI, [10H], SI and DS will contain 0200H and 0100H, respectively.

- In the 8086, the SP is decremented by 2 for PUSH and incremented by 2 for POP. For example, consider PUSH [BX]. If [DS] = 2000_{16}, [BX] = 0200_{16}, [SP] = 3000_{16}, [SS] = 4000_{16}, and [20200] = 0120_{16}, then, after execution of PUSH [BX], memory locations 42FFF and 42FFE will contain 01_{16} and 20_{16}, respectively, and the contents of SP will be $2FFE_{16}$.

- XCHG has two variations. These are XCHG reg, reg and XCHG mem, reg. For example, XCHG AX, BX exchanges the contents of a 16-bit register such as BX with the contents of AX. XCHG mem, reg

TABLE 5-2
8086 Data Transfer Instructions (Courtesy of Intel Corporation)

General Purpose	
MOV d,s	[d] ← [s] MOV byte or word
PUSH d	PUSH word into stack
POP d	POP word off stack
XCHG d,s	[d] ↔ [s] Exchange byte or word
XLAT	AL ← [20-bit address computed from AL, BX, and DS]
Input/Output	
IN A, DX or Port	Input byte or word
OUT DX or Port, A	Output byte or word
Address Object	
LEA reg, mem	LOAD Effective Address
LDS reg, mem	LOAD pointer using DS
LES reg, mem	LOAD pointer using ES
Flag Transfer	
LAHF	LOAD AH register from flags
SAHF	STORE AH register in flags
PUSHF	PUSH flags onto stack
POPF	POP flags off stack

d = "mem" or "reg" or "segreg," s = "data" or "mem" or "reg" or "segreg," A = AX or AL.

exchanges 8- or 16-bit data in reg or mem with 8- or 16-bit reg.

- XLAT can be used to employ an index in a table. This instruction utilizes BX to hold the starting address of the table in memory consisting of 8-bit data elements. The index in the table is assumed to be in the AL register. For example, if $[BX] = 0200_{16}$, $[AL] = 04_{16}$, and $[DS] = 3000_{16}$, then, after XLAT, the contents of location 30204_{16} will be loaded into AL. Note that the XLAT instruction is the same as MOV AL, [AL] [BX].

- Consider fixed port addressing in which the 8-bit port address is directly specified as part of the instruction. IN AL, 38H inputs 8-bit data from port 38H into AL. IN AX, 38H inputs 16-bit data from ports 38H and 39H into AX. OUT 38H, AL outputs the contents of AL to port 38H. OUT 38H, AX, on the other hand, outputs the 16-bit contents of AX to ports 38H and 39H.

- For variable port addressing, the port address is 16-bit and is specified in the DX register. Consider ports addressed by the 16-bit address contained in DX. Assume $[DX] = 3124_{16}$ in all the following examples:

IN AL, DX inputs 8-bit data from 8-bit port 3124_{16} into AL.

IN AX, DX inputs 16-bit data from ports 3124_{16} and 3125_{16} into AX.

OUT DX, AL outputs 8-bit data from AL into port 3124_{16} data.

OUT DX, AX outputs 16-bit data from AX into ports 3124_{16} and 3125_{16}.

Variable port addressing allows up to 65,536 ports with addresses from 0000H to FFFFH. The port addresses in variable port addressing can be calculated dynamically in a program. For example, assume that an 8086-based microcomputer is connected to three printers via three separate ports. Now, in order to output to each one of the printers, separate programs are required if fixed port addressing is used. However, with variable port addressing, one can write a general subroutine to output to the printers and then supply the address of the port for a particular printer in which data output is desired to register DX in the subroutine.

Arithmetic Instructions Table 5–3 shows the 8086 arithmetic instructions. These operations can be performed on four types of numbers: unsigned binary, signed binary, unsigned packed decimal, and signed packed decimal numbers. Binary numbers can be 8 or 16 bits wide. Decimal numbers are stored in bytes—two digits per byte for packed decimal and one digit per byte for unpacked decimal with the high 4 bits filled with zeros.

Let us explain some of the instructions in Table 5–3.

- Consider ADC mem/reg, mem/reg. This instruction adds data with carry from reg to reg or from reg to mem or from mem to reg. There is no ADC mem, mem instruction. For example, if $[AX] = 0020_{16}$, $[BX] = 0300_{16}$, $CF = 1$, $[DS] = 2020_{16}$, and $[20500] = 0100_{16}$, then, after ADC AX, [BX], the contents of register $AX = 0020 + 0100 + 1 = 0121_{16}$. All flags are affected.

- DIV mem/reg divides [AX] or [DX:AX] registers by reg or mem. For example, if $[AX] = 0005_{16}$ and $[CL] = 02_{16}$, then, after DIV CL, $[AH] = 01_{16}$ and $[AL] = 02_{16}$.

- Consider MUL BL. If $[AL] = 20_{16}$ and $[BL] = 02_{16}$, then, after MUL BL, register AX will contain 0040_{16}.

- Consider CBW. This instruction extends the sign from the AL register to AH register. For example, if $AL = F1_{16}$, then, after execution of CBW, register AH will contain FF_{16} since the most significant bit of $F1_{16}$ is 1. Note that the sign extension is very useful when one wants to perform an arithmetic operation on two numbers of different lengths. For example, the 16-bit number 0020_{16} can be added with

TABLE 5–3
8086 Arithmetic Instructions (Courtesy of Intel Corporation)

	Addition	
ADD a, b	Add byte or word	
ADC a, b	Add byte or word with carry	
INC reg/mem	Increment byte or word by one	
AAA	ASCII adjust for addition	
DAA	Decimal adjust [AL] to be used after ADD or ADC	

	Subtraction	
SUB a, b	Subtract byte or word	
SBB a, b	Subtract byte or word with borrow	
DEC reg/mem	Decrement byte or word by one	
NEG reg/mem	Negate byte or word	
CMP a, b	Compare byte or word	
AAS	ASCII adjust for subtraction	
DAS	Decimal adjust [AL] to be used after SUB or SBB	

	Multiplication	
MUL reg/mem	Multiply byte or word unsigned	for byte $[AX] \leftarrow [AL] \cdot [mem/reg]$
IMUL reg/mem	Integer multiply byte or word (signed)	for word $[DX][AX] \leftarrow [AX] \cdot [mem/reg]$

	Division	
DIV reg/mem	Divide byte or word unsigned	$16 \div 8$ bit
IDIV reg/mem	Integer divide byte or word (signed)	$[AH] \leftarrow$ remainder $\leftarrow \dfrac{[AX]}{[mem/reg]}$
		$[AL] \leftarrow$ quotient
		$32 \div 16$ bit
AAD	ASCII adjust for division	
CBW	Convert byte to word	$[DX] \leftarrow$ remainder $\leftarrow \dfrac{[DX:AX]}{[mem/reg]}$
CWD	Convert word to double word	$[AX] \leftarrow$ quotient

a = "reg" or "mem," b = "reg" or "mem" or "data."

the 8-bit number $E1_{16}$ by sign-extending El as follows:

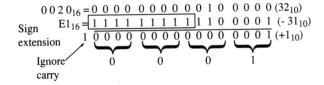

Another example of sign extension is that, in order to multiply a signed 8-bit number by a signed 16-bit number, one must first sign-extend the signed 8-bit into a signed 16-bit number and then the instruction IMUL can be used for 16 × 16 signed multiplication.

• CWD sign-extends the AX register into the DX register. That is, if the most significant bit of AX is 1, then store $FFFF_{16}$ into DX.

• The distinction between the byte or word operations on memory is usually made by the assembler by using B for byte or W for word as trailing characters with the instructions. Typical examples are MULB or MULW.

• Numerical data received by an 8086-based microcomputer from a terminal is usually in ASCII code. The ASCII codes for numbers 0 to 9 are 30H through 39H. Two 8-bit data can be entered into an 8086-based microcomputer via a terminal. The ASCII codes for these data (with 3 as the upper nibble for each type) can be added. AAA instruction can then be used to provide the correct unpacked BCD. Suppose that ASCII codes for 2 (32_{16}) and 5 (35_{16}) are entered into an 8086-based microcomputer via a terminal. These ASCII codes can be added and then the result can be adjusted to provide the correct unpacked BCD using the AAA instruction as follows:

```
ADD CL, DL    ; [CL] = 32₁₆ = ACSII for 2
```
$$\text{ADD CL, DL} \quad ; [CL] = 32_{16} = \text{ACSII for 2}$$
$$\quad ; [DL] = 35_{16} = \text{ASCII for 5}$$
$$\quad ; \text{Result } [CL] = 67_{16}$$
$$\text{MOV AL, CL} \quad ; \text{Move ASCII result}$$
$$\quad ; \text{into AL since AAA}$$
$$\quad ; \text{adjust only } [AL]$$
$$\text{AAA} \quad ; [AL] = 07, \text{unpacked}$$
$$\quad ; \text{BCD for 7}$$

Note that, in order to send the unpacked BCD result 07_{16} back to the terminal, $[AL] = 07$ can be ORed with 30H to provide 37H, the ASCII code for 7.

- DAA is used to adjust the result of adding two packed BCD numbers in AL to provide a valid BCD number. If after the addition, the low 4 bits of the result in AL is greater than 9 (or if AF = 1), then the DAA adds 6 to the low 4 bits of AL. On the other hand, if the high 4 bits of the result in AL is greater than 9 (or if CF = 1), then DAA adds 60H to AL.

- DAS may be used to adjust the result of subtraction in AL of two packed BCD numbers to provide the correct packed BCD.

While performing these subtractions, any borrows from low and high nibbles are ignored. For example, consider subtracting BCD 55 in DL from BCD 94 in AL:

$$\text{SUB AL, DL} \quad ; [AL] = 3FH \rightarrow \text{low nibble} = 1111$$
$$\text{DAS} \quad ; CF = 0 \qquad\qquad -6 = 1010$$
$$\qquad\qquad\qquad\qquad\qquad\qquad\qquad \overline{1001}$$
$$\quad ; [AL] = 39 \text{ BCD} \qquad\nearrow 1$$
$$\qquad\qquad\qquad\qquad\text{Ignore 1}$$

- IMUL mem/reg provides signed 8 × 8 or signed 16 × 16 multiplication. As an example, if $[CL] = FDH = -3_{10}$, $[AL] = FEH = -2_{10}$, then, after IMUL CL, register AX contains 0006H.

- Consider 16 × 16 unsigned multiplication, MUL WORD PTR [BX]. If [BX] = 0050H, [DS] = 3000H, [30050H] = 0002H, and [AX] = 0006H, then, after MUL WORD PTR [BX], [DX] = 0000H and [AX] = 000CH.

- Consider DIV BL. If [AX] = 0009H and [BL] = 02H, then, after DIV BL,

$$[AH] = \text{remainder} = 01H$$
$$[AL] = \text{quotient} = 04H$$

- Consider IDIV WORD PTR [BX]. If [BX] = 0020H, [DS] = 2000H, [20020H] = 0004H, and [DX] [AX] = 00000011H, then, after IDIV WORD PTR [BX],

$$[DX] = \text{remainder} = 0001H$$
$$[AX] = \text{quotient} = 0004H$$

- AAD converts two unpacked BCD digits in AH and AL to an equivalent binary number in AL. AAD must be used before dividing two unpacked BCD digits in AX by an unpacked BCD byte. For example, consider dividing [AX] = unpacked BCD 0508 (58 decimal) by [DH] = 07H. [AX] must first be converted to binary by using AAD. The register AX will then contain 003AH = 58 decimal. After DIV DH, [AL] = quotient = 08 unpacked BCD, [AH] = remainder = 02 unpacked BCD.

- AAM adjusts the product of two unpacked BCD digits in AX. If $[AL] = BCD3 = 00000011_2$ and $[CH] = BCD8 = 0000\,1000_2$, then, after MUL CH, $[AX] = 0000000000011000_2 = 0018H$, and, after using AAM, $[AX] = 00000010\,00000100_2 =$ unpacked 24. The following instruction sequence accomplishes this:

$$\text{MUL CH}$$
$$\text{AAM}$$

Note that the 8086 does not allow multiplication of two ASCII codes. Therefore, before multiplying two ASCII bytes received from a terminal, one must mask the upper 4 bits of each one of these bytes and then multiply them as two unpacked BCD digits and then use AAM for adjustment. In order to convert the unpacked BCD product back to ASCII, for sending back to the terminal, one must OR the product with 3030H.

Bit Manipulation Instructions The 8086 provides three groups of bit manipulation instructions. These are logicals, shifts, and rotates as shown in Table 5–4. The operand to be shifted or rotated can be either 8- or 16-bit.

Let us explain some of the instructions in Table 5–4.

- TEST CL, 05H logically ANDs [CL] with $0000\,0101_2$ but does not store the result in CL. All flags are affected.

- ROL mem/reg, CNT rotates [mem/reg] left by the specified number of bits. The number of bits to be rotated is either 1 or contained in CL. For example, if CF = 0, $[BX] = 0010_{16}$, and $[CL] = 03_{16}$, then, after ROL BX, CL, register BX will contain 0080_{16} and CF = 0. On the other hand, ROL BL, 1 rotates the 8-bit contents of BL 1 bit to the left.

- Consider SHR mem/reg, CNT or SHL mem/reg, CNT. These instructions are logical right or left shifts, respectively. The CL register contains the number of shifts if the shift is greater than 1. If CNT = 1, the shift is fast. In both cases, the last bit shifted out goes to CF (carry flag). Figures 5–4, 5–5, and 5–6 illustrate the shift and rotate instructions.

- Consider SAR mem/reg, CNT or SAL mem/reg, CNT (Figure 5–4). Note that a true arithmetic left shift does not exist in 8086 because the sign bit is not retained in SAL.

TABLE 5–4
8086 Bit Manipulation Instructions (Courtesy of Intel Corporation)

	Logicals
NOT mem/reg	NOT byte or word
AND a, b	AND byte or word
OR a, b	OR byte or word
XOR a, b	Exclusive OR byte or word
TEST a, b	Test byte or word
	Shifts
SHL/SAL mem/reg, CNT	Shift logical/arithmetic left byte or word
SHR/SAR mem/reg, CNT	Shift logical/arithmetic right byte or word
	Rotates
ROL mem/reg, CNT	Rotate left byte or word
ROR mem/reg, CNT	Rotate right byte or word
RCL mem/reg, CNT	Rotate through carry left byte or word
RCR mem/reg, CNT	Rotate through carry right byte or word

a = "reg" or "mem," b = "reg" or "mem" or "data," CNT = number of times to be shifted. If CNT > 1, then CNT is contained in CL. Zero or negative shifts and rotates are illegal. If CNT = 1, then CNT is immediate data. Up to 255 shifts allowed.

- Consider ROL mem/reg, CNT or ROR mem/reg, CNT (Figure 5–5).
- Consider RCL mem/reg, CNT and RCR mem/reg, CNT (Figure 5–6).

String Instructions String instructions are available to MOVE, COMPARE, or SCAS for a value as well as to move string elements to and from the accumulator. These instructions, listed in Table 5–5, contain prefixes that cause the instruction to be repeated in hardware, allowing long strings to be processed much faster than if done in a software loop.

Let us explain some of the instructions in Table 5–5.

- MOVS word or byte moves 8- or 16-bit data from the memory location addressed by SI to the memory location addressed by DI. SI and DI are incremented or decremented depending on the DF flag. For example, if [DF] = 0, [DS] = 1000_{16}, [ES] = 3000_{16}, [SI] = 0002_{16}, [DI] = 0004_{16}, and [10002] = 1234_{16}, then, after MOVS WORD, [30004] = 1234_{16}, [SI] = 0004_{16}, and [DI] = 0006_{16}.
- REP repeats the instruction that follows until the CX register is decremented to 0.
- REPE/REPZ or REPNE/REPNZ prefix can be used with CMPS or SCAS to cause one of these instructions to continue executing until ZF = 0 (for REPNE/REPNZ prefix) and CX = 0. Note that REPE and REPZ are two mnemonics for the same prefix byte. Similarly, REPNE and REPNZ also provide the same purpose.
- If CMPS is prefixed with REPE or REPZ, the operation is interpreted as "compare while not end-of-string (CX ≠ 0) and strings are equal (ZF = 1)." If CMPS is preceded by REPNE or REPNZ, the operation is interpreted as "compare while not end-of-string (CX ≠ 0) and strings not equal (ZF = 0)." Thus, repeated CMPS can be used to find matching or differing string elements.

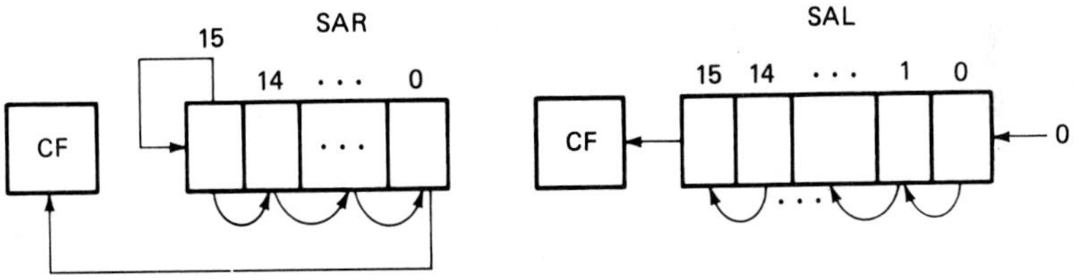

Figure 5–4 8086 SAR and SAL instructions

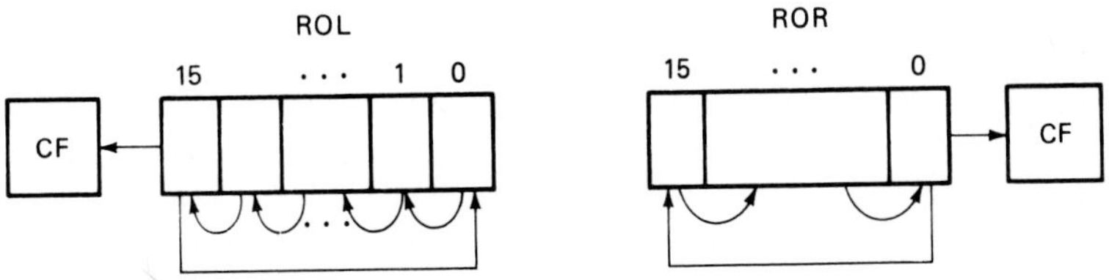

Figure 5–5 8086 ROL and ROR instructions

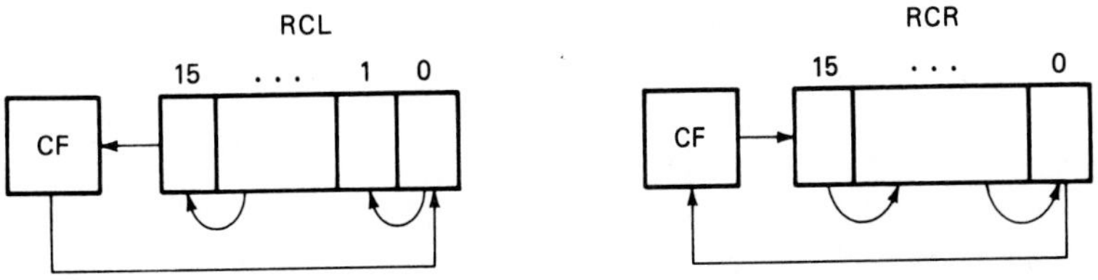

Figure 5–6 8086 RCL and RCR instructions

TABLE 5–5
8086 String Instructions (Courtesy of Intel Corporation)

REP	Repeat MOVS or STOS until CX = 0
REPE/REPZ	Repeat CMPS or SCAS until ZF = 0
REPNE/REPNZ	Repeat CMPS or SCAS until ZF = 1
MOVS BYTE/WORD	Move byte or word string
CMPS BYTE/WORD	Compare byte or word string
SCAS BYTE/WORD	Scan byte or word string
LODS BYTE/WORD	Load from memory into AL or AX
STOS BYTE/WORD	Store AL or AX into memory

- If SCAS is prefixed with REPE or REPZ, the operation is interpreted as "scan while not end-of-string (CX ≠ 0) and string-element = scan-value (ZF = 1)." This form may be used to scan for departure from a given value. If SCAS is prefixed with REPNE or REPNZ, the operation is interpreted as "scan while not end-of-string (CX ≠ 0) and string-element is not equal to scan-value (ZF = 0)." This form may be used to locate a value in a string.

- Repeated string instructions are interruptible; the processor recognizes the interrupt before processing the next string element. Upon return from the interrupt, the repeated operation is resumed from the point of interruption. When multiple prefixes (such as LOCK and segment override) are specified in addition to any of the repeat prefixes, program execution does not resume properly upon return from interrupt. The processor remembers only one prefix in effect at the time of the interrupt, the prefix that immediately precedes the string instruction.

- Consider SCAS word or byte. This compares the memory with AL or AX. If [DI] = 0000_{16}, [ES] = 2000_{16}, [DF] = 0, [20000] = 05_{16}, and [AL] = 03_{16}, then, after SCAS BYTE, DI wil contain 0001_{16} because [DF] = 0 and all flags are affected based on the operation [AL] − [20000].

Unconditional Transfers   Unconditional transfer instructions transfer control to a location either in the current executing memory segment (intrasegment) or to a different code segment (intersegment). Table 5–6 lists the unconditional transfer instructions.

The jump instruction in Table 5–6 has a few variations. Some of these are JMP mem, JMP disp8, JMP disp16, and JMP reg. Note that for intersegment jumps, both IP and CS change. For intrasegment jumps, IP changes and CS is fixed. JMP disp8 adds the second object code byte (signed 8-bit displacement) to [IP + 2], and [CS] is unchanged.

TABLE 5–6
8086 Unconditional Transfers (Courtesy of Intel Corporation)

CALL reg/mem/disp16	Call subroutine
RET	Return from subroutine
JMP reg/mem/disp8/disp16	Unconditional jump

JMP mem moves the contents of next two words to IP and CS, respectively. JMP disp16 adds the next word (16-bit unsigned displacement) to IP + 2, and CS is unchanged. JMP mem moves the next two words to IP and CS, respectively. JMP reg moves the [reg] into IP, and [CS] is unchanged.

Conditional Branch Instructions   All 8086 conditional branch instructions use 8-bit signed displacement. That is, the displacement covers a branch range of -128_{10} to $+127_{10}$ with 0 being positive. The structure of a typical conditional branch instruction is as follows:

If condition is true,
  then PC ← PC + disp8
  otherwise PC ← PC + 2 and execute
  next instruction

There are two types of conditional branch instructions. In one type, the various relationships that exist between two numbers such as equal, above, below, less than, or greater than can be determined by the appropriate conditional branch instruction after a COMPARE instruction. These instructions can be used for both signed and unsigned numbers. While comparing signed numbers, terms such as "less than" and "greater than" are used. On the other hand, while comparing unsigned numbers, terms such as "below zero" or "above zero" are used.

Table 5–7 lists the 8086 signed and unsigned conditional branch instructions. Note that in Table 5–7, the instructions for checking which two numbers are "equal" or "not equal" are the same for both signed and unsigned numbers. This is because when two numbers are compared for equality, irrespective of whether they are signed or unsigned, they will provide a zero result (Z = 1) if equal or a nonzero result (Z = 0) if not equal. Therefore, the same instructions apply for both signed and unsigned numbers for "equal to" or "not equal to" conditions.

The second type of conditional branch instructions is concerned with the setting of flags rather than the relationship between two numbers. Table 5–8 lists these instructions.

Now, in order to check whether the result of an arithmetic or logic operation is zero, nonzero, positive or negative, did or did not produce a carry, did or did not produce parity, or did or did not cause overflow, the following instructions should be used: JZ, JNZ, JS, JNS, JC, JNC, JP, JNP, JO, JNO. However, in order to compare two signed or unsigned numbers (a in A or b

TABLE 5–7
8086 Signed and Unsigned Conditional Branch Instructions

Signed		Unsigned	
Name	Alternate Name	Name	Alternate Name
JE disp 8 (JUMP if equal)	JZ disp8 (JUMP if result zero)	JE disp8 (JUMP if equal)	JZ disp8 (JUMP if zero)
JNE disp8 (JUMP if not equal)	JNZ disp 8 (JUMP if not zero)	JNE disp8 (JUMP if not equal)	JNZ disp8 (JUMP if not zero)
JG disp8 (JUMP if greater)	JNLE disp8 (JUMP if not less or equal)	JA disp8 (JUMP if above)	JNBE disp8 (JUMP if not below or equal)
JGE disp8 (JUMP if greater or equal)	JNL disp8 (JUMP if not less)	JAE disp8 (JUMP if above or equal)	JNB disp8 (JUMP if not below)
JL disp8 (JUMP if less than)	JNGE disp8 (JUMP if not greater or equal)	JB disp8 (JUMP if below)	JNAE disp8 (JUMP if not above or equal)
JLE disp8 (JUMP if less or equal)	JNG disp8 (JUMP if not greater)	JBE disp8 (JUMP if below or equal)	JNA disp8 (JUMP if not above)

TABLE 5–8
8086 Conditional Branch Instructions Affecting Individual Flags

JC disp8	JUMP if carry, i.e., CF = 1
JNC disp8	JUMP if no carry, i.e., CF = 0
JP disp8	JUMP if parity, i.e., PF = 1
JNP disp8	JUMP if no parity, i.e., PF = 0
JO disp8	JUMP if overflow, i.e., OF = 1
JNO disp8	JUMP if no overflow, i.e., OF = 0
JS disp8	JUMP if sign, i.e., SF = 1
JNS disp8	JUMP if no sign, i.e., SF = 0
JZ disp8	JUMP if result zero, i.e., Z = 1
JNZ disp8	JUMP if result not zero, i.e., Z = 0

TABLE 5–9
8086 Instructions To Be Used after CMP A, B

Signed "a" and "b"		Unsigned "a" and "b"	
JGE disp8	if a ≥ b	JA disp8	if a > b
JL disp8	if a < b	JAE disp8	if a ≥ b
JG disp8	if a > b	JB disp8	if a < b
JLE disp8	if a ≤ b	JBE disp8	if a ≤ b

in B) for various conditions, we use CMP A, B, which will form a-b, and then one of the instructions in Table 5–9.

Now let us illustrate the concept of using the preceding signed or unsigned instructions by an example. Consider clearing a section of memory starting at B up to and including A, where $[A] = 3000_{16}$ and $[B] = 2000_{16}$ using the following program:

```
          MOV DS, AX      ;   Initialize DS
          MOV BX, 2000H
          MOV CX, 3000H
LOOP      MOV [BX], 0000H
          INC BX
          INC BX
          CMP CX, BX
          JGE LOOP
            •
            •
            •
```

JGE treats CMP operands as 2's complement numbers. The loop will terminate when BX = 3002H.

Now, suppose that the contents of A and B are as follows:

$$[A] = 8500_{16}$$
$$[B] = 0500_{16}$$

In this case, after CMP CX, BX is first executed,

$$
\begin{aligned}
[CX] - [BX] &= 8500 - 0500 \\
&= 8000_{16} \\
&= 1000\ 000\ 000\ 000 \\
&\qquad\uparrow \\
&\quad SF = 1, \text{ i.e., a} \\
&\quad \text{negative number}
\end{aligned}
$$

Since 8000_{16} is a negative number, the loop terminates. The correct approach is to use a branch instruction that treats operands as unsigned numbers (addresses are always positive numbers) and uses the following program segment:

```
LOOP      MOV   [BX],   0000H
          INC   BX
          INC   BX
```

                    CMP   CX,   BX
                    JAE   LOOP

JAE will work regardless of the values of A and B.

Iteration Control Instructions Table 5–10 lists
these instructions. In Table 5–10, LOOP disp8 decrements the CX register by 1 without affecting the flags
and then acts in the same way as the JMP disp8 instruction
except that if CX ≠ 0, then the JMP is performed;
otherwise, the next instruction is executed.

Interrupt Instructions Table 5–11 shows the interrupt instructions.

Processor Control Instructions Table 5–12
shows the processor control functions. Let us explain
some of the instructions in Table 5–12.

- ESC mem places the contents of the specified memory location on the data bus at the time when the
  8086 ready pin is asserted by the addressed memory
  device. This instruction allows the 8086 to invoke
  other processors such as the 8087 floating-point processor.

- LOCK outputs a LOW on the LOCK pin of the 8086
  for the duration of the next instruction. This signal
  is used in multiprocessing.

- WAIT causes the 8086 to enter an idle state if the
  signal on the TEST pin is not asserted. By placing
  the WAIT before ESC, the 8086 can do other things

TABLE 5–10
8086 Iteration Control Instructions (Courtesy of Intel
Corporation)

LOOP disp8	Decrement CX by 1 without affect-ing flags and LOOP if CX ≠ 0; otherwise, go to the next instruction
LOOPE/LOOPZ disp8	Decrement CX by 1 without affect-ing flags and LOOP if CX not equal/not zero and ZF = 1; other-wise, go to the next instruction
LOOPNE/LOOPNZ disp 8	Decrement CX by 1 without affect-ing flags and LOOP if CX not equal/not zero and ZF = 0; other-wise, go to the next instruction
JCXZ disp8	JMP if register CX = 0

TABLE 5–11
8086 Interrupt Instructions (Courtesy of Intel
Corporation)

INT interrupt number (can be 0–255$_{10}$)	Software interrupt instructions (INT 32$_{10}$–255$_{10}$ available to the user)
INTO	Interrupt on overflow
IRET	Interrupt return

TABLE 5–12
8086 Processor Control Instructions (Courtesy of Intel
Corporation)

STC	Set carry CF ← 1
CLC	Clear carry CF ← 0
CMC	Complement carry CF ← CF'
STD	Set direction flag
CLD	Clear direction flag
STI	Set interrupt enable flag
CLI	Clear interrupt enable flag
NOP	No operation
HLT	Halt after interrupt is set
WAIT	Wait for TEST pin active
ESC mem	Escape to external processor
LOCK	Lock bus during next instruction

while a subordinate processor such as a floating-point
processor is executing an instruction.

5–5 8086 ASSEMBLER-DEPENDENT INSTRUCTIONS

Some 8086 instructions do not define whether an 8-bit
or a 16-bit operation is to be executed. Instructions with
one of the 8086 registers as an operand typically define
the operation as 8-bit or 16-bit based on the register size.
An example is MOV CL, [BX], which moves an 8-bit
number with the offset defined by [BX] in DS into register
CL; MOV CX, [BX], on the other hand, moves the
number from offsets [BX] and [BX + 1] in DS into CX.

Instructions with a single-memory operand may define an 8-bit or a 16-bit operation by adding B for byte
or W for word with the mnemonic. Typical examples are
MULB [BX] and CMPW [ADDR]. The string instructions may define this in two ways. Typical examples are
MOVSB or MOVS BYTE for 8-bit and MOVSW or
MOVS WORD for 16-bit. Memory offsets can also be
specified by including BYTE PTR for 8-bit and WORD
PTR for 16-bit with the instruction. Typical examples
are INC BYTE PTR [BX] and INC WORD PTR [BX].

5–6 TYPICAL 8086 ASSEMBLER PSEUDO-INSTRUCTIONS

Examples of typical assemblers include the Intel ASM-
86 assembler and the microsoft 8086 assembler written
for the IBM PC. These assemblers allow the programmer
to assign the values of CS, DS, SS, and ES. One of the
requirements of these assemblers is that a variable's type
must be declared as a byte (8-bit), word (16-bit), or
double word (4 bytes or 2 words) before using a program.
Some examples are as follows:

       JOHN DB 0   JOHN is declared as a byte offset
                      with contents zero.

BOB DW 25FIH	BOB is declared as a word offset with contents 25FIH.
DICK DD 0	DICK is declared as a double word (4 bytes) offset with zero contents.

The EQU directive can be used to assign a name to constants. For example, the statement JOHN EQU 21H directs the assembler to assign the value 21H every time it finds JOHN in the program. This means that the assembler reads the statement MOV BH, JOHN as MOV BH, 21H. As mentioned before, DB, DW, and DD are the directives used to assign names and specific data types for variables in a program. For example, after execution of the statement BOB DW 2050H, the assembler assigns 50H to the offset name BOB and 20H to the offset name BOB + 1. This means that the program can use the instruction MOV BX, [BOB] to load the 16-bit contents of memory starting at the offset BOB in DS into BX. The DW sets aside storage for a word in memory and gives the starting address of this word the name BOB.

As an example, consider 16×16 multiplication. The size of the product should be 32 bits and must be initialized to zero. The following will accomplish this:

Multiplicand	DW 2A05H
Multiplier	DW 052AH
Product	DD 0

Typical 8086 addressing mode examples for the typical ASM-86 assembler are given next:

MOV AH, BL	Both source and destination are in register mode.
MOV CH, 8	Source is in immediate mode and destination is in register mode.
MOV AX, [START]	Source is in memory direct mode and destination is in register mode.
MOV CH, [BX]	Source is in register indirect mode and destination is in register mode.
MOV [SI], AL	Source is in register mode and destination is in register indirect mode.
MOV [DI], BH	Source is in register mode and destination is in register indirect mode.
MOV BH, VALUE [DI]	Source is in register indirect with displacement mode and destination is in register mode; VALUE is typically de-

	fined by the EQU directive prior to this instruction.
MOV AX, 4[DI]	Source is in indexed with displacement mode and destination is in register mode.
MOV SI, 2[BP] [DI]	Source is in based indexed with displacement mode and destination is in register mode.
OUT 30H, AL	Source is in register mode and destination is in direct port mode.
IN AX, DX	Source is in indirect port mode and destination is in register mode.

In the following paragraphs, more assembler directives such as SEGMENT, ENDS, ASSUME, and DUP will be discussed.

SEGMENT and ENDS Directives A section of a program or a data array can be defined by the SEGMENT and ENDS directives as follows:

BOB	SEGMENT	
XI	DB	0F1H
X2	DB	50H
X3	DB	25H
BOB	ENDS	

The segment name is BOB. The assembler will assign a numeric value to BOB corresponding to the base value of the data segment. The programmer must use the 8086 instructions to load BOB into DS as follows:

MOV BX, BOB
MOV DS, BX

Note that the segment registers must be loaded via a 16-bit register such as AX or by the contents of a memory location. A data array or an instruction sequence between the SEGEMENT and ENDS directives is called a *logical segment*. These two directives are used to set up a logical segment with a specific name. The Intel or microsoft 8086 assembler allows one to use up to 31 characters for the name without any spaces. An underscore can be used to separate words in a name. An example is PROGRAM_JOHN.

ASSUME Directive As mentioned before, the 8086, at any time, can directly address four physical segments, which include a code segment, a data segment, a stack segment, and an extra segment. The 8086 may contain a number of logical segments containing codes, data, and stack. The ASSUME pseudo-instruction assigns a logical segment to a physical segment at any given time. That is, the ASSUME directive tells the assembler what addresses will be in the segment registers at execution time.

For example, the statement ASSUME CS: PROGRAM_1, DS: DATA_1, SS: STACK_1 directs the assembler to use the logical code segment PROGRAM_1 as CS containing the instructions, the logical data segment DATA_1 as DS containing data, and the logical stack segment STACK_1 as SS containing the stack.

DUP Directive The DUP directive can be used to initialize several locations to zero. For example, the statement START DW 4 DUP (0) reserves four words starting at the offset START in DS and initializes them to zero. The DUP directive can also be used to reserve several locations that need not be initialized. A question mark must be used with DUP in this case. For example, the statement BEGIN DB 100 DUP (?) reserves 100 bytes of uninitialized data space to an offset BEGIN in DS. Note that BEGIN should be typed in the label field, DB in the code field, and 100 DUP (?) in the operand field.

A typical example illustrating the use of these directives is given next:

```
DATA_1      SEGMENT
ADDR_1      DW   3005H
ADDR_2      DW   2003H
DATA_1      ENDS
STACK_1     SEGMENT
            DW 60 DUP (0)        ;   Assign 60₁₀
                                 ;   words of stack
                                 ;   with zeros
STACK_TOP   LABEL WORD           ;   Initialize stack-
                                 ;   top to next lo-
STACK_1     ENDS                 ;   cation after top
                                 ;   of stack.
CODE_1      SEGMENT
            ASSUME CS: CODE_1, DS: DATA_1,
               SS: STACK_1
            MOV AX, STACK_1
            MOV SS, AX
            LEA SP, STACK_TOP
            MOV AX, DATA_1
            MOV DS, AX
            LEA SI, ADDR_1
            LEA DI, ADDR_2
                —                Main program
                —                body
CODE_1      ENDS     —
```

Note that LABEL is a directive used to initialize STACK_TOP to the next location after the top of the stack. The statement STACK_TOP LABEL WORD gives the name STACK_TOP to the next address after the 60 words are set aside for the stack. The WORD in this statement indicates that PUSH into and POP from the stack are done as words.

Also note that the ASSUME directive tells the assembler the names of the logical segments to use as the code segment, data segment, and stack segment. The extra segment can be assigned a name in a similar manner. When the instructions are executed, the displacements in the instructions along with the segment register contents are used by the assembler to generate the 20-bit physical addresses. The segment register, other than the code segment, must be initialized before they are used to access data.

When the assembler translates an assembly language program, it computes the displacement, or offset, of each instruction code byte from the start of a logical segment that contains it. For example, in the preceding program, the CS: CODE_1 in the ASSUME statement directs the assembler to compute the offsets or displacements by the following instructions from the start of the logical segment CODE_1. This means that when the program is run, the CS will contain the 16-bit value where the logical segment CODE_1 is located in memory. The assembler keeps track of the instruction byte displacements, which are loaded into IP. The 20-bit physical address generated from CS and IP are used to fetch each instruction.

Another example to store data bytes in a data segment and to allocate stack is as follows:

```
DSEG     SEGMENT
ARRAY    DB 02H, 0F1H, 0A2H    ;  Store 3 bytes of
DSEG     ENDS                  ;  data in an ad-
            —                  ;  dress defined by
            —                  ;  DSEG as DS and
            —                  ;  ARRAY as off-
                               ;  set
SSEG     SEGMENT
            DW 10 DUP (0)       ;  Allocate
                                ;  10 word stack
STACK    LABEL WORD             ;  Label initial TOS
_TOP
SSEG     ENDS
            —
            —
            —
            MOV AX, DSEG        ;  Initialize
            MOV DS, AX          ;  DS
            MOV AX, SSEG        ;  Initialize
            MOV SS, AX          ;  SS
            MOV SP, STACK_TOP   ;  Initialize SP
            —
            —
            —
```

A logical segment is not normally given a physical starting address when it is declared. After the program is assembled, the programmer uses the linker to assign physical address. Note that all segment registers used in a program, except CS, must be initialized by instructions before they are used to access data. This is because when the assembler reads through the program, it calculates the offset of each instruction from the start of the logical segment and places it into IP and places the 16-bit address where the logical code segment is located in CS.

Example 5-1

Determine the effect of each of the following 8086 instructions:

1. DIV CH
2. CBW
3. MOVSW

Assume the following data prior to execution of each of these instructions independently (assume all numbers in hexadecimal):

[DS]	= 2000H
[ES]	= 4000H
[CX]	= 0300H
[SP]	= 4000H
[SS]	= 6000H
[AX]	= 0091H
[20300H]	= 05H, [20301H] = 02H
[40200H]	= 06H, [40201H] = 07H
[SI]	= 0300H
[DI]	= 0200H
DF	= 0

Solution

1. Before unsigned division, CH contains 03_{10} and AX contains 145_{10}. Therefore, after DIV CH,

   $$[AH] = \text{remainder} = 01H$$
   $$[AL] = \text{quotient} = 48_{10} = 30H$$

2. CBW sign-extends AL register into AH register. Since the contents of AL is 91H, the sign bit is 1. Therefore, after CBW,

   $$[AX] = FF91H$$

3. Before MOVSW,

   Source String
   [SI] = 0300H, [DS] = 2000H

   Physical address = 20300H

   Destination String
   [DI] = 0200H, [ES] = 4000H

   Physical address = 40200H

   After MOVSW,

   $$[40200H] = 05H, [40201H] = 02H$$

   Since DF = 0,

   $$[SI] = 0302H, [D0] = 0202H$$

Example 5-2

Write an 8086 assembly language program to add two 16-bit numbers in CX and DX and store the result in location 0500H addressed by DI.

Solution

```
DATA    SEGMENT
        DW 7FA1H              ; Number 1 here
        DW 0371H              ; Number 2 here
DATA    ENDS
CODE    SEGMENT
        ASSUME CS: CODE, DS: DATA
        MOV AX, DATA          ; Initialize DS
        MOV DS, AX            ; Initialize DI
        MOV DI, 0500H
        ADD CX, DX            ; Add
        MOV [DI], CX          ; Store
        HLT
CODE    ENDS
        END
```

Example 5-3

Write an 8086 assembly language program to add two 64-bit numbers. Assume SI and DI contain the starting addresses of the numbers. Store the result in memory pointed to by [DI].

Solution

```
DATA_ARRAY SEGMENT
DATA1      DD  0A71 F218H  ; DATA1 low
           DD  2F17 6200H  ; DATA1 high
DATA2      DD  7A24 1601H  ; DATA2 low
           DD  152A 671FH  ; DATA2 high
DATA_ARRAY ENDS
PROG_CODE  SEGMENT
           ASSUME CS: PROG_CODE, DS:
               DATA_ARRAY
           MOV AX,
               DATA_ARRAY
           MOV DS, AX       ; Initialize DS
           MOV DX, 4        ; Load 4 into DX
           MOV BX, 2        ; Initialize BX
           MOV SI, DATA1    ; Initialize SI
           MOV DI, DATA2    ; Initialize DI
           CLC              ; Clear carry
START      MOV AX, [SI]     ; Load DATA1
           ADC [DI], AX     ; Add DATA2 with
                            ; carry
           ADD SI, BX       ; Update
           DEC DX           ; pointers
```

```
              JNZ START        ;   Decrement
                               ;   pointer
              HLT
PROG_CODE     ENDS
              END
```

Example 5-4

Write an 8086 assembly language program to multiply
two 16-bit unsigned numbers to provide a 32-bit result.
Assume that the two numbers are stored in CX and DX.

Solution

```
CODE_SEG SEGMENT
         ASSUME CS: CODE_SEG
         MOV AX, DX   ; Move first data
         MUL CX       ; [DX] [AX] ← [AX] * [CX]
         HLT
CODE_SEG ENDS
         END
```

Example 5-5

Write an 8086 assembly language program that will move
50_{10} 8-bit data elements from a source string, pointed to
by SI, to a destination string pointed to by DI. Assume
DS, SI, and DI are initialized.

Solution

```
CODE_SEG   SEGMENT
           ASSUME CS: CODE_SEG
           MOV CX, 50      ;   Load 50 into
                           ;   CS
           REPMOVSB        ;   Move until
                           ;   CX = 0
           HLT
CODE_SEG   ENDS
           END
```

Example 5-6

Write an 8086 assembly language program to clear 50_{10}
consecutive bytes. Assume DS is already initialized.

Solution

```
CODE_SEG   SEGMENT
           ASSUME CS: CODE_SEG
           LEA BX, ADDR    ;   Initialize BX
           MOV CX, 50      ;   Initialize
                           ;   loop count
```

```
START      MOV [BX], 00H   ;   Clear mem-
                           ;   ory byte
           INC BX          ;   Update
                           ;   pointer
           LOOP START      ;   Decrement
                           ;   CX and loop
           HLT
CODE_SEG   ENDS
           END
```

Example 5-7

Write an 8086 assembly language program to compute

$$\sum_{i=1}^{n} X_i Y_i$$

where X_i and Y_i are signed 8-bit numbers and $n = 100$.
Assume DS is already initialized and X_i's and Y_i's are
already stored in memory. Also, assume no overflow.

Solution

```
PROG    SEGMENT
        ASSUME CS: PROG
        MOV CX, 100     ;   Initialize loop count
        LEA BX, ADDR1   ;   Load ADDR1 into BX
        LEA SI, ADDR2   ;   Load ADDR2 into SI
        MOV DX, 0000H   ;   Initialize sum to zero
START   MOV AL, [BX]    ;   Load data into AL
        IMUL [SI]       ;   Signed multiplication
        ADD DX, AX      ;   Sum X_iY_i
        INC BX          ;   Update
        INC SI          ;   pointers
        LOOP START      ;   Decrement CX and
                        ;   loop
        HLT
PROG    ENDS
        END
```

Example 5-8

Write an 8086 assembly language program to add two
words; each word contains four packed BCD digits. The
first word is stored in two consecutive locations with the
low byte pointed to by SI at the offset DIGIT1, while
the second word is stored in two consecutive locations
with the low byte pointed to by BX at the offset DIGIT2.
Store the result in memory pointed to by BX.

Solution

```
DATA_SEG   SEGMENT
```

```
DIGIT1      DW   3125H
DIGIT2      DW   7391H
DATA_SEG    ENDS
CODE        SEGMENT
            ASSUME CS: CODE, DS: DATA_SEG
            MOV AX, DATA_SEG   ;  Initialize DS
            MOV DS, AX
            MOV CX, 2          ;  Initialize loop
                               ;  count
            MOV SI, DIGIT1     ;  Initialize SI
            MOV BX, DIGIT2     ;  Initialize BX
            CLC                ;  Clear carry
START       MOV AL, [SI]       ;  Move data
            ADC AL, [BX]       ;  Perform addi-
                               ;  tion
            DAA                ;  BCD adjust
            MOV [BX], AL       ;  Store result
            INC SI             ;  Update
            INC BX             ;  pointers
            LOOP START         ;  Decrement CX
                               ;  and loop
            HLT
CODE        ENDS
            END
```

Example 5-9

Write an 8086 assembly language program to add two
words; each word contains two ASCII digits. The first
word is stored in two consecutive locations with the low
byte pointed to by SI at the offset DIGIT1, while the
second word is stored in two consecutive locations with
the low byte pointed to by DI at the offset DIGIT2. Store
the result in locations pointed to by DI.

Solution

```
DATA    SEGMENT
DIGIT1  DW   2422H
DIGIT2  DW   3134H
DATA    ENDS
CODE    SEGMENT
        ASSUME CS: CODE, DS: DATA
        MOV AX, DATA   ;  Initialize DS
        MOV CX, 2      ;  Initialize loop count
        MOV SI, DIGIT1 ;  Initialize SI
        MOV DI, DIGIT2 ;  Initialize DI
        CLC            ;  Clear carry
START   MOV AL, [SI]   ;  Move data
        ADC AL, [DI]   ;  Perform addition
        AAA            ;  ASCII adjust
        MOV [DI], AL   ;  Store result
```

```
            INC SI        ;  Update
            INC DI        ;  pointers
            LOOP START    ;  Decrement CX and loop
            HLT
CODE        ENDS
            END
```

Example 5-10

Write an 8086 assembly language program to compare
a source string of 50_{10} words pointed to by an offset of
2000H in DS with a destination string pointed to by an
offset 3000H in ES. The program should be halted as
soon as a match is found or the end of the string is reached.
Assume DS is initialized and strings are already stored
in memory.

Solution

```
CODE    SEGMENT
        ASSUME CS: CODE
        MOV SI, 2000H    ;  Initialize SI
        MOV DI, 3000H    ;  Initialize DI
        MOV CX, 50       ;  Initialize CX
        CLD              ;  DF is cleared so
                         ;  that SI and DI will
                         ;  auto-increment after
                         ;  compare
        REPNECMPSW       ;  Repeat CMPSW until
                         ;  CX = 0 or until
                         ;  compared words are
                         ;  equal
        HLT              ;  Stop
CODE    ENDS
        END
```

Example 5-11

Write a subroutine in 8086 assembly language that can
be called by a main program in a different code segment.
The subroutine will multiply a signed 16-bit number by
a signed 8-bit number. The main program will call this
subroutine, store the results in two consecutive memory
words, and stop. Assume SI and DI point to the signed
8-bit and 16-bit data, respectively.

Solution

Main Program

```
MAIN_PROG  SEGMENT            ;  Give
                              ;  assembler
           ASSUME CS: MAIN_PROG  ;  CS name
           MOV AX, 5000H      ;  Initialize
```

```
          MOV DS, AX              ; DS to
                                  ; 5000H
          MOV AX, 6000H           ; Initialize
          MOV SS, AX              ; SS to
                                  ; 6000H
          MOV SP, 0020H           ; Initialize
                                  ; SP
          MOV BX, 2000H           ; Initialize
                                  ; BX
          MOV AL, [SI]            ; Move
                                  ; 8-bit data
          MOV CX, [DI]            ; Move 16-
                                  ; bit data
          CALL MUL                ; Call mul-
                                  ; tiplication
                                  ; subrou-
                                  ; tine
          MOV [BX], DX            ; Store
                                  ; high
                                  ; word of
                                  ; result
          MOV 2[BX], AX           ; Store low
                                  ; word
                                  ; of result
          HLT
MAIN_PROG ENDS
          END
```

Subroutine

```
SUBR      SEGMENT
          ASSUME CS: SUBR
MUL       PROC FAR       ; Must be called
                         ; from another code
                         ; segment
          CBW            ; Sign-extend AL
          IMUL CX        ; [DX] [AX] ← [AX]
                         ; * [CX]
          RET            ; Return
MUL       ENDP           ; End of procedure
                         ; MUL
SUBR      ENDS
END
```

5-7 8086 INPUT/OUTPUT

5-7-1 Programmed I/O

The 8086 uses either standard I/O or memory-mapped I/O. The standard I/O uses the instructions IN and OUT and is able to provide up to 64K bytes of I/O locations. The standard I/O can transfer either 8-bit data or 16-bit data to or from a peripheral device. The 64K-byte I/O locations can then be configured as 64K 8-bit ports or 32K 16-bit ports. All I/O transfers between the 8086 and peripheral devices take place via AL for 8-bit ports (AH

is not involved) and AX for 16-bit ports. The I/O port addressing can be done either directly or indirectly.

- *Direct:*

  IN AX, PORTA or IN AL, PORTA inputs 16-bit contents of port A into AX or 8-bit contents of port A into AL, respectively.

  OUT PORTA, AX or OUT PORTA, AL outputs 16-bit contents of AX into port A or 8-bit contents of AL into port A, respectively.

- *Indirect:*

  IN AX, DX or IN AL, DX inputs 16-bit data addressed by DX into AX or 8-bit data addressed by DX into AL, respectively.

  OUT DX, AX or OUT DX, AL outputs 16-bit contents of AX into the port addressed by DX or 8-bit contents of AL into the port addressed by DX, respectively.

Memory-mapped I/O is basically accomplished by using the memory instructions such as MOV AX or AL, [BX] and MOV [BX], AX or AL for inputting or outputting 8- or 16-bit data into AL or AX addressed by the 20-bit address computed from DS and BX.

The 8086 programmed I/O capability will be explained in the following paragraphs using the 8255 I/O chip. The 8255 is a general-purpose programmable I/O chip. The 8255 has three 8-bit I/O ports: ports A, B, and C. Ports A and B are latched 8-bit ports for both input and output. Port C is also an 8-bit port with latched output, but the inputs are not latched. Port C can be used in two ways: It can be used either as a simple I/O port or as a control port for data transfer using handshaking as via ports A and B.

The 8086 configures the three ports by outputting appropriate data to the 8-bit control register. The ports can be decoded by two 8255 input pins A_0 and A_1 as follows:

A_1	A_0	Port Name
0	0	Port A
0	1	Port B
1	0	Port C
1	1	Control register

The structure of the control register is shown in the diagram at top of page 139.

Bit 7 (D_7) of the control register must be 1 to send the definitions for bits 0–6 (D_0–D_6) as shown in the diagram. In this format, bits D_0–D_6 are divided into two groups: groups A and B. Group A configures all 8 bits of port A and the upper 4 bits of port C, while group B defines all 8 bits of port B and the lower 4 bits of port C. All bits in a port can be configured as a parallel input port by writing a 1 at the appropriate bit in the control register by the 8086 OUT instruction, and a 0 in a par-

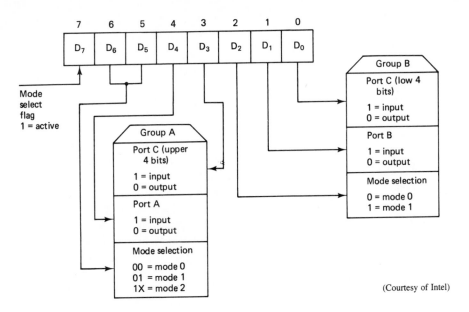

(Courtesy of Intel)

ticular bit position will configure the appropriate port as a parallel output port.

Group A has three modes of operation: modes 0, 1, and 2. Group B has two modes: modes 0 and 1. Mode 0 for both groups provides simple I/O operation for each of the three ports. No handshaking is required. Mode 1 for both groups is the strobed I/O mode used for transferring I/O data to or from a specified port in conjunction with strobes or handshaking signals. Ports A and B use the lines on port C to generate or accept these handshaking signals. Mode 2 of group A is the strobed bidirectional bus I/O and may be used for communicating with a peripheral device on a single 8-bit data bus for both transmitting and receiving data (bidirectional bus I/O). Handshaking signals are required. Interrupt generation and enable/disable functions are also available.

When $D_7 = 0$, the bit set/reset control word format is used for the control register as follows:

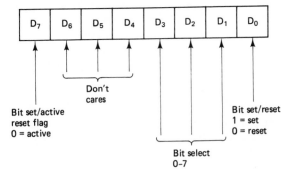

(Courtesy of Intel)

This format is used to set or reset the output on a pin of port C or when enabling of the interrupt output signals for handshake data transfer is desired. For example, the 8 bits

0	X X X	1 1 0	0
↑	Don't	↑	↑
Bit set/reset mode	cares	Bit 6	Clear

will clear bit 6 of port C to zero. Note that the control word format can be outputted to the 8255 control register by using the 8086 OUT instruction.

Now, let us define the control word format for mode 0 more precisely by means of a numerical example. Consider that the control word format is $1000\ 0010_2$. With this data in the control register, all 8 bits of port A are configured as outputs and that the 8 bits of port C are also configured as outputs. All 8 bits of port B, however, are defined as inputs. On the other hand, outputting $1001\ 1011_2$ into the control register will configure all three 8-bit ports (ports A, B, and C) as inputs.

5-7-2 8089 Input/Output Processor (IOP)

The 8089 IOP is designed for the 8086 and can service I/O devices directly, removing this task from the 8086.

The 8089 is a general-purpose I/O system implemented on a single 40-pin chip. Two independent I/O channels with DMA capabilities are provided. The 8089 has about 50 different types of instructions for performing efficient I/O operations. The 8089 is directly compatible with the Intel 8086 and 8088 16-bit microprocessors. A typical 8086/8089 configuration block diagram is shown in Figure 5-7.

The 8086 performs an I/O operation by forming a message for the 8089 in main memory. The 8086 activates the channel attention line to indicate to the IOP that an I/O operation is to be performed. Note that the message provided by the 8086 specifies the function to be performed by the 8089. The 8089 reads the message and executes the specified operation by activating the required

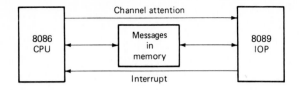

Figure 5-7 8086/8089 block diagram (Courtesy of Intel Corporation)

channel program. The 8089 informs the 8086 of completion of the channel program by activating the interrupt request line. Typical 8086 I/O commands include starting or stopping an I/O program.

Some of the applications of the 8089 IOP include operating system support, graphic display functions, and interfacing to a high-performance hard disk. For example, the 8089 has the instructions to search and update the disk directory. This provides significant support to operating system implementation in an 8086-based system. The 8089 also has the capability of supporting graphic display functions such as screen refresh. Finally, the 8089 can provide all the major I/O functions for interfacing a high-performance hard disk such as Winchester-type to an 8086-based microcomputer.

5-7-3 8086 Interrupts

The 8086 assigns every interrupt a type code so that the 8086 can identify it. Interrupts can be initiated by external devices or internally by software instructions or by exceptional conditions such as attempting to divide by zero.

Predefined Interrupts The first five interrupt types are reserved for specific functions.

- Type 0: INT0 Divide by zero
- Type 1: INT1 Single step
- Type 2: INT2 Nonmaskable interrupt (NMI pin)
- Type 3: INT3 Breakpoint
- Type 4: INT4 Interrupt on overflow

The interrupt vectors for these five interrupts are predefined by Intel. The user must provide the desired IP and CS values in the interrupt pointer table. The user may also initiate these interrupts through hardware or software. If a predefined interrupt is not used in a system, the user may assign some other function to the associated type.

The 8086 is automatically interrupted whenever a division by zero is attempted. This interrupt is nonmaskable and is implemented by Intel as part of the execution of the divide instruction.

When the TF (trap flag) is set by an instruction, the 8086 goes into the single-step mode. The TF can be cleared to zero as follows:

PUSHF	; Save flags
MOV BP, SP	; Move [SP] ← [BP]
AND 0[BP], 0FEFFH	; Clear TF
POPF	; Pop flags

Note here that 0[BP] rather than [BP] is used since BP cannot be used without displacement in the 8086 assembler. Now, to set TF, the AND instruction just shown should be replaced by OR 0[BP], 0100H. Once TF is set to 1, the 8086 automatically generates a Type 1 interrupt after execution of each instruction. The user can write a service routine at the interrupt address vector to display memory locations and/or register to debug a program. Single step is nonmaskable and cannot be enabled by the STI (enable interrupt) or the CLI (disable interrupt) instruction.

The nonmaskable interrupt is initiated via the 8086 NMI pin. It is edge triggered (LOW to HIGH) and must be active for 2 clock cycles to guarantee recognition. It is normally used for catastrophic failures such as a power failure. The 8086 obtains the interrupt vector address by automatically executing the INT2 (type 2) instruction internally.

The type 3 interrupt is used for breakpoint and is nonmaskable. The user inserts the 1-byte instruction INT3 into a program by replacing an instruction. Breakpoints are useful for program debugging.

The interrupt on overflow is a type 4 interrupt. This interrupt occurs if the overflow flag (OF) is set and the INTO instruction is executed. The overflow flag is affected, for example, after execution of a signed arithmetic (such as IMUL, signed multiplication) instruction. The user can execute an INTO instruction after the IMUL. If there is an overflow, an error service routine written by the user at the type 4 interrupt address vector is executed.

Internal Interrupts The user can generate an interrupt by executing a 2-byte interrupt instruction INTnn. The INTnn instruction is not maskable by the interrupt enable flag (IF). The INTnn instruction can be used to test an interrupt service routine for external interrupts. Type codes 0–255 can be used. If a predefined interrupt is not used in a system, the associate-type code can be utilized with the INTnn instruction to generate software (internal) interrupts.

External Maskable Interrupts The 8086 maskable interrupts are initiated via the INTR pin. These interrupts can be enabled or disabled by STI (IF = 1) or CLI (IF = 0), respectively. If IF = 1 and INTR is active (HIGH) without occurrence of any other interrupts, the 8086, after completing the current instruction, generates INTA LOW twice, each time for about 2 cycles.

The state of the INTR pin is sampled during the last clock cycle of each instruction. In some instances, the 8086 samples the INTR pin at a later time. An example is execution of POP to a segment register. In this case, the interrupts are sampled until completion of the following instruction. This allows a 32-bit pointer to be loaded to SS and SP without the danger of an interrupt occurring between the two loads.

$\overline{\text{INTA}}$ is only generated by the 8086 in response to INTR, as shown in Figure 5–8. The interrupt acknowledge sequence includes two $\overline{\text{INTA}}$ cycles separated by 2 idle clock cycles. ALE is also generated by the 8086 and will load the address latches with indeterminate information. The ALE is useful in maximum systems with multiple 8259A priority interrupt controllers. During the $\overline{\text{INTA}}$ bus cycles, DT/$\overline{\text{R}}$ and $\overline{\text{DEN}}$ are LOW (see 8086 minimum mode bus cycle). The first $\overline{\text{INTA}}$ bus cycle indicates that an interrupt acknowledge cycle is in progress and allows the system to be ready to place the interrupt-type code on the next $\overline{\text{INTA}}$ bus cycle. The 8086 does not obtain the information from the bus during the first cycle. The external hardware must place the type code on the lower half of the 16-bit data bus (D_0–D_7) during the second cycle.

In the minimum mode, the M/IO is LOW indicating I/O operation during the $\overline{\text{INTA}}$ bus cycles. The 8086 internal $\overline{\text{LOCK}}$ signal is also LOW from T_2 of the first bus cycle until T_2 of the second bus cycle to avoid the BIU from accepting a hold request between the two $\overline{\text{INTA}}$ cycles. Figure 5–9 shows a simplified interconnection between the 8086 and 74LS244 for servicing the INTR.

$\overline{\text{INTA}}$ enables the 74LS244 to place type code nn on the 8086 data bus.

In the maximum mode, the status lines S_0–S_2 will enable the $\overline{\text{INTA}}$ output for each cycle via the 8282. The 8086 $\overline{\text{LOCK}}$ output will be active from T_2 of the first cycle until T_2 of the second to prevent the 8086 from accepting a hold request on either $\overline{\text{RQ}}/\overline{\text{GT}}$ input and to prevent bus arbitration logic from releasing the bus between $\overline{\text{INTA}}$s in multimaster systems. The $\overline{\text{LOCK}}$ output can be used in external logic to lock other devices off the system bus, thus ensuring the $\overline{\text{INTA}}$ sequence to be completed without intervention.

Interrupt Procedures Once the 8086 has the interrupt-type code (via the bus for hardware interrupts, from software interrupt instructions INTnn, or from the predefined interrupts), the type code is multiplied by 4 to obtain the corresponding interrupt vector in the interrupt vector table. The 4 bytes of the interrupt vector are the least significant byte of the instruction pointer, most significant byte of the pointer, least significant byte of the code segment register, and most significant byte of the code segment register. During the transfer of control, the 8086 pushes the flags and current code segment register and instruction pointer onto the stack. The new CS and IP values are loaded. Flags TF and IF are then cleared to zero. The CS and IP values are read by the 8086 from the interrupt vector table. No segment registers are used

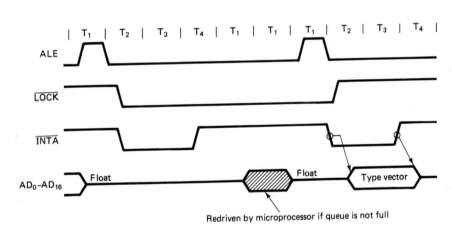

Figure 5–8 $\overline{\text{INTA}}$ cycle.
(Courtesy of Intel)

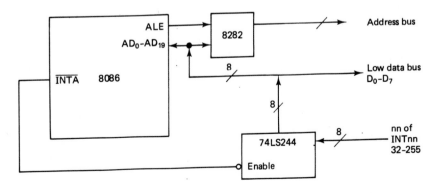

Figure 5–9 Servicing the INTR in the minimum mode

when accessing the interrupt pointer table. $S_4 S_3$ has the value 10_2 to indicate no segment register selection.

Interrupt Priorities As far as the 8086 interrupt priorities are concerned, the single-step interrupt has the highest priority, followed by NMI, followed by the software interrupts (all interrupts except single step, NMI, and INTR interrupts). This means that a simultaneous NMI and single step will cause the NMI service routine to follow single step; a simultaneous software interrupt and single step will cause the software interrupt service routine to follow single step; and a simultaneous NMI and software interrupt will cause the NMI service routine to be executed prior to the software interrupt service routine. An exception to this priority scheme occurs if all three nonmaskable interrupts (single step, software, and NMI) are pending. For this case, the software interrupt service routine will be executed first followed by the NMI service routine, and single stepping will not be serviced. However, if software interrupt and single stepping are pending, single stepping resumes upon execution of the instruction causing the software interrupt (the next instruction in the routine being single stepped).

The INTR is maskable and has the lowest priority. If the user does wish to single step before INTR is serviced, the single-step routine must disable interrupts during execution of the program being single stepped and reenable interrupts on entry to the single-step routine. To avoid single stepping before the NMI service routine, the single-step routine must check the return address on the stack for the NMI service routine address and return control to that routine without single step enabled. Figure 5–10(a) and 5–10(b) illustrate this. In Figure 5–10(a), single step and NMI occur at the same time, whereas in Figure 5–10(b), NMI, INTR, and a divide error occur during a divide instruction being single stepped.

A priority interrupt controller such as the 8259A can be used with the 8086 INTR to provide eight levels of interrupts. The 8259A has built-in features for expansion of up to 64 levels with additional 8259s. The 8259A is programmable and can be readily used with the 8086 to obtain multiple interrupts from the single 8086 INTR pin.

Interrupt Pointer Table The interrupt pointer table provides interrupt address vectors (IP and CS contents) for all the interrupts. There may be up to 256 entries for the 256 type codes. Each entry consists of two addresses—one for storing IP and the other for storing CS. Note that in the 8086 each interrupt address vector is a 20-bit address obtained from IP and CS.

In order to service an interrupt, the 8086 calculates the two addresses in the pointer table where IP and CS are stored for a particular interrupt type as follows:

For INTnn

⌐—— Type code

The table address for IP = 4 × nn, and the table address for CS = 4 × nn + 2.

For example, consider INT2:

$$\text{Address for IP} = 4 \times 2 = 00008\text{H}$$

$$\text{Address for CS} = 00008 + 2 = 0000\text{AH}$$

The values of IP and CS are loaded from locations 00008H and 0000AH in the pointer table. Similarly, the IP and CS addresses for other INTnn are calculated, and their values are obtained from the contents of these addresses in the pointer table (Table 5–13).

The 8086 interrupt vectors are defined as follows:

Vectors 0–4	For predefined interrupts
Vectors 5–31	For Intel's future use
Vectors 32–255	For user interrupts

Interrupt service routines should be terminated with an IRET (interrupt return) instruction, which pops the top three stack words into the IP, CS, and flags, thus returning to the right place in the main program.

5–7–4 8086 DMA

When configured in minimum mode (MN/$\overline{\text{MX}}$ HIGH), the 8086 provides HOLD and HLDA (hold acknowledge) signals to control the system bus for DMA applications. In this type of DMA, the peripheral device can request the DMA transfer via the DMA request (DRQ) line connected to a DMA controller chip such as the 8257. In response to this request, the 8257 sends a HOLD signal to the 8086. The 8257 then WAITs for the HLDA signal from the 8086. On receipt of this HLDA, the 8257 sends a DMACK signal to the peripheral device. The 8257 then takes over the bus and controls data transfer between the RAM and peripheral device. On completion of data transfer, the 8257 returns control to the 8086 by disabling the HOLD and DMACK signals.

5–8 SYSTEM DESIGN USING 8086

This section covers the basic concepts associated with interfacing the 8086 to its support chips such as memory and I/O. Topics such as timing diagrams and 8086 pins and signals will also be included.

5–8–1 Pins and Signals

The 8086 pins and signals are shown in Figure 5–11. Unless otherwise indicated, all 8086 pins are TTL compatible. As mentioned before, the 8086 can operate in two modes. These are minimum mode (uniprocessor system with a single 8086) and maximum mode (multiprocessor system with more than one 8086). MN/$\overline{\text{MX}}$ is an input pin used to select one of these modes. When MN/$\overline{\text{MX}}$ is HIGH, the 8086 operates in the minimum mode. In this mode, the 8086 is configured (that is, pins are

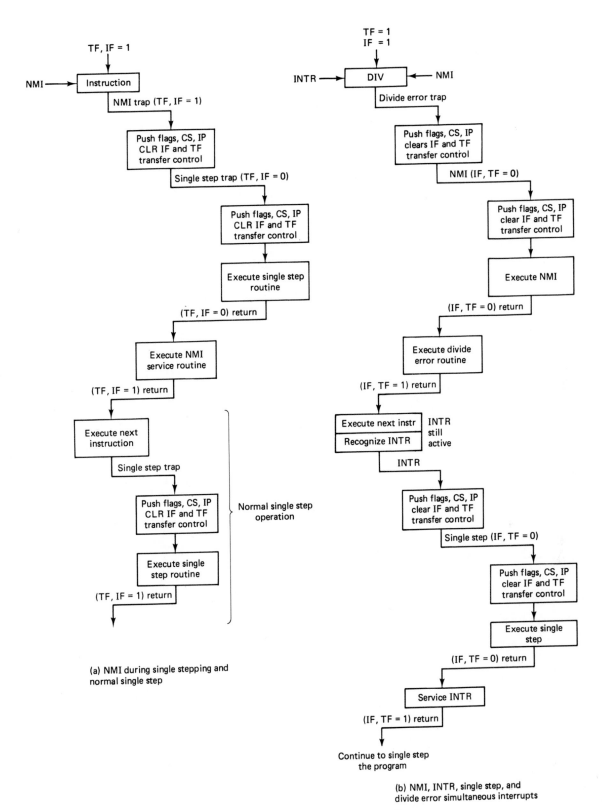

(a) NMI during single stepping and normal single step

(b) NMI, INTR, single step, and divide error simultaneous interrupts

Figure 5-10   NMI service routine

TABLE 5–13
8086 Interrupt Pointer Table

Interrupt Type Code			20-Bit Memory Address
0	IP		00000H
	CS		00002H
1	IP		00004H
	CS		00006H
2			00008H
			0000AH
.			.
.			.
.			.
255	IP		003FEH
	CS		00400H

Common Signals		
Name	**Function**	**Type**
AD15–AD0	Address/Data Bus	Bidirectional, 3-state
A19/S6-A16/S3	Address/Status	Output, 3-state
$\overline{BHE}$/S7	Bus High Enable/Status	Output, 3-State
MN/$\overline{MX}$	Minimum/Maximum Mode Control	Input
$\overline{RD}$	Read Control	Output, 3-state
$\overline{TEST}$	Wait On Test Control	Input
READY	Wait State Control	Input
RESET	System Reset	Input
NMI	Non-Maskable Interrupt Request	Input
INTR	Interrupt Request	Input
CLK	System Clock	Input
Vcc	+5 V	Input
GND	Ground	

Minimum Mode Signals (MN/MX = Vcc)		
Name	**Function**	**Type**
HOLD	Hold Request	Input
HLDA	Hold Acknowledge	Output
$\overline{WR}$	Write Control	Output, 3-state
M/$\overline{IO}$	Memory/IO Control	Output, 3-State
DT/$\overline{R}$	Data Transmit/Receive	Output, 3-state
$\overline{DEN}$	Data Enable	Output, 3-state
ALE	Address Latch Enable	Output
$\overline{INTA}$	Interrupt Acknowledge	Output

Maximum Mode Signals (MN/$\overline{MX}$ = GND)		
Name	**Function**	**Type**
$\overline{RQ}/\overline{GT}1, 0$	Request/Grant Bus Access Control	Bidirectional
$\overline{LOCK}$	Bus Priority Lock Control	Output, 3-State
$\overline{S2}$-$\overline{S0}$	Bus Cycle Status	Output, 3-State
QS1, QS0	Instruction Queue Status	Output

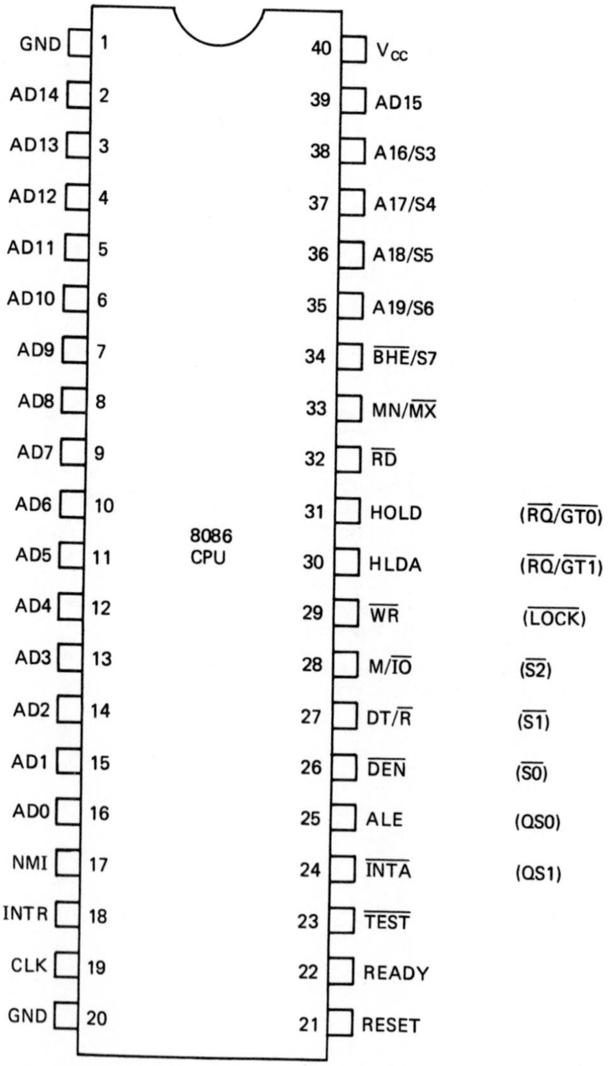

8086 CPU pin diagram (40-pin):

Left pin	#		#	Right pin
GND	1		40	Vcc
AD14	2		39	AD15
AD13	3		38	A16/S3
AD12	4		37	A17/S4
AD11	5		36	A18/S5
AD10	6		35	A19/S6
AD9	7		34	$\overline{BHE}$/S7
AD8	8		33	MN/$\overline{MX}$
AD7	9		32	$\overline{RD}$
AD6	10		31	HOLD ($\overline{RQ}/\overline{GT0}$)
AD5	11		30	HLDA ($\overline{RQ}/\overline{GT1}$)
AD4	12		29	$\overline{WR}$ ($\overline{LOCK}$)
AD3	13		28	M/$\overline{IO}$ ($\overline{S2}$)
AD2	14		27	DT/$\overline{R}$ ($\overline{S1}$)
AD1	15		26	$\overline{DEN}$ ($\overline{S0}$)
AD0	16		25	ALE (QS0)
NMI	17		24	$\overline{INTA}$ (QS1)
INTR	18		23	$\overline{TEST}$
CLK	19		22	READY
GND	20		21	RESET

Maximum mode pin functions (e.g., $\overline{LOCK}$) are shown in parentheses

Figure 5–11 Pin definitions. (Courtesy of Intel)

defined) to support small, single-processor systems using a few devices that use the system bus. When MN/$\overline{\text{MX}}$ is LOW, the 8086 is configured (that is, pins are defined in the maximum mode) to support multiprocessor systems. In this case, the Intel 8288 bus controller is added to the 8086 to provide bus controls and compatibility with the multibus architecture. Note that, in a particular application, MN/$\overline{\text{MX}}$ must be tied to either HIGH or LOW.

The AD_0–AD_{15} lines are a 16-bit multiplexed address/data bus. During the first clock cycle, AD_0–AD_{15} are the low-order 16 bits of address. The 8086 has a total of 20 address lines. The upper four lines are multiplexed with the status signals for the 8086. These are the A_{16}/S_3, A_{17}/S_4, A_{18}/S_5, and A_{19}/S_6. During the first clock period of a bus cycle (read or write cycle), the entire 20-bit address is available on these lines. During all other clock cycles for memory and I/O operations, AD_{15}–AD_0 contain the 16-bit data and S_3, S_4, S_5, and S_6 become status lines. S_3 and S_4 lines are decoded as follows:

A_{17}/S_4	A_{16}/S_3	Function
0	0	Extra segment
0	1	Stack segment
1	0	Code or no segment
1	1	Data segment

Therefore, after the first clock cycle of an instruction execution, the A_{17}/S_4 and A_{16}/S_3 pins specify which segment register generates the segment portion of the 8086 address. Thus, by decoding these lines and then using the decoder outputs as chip selects for memory chips, up to 4 megabytes (1 megabyte per segment) can be provided. This provides a degree of protection by preventing erroneous write operations to one segment from overlapping into another segment and destroying information in that segment. A_{18}/S_5 and A_{19}/S_6 are used as A_{18} and A_{19}, respectively, during the first clock period of an instruction execution. If an I/O instruction is executed, they stay LOW during the first clock period. During all other cycles, A_{18}/S_5 indicates the status of the 8086 interrupt enable flag and A_{19}/S_6 becomes S_6, and a LOW A_{19}/S_6 pin indicates that the 8086 is on the bus. During a hold acknowledge clock period, the 8086 tristates the A_{19}/S_6 pin and thus allows another bus master to take control of the system bus.

The 8086 tristates AD_0–AD_{15} during interrupt acknowledge or hold acknowledge cycles.

$\overline{\text{BHE}}$/S_7 is used as $\overline{\text{BHE}}$ (bus high enable) during the first clock cycle of an instruction execution. The 8086 outputs a LOW on this pin during read, write, and interrupt acknowledge cycles in which data are to be transferred in a high-order byte (AD_{15}–AD_8) of the data bus. $\overline{\text{BHE}}$ can be used in conjunction with AD_0 to select memory banks. A thorough discussion is provided later. During all other cycles, $\overline{\text{BHE}}$/S_7 is used as S_7, and the 8086

maintains the output level ($\overline{\text{BHE}}$) of the first clock cycle on this pin.

$\overline{\text{RD}}$ is LOW whenever the 8086 is reading data from memory or an I/O location.

$\overline{\text{TEST}}$ is an input pin and is only used by the WAIT instruction. The 8086 enters a wait state after execution of the WAIT instruction until a LOW is seen on the $\overline{\text{TEST}}$ pin. This input is synchronized internally during each clock cycle on the leading edge of the CLK pin.

INTR is the maskable interrupt input. This line is not latched, and, therefore, INTR must be held at a HIGH level until recognized to generate an interrupt.

NMI is the nonmaskable interrupt input activated by a leading edge.

RESET is the system reset input signal. This signal must be HIGH for at least 4 clock cycles to be recognized, except after power-on, which requires a 50-μs reset pulse. It causes the 8086 to initialize registers DS, SS, ES, IP, and flags to all zeros. It also initializes CS to FFFFH. Upon removal of the RESET signal from the RESET pin, the 8086 will fetch its next instruction from 20-bit physical address FFFF0H (CS = FFFFH, IP = 0000H).

When the 8086 detects the positive-going edge of a pulse on RESET, it stops all activities until the signal goes LOW. When RESET is LOW, the 8086 initializes the system as follows:

8086 Component	Content
Flags	Clear
IP	0000H
CS	FFFFH
DS	0000H
SS	0000H
ES	0000H
Queue	Empty

The RESET signal to the 8086 can be generated by the 8284. The 8284 has a Schmitt trigger input ($\overline{\text{RES}}$) for generating RESET from a LOW active external reset.

To guarantee reset from power-up, the reset input must remain below 1.05 V for 50 μs after V_{CC} has reached the minimum supply voltage of 4.5 V. The $\overline{\text{RES}}$ input of the 8284 can be driven by a simple RC circuit as shown in Figure 5–12.

The values of R and C can be selected as follows:

$$V_C\,(t) = V\,[1 - \exp - (t/RC)]$$

where t = 50 μs, V = 4.5 V, V_C = 1.05 V, and RC = 188 μs. For example, if C is chosen arbitrarily to be 0.1 μF, then R = 1.88 kΩ.

As mentioned before, the 8086 can be configured in either minimum or maximum mode using the MN/$\overline{\text{MX}}$ input pin. In minimum mode, the 8086 itself generates all bus control signals. These signals are as follows:

- DT/$\overline{\text{R}}$ (data transmit/receive) is an output signal required in a minimum system that uses an 8286/8287

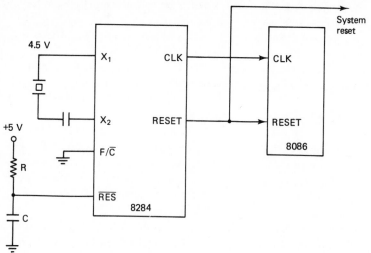

Figure 5–12 8086 reset and system reset. (Courtesy of Intel)

data bus transceiver. It is used to control direction of data flow through the transceiver.

- $\overline{\text{DEN}}$ (data enable) is provided as an output enable for the 8286/8287 in a minimum system that uses the transceiver.
  $\overline{\text{DEN}}$ is active LOW during each memory and I/O access and for $\overline{\text{INTA}}$ cycles.

- ALE (address latch enable) is an output signal provided by the 8086 and can be used to demultiplex the AD_0–AD_{15} into A_0–A_{15} and D_0–D_{15} at the falling edge of ALE. The 8086 ALE signal is the same as the 8085 ALE.

- $M/\overline{\text{IO}}$ is an 8086 output signal similar to the 8085 $\text{IO}/\overline{\text{M}}$. It is used to distinguish a memory access ($M/\overline{\text{IO}}$ = HIGH) from an I/O access ($M/\overline{\text{IO}}$ = LOW). When the 8086 executes an I/O instruction such as IN or OUT, it outputs a LOW on this pin. On the other hand, the 8086 outputs HIGH on this pin when it executes a memory reference instruction such as MOVE AX, [SI].

- $\overline{\text{WR}}$ is used by the 8086 for outputting a LOW to indicate that the processor is performing a write memory or write I/O operation, depending on the $M/\overline{\text{IO}}$ signal.

- $\overline{\text{INTA}}$ is similar to the 8085 $\overline{\text{INTA}}$. For interrupt acknowledge cycles (for INTR pin), the 8086 outputs LOW on this pin.

- HOLD (input) and HLDA (output) have the same purpose as the 8085 HOLD/HLDA pins and are used for DMA. A HIGH on the HOLD pin indicates that another master is requesting to take over the system bus. The processor receiving the HOLD request will output HLDA HIGH as an acknowledgment. At the same time, the processor tristates the system bus. Upon receipt of LOW on the HOLD pin, the processor places LOW on the HLDA pin. HOLD is not an asynchronous input. External synchronization should be provided if the system cannot otherwise guarantee the setup time.

- CLK (input) provides the basic timing for the 8086 and bus controller.

The maximum clock frequencies of the 8086-4, 8086, and 8086-2 are 4 MHz, 5 MHz, and 8 MHz, respectively. Since the design of these processors incorporates dynamic cells, a minimum frequency of 2 MHz is required to retain the state of the machine. The 8086-4, 8086, and 8086-2 will be referred to as 8086 in the the following discussion.

Minimum frequency requirement, single stepping, or cycling of the 8086 may not be accomplished by disabling the clock. Since the 8086 does not have on-chip clock generation circuitry, an 8284 clock generator chip must be connected to the 8086 CLK pin as shown in Figure 5–13. The crystal must have a frequency 3 times the 8086 internal frequency. That is, the 8284 divides the crystal clock frequency by 3. In other words, to generate 5-MHz 8086 internal clock, the crystal clock must be 15 MHz. To select the crystal inputs of the 8284 as the frequency source for clock generation, the $F/\overline{C}$ input must be strapped to ground. This strapping option allows either the crystal or the external frequency input

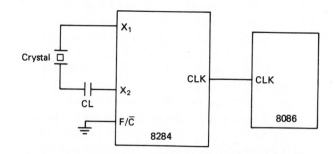

Figure 5–13 8284 clock generator connections to the 8086. (Courtesy of Intel)

as the source for clock generation. When selecting a crystal for use with the 8284, the crystal series resistance should be as low as possible. The oscillator delays in the 8284 appear as inductive elements to the crystal and cause the 8284 to run at a frequency below that of the pure series resonance; a capacitor CL should be placed in series with the crystal and the X_2 pin of the 8284. This capacitor cancels the inductive element. The impedance of the capacitor $XC = 1/2\pi f CL$, where f is the crystal frequency. It is recommended that the crystal series resistance plus XC be kept less than 1 kΩ. As the crystal frequency increases, CL should be decreased. For example, a 12-MHz crystal may require CL $\approx$ 24 pF, while 22 MHz may require CL $\approx$ 8 pF. If very close correlation with the pure series resonance is not necessary, a nominal CL value of 12 to 15 pF may be used with a 15-MHz crystal. Two crystal manufacturers recommended by Intel are Crystle Corp. model CY 15A (15 MHz) and CTS Knight, Inc. model CY 24 A (24 MHz).

Note that the 8284 can be used to generate the 8086 READY input signal based on inputs from slow memory and I/O devices that are not capable of transferring information at the 8086 rate.

In the maximum mode, some of the 8086 pins in the minimum mode are redefined. For example, pins HOLD, HLDA, $\overline{WR}$, M/$\overline{IO}$, DT/$\overline{R}$, $\overline{DEN}$, ALE, and $\overline{INTA}$ in the minimum mode are redefined as $\overline{RQ}/\overline{GT0}$, $\overline{RQ}/\overline{GT1}$, $\overline{LOCK}$, $\overline{S_2}$, $\overline{S_1}$, $\overline{S_0}$, QS0, and QS1, respectively. In maximum mode, the 8288 bus controller decodes the status information from $\overline{S_0}$, $\overline{S_1}$, and $\overline{S_2}$ to generate bus timing and control signals required for a bus cycle. $\overline{S_2}$, $\overline{S_1}$, and $\overline{S_0}$ are 8086 outputs and are decoded as follows:

$\overline{S_2}$	$\overline{S_1}$	$\overline{S_0}$	Function
0	0	0	Interrupt acknowledge
0	0	1	Read I/O port
0	1	0	Write I/O port
0	1	1	Halt
1	0	0	Code access
1	0	1	Read memory
1	1	0	Write memory
1	1	1	Inactive

The $\overline{RQ}/\overline{GT0}$, $\overline{RQ}/\overline{GT1}$ request/grant pins are used by other local bus masters to force the processor to release the local bus at the end of the processor's current bus cycle. Each pin is bidirectional, with $\overline{RQ}/\overline{GT0}$ having higher priority than $\overline{RQ}/\overline{GT1}$. These pins have internal pull-up resistors so that they may be left unconnected. The request/grant function of the 8086 works as follows:

1. A pulse (one clock wide) from another local bus master ($\overline{RQ}/\overline{GT0}$ or $\overline{RQ}/\overline{GT1}$ pins) indicates a local bus request to the 8086.
2. At the end of 8086 current bus cycle, a pulse (one clock wide) from the 8086 to the requesting master

indicates that the 8086 has relinquished the system bus and tristated the outputs. Then the new bus master subsequently relinquishes control of the system bus by sending a LOW on $\overline{RQ}/\overline{GT0}$ or $\overline{RQ}/\overline{GT1}$ pins. The 8086 then regains bus control.

The 8086 outputs LOW on the $\overline{LOCK}$ pin to prevent other bus masters from gaining control of the system bus.

5-8-2 8086 Basic System Concepts

This section describes basic concepts associated with the 8086 bus cycles, address and data bus, system data bus, and multiprocessor environment.

8086 Bus Cycle In order to communicate with external devices via the system for transferring data or fetching instructions, the 8086 executes a bus cycle. The 8086 basic bus cycle timing diagram is shown in Figure 5-14. The minimum bus cycle contains four microprocessor clock periods called *T states*. The bus cycle timing diagram depicted in Figure 5-14 can be described as follows:

1. During the first T state (T_1), the 8086 outputs the 20-bit address computed from a segment register and an offset on the multiplexed address/data/status bus.
2. For the second T state (T_2), the 8086 removes the address from the bus and either tristates or activates the AD_{15}–AD_0 lines in preparation for reading data via the AD_{15}-AD_0 lines during the T_3 cycle. In the case of a write bus cycle, the 8086 outputs data on the AD_{15}–AD_0 lines. Also, during T_2, the upper four multiplexed bus lines switch from address (A_{19}–A_{16}) to bus cycle status (S_6, S_5, S_4, S_3). The 8086 outputs a LOW on $\overline{RD}$ (for a read cycle) or $\overline{WR}$ (for a write cycle) during portions of T_2, T_3, and T_4.
3. During T_3, the 8086 continues to output status information on the four A_{19}–A_{16}/S_6–S_3 lines and will either continue to output write data or input read data to or from the AD_{15}–AD_0 lines. If the selected memory or I/O device is not fast enough to transfer data to the 8086, the memory or I/O device activates the 8086's READY input line LOW by the start of T_3. This will force the 8086 to insert additional clock cycles (wait states T_W) after T_3. Bus activity during T_W is the same as that during T_3. When the selected device has had sufficient time to complete the transfer, it must activate the 8086 READY pin HIGH. As soon as the T_W clock periods end, the 8086 executes the last bus cycle (T_4). The 8086 will latch data on the AD_{15}–AD_0 lines during the last wait state or during T_3 if no wait states are requested.
4. During T_4, the 8086 disables the command lines and the selected memory and I/O devices from the bus. Thus, the bus cycle is terminated in T_4. The bus cycle appears to devices in the system as a syn-

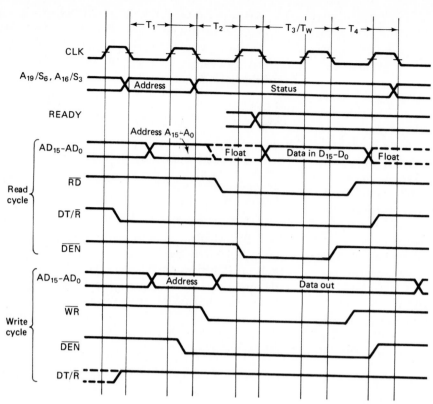

Figure 5-14 Basic 8086 bus cycle. (Courtesy of Intel)

chronous event consisting of an address to select the device, a register or memory location within the device, a read strobe, or a write strobe along with data.

5. The $\overline{\text{DEN}}$ and DT/$\overline{\text{R}}$ pins are used by the 8286/8287 transceiver in a minimum system. During the read cycle, the 8086 outputs $\overline{\text{DEN}}$ LOW during part of the T_2 and all of the T_3 cycles. This signal can be used to enable the 8286/8287 transceiver. The 8086 outputs a LOW on the DT/$\overline{\text{R}}$ pin from the start of the T_1 and part of the T_4 cycles. The 8086 uses this signal to receive (read) data from the receiver during T_3–T_4. During a write cycle, the 8086 outputs $\overline{\text{DEN}}$ LOW during part of the T_1, all of the T_2 and T_3, and part of the T_4 cycles. The signal can be used to enable the transceiver. The 8086 outputs a HIGH on DT/$\overline{\text{R}}$ throughout the 4 bus cycles to transmit (write) data to the transceiver during T_3–T_4.

8086 Address and Data Bus Concepts The majority of memory and I/O chips capable of interfacing to the 8086 require a stable address for the duration of the bus cycle. Therefore, the address on the 8086 multiplexed address/data bus during T_1 should be latched. The latched address is then used to select the desired I/O or memory location. Note that the 8086 has a 16-bit multiplexed address and data bus, while the 8085's 8-bit data lines and LOW address byte are multiplexed. Hence, the multiplexed bus components of the 8085 family are not applicable to the 8086.

To demultiplex the bus, the 8086 provides an ALE (address latch enable) signal to capture the address in either the 8282 (noninverting) or 8283 (inverting) 8-bit bistable latches. These latches propagate the address through to the outputs while ALE is HIGH and latch the address in the following edge of ALE. This only delays address access and chip select decoding by the propagation delay of the latch. Figure 5–15 shows how the 8086 demultiplexes the address and data buses.

The programmer views the 8086 memory address space as a sequence of one million bytes in which any byte may contain an 8-bit data element and any two consecutive bytes may contain a 16-bit data element. There is no constraint on byte or word addresses (boundaries). The address space is physically implemented on a 16-bit data bus by dividing the address space into two banks of up to 512K bytes as shown in Figure 5–16. These banks can be selected by $\overline{\text{BHE}}$ and A_0 as follows:

$\overline{\text{BHE}}$	A_0	Byte Transferred
0	0	Both bytes
0	1	Upper byte to/from odd address
1	0	Lower byte to/from even address
1	1	None

One bank is connected to D_7–D_0 and contains all even-addressed bytes ($A_0 = 0$). The other bank is connected to D_{15}–D_8 and contains odd-addressed bytes ($A_0 = 1$). A particular byte in each bank is addressed by A_{19}–A_1. The even-addressed bank is enabled by a LOW on A_0,

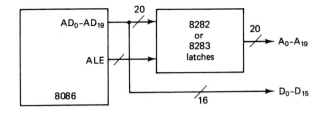

Figure 5–15 Separate address and data buses

and data bytes are transferred over the D_7–D_0 lines. The 8086 outputs a HIGH on $\overline{BHE}$ (bus high enable) and thus disables the odd-addressed bank. The 8086 outputs a LOW on $\overline{BHE}$ to select the odd-addressed bank and a HIGH on A_0 to disable the even-addressed bank. This directs the data transfer to the appropriate half of the data bus.

Activation of A_0 and $\overline{BHE}$ is performed by the 8086 depending on odd or even addresses and is transparent to the programmer. As an example, consider execution of the instruction MOV DH, [BX]. Suppose the 20-bit address computed by BX and DS is even. The 8086 outputs a LOW on A_0 and a HIGH on $\overline{BHE}$. This will select the even-addressed bank. The content of the selected memory is placed on the D_7–D_0 lines by a memory chip. The 8086 reads this data via D_7–D_0 and automatically places it in DH. Next, consider accessing a 16-bit word by the 8086 with the low byte at an even address as shown in Figure 5–17. For example, suppose that the 8086 executes the instruction MOV [BX], CX. Assume [BX] = 0004H and [DS] = 2000H. The 20-bit physical address for the word is 20004H. The 8086 outputs a LOW on both A_0 and $\overline{BHE}$, enabling both banks simultaneously. The 8086 outputs [CL] to the D_7–D_0 lines and [CH] to the D_{15}–D_8 lines, with $\overline{WR}$ LOW and M/$\overline{IO}$ HIGH. The enabled memory banks obtain the 16-bit data and write [CL] to location 20004H and [CH] to location 20005H.

Next, consider accessing an odd-addressed 16-bit word by the 8086 using MOV [BX], CX. For example, suppose the 20-bit physical address computed by the 8086 is 20005H. The 8086 accomplishes this transfer in 2 bus cycles. In the first bus cycle, the 8086 outputs a HIGH on A_0 and a LOW on $\overline{BHE}$ and thus enables the odd-addressed bank and disables the even-addressed bank. The 8086 also outputs a LOW on the $\overline{RD}$ and a HIGH on the M/$\overline{IO}$ pins. In this bus cycle, the odd memory bank places [20005H] on the D_{15}–D_8 lines. The 8086 reads this data into CL. In the second bus cycle, the 8086 outputs a LOW on A_0 and a HIGH on $\overline{BHE}$ and thus enables the even-addressed bank and disables the odd-addressed bank. The 8086 also outputs a LOW on the $\overline{RD}$ and a HIGH on the M/$\overline{IO}$ pins. The selected even-addressed memory bank places [20006H] on the D_7–D_0 lines. The 8086 reads this data into CH. This odd-addressed word transfer is shown in Figure 5–18.

During a byte read, the 8086 floats the entire D_{15}–D_0 lines during portions of the T_2 cycle even though data are expected on the upper or lower half of the data bus. As will be shown later, this action simplifies the chip select decoding requirements for ROMs and EPROMs. During a byte write, the 8086 will drive the entire 16-bit data bus. The information on the half of the data bus not transferring data is indeterminate. These concepts also apply to I/O transfers.

If memory or I/O devices are directly connected to the multiplexed bus, the designer must guarantee that the devices do not corrupt the address on the bus during T_1. To avoid this, the memory or I/O devices should have an output enable controlled by the 8086 read signal. This is shown in Figure 5–19. The 8086 timing guarantees that the read is not valid until after the address is latched by ALE as shown in Figure 5–20.

All Intel peripherals, EPROMs, and RAMs for microprocessors provide output enable for read inputs to allow connection to the multiplexed bus. Several tech-

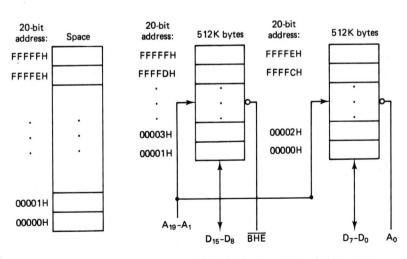

Figure 5–16 8086 memory. (Courtesy of Intel)

(a) One-megabyte address

(b) Physical implementation of address space

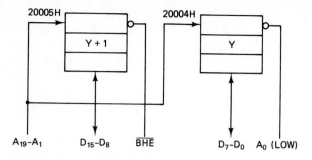

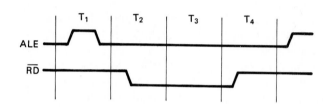

Figure 5–17 Even-addressed word transfer. (Courtesy of Intel)

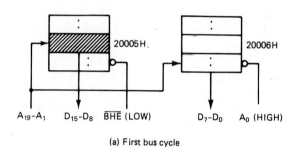

(a) First bus cycle

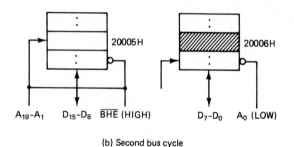

(b) Second bus cycle

Figure 5–18 Odd-addressed word transfer. (Courtesy of Intel)

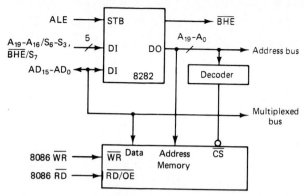

Figure 5–19 Devices with output enabling the multiplexed bus. (Courtesy of Intel)

Figure 5–20 Relationship of ALE and read. (Courtesy of Intel)

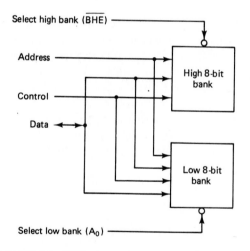

Figure 5–21 8086 memory array. (Courtesy of Intel)

niques are available for interfacing the devices without output enables to the 8086 multiplexed bus. However, these techniques will not be discussed here.

5–8–3 Interfacing with Memories

Figure 5–21 shows a general block diagram of an 8086 memory array. In Figure 5–21, the 16-bit word memory is partitioned into HIGH and LOW 8-bit banks on the upper and lower halves of the data bus selected by $\overline{BHE}$ and A_0.

ROMs and EPROMs ROMs and EPROMs are the simplest memory chips to interface to the 8086. Since ROMs and EPROMs are read-only devices, A_0 and $\overline{BHE}$ are not required to be part of the chip enable/select decoding (chip enable is similar to chip select except chip enable also provides whether the chip is in active or standby power mode). The 8086 address lines must be connected to the ROM/EPROM chips starting with A_1 and higher to all the address lines of the ROM/EPROM

chips. The 8086 unused address lines can be used as chip enable/select decoding. To interface the ROMs/EPROMs directly to the 8086 multiplexed bus, they must have output enable signals. Figure 5–22 shows the 8086 interfaced to two 2716 chips.

Byte accesses are obtained by reading the full 16-bit word onto the bus with the 8086 discarding the unwanted byte and accepting the desired byte. If $\overline{RD}$, $\overline{WR}$, and $M/\overline{IO}$ are not decoded to generate separate memory and I/O commands for memory and I/O chips and the I/O space overlaps with the memory space of ROM/

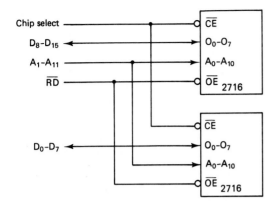

Figure 5-22 ROM/EPROM interface to the 8086. (Courtesy of Intel)

EPROM, then M/$\overline{\text{IO}}$ must be a condition of chip select decoding.

Static RAMs Since static RAMs are read/write memories, both A_0 and $\overline{\text{BHE}}$ must be included in the chip select/enable decoding of the devices, and write timing must be considered in the compatibility analysis. For each static RAM, the memory data lines must be connected to either the upper half (AD_{15}–AD_8) or lower half (AD_7–AD_0) of the 8086 data lines.

For static RAMs without output enable pins, read and write lines must be used as enables for chip select generation to avoid bus contention. If read and write lines are not used to activate the chip selects, static RAMs with common input/output pins (such as the 2114) will face extreme bus contentions between chip selects and write active. The 8086 A_0 and $\overline{\text{BHE}}$ pins must be used to enable the chip selects. A possible way of generating chip selects for high and low static RAM banks is given in Figure 5–23. Note that the Intel 8205 has three enables ($\overline{E_1}$, $\overline{E_2}$, and E_3), three inputs (A_0–A_2), and eight outputs (O_0–O_7).

For devices with output enables (such as the 2142), one way to generate chip selects for the static RAMs is by gating the 8086 $\overline{\text{WR}}$ signal with $\overline{\text{BHE}}$ and A_0 to provide upper and lower bank write strobes.

Dynamic RAMs Dynamic RAMs store information as charges in capacitors. Since capacitors can hold charges for a few milliseconds, refresh circuitry is necessary in dynamic RAMs for retaining these charges. Therefore, dynamic RAMs are complex devices to design a system. To relieve the designer of most of these complicated interfacing tasks, Intel provides the 8202 dynamic RAM controller as part of the 8086 family of peripheral devices. The 8202 can be interfaced with the 8086 to build a dynamic memory system. A thorough discussion on this topic can be found in Intel manuals.

5-8-4 I/O Ports

Devices with 8-bit I/O ports can be connected to either the upper or lower half of the data bus. Bus loading is distributed by connecting an equal number of devices to the upper and lower halves of the data bus. If the I/O port chip is connected to the lower half of the 8086 data lines (AD_0–AD_7), the port addresses will be even (A_0 = 0). On the other hand, the port addresses will be odd (A_0 = 1) if the I/O port chip is connected to the upper half of the 8086 data lines (AD_8–AD_{15}). A_0 will always be 1 or 0 for the partitioned I/O chip. Therefore, A_0 cannot be used as an address input to select registers within a particular I/O chip. If two chips are connected to the lower and upper halves of the 8086 address bus that differ only in A_0 (consecutive odd and even addresses), A_0 and $\overline{\text{BHE}}$ must be used as conditions of chip select decoding to avoid a write to one I/O chip from erroneously performing a write to the other.

Figure 5–24 shows two ways of generating chip selects for I/O port chips. The first method shown in Figure 5–24(a) uses separate 8205 chips to generate chip selects for odd- and even-addressed byte peripherals. If a 16-bit word transfer is performed to an even-addressed I/O chip, the adjacent odd-addressed I/O chip is also selected. Figure 5–24(b) generates chip selects for byte transfers only.

For efficient bus utilization and simplicity of I/O chip selection, 16-bit I/O ports should be assigned even addresses. Both A_0 and $\overline{\text{BHE}}$ should be the chip select conditions to ensure that the I/O chip is selected only for

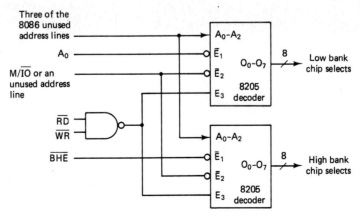

Figure 5-23 Generating chip selects for static RAMs without output enables. (Courtesy of Intel)

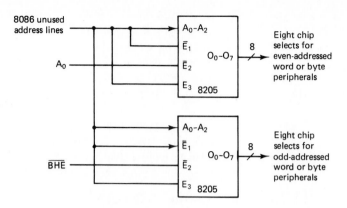

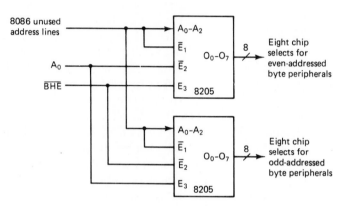

(a) Generating chip selects for odd- and even-addressed byte peripherals

(b) Generating chip selects for byte transfers only

Figure 5–24 Techniques for generating I/O device chip selects. (Courtesy of Intel)

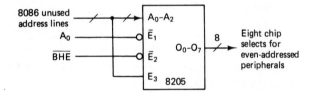

Figure 5–25 Chip selects for 16-bit ports. (Courtesy of Intel)

word operations. Figure 5–25 shows a method of generating chip selects for 16-bit ports. Note that in Figure 5–25 the 8086 will output a LOW on both A_0 and $\overline{BHE}$ when it executes a 16-bit I/O instruction with an even port address. For example, IN AX, 0006H inputs the 16-bit contents of ports 0006H and 0007H in AX.

5–8–5 8086-Based Microcomputer

In this section, an 8086 will be interfaced in the minimum mode to provide 2K × 16 EPROM, 1K × 16 static RAM, and six 8-bit I/O ports. The 2716 EPROM, 2142 static RAM, and 8255 I/O chips will be used for this purpose. Memory and I/O maps will also be determined. Figure 5–26 shows a hardware schematic for accomplishing this.

Three 8282 octal latches, numbered as 8282-1, 8282-2, and 8282-3, are used. The STB input of the 8282 strobes the eight inputs at the DI_{0-7} pins into the internal data latches. When $\overline{OE}$ is LOW, the 8-bit data at the data latches are transferred to the output pins DO_{0-7}. The 8086 ALE pin is used as the STB input for all three latches, and $\overline{OE}$ is tied to ground. The 8282-1 latches A_{16}–A_9 and $\overline{BHE}$. Pins DI_{5-7} and pins DO_{5-7} are not used for the 8282-1 chip. The 8282-2 and 8282-3 chips provide the A_{15}–A_8 and A_7–A_0 address pins, respectively.

The 2716 is a 2K × 8 ultraviolet EPROM with eleven address pins (A_0–A_{10}) and eight data pins (O_{0-7}). Two 2716 chips, numbered as 2716-1 and 2716-2, are used. The 2716-1 provides all the even-addressed data, and the 2716-2 contains all the odd-addressed data. The 8086 A_1–A_{11} pins are connected to the A_0–A_{10} pins of these chips. The 2716-1 even EPROM's O_{0-7} pins are connected to the 8086 D_0–D_7 pins because the 8086 reads data via the D_0–D_7 pins for even addresses. On the other hand, the O_{0-7} pins of the 2716-2 are connected to the 8086 D_8–D_{15} pins. The 8086 reads data via the D_8–D_{15} pins for odd addresses.

The 8205 is a 3-to-8 decoder with three enable pins ($\overline{E_1}$, $\overline{E_2}$, and E3). E3 is tied to HIGH. $\overline{E_1}$ and $\overline{E_2}$ are

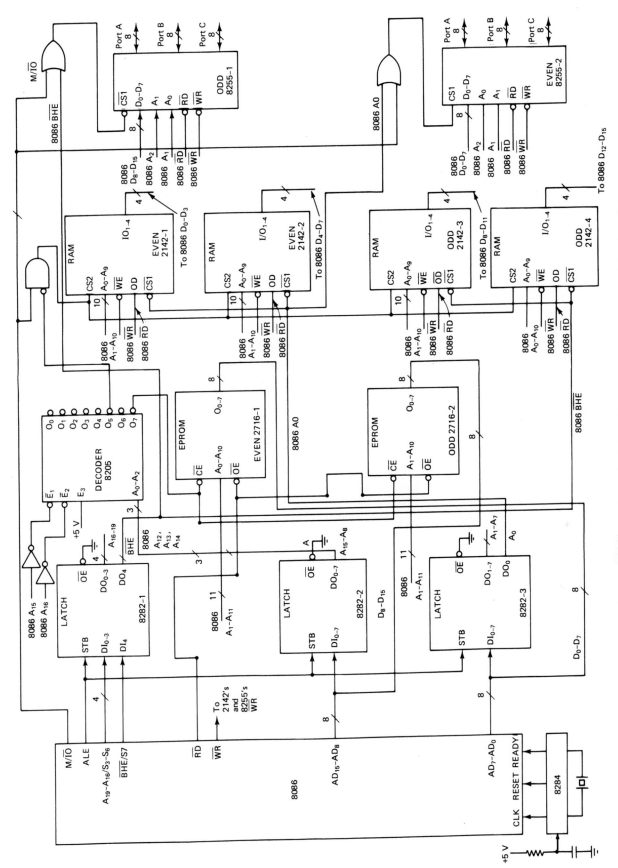

Figure 5-26 8086 interface to memory and I/O. (Reprinted with permission from *Microprocessors and Microcomputer-Based System Design* by M. Rafiquzzaman. Copyright 1990 by CRC Press, Inc., Boca Raton, FL.)

153

enabled by the 8086 A_{15} and A_{16} pins. The 8205 is used to provide the fully decoding technique for addressing the 2716 and 2142 chips. The 8205 3-to-8 decoder is used for future expansion.

Next, the memory map for the 2142 RAMs will be determined. The 2142 is a 1K × 4-bit static RAM. Therefore, four 2142 RAM chips, numbered as 2142-1, 2142-2, 2142-3, and 2142-4, are required. The 4-bit data are read from the 2142 when $\overline{CS1} = 0$, CS2 = 1, $\overline{WE} = 1$, and OD = 0. On the other hand, the 4-bit data are written into the 2142 when $\overline{CS1} = 0$, CS2 = 1, $\overline{WE} = 0$, and OD = 1. The 2142-1 and 2142-2 RAM chips provide the even addresses since the 8086 A_0 pin is used to enable them. The 8086 A_1–A_{10} pins are connected to the A_0–A_9 pins of these chips. The 8086 D_0–D_3 and D_4–D_7 pins are connected, respectively, to the I/O_{1-4} pins of the 2142-1 and 2142-2. Both chips are enabled simultaneously by enabling CS2 via ANDing the 8205 decoder output $\overline{O}_5$ and $M/\overline{IO}$. The 2142-3 and 2142-4 chips contain the odd addresses since the 8086 $\overline{BHE}$ pin is used to enable them. Also, these chips are simultaneously enabled by CS2 via ANDing $\overline{O}_5$ and $M/\overline{IO}$. The 8086 A_{11} pin is not required for the 2142 chips and is assumed to be 1. The 2142-1 and 2142-2 chips contain all even addresses FD800H, FD802H, . . . , FDFFEH. The memory map for the 2142-3 and 2142-4 chips includes all odd addresses FD801H, FD803H, . . . , FDFFFH, assuming the A_{11} pin to be 1.

In order to determine the memory map for the 2716 EPROM, consider Figure 5–27 (obtained from Figure 5–26) showing pertinent connections for the even EPROM 2716-1. In Figure 5–27, the 8086 address lines A_{19}–A_{17} are not used and are, therefore, don't cares. Assume the don't cares to be HIGH. The even memory map for the 2716-1 in Figure 5–27 is as follows:

A_{19}	A_{18}	A_{17}	A_{16}	A_{15}	A_{14}	A_{13}	A_{12}	A_{11} A_{10} . . .	A_1	A_0
1	1	1	1	1	1	1	1	All 0's to all 1's	↑	0

The first group of four (1 1 1 1) is labeled F; the second group of four (1 1 1 1) is labeled F.

Therefore, the memory map of the 2716-1 contains all even addresses FF000H, FF002H, . . . , FFFFEH. Note that the 8086 reset vector FFFF0H (CS = FFFFH, IP = 0000H) is included in this map. For any 8086-based design, the memory map must include the reset vector FFFF0H. The memory map of the odd EPROM 2716-2 contains the odd addresses FF001H, FF003H, . . . , FFFFFH.

Let us verify the memory map for the odd RAMs 2142-3 and 2142-4. Consider Figure 5–28 (obtained from Figure 5–26) showing pertinent connections for the odd RAMs 2142-3 and 2142-4. From Figure 5–28, the odd memory map can be obtained as follows:

A_{19}	A_{18}	A_{17}	A_{16}	A_{15}	A_{14}	A_{13}	A_{12}	A_{11}	$A_{10}A_9$ . . . A_1A_0
1	1	1	1	1	1	0	1	1	Can be 0's to all 1's
		F				D		Don't care assumed 1	1

Therefore, the 2142-3 and 2142-4 RAMs contain the odd addresses FD801H, FD803H, . . . , FDFFFH. Similarly, the 2142-1 and 2142-2 RAMs contain the even addresses FD800H, FD802H, . . . , FDFFEH.

The memory maps can be summarized as shown in Table 5–14. In the table, the physical address FFFF0H can also be translated into the logical address with segment register value FFFFH and offset 0000H (reset vector).

Let us now decode the I/O port addresses. The 8255-1 will contain the odd-addressed ports since it is enabled

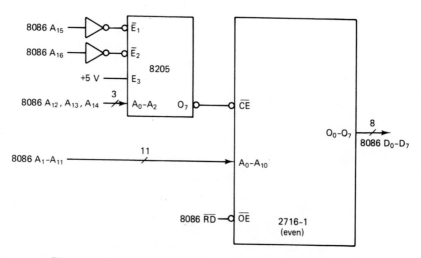

Figure 5–27 Even EPROM 2716-1 with pertinent connections

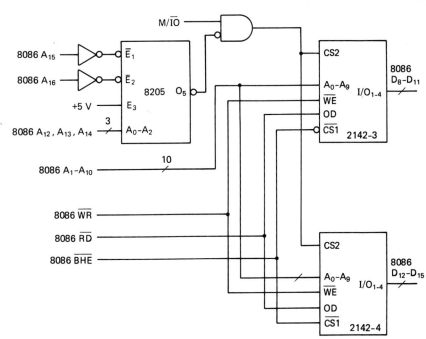

Figure 5–28 Odd RAMs 2142-3 and 2142-4 with pertinent connections

TABLE 5–14
Memory Map Summary

Chip	Physical Address (20-Bit)	Logical Address	
		Segment Register (16-Bit)	Offset Register (16-Bit)
2716-1 (even)	FF000H, FF001H, . . . , FFFFEH	FF00H	0000H, 0002H, . . . , 0FFEH
2716-2 (odd)	FF001H, FF003H, . . . , FFFFFH	FF00H	0001H, 0003H, . . . , 0FFFH
2142-1, 2142-2 (even)	FD800H, FD802H, . . . , FDFFEH	FD00H	0800H, 0802H, . . . , 0FFEH
2142-3, 2142-4 (odd)	FD801H, FD803H, . . . , FDFFFH	FD00H	0801H, 0803H, . . . , 0FFFH

by $\overline{\text{BHE}}$, while the 8255-2 will include the even-addressed ports since it is enabled by A_0.

Since the 8086 A_1 and A_2 pins are utilized in addressing the ports, bits A_3–A_7 are don't cares and are assumed to be 1's here. Note that $A_0 = 1$ for odd-addressed ports, while $A_0 = 0$ for even-addressed ports.

For the 8255-1 odd-addressed ports,

Port Name	Address									
	A_7	A_6	A_5	A_4	A_3	A_2	A_1	A_0		
Port A	1	1	1	1	1	0	0	1	=	F9H
Port B	1	1	1	1	1	0	1	1	=	FBH
Port C	1	1	1	1	1	1	0	1	=	FDH
Control register	1	1	1	1	1	1	1	1	=	FFH

For the 8255-2 even-addressed ports,

Port Name	Address									
	A_7	A_6	A_5	A_4	A_3	A_2	A_1	A_0		
Port A	1	1	1	1	1	0	0	0	=	F8H
Port B	1	1	1	1	1	0	1	0	=	FAH
Port C	1	1	1	1	1	1	0	0	=	FCH
Control register	1	1	1	1	1	1	1	0	=	FEH

In the preceding decode tables, the standard I/O technique is used. The 8255 I/O chips can also be interfaced to the 8086 using memory-mapped I/O. In this case, the 8086 $M/\overline{\text{IO}}$ pin will not be used. The 20-bit physical addresses for the ports can be determined in a similar way by considering any unused 8086 address bits (A_3–A_{19}) as don't cares.

Example 5-12

An 8086–8255-based microcomputer is required to drive an LED connected to bit 2 of port B based on two switch inputs connected to bits 6 and 7 of port A. If both switches are either HIGH or LOW, turn the LED ON; otherwise, turn it OFF. Assume a HIGH will turn the LED ON and a LOW will turn it OFF. Write an 8086 assembly language program to accomplish this.

Solution

```
PROG    SEGMENT
        ASSUME CS: PROG
        MOV AL, 90H       ; Configure port A
        OUT CNTRL, AL     ; as input and port B
                          ; as output
BEGIN   IN AL, PORT A     ; Input port A
        AND AL, 0C0H      ; Retain bits 6 and 7
        JPE LEDON         ; If both switches
                          ; HIGH, turn LED ON
        MOV AL, 00H       ; Otherwise, turn
        OUT PORT B, AL    ; LED OFF
        JMP BEGIN         ; Repeat
LEDON   MOV AL, 04H       ; Turn LED
        OUT PORT B, AL    ; ON
        JMP BEGIN
PROG    ENDS
        END
```

QUESTIONS AND PROBLEMS

5–1. What is the basic difference between the 8086, 8086-2, and 8086-4?

5–2. Consider MOV AX, [START]. How many cycles are required by the 8086 to perform the transfer if:
(a) START = 5000H
(b) START = 5001H

5–3. What is the purpose of the 8086 MN/$\overline{\text{MX}}$ pin?

5–4. IF [DS] = 205FH and OFFSET = 0051H, what is the physical address? Does the EU or BIU compute this physical address?

5–5. In an 8086 system, SEGMENT 1 contains addresses 05000H–050FFH and SEGMENT 2 contains address FF000H–FFFFFH. What are these segments called?

5–6. Determine the addressing modes for the following instructions:
(a) AAA
(b) CALL BYTE PTR [BX]
(c) MOV AX, CX
(d) ADD [SI], CX

5–7. Find the overflow, direction, interrupt, trap, sign, zero, parity, and carry flags after execution of the following instruction sequence:

```
MOV   AH,   0FFH
SAHF
```

5–8. What is the content of AL after execution of the following instruction sequence?

```
MOV   BH,   33H
MOV   AL,   32H
ADD   AL,   BH
AAA
```

5–9. What is the content of AX after execution of the following instruction sequence?

```
MOV   CH, –5
MOV   AL,   CH
IMUL  CH
```

5–10. What are the remainder, quotient, and registers containing them after execution of the following instruction sequence?

```
MOV   DX,   0030H
MOV   AX,   0055H
MOV   CX,   2
IDIV  CX
```

5–11. Write an 8086 instruction sequence to set the trap flag for single stepping.

5–12. Write 8086 assembly programs to perform the following:
(a) Subtract two 64-bit numbers.
(b) Multiply two 16-bit unsigned numbers.
(c) Logically shift a 64-bit number twice to the right.

5–13. Write an 8086 assembly program to add a 16-bit number stored in CX (bits 0 to 7 containing the high-order byte of the number and bits 8 to 15 containing the low-order byte) with another 16-bit number stored in AX (bits 0 to 7 containing the low-order 8 bits of the number and bits 8 through 15 containing the high-order 8 bits). Store the result in DX.

5–14. Write an 8086 assembly program to multiply the top two 16-bit unsigned words of the stack. Store the 32-bit result onto the stack.

5–15. Write an 8086 assembly program to divide an 8-bit signed number in DH by an 8-bit signed number in DL. Store the quotient in DH and the remainder in DL.

5–16. Write an 8086 assembly program to add fifty 16-bit numbers stored in consecutive memory locations starting at displacement 0500H in DS = 0200H. Store the 16-bit result onto the stack.

5–17. Write an 8086 assembly program to find the minimum value of a string of 20 signed 16-bit numbers using indexed addressing.

5–18. Write an 8086 assembly program to move 50_{16} words from a source with displacement 0020H in ES = 5000H to a destination with displacement 1000H in the same extra segment.

5–19. Write an 8086 assembly program to divide a 28-bit unsigned number in the high 28 bits of DX AX by 8_{10}. Do not use any divide instruction. Store the quotient in the low 28 bits of DX AX.

5–20. Write an 8086 assembly program to compare two strings of 15 ASCII characters. The first string (string 1) is stored starting at offset 5000H in DS = 0020H followed by the string. The first character of the second string (string 2) is stored starting at 6000H in ES = 1000H. The ASCII character in the first location of string 1 will be compared with the first ASCII character of string 2, and so on. Each time a match is found, store EE_{16} onto the stack; otherwise, store 00_{16} onto the stack.

5–21. Write a subroutine in 8086 assembly language that can be called up by a main program in a different code segment. The subroutine will compute

$$\sum_{i=1}^{100} X_i^2$$

Assume X_i's are signed 8-bit and stored in consecutive locations starting at displacement 0050H in DS = 2020H. Also, write the main program that will call this subroutine to compute

$$\sum_{i=1}^{100} \frac{X_i^2}{100}$$

and store the 16-bit result in two consecutive memory words starting at displacement 0400H is DS = 2020H.

5–22. Write a subroutine in 8086 assembly language to convert a 2-digit unsigned BCD number to binary. The most significant digit is stored in a memory location starting at offset 4000H in DS = 0020H, and the least significant is stored at offset 4001H in the same DS. Store the binary result in DX. Use the value of the 2-digit BCD number, $V = D_1 \times 10^1 + D_0$.

5–23. Assume an 8086–8255-based microcomputer. Suppose that four switches are connected at bits 0 through 3 of port A and an LED is connected at bit 4 of port B. If the number of LOW switches is even, turn the port B LED ON; otherwise, turn the Port B LED OFF. Write an 8086 assembly language program to accomplish this.

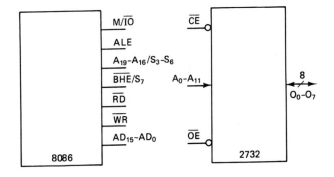

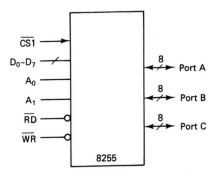

Figure P5-24

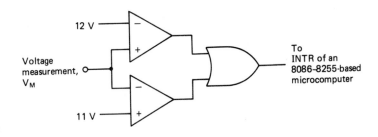

Figure P5-25

5-24. Interface one 2732 and one 8255 to an 8086 to obtain odd 2732 locations and even addresses for the 8255's port A, port B, port C, and control registers. Show only the connections for the pins shown in Figure P5–24. Assume all unused address lines to be zeros.

5-25. In Figure P5–25, if $V_M > 12$ V, turn the LED ON connected at bit 4 of port A. On the other hand, if $V_M < 11$ V, turn the LED OFF. Use ports, registers, and memory locations of your choice.

(a) Draw a hardware block diagram showing the microcomputer and the connections of the figure to its ports.

(b) Write a service routine in 8086 assembly language.

6

Motorola MC68000

This chapter contains the details of the Motorola 68000 microprocessor. Topics include architecture, addressing modes, instruction set, and interfacing features of the Motorola 68000.

6–1 INTRODUCTION

The MC68000 is Motorola's first 16-bit microprocessor. Its address and data registers are all 32 bits wide, and its ALU is 16 bits wide. The 68000 is designed using HMOS technology. The 68000 requires a single 5 V supply. The processor can be operated from a maximum internal clock frequency of 25 MHz. The 68000 is available in several frequencies, including 6, 10, 12.5, 16.67, and 25 MHz. The 68000 does not have on-chip clock circuitry and, therefore, requires a crystal oscillator or external clock generator/driver circuit to generate the clock.

The 68000 has several different versions, which include the 68008, 68010, and 68012. The 68000 and 68010 are packaged either in a 64-pin DIP (dual in-line package) with all pins assigned or in a 68-pin quad pack or PGA (pin grid array) with some unused pins. The 68000 is also packaged in 68-terminal chip carrier. The 68008 is packaged in a 48-pin dual in-line package, while the 68012 is packaged in an 84-pin grid array. The 68008 provides the basic 68000 capabilities with inexpensive packaging. It has an 8-bit data bus, which facilitates the interfacing of this chip to inexpensive 8-bit peripheral chips. The 68010 provides hardware-based virtual memory support and efficient looping instructions. Like the 68000, it has a 16-bit data bus and a 24-bit address bus. The 68012 includes all the 68010 features with a 31-bit address bus. The clock frequencies of the 68008, 68010, and 68012 are the same as those of the 68000. The following table summarizes the basic differences among the 68000 family members:

	68000	68008	68010	68012
Data size (bits)	16	8	16	16
Address bus size (bits)	24	20	24	31
Virtual memory	No	No	Yes	Yes
Control registers	None	None	3	3
Directly addressable memory (bytes)	16M	1M	16M	2G

In order to implement operating systems and protection features, the 68000 can be operated in two modes: supervisor and user. The *supervisor mode* is also called the *operating system mode*. In this mode, the 68000 can execute all instructions. The 68000 operates in one of these modes based on the S bit of the status register. When the S bit is 1, the 68000 operates in the supervisor mode; when the S bit is 0, the 68000 operates in the user mode.

Table 6–1 lists the basic differences between the 68000 user and supervisor modes. From Table 6–1, it can be seen that the 68000 executing a program in the supervisor mode can enter the user mode by modifying the S bit of the status register to 0 via an instruction. Instructions such as MOVE to/from SR, ORI to/from SR, and EORI to/from SR can be used to accomplish this. On the other hand, the 68000 executing a program in the user mode can enter the supervisor mode only via recognition of a trap, reset, or interrupt. Note that, upon hardware reset, the 68000 operates in the supervisor mode and can execute all instructions. An attempt to execute *privileged instructions* (instructions that can only be executed in the supervisor mode) in the user mode will automatically generate an internal interrupt (trap) by the 68000. The logical level in the 68000 function code pin (FC2) indicates to the external devices whether the 68000 is currently operating in the user or supervisor mode. The 68000 has three function

TABLE 6–1
68000 User and Supervisor Modes (Courtesy of Motorola)

	Supervisor Mode	User Mode
Enter mode by	Recognition of a trap, reset, or interrupt	Clearing status bit S
System stack pointer	Supervisor stack pointer	User stack pointer
Other stack pointers	User stack pointer and registers A0–A6	Registers A0–A6
Instructions available	All including: STOP RESET MOVE to/from SR ANDI to/from SR ORI to/from SR EORI to/from SR MOVE USP to (An) MOVE to USP RTE	All except those listed under Supervisor mode
Function code pin FC2	1	0

code pins (FC2, FC1, and FC0), which indicate to the external devices whether the 68000 is accessing supervisor program/data or user/data or performing an interrupt acknowledge cycle.

The 68000 can operate on five different data types: bits, 4-bit binary-coded decimal (BCD) digits, bytes, 16-bit words, and 32-bit long words. The 68000 instruction set includes 56 basic instruction types. With 14 addressing modes, 56 instructions, and 5 data types, the 68000 contains over 1000 OP codes. The fastest instruction is one that copies the contents of one register into another register. It is executed in 500 ns at an 8-MHz clock rate. The slowest instruction is 32-bit by 16-bit divide, which is executed in 21.25 μs at 8 MHz.

The 68000 has no I/O instructions. Thus, all I/O is memory-mapped.

The MC68000 is a general-purpose register processor because any data register can be configured as an accumulator or as a scratchpad register. Any data or address register can be used as an index register. Although the 68000 PC is 32 bits wide, only the low-order 24 bits are used. Since this is a byte-addressable machine, it follows that the 68000 microprocessor can directly address 16 megabytes of memory.

6–2 68000 REGISTERS

Figure 6–1 shows the 68000 registers. This microprocessor includes eight 32-bit data registers (D0–D7) and nine 32-bit address registers (A0–A7 plus A7'). Data registers normally hold data items such as 8-bit bytes, 16-bit words, 32-bit long words, and 4-bit BCD numbers. On the other hand, an address register usually holds the memory address of an operand. Since the 68000 uses 24-bit addresses, it discards the uppermost 8 bits (bits 24–31), while using the address register to hold memory addresses. The 68000 uses A7 or A7' as the user or supervisor stack pointer (USP or SSP), respectively, depending on the mode of operation.

The 68000 status register is composed of two bytes: a user byte and a system byte (Figure 6–2).

The user byte includes typical condition codes such as C, V, N, Z, and X. The meaning of the C, V, N, and Z flags is obvious. Let us explain the meaning of the X bit. Note that the 68000 does not have any ADDC or SUBC instructions; rather, it has ADDX and SUBX instructions. Since the carry flag C and extend flag X are usually affected in an identical manner, one can use ADDX or SUBX to reflect the carries in multiprecision arithmetic. The contents of the system byte include a 3-bit interrupt mask (I2, I1, I0), a supervisory flag (S), and a trace flag (T). When the supervisory flag is 1, then the system operates in the supervisory mode; otherwise, the user mode of operation is assumed. When the trace flag is set to 1, the processor generates a trap (internal interrupt) after executing each instruction. A debugging routine can be written at the interrupt address vector to display registers and/or memory after execution of each instruction. Thus, this will provide single-stepping facility. Note that the trace flag can be set to one in the supervising mode by executing the instruction ORI# $8000, SR.

The interrupt mask bits (I2, I1, I0) provide the status of the 68000 interrupt pins $\overline{IPL2}$, $\overline{IPL1}$, $\overline{IPL0}$. I2I1I0 = 000 indicates that all interrupts are enabled. I2I1I0 = 111 indicates that all maskable interrupts except the nonmaskable interrupt (Level 7) are disabled. The other combinations of I2, I1, and I0 provide the maskable interrupt levels. Note that the signals on the $\overline{IPL2}$, $\overline{IPL1}$, and $\overline{IPL0}$ pins are inverted and then compared with I2, I1, and I0, respectively.

6–3 68000 MEMORY ADDRESSING

The MC68000 supports bytes (8 bits), words (16 bits), and long words (32 bits) as shown in Figure 6–3. Byte addressing includes both odd and even addresses (0, 1, 2, 3, . . .); word addressing includes only even addresses in increments of 2 (0, 2, 4, . . .); and long word addressing contains even addresses in increments of 4 (0, 4, 8, . . .).

As an example of 68000 addressing structure, consider MOVE.L D0, $506080. If [D0] = $07F12481, then, after this MOVE, [$506080] = $07, [$506081] = $F1, [$506082] = $24, and [$506083] = $81.

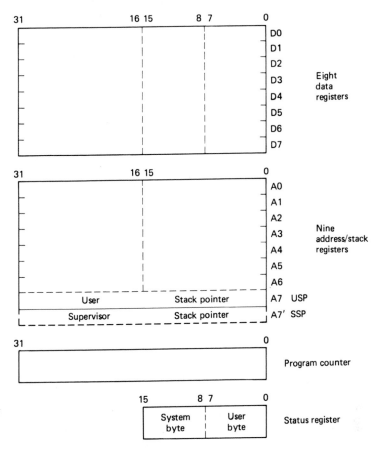

Figure 6–1 MC68000 programming model (Reprinted with permission of Motorola)

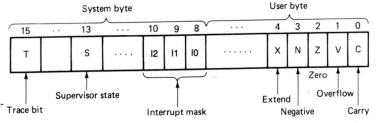

Figure 6–2 68000 status register (Reprinted with permission of Motorola)

6–4 68000 INSTRUCTION FORMAT

All 68000 instructions occupy one to five words, and they always start on the word boundary and even-addressed byte. The first word is called the *operation word,* and it specifies the operation type, operand sizes, and their addressing modes. The remaining words include other information such as immediate operands or extensions to the effective address mode specified in the operation word (see Figure 6–4).

In the 68000, there are more than 18 different instruction formats. A detailed description of some of them is provided in Table 6–2.

Consider instruction format 1. Here, the 2-bit operand type field specifies the operand size in the following manner: 01—byte, 11—word, and 10—long word. The 6-bit operand field is further divided into a 3-bit mode field and a 3-bit register field. In the 68000, we cannot

use all registers in all modes. In other words, a particular mode forces a programmer to use only a set of registers in that mode. For example, we cannot use an address register as a destination in an 8-bit MOVE. Because of this restriction, a 3-bit register field is adequate to take care of 16 registers (D0–D7 plus A0–A7).

Also, many two-address instructions expect one of the operands to be in the register mode. For example, consider the 68000 ADD instruction (see format 2). In this case, we have only three possibilities, namely, register to register, memory to register, and vice versa. This means that we cannot perform memory to memory addition.

Some 68000 instructions have multiple formats. For example, the ROR (rotate right) instruction has two different formats: one for the register rotate and the other for the memory rotate.

Small constants are represented using formats 4 and

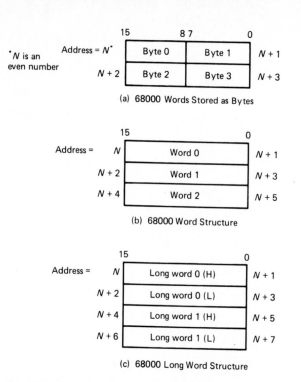

(a) 68000 Words Stored as Bytes

(b) 68000 Word Structure

(c) 68000 Long Word Structure

For byte addressing (not shown in this figure), each byte can be uniquely addressed with bit 0 as the least significant bit and bit 7 as the most significant bit.

Figure 6–3 68000 addressing structure (Reprinted with permission of Motorola)

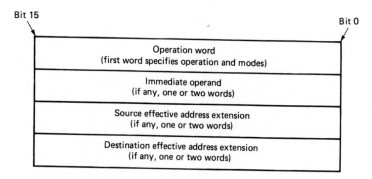

Figure 6–4 68000 instruction format (Reprinted with permission of Motorola)

5. Typically, constants in the range from 0 to 7 may be specified using format 5. On the other hand, format 4 allows one to specify an 8-bit 2's complement number. In this case, the destination must be a data register, and the 8-bit data is actually sign-extended to obtain a 32-bit long word. This result is then transferred to the specified data register.

6–5 68000 ADDRESSING MODES

The 14 addressing modes of the 68000 shown in Table 6–3 can be divided into 6 basic groups: register direct, address register indirect, absolute, program counter relative, immediate, and implied.

As mentioned, the 68000 has three types of instructions: no operand, single operand, and double operand. The single-operand instructions contain the effective ad-dress (EA) in the operand field. The EA for these instructions is calculated by the 68000 using the addressing mode used for this operand. In case of two-operand instructions, one of the operands usually contains the EA and the other operand is usually a register or memory location. The EA in these instructions is calculated by the 68000 based on the addressing mode used for the EA. Some two-operand instructions have the EA in both operands. This means that the operands in these instructions can use two different addressing modes. Note that the 68000 address registers do not support byte-sized operands. Therefore, when an address register is used as a source operand, either the low-order word or the entire long word operand is used, depending on the operation size. When an address register is used as the destination operand, the entire register is affected regardless of the operation size. If the operation size is a word, any other operands are sign-extended to 32 bits after the operation

TABLE 6-2
Some 68000 Instruction Formats

Format Number	Number of Fields	Name of the Field	Field Size (in Bits)	Instructions That Use This Format
1	4	OP code	2	MOVE
		operand type	2	
		operand 1	6	
		operand 2	6	
2	4	OP code	4	ADD, AND, CMP, SUB
		register	3	
		mode	3	
		operand	6	
3	5	OP code 1	4	MOVEP
		register 1	3	
		mode	3	
		OP code 1	3	
		register	3	
4	4	OP code 1	4	MOVEQ
		register	3	
		OP code 2	1	
		data	8	
5	5	OP code 1	4	ADDQ, SUBQ
		data (small constant)	3	
		OP code 2	1	
		operand type	2	
		operand	6	

is performed. Data registers, on the other hand, support data operands of byte, word, or long word size.

Register Direct Addressing In this mode, the eight data registers (D0–D7) or seven address registers (A0–A6) contain the data operand. For example, consider ADD $005000, D0. The destination operand of this instruction is in data register direct mode.

Now, if $[005000] = 0002_{16}$ and $[D0] = 0003_{16}$, then, after execution of ADD $005000, D0, the contents of D0 = 0002 + 0003 = 0005. Note that in this instruction, the $ symbol is used to represent hexadecimal numbers by Motorola. Also note that instructions are not available for byte operations using address registers.

Address Register Indirect Addressing There are five different types of address register indirect mode.

In the register indirect mode, an address register contains the effective address. For example, consider CLR (A1). If [A1] = $003000, then, after execution of CLR (A1), the contents of memory location $003000 will be cleared to zero.

The postincrement address register indirect mode increments an address register by 1 for byte, 2 for word, and 4 for long word after it is used. For example, consider CLR.L (A0)+. If $[A0] = 005000_{16}$, then, after execution of CLR.L (A0)+, the contents of memory locations 005000_{16} and 005002_{16} are cleared to zero and [A0] = 005000 + 4 = 005004. The postincrement mode is typically used with memory arrays stored from LOW to HIGH memory locations. For example, in order to clear 1000_{16} words starting at memory location 003000_{16}, the following instruction sequence can be used:

TABLE 6–3
68000 Addressing Modes (Courtesy of Motorola)

Mode	Generation	Assembler Syntax
Register direct addressing		
Data register direct	EA = Dn	Dn
Address register direct	EA = An	An
Address register indirect addressing		
Register indirect	EA = (An)	(An)
Postincrement register indirect	EA = (An), An ← An + N	(An)+
Predecrement register indirect	An ← An − N, EA = (An)	−(An)
Register indirect with offset	EA = (An) + d_{16}	d(An)
Indexed register indirect with offset	EA = (An) + (Ri) + d_8	d(An, Ri)
Absolute data addressing		
Absolute short	EA = (Next word)	xxxx
Absolute long	EA = (Next two words)	xxxxxxxx
Program counter relative addressing		
Relative with offset	EA = (PC) + d_{16}	d
Relative with index and offset	EA = (PC) + (Ri) + d_8	d(Ri)
Immediate data addressing		
Immediate	DATA = Next word(s)	#xxxx
Quick immediate	Inherent data	#xx
Implied addressing		
Implied register	EA = SR, USP, SP, PC	

Notes:
EA = effective address
An = address register
Dn = data register
Ri = address or data register used as index register
SR = status register
PC = program counter
SP = active system stack pointer

USP = user stack pointer
d_8 = 8-bit offset (displacement)
d_{16} = 16-bit offset (displacement)
N = 1 for byte, 2 for words, and 4 for long words
( ) = contents of
← = replaces

```
            MOVE.W  #$1000, D0       ; Load length of
                                       data into D0

            MOVEA.L #$003000, A0     ; Load starting ad-
                                       dress into A0

REPEAT      CLR.W   (A0)+            ; Clear a location
                                       pointed to by A0
                                       and increment
                                       A0 by 2

            SUBQ    #1, D0           ; Decrement D0
                                       by 1

            BNE     REPEAT           ; Branch to RE-
            —                          PEAT if Z = 0;
            —                          otherwise, go to
            —                          next instruction
```

Note that in this instruction sequence, CLR.W (A0)+ automatically points to the next location by incrementing A0 by 2 after clearing a memory location.

The predecrement address register indirect mode, on the other hand, decrements an address register by 1 for byte, 2 for word, and 4 for long word before using a register. For example, consider CLR.W −(A0). If [A0] = 002004, then, after execution of CLR.W −(A0), the contents of A0 is first decremented by 2—that is, [A0] = 002002_{16}. The contents of memory location 002002 is then cleared to zero. The predecrement mode

is used with arrays stored from HIGH to LOW memory locations. For example, in order to clear 1000_{16} words starting at memory location 4000_{16}, the following instruction sequence can be used:

```
            MOVE.W  #$1000, D0       ; Load length of
                                       data into D0

            MOVEA.L #$004002, A0     ; Load starting ad-
                                       dress plus 2 into
                                       A0

REPEAT      CLR.W   −(A0)            ; Decrement A0
                                       by 2 and clear
                                       memory location
                                       addressed by A0

            SUBQ    #1, D0           ; Decrement D0
                                       by 1

            BNE     REPEAT           ; If Z = 0, branch
            —                          to REPEAT;
            —                          otherwise, go to
            —                          next instruction
```

In this instruction sequence, CLR.W −(A0) first decrements A0 by 2 and then clears the location. Since the starting address is 004000_{16}, A0 must initially be initialized with 004002_{16}.

It should be pointed out that the predecrement and

postincrement modes can be combined in a single instruction. A typical example is MOVE.W (A5)+, −(A3).

The two other address register modes provide accessing of the tables by allowing offsets and indexes to be included to an indirect address pointer. The address register indirect with offset mode determines the effective address by adding a 16-bit signed integer to the contents of an address register. For example, consider MOVE.W $10(A5), D3 in which the source operand is an address register indirect with offset mode. If $[A5] = 00002000_{16}$ and $[002010]_{16} = 0014_{16}$, then, after execution of MOVE.W $10(A5), D3, register D3 will contain 0014_{16}.

The indexed register indirect with offset determines the effective address by adding an 8-bit signed integer and the contents of a register (data or address register) to the contents of an address (base) register. This mode is usually used when the offset from the base address register needs to be varied during program execution. The size of the index register can be a sign-extended 16-bit integer or a 32-bit value. As an example, consider MOVE.W $10(A4, D3.W), D4 in which the source is in the indexed register indirect with offset mode. Note that in this instruction A4 is the base register and D3.W is the 16-bit index register (sign-extended to 32 bits). This register can be specified as 32 bits by using D3.L in the instruction, and 10_{16} is the 8-bit offset that is sign-extended to 32 bits. If $[A4] = 00003000_{16}$, $[D3] = 0200_{16}$, and $[003210_{16}] = 0024_{16}$, then this MOVE instruction will load 0024_{16} into the low 16 bits of register D4.

The address register indirect with offset mode can be used to access a single table where the offset (maximum 16 bits) can be the starting address of the table (fixed number) and the address register can hold the index number in the table to be accessed. Note that the starting address, plus the index number, provides the address of the element to be accessed in the table. For example, consider MOVE.W $3400(A5), D1. If A5 contains 04, then this MOVE instruction transfers the contents of 3404 (i.e., the fifth element, 0 being the first element) into the low 16 bits of D1.

The indexed register indirect with offset, on the other hand, can be used to access multiple tables where the offset (maximum 8 bits) can be the element number to be accessed. The address register pointer can be used to hold the starting address of the table containing the lowest starting address, and the index register can be used to hold the difference between the starting address of the table being accessed and the table with the lowest starting address. For example, consider three tables with table 1 starting at 002000_{16}, table 2 at 003000_{16}, and table 3 at 004000_{16}. Now, in order to transfer the seventh element (0 being the first element) in table 2 to the low 16 bits of register D0, the instruction MOVE.W $06(A2, D1.W), D0 can be used, where [A2] = starting address of table with lowest address = 002000_{16} in this case and $[D1]_{low\ 16\ bits}$ = difference between starting address of table being accessed and starting address of table with lowest address = $003000_{16} - 002000_{16} = 1000_{16}$. Therefore, this MOVE instruction will transfer the contents of address 003006_{16} (seventh element in table 2) to register D0.

Absolute Addressing In this mode, the effective address is part of the instruction. The 68000 has two modes: absolute short addressing, in which a 16-bit address is used (the address is sign-extended to 24 bits before use), and absolute long addressing, in which a 24-bit address is used. For example, consider ADD $2000, D2 as an example of the absolute short mode. If $[2000] = 0012_{16}$ and $[D2] = 0010_{16}$, then, after executing ADD $2000, D2, register D2 will therefore contain 0022_{16}. The absolute long addressing mode is used when the address size is more than 16 bits. For example, MOVE.W $240000, D5 loads the 16-bit contents of memory location 240000_{16} into the low 16 bits of D5. The absolute short mode includes an address ADDR in the range $0 \le ADDR \le \$7FFF$ or $\$FF800 \le ADDR \le \$FFFFFF$.

Note that a single instruction may use both short and long absolute modes, depending on whether the source or destination address is less than, equal to, or greater than the 16-bit address. A typical example is MOVE.W $500002, $1000.

Program Counter Relative Addressing The 68000 has two program counter relative addressing modes: relative with offset and relative with index and offset. In relative with offset, the effective address is obtained by adding the contents of the current PC with a sign-extended 16-bit displacement. This mode can be used when the displacement needs to be fixed during program execution. Typical branch instructions such as BEQ, BRA, and BLE use the relative mode with offset. This mode can also be used by some other instructions. For example, consider ADD *+$30, D5 in which the source operand is in relative with offset mode. Note that typical assemblers use the symbol * to indicate offset. Now suppose that the current PC contents is $002000, the contents of 002030_{16} is 0005, and the low 16 bits of D5 contain 0010_{16}. Then, after execution of this ADD instruction, D5 will contain 0015_{16}.

In relative with index and offset, the effective address is obtained by adding the contents of the current PC, a signed 8-bit displacement (sign-extended to 32 bits), and the contents of an index register (address or data register). The size of the index register can be 16 or 32 bits wide. For example, consider ADD.W $4(PC, D0.W), D2. If $[D2] = 00000012_{16}$, $[PC] = 002000_{16}$, $[D0]_{low\ 16\ bits} = 0010_{16}$, and $[002014] = 0002_{16}$, then, after this ADD, $[D2]_{low\ 16\ bits} = 0014_{16}$. This mode is used when the displacement needs to be changed during program execution.

Immediate Data Addressing There are two immediate modes available with the 68000. These are the immediate and quick immediate modes. In the immediate mode, the operand data is constant data, which is part of the instruction. For example, consider ADD #$0005, D0. If [D0] = 0002_{16}, then, after this ADD instruction, [D0] = $0002_{16} + 0005_{16} = 0007_{16}$. Note that the # symbol is used by Motorola to indicate the immediate mode.

The quick immediate mode allows one to increment or decrement a register by a number from 0 to 7. For example, ADDQ #1, D0 increments the contents of D0 by 1. Note that the data 1 is inherent in the instruction.

Implied Addressing There are two types of implied addressing modes: implicit and explicit. The instructions using the implicit mode do not require any operand, and registers such as PC, SP, or SR are implicitly referenced in these instructions. For example, RTE returns from an exception routine to the main program by using implicitly the PC and SR. The JMP add instruction, on the other hand, allows loading a value into the PC, although the PC is not explicitly defined in the instruction.

It should be pointed out that in the 68000 the first operand of a two-operand instruction is the source and the second operand is the destination. Recall that in the case of the 8086, the first operand is the destination and the second operand is the source.

All of the 68000 addressing modes in Table 6–3 can be further divided into four functional categories as shown in Table 6–4.

Data Addressing Mode An addressing mode is said to be a data addressing mode if it references data objects. For example, all 68000 addressing modes except the address register direct mode fall into this category.

Memory Addressing Mode An addressing mode that is capable of accessing a data item stored in memory is classified as a memory addressing mode. For example, the data and address register direct addressing modes cannot satisfy this definition.

Control Addressing Mode This refers to an addressing mode that has the ability to access a data item stored in memory without the need to specify its size. For example, all 68000 addressing modes except the following are classified as control addressing modes: data register direct, address register direct, address register indirect with postincrement, address register indirect with predecrement, and immediate.

Alterable Addressing Mode If the effective address of an addressing mode is written into, then that mode is an alterable addressing mode. For example, the immediate and the program counter relative addressing modes will not satisfy this definition.

6–6 68000 INSTRUCTION SET

The 68000 instruction set contains 56 basic instructions. Table 6–5 lists them in alphabetical order. Table 6–6 lists those affecting the condition codes. The repertoire is very versatile and offers an efficient means to handle high-level language structures (such as arrays and linked

TABLE 6–4
68000 Addressing Modes — Functional Categories (Courtesy of Motorola)

Addressing Mode	Addressing Category			
	Data	Memory	Control	Alterable
Data register direct	X	—	—	X
Address register direct	—	—	—	X
Address register indirect	X	X	X	X
Address register indirect with postincrement	X	X	—	X
Address register indirect with predecrement	X	X	—	X
Address register indirect with displacement	X	X	X	X
Address register indirect with index	X	X	X	X
Absolute short	X	X	X	X
Absolute long	X	X	X	X
Program counter with displacement	X	X	X	—
Program counter with index	X	X	X	—
Immediate	X	X	—	—

TABLE 6-5
68000 Instruction Set

Instruction	Size	Length (Words)	Operation
ABCD − (Ay), −(Ax)	B	1	$-(Ay)_{10} + -(Ax)_{10} + X \rightarrow (Ax)$
ABCD Dy, Dx	B	1	$(Dy)_{10} + (Dx)_{10} + X \rightarrow Dx$
ADD (EA), (EA)	B,W,L	1	$(EA) + (EA) \rightarrow EA$
ADD (EA), Dn	B,W,L	1	$(EA) + Dn \rightarrow Dn$
ADDA (EA), An	W,L	1	$(EA) + (An) \rightarrow An$
ADDI # data, (EA)	B,W,L	2 for B,W 3 for L	$data + (EA) \rightarrow EA$
ADDQ#data, (EA)	B,W,L	1	$data + (EA) \rightarrow EA$
ADDX − (Ay), −(Ax)	B,W,L	1	$-(Ay) + -(Ax) + X \rightarrow (Ax)$
ADDX Dy, Dx	B,W,L	1	$Dy + Dx + X \rightarrow Dx$
AND (EA), (EA)	B,W,L	1	$(EA) \wedge (EA) \rightarrow EA$
ANDI #data, (EA)	B,W,L	2 for B,W 3 for L	$data \wedge (EA) \rightarrow EA$
ANDI #data$_8$, CCR	B	2	$data_8 \wedge (CCR) \rightarrow CCR$
ANDI # data$_{16}$, SR	W	2	$data_{16} \wedge SR \rightarrow SR$
ASL Dx, Dy	B,W,L	1	number of shifts determined by [D$_x$]
ASL #data, Dy	B,W,L	1	number of shifts determined by # data
ASL (EA)	B,W,L	1	shift once
ASR Dx, Dy	B,W,L	1	number of shifts determined by [D$_x$]
ASR#data, Dy	B,W,L	1	number of shifts determined by immediate data
ASR (EA)	B,W,L	1	shift once
BCC d	B,W	1 for B 2 for W	Branch to PC + d if carry = 0; else next instruction
BCHG Dn, (EA)	B,L	1	[bit of (EA), specified by Dn]′ → Z [bit of (EA) specified by Dn]′ → bit of (EA)
BCHG #data, (EA)	B,L	2	Same as BCHG Dn, (EA) except bit number is specified by immediate data
BCLR Dn, (EA)	B,L	1	[bit of (EA)]′ →Z 0 →bit of (EA) specified by Dn

Continued.

TABLE 6–5
68000 Instruction Set (cont.)

Instruction	Size	Length (Words)	Operation
BCLR #data, (EA)	B,L	2	Same as BCLR Dn, (EA) except the bit is specified by immediate data.
BCS d	B,W	1 for B 2 for W	Branch to PC + d if carry = 1; else next instruction
BEQ d	B,W	1 for B 2 for W	Branch to PC + d if Z = 1; else next instruction
BGE d	B,W	1 for B 2 for W	Branch to PC + d if greater than or equal; else next instruction
BGT d	B,W	1 for B 2 for W	Branch to PC + d if greater than; else next instruction
BHI d	B,W	1 for B 2 for W	Branch to PC + d if higher; else next instruction
BLE d	B,W	1 for B 2 for W	Branch to PC + d if less or equal; else next instruction
BLS d	B,W	1 for B 2 for W	Branch to PC + d if low or same; else next instruction
BLT d	B,W	1 for B 2 for W	Branch to PC + d if less than; else next instruction
BMI d	B,W	1 for B 2 for W	Branch to PC + d if N = 1; else next instruction
BNE d	B,W	1 for B 2 for W	Branch to PC + d if Z = 0; else next instruction
BPL d	B,W	1 for B 2 for W	Branch to PC + d if N = 0; else next instruction
BRA d	B,W	1 for B 2 for W	Branch always to PC + d
BSET Dn, (EA)	B,L	1	[bit of (EA)]′→Z 1 → bit of (EA) specified by Dn
BSET #data, (EA)	B,L	2	Same as BSET Dn, (EA) except the bit is specified by immediate data
BSR d	B,W	1 for B 2 for W	PC → −(SP) PC + d → PC
BTST Dn, (EA)	B,L	1	[bit of (EA) specified by Dn]′ → Z
BTST #data, (EA)	B,L	2	Same as BTST Dn, (EA) except the bit is specified by immediate data
BVC d	B,W	1 for B 2 for W	Branch to PC + d if V = 0; else next instruction
BVS d	B,W	1 for B 2 for W	Branch to PC + d if V = 1; else next instruction
CHK (EA), Dn	W	1	If Dn < 0 or Dn > (EA), then trap
CLR (EA)	B,W,L	1	0 → EA
CMP (EA), Dn	B,W,L	1	Dn − (EA) ⇒ Affect all condition codes except X
CMP (EA), An	W,L	1	An − (EA) ⇒ Affect all condition codes except X
CMPI #data, (EA)	B,W,L	2 for B,L 3 for L	(EA) − data ⇒ Affect all flags except X-bit
CMPM (Ay)+, (Ax)+	B,W,L	1	(Ax)+ − (Ay)+ ⇒ Affect all flags except X
DBCC Dn, d	W	2	If condition false, i.e., C = 1, then Dn − 1 → Dn; if Dn ≠ −1, then PC + d → PC, else PC + 2 → PC
DBCS Dn, d	W	2	Same as DBCC except condition is C = 1
DBEQ Dn, d	W	2	Same as DBCC except condition is Z = 1
DBF Dn, d	W	2	Same as DBCC except condition is always false
DBGE Dn, d	W	2	Same as DBCC except condition is greater or equal
DBGT Dn, d	W	2	Same as DBCC except condition is greater than
DBHI Dn, d	W	2	Same as DBCC except condition is high
DBLE Dn, d	W	2	Same as DBCC except condition is less than or equal

TABLE 6–5
68000 Instruction Set (cont.)

Instruction	Size	Length (Words)	Operation
DBLS Dn, d	W	2	Same as DBCC except condition is low or same
DBLT Dn, d	W	2	Same as DBCC except condition is less than
DBMI Dn, d	W	2	Same as DBCC except condition is N = 1
DBNE Dn, d	W	2	Same as DBCC except condition Z = 0
DBPL Dn, d	W	2	Same as DBCC except condition N = 0
DBT Dn, d	W	2	Same as DBCC except condition is always true
DBVC Dn, d	W	2	Same as DBCC except condition is V = 0
DBVS Dn, d	W	2	Same as DBCC except condition is V = 1
DIVS (EA), Dn	W	1	signed Division $(Dn)_{32}/(EA)_{16} \Rightarrow$ $(Dn)_{0-7}$ = quotient $(Dn)_{8-15}$ = remainder
DIVU (EA), Dn	W	1	Same as DIVS except division is unsigned
EOR Dn, (EA)	B,W,L	1	$Dn \oplus (EA) \to EA$
EORI #data, (EA)	B,W,L	3 for L / 2 for B,W	$data \oplus (EA) \to EA$
EORI #d_8, CCR	B	2	$d_8 \oplus CCR \to CCR$
EORI #d_{16}, SR	W	2	$d_{16} \oplus SR \to SR$; Privileged instructions (S = 1)
EXG Rx, Ry	L	1	$Rx \leftrightarrow Ry$
EXT Dn	W,L	1	Extend sign bit of Dn from 8-bit to 16-bit or from 16-bit to 32-bit depending on whether the operand size is B or W
JMP (EA)	unsized	1	$(EA) \to PC$ Unconditional jump using address in operand
JSR (EA)	unsized	1	$PC \to -(SP);$ $(EA) \to PC$ Jump to subroutine using address in operand
LEA (EA), An	L	1	$(EA) \to An$
LINK An, # −d	unsized	2	$An \to (SP); SP \to An;$ $SP - d \to SP$
LSL Dx, Dy	B,W,L	1	[diagram: $c \leftarrow$, $x \leftarrow$ D_y $\leftarrow 0$] number of shifts specified by [Dx] from 0 to 63
LSL # data, Dy	B,W,L	1	Same as LSL Dx, Dy except immediate data specifies the number of shifts from 0 to 7
LSL (EA)	B,W,L	1	Same as LSL Dx, Dy except left shift is performed only once
LSR Dx, Dy	B,W,L	1	[diagram: $0 \to$ D_y $\to c$, $\to x$] Number of shifts specified by Dx from 0 to 63
LSR # data, Dy	B,W,L	1	Same as LSR except immediate data specifies the number of shifts from 0 to 7
LSR (EA)	B,W,L	1	Same as LSR, Dx, Dy except the right shift is performed once only.
MOVE (EA), (EA)	B,W,L	1	$(EA)_{source} \to (EA)_{destination}$
MOVE (EA), CCR	W	1	$(EA) \to CCR$
MOVE(EA), SR	W	1	If S = 1, then $(EA) \to SR$; else TRAP
MOVE SR, (EA)	W	1	$SR \to (EA)$ is S = 1; else TRAP
MOVE An, USP	L	1	If S = 1, then $An \to USP$; else TRAP

Continued.

TABLE 6–5
68000 Instruction Set (cont.)

Instruction	Size	Length (Words)	Operation
MOVE USP, An	L	1	If S = 1, then USP → An; else TRAP
MOVEA (EA), An	W,L	1	(EA) → An
MOVEM register list, (EA)	W,L	2	Registers → (EA)
MOVEM (EA), register list	W,L	2	(EA) → registers
MOVEP Dx, d (Ay)	W,L	2	Dx → d(Ay)
MOVEP d(Ay), Dx	W,L	2	d(Ay) → Dx
MOVEQ #d_8, Dn	L	1	d_8 sign extended to 32-bit → Dn
MULS $(EA)_{16}$, Dn_{16}	W	1	Signed 16 × 16 multiplication $(EA)_{16}$ *$(Dn)_{16}$ → $(Dn)_{32}$
MULU $(EA)_{16}$, $(Dn)_{16}$	W	1	Unsigned 16 × 16 multiplication $(EA)_{16}$ *$(Dn)_{16}$ → $(Dn)_{32}$
NBCD (EA)	B	1	$0 - (EA)_{10} - X → EA$
NEG (EA)	B,W,L	1	0 − (EA) → EA
NEGX (EA)	B,W,L	1	0 − (EA) − X → EA
NOP	unsized	1	No operation
NOT (EA)	B,W,L	1	{(EA)}′ → EA
OR (EA), Dn	B,W,L	1	(EA) ∨ Dn → Dn
OR Dn, (EA)	B,W,L	1	Dn ∨ (EA) → EA
ORI #data, (EA)	B,W,L	2 for B,W 3 for L	data ∨ (EA) → EA
ORI #d_8, CCR	B	2	d_8 ∨ CCR → CCR
ORI #d_{16}, SR	W	2	If S = 1, then d_{16} ∨ SR → SR; else TRAP
PEA (EA)	L	1	$(EA)_{16}$ sign extend to 32-bits → − (SP)
RESET	unsized	1	If S = 1, then assert RESET line; else TRAP
ROL Dx, Dy	B,W,L	1	 D_x specifies number of times to be rotated from 0 to 63
ROL #data, Dy	B,W,L	1	Same as ROL Dx, Dy except immediate data specifies number of times to be rotated from 0 to 7
ROL (EA)	B,W,L	1	Same as ROL Dx, Dy except (EA) is rotated once Dx specifies number of rotates from 0 to 63
ROR Dx, Dy	B,W,L	1	
ROR #data, Dy	B,W,L	1	Same as ROR Dx, Dy except the number of rotates is specified by immediate data from 0 to 7
ROR (EA)	B,W,L	1	Same as ROR Dx, Dy except (EA) is rotated once
ROXL Dx, Dy	B,W,L	1	Same as ROR Dx, Dy except (EA) is rotated once Dx specifies the number of rotates 0 to 63
ROXL #data, Dy	B,W,L	1	Same as ROXL Dx, Dy except immediate data specifies number of rotates from 0 to 7

TABLE 6–5
68000 Instruction Set (cont.)

Instruction	Size	Length (Words)	Operation
ROXL (EA)	B,W,L	1	Same as ROXL Dx, Dy except (EA) is rotated once

Instruction	Size	Length (Words)	Operation
			Dx specifies number of rotates from 0 to 63
ROXR Dx, Dy	B,W,L	1	
ROXR #data, Dy	B,W,L	1	Same as ROXR Dx, Dy except immediate data specifies number of rotates from 0 to 7
ROXR (EA)	B,W,L	1	Same as ROXR Dx, Dy except (EA) is rotated once
RTE	unsized	1	If S = 1, then (SP)+ → SR; (SP)+ → PC, else TRAP
RTR	unsized	1	(SP) + → CC; (SP) + → PC
RTS	unsized	1	(SP) + → PC
SBCD − (Ay), − (Ax)	B	1	$-(Ax)_{10} - -(Ay)_{10} - X \rightarrow (Ax)$
SCC (EA)	B	1	If C = 0, then 1s → (EA) else 0s → (EA)
SCS (EA)	B	1	Same as SCC except the condition is C = 1
SEQ (EA)	B	1	Same as SCC except if Z = 1
SF (EA)	B	1	Same as SCC except condition is always false
SGE (EA)	B	1	Same as SCC except if greater or equal
SGT (EA)	B	1	Same as SCC except if greater than
SHI (EA)	B	1	Same as SCC except if high
SLE (EA)	B	1	Same as SCC except if less or equal
SLS (EA)	B	1	Same as SCC except if low or same
SLT (EA)	B	1	Same as SCC except if less than
SMI (EA)	B	1	Same as SCC except if N = 1
SNE (EA)	B	1	Same as SCC except if Z = 0
SPL (EA)	B	1	Same as SCC except if N = 0
ST (EA)	B	1	Same as SCC except condition always true
STOP #data	unsized	2	If S = 1, then data → SR and stop; TRAP if executed in user mode
SUB (EA), (EA)	B,W,L	1	(EA) − (EA) → EA
SUBA (EA), An	W,L	1	An − (EA) → An
SUBI #data, (EA)	B,W,L	2 for B,W 3 for L	(EA) − data → EA
SUBQ # data, (EA)	B,W,L	1	(EA) − data → EA
SUBX − (Ay), − (Ax)	B,W,L	1	−(Ax) − −(Ay) − X → (Ax)
SUBX Dy, Dx	B,W,L	1	Dx − Dy − X → Dx
SVC (EA)	B	1	Same as SCC except if V = 0
SVS (EA)	B	1	Same as SCC except if V = 1
SWAP Dn	W	1	Dn [31:16] ↔ Dn [15:0]
TAS (EA)	B	1	(EA) tested; N and Z are affected accordingly; 1 → bit 7 of (EA)
TRAP #vector	unsized	1	PC → −(SSP), SR → −(SSP), (vector) → PC; 16 TRAP vectors are available
TRAPV	unsized	1	If V = 1, then TRAP
TST (EA)	B,W,L	1	(EA) − 0 ⇒ condition codes affected. No result provided
UNLK An	unsized	1	An → SP; (SP)+ → An

TABLE 6–6
68000 Instructions Affecting Condition Codes

Instruction	X	N	Z	V	C
ABCD	√	U	√	U	—
ADD, ADDI, ADDQ, ADDX	√	√	√	√	√
AND, ANDI	—	√	√	0	0
ASL, ASR	√	√	√	√	√
BCHG, BCLR, BSET, BTST	—	—	√	—	—
CHK	—	√	U	U	U
CLR	—	0	1	0	0
CMP, CMPA, CMPI, CMPM	—	√	√	√	√
DIVS, DIVU	—	√	√	√	0
EOR, EORI	—	√	√	0	0
EXT	—	√	√	0	0
LSL, LSR	√	√	√	0	√
MOVE (ea), (ea)	—	√	√	0	0
MOVE TO CC	√	√	√	√	√
MOVE TO SR	√	√	√	√	√
MOVEQ	—	√	√	0	0
MULS, MULU	—	√	√	0	0
NBCD	√	U	√	U	√
NEG, NEGX	√	√	√	√	√
NOT, OR, ORI	—	√	√	0	0
ROL, ROR	—	√	√	0	√
ROXL, ROXR	√	√	√	0	√
RTE, RTR	√	√	√	√	√
SBCD	√	U	√	U	√
STOP	√	√	√	√	√
SUB, SUBI, SUBQ, SUBX	√	√	√	√	√
SWAP	—	√	√	0	0
TAS	—	√	√	0	0
TST	—	√	√	0	0

√ Affected, — Not Affected, U—Undefined

lists). Note that in order to identify the operand size of an instruction, the following notation is placed after a 68000 mnemonic: .B for byte, .W or none for word, .L for long word. For example,

ADD.B   D0, D1 ; $[D1]_8 \leftarrow [D0]_8 + [D1]_8$

ADD.W
or   D0, D1 ; $[D1]_{16} \leftarrow [D0]_{16} + [D1]_{16}$
ADD

ADD.L   D0, D1 ; $[D1]_{32} \leftarrow [D0]_{32} + [D1]_{32}$

All 68000 instructions may be classified into eight groups as follows:

1. Data movement instructions
2. Arithmetic instructions
3. Logical instructions
4. Shift and rotate instructions
5. Bit manipulation instructions
6. Binary-coded decimal instructions
7. Program control instructions
8. System control instructions

Data Movement Instructions These instructions allow data transfers from register to register, register to memory, memory to register, and memory to memory. In addition, there are also special data movement instructions such as MOVEM (move multiple registers). Typically, byte, word, or long word data can be transferred. A list of the 68000 data movement instructions is given in Table 6–7. Let us now explain the data movement instructions.

MOVE Instructions The format for the basic MOVE instruction is MOVE.S (EA), (EA), where S = L, W, or B. (EA) can be a register or memory location, depending on the addressing mode used. Consider MOVE.B D3, D1, which uses the data register direct mode for both the source and destination. If $[D3] = 05_{16}$ and $[D1] = 01_{16}$, then, after execution of this MOVE instruction, $[D1] = 05_{16}$ and $[D3] = 05_{16}$.

There are several variations of the MOVE instruction. For example, MOVE.W CCR, (EA) moves the contents of the low-order byte of SR, i.e., CCR, to the low-order byte of the destination operand; the up-

TABLE 6–7
68000 Data Movement Instructions

Instruction	Size	Comment
EXG Rx, Ry	L	Exchange the contents of two registers. Rx or Ry can be any address or data register. No flags are affected.
LEA (EA), An	L	The effective address (EA) is calculated using the particular addressing mode used and then loaded into the address register. (EA) specifies the actual data to be loaded into An.
LINK An, #-displacement	Unsized	The current contents of the specified address register are pushed onto the stack. After the push, the address register is loaded from the updated SP. Finally, the 16-bit sign-extended displacement is added to the SP. A negative displacement is specified to allocate stack.
MOVE (EA), (EA)	B, W, L	(EA)s are calculated by the 68000 using the specific addressing mode used. (EA)s can be register or memory location. Therefore, data transfer can take place between registers, between a register and a memory location, and between different memory locations. Flags are affected. For byte-size operation, address register direct is not allowed. An is not allowed in the destination (EA). The source (EA) can be An for word or long word transfers.
MOVEM reg list, (EA) or (EA), reg list	W, L	Specified registers are transferred to or from consecutive memory locations starting at the location specified by the effective address.
MOVEP Dn, d (Ay) or d (Ay), Dn	W, L	Two (W) or four (L) bytes of data are transferred between a data register and alternate bytes of memory, starting at the location specified and incrementing by 2. The high-order byte of data is transferred first, and the low-order byte is transferred last. This instruction has the address register indirect with displacement only mode.
MOVEQ # data, Dn	L	This instruction moves the 8-bit inherent data into the specified data register. The data is then sign-extended to 32 bits.
PEA (EA)	L	Computes an effective address and then pushes the 32-bit address onto the stack.
SWAP Dn	W	Exchanges 16-bit halves of a data register.
UNLK An	Unsized	An → SP; (SP)+ → An

• (EA) in LEA (EA), An can use all addressing modes except Dn, An, (An)+, −(An), and immediate.
• Destination (EA) in MOVE (EA), (EA) can use all modes except An, relative, and immediate.
• Source (EA) in MOVE (EA), (EA) can use all modes.
• Destination (EA) in MOVEM reg list, (EA) can use all modes except, An, (An)+, relative, and immediate.
  Source (EA) in MOVEM (EA), reg list can use all modes except Dn, An, −(An), and immediate.
• (EA) in PEA (EA) can use all modes except, An, (An)+, −(An), and immediate.

per byte of SR is considered to be zero. The source operand is a word. Similarly, MOVE.W (EA), CCR moves an 8-bit immediate number, or low-order 8-bit data, from a memory location or register into the condition code register; the upper byte is ignored. The source operand is a word. Data can also be transferred between (EA) and SR or USP using the following instructions:

MOVE.W (EA), SR
MOVE.W SR, (EA)
MOVE.L USP, An
MOVE.L An, USP

MOVEA.W or .L (EA), An can be used to load an address into an address register. Word-size source operands are sign-extended to 32 bits. Note that (EA) is obtained using an addressing mode. As an example, MOVEA.W #$2000, A5 moves the 16-bit word 2000_{16} into the low 16 bits of A5 and then sign-extends 2000_{16} to the 32-bit number 00002000_{16}. Note that sign extension means extending bit 15 of 2000_{16} from bit 16 through bit 31. As mentioned before, sign extension is required when an arithmetic operation between two signed binary numbers of different size is performed. (EA) in MOVEA can use all addressing modes.

The MOVEM instruction can be used to push or pop multiple registers to or from the stack. For example, MOVEM.L D0–D7/A0–A6, –(SP) saves the contents of all eight data registers and seven address registers in the stack. This instruction stores address registers in the order A6–A0 first, followed by data registers in the order D7–D0, regardless of the order in the register list. MOVEM.L (SP)+ , D0–D7/A0–A6 restores the contents of the registers in the order D0–D7, A0–A6, regardless of the order in the register list. The MOVEM instruction can also be used to save a set of registers in memory. In addition to the preceding predecrement and postincrement modes for the effective address, the MOVEM instruction allows all of the control modes. If the effective address is in one of the control modes, such as absolute short, then the registers are transferred starting at the specified address and up through higher addresses. The order of transfer is from D0 to D7 and then from A0 to A7. For example, MOVEM.W A5/D1/D3/A1–A3, $2000 transfers the low 16-bit contents of D1, D3, A1, A2, A3, and A5 to locations $2000, $2002, $2004, $2006, $2008, and $200A, respectively.

The MOVEQ.L #d8, Dn instruction moves the immediate 8-bit data into the low byte of Dn. The 8-bit data is then sign-extended to 32 bits. This is a one-word instruction. For example, MOVEQ.L #$8F, D5 moves $FFFFFF8F into D5.

In order to transfer data between the 68000 data registers and 6800 (8-bit) peripherals, the MOVEP instruction can be used. This instruction transfers 2 or 4 bytes of data between a data register and alternate byte locations in memory, starting at the location specified and incrementing by 2. Register indirect with displacement is the only addressing mode used with this instruction. If the address is even, all the transfers are made on the high-order half of the data bus; if the address is odd, all the transfers are made on the low-order half of the data bus. The high-order byte from the register is transferred first, and the low-order byte is transferred last. For example, consider MOVEP.L $0020(A2), D1. If [A2] = $00002000, [002020] = 02, [002022] = 05, [002024] = 01, and [002026] = 04, then, after execution of this MOVEP instruction, D1 will contain 02050104_{16}.

EXG and SWAP Instructions

The EXG Rx, Ry instruction exchanges the 32-bit contents of Rx with that of Ry. The exchange is between two data registers, or two address registers, or an address and a data register. The EXG instruction exchanges only 32-bit long words. The data size (L) does not have to be specified after the EXG instruction since this instruction has only one data size (L) and it is assumed that the default is this single data size. No flags are affected.

The SWAP Dn instruction, on the other hand, exchanges the low 16 bits of Dn with the high 16 bits of Dn. All condition codes are affected.

LEA and PEA Instructions

The LEA.L (EA), An instruction moves an effective address (EA) into the specified address register. The (EA) can be calculated based on the addressing mode of the source. For example, LEA $00256022, A5 moves $00256022 into A5. This instruction is equivalent to MOVEA.L #$00256022, A5. Note that $00256022 is contained in PC. It should be pointed out that the LEA instruction is very useful when address calculation is desired during program execution. (EA) in LEA specifies the actual data to be loaded into An, whereas (EA) in MOVEA specifies the address of actual data. For example, consider LEA $04(A5, D2.W), A3. If [A5] = 00002000_{16} and [D2] = 0028_{16}, then the LEA instruction moves $0000202C_{16}$ into A3. On the other hand, MOVEA $04(A5, D2.W), A3 moves the contents of $0000202C_{16}$ into A3. Therefore, it is obvious that if address calculation is required, the instruction LEA is very useful.

The PEA (EA) instruction computes an effective address and then pushes it onto the stack. This instruction can be used when the 16-bit address used in the absolute short mode is required to be pushed onto the stack. For example, consider PEA $2000 and [USP] = 00003004_{16}. Then, after this PEA instruction, $2000 is sign-extended to 32 bits and pushed onto the stack. The low-order 16 bits are stored at 00003002_{16}, and the high-order 16 bits are pushed onto the stack at 00003000_{16}.

LINK and UNLK Instructions

Before calling a subroutine, the main program quite often transfers values of certain parameters to the subroutine. It is convenient to save these variables onto the stack before calling the subroutine. These variables can then be read from the stack and used by the subroutine for computations. The 68000 LINK and UNLK instructions are used for this purpose. In addition, the 68000 LINK instruction allows one to reserve temporary storage for the local variables of a subroutine. This storage can be accessed as needed by the subroutine and can be released using UNLK before returning to the main program. The LINK instruction is usually used at the beginning of a subroutine to allocate stack space for storing local variables and parameters for nested subroutine calls. The UNLK instruction is usually used at the end of a subroutine before the RETURN instruction to release the local area and restore the stack pointer contents so that it points to the return address.

The LINK An, # – displacement instruction causes the current contents of the specified An to be pushed onto the system stack. The updated SP contents are then loaded into An. Finally, a sign-extended 2's complement displacement value is added to the SP. No flags are affected. For example, consider LINK A5, # – 100. If $[A5] = 00002100_{16}$ and $[USP] = 00004104_{16}$, then, after execution of the LINK instruction, the situation shown in Figure 6–5 occurs. This means that after the LINK instruction, $[A5] = 00002100$ is pushed onto the stack and the [updated USP] = 004100 is loaded into A5. USP is then loaded with 004000 and therefore 100 locations are allocated to the subroutine at the beginning of which this particular LINK instruction can be used. Note that A5 cannot be used in the subroutine.

The UNLK instruction at the end of this subroutine before the RETURN instruction releases the 100 locations and restores the contents of A5 and USP to those prior to using the LINK instruction. For example, UNLK A5 will load $[A5] = 00004100$ into USP and the two stack words 00002100 into A5. USP is then incremented by 4 to contain 00004104. Therefore, the contents of A5 and USP prior to using the LINK instruction are restored.

In this example, after execution of the LINK, addresses $003FFF and below can be used as the stack. One hundred locations starting at $004000 and above can be reserved for storing the local variables of the subroutine. These variables can then be accessed with an address register such as A5 as a base pointer using the address register indirect with displacement mode. MOVE.W d(A5), D1 for read and MOVE.W D1, d(A5) for write are typical examples.

Arithmetic Instructions   These instructions allow:

- 8-, 16-, or 32-bit additions and subtractions.
- 16-bit by 16-bit multiplication (both signed and unsigned) and 32-bit by 16-bit division (both signed and unsigned).
- Compare, clear, and negate instructions.
- Extended arithmetic instructions for performing multiprecision arithmetic.
- Test (TST) instruction for comparing the operand with zero.

- Test and set (TAS) instruction, which can be used for synchronization in a multiprocessor system.

The 68000 arithmetic instructions are summarized in Table 6–8. Let us now explain the arithmetic instructions.

Addition and Subtraction Instructions

- Consider ADD.W $122000, D0. If $[122000_{16}] = 0012_{16}$ and $[D0] = 0002_{16}$, then, after execution of this ADD, the low 16 bits of D0 will contain 0014_{16}.
- The ADDI instruction can be used to add immediate data to a register or memory location. The immediate data follows the instruction word. For example, consider ADDI.W #$0012, $100200. If $[100200_{16}] = 0002_{16}$, then, after execution of this ADDI, memory location 100200_{16} will contain 0014_{16}.
- ADDQ adds a number from 0 to 7 to the register or memory location in the destination operand. This instruction occupies 16 bits, and the immediate data 0 to 7 is specified by 3 bits in the instruction word. For example, consider ADDQ.B #2, D1. If $[D1]_{low byte} = 20_{16}$, then, after execution of this ADDQ, the low byte of register D1 will contain 22_{16}.
- All subtraction instructions subtract the source from the destination. For example, consider SUB.W D2, $122200. If $[D2]_{low word} = 0003_{16}$ and $[122200_{16}] = 0007_{16}$, then, after execution of this SUB, memory location 122200_{16} will contain 0004_{16}.
- Consider SUBI.W #$0003, D0. If $[D0]_{low word} = 0014_{16}$, then, after execution of this SUBI, D0 will contain 0011_{16}. Note that the same result can be obtained by using a SUBQ.W #$3, D0. However, in this case, the data 3 is inherent in the instruction word.

Multiplication and Division Instructions   The
68000 instruction set includes both signed and unsigned multiplication of integer numbers.

- MULS (EA), Dn multiplies two 16-bit signed numbers and provides a 32-bit result. For example, consider MULS # – 2, D5. If $[D5] = 0003_{16}$, then,

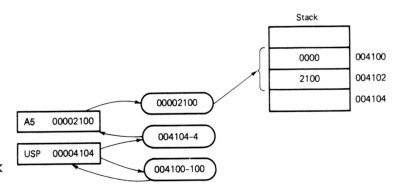

Figure 6–5   Execution of the LINK instruction

TABLE 6-8
68000 Arithmetic Instructions

Instruction	Size	Operation
Addition and Subtraction Instructions		
ADD (EA), (EA)	B, W, L	(EA) + (EA) → (EA)
ADDI #Data, (EA)	B, W, L	(EA) + data → EA
ADDQ #d_8, (EA)	B, W, L	(EA) + d_8 → EA
		d_8 can be an integer from 0 to 7
ADDA (EA), An	W, L	An + (EA) → An
SUB (EA), (EA)	B, W, L	(EA) − (EA) → (EA)
SUBI # data, (EA)	B, W, L	(EA) − data → EA
SUBQ #d_8, (EA)	B, W, L	(EA) − d_8 → EA
		d_8 can be an integer from 0 to 7
SUBA (EA), An	W, L	An − (EA) → An
Multiplication and Division Instructions		
MULS (EA), Dn	W	$(Dn)_{16} * (EA)_{16} → (Dn)_{32}$ (signed multiplication)
MULU (EA), Dn	W	$(Dn)_{16} * (EA)_{16} → (Dn)_{32}$ (unsigned multiplication)
DIVS (EA), Dn	W	$(Dn)_{32}/(EA)_{16} → (Dn)_{32}$ (signed division, high word of Dn contains remainder and low word of Dn contains the quotient)
DIVU (EA), Dn	W	$(Dn)_{32}/(EA)_{16} → (Dn)_{32}$ (unsigned division, remainder is in high word of Dn and quotient is in low word of Dn)
Compare, Clear, and Negate Instructions		
CMP (EA), Dn	B, W, L	Dn − (EA) ⇒ No result. Affects flags.
CMPA (EA), An	W, L	An − (EA) ⇒ No result. Affects flags.
CMPI # data, (EA)	B, W, L	(EA) − data ⇒ No result. Affects flags.
CMPM (Ay) + , (Ax) +	B, W, L	(Ax)+ − (Ay)+ ⇒ No result. Affects flags.
CLR (EA)	B, W, L	0 → EA
NEG (EA)	B, W, L	0 − (EA) → EA

after this MULS, D5 will contain the 32-bit result $FFFFFFFA_{16}$, which is −6 in decimal.

- MULU (EA), Dn performs unsigned multiplication. Consider MULU (A0), D1. If [A0] = 00102000_{16}, [102000] = 0300_{16}, and [D1] = 0200_{16}, then, after this MULU, D1 will contain the 32-bit result 00060000_{16}.

- Consider DIVS #2, D1. If [D1] = -5_{10} = $FFFFFFFB_{16}$, then, after this DIVS, register D1 will contain

D1	FFFF	FFFE
	16-bit remainder = -1_{10}	16-bit quotient = -2_{10}

Note that in the 68000, after DIVS, the sign of the remainder is always the same as the dividend unless

the remainder is equal to zero. Therefore, in this example, since the dividend is negative (-5_{10}), the remainder is negative (-1_{10}). Also, division by zero causes an internal interrupt automatically. A service routine can be written by the user to indicate an error. N = 1 if the quotient is negative, and V = 1 if there is an overflow.

- DIVU is the same as the DIVS instruction except that the division is unsigned. For example, consider DIVU #4, D5. If [D5] = 14_{10} = $0000000E_{16}$, then, after this DIVU, register D5 will contain

D5	0002	0003
	16-bit remainder	16-bit quotient

As with the DIVS instruction, division by zero using

TABLE 6–8
68000 Arithmetic Instructions (cont.)

Instruction	Size	Operation
		Extended Arithmetic Instructions
ADDX Dy, Dx	B, W, L	Dx + Dy + X → Dx
ADDX − (Ay), − (Ax)	B, W, L	−(Ax) + −(Ay) + X → (Ax)
EXT Dn	W, L	If size is W, then sign extend low byte of Dn to 16 bits. If size is L, then sign extend low 16 bits of Dn to 32 bits.
NEGX (EA)	B, W, L	0 − (EA) − X → EA
SUBX Dy, Dx	B, W, L	Dx − Dy − X → Dx
SUBX − (Ay), −(Ax)	B, W, L	−(Ax) − −(Ay) − X → (Ax)
		Test Instruction
TST (EA)	B, W, L	(EA) − 0 ⇒ Flags affected.
		Test and Set Instruction
TAS (EA)	B	If (EA) = 0, then set Z = 1; else Z = 0, N = 1 and then always set bit 7 of (EA) to 1.

NOTE: If (EA) in the ADD or SUB instruction is an address register, the operand length is WORD or LONG WORD.

(EA) in any instruction is calculated using the addressing mode used.

All instructions except ADDA and SUBA affect condition codes.

- Source (EA) in the above ADD, ADDA, SUB, and SUBA can use all modes. Destination (EA) in the above ADD and SUB instructions can use all modes except An, relative, and immediate.
- Destination (EA) in ADDI and SUBI can use all modes except An, relative, and immediate.
- Destination (EA) in ADDQ and SUBQ can use all modes except relative and immediate.
- (EA) in all multiplication and division instructions can use all modes except An.
- Source (EA) in CMP and CMPA instructions can use all modes.
- Destination (EA) in CMPI can use all modes except An, relative, and immediate.
- (EA) in CLR and NEG can use all modes except An, relative, and immediate.
- (EA) in NEGX can use all modes except An, relative and immediate.
- (EA) in TST can use all modes except An, relative, and immediate.
- (EA) in TAS can use all modes except An, relative, and immediate.

DIVU causes a trap (internal interrupt), and V = 1 if there is an overflow.

Compare, Clear, and Negate Instructions

- The compare instructions affect condition codes but do not provide the subtraction result. Consider CMPM.W (A0)+, (A1)+. If [A0] = 00100000_{16}, [A1] = 00200000_{16}, [100000] = 0005_{16}, and [200000] = 0006_{16}, then, after this CMP instruction, N = 0, C = 0, X = 0, V = 0, Z = 0, [A0] = 00100002_{16}, and [A1] = 00200002_{16}.
- CLR.L D5 clears all 32 bits of D5 to zero.
- Consider NEG.W (A0). If [A0] = 00200000_{16} and [200000] = 5_{10}, then, after this NEG instruction, the low 16 bits of location 200000_{16} will contain $FFFB_{16}$.

Extended Arithmetic Instructions

- The ADDX and SUBX instructions can be used in performing multiprecision arithmetic since there are

no ADDC (add with carry) or SUBC (subtract with borrow) instructions. For example, in order to perform a 64-bit addition, the following two instructions can be used:

ADD.L D0, D5	Add low 32 bits of data and store in D5.
ADDX.L D1, D6	Add high 32 bits of data along with any carry from the low 32-bit addition and store result in D6.

Note that in this example, D1 D0 contain one 32-bit data and D6 D5 contain the other 32-bit data. The 32-bit result is stored in D6 D5.

- Consider EXT.W D2. If $[D2]_{low\ byte}$ = $F3_{16}$, then, after the EXT, [D2] = $FFF3_{16}$.

Test Instructions Consider TST.W (A0). If [A0] = 00300000_{16} and [300000] = $FFFF_{16}$, then, after the TST.W (A0), the operation $FFFF_{16}$ − 0000_{16} is performed internally by the 68000, Z is cleared to 0, and N is set to 1. V and C flags are always cleared to 0.

Test and Set Instructions

TAS (EA) is usually used to synchronize two processors in multiprocessor data transfers. For example, consider two 68000-based microcomputers with shared RAM as shown in Figure 6–6.

Suppose that it is desired to transfer the low byte of D0 from processor 1 to the low byte of D2 in processor 2. A memory location, namely, TRDATA, can be used to accomplish this. First, processor 1 can execute the TAS instruction to test the byte in the shared RAM with address TEST for zero value. If it is, processor 1 can be programmed to move the low byte of D0 into location TRDATA in the shared RAM. Processor 2 can then execute an instruction sequence to move the contents of TRDATA from the shared RAM into the low byte of D2. The following instruction sequence will accomplish this:

Processor 1 Routine		Processor 2 Routine	
Proc 1	TAS TEST	Proc 2	TAS TEST
	BNE Proc 1		BNE Proc 2
	MOVE.B D0,		MOVE.B
	TRDATA		TRDATA, D2
	CLR.B TEST		CLR.B TEST
	—		—
	—		—
	—		—

Note that in these instruction sequences, TAS TEST checks the byte addressed by TEST for zero. If [TEST] = 0, then Z is set to 1; else Z = 0, N = 1. After this, bit 7 of [TEST] is set to 1. Note that a zero value of TEST indicates that the shared RAM is free for use and the Z bit indicates this after the TAS is executed. In each of the instruction sequences, after a data transfer using the MOVE instruction, TEST is cleared to zero so that the shared RAM is free for use by the other processor. In order to avoid testing the TEST byte simultaneously by two processors, the TAS is executed in a read-modify-write cycle. This means that once the operand is addressed by the 68000 executing the TAS, the system bus is not available to the other 68000 until the TAS is completed.

Logical Instructions

These instructions include logical OR, EOR, AND, and NOT as shown in Table 6–9.

- Consider AND.W D1, D5. If [D1] = 0001_{16} and [D5] = $FFFF_{16}$, then, after execution of this AND, the low 16 bits of both D1 and D5 will contain 0001_{16}.

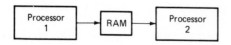

Figure 6–6 Two 68000s interfaced via shared RAM

- Consider ANDI.B #$00, CCR. If [CCR] = 01_{16}, then, after this ANDI, register CCR will contain 00_{16}.
- Consider EOR.W D1, D2. If [D1] = $FFFF_{16}$ and [D2] = $FFFF_{16}$, then, after execution of this EOR, register D2 will contain 0000_{16} and D1 will remain unchanged at $FFFF_{16}$.
- Consider NOT.B D5. If [D5] = 02_{16}, then, after execution of this NOT, the low byte of D5 will contain FD_{16}.
- Consider ORI #$E002, SR. If [SR] = $111D_{16}$, then, after execution of this ORI, register SR will contain F11F. Note that this is a privileged instruction since the high byte of SR containing the control bits is changed and therefore can be executed only in the supervisory mode.

Shift and Rotate Instructions

The 68000 shift and rotate instructions are listed in Table 6–10.

- All the instructions in Table 6–10 affect N and Z flags according to the result. V is reset to zero except for ASL.
- Note that in the 68000 there is no true arithmetic shift left instruction. In true arithmetic shifts, the sign bit of the number being shifted is retained. In the 68000, the instruction ASL does not retain the sign bit, whereas the instruction ASR retains the sign bit after performing the arithmetic shift operation.
- Consider ASL.W D1, D5. If [D1]$_{low\ 16\ bits}$ = 0002_{16} and [D5]$_{low\ 16\ bits}$ = $9FF0_{16}$, then, after this ASL instruction, [D5]$_{low\ 16\ bits}$ = $7FC0_{16}$, C = 0, and X = 0. Note that the sign of the contents of D5 is changed from 1 to 0, and therefore the overflow is set. The sign bit of D5 is changed after shifting [D5] twice. The contents of D5 are not updated after each shift.
- ASR, retains the sign bit. For example, consider ASR.W #2, D1. If [D1] = $FFE2_{16}$, then, after this ASR, the low 16 bits of [D1] = $FFF0_{16}$, C = 1, and X = 1. Note that the sign bit is retained.
- ASL (EA) or ASR (EA) shifts (EA) 1 bit to left or right, respectively. For example, consider ASL.W (A0). If [A0] = 00002000_{16} and [002000] = 9001_{16}, then, after execution of this ASL, [002000] = 2002_{16}, X = 1, and C = 1. On the other hand, after ASR.W (A0), memory location 002000_{16} will contain $C800_{16}$, C = 1, and X = 1. Note that only memory-alterable modes are allowed for (EA). Also, only 16-bit operands are allowed for (EA) when the destination is a memory location.
- The LSL and ASL instructions are the same in the 68000 except that with the ASL, V is set to 1 if there is a sign change of the result from the original value.
- Consider LSR.W #0003, D1. If [D1] = 8000_{16}, then, after this LSR, [D1] = 1000_{16}, X = 0, and C = 0.

TABLE 6–9
68000 Logical Instructions

Instruction	Size	Operation
AND (EA), (EA)	B, W, L	$(EA) \wedge (EA) \to (EA)$; (EA) cannot be address register
ANDI # data, (EA)	B, W, L	$(EA) \wedge \# data \to EA$; (EA) cannot be address register
ANDI # data$_8$, CCR	B	$CCR \wedge \# data \to CCR$
ANDI # data$_{16}$, SR	W	$SR \wedge \# data \to SR$
EOR Dn, (EA)	B, W, L	$Dn \oplus (EA) \to EA$; (EA) cannot be address register
EORI # data, (EA)	B, W, L	$(EA) \oplus \# data \to EA$; (EA) cannot be address register
NOT (EA)	B, W, L	One's complement of $(EA) \to EA$;
OR (EA), (EA)	B, W, L	$(EA) \vee (EA) \to (EA)$ (EA) cannot be address register
ORI # data, (EA)	B, W, L	$(EA) \vee \# data \to EA$; (EA) cannot be address register
ORI # data$_8$, CCR	B	$CCR \vee \# data_8 \to CCR$
ORI # data$_{16}$, SR	W	$SR \vee \# data \to SR$

- Source (EA) in AND and OR can use all modes except An.
- Destination (EA) in AND or OR or EOR can use all modes except An, relative, and immediate.
- Destination (EA) in ANDI, ORI, and EORI can use all modes except An, relative, and immediate.
- (EA) in NOT can use all modes except An, relative, and immediate.

TABLE 6–10
68000 Shift and Rotate Instructions

Instruction	Size	Operation
ASL, Dx, Dy	B, W, L	 Shift [Dy] by the number of times to left specified in Dx; the low 6 bits of Dx specify the number of shifts from 0 to 63
ASL # data, Dn	B, W, L	Same as ASL Dx, Dy except that the number of shifts is specified by immediate data from 0 to 7
ASL (EA)	B, W, L	(EA) is shifted one bit to left; the most significant of (EA) goes to x and c, and zero moves into the least significant bit
ASR Dx, Dy	B, W, L	 Arithmetically shift [Dy] to the right by retaining the sign bit; the low 6 bits of Dx specify the number of shifts from 0 to 63
ASR # data, Dn	B, W, L	Same as above except the number of shifts is from 0 to 7
ASR (EA)	B, W, L	Same as above except (EA) is shifted once to the right

TABLE 6–10
68000 Shift and Rotate Instructions (cont.)

Instruction	Size	Operation
LSL Dx, Dy	B, W, L	 Low 6 bits of Dx specify the number of shifts from 0 to 63
LSL # data, Dn	B, W, L	Same as above except the number of shifts is specified by immediate data from 0 to 7
LSL (EA)	B, W, L	(EA) is shifted one bit to the left
LSR Dx, Dy	B, W, L	 Same as LSL Dx, Dy except shift is to the right
LSR #data, Dn	B, W, L	Same as LSL # data, Dn, except shift is to the right by immediate data from 0 to 7.
LSR (EA)	B, W, L	Same as LSL (EA) except shift is to the right
ROL Dx, Dy	B, W, L	 Low 6 bits of Dx specify the number of times [Dy] to be shifted

Continued.

6–6 68000 INSTRUCTION SET **179**

TABLE 6-10
68000 Shift and Rotate Instructions (cont.)

Instruction	Size	Operation
ROL # data, Dn	B, W, L	Same as above except that the immediate data specifies that [Dn] to be shifted from 0 to 7
ROL (EA)	B, W, L	(EA) is rotated once to the left
ROR Dx, Dy	B, W, L	

Low 6 bits of Dx specify the number of shifts from 0 to 63

Instruction	Size	Operation
ROR # data, Dn,	B, W, L	Same as ROL # data, Dn except the shift is to the right by immediate data from 0 to 7
ROR (EA)	B, W, L	(EA) is rotated once to the right
ROXL Dx, Dy	B, W, L	

Low 6 bits of Dx contain the number of rotates from 0 to 63.

Instruction	Size	Operation
ROXL # data, Dy	B, W, L	Same as above except immediate data specifies number of rotates from 0 to 7
ROXL (EA)	B, W, L	(EA) is rotated one bit to right
ROXR Dx, Dy	B, W, L	

Same as ROXL Dx, Dn except the rotate is to the right

Instruction	Size	Operation
ROXR #data, Dn	B, W, L	Same as ROXL # data, Dy, except rotate is to the right by immediate data from 0 to 7
ROXR (EA)	B, W, L	Same as ROXL (EA) except rotate is to the right

•(EA) in ASL, ASR, LSL, LSR, ROL, ROR, ROXL, and ROXR can use all modes except Dn, An, relative, and immediate.

- Consider ROL.B #02, D2. If $[D2] = B1_{16}$ and $C = 1$, then, after this ROL, the low byte of $[D2] = C6_{16}$ and $C = 0$. On the other hand, with $[D2] = B1_{16}$ and $C = 1$, consider ROR.B #02, D2. After this ROR, register D2 will contain $6C_{16}$ and $C = 0$.

- Consider ROXL.W D2, D1. If $[D2] = 0003_{16}$, $[D1] = F201_{16}$, $C = 0$, and $X = 1$, then the low 16 bits after execution of this ROXL are $[D1] = 900F_{16}$, $C = 1$, and $X = 1$.

Bit Manipulation Instructions The 68000 has four bit manipulation instructions, and these are listed in Table 6-11.

- In all of the instructions in Table 6-11, the 1's complement of the specified bit is reflected in the Z flag.

TABLE 6-11
Bit Manipulation Instructions

Instruction	Size	Operation
BCHG Dn, (EA) BCHG # data, (EA)	B,L	A bit in (EA) specified by Dn or immediate data is tested; the 1's complement of the bit is reflected in both the Z flag and the specified bit position
BCLR Dn, (EA) BCLR # data, (EA)	B,L	A bit in (EA) specified by Dn or immediate data is tested and the 1's complement of the bit is reflected in the Z flag; the specified bit is cleared to zero
BSET Dn, (EA) BSET # data, (EA)	B,L	A bit in (EA) specified by Dn or immediate data is tested and the 1's complement of the bit is reflected in the Z flag; the specified bit is then set to one
BTST Dn, (EA) BTST # data, (EA)	B,L	A bit in (EA) specified by Dn or immediate data is tested. The 1's complement of the specified bit is reflected in the Z flag.

•(EA) in the above instructions can use all modes except An, relative, and immediate.
•If (EA) is memory location then data size is byte; if (EA) is Dn then data size is long word.

The specified bit is then 1's complemented, cleared to 0, set to 1, or unchanged by BCHG, BCLR, BSET, or BTST, respectively. In all the instructions in Table 6-11, if (EA) is Dn, then the length of Dn is 32 bits; otherwise, the length of the destination is 1 byte.

- Consider BCHG.B #2, $003000. If $[003000] = 05_{16}$, then, after execution of this BCHG, $Z = 0$ and $[003000] = 01_{16}$.

- Consider BCLR.L #3, D1. If $[D1] = F210E128_{16}$, then, after execution of this BCLR, register D1 will contain $F210E120_{16}$ and $Z = 0$.

- Consider BSET.B #0, (A1). If $[A1] = 00003000_{16}$ and $[003000] = 00_{16}$, then, after execution of this BSET, memory location 003000 will contain 01_{16} and $Z = 1$.

- Consider BTST.B #2, $002000. If $[002000] = 02_{16}$, then, after execution of this BTST, $Z = 1$ and $[002000] = 02_{16}$.

Binary-Coded Decimal Instructions The 68000 instruction set contains three BCD instructions, namely, ABCD for adding, SBCD for subtracting, and NBCD for negating. These instructions always include

TABLE 6–12
68000 Binary-Coded Decimal Instructions

Instruction	Operand Size	Operation
ABCD Dy, Dx	B	$(Dx)_{10} + (Dy)_{10} + X \rightarrow Dx$
ABCD $-(Ay), -(Ax)$	B	$-(Ax)_{10} + -(Ay)_{10} + X \rightarrow (Ax)$
SBCD Dy, Dx	B	$(Dx)_{10} - (Dy)_{10} - X \rightarrow Dx$
SBCD $-(Ay), -(Ax)$	B	$-(Ax)_{10} - -(Ay)_{10} - X \rightarrow (Ax)$
NBCD (EA)	B	$0 - (EA)_{10} - X \rightarrow EA$

•(EA) in NBCD can use all modes except An, relative, and immediate.

the extend (X) bit in the operation. The BCD instructions are listed in Table 6–12.

- Consider ABCD D1, D2. If $[D1] = 25_{16}$, $[D2] = 15_{16}$, and $X = 0$, then, after execution of this ABCD instruction, $[D2] = 40_{16}$, $X = 0$, and $Z = 0$.
- Consider SBCD $-(A2), -(A3)$. If $(A2) = 00002004_{16}$, $(A3) = 00003003_{16}$, $(002003) = 05_{16}$, $(003002) = 06_{16}$, and $X = 1$, then, after execution of this SBCD instruction, $[003002] = 00_{16}$, $X = 0$, and $Z = 1$.
- Consider NBCD (A1). If $[A1] = [00003000_{16}]$, $[003000] = 05$, and $X = 1$, then, after execution of this NBCD instruction, $[003000] = FA_{16}$.

Program Control Instructions These instructions include branches, jumps, and subroutine calls as listed in Table 6–13.

- Consider Bcc d. There are 14 branch conditions. This means that cc in Bcc can be replaced by 14 conditions providing 14 instructions. These are BCC, BCS, BEQ, BGE, BGT, BHI, BLE, BLS, BLT, BMI, BNE, BPL, BVC, and BVS. It should be mentioned that some of these instructions are applicable to both signed and unsigned numbers, some can be used with only signed numbers, and some instructions are applicable to only unsigned numbers as shown at the bottom of this page.

  After signed arithmetic operations such as ADD or SUB, instructions such as BEQ, BNE, BVS, BVC, BMI, and BPL can be used. On the other hand, after unsigned arithmetic operations, instructions such as BCC, BCS, BEQ, and BNE can be used. It should be pointed out that if $V = 0$, BPL and BGE have the same meaning. Likewise, if $V = 0$, BMI and BLT perform the same function.

The conditional branch instructions can be used after typical arithmetic instructions such as subtraction to branch to a location if cc is true. For example, consider SUB.W D1, D2. Now if [D1] and [D2] are unsigned numbers, then

BCC d	can be used if	$[D2] > [D1]$
BCS d	can be used if	$[D2] \leq [D1]$
BEQ d	can be used if	$[D2] = [D1]$
BNE d	can be used if	$[D2] \neq [D1]$
BHI d	can be used if	$[D2] > [D1]$
BLS d	can be used if	$[D2] \leq [D1]$

On the other hand, if [D1] and [D2] are signed numbers, then after SUB.W D1, D2, the following branch instructions can be used:

BEQ d	can be used if	$[D2] = [D1]$
BNE d	can be used if	$[D2] \neq [D1]$
BLT d	can be used if	$[D2] < [D1]$
BLE d	can be used if	$[D2] \leq [D1]$
BGT d	can be used if	$[D2] > [D1]$
BGE d	can be used if	$[D2] \geq [D1]$

For Both Signed and Unsigned Numbers	For Signed Numbers	For Unsigned Numbers
BCC d (branch if C = 0)	BGE d (branch if greater or equal)	BHI d (branch if high)
BCS d (branch if C = 1)	BGT d (branch if greater than)	BLS d (branch if low or same)
BEQ d (branch if Z = 1)	BLE d (branch if less than or equal)	
BNE d (branch if Z = 0)	BLT d (branch if less than)	
	BMI d (branch if N = 1)	
	BPL d (branch if N = 0)	
	BVC d (branch if V = 0)	
	BVS d (branch if V = 1)	

TABLE 6-13
68000 Program Control Instructions

Instruction	Size	Operation
Bcc d	B,W	If condition code cc is true, then PC + d → PC. The PC value is current instruction location plus 2. d can be 8- or 16-bit signed displacement. If 8-bit displacement is used, then the instruction size is 16 bits with the 8-bit displacement as the low byte of the instruction word. If 16-bit displacement is used, then the instruction size is two words with 8-bit displacement field (low byte) in the instruction word as zero and the second word following the instruction word as the 16-bit displacement. There are 14 conditions such as BCC (Branch if Carry Clear), BEQ (Branch if result equal to zero, i.e., Z = 1), and BNE (Branch if not equal, i.e., Z = 0). Note that the PC contents will always be even since the instruction length is either one word or two words depending on the displacement widths.
BRA d	B,W	Branch always to PC + d where PC value is current instruction location plus 2. As with Bcc, d can be signed 8 or 16 bits. This is an unconditional branching instruction with relative mode. Note that the PC contents are even since the instruction is either one word or two words.
BSR d	B,W	PC → - (SP) PC + d → PC The address of the next instruction following PC is pushed onto the stack. PC is then loaded with PC + d. As before, d can be signed 8 or 16 bits. This is a subroutine call instruction using relative mode.
DBcc Dn, d	W	If cc is false, then Dn - 1 → Dn, and if Dn = -1, then PC + 2 → PC If Dn ≠ -1, then PC + d → PC; else PC + 2 → PC.
JMP (EA)	unsized	(EA) → PC This is an unconditional jump instruction which uses control addressing mode
JSR (EA)	unsized	PC → - (SP) (EA) → PC This is a subroutine call instruction which uses control addressing mode
RTR	unsized	(SP) + → CCR (SP) + → PC Return and restore condition codes
RTS	unsized	Return from subroutine (SP) + → PC
Scc (EA)	B	If cc is true, then the byte specified by (EA) is set to all ones; otherwise the byte is cleared to zero.

•(EA) in JMP and JSR can use all modes except Dn, An, (An)+, -(An), and immediate.
•(EA) in Scc can use all modes except An, relative, and immediate.

Now, as a specific example, consider BEQ * + \$20. If [PC] = 000200_{16}, then, after execution of this BEQ, program execution starts at 000220_{16} if Z = 1; if Z = 0, program execution continues at 000200_{16}. Note that * is used by some assemblers to indicate displacement.

- The instructions BRA and JMP are unconditional jump instructions. BRA uses the relative addressing mode, whereas JMP uses only control addressing modes. For example, consider BRA*

+ \$20. If [PC] = 000200_{16}, then, after execution of this BRA, program execution starts at 000220_{16}.

Now, consider JMP (A1). If [A1] = 00000220_{16}, then, after execution of this JMP, program execution starts at 000220_{16}.

- The instructions BSR and JSR are subroutine call instructions. BSR uses the relative mode, whereas JSR uses the control addressing mode. Consider the following program segment:

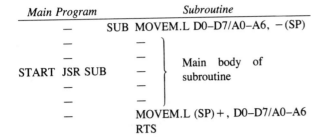

Main Program	Subroutine
—	SUB MOVEM.L D0–D7/A0–A6, –(SP)
—	—
—	—
START JSR SUB	— Main body of subroutine
—	—
—	—
—	MOVEM.L (SP)+, D0–D7/A0–A6
	RTS

Here, the JSR SUB instruction calls the subroutine called SUB. In response to JSR, the 68000 pushes the current PC contents called START onto the stack and loads the starting address SUB of the subroutine into PC. The first MOVEM in the SUB pushes all registers onto the stack and, after the subroutine is executed, the second MOVEM instruction pops all the registers back. Finally, RTS pops the address START from the stack into PC, and program control is returned to the main program. Note that BSR SUB could have been used instead of JSR SUB in the main program. In that case, the 68000 assembler would have considered the SUB with BSR as a displacement rather than as an address with the JSR instruction.

- DBcc Dn, d tests both the condition codes and the value in a data register. DBcc first checks if cc (NE, EQ, GT, etc.) is satisfied. If cc is satisfied, the next instruction is executed. If cc is not satisfied, the specified data register is decremented by 1. If $[Dn] = -1$, then the next instruction is executed. Finally, if $Dn \neq -1$, then branch to PC + d. For example, consider DBNE D5, *−4 with $[D5] = 00003002_{16}$ and $[PC] = 002006_{16}$. If $Z = 1$, then $[D5] = 00003001_{16}$. Since $[D5] \neq -1$, program execution starts at 002002_{16}.

  It should be pointed out that there is a false condition in the DBcc instruction and that this instruction is the DBF (some assemblers use DBRA for this). In this case, the condition is always false. This means that, after execution of this instruction, Dn is decremented by 1 and if $[Dn] = -1$, then the next instruction is executed. If $[Dn] \neq -1$, then branch to PC + d.

- Consider SPL (A5). If $[A5] = 00200020_{16}$ and $N = 0$, then, after execution of this SPL, memory location 200020_{16} will contain 11111111_2.

System Control Instructions The 68000 system control instructions include privileged instructions, trap and check instructions, and instructions that use or modify CCR. Note that the privileged instructions can be executed only in the supervisor mode. The system control instructions are listed in Table 6–14.

- The RESET instruction when executed in the su-

TABLE 6–14
68000 System Control Instructions

Instruction	Size	Operation
Privileged Instructions		
RESET	Unsized	If supervisory state, then assert reset line; else TRAP
RTE	Unsized	If supervisory state, then restore SR and PC; else TRAP
STOP # data	Unsized	If supervisory state, then load immediate data to SR and then STOP; else TRAP
ORI to SR MOVE USP ANDI to SR EORI to SR MOVE (EA) to SR		These instructions were discussed earlier
Trap and Check Instructions		
TRAP # vector	Unsized	PC → – (SSP) SR → – (SSP) Vector address → PC
TRAPV	Unsized	TRAP if V = 1
CHK (EA), Dn	W	If Dn < 0 or Dn > (EA), then TRAP
Status Register		
ANDI to CCR EORI to CCR MOVE (EA) to/from CCR ORI to CCR MOVE SR to (EA)		Already explained earlier

•(EA) in CHK can use all modes except An.

pervisor mode outputs a signal on the reset pin of the 68000 in order to initialize the external peripheral chips. The 68000 reset pin is bidirectional. The 68000 can be reset by asserting the reset pin using hardware, whereas the peripheral chips can be reset using the software RESET instruction.

- MOVE.L USP, (An) or MOVE.L (An), USP can be used to save, restore, or change the contents of USP in supervisor mode. The USP must be loaded in supervisor mode since MOVE USP is a privileged instruction.

- Consider TRAP # n. There are 16 TRAP instructions with n ranging from 0 to 15. The hexadecimal vector address is calculated using the following equation:

Hexadecimal vector address $= 80 + 4*n$

The TRAP instruction first pushes the contents of the PC and then the SR onto the system (user or supervisor) stack. The hexadecimal vector address is then loaded into PC. TRAP is basically a software interrupt.

One of the 16 trap instructions can be executed in the user mode to execute a supervisor program located at the specified trap routine. Using the TRAP instruction, control can be transferred to the supervisor mode from the user mode.

There are other traps that occur due to certain arithmetic errors. For example, division by zero automatically traps to location 14_{16}. On the other hand, an overflow condition, i.e., if V = 1, will trap to address $1C_{16}$ if the instruction TRAPV is executed.

- The CHK (EA), Dn instruction compares [Dn] with (EA). If $[Dn]_{low\ 16\ bits} < 0$ or if $[Dn]_{low\ 16\ bits} > (EA)$, then a trap to location 0018_{16} is generated. Also, N is set to 1 if $[Dn]_{low\ 16\ bits} < 0$, and N is reset to 0 if $[Dn]_{low\ 16\ bits} > (EA)$. (EA) is treated as a 16-bit 2's complement integer. Note that program execution continues if $[Dn]_{low\ 16\ bits}$ lies between 0 and (EA).

Consider CHK (A5), D2. If $[D2]_{low\ 16\ bits} = 0200_{16}$, $[A5] = 00003000_{16}$, and $[003000_{16}] = 0100_{16}$, then, after execution of this CHK, the 68000 will trap since $[D2] = 0200_{16}$ is greater than $[003000] = 0100_{16}$.

The purpose of the CHK instruction is to provide boundary checking by testing if the contents of a data register is in the range from zero to an upper limit. The upper limit used in the instruction can be set equal to the length of the array. Then, every time the array is accessed, the CHK instruction can be executed to make sure that the array bounds have not been violated.

The CHK instruction is usually placed following the computation of an index value to ensure that the index value is not violated. This permits a check of whether or not the address of an array being accessed is within the array boundaries when the address register indirect with index mode is used to access an array element. For example, the following instruction sequence permits accessing of an array with base address in A2 and array length of 50_{10} bytes:

```
—
—

—

CHK #49,D2
MOVE.B 0(A2,D2 · W),D3
—

—
```

In the above, if low 16 bits of D2 is greater than 49, the 68000 will trap to location 0018_{16}. It is assumed that D2 is computed prior to execution of the CHK instruction.

6–7 68000 STACK

The 68000 supports stacks with the address register indirect postincrement and predecrement addressing modes. In addition to SP, all seven address registers (A0–A6) can be used as stack pointers by using appropriate addressing modes. Subroutine calls, traps, and interrupts automatically use the system stack pointers: USP when S = 0 and SSP when S = 1. Subroutine calls push the PC onto the system stack, while RTS pops the PC from the stack. Traps and interrupts push both the PC and SR onto the system stack, while RTE pops the PC and SR from the stack.

These stack operations fill data from HIGH to LOW memory. This means that the system SP is decremented by 2 for word or 4 for long word after a push and incremented by 2 for word or 4 for long word after a pop. As an example, suppose that a 68000-CALL instruction (JSR or BSR) is executed when PC = $0031F200; then, after execution of the subroutine call, the stack will push the PC as follows:

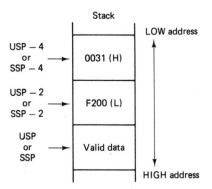

Note that the system SP always points to valid data.

Stacks can be created by the user by using address register indirect with postincrement or predecrement modes. Using one of the seven address registers (A0–A6), the user may create stacks that can be filled from either HIGH to LOW memory or vice versa:

1. Filling a stack from HIGH to LOW memory is implemented with predecrement mode for push and postincrement mode for pop.
2. Filling a stack from LOW to HIGH memory is implemented with postincrement for push and predecrement for pop.

For example, consider the following stack growing from HIGH to LOW memory addresses in which A5 is used as the stack pointer:

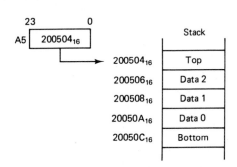

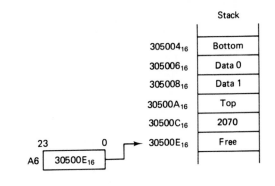

In order to push the 16-bit contents 0504_{16} of memory location 305016_{16}, the instruction MOVE.W $305016, $-(A5)$ can be used as follows:

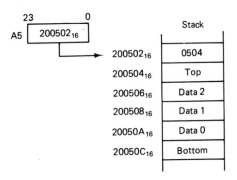

The 16-bit data 0504_{16} can be popped from the stack into the low 16 bits of D0 by using MOVE.W (A5)+, D0. A5 will contain 200504_{16} after the pop. Note that, in this case, the stack pointer A5 points to valid data.

Next, consider the stack growing from LOW to HIGH memory addresses in which A6 is used as the stack pointer:

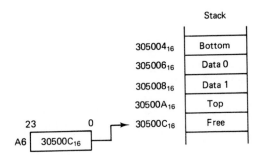

Now, in order to push the 16-bit contents 2070_{16} of the low 16 bits of D5, the instruction MOVE.W D5, (A6)+ can be used as follows at the top of next column.

The 16-bit data 2070_{16} can be popped from the stack into the 16-bit memory location 417024_{16} by using MOVE.W $-(A6), \$417024$. Note that, in this case, the stack pointer A6 points to the free location above the valid data.

Example 6-1

Determine the effect of each of the following 68000 instructions:

- CLR D0
- MOVE.L D1, D0
- CLR.L (A0)+
- MOVE $-(A0)$, D0
- MOVE 20(A0), D0
- MOVEQ.L #$D7, D0
- MOVE 21(A0, A1.L), D0

Assume the following initial configuration before each instruction is executed; also assume all numbers in hex:

$$(D0) = 22224444, (D1) = 55556666$$
$$(A0) = 00002224, (A1) = 00003333$$
$$(002220) = 8888, (002222) = 7777$$
$$(002224) = 6666, (002226) = 5555$$
$$(002238) = AAAA, (00556C) = FFFF$$

See Solution at top of page 186.

Example 6-2

Write a 68000 program segment that implements each of the following Pascal segments:
(a) If $X \geq Y$, then $X := X + 10$;
    else $Y := Y - 12$.

    . . .

    . . .

(b) SUM := 0; for $i := 0$ to 9, do
    SUM := SUM + A (i).

    . . .

    . . .

Assume the following information about the variables involved in this problem:

Variable	Comments
(a) X	Address of a 16-bit signed integer
Y	Address of a 16-bit signed integer
(b) A0	Address of the first element of unsigned integers, array of 10 elements
SUM	Address of the sum

Solution to Example 6—1

Instruction	Effective Address	Net Effect (Hex)
CLR D0	Destination EA = D0	D0 ← 22220000
MOVE.L D1, D0	Destination EA = D0	D0 ← 55556666
	Source EA = D1	
CLR.L (A0)+	Destination EA = (A0)	(002224) ← 0000
		(002226) ← 0000
		A0 ← 00002228
MOVE −(A0), D0	Source EA = (A0) − 2	A0 ← 00002222
	Destination EA = D0	D0 ← 22227777
MOVE 20(A0), D0	Source EA = (A0) + 20_{10}	D0 ← 2222AAAA
	(or 14_{16}) = 002238	
	Destination EA = D0	
MOVEQ.L #$D7, D0	Source data = $D7_{16}$	D0 ← FFFFFFD7
	Destination EA = D0	
MOVE 21 (A0, A1.L), D0	Source EA = (A0) + (A1) + 21_{10}	D0 ← 2222FFFF
	= 556C	
	Destination EA = D0	

Solution to Example 6—2

(a)
```
        LEA X, A0       ; Point A0 to X
        LEA Y, A1       ; Point A1 to Y
        MOVE (A0), D0   ; Move [X] into D0
        CMP (A1), D0    ; Compare [X] with [Y]
        BGE THPRT
        SUBI #12, (A1)  ; Execute else part
        BRA NEXT
THPRT   ADDI #10, (A0)  ; Execute then part
NEXT    . . .
```

(b)
```
        LEA SUM, A1     ; Point to SUM
        LEA Y, A0       ; Point A0 to Y [0]
        CLR D0          ; Clear the sum to zero
        MOVE #9, D1     ; Initialize D1 with loop
                        ;   limit
LOOP    ADD (A0)+, D0   ; Perform the iterative
        DBF D1, LOOP    ; Summation
        MOVE D0, (A1)   ; Transfer the result
        . . .
```

Note that condition F in DBF is always false and thus we exit from the loop only when the contents of register D1 becomes − 1. Therefore, we repeat the addition process for 10 times as desired.

Example 6–3

Write a 68000 assembly program to clear 100_{10} consecutive bytes.

Solution

```
        ORG $2000
        MOVEA.L #$3000, A0  ; Load A0 with $3000
        MOVE #99, D0        ; Move 99₁₀ into D0
```

```
LOOP    CLR.B (A0)+     ; Clear [3000₁₆] and
                        ; point to next address
        DBF D0, LOOP    ; decrement and
                        ;   branch
FINISH  JMP FINISH      ; Halt
```

Note that the 68000 has no halt instruction in the user mode. The 68000 has the STOP instruction in the supervisor mode. Therefore, the unconditional jump to same location such as JMP FINISH in this program must be used. Since DBF is a word instruction and considers D0's low 16-bit word as the loop count, one should be careful about initializing D0 using the MOVEQ.B.

Example 6–4

Write a 68000 assembly program to compute $\sum_{i=1}^{N} X_i Y_i$, where X_i and Y_i are signed 16-bit numbers and $N = 100$.

Solution

```
        ORG $1000
        MOVE #99, D0    ; Move 99₁₀ into D0
        LEA P, A0       ; Load address P into A0
        LEA Q, A1       ; Load address Q into A1
        CLR.L D1        ; Initialize D1 to zero
LOOP    MOVE (A0)+, D2  ; Move [X] to D2
        MULS (A1)+, D2  ; D2 ← [X] * [Y]
        ADD.L D2, D1    ; D1 ← ΣXᵢYᵢ
        DBF D0, LOOP    ; Decrement and branch
FINISH  JMP FINISH      ; Halt
```

Example 6–5

Write a 68000 subroutine to compute $Y = \sum_{i=1}^{N} X_i^2 / N$. Assume the X_i's are 16-bit signed integers and $N = 100$.

The numbers are stored in consecutive locations. Assume A0 points to the X_i's and SP is already initialized.

Solution

```
SQRE    MOVEM.L D2, D3/A0, -(SP)    ; Save registers
        CLR.L D1                    ; Clear sum
        MOVE #99, D2                ; Initialize loop
                                      count
LOOP    MOVE.W (A0)+, D3            ; Move X_i's into
                                      D3
        MULS D3, D3                 ; Compute X_i^2
        ADD.L D3, D1
        DBF D2, LOOP               ; Store X_i^2 into
                                      D1
        DIVS #100, D1              ; Compute ΣX_i^2/
                                      N
        MOVEM.L (SP)+, D2, D3/A0   ; Restore regis-
                                      ters
        RTS
```

Example 6–6

Write a 68000 assembly language program to move a block of data of length 100_{10} from the source block starting at location 002000_{16} to the destination block starting at location 003000_{16}.

Solution

```
        MOVEA.L #$2000, A4         ; Load A4 with
                                     source address
        MOVEA.L #$3000, A5         ; Load A5 with des-
                                     tination address
        MOVE #99, D0               ; Load D0 with
                                     count - 1 = 99_10
START   MOVE.W (A4)+, (A5)+        ; Move source data
                                     to destination
        DBF D0, START              ; Branch if
                                     D0 ≠ -1
END     JMP END                    ; Halt
```

6–8 68000 PINS AND SIGNALS

The 68000 is packaged in one of the following:

- 64-pin dual in-line package (DIP)
- 68-terminal chip carrier
- 68-pin quad pack
- 68-pin grid array (PGA)

Figure 6–7 shows the 68000 pin diagram for the DIP.

The 68000 is provided with two V_{CC} (+5 V) and two ground pins. Power is thus distributed in order to reduce noise problems at high frequencies. Also, in order to build a prototype to demonstrate that the paper design for the 68000-based microcomputer is correct, one must use either wire-wrap or solder for the actual construction. Prototype board must not be used because, at high fre-

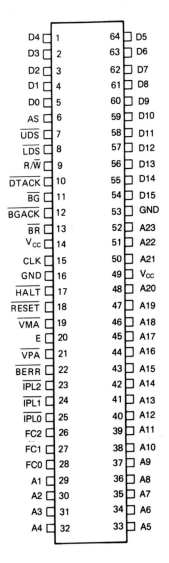

Figure 6–7 68000 pins and signals (Reprinted with permission of Motorola)

quencies above 4 MHz, there will be noise problems due to stray capacitances. The 68000 consumes about 1.5 W of power.

D0–D15 are the 16 data bus pins. All transfers to and from memory and I/O devices are conducted over the 16-bit data bus. A1–A23 are the 23 address lines. A0 is obtained by encoding the $\overline{UDS}$ (upper data strobe) and $\overline{LDS}$ (lower data strobe) lines.

The 68000 operates on a single-phase TTL-level clock at 6, 8, 10, 12.5, 16.67, or 25 MHz. The clock signal must be generated externally and applied to the 68000 clock input line. An external crystal oscillator chip is required to generate the clock.

Figure 6–8 shows the 68000 CLK waveform and clock timing specifications. The clock is at TTL-compatible voltage. The clock timing specifications provide data for three different clock frequencies: 8 MHz, 10 MHz, and 12.5 MHz.

The 68000 CLK input can be provided by a crystal

Characteristic	Symbol	8 MHz Min	8 MHz Max	10 MHz Min	10 MHz Max	12.5 MHz Min	12.5 MHz Max	Unit
Frequency of operation	f	4.0	8.0	4.0	10.0	4.0	12.5	MHz
Cycle time	t_{cyc}	125	250	100	250	80	250	ns
Clock pulse width	t_{CL} t_{CH}	55 55	125 125	45 45	125 125	35 35	125 125	ns
Rise and fall times	t_{Cr} t_{Cf}	— —	10 10	— —	10 10	— —	5 5	ns

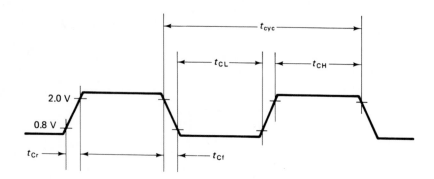

Figure 6–8 68000 clock input timing diagram and ac electrical specifications. (Reprinted with permission of Motorola)

oscillator or by designing an external circuit. Figure 6–9 shows a simple oscillator to generate the 68000 CLK input. This circuit uses two inverters connected in series. Inverter 1 is biased in its transition region by the resistor R. Inverter 1 inputs the crystal output (sinusoidal) to produce a logic pulse train at the output of inverter 1. Inverter 2 sharpens the wave and drives the crystal. For this circuit to work, HCMOS logic (74HC00, 74HC02, or 74HC04) must be used and a coupling capacitor should be connected across the supply terminals to reduce the ringing effect during high-frequency switching of the HCMOS devices. Additionally, the output of this oscillator is fed to the CLK input of a D flip-flop (74LS74) to further reduce the ringing. Hence, a clock signal of 50% duty cycle at a frequency of 1/2 the crystal frequency is generated.

The 68000 signals can be divided into five functional categories:

1. Synchronous and asynchronous control lines
2. System control lines
3. Interrupt control lines
4. DMA control lines
5. Status lines

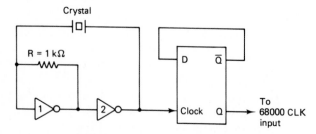

Figure 6–9 External clock circuitry

Synchronous and Asynchronous Control Lines The 68000 bus control is asynchronous. This means that once a bus cycle is initiated, the external device must send a signal back in order to complete it. The 68000 also contains three synchronous control lines that facilitate interfacing to synchronous peripheral devices such as Motorola's inexpensive MC6800 family.

Synchronous operation means that bus control is synchronized or clocked using a common system clock signal. In 6800 family peripherals, this common clock is a phase-two ($\varphi 2$) or an E clock signal depending on the particular chip used. With synchronous control, all READ and WRITE operations must be synchronized with the common clock. However, this may create problems when interfacing slow peripheral devices. This problem does not arise with asynchronous bus control.

Asynchronous operation is not dependent on a common clock signal. The 68000 utilizes the asynchronous control lines to transfer data between the 68000 and peripheral devices via handshaking. Using asynchronous operation, the 68000 can be interfaced to any peripheral chip regardless of the speed.

The 68000 has three control lines to transfer data over its bus in a synchronous manner: E (enable), $\overline{VPA}$ (valid peripheral address), and $\overline{VMA}$ (valid memory address). The E clock corresponds to the phase-two clock of the 6800. The E clock is outputted at a frequency that is 1/10 the 68000 input clock. $\overline{VPA}$ is an input and tells the 68000 that a 6800 device is being addressed and therefore data transfer must be synchronized with the E clock. $\overline{VMA}$ is the processor's response to $\overline{VPA}$. $\overline{VMA}$ is asserted when the memory address is valid. This also tells the external device that the next data transfer over the data bus will be synchronized with the E clock.

$\overline{VPA}$ can be generated by decoding the address pins and address strobe ($\overline{AS}$). Note that the 68000 asserts $\overline{AS}$ LOW when the address on the address bus is valid. $\overline{VMA}$ is typically used as the chip select of the 6800 peripherals. This ensures that the 6800 peripherals are selected and deselected at the correct time. The 6800 peripheral interfacing sequence is as follows:

1. The 68000 initiates a cycle by starting a normal read or write cycle.

2. The 6800 peripheral defines the 68000 cycle by asserting the 68000 $\overline{VPA}$ input. If $\overline{VPA}$ is asserted as soon as possible after assertion of $\overline{AS}$, then $\overline{VPA}$ will be recognized as being asserted on the falling edge of S4. If $\overline{VPA}$ is not asserted at the falling edge of S4, the 68000 inserts wait states until $\overline{VPA}$ is recognized by the 68000 as asserted. $\overline{DTACK}$ should not be asserted while $\overline{VPA}$ is asserted. The 6800 peripheral must remove $\overline{VPA}$ within 1 clock period after $\overline{AS}$ is negated.

3. The 68000 monitors enable (E) until it is LOW. The 68000 then synchronizes all READ and WRITE operations with the E clock. The $\overline{VMA}$ output pin is asserted LOW by the 68000.

4. The 6800 peripheral waits until E is active (HIGH) and then transfers the data.

5. The 68000 waits until E goes LOW (on a read cycle the data is latched as E goes LOW internally). The 68000 then negates $\overline{VMA}$, $\overline{AS}$, $\overline{UDS}$, and $\overline{LDS}$. The 68000 thus terminates the cycle and starts the next cycle.

The 68000 utilizes five lines to control address and data transfers asynchronously: $\overline{AS}$ (address strobe), R/$\overline{W}$ (read/write), $\overline{DTACK}$ (data acknowledge), $\overline{UDS}$ (upper data strobe), and $\overline{LDS}$ (lower data strobe).

The 68000 outputs $\overline{AS}$ to notify the peripheral device when data is to be transferred. $\overline{AS}$ is active LOW when the 68000 provides a valid address on the address bus. The R/$\overline{W}$ output line indicates whether the 68000 is reading data from or writing data into a peripheral device. R/$\overline{W}$ is HIGH for read and LOW for write. $\overline{DTACK}$ is used to tell the 68000 that a transfer is to be performed. When the 68000 wants to transfer data asynchronously, it first activates the $\overline{AS}$ line and, at the same time, the 68000 generates the required address on the address lines in order to select the peripheral device.

Since the $\overline{AS}$ line tells the peripheral chip when to transfer data, the $\overline{AS}$ line should be part of the address decoding scheme. After enabling $\overline{AS}$, the 68000 enters the wait state until it receives $\overline{DTACK}$ from the selected peripheral device. On receipt of $\overline{DTACK}$, the 68000 knows that the peripheral device is ready for data transfer. The 68000 then utilizes the R/$\overline{W}$ and data lines to transfer data. $\overline{UDS}$ and $\overline{LDS}$ are defined as follows:

$\overline{UDS}$	$\overline{LDS}$	Data Transfer Occurs Via:	Address
1	0	D0–D7 pins for byte	Odd
0	1	D8–D15 pins for byte	Even
1	1	D0–D15 pins for word or long word	Even

$\overline{UDS}$ and $\overline{LDS}$ are used to segment the memory into bytes instead of words. When $\overline{UDS}$ is asserted, contents of even addresses are transferred on the high-order eight lines of the data bus, D8–D15. The 68000 internally shifts this data to the low byte of the specified register. When $\overline{LDS}$ is asserted, contents of odd addresses are transferred on the low-order eight lines of the data bus, D0–D7. During word and long word transfers, both $\overline{UDS}$ and $\overline{LDS}$ are asserted and information is transferred on all 16 data lines, D0–D15. Note that during byte memory transfers, A0 corresponds to $\overline{UDS}$ for even addresses (A0 = 0) and to $\overline{LDS}$ for odd addresses (A0 = 1). The circuit in Figure 6–10 shows how even and odd addresses are interfaced to the 68000.

System Control Lines The 68000 has three control lines, namely, $\overline{BERR}$ (bus error), $\overline{HALT}$, and $\overline{RESET}$, that are used to control system-related functions.

$\overline{BERR}$ is an input to the 68000 and is used to inform the processor that there is a problem with the instruction cycle currently being executed. With asynchronous operation, this problem may arise if the 68000 does not receive $\overline{DTACK}$ from a peripheral device. An external timer can be used to activate the $\overline{BERR}$ pin if the external device does not send $\overline{DTACK}$ within a certain period of time. On receipt of $\overline{BERR}$, the 68000 does one of the following:

- Reruns the instruction cycle that caused the error.

- Executes an error service routine.

The troubled instruction cycle is rerun by the 68000 if it receives a $\overline{HALT}$ signal along with the $\overline{BERR}$ signal. On receipt of LOW on both the $\overline{HALT}$ and $\overline{BERR}$ pins, the 68000 completes the current instruction cycle and then goes into the high-impedance state. On removal of both $\overline{HALT}$ and $\overline{BERR}$ (that is, when both $\overline{HALT}$ and $\overline{BERR}$ are HIGH), the 68000 reruns the troubled instruction cycle. The cycle can be rerun repeatedly if both $\overline{BERR}$ and $\overline{HALT}$ are enabled/disabled continually.

On the other hand, an error service routine is executed only if the $\overline{BERR}$ signal is received without $\overline{HALT}$. In this case, the 68000 will branch to a bus error vector address where the user can write a service routine. If two simultaneous bus errors are received via the $\overline{BERR}$ pin without $\overline{HALT}$, the 68000 automatically goes into the halt state until it is reset.

The $\overline{HALT}$ line can also be used by itself to perform single-stepping or to provide $\overline{DMA}$. When the $\overline{HALT}$ input is activated, the 68000 completes the current in-

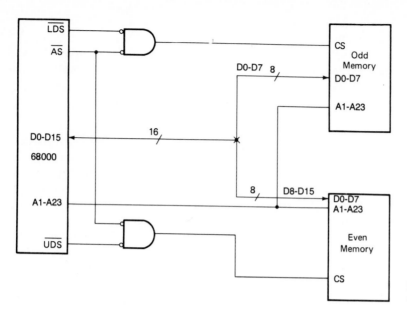

Figure 6–10 Interfacing of the 68000 to even and odd addresses

struction and goes into a high-impedance state until HALT is returned to HIGH. By enabling/disabling the HALT line continually, the single-stepping debugging can be accomplished. However, since most 68000 instructions consist of more than one clock cycle, single-stepping using HALT is not normally used. Rather, the trace bit in the status register is used to single-step the complete instruction.

One can also use HALT to perform microprocessor-halt DMA. Since the 68000 has separate DMA control lines, DMA using the HALT line will not normally be used.

The HALT pin can also be used as an output signal. The 68000 will assert the HALT pin LOW when it goes into a halt state as a result of a catastrophic failure. The double bus error (activation of BERR twice) is an example of this type of error. When this occurs, the 68000 goes into a high-impedance state until it is reset. The HALT line informs the peripheral devices of the catastrophic failure.

The RESET line of the 68000 is also bidirectional. In order to reset the 68000, both the RESET and HALT pins must be asserted for 10 clock cycles at the same time except when V_{cc} is initially applied to the 68000. In this case, an external reset must be applied for at least 100 ms. The 68000 executes a reset service routine automatically for loading the PC with the starting address of the program.

The 68000 RESET pin can also be used as an output line. A LOW can be sent to this output line by executing the RESET instruction in the supervisor mode in order to reset external devices connected to the 68000. Upon execution of the RESET instruction, the 68000 drives the RESET pin LOW for 124 clock periods and does not affect any data, address, or status register. Therefore, the RESET instruction can be placed anywhere in the program whenever the external devices need to be reset.

An RC circuit such as the simple RESET circuit shown in Figure 6–11 can be used for 68000 hardware reset. Upon hardware reset, the 68000 loads the supervisor stack pointer from locations $000000 (high 16 bits) and $000002 (low 16 bits) and loads the PC from $000004 (high 16 bits) and $000006 (low 16 bits). In addition, the 68000 clears the trace bit in SR to 0 and sets bits I2I1I0 in SR to 111. All other registers are unaffected.

The circuit in Figure 6–11 is similar to the 8085 RESET circuit except that the output goes to both RESET and HALT lines of the 68000. A more accurate RESET circuit for the 68000 is shown in Figure 6–12.

The Motorola MC1455 in Figure 6–12 is a timer chip that provides accurate time delays or oscillation. The timer is precisely controlled by external resistors and capacitors. The time may be triggered by an external trigger input (falling waveform) and can be reset by an external reset input (falling waveform). The RESET circuit in Figure 6–12 will assert the 68000 RESET pin for at least 10 clock cycles. From the MC1455 data sheet,

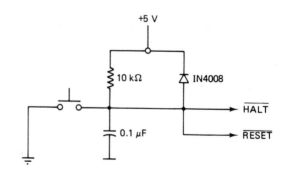

Figure 6–11 68000 RESET circuit (simple)

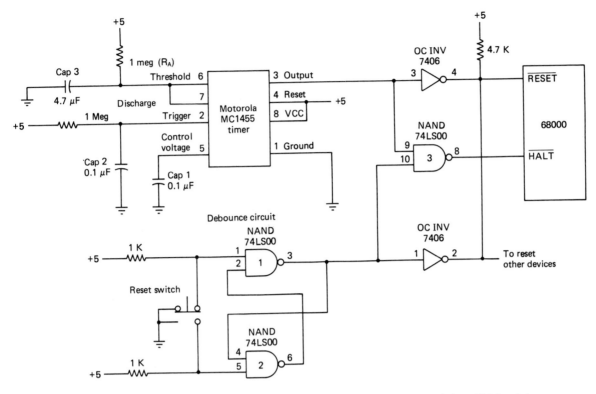

Figure 6–12 68000 $\overline{\text{RESET}}$ circuit (more accurate). (Reprinted by permission of Motorola)

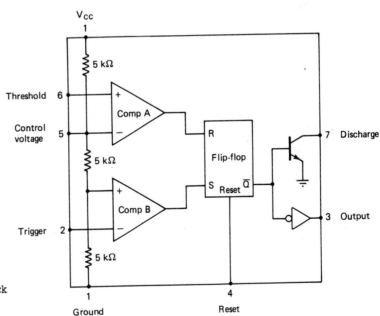

Figure 6–13 MC1455 internal block diagram. (Reprinted by permission of Motorola)

the internal block diagram of the MC1455 is as shown in Figure 6–13.

In Figure 6–13, when input voltage V_{CC} to trigger comparator falls below $1/3 V_{CC}$, comparator output triggers the flip-flop so that its output becomes LOW. This turns the capacitor discharge transistor OFF and drives the digital output ($\overline{Q}$) to the HIGH state. This condition permits the capacitor to charge at an exponential rate set

by the RC time constant. When the capacitor voltage reaches $2/3 V_{CC}$, the threshold comparator resets the flip-flop. The action discharges the timing capacitor and returns the digital output to the LOW state. The output will be HIGH for $t = 1.1R_A C$ s, where $R_A = 1$ MΩ and $C = 4.7$ μF.

The MC1455 can be connected so that it will trigger itself and the capacitor voltage will oscillate between

1/3 V_{CC} and 2/3 V_{CC}. Once the flip-flop has been triggered by an input signal, it cannot be retriggered until the present timing period has been completed. A reset pin is provided to discharge the capacitor, thus interrupting the timing cycle. The reset pin should be tied to V_{CC} when not in use. With proper trigger input as shown in Figure 6–12, the MC1455 output will stay HIGH for $1.1R_AC = 5.17$ s $(1.1 \times 10^6 \times 4.7 \times 10^{-6})$. The 68000 requires the $\overline{\text{RESET}}$ and $\overline{\text{HALT}}$ lines to be LOW for at least 10 cycles. If the 68000 clock cycle is 0.125 μs (8-MHz clock), then the 68000 $\overline{\text{RESET}}$ and $\overline{\text{HALT}}$ pins must be LOW for at least 0.125 μs $\times$ 10 = 1.25 μs. Since the MC1455 output is connected to the 68000 $\overline{\text{RESET}}$ pin through an inverter, the $\overline{\text{RESET}}$ pin will be held LOW for 5.17 s (greater than 1.25 μs). Hence, the timing requirement for the 68000 $\overline{\text{RESET}}$ pin is satisfied. The $\overline{\text{HALT}}$ pin is activated by NANDing the MC1455 true output and the debouncing circuit output. The $\overline{\text{HALT}}$ pin is LOW when both inputs to NAND gate 3 are HIGH. The MC1455 output is HIGH for 5.17 s and the output of the debounce circuit is HIGH when the push button is activated. This will generate a LOW at the $\overline{\text{HALT}}$ pin for 5.17 s (greater than 1.25 μs). The timing requirements of the 68000 $\overline{\text{RESET}}$ and $\overline{\text{HALT}}$ pins will be satisfied by the $\overline{\text{RESET}}$ circuit of Figure 6–12.

Note that when the $\overline{\text{RESET}}$ circuit is not activated, the top input of AND gate 1 is HIGH and the bottom input of AND gate 2 is LOW (HIGH is grounded to LOW, see Figure 6–12). Since a NAND gate always produces a HIGH output when one of the inputs is LOW, the output of NAND gate 2 will be HIGH. This will make the bottom input of NAND gate 1 HIGH, and thus the output of NAND gate 1 will be LOW, which in turn will make the output of NAND gate 3 HIGH. Therefore, the 68000 will not be reset when the push button is not activated. Upon activation of the push button, the top input of NAND gate 1 is LOW (HIGH is grounded to LOW); this will make the output of NAND gate 1 HIGH. Hence, both inputs of NAND gate 3 will be HIGH, thus

providing a LOW at the $\overline{\text{HALT}}$ pin for 5.17 s (greater than 1.25 μs).

Interrupt Control Lines $\overline{\text{IPL0}}$, $\overline{\text{IPL1}}$, and $\overline{\text{IPL2}}$ are the three interrupt control lines. These lines provide for seven interrupt priority levels ($\overline{\text{IPL2}}$, $\overline{\text{IPL1}}$, $\overline{\text{IPL0}}$ = 111 means no interrupt and $\overline{\text{IPL2}}$, $\overline{\text{IPL1}}$, $\overline{\text{IPL0}}$ = 000 means nonmaskable interrupt with the highest priority). The 68000 interrupts will be discussed later in this chapter.

DMA Control Lines The $\overline{\text{BR}}$ (bus request), $\overline{\text{BG}}$ (bus grant), and $\overline{\text{BGACK}}$ (bus grant acknowledge) lines are used for DMA purposes. The 68000 $\overline{\text{DMA}}$ will be discussed later in this chapter.

Status Lines The 68000 has the three output lines or function code pins FC2, FC1, and FC0. These lines tell external devices whether user data/program or supervisor data/program is being addressed. These lines can be decoded to provide user or supervisor programs/data and interrupt acknowledge as shown in Table 6–15.

The FC2, FC1, and FC0 pins can be used to partition memory into four functional areas: user data memory, user program memory, supervisor data memory, and supervisor program memory. Each memory partition can directly access up to 16 megabytes, and thus the 68000 can be made to directly address up to 64 megabytes of memory. This is shown in Figure 6–14.

TABLE 6–15
Function Code Lines (Courtesy of Motorola)

FC2	FC1	FC0	Operation
0	0	0	Unassigned
0	0	1	User data
0	1	0	User program
0	1	1	Unassigned
1	0	0	Unassigned
1	0	1	Supervisor data
1	1	0	Supervisor program
1	1	1	Interrupt acknowledge

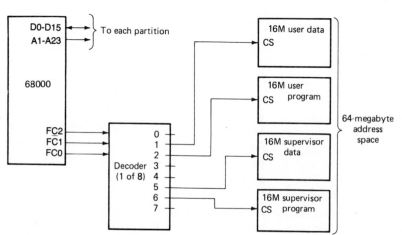

Figure 6–14 Partitioning 68000 address space using FC2, FC1, and FC0 pins

6–9 68000 READ AND WRITE CYCLE TIMING DIAGRAMS

The 68000 family of processors (68000, 68008, 68010, and 68012) uses a handshaking mechanism to transfer data between the processors and peripheral devices. This means that all these processors can transfer data asynchronously to and from peripherals of varying speeds.

Figure 6–15 shows 68000 read and write cycle timing diagrams. During the read cycle, the 68000 obtains data from a memory location or an I/O port. If the instruction specifies a word (such as MOVE.W $020504, D1) or a long word (such as MOVE.L $030808, D0), the 68000 reads both upper and lower bytes at the same time by asserting the $\overline{UDS}$ and $\overline{LDS}$ pins. When the instruction is for a byte operation, the 68000 utilizes an internal bit to find which byte to read and then outputs the data strobe required for that byte.

For byte operations, when the address is even (A0 = 0), the 68000 asserts $\overline{UDS}$ and reads data via the D8–D15 pins into the low byte of the specified data register. On the other hand, when the address is odd (A0 = 1), the 68000 outputs a LOW on $\overline{LDS}$ and reads data via the D0–D7 pins into the low byte of the specified data register. For example, consider MOVE.B $507144, D5. The 68000 outputs a LOW on $\overline{UDS}$ (since A0 = 0) and a HIGH on $\overline{LDS}$. The memory chip's eight data lines must be connected to the 68000 D8–D15 pins. The 68000 reads the data byte via the D8–D15 pins into the low byte of D5. Note that, for reading a data byte from an odd location by executing an instruction such as MOVE.B $507145, D5, the eight data lines of the memory chip must be connected to the 68000 D0–D7 pins. The 68000, in this case, outputs a LOW on $\overline{LDS}$ (since A0 = 1) and a HIGH on $\overline{UDS}$ and then reads the data byte into the low byte of D5.

Let us now discuss the read timing diagram of Figure 6–15. Consider Figure 6–15 for word read timing. During S0, address and data signals are in the high-impedance state. At the start of S1, the 68000 outputs the address on its address pins (A1–A23). During S0, the 68000 outputs FC2–FC0 signals. $\overline{AS}$ is asserted at the start of S2 to indicate a valid address on the bus. $\overline{AS}$ can be used at this point to latch the signals on the address pins. The 68000 asserts the $\overline{UDS}$ and $\overline{LDS}$ pins to indicate a READ operation. The 68000 now waits for the peripheral device to assert $\overline{DTACK}$. Upon placing data on the data bus, the peripheral device asserts $\overline{DTACK}$. The 68000 samples the $\overline{DTACK}$ signal at the end of S4. If $\overline{DTACK}$ is not asserted by the peripheral device, the processor automatically inserts a wait state(s) (W).

However, upon assertion of $\overline{DTACK}$, the 68000 negates the $\overline{AS}$, $\overline{UDS}$, and $\overline{LDS}$ signals and then latches the data from the data bus into an internal register at the end of the next cycle. Once the selected peripheral device senses that the 68000 has obtained data from the data bus (by recognizing the negation of $\overline{AS}$, $\overline{UDS}$, or $\overline{LDS}$), the peripheral device must negate $\overline{DTACK}$ immediately so that it does not interfere with the start of the next cycle.

If $\overline{DTACK}$ is not asserted by the peripheral at the end of S4 (Figure 6–15 SLOW READ), the 68000 inserts wait states. The 68000 outputs valid addresses on the address pins and keeps asserting $\overline{AS}$, $\overline{UDS}$, and $\overline{LDS}$ until the peripheral asserts $\overline{DTACK}$. The 68000 always inserts an even number of wait states if $\overline{DTACK}$ is not asserted by the peripheral since all 68000 operations are performed using the clock with two states per clock cycle. Note, in Figure 6–15, that the 68000 inserts 4 wait states or 2 cycles.

As an example of word read, consider that the 68000 is ready to execute the MOVE.W $602122, D0 instruction. The 68000 performs as follows:

1. The 68000, at the end of S0, places the upper 23 bits of the address 602122_{16} on A1–A23.

2. At the end of S1 state, the 68000 asserts $\overline{AS}$, $\overline{UDS}$, and $\overline{LDS}$.

3. The 68000 continues to output a HIGH on the R/$\overline{W}$ pin from the beginning of the read cycle to indicate a READ operation.

4. At the end of S0, the 68000 places appropriate outputs on the FC2–FC0 pins to indicate either supervisor or user read.

5. If the peripheral asserts $\overline{DTACK}$ at the end of S4, the 68000 reads the contents of 602122_{16} and 602123_{16} via the D8–D15 and D0–D7 pins, respectively, into the high and low bytes of D0 at the end of S6. If the peripheral does not assert $\overline{DTACK}$ at the end of S4, the 68000 continues to insert wait states.

6–10 68000 MEMORY INTERFACE

One of the advantages of the 68000 is that it can easily be interfaced to memory chips since it goes into a wait state if $\overline{DTACK}$ is not asserted by the memory devices at the end of S4. A simplified schematic showing an interface of a 68000 to two 2732's and two 6116's is shown in Figure 6–16. The 2732 is a 4K × 8 EPROM, and the 6116 is a 2K × 8 static RAM. For a 4-MHz clock, each cycle is 250 ns. The 68000 samples $\overline{DTACK}$ at the falling edge of S4 (third clock cycle) and latches data at the falling edge of S6 (fourth clock cycle). $\overline{AS}$ is used to assert $\overline{DTACK}$. $\overline{AS}$ goes to LOW after 500 ns (2 clock cycles). The time delay between $\overline{AS}$ going LOW and the falling edge of S6 is 500 ns. Note that $\overline{LDS}$ and $\overline{UDS}$ must be used as chip selects as in Figure 6–16. They must not be connected to A0 of the memory chips since, in that case, half of the memory in each chip would be wasted.

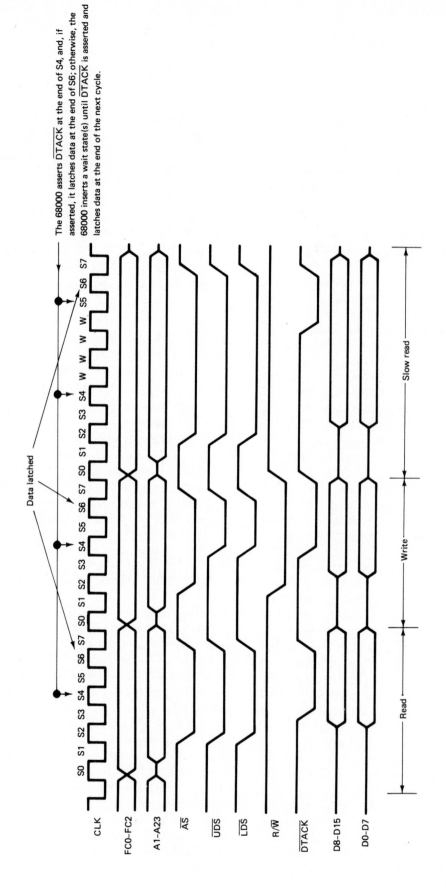

The 68000 asserts $\overline{\text{DTACK}}$ at the end of S4, and, if asserted, it latches data at the end of S6; otherwise, the 68000 inserts a wait state(s) until $\overline{\text{DTACK}}$ is asserted and latches data at the end of the next cycle.

Data latched

CLK

FC0–FC2

A1–A23

$\overline{\text{AS}}$

$\overline{\text{UDS}}$

$\overline{\text{LDS}}$

R/$\overline{\text{W}}$

$\overline{\text{DTACK}}$

D8–D15

D0–D7

Read   Write   Slow read

Figure 6–15 68000 interface to 2732/6116. (Reprinted by permission of Motorola)

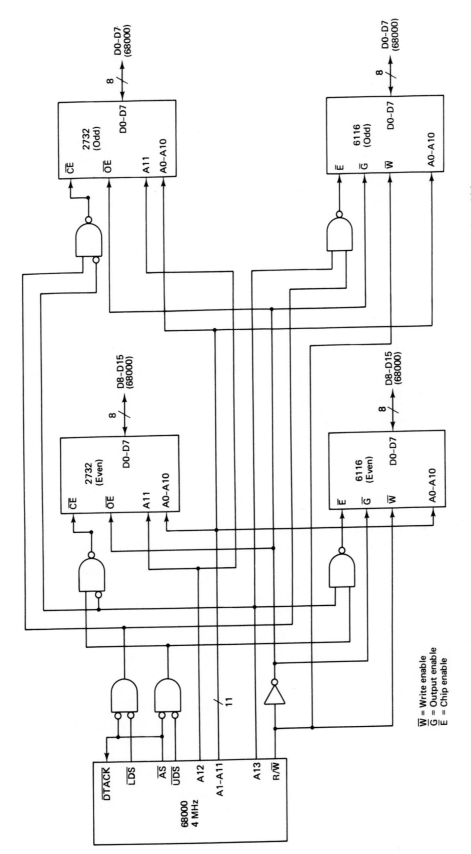

Figure 6–16 68000 read and write cycle timing diagrams. (Reprinted by permission of Motorola)

$\overline{W}$ = Write enable
$\overline{G}$ = Output enable
$\overline{E}$ = Chip enable

195

In Figure 6–16, a delay circuit for $\overline{\text{DTACK}}$ is not required since the 2732 and 6116 both place data on the bus lines before the 68000 samples $\overline{\text{DTACK}}$. This is due to the 68000 clock frequency of 4 MHz in this case, and thus $t_{cyc} = 250$ ns. The access times of the 2732 and 6116 are 450 ns and 120 ns, respectively. Since $\overline{\text{DTACK}}$ is sampled after 3 clock cycles (3×250 ns $= 750$ ns), both the 2732 and 6116 will have adequate time to place data on the bus for the 68000 to latch.

Consider the 68000–2732 timing parameters with various 68000 clock frequencies as follows:

Case	68000 Frequency	Clock Cycle (t_{cyc})	Time before First DTACK Is Sampled	Comment
1	6 MHz	166.7 ns	$3(166.7) = 500.1$ ns	No timing problems
2	8 MHz	125 ns	$3(125) = 375$ ns	No timing problems since 68000 latches data after 500 ns
3	10 MHz	100 ns	$3(100) = 300$ ns	Not enough time for 2732 to place data on bus; needs delay circuit
4	12.5 MHz	80 ns	$3(80) = 240$ ns	Same as case 3
5	16.67 MHz	60 ns	$3(60) = 180$ ns	Same as case 3
6	25 MHz	40 ns	$3(40) = 120$ ns	Same as case 3

In cases 3–6, delay circuits must be added to ensure that the 2732 has enough time to place data on the bus before the 68000 latches data. A ring counter using D flip-flops can be used as the delay circuit.

Let us now determine the memory maps. Assume the don't care values of A23–A14 to be 0's. Note that A13 = 0 selects the 2732 and deselects the 6116, while A13 = 1 deselects the 2732 and selects the 6116. Also, when the 6116 is accessed, A12 has a don't care value (assume 0). The memory maps are as follows:

• *2732 even*

A23 A22 . . . A14 A13 A12 A11 . . . A1 A0

| 0 | 0 . . . 0 | 0 | Connected to A11–A0 of 2732 | 0 |

Address range: $000000, $000002, . . . , $001FFE

• *2732 odd*

A23 A22 . . . A14 A13 A12 A11 . . . A1 A0

| 0 | 0 . . . 0 | 0 | Connected to A11–A0 of 2732 | 1 |

Address range: $000001, $000003, . . . , $001FFF

• *6116 even*

A23 A22 . . . A14 A13 A12 A11 A10 . . . A1 A0

| 0 | 0 . . . | 1 | 0 | Connected to A10–A0 of 6116 | 0 |

Address range: $002000, $002002, . . . , $002FFE

• *6116 odd*

A23 A22 . . . A14 A13 A12 A11 A10 . . . A1 A0

| 0 | 0 . . . 0 | 1 | 0 | Connected to A10–A0 of 6116 | 1 |

Address range: $002001, $002003, . . . , $002FFF

6–11   68000 SYSTEM DIAGRAM

Figure 6–17 shows a simplified version of the 68000 basic system diagram.

6–12   68000 I/O

In this section, I/O techniques associated with the Motorola 68000 are considered.

6–12–1   68000 Programmed I/O

As mentioned before, the 68000 uses memory-mapped I/O. Programmed I/O can be achieved in the 68000 in one of the following ways:

1. By interfacing the 68000 synchronously with 6800 peripherals such as the MC6821. Note that synchronous operation means that we have to synchronize every READ or WRITE operation with the clock.
2. By interfacing the 68000 asynchronously with its own family of peripheral devices such as the MC68230, parallel interface/timer chip.

It should be pointed out that 68000 peripherals are very expensive. Also, it is both sufficient and economical in most applications these days to use 6800 peripherals to perform 68000 programmed I/O. We first illustrate 68000 programmed I/O by interfacing it with the 6821.

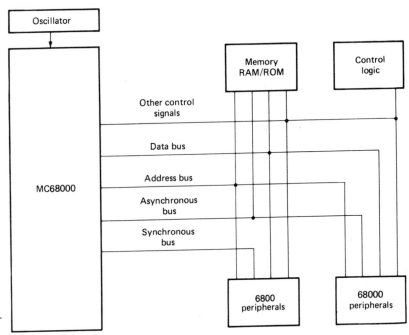

Figure 6-17 68000 basic system (Reprinted by permission of Motorola)

68000/6821 Interface The Motorola 6821 is a 40-pin peripheral interface adapter (PIA) chip. It is provided with an 8-bit bidirectional data bus (D0–D7), two register select lines (RS0, RS1), a read/write line (R/$\overline{W}$), a reset line ($\overline{RES}$), an enable line (E), two 8-bit I/O ports (PA0–PA7) and (PB0–PB7), and other pins.

There are six 6821 registers. These include two 8-bit ports (ports A and B), two data direction registers, and two control registers. Selection of these registers is controlled by the RS0 and RS1 inputs together with bit 2 of the control register. Table 6–16 shows how the registers are selected.

In Table 6–16, bit 2 in each control register (CRA-2 and CRB-2) determines selection of either an I/O port or the corresponding data direction register when the proper register select signals are applied to RS0 and RS1. A 1 in bit 2 allows access of I/O ports, while a 0 selects the data direction registers.

Each I/O port bit can be configured to act as an input or output. This is accomplished by setting a 1 in the corresponding data direction register bit for those bits that are to be output and a 0 for those bits that are to be inputs.

A $\overline{RESET}$ signal sets all PIA registers to 0. This has the effect of setting PA0–PA7 and PB0–PB7 as inputs.

There are three built-in signals in the 68000 that provide the interface with the 6821. These are the enable (E), valid memory address ($\overline{VMA}$), and valid peripheral address ($\overline{VPA}$).

The enable signal (E) is an output from the 68000. It corresponds to the E signal of the 6821. This signal is the clock used by the 6821 to synchronize data transfer.

TABLE 6-16
6821 Register Definition (Courtesy of Motorola)

| RS1 | RS0 | Control Register Bits 2 | | Register Selected |
		CRA-2	CRB-2	
0	0	1	X	I/O port A
0	0	0	X	Data direction register A
0	1	X	X	Control register A
1	0	X	1	I/O port B
1	0	X	0	Data direction register B
1	1	X	X	Control register B

X = Don't care

The frequency of the E signal is 1/10 the 68000 clock frequency. Therefore, this allows one to interface the 68000 (which operates much faster than the 6821) with the 6821. The valid memory address ($\overline{VMA}$) signal is outputted by the 68000 to indicate to the 6800 peripherals that there is a valid address on the address bus. The valid peripheral address ($\overline{VPA}$) is an input to the 68000. This signal is used to indicate that the device addressed by the 68000 is a 6800 peripheral. This tells the 68000 to synchronize data transfer with the enable signal (E).

Let us now discuss how the 68000 instructions can be used to configure the 6821 ports. As an example, bit 7 and bits 0–6 of port A can be configured, respectively, as input and outputs using the following instruction sequence:

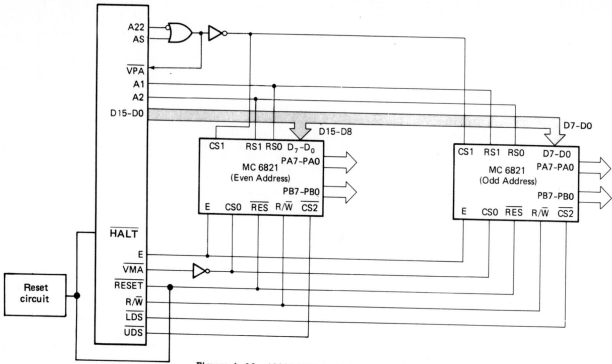

Figure 6-18 68000 I/O port block diagram

BCLR.B #$2, CRA   ; Address DDRA
MOVE.B #$7F, DDRA   ; Configure port A
BSET.B #$2, CRA   ; Address port A

Once the ports are configured to the designer's specification, the 6821 can be used to transfer data from an input device to the 68000 or from the 68000 to an output device by using the MOVE.B instruction as follows:

MOVE.B (EA), Dn   Transfer 8-bit data from an input port to the specified data register Dn.

MOVE.B Dn, (EA)   Transfer 8-bit data from the specified data register Dn to an output port.

Figure 6-18 shows a block diagram of how two 6821's are interfaced to the 68000 in order to generate four 8-bit I/O ports. Note that the least significant bit, A0, of the 68000 address pins is internally encoded to generate two signals, the upper data strobe ($\overline{\text{UDS}}$) and lower data strobe ($\overline{\text{LDS}}$). For byte transfers, $\overline{\text{UDS}}$ is asserted if an even-numbered byte is being transferred and $\overline{\text{LDS}}$ is asserted for an odd-numbered byte.

In Figure 6-18, I/O port addresses can be obtained as follows. When A22 = 1 and $\overline{\text{AS}}$ = 0, the OR gate output will be LOW. This OR gate output is used to provide $\overline{\text{VPA}}$. The inverted OR gate output, in turn, makes CS1 HIGH on both 6821's. Note that A22 is arbitrarily chosen. A22 is chosen to be HIGH to enable CS1 so that the addresses for the ports and the reset vector are not the same. Assuming that the don't care address lines A23 and A21–A3 are 0's, the addresses for the I/O ports, control registers, and data direction registers for the even 6821 (A0 = 0) can be obtained as seen at the bottom of the page.

Similarly, the addresses for the ports, control registers, and data direction registers for the odd 6821 (A0 = 1) can be determined as follows:

Port Name	Odd 6821 Address
Port A or DDRA	$400001
CRA	$400003
Port B or DDRB	$400005
CRB	$400007

Port Name	Even 6821 Address							
	A23	A22	A21	...	A3	A2	A1	A0
Port A or DDRA	0	1	0	...	0	0	0	0	= $400000
CRA	0	1	0	...	0	0	1	0	= $400002
Port B or DDRB	0	1	0	...	0	1	0	0	= $400004
CRB	0	1	0	...	0	1	1	0	= $400006

68000/68230 Interface The 48-pin parallel interfaces provided by the 68230 can be 8 or 16 bits wide with unidirectional or bidirectional modes. In the unidirectional mode, a data direction register configures each port as an input or output. In the bidirectional mode, the data direction registers are ignored and the direction is determined by the state of four handshake pins.

The 68230 allows use of interrupts and also provides a DMA request pin for connection to a DMA controller chip such as the MC68450. The timer contains a 24-bit-wide counter. This counter can be clocked by the output of a 5-bit (divide by 32) prescaler or by an external timer input pin (TIN).

The 68230 ports can be configured for various modes of operation. For example, consider ports A and B. Bits 6 and 7 of the port general control register, PGCR (R0), are used for configuring ports A and B in one of four modes as follows:

PGCR
Bits

7	6	Mode	
0	0	0	(unidirectional 8-bit)
0	1	1	(unidirectional 16-bit)
1	0	2	(bidirectional 8-bit)
1	1	3	(bidirectional 16-bit)

The other pins of the PGCR are defined for handshaking.

Modes 0 and 2 configure ports A and B as unidirectional or bidirectional 8-bit ports. Modes 1 and 3, on the other hand, combine ports A and B together to form a 16-bit unidirectional or bidirectional port. Ports configured as unidirectional 8-bit must be programmed further as submodes of operation using bits 7 and 6 of PACR (R6) and PBCR (R7) as follows:

Submode	Bit 7 of PACR or PBCR	Bit 6 of PACR or PBCR	Comment
00	0	0	Pin-definable double-buffered input or single-buffered output
01	0	1	Pin-definable double-buffered output or nonlatched input
1X	1	X	Bit I/O (pin-definable single-buffered output or nonlatched input)

Note that X means don't care. Nonlatched inputs are latched internally, but the bit values are not available at the port.

The submodes define the ports as parallel input ports, parallel output ports, or bit-configurable I/O ports. In addition to these, the submodes further define the ports as latched input ports, interrupt-driven ports, DMA ports, and ports with various I/O handshake operations. Table 6–17, lists some of the 68230 registers. Some of these registers are considered in detail in the following discussion.

Figure 6–19 shows a simplified schematic for the 68000/68230 interface. A23 is chosen to be HIGH to select the 68230 chips so that the port addresses are different from the 68000 reset vector addresses 000000_{16}–000006_{16}. The configuration in the figure will provide

TABLE 6–17
Some of the 68230 Registers

Register Select Bits					
RS5	RS4	RS3	RS2	RS1	Register Selected
0	0	0	0	0	PGCR, Port General Control Register (R0)
0	0	0	1	0	PADDR, Port A Data Direction Register (R2)
0	0	0	1	1	PBDDR, Port B Data Direction Register (R3)
0	0	1	0	0	PCDDR, Port C Data Direction Register (R4)
0	0	1	1	0	PACR, Port A Control Register (R6)
0	0	1	1	1	PBCR, Port B Control Register (R7)
0	1	0	0	0	PADR, Port A Data Register (R8)
0	1	0	0	1	PBDR, Port B Data Register (R9)
0	1	1	0	0	PCDR, Port C Data Register (R12)

Reprinted by permission of Motorola

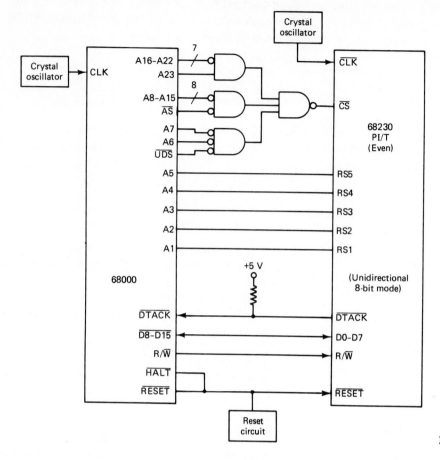

Figure 6-19 68000/68230 interface

even port addresses since $\overline{\text{UDS}}$ is used for enabling the 68230 $\overline{\text{CS}}$.

From the figure, addresses are for registers PGCR (R0), PADDR (R2), PBDDR (R3), PACR (R6), PBCR (R7), PADR (R8), and PBDR (R9). Consider PGCR at bottom of page.

Similarly,

Address	for	PADDR	= $800004
Address	for	PBDDR	= $800006
Address	for	PACR	= $80000C
Address	for	PBCR	= $80000E
Address	for	PADR	= $800010
Address	for	PBDR	= $800012

As an example, the following instruction sequence will select mode 0, submode 1X and configure bits 0–5 as outputs, bits 6 and 7 as inputs, and port B as an input port:

```
PGCR    EQU $800000
PADDR   EQU $800004
```

PBDDR   EQU $800006
PACR   EQU $80000C
PBCR   EQU $80000E
```
        MOVE.B #$00, PGCR    ; Select mode 0
        MOVE.B #$FF, PACR    ; Port A bit I/O sub-
                               mode
        MOVE.B #$FF, PBCR    ; Port B bit I/O sub-
                               mode
        MOVE.B #$3F, PADDR   ; Configure port A
                               bits 0–5 as outputs
                               and bits 6, 7 as in-
                               puts
        MOVE.B #$00, PBDDR   ; Configure port B
                               as an input port
```

Example 6-7

A 68000/68230-based microcomputer is required to drive an LED connected at bit 7 of port A based on two switch inputs connected at bits 0 and 1 of port B. If both switches are either HIGH or LOW, turn the LED ON; otherwise,

A23	A22	A21	A20	. . .	A6	A5	A4	A3	A2	A1	A0	
1	0	0	0	. . .	0	0	0	0	0	0	0	= $800000

RS5–RS1 span A5–A1; $\overline{\text{UDS}}$ points to A0

turn it OFF. Assume that a HIGH will turn the LED ON and a LOW will turn it OFF. Write a 68000 assembly program to accomplish this.

Solution

```
           MOVE.B #0, PGCR     ;  Select mode 0
           MOVE.B #$0FF, PACR  ;  Port A bit I/O sub-
                                  mode
           MOVE.B #$0FF, PBCR  ;  Port B bit I/O sub-
                                  mode
           MOVE.B #$80, PADDR  ;  Configure port A bit
                                  7 as output
           MOVE.B #0, PBDDR    ;  Configure port B as
                                  input
           MOVE.B Port B, D0   ;  Input port B
           ANDI.B #$0C0, D0    ;  Retain bits 6 and 7
           BEQ LEDON           ;  If both switches
                                  LOW, turn LED ON
           CMPI.B #$0C0, D0    ;  If both switches
                                  HIGH, turn LED
                                  ON
           MOVE.B #$00, Port A ;  Turn LED OFF
           JMP STOP
LEDON      MOVE.B #$80, Port A ;  Turn LED ON
STOP       JMP STOP
```

6-12-2 68000 Interrupt System

The 68000 interrupt I/O can be divided into two types: external interrupts and internal interrupts.

External Interrupts The 68000 provides seven levels of external interrupts, 0 through 7. The external hardware provides an interrupt level using the pins $\overline{IPL0}$, $\overline{IPL1}$, $\overline{IPL2}$. Like other microprocessors, the 68000 checks for and accepts interrupts only between instructions. It compares the value of inverted $\overline{IPL0}$–$\overline{IPL2}$ with the current interrupt mask contained in the bits 10, 9, and 8 of the status register.

If the value of the "inverted" $\overline{IPL0}$–$\overline{IPL2}$ is greater than the value of the current interrupt mask, then the CPU acknowledges the interrupt and initiates interrupt processing. Otherwise, the CPU continues with the current interrupt. Interrupt request level 0 ($\overline{IPL0}$–$\overline{IPL2}$ all HIGH) indicates that no interrupt service is requested. An inverted $\overline{IPL2}$, $\overline{IPL1}$, $\overline{IPL0}$ of 7 is always acknowledged. Therefore, interrupt level 7 is "nonmaskable." Note that the interrupt level is indicated by the interrupt mask bits (inverted $\overline{IPL2}$, $\overline{IPL1}$, $\overline{IPL0}$).

To ensure that an interrupt will be recognized, the following interrupting rules should be considered:

1. The incoming interrupt request level must be at a higher priority level than the mask level set in the interrupt mask bits (except for level 7, which is always recognized).

2. The $\overline{IPL2}$–$\overline{IPL0}$ pins must be held at the interrupt request level until the 68000 acknowledges the interrupt by initiating an interrupt acknowledge ($\overline{IACK}$) bus cycle.

Interrupt level 7 is edge-triggered. On the other hand, interrupt levels 1–6 are level-sensitive. But as soon as one of them is acknowledged, the processor updates its interrupt mask at the same level.

The 68000 does not have any EI (enable interrupt) or DI (disable interrupt) instructions. Instead, the level indicated by I2I1I0 in the SR disables all interrupts below or equal to this value and enables all interrupts above this. For example, if I2I1I0 = 100, then interrupt levels 1–4 are disabled and 5–7 are enabled. Note that I2I1I0 = 000 enables all interrupts and I2I1I0 = 111 disables all interrupts.

Once the 68000 has decided to acknowledge an interrupt, it performs several steps:

1. Makes an internal copy of the current status register.
2. Updates the priority mask and address lines A3–A1 with the level of the interrupt recognized (inverted $\overline{IPL}$ pins) and then asserts $\overline{AS}$ to inform the external devices that A1–A3 has the interrupt level.
3. Enters the supervisor state by setting the S bit in SR to 1.
4. Clears the T bit in SR to inhibit tracing.
5. Pushes the program counter (PC) onto the system stack.
6. Pushes the internal copy of the old SR onto the system stack.
7. Runs an $\overline{IACK}$ bus cycle for vector number acquisition (to provide the address of the service routine).
8. Multiplies the 8-bit interrupt vector by 4. This points to the location that contains the starting address of the interrupt service routine.
9. Jumps to the interrupt service routine.
10. The last instruction of the service routine should be RTE, which restores the original status word and program counter by popping them from the stack.

External logic can respond to the interrupt acknowledge in one of three ways: by requesting automatic vectoring (autovector), by placing a vector number on the data bus (nonautovector), or by indicating that no device is responding (spurious interrupt).

Autovector If the hardware asserts $\overline{VPA}$ to terminate the $\overline{IACK}$ bus cycle, the 68000 directs itself automatically to the proper interrupt vector corresponding to the current interrupt level. No external hardware is required for providing the interrupt address vector.

		I2	I1	I0
Level 1 ← Interrupt vector $19 for		0	0	1
Level 2 ← Interrupt vector $1A for		0	1	0
Level 3 ← Interrupt vector $1B for		0	1	1
Level 4 ← Interrupt vector $1C for		1	0	0
Level 5 ← Interrupt vector $1D for		1	0	1
Level 6 ← Interrupt vector $1E for		1	1	0
Level 7 ← Interrupt vector $1F for		1	1	1

Nonautovector The interrupting device uses external hardware to place a vector number on data lines D0–D7 and then performs a $\overline{\text{DTACK}}$ handshake to terminate the $\overline{\text{IACK}}$ bus cycle. The vector numbers allowed are $40 to $FF, but Motorola has not implemented a protection on the first 64 entries so that user-interrupt vectors may overlap at the discretion of the system designer.

Spurious Interrupt Another way to terminate an interrupt acknowledge bus cycle is with the $\overline{\text{BERR}}$ (bus error) signal. Even though the interrupt control pins are synchronized to enhance noise immunity, it is possible that external system interrupt circuitry may initiate an $\overline{\text{IACK}}$ bus cycle as a result of noise. Since no device is requesting interrupt service, neither $\overline{\text{DTACK}}$ nor $\overline{\text{VPA}}$ will be asserted to signal the end of the nonexisting $\overline{\text{IACK}}$ bus cycle. When there is no response to an $\overline{\text{IACK}}$ bus cycle after a specified period of time (monitored by the user using an external timer), $\overline{\text{BERR}}$ can be asserted by an external timer. This indicates to the processor that it has recognized a spurious interrupt. The 68000 provides 18H as the vector to fetch for the starting address of this exception-handling routine.

Then, from the vector *n* provided by the above, the 68000 reads the long word located at memory 4*n. This long word is the address of the service routine. We see that the address is found using indirect addressing.

It should be pointed out that the spurious interrupt and bus error interrupt due to troubled instruction cycle (when no $\overline{\text{DTACK}}$ is received by the 68000) have two different interrupt vectors. Spurious interrupt occurs when the $\overline{\text{BERR}}$ pin is asserted during interrupt processing.

Internal Interrupts The internal interrupt is a software interrupt. This interrupt is generated when the 68000 executes a software interrupt instruction (TRAP) or by some undesirable events such as division by zero or execution of an illegal instruction.

68000 Interrupt Map Figure 6–20 shows an interrupt map of the 68000. Vector addresses $00 through $2E (not shown in the figure) include vector addresses for reset, bus error, trace, divide by 0, etc., and addresses $30 through $5C are unassigned. The RESET vector requires four words (addresses 0, 2, 4, and 6), while the other vectors require only two words. After hardware reset, the 68000 loads the supervisor SP high and low words, respectively, from addresses 000000_{16} and

Vector Address		Vector Number
$60, $62	Spurious interrupt	$18
$64, $66	Autovector 1	$19
$68, $6A	Autovector 2	$1A
$6C, $6E	Autovector 3	$1B
$70, $72	Autovector 4	$1C
$74, $76	Autovector 5	$1D
$78, $7A	Autovector 6	$1E
$7C, $7E	Autovector 7	$1F
$80 to $BC	TRAP instructions	$20 to $2F
$C0 to $FC	Unassigned	$30 to $3F
$100 to $3FC	User interrupts (nonautovector)	$40 to $FF

Figure 6–20 68000 interrupt map

000002_{16}, and the PC high and low words, respectively, from 000004_{16} and 000006_{16}. The typical assembler directive DC (define constant) can be used to load the PC and SSP. For example, the following will load SSP with $16F128 and PC with $781624:

```
ORG     $000000
DC.L    $0016F128
DC.L    $00781624
```

68000 Interrupt Address Vector   Suppose that the user decides to write a service routine starting at location $123456 using autovector 1. Since the autovector 1 address is $000064 and $000066, the numbers $0012 and $3456 must be stored in locations $000064 and $000066, respectively.

An Example of Autovector and Nonautovector Interrupts   As an example to illustrate the concept of autovector and nonautovector interrupts, consider Figure 6–21. In this figure, I/O device 1 uses nonautovector and I/O device 2 uses autovector interrupts. The system is capable of handling interrupts from eight devices since an 8-to-3 priority encoder such as the 74LS148 is used.

Suppose that I/O device 2 drives $\overline{I/O2}$ LOW in order to activate line 3 of this encoder. This, in turn, interrupts the processor. When the 68000 decides to acknowledge the interrupt, it drives FC0–FC2 HIGH. The interrupt level is reflected on A1–A3 when $\overline{AS}$ is activated by the 68000. The $\overline{IACK3}$ and $\overline{I/O2}$ signals are used to generate $\overline{VPA}$. Once $\overline{VPA}$ is asserted, the 68000 obtains the interrupt vector address using autovectoring.

In the case of $\overline{I/O1}$, line 5 of the priority encoder is activated to initiate the interrupt. By using appropriate logic, $\overline{DTACK}$ is asserted using $\overline{IACK5}$ and $\overline{I/O1}$. The vector number is placed on D0–D7 by enabling an octal buffer such as the 74LS244 using $\overline{IACK5}$. The 68000 inputs this vector number and multiplies it by 4 to obtain the interrupt address vector.

Interfacing a Typical A/D Converter to the 68000 Using Autovector and Nonautovector Interrupts   Figure 6–22 shows the interfacing of a typical A/D converter to the 68000-based microcomputer using the autovector interrupt. In the figure, the A/D converter can be started by sending a START pulse. The $\overline{BUSY}$ signal can be connected to line 4 (for example) of the encoder. Note that line 4 is 100_2 for $\overline{IPL2}$, $\overline{IPL1}$, $\overline{IPL0}$, which is a level 3 (inverted 100_2) interrupt. $\overline{BUSY}$ can be used to assert $\overline{VPA}$ so that, after acknowledgment of the interrupt, the 68000 will service the interrupt as a level 3 autovector interrupt. Note that the encoder in Figure 6–22 is used for illustrative purposes. This encoder is not required for a single device such as the A/D converter in the example.

Figure 6–23 shows the interfacing of a typical A/D converter to the 68000-based microcomputer using the nonautovector interrupt. In the figure, the 68000 starts the A/D converter as before. Also, the $\overline{BUSY}$ signal is used to interrupt the microcomputer using line 5 ($\overline{IPL2}$, $\overline{IPL1}$, $\overline{IPL0}$ = 101, which is a level 2 interrupt) of the encoder. $\overline{BUSY}$ can be used to assert $\overline{DTACK}$ so that, after acknowledgment of the interrupt, FC2, FC1, FC0

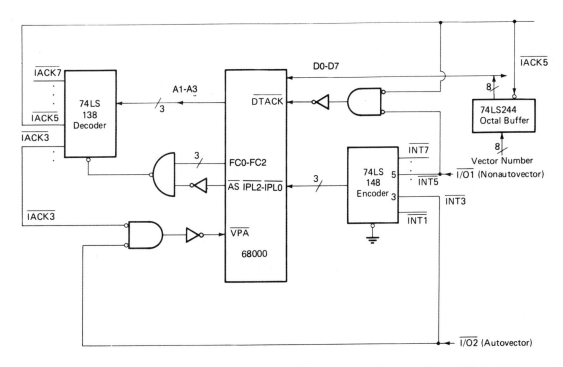

Figure 6–21   Autovector and nonautovector interrupts (Reprinted by permission of Motorola)

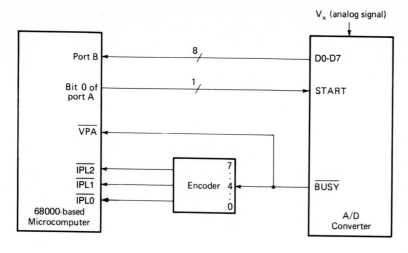

Figure 6-22 Interfacing of a typical 8-Bit A/D converter to 68000-based microcomputer using auto-vector interrupt

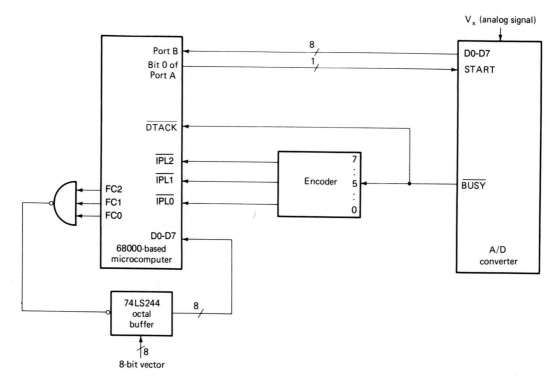

Figure 6-23 Interfacing of a typical 8-Bit A/D converter to 68000-based microcomputer using nonautovector interrupt

will become 111_2, which can be ANDed and inverted to enable an octal buffer such as the 74LS244 in order to transfer an 8-bit vector from the input of the buffer to the D0–D7 lines of the 68000. The 68000 can then multiply this vector by 4 to determine the interrupt address vector. As before, the encoder in Figure 6–23 is not required for the single A/D converter.

6–12–3 68000 DMA

Three DMA control lines are provided with the 68000. These are $\overline{BR}$ (bus request), $\overline{BG}$ (bus grant), and $\overline{BGACK}$ (bus grant acknowledge).

The $\overline{BR}$ line is an input to the 68000. The external device activates this line to tell the 68000 to release the system bus.

At least 1 clock period after receiving $\overline{BR}$, the 68000 will enable its $\overline{BG}$ output line to acknowledge the DMA request. However, the 68000 will not relinquish the bus until it has completed the current instruction cycle. The external device must check the $\overline{AS}$ (address strobe) line to determine the completion of the instruction cycle by the 68000. When $\overline{AS}$ becomes HIGH, the 68000 will tristate its address and date lines and will give up the bus to the external device.

After taking over the bus, the external device must

enable the $\overline{BGACK}$ line. The $\overline{BGACK}$ line tells the 68000 and other devices connected to the bus that the bus is being used. The 68000 stays in a tristate condition until $\overline{BGACK}$ becomes HIGH.

6–12–4 68000 Exception Handling

A 16-bit microcomputer is usually capable of handling unusual or exceptional conditions. These conditions include situations such as execution of illegal instruction or division by zero. In this section, the exception-handling capabilities of the 68000 are described.

The 68000 exceptions can be divided into three groups, namely, groups 0, 1, and 2. Group 0 has the highest priority, and group 2 has the lowest priority. Within each group, there are additional priority levels. A list of 68000 exceptions along with individual priorities is as follows:

Group 0   Reset (highest level in this group), address error (next level), and bus error (lowest level)

Group 1   Trace (highest level), interrupt (next level), illegal OP code (next level), and privilege violation (lowest level)

Group 2   TRAP, TRAPV, CHK, and ZERO DIVIDE (no individual priorities assigned in group 2)

Exceptions from group 0 always override an active exception from group 1 or group 2.

Group 0 exception processing begins at the completion of the current bus cycle (2 clock cycles). Note that the number of cycles required for a READ or WRITE operation is called a *bus cycle*. This means that during an instruction fetch if there is a group 0 interrupt, the 68000 will complete the instruction fetch and then service the interrupt.

Group 1 exception processing begins at the completion of the current instruction.

Group 2 exceptions are initiated through execution of an instruction. Therefore, there are no individual priority levels within group 2. Exception processing occurs when a group 2 interrupt is encountered, provided there are no group 0 or group 1 interrupts.

When an exception occurs, the 68000 saves the contents of the program counter and status register onto the stack and then executes a new program whose address is provided by the exception vectors. Once this program is executed, the 68000 returns to the main program using the stored values of program counter and status register.

Exceptions can be of two types: internal or external. The internal exceptions are generated by situations such as division by zero, execution of illegal or unimplemented instructions, and address error. As mentioned before, internal interrupts are called *traps*. The external exceptions are generated by bus error, reset, or interrupts. The basic concepts associated with interrupts relating them

to the 68000 have already been described. In this section, we will discuss the other exceptions.

In response to an exceptional condition, the processor executes a user-written program. In some microcomputers, one common program is provided for all exceptions. The beginning section of the program determines the cause of the exception and then branches to the appropriate routine. The 68000 utilizes a more general approach. Each exception can be handled by a separate program.

As mentioned before, the 68000 has two modes of operation: user state and supervisor state. The operating system runs in supervisor mode, and all other programs are executed in user mode. The supervisor state is, therefore, more privileged. Several privileged instructions such as MOVE to SR can be executed only in supervisor mode. Any attempt to execute them causes a trap.

We will now discuss how the 68000 handles exceptions caused by external reset, instructions causing traps, bus and address errors, tracing, execution of privileged instructions in user mode, and execution of illegal/unimplemented instructions.

- The reset exception is generated externally. In response to this exception, the 68000 automatically loads the initial starting address into the processor.

- The 68000 has a TRAP instruction, which always causes an exception. The operand for this instruction varies from 0 to 15. This means that there are 16 TRAP instructions. Each TRAP instruction has an exception vector. TRAP instructions are normally used to call subroutines in an operating system. Note that this automatically places the 68000 in supervisor state. TRAPs can also be used for inserting breakpoints in a program. Two other 68000 instructions cause traps if a particular condition is true. These are TRAPV and CHK. TRAPV generates an exception if the overflow flag is set. The TRAPV instruction can be inserted after every arithmetic operation in a program for causing a trap whenever there is the possibility of an overflow. A routine can be written at the vector address for the TRAPV to indicate to the user that an overflow has occurred. The CHK instruction is designed to ensure that access to an array in memory is within the range specified by the user. If there is a violation of this range, the 68000 generates an exception.

- A bus error occurs when the 68000 tries to access an address that does not belong to the devices connected to the bus. This error can be detected by asserting the $\overline{BERR}$ pin on the 68000 chip by an external timer when no $\overline{DTACK}$ is received from the device after a certain period of time. In response to this, the 68000 executes a user-written routine located at an address obtained from the exception vectors. An address error, on the other hand, occurs

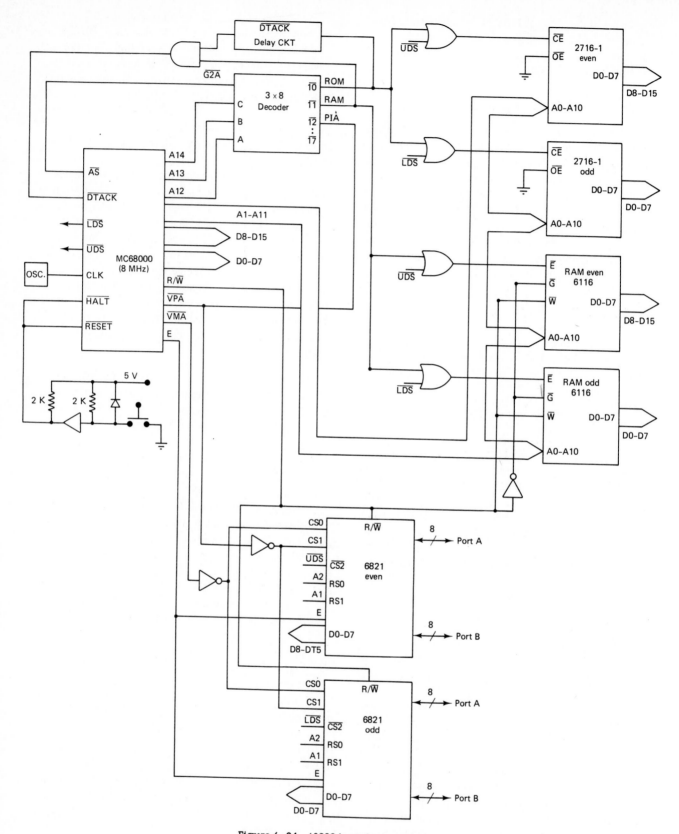

Figure 6–24 68000-based microcomputer

when the 68000 tries to read or write a word (16-bit) or long word (32-bit) in an odd address. This address error has a different exception vector from the bus error.

- The trace exception in the 68000 can be generated by setting the trace bit in the status register. In response to the trace exception, the 68000 causes an internal exception after execution of every instruction. The user can write a routine at the exception vectors for the trace instructiton to display registers and memory. The trace exception provides the 68000 with the single-stepping debugging feature.

- As mentioned before, the 68000 has privileged instructions, which must be executed in supervisor mode. An attempt to execute these instructions causes privilege violation.

- Finally, the 68000 causes an exception when it tries to execute an illegal or unimplemented instruction.

6–13   68000/2716/6116/6821-BASED MICROCOMPUTER

Figure 6–24 shows the schematic of a 68000-based microcomputer with a 4K EPROM, a 4K static RAM, and four 8-bit I/O ports. Let us explain the various sections of the hardware schematic.

Two 2716-1 and two 6116 chips are required to obtain the 4K EPROM and 4K RAM. The $\overline{LDS}$ and $\overline{UDS}$ pins are ORed with the memory select signal to enable the chip selects for the EPROMs and the RAMs.

Address decoding is accomplished by using a 3×8 decoder. The decoder enables the memory of the I/O chips depending on the status of address lines A12–A14 and the $\overline{AS}$ line of the 68000. $\overline{AS}$ is used to enable the decoder. $\overline{I0}$ selects the EPROMs, $\overline{I1}$ selects the RAMs, and $\overline{I2}$ selects the I/O ports.

When addressing memory chips, the $\overline{DTACK}$ input of the 68000 must be asserted for data acknowledge. The 68000 clock in the hardware schematic is 8 MHz. Therefore, each clock cycle is 125 ns. In Figure 6–25, $\overline{AS}$ is used to enable the 3×8 decoder. The outputs of the decoder are gated to assert 68000 $\overline{DTACK}$. This means that $\overline{AS}$ is indirectly used to assert $\overline{DTACK}$. From the 68000 read timing diagram of Figure 6–15, $\overline{AS}$ goes to LOW after approximately 2 cycles (250 ns for the 8-MHz clock) from the beginning of the bus cycle. With no wait states, the 68000 samples $\overline{DTACK}$ at the falling edge of S4 (375 ns), and, if recognized, the 68000 latches data at the falling edge of S6 (500 ns). If $\overline{DTACK}$ is not recognized at the falling edge of S4, the 68000 inserts a 1-cycle (125 ns in this case) wait state, samples $\overline{DTACK}$ at the end of S6, and, if recognized, latches data at the end of S8 (625 ns); and the process continues. Since the

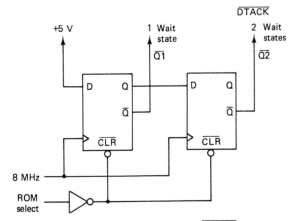

Figure 6–25   Delay circuit for $\overline{DTACK}$

access time of the 2716-1 is 350 ns, $\overline{DTACK}$ recognition by the 68000 at the falling edge of S6 (500 ns) and, hence, latching of data at the falling edge of S8 (625 ns) will satisfy the timing requirement. This means that the decoder output $\overline{I0}$ for ROM select must go LOW at the end of S6. Therefore, $\overline{DTACK}$ must be delayed by 250 ns, i.e., 2 cycles (S2 through S6).

A delay circuit, as shown in Figure 6–25, is designed using a 74LS175 D flip-flop. ROM select activates the delay circuit. The input is then shifted right 2 bits to obtain a 2-cycle wait state to allow sufficient time for data transfer. $\overline{DTACK}$ assertion and recognition are delayed by 2 cycles during data transfer with EPROMs.

When ROM is not selected by the decoder, then the clear ($\overline{CLR}$) pin is asserted (output of the inverter). Q is forced LOW, and $\overline{Q}$ is HIGH; therefore, $\overline{DTACK}$ is not asserted. When the processor is addressing the ROMs, then the output of the inverter is HIGH and the clear pin is not asserted. Now, the D flip-flop will accept a HIGH at the input, Q will output HIGH, and $\overline{Q}$ will output LOW. Now that $\overline{Q}$ is LOW, it can assert $\overline{DTACK}$. $\overline{Q1}$ will provide one wait state, and $\overline{Q2}$ will provide two wait states. Since the 2716-1 EPROM has a 350-ns access time and the microprocessor is operating at 8 MHz (125-ns clock cycle), two wait states are inserted before asserting $\overline{DTACK}$ ($2 \times 125 = 250$ ns). Therefore, $\overline{Q2}$ can be connected to $\overline{DTACK}$ pin. Note that no wait state is required for RAMs since the access time for RAMs is only 120 ns.

Four 8-bit I/O ports are obtained by using two 6821 chips. When the I/O ports are selected, the $\overline{VPA}$ pin is asserted instead of $\overline{DTACK}$. This will acknowledge to the 68000 that it is addressing a 6800-type peripheral. In response, the 68000 will synchronize all data transfer with the E clock.

The memory and I/O maps for the schematic (Figure 6–24) are as follows:

• *Memory Maps (all numbers in hex)*

					$\overline{\text{LDS}}$ or $\overline{\text{UDS}}$	
A23–A15	A14	A13	A12	A11–A1	A0	
0–0	0	0	0	0–0	0	ROM (even) = 2K
0–0	0	0	0	1–1	0	$000000, $000002, $000004, . . . , $000FFE
0–0	0	0	0	0–0	1	ROM (odd) = 2K
0–0	0	0	0	1–1	1	$000001, $000003, $000005, . . . , $000FFF
0–0	0	0	1	0–0	0	RAM (even) = 2K
0–0	0	0	1	1–1	0	$001000, $001002, . . . , $001FFE
0–0	0	0	1	0–0	1	RAM (odd) = 2K
0–0	0	0	1	1–1	1	$001001, $001003, . . . , $001FFF

• *Memory-Mapped I/O (all numbers in hex)*

					RS1	RS0	$\overline{\text{UDS}}$ or $\overline{\text{LDS}}$	
A23–A15	A14	A13	A12	A11–A3	A2	A1	A0	Register Selected (Address)—Even
0–0	0	1	0	0–0	0	0	0	Port A or DDRA = $002000
0–0	0	1	0	0–0	0	1	0	CRA = $002002
0–0	0	1	0	0–0	1	0	0	Port B or DDRB = $002004
0–0	0	1	0	0–0	1	1	0	CRB = $002006
								Register Selected (Address)—Odd
0–0	0	1	0	0–0	0	0	1	Port A or DDRA = $002001
0–0	0	1	0	0–0	0	1	1	CRA = $002003
0–0	0	1	0	0–0	1	0	1	Port B or DDRB = $002005
0–0	0	1	0	0–0	1	1	1	CRB = $002007

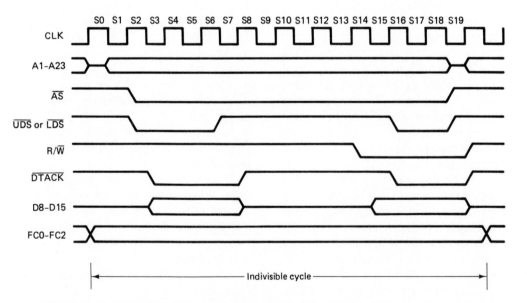

Figure 6–26 MC68000 read-modify-write cycle for TAS. (Reprinted by permission of Motorola)

Note that, upon hardware reset, the 68000 loads the supervisor SP high and low words, respectively, from addresses \$000000 and \$000002 and the PC high and low words, respectively, from locations \$000004 and \$000006. The memory map of Figure 6–26 contains these reset vector addresses in the even and odd 2716 − 1 chips.

6–14 MULTIPROCESSING WITH 68000 USING TAS INSTRUCTION AND $\overline{\text{AS}}$ SIGNAL

Earlier, the 68000 TAS instruction was discussed. The TAS instruction supports the software aspects of interfacing two or more 68000's via shared RAM. When TAS is executed, an indivisible read-modify-write cycle is performed. The timing diagram for this specialized cycle is shown in Figure 6–26.

During both the read and write portions of the cycle, $\overline{\text{AS}}$ remains LOW, and the cycle starts as the normal read cycle. However, in the normal read, $\overline{\text{AS}}$ going inactive indicates the end of the read. During execution of TAS, $\overline{\text{AS}}$ stays LOW throughout the cycle, and therefore $\overline{\text{AS}}$ can be used in the design as a bus-locking circuit. Due to bus locking, only one processor at a time can perform a TAS operation in a multiprocessor system.

The TAS instruction supports multiprocessor operations (globally shared resources) by checking a resource for availability and reserving or locking it for use by a single processor. The TAS instruction can, therefore, be used to allocate memory space reservations. The TAS instruction execution flowchart for allocating memory is shown in Figure 6–27.

The shared RAM of Figure 6–27 is divided into M sections. The first byte of each section will be pointed to by (EA) of the TAS (EA) instruction. In the flowchart of Figure 6–27 (EA) first points to the first byte of section 1. The instruction TAS (EA) is then executed.

The TAS instruction checks the most significant bit (N bit) in (EA). N = 0 indicates that section 1 is free; N = 1 means section 1 is busy. If N = 0, then section 1 will be allocated for use. If N = 1 (section 1 is busy), then a program will be written to subtract one section length from (EA) to check the next section for availability. Also, (EA) must be checked with the value TASLOCM. If (EA) < TASLOCM, then no space is available for allocation. However, if (EA) > TASLOCM, then TAS is executed and the availability of that section is determined.

In a multiprocessor environment, the TAS instruction provides software support for interfacing two or more 68000's via shared RAM. The $\overline{\text{AS}}$ signal can be used to provide the bus-locking mechanism.

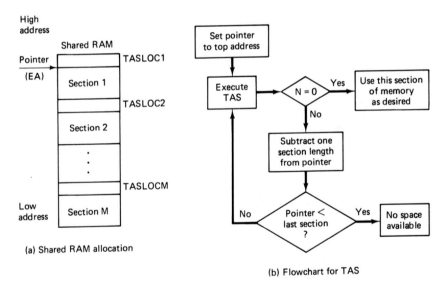

Figure 6–27 Memory allocation using TAS. (Reprinted by permission of Motorola)

(a) Shared RAM allocation

(b) Flowchart for TAS

QUESTIONS AND PROBLEMS

6–1. What are the basic differences between the 68000, 68008, 68010, and 68012?

6–2. What does a HIGH on the 68000 FC2 pin indicate?

6–3. (a) If a 68000-based system operates in the user mode and an interrupt occurs, what will the 68000 mode be?

(b) If a 68000-based system operates in the supervisor mode, how can the mode be changed to user mode?

6–4. (a) What is the purpose of the trace and X flags?

(b) How can you set or reset them?

6–5. Indicate whether the following 68000 instructions are valid or not valid. Justify your answers.

(a) MOVE.B D0, (A1)

(b) MOVE.B D0, A1

6-6. Identify the following instructions as privileged or nonprivileged:
   (a) MOVE (A2), SR
   (b) MOVE CCR, (A5)
   (c) MOVE.L USP, A2

6-7. (a) Find the contents of locations $305020 and $305021 after execution of MOVE D5, $305020. Assume [D5] = $6A2FA150 prior to execution of this MOVE instruction.
   (b) If [A0] = $203040FF and [D0] = $40F12560, what happens after execution of MOVE (A0), D0?

6-8. Identify the addressing modes for each of the following instructions:
   (a) CLR D0
   (b) MOVE.L (A0)+, -(A5)
   (c) MOVE $2000 (A2), D1

6-9. Determine the contents of registers and locations affected by each of the following instructions:
   (a) MOVE (A0)+, D1
      Assume the following data prior to execution of this MOVE:

$$[A0] = \$105020$$
$$[D1] = \$70801F25$$
$$[\$105020] = \$50$$
$$[\$105021] = \$51$$
$$[\$105022] = \$52$$
$$[\$105023] = \$7F$$

   (b) MOVEA D5, A2
      Assume the following data prior to execution of this MOVEA:

$$[D5] = \$A725B600$$
$$[A2] = \$5030801F$$

6-10. Find the contents of register D0 after execution of the following two instructions:

EXT D0
EXT.L D0

   Assume [D0] = $F215A700 prior to execution of the instruction sequence.

6-11. Find the contents of D1 after execution of DIVS #6, D1. Assume [D1] = $FFFFFFF7 prior to execution of the instruction. Identify the quotient and remainder. Comment on the sign of the remainder.

6-12. Write a 68000 assembly program to multiply a 16-bit signed number in the low word of D0 by an 8-bit signed number in the highest byte (bits 31-24) of D0.

6-13. Write a 68000 assembly program to divide a 16-bit signed number in the high word of D1 by an 8-bit signed number in the lowest byte of D1.

6-14. Write a 68000 assembly program to add the top two 16 bits of the stack. Store the 16-bit result onto the stack. Assume supervisor mode.

6-15. Write a 68000 assembly program to add a 16-bit number in the low word (bits 0-15) of D1 with another 16-bit number in the high word (bits 16-31) of D1. Store the result in the high word of D1.

6-16. Write a 68000 assembly program to add two 48-bit data in memory as shown in figure below:

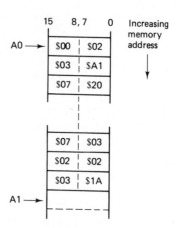

Store result pointed to by A1. The operation is given by:

$00	02	03	A1	07	20
$07	03	02	02	03	1A
$07	05	05	A3	0A	3A

Assume data pointers along with data are already initialized.

6-17. Write a 68000 assembly program to divide a 9-bit unsigned number in the high 9 bits (bits 31-23) of D0 by 8_{10}. Do not use any division instruction. Store the result in D0. Neglect remainder.

6-18. Write a 68000 assembly program to compare two strings of 15 ASCII characters. The first string is stored starting at $502030 followed by the string. The second string is stored at location $302510. The ASCII character in location $502030 of string 1 will be compared with the ASCII character in location $302510 of string 2, [$502031] will be compared with [$302511], and so on. Each time there is a match, store $EEEE onto the stack; otherwise, store $0000 onto the stack.

6-19. Write a subroutine in 68000 assembly language to subtract two unsigned 4-digit BCD numbers. BCD number 1 is stored at a location starting from $500000 through $500003, with the least significant digit at $500003 and the most significant digit at $500000. BCD number 2 is stored at a location starting from $700000 through $700003, with the least significant digit at $700003 and the most significant digit at $700000. BCD number 2 is to be subtracted from BCD number 1. Store the result in D5.

6–20. Write a subroutine in 68000 assembly language to compute

$$Z = \sum_{i=1}^{100} Xi$$

Assume the Xi's are signed 8-bit and stored in consecutive locations starting at $504020. Assume A0 points to the Xi's. Also, write the main program in 68000 assembly language to perform all initializations, call the subroutine, and then compute $Z/100$.

6–21. Write a subroutine in 68000 assembly language to convert a 3-digit unsigned BCD number to binary. The most significant digit is stored in a memory location starting at $3000, the next digit is stored at $3001, and so on. Store the result in D3. Use the value of the 3-digit BCD number

$$N = N2 \times 10^2 + N1 \times 10^1 + N0$$
$$= ((10 \times N2 + N1) \times 10 + N0$$

6–22. Write a 68000 assembly program to compute the following:

$$I = 6 * J + K/M$$

where locations $6000, $6002, and $6004 contain the 16-bit signed integers J, K, and M. Store the result into a long word starting at $6006. Discard the remainder of K/M.

6–23. Determine the status of $\overline{AS}$, FC2–FC0, $\overline{LDS}$, $\overline{UDS}$, and address lines immediately after execution of the following instruction sequence (before the 68000 tristates these lines to fetch the next instruction):

MOVE #$2050, SR
MOVE.B D0, $405060

Assume the 68000 is in supervisor mode prior to execution of this instruction sequence.

6–24. Suppose that three switches are connected to bits 0–2 of port A and an LED to bit 6 of port B. If the number of HIGH switches is even, turn the LED ON; otherwise, turn the LED OFF. Write a 68000 assembly language program to accomplish this.
  (a) Assume a 68000/6821 system.
  (b) Assume a 68000/68230 system.

6–25. Assume the pins and signals shown in Figure P6–25 for the 68000, 68230, and 2716. Connect the chips and draw a neat schematic. Determine the memory and I/O maps. Assume a 16.67-MHz internal clock for the 68000.

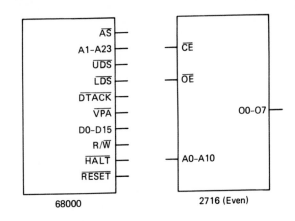

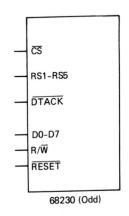

Figure P6–25

6–26. Find $\overline{LDS}$ and $\overline{UDS}$ after execution of the 68000 instruction sequence:

MOVEA.L #$05A123, A2
MOVE.W (A2), D1

6–27. Write a service routine for a reset that will initialize all data registers to zero, address registers to $FFFFFFFF, supervisor SP to $502078, and user SP to $1F0524, and then jump to $7020F0.

6–28. Assume the stack and register values shown in Figure P6-28 before occurrence of an interrupt. If an external device requests an interrupt by asserting the $\overline{IPL2}$, $\overline{IPL1}$, $\overline{IPL0}$, pins with the value

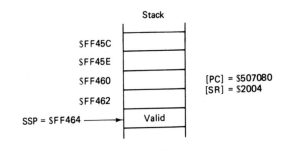

Figure P6–28

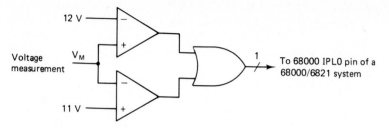

000_2, determine the contents of SSP and SR during interrupt and after execution of RTE at the end of the service routine of the interrupt. Draw the memory layouts and show where SSP points to and the stack contents during and after interrupt. Assume that the stack is not used by the service routine.

6–29. Consider the following data prior to a 68000 hardware reset:

$$[D0] = \$7F2A1620$$
$$[A1] = \$6AB11057$$
$$[SR] = \$001F$$

What are the contents of D0, A1, and SR after hardware reset?

6–30. In Figure P6–30, if VM > 12 V, turn an LED ON connected at bit 3 of port A. If VM < 11 V, turn the LED OFF. Use ports, registers, and memory locations as needed. Use a level 1 autovectored interrupt.

(a) Draw a neat block diagram showing the 68000/6821 microcomputer and the connections to the diagram in Figure P6–30 to ports.

(b) Write a service routine in 68000 assembly language.

6–31. Write a subroutine in 68000 assembly language using the TAS instruction to find, reserve, and lock a memory segment for the main program. The memory is divided into three segments (0, 1, 2) of 16 bytes each. The first byte of each segment includes a flag byte to be used by the TAS instruction. In the subroutine, a maximum of three 16-byte memory segments must be checked for a free segment (flag byte = 0). Once a free segment is found, the TAS instruction is used to set the flag byte to $FF. The starting address of the free segment must be stored in A0 and the low byte D0 must be cleared to zero to indicate a free segment. If no free block is found, $FF must be stored in the low byte of D0.

the 8086. Also, on the 80386 in protected mode, the semantics of all instructions that affect segment registers (PUSH, POP, MOV, LES, LDS) and those that affect program flow (CALL, INTO, INT, IRET, JMP, RET) are quite different from the 8086.

The main differences between the 80286 and the 80386 are the 32-bit addresses and data types and paging and memory management. To provide these features and other applications, several new instructions are added in the 80386 instruction set beyond those of the 80286.

Internal Architecture   The internal architecture of the 80386 includes six functional units that operate in parallel, as shown in Figure 7–1. The parallel operation is known as *pipelined processing*. Fetching, decoding, execution, memory management, and bus access for several instructions are performed simultaneously. The six functional units of the 80386 are as follows:

1. Bus interface unit
2. Code prefetch unit
3. Decoding unit
4. Execution unit
5. Segmentation unit
6. Paging unit

The bus interface unit interfaces between the 80386 with memory and I/O. Based on internal requests for fetching instructions and transferring data from the code prefetch unit, the 80386 generates the address, data, and control signals for the current bus cycles.

The code prefetch unit prefetches instructions when the bus interface unit is not executing bus cycles. It then stores them in a 16-byte instruction queue for execution by the instruction decoding unit.

The instruction decoding unit translates instructions from the prefetch queue into microcodes. The decoded instructions are then stored in an instruction queue (FIFO) for processing by the execution unit.

The execution unit processes the instructions from the instruction queue. It contains a control unit, a data unit, and a protection test unit. The control unit contains microcode and parallel hardware for fast multiply, divide, and effective address calculation. The data unit includes an ALU, 8 general-purpose registers, and a 64-bit barrel shifter for performing multiple bit shifts in 1 clock cycle. The data unit carries out data operations requested by the control unit. The protection test unit checks for segmentation violations under the control of the microcode.

The segmentation unit translates logical addresses into linear addresses at the request of the execution unit. The translated linear address is sent to the paging unit.

Upon enabling of the paging mechanism, the 80386 translates the linear addresses into physical addresses. If paging is not enabled, the physical address is identical to the linear address and no translation is necessary.

System Block Diagram   Figure 7–2 shows a typical 80386 system block diagram. Besides the 80386 microprocessor itself, the following components are shown:

- 80287 or 80387 numeric coprocessor
- 82384 clock generator
- 8259A interrupt controller
- 82258 advanced DMA controller

The function of each of these components is described next.

The 80287 or 80387 numeric coprocessor extends the instruction set of the 80386 to include instructions such as floating-point operations. These instructions are executed in parallel by the 80287 or 80387 with the 80386 and thus off-load the 80386 of these functions.

The 82384 clock generator provides system clock and reset signals. The 82384 generates both the 80386

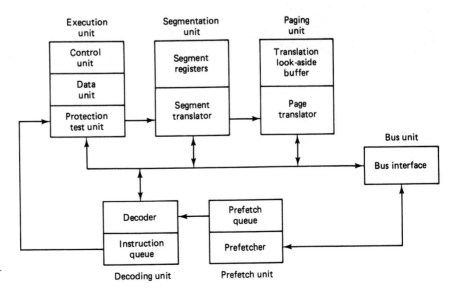

Figure 7–1   80386 functional units.
(Courtesy of Intel Corp.)

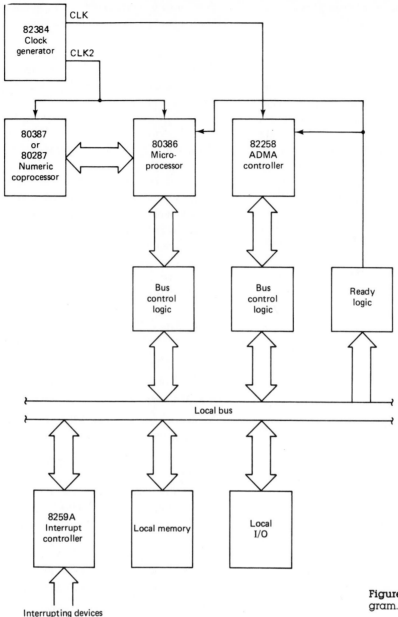

Figure 7–2 80386 system block diagram. (Courtesy of Intel Corp.)

clock (CLK2) and a half-frequency clock (CLK) to drive the 80286-compatible devices that may be included in the system. It also generates the 80386 RESET signal.

The 8259A interrupt controller provides interrupt control and management functions. Interrupts from as many as 8 external sources are accepted by one 8259A and up to 64 interrupt requests can be handled by connecting several 8259A chips. The 8259A manages priorities between several interrupts; it then interrupts the 80386 and sends a code to the 80386 to identify the source of the interrupt.

The 82258 DMA controller performs DMA transfers between the main memory and an I/O device such as a hard disk or floppy disk. The 82258 advanced DMA (ADMA) controller provides four channels and all signals necessary to perform DMA transfers.

Processing Modes The 80386 has three processing modes: protected mode, real-address mode, and virtual 8086 mode.

Protected mode is the normal 32-bit application of the 80386. All instructions and features of the 80386 are available in this mode.

Real-address mode (also known as "real mode") is the mode of operation of the processor upon hardware reset. This mode appears to programmers as a fast 8086 with a few new instructions. This mode is utilized by most applications for initialization purposes only.

Virtual 8086 mode (also called "V86 mode") is a mode in which the 80386 can go back and forth repeatedly between V86 mode and protected mode at a fast speed. The 80386, when entering into V86 mode, can execute an 8086 program. The processor can then leave

V86 mode and enter protected mode to execute an 80386 program.

As mentioned, the 80386 enters real-address mode upon hardware reset. In this mode, the protection enable (PE) bit in a control register—the control register 0 (CR0)—is cleared to zero. Setting the PE bit in CR0 places the 80386 in protected mode. When the 80386 is in protected mode, setting the VM (virtual mode) bit in the flag register (the EFLAGS register) places the 80386 in V86 mode.

7-2-1 Basic 80386 Programming Model

The 80386 basic programming model includes the following aspects:

- Memory organization and segmentation
- Data types
- Registers
- Instruction format
- Addressing modes
- Features of interrupts and exceptions of interest to application programmers

I/O is not included as part of the basic programming model because systems designers may select to use I/O instructions for application programs or may select to reserve them for the operating system. Therefore, 80386 I/O capabilities will be covered during the discussion of systems programming.

Memory Organization and Segmentation

The 4-gigabyte physical memory of the 80386 is structured as 8-bit bytes. Each byte can be uniquely accessed by a 32-bit address. The programmer can write assembly language programs without knowledge of physical address space.

The memory organization model available to applications programmers is determined by the system software designers. The memory organization model available to the programmer for each task can vary between the following possibilities:

1. A "flat" address space includes a single array of up to 4 gigabytes. Even though the physical address space can be up to 4 gigabytes, in reality it is much smaller. The 80386 maps the 4-gigabyte flat space into the physical address space automatically by using an address-translation scheme transparent to the applications programmers.

2. A segmented address space includes up to 16,383 linear address spaces of up to 4 gigabytes each. In a segmented model, the address space is called the "logical" address space and can be up to 2^{46} bytes (64 tetrabytes). The processor maps this address

space onto the physical address space (up to 4 gigabytes by an address-translation technique).

To applications programmers, the logical address space appears as up to 16,383 one-dimensional subspaces, each with a specified length. Each of these linear subspaces is called a *segment*. A segment is a unit of contiguous address space with sizes varying from 1 byte up to a maximum of 4 gigabytes. A pointer in the logical address space consists of a 16-bit segment selector identifying a segment and a 32-bit offset addressing a byte within a segment.

Data Types Data types can be byte (8-bit), word (16-bit with the low byte addressed by n and the high byte addressed by $n + 1$), and double word (32-bit with byte 0 addressed by n and byte 3 addressed by $n + 3$). All three data types can start at any byte address. Therefore, the words are not required to be aligned at even-numbered addresses, and double words need not be aligned at addresses evenly divisible by 4. However, for maximum performance, data structures (including stacks) should be designed in such a way that, whenever possible, word operands are aligned at even addresses and double word operands are aligned at addresses evenly divisible by 4.

Depending on the instruction referring to the operand, the following additional data types are available: integer (signed 8-, 16-, or 32-bit), ordinal (unsigned 8-, 16-, or 32-bit), near pointer (a 32-bit logical address that is an offset within a segment), far pointer (a 48-bit logical address consisting of a 16-bit selector and a 32-bit offset), string (8-, 16-, or 32-bit from 0 bytes to $2^{32} - 1$ bytes), bit field (a contiguous sequence of bits starting at any bit position of any byte and containing up to 32 bits), bit string (a contiguous sequence of bits starting at any position of any byte and containing up to $2^{32} - 1$ bits), and packed/unpacked BCD. When the 80386 is interfaced to a coprocessor such as the 80287 or 80387, then floating-point numbers (signed 32-, 64-, or 80-bit real numbers) are supported. Note that the 80486 contains on-chip floating-point hardware.

Registers Figure 7–3 shows the 80386 registers. As shown in Figure 7–3(a), the 80386 has 16 registers classified as general, segment, status, and instruction pointer.

The eight general registers are the 32-bit registers EAX, EBX, ECX, EDX, EBP, ESP, ESI, and EDI. The low-order word of each of these eight registers has the 8086/80186/80286 register names AX (AH or AL), BX (BH or BL), CX (CH or CL), DX (DH or DL), BP, SP, SI, and DI. They are useful for making the 80386 compatible with the 8086, 80186, and 80286 processors.

The six 16-bit segment registers—CS, SS, DS, ES, FS, and GS allow systems software designers to select either a flat or segmented model of memory organization. The purpose of CS, SS, DS, and ES is obvious. The two additional data segment registers FS and GS are included

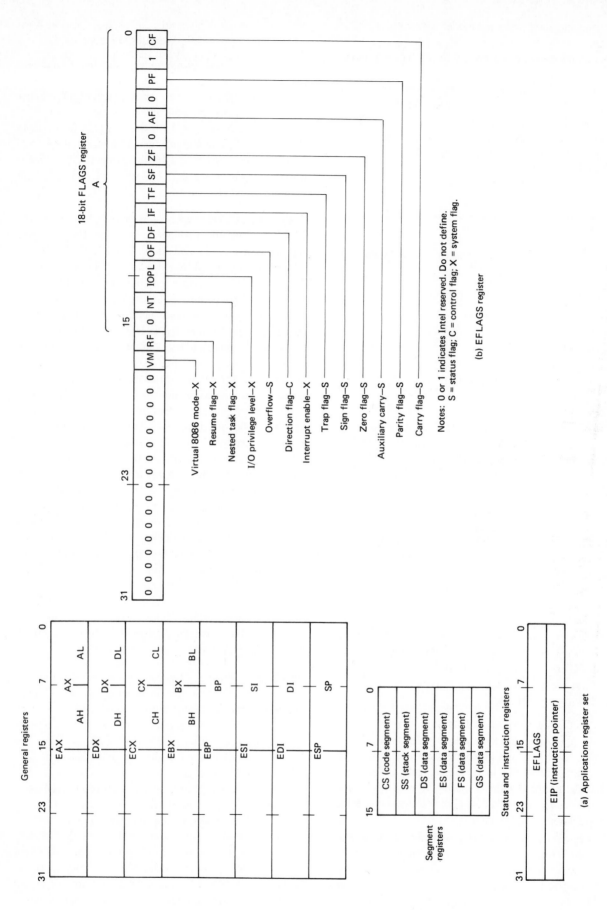

Figure 7–3 80386 registers. (Courtesy of Intel Corp.)

218

in the 80386 so that the four data segment registers (DS, ES, FS, and GS) can access four separate data areas and allow programs to access different types of data structures. For example, one data segment register can point to the data structures of the current module, another to the exported data of a higher-level module, another to a dynamically created data structure, and another to data shared with another task.

The flag register is a 32-bit register named EFLAGS. Figure 7–3(b) shows the meaning of each bit in this register. The low-order 16 bits of EFLAGS is named FLAGS and can be treated as a unit. This is useful when executing 8086/80186/80286 code because this part of EFLAGS is similar to the FLAGS register of the 8086/80186/80286. The 80386 flags are grouped into three types: status flags, control flags, and system flags.

The status flags include CF, PF, AF, ZF, SF, and OF like the 8086/80186/80286. The control flag DF is used by strings like the 8086/80186/80286. The system flags control I/O, maskable interrupts, debugging, task switching, and enabling of virtual 8086 execution in a protected, multitasking environment. The purpose of IF and TF is identical to the 8086/80186/80286. Let us explain the other flags:

- IOPL (I/O privilege level)—This 2-bit field supports the 80386 protection feature. The IOPL field defines the privilege level needed to execute I/O instructions. If the present privilege level is less than or equal to IOPL (privilege level is specified by numbers), the 80386 can execute I/O instructions; otherwise, it takes a protection exception.

- NT (nested task)—The NT bit controls the IRET operation. If NT = 0, a usual return from interrupt is taken by the 80386 by popping EFLAGS, CS, and EIP from the stack. If NT = 1, the 80386 returns from an interrupt via task switching.

- RF (resume flag)—If RF = 1, the 80386 ignores debug faults and does not take another exception so that an instruction can be restarted after a normal debug exception. If RF = 0, the 80386 takes another debug exception to service debug faults.

- VM (virtual 8086 mode)—When the VM bit is set to 1, the 80386 executes 8086 programs. When the VM bit is 0, the 80386 operates in the protected mode.

The RF, NT, DF, and TF bits can be set or reset by an 80386 program executing at any privilege level. The VM and IOPL bits can be modified by a program running at only privilege level 0 (the highest privilege level). An 80386 with I/O privilege level can modify only the IF bit. The IRET instruction or a task switch can set or reset the RF and VM bits. The other control bits can also be modified by the POPF instruction.

The instruction pointer register (EIP) contains the offset address relative to the start of the current code segment of the next sequential instruction to be executed. The EIP is not directly accessible by the programmer; it is controlled implicitly by control-transfer instructions, interrupts, and exceptions. The low-order 16 bits of EIP is named IP and is useful when the 80386 executes 8086/80186/80286 instructions.

7–2–2 80386 Addressing Modes

The 80386 has 11 addressing modes, classified into register/immediate and memory addressing modes. The register/immediate type includes 2 addressing modes, while the memory addressing type contains 9 modes.

Register/Immediate Modes   Instructions using the register or immediate modes operate on either register or immediate operands.

1. Register mode—The operand is contained in one of the 8-, 16-, or 32-bit general registers. An example is DEC ECX, which decrements the 32-bit register ECX by 1.

2. Immediate mode—The operand is included as part of the instruction. An example is MOVE EDX, 5167812FH, which moves the 32-bit data $5167812F_{16}$ to the EDX register. Note that the source operand in this case is in immediate mode.

Memory Addressing Modes   The other 9 addressing modes specify the effective memory address of an operand. These modes are used when accessing memory. An 80386 address consists of two parts: a segment base address and an effective address. The effective address is computed by adding any combination of the following four elements:

- *Displacement*—The 8- or 32-bit immediate data following the instruction is the displacement; 16-bit displacements can be used by inserting an address prefix before the instruction.

- *Base*—The contents of any general-purpose register can be used as a base. Compilers normally use these base registers to point to the beginning of the local variable area.

- *Index*—The contents of any general-purpose register except ESP can be used as an index register. The elements of an array or a string of characters can be accessed via the index register.

- *Scale*—The index register's contents can be multiplied (scaled) by a factor of 1, 2, 4, or 8. A scaled index mode is efficient for accessing arrays or structures.

As shown in Figure 7–4, the effective address (EA) of an operand is computed according to the following formula:

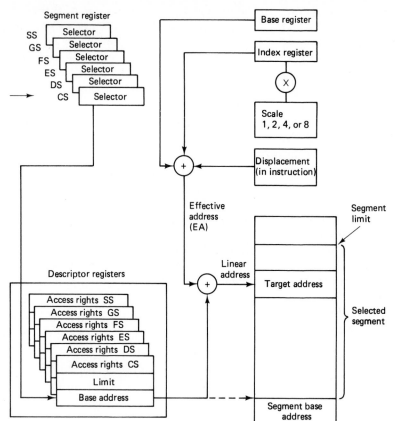

Figure 7-4 Addressing mode calculations. (Courtesy of Intel Corp.)

$$EA = \text{base register} + (\text{index register} \times \text{scale}) + \text{displacement}$$

The 9 memory addressing modes are a combination of these four elements. Of the 9 modes, 8 of them are executed with the same number of clock cycles since the effective address calculation is pipelined with the execution of other instructions; the mode containing base, index, and displacement elements requires 1 additional clock cycle.

1. Direct mode—The operand's effective address is included as part of the instruction as an 8-, 16-, or 32-bit displacement. An example is DEC.WORD PTR [4000H].

2. Register indirect mode—A base or index register contains the operand's effective address. An example is MOV EBX, [ECX].

3. Base mode—The contents of a base register is added to a displacement to obtain the operand's effective address. An example is MOV [EDX + 16], EBX.

4. Index mode—The contents of an index register is added to a displacement to obtain the operand's effective address. An example is ADD START [EDI], EBX.

5. Scaled index mode—The contents of an index register is multiplied by a scaling factor (1, 2, 4, or 8), and the result is added to a displacement to obtain the operand's effective address. An example is MOV START [EBX * 8], ECX.

6. Based index mode—The contents of a base register is added to the contents of an index register to obtain the operand's effective address. An example is MOV ECX, [ESI] [EAX].

7. Based scaled index mode—The contents of an index register is multiplied by a scaling factor (1, 2, 4, or 8), and the result is added to the contents of a base register to obtain the operand's effective address. An example is MOV [ECX * 4] [EDX], EAX.

8. Based index mode with displacement —The operand's effective address is obtained by adding the contents of a base register and an index register with a displacement. An example is MOV [EBX] [EBP + 0F24782AH], ECX.

9. Based scaled index mode with displacement—The contents of an index register is multiplied by a scaling factor, and the result is added to the contents of a base register and a displacement to obtain the operand's effective address. An example is MOV [ESI * 8] [EBP + 60H], ECX.

7-2-3 80386 Instruction Set

The 80386 can execute 8086/80186/80286 16-bit instructions in real and protected modes. This is provided in order to make the 80386 software compatible with the 80286, 80186, and 8086. The 80386 uses the D bit in the segment descriptor register (8 bytes wide) to determine whether the instruction size is 16 or 32 bits wide. If D = 0, the 80386 uses all operand lengths and effective addresses as 16 bits long. If D = 1, then the default length for operands and addresses is 32 bits. Note that, in protected mode, the operating system can set or reset the D bit using proper instructions. In real mode, the default size for operands and addresses is 16 bits. Note also that the real-address mode does not use descriptors.

Irrespective of the D-bit definition, the 80386 can execute either 16- or 32-bit instructions via the use of two override prefixes such as the operand size prefix and address length prefix. These prefixes override the D bit on an individual instruction basis. These prefixes are automatically included by Intel assemblers. For example, if D = 1 and the 80386 wants to execute INC WORD PTR [BX] to increment a 16-bit memory location, the assembler automatically adds the operand size prefix to specify only a 16-bit value.

The 80386 uses either 8- or 32-bit displacements and any register as the base or index register while executing 32-bit code. However, the 80386 uses either 8- or 16-bit displacements with the base and index registers conforming to the 80286 while executing 16-bit code. The base and index registers utilized by the 80386 for 16- and 32-bit addresses are as follows:

	16-Bit Addressing	32-Bit Addressing
Base register	BX, BP	Any 32-bit general-purpose register
Index register	SI, DI	Any 32-bit general-purpose register except ESP
Scale factor	None	1, 2, 4, 8
Displacement	0, 8, 16 bits	0, 8, 32 bits

A description of some of the new 80386 instructions is given next.

Arithmetic Instructions

There are two new instructions beyond those of the 80286:

CWDE — Sign-extend 16-bit contents of AX to a 32-bit double word in EAX.
CDQ — Sign-extend a double word (32 bits) in EAX to a quadword (64 bits) in EDX:EAX.

The 80386 includes all of the 8086 arithmetic instructions plus some new ones. Two of the instructions are as follows:

Instruction	Operation
ADC reg32/mem32, imm32	[reg32 or mem32] ← [reg32 or mem32] + 32-bit immediate data + CF

Instruction	Operation
ADC reg32/mem32, imm8	[reg32 or mem32] ← [reg32 or mem32] + 8-bit immediate data sign-extended to 32 bits + CF

Similarly, the other add instructions include the following:

ADC	reg32/mem32,	reg32/mem32
ADD	reg32/mem32,	imm32
ADD	reg32/mem32,	imm8
ADD	reg32/mem32,	reg32/mem32

The 80386 SUB/SBB instructions have the same operands as the ADD/ADC instructions.

The 80386 multiply instructions include all of the 8086 instructions plus some new ones. Some of them are listed next:

Instruction	Operation
IMUL EAX, reg32/mem32	EDX:EAX ← EAX * reg32 or mem32 (signed multiplication) CF and OF flags are cleared to 0 if EDX value is 0; otherwise, they are set.
IMUL AX, reg16/mem16	DX:AX ← AX * reg16/mem 16 (signed multiplication)
IMUL AL, reg8/mem8	(signed multiplication) AX ← AL * reg8/mem8
IMUL reg16, reg16/mem16, imm8	reg16 ← reg16/mem16 * (imm8 sign-extended to 16 bits) (signed multiplication) Result is low 16 bits of product.
IMUL reg32, reg32/mem32, imm8	reg32 ← reg32/mem32 * (imm8 sign-extended to 32 bits) (signed multiplication) Result is low 32 bits of product.

The unsigned multiplication MUL instruction has the same operands.

The 80386 divide instructions include all of the 8086 instructions plus some new ones. Some of them are listed next:

Instruction	Operation
IDIV EAX, reg32/mem32	EDX:EAX ÷ reg32 or mem32 (signed division) EAX = quotient and EDX = remainder.
IDIV AL, reg8/mem8	AX ÷ reg8 or mem8 (signed division) AL = quotient and AH = remainder.
IDIV AX, reg16/mem16	DX:AX ÷ reg16 or mem16 (signed division) AX = quotient and DX = remainder.

The DIV instruction performs unsigned division, and the operation is the same as IDIV.

Bit Instructions

The 80386 six bit instructions are as follows:

BSF — Bit scan forward
BSR — Bit scan reverse
BT — Bit test

BTC   Bit test and complement
BTR   Bit test and reset
BTS   Bit test and set

These instructions are discussed separately next.

- BSF (bit scan forward) takes the form

         BSF   d,   s
                reg16, reg16
                reg16, mem16
                reg32, reg32
                reg32, mem32

BSF scans (checks) the 16-bit (word) or 32-bit (double word) number defined by s from right to left (bit 0 to bit 15 or bit 31). The bit number of the first 1 found is stored in d. If the whole 16-bit or 32-bit number is 0, the zero flag is set to 1; if a 1 is found, the zero flag is reset to 0. For example, consider BSF EBX, EDX. If $[EDX] = 01241240_{16}$, then $[EBX] = 00000006_{16}$ and $ZF = 0$. The bit number 6 in EDX (contained in second nibble of EDX) is the first 1 found when [EDX] is scanned from the right.

- BSR (bit scan reverse) takes the form

         BSR   d,   s
                reg16, reg16
                reg16, mem16
                reg32, reg32
                reg32, mem32

BSR scans (checks) the 16-bit or 32-bit number defined by s from the most significant bit (bit 15 or bit 31) to the least significant bit (bit 0). The destination operand d is loaded with the bit index (bit number) of the first set bit. If the bits in the number are all 0's, ZF is set to 1 and operand d is undefined; ZF is reset to 0 if a 1 is found.

- BT (bit test) takes the form

         BT   d,   s
                reg16, reg16
                mem16, reg16
                reg16, imm8
                mem16, imm8
                reg32, reg32
                mem32, reg32
                reg32, imm8
                mem32, imm8

BT assigns the bit value of operand d (base) specified by operand s (bit offset) to the carry flag. Only CF is affected. If operand s is an immediate data, only 8 bits are allowed in the instruction. This operand is taken modulo 32 so that the range of immediate bit offset is from 0 to 31. This permits any bit within a register to be selected. If d is a register, the bit value assigned to CF is defined by the value of the bit number defined by s taken modulo the register

size (16 or 32). If d is a memory bit string, the desired 16 bits or 32 bits can be determined by adding s (bit index) divided by operand size (16 or 32) to the memory address of d. The bit within this 16- or 32-bit word is defined by d taken modulo the operand size (16 or 32). If d is a memory operand, the 80386 may access 4 bytes in memory starting at effective address plus $4 \times$ [bit offset divided by 32]. As an example, consider BT CX, DX. If $[CX] = 081F_{16}$ and $[DX] = 0021_{16}$, then, since the contents of DX is 33_{10}, the bit number 1 (remainder of $33/16 = 1$) of CX (value 1) is reflected in CF and therefore $CF = 1$.

- BTC (bit test and complement) takes the form

         BTC   d, s

where d and s have the same definitions as for the BT instruction. The bit of d defined by s is reflected in CF. After CF is assigned, the same bit of d defined by s is 1's complemented. The 80386 determines the bit number from s (whether s is immediate data or register) and d (whether d is register or memory bit string) in the same way as for the BT instruction.

- BTR (bit test and reset) takes the form

         BTR   d, s

where d and s have the same definitions as for the BT instruction. The bit of d defined by s is reflected in CF. After CF is assigned, the same bit of d defined by s is reset to 0. Everything else applicable to the BT instruction also applies to BTR.

- BTS (bit test and set) takes the form

         BTS   d, s

BTS is the same as BTR except the specified bit in d is set to 1 after the bit value of d defined by s is reflected in CF. Everything else applicable to the BT instruction also applies to BTS.

Byte-Set-on-Condition Instructions   These instructions set a byte to 1 or reset a byte to 0 depending on any of the 16 conditions defined by the status flags. The byte may be located in memory or in a 1-byte general register. These instructions are very useful in implementing Boolean expressions in high-level languages such as Pascal. The general structure of these instructions is SETcc (set byte on condition cc), which sets a byte to 1 if condition cc is true or else resets the byte to 0. A list of these instructions is given in Table 7–1.

As an example, consider SETB BL. If $[BL] = 52_{16}$ and $CF = 1$, then, after this instruction is executed, $[BL] = 01_{16}$ and CF remains at 1; all other flags (OF, SF, ZF, AF, PF) are undefined. On the other hand, if $CF = 0$, then, after execution of this instruction, $[BL] = 00_{16}$, $CF = 0$, and $ZF = 1$; all other flags are

TABLE 7–1
80386 Byte-Set-on-Condition Instructions

Instruction	Condition Codes	Description
SETA/SETNBE reg8 mem8	CF = 0 and ZF = 0	Set byte if above or set if not below/equal
SETAE/SETNB/SETNC reg8/mem8	CF = 0	Set if above/equal, set if not below, or set if not carry
SETB/SETNAE/SETC reg8/mem8	CF = 1	Set if below, set if not above/equal, or set if carry
SETBE/SETNA reg8/ mem8	CF = 1 or ZF = 1	Set if below/equal or set if not above
SETE/SETZ reg8/mem8	ZF = 1	Set if equal or set if zero
SETG/SETNLE reg8/ mem8	ZF = 0 or SF = OF	Set if greater or set if not less/equal
SETGE/SETNL reg8/ mem8	SF = OF	Set if greater/equal or set if not less
SETL/SETNGE reg8/ mem8	SF ≠ OF	Set if less or set if not greater/equal
SETLE/SETNG reg8/ mem8	ZF = 1 and SF ≠ OF	Set if less/equal or set if not greater
SETNE/SETNZ reg8/ mem8	ZF = 0	Set if not equal or set if not zero
SETNO reg8/mem8	OF = 0	Set if no overflow
SETNP/SETPO reg8/mem8	PF = 0	Set if no parity or set if parity odd
SETNS reg8/mem8	SF = 0	Set if not sign
SETO reg8/mem8	OF = 1	Set if overflow
SETP/SETPE reg8/mem8	PF = 1	Set if parity or set if parity even
SETS reg8/mem8	SF = 1	Set if sign

Courtesy of Intel Corp.

undefined. The other SETcc instructions can similarly be explained.

Conditional Jumps and Loops

JECXZ disp8 jumps if [ECX] = 0; disp8 means a relative address. JECXZ tests the contents of the ECX register for zero and not the flags. If [ECX] = 0, then, after execution of the JECXZ instruction, the program branches with a signed 8-bit relative offset ($+127_{10}$ to -128_{10} with 0 being positive) defined by disp8. The JECXZ instruction is useful at the beginning of a conditional loop that terminates with a conditional loop instruction such as LOOPNE label. JECXZ prevents entering the loop with [ECX] = 0, which would cause the loop to execute up to 2^{32} times instead of zero times.

The loop instructions are listed next:

LOOP disp8	Decrement CX/ECX by 1 and jump if CX/ECX ≠ 0.
LOOP/LOOPZ disp8	Decrement CX/ECX by 1 and jump if CX/ECX ≠ 0 and ZF = 1.
LOOPNE/LOOPNZ disp8	Decrement CX/ECX by 1 and jump if CX/ECX ≠ 0 and ZF = 0.

The 80386 loop instructions are similar to those of the 8086/80186/80286 except that if the counter is more than 16 bits, the ECX register is used as the counter.

Data Transfer Instructions

Move Instructions   The move instructions are described as follows:

MOVSX	d,	s	Move and sign-extend
MOVZX	d,	s	Move and zero-extend
	reg16,	reg8	
	reg16,	mem8	
	reg32,	reg8	
	reg32,	mem8	
	reg32,	reg16	
	reg32,	mem16	

MOVSX reads the contents of the effective address or register as a byte or a word from the source, sign-extends the value to the operand size of the destination (16 or 32 bits), and stores the result in the destination. No flags are affected. MOVZX, on the other hand, reads the contents of the effective address or register as a byte or a word, zero-extends the value to the operand size of the destination (16 or 32 bits), and stores the result in the destination. No flags are affected. For example, consider MOVSX BX, CL. If CL $= 81_{16}$ and $[BX] = 21AF_{16}$, then, after execution of this MOVSX, register BX contains $FF81_{16}$ and CL contents do not change. Now, consider MOVZX CX, DH. If CX $= F237_{16}$ and $[DH] = 85_{16}$, then, after execution of this MOVZX, register CX contains 0085_{16} and DH contents do not change.

Push and Pop Instructions There are two new push and pop instructions in the 80386 beyond those of the 80286: PUSHAD and POPAD. PUSHAD saves all 32-bit general registers (the order is EAX, ECX, EDX, EBX, original ESP, EBP, ESI, and EDI) onto the 80386 stack. PUSHAD decrements the stack pointer (ESP) by 32_{10} to hold the eight 32-bit values. No flags are affected. POPAD reverses a previous PUSHAD. It pops the eight 32-bit registers (the order is EDI, ESI, EBP, ESP, EBX, EDX, ECS, and EAX). The ESP value is discarded instead of loading onto ESP. No flags are affected. Note that ESP is actually popped but thrown away so that [ESP], after popping all the registers, will be incremented by 32_{10}.

Load Pointer Instructions There are five instructions in the load pointer instruction category: LDS, LES, LFS, LGS, and LSS. The first two instructions, LDS and LES, are available in the 80286. The 80286 loads 32 bits from a specified location (16-bit offset and DS) into a specified 16-bit register such as BX and (the other 16 bits) into DS for LDS or ES for LES. The 80386, on the other hand, can have four versions of these instructions as follows:

```
LDS   reg16,   mem16:mem16
LDS   reg32,   mem16:mem32
LES   reg16,   mem16:mem16
LES   reg32,   mem16:mem32
```

Note that mem16:mem16 or mem16:mem32 defines a memory operand containing four pointers composed of two numbers. The number to the left of the colon corresponds to the pointer's segment selector; the number to the right corresponds to the offset. These instructions read a full pointer from memory and store it in the selected segment register:specified register. The instruction loads 16 bits into DS (for LDS) or into ES (for LES). The other register loaded is 32 bits for 32-bit operand size and 16 bits for 16-bit operand size. The 16- and 32-bit registers to be loaded are determined by the reg16 or reg32 register specified.

The three new instructions LFS, LGS, and LSS associated with segment registers FS, GS, and SS can similarly be explained.

Flag Control Instructions

There are two new flag control instructions in the 80386 beyond those of the 80286: PUSHFD and POPFD. PUSHFD decrements the stack pointer by 4 and saves the 80386 EFLAGS register to the new top of the stack. No flags are affected. POPFD pops the 32 bits (double word) from the top of the stack and stores the value in EFLAGS. All flags except VM and RF are affected.

Logical Instructions

There are two new logical instructions in the 80386 beyond those of the 80286:

SHLD	d,	s,	count	Shift left double
SHRD	d,	s,	count	Shift right double
	d	s	count	
	reg16,	reg16,	imm8	
	mem16,	reg16,	imm8	
	reg16,	reg16,	CL	
	mem16,	reg16,	CL	
	reg32,	reg32,	CL	
	mem32,	reg32,	imm8	
	reg32,	reg32,	CL	
	mem32,	reg32,	CL	

For both SHLD and SHRD, the shift count is defined by the low 5 bits and, therefore, shifts from 0 to 31 can be obtained.

SHLD shifts the contents of d:s by the specified shift count with the result stored back into d; d is shifted to the left by the shift count with the low-order bits of d filled from the high-order bits of s. The bits in s are not altered after shifting. The carry flag becomes the value of the bit shifted out of the most significant bit of d. If the shift count is zero, this instruction works as an NOP. For the specified shift count, the SF, ZF, and PF flags are set according to the result in d. CF is set to the value of the last bit shifted out. OF and AF are undefined.

SHRD shifts the contents of d:s by the specified shift count to the right with the result stored back into d. The bits in d are shifted right by the shift count with the high-order bits filled from the low-order bits of s. The bits in s are not altered after shifting. If the shift count is zero, this instruction operates as an NOP. For the specified shift count, the SF, ZF, and PF flags are set according to the value of the result. CF is set to the value of the last bit shifted out. OF and AF are undefined.

As an example, consider SHLD BX, DX, 2. If $[BX] = 183F_{16}$ and $[DX] = 01F1_{16}$, then, after this SHLD, $[BX] = 60FC_{16}$, $[DX] = 01F1_{16}$, CF $= 0$, SF $= 0$, ZF $= 0$, and PF $= 1$. Similarly, the SHRD instruction can be illustrated.

String Instructions

Compare String Instructions There is a new 80386 instruction CMPS mem32, mem32 (or CMPSD) beyond the compare string instruction available with the 80286. This instruction compares 32-bit words ES:EDI (second operand) with DS:ESI and affects the flags. The direction of subtraction of CMPS is [[ESI]] − [[EDI]]. The left operand (ESI) is the source, and the right operand (EDI) is the destination. This is a reverse of the normal Intel convention in which the left operand is the destination and the right operand is the source. This is true for byte (CMPSB) or word (CMPSW) compare instructions. The result of subtraction is not stored; only the flags are affected. For the first operand (ESI), DS is used as the segment register unless a segment override byte is present; for the second operand (EDI), ES must be used as the segment register and cannot be overridden. ESI and EDI are incremented by 4 if DF = 0 and are decremented by 4 if DF = 1. CMPSD can be preceded by the REPE or REPNE prefix for block comparison. All flags affected.

Load and Move String Instructions   There are two new load and move instructions in the 80386 beyond those of 80286. These are LODS mem32 (or LODSD) and MOVS mem32, mem32 (or MOVSD). LODSD loads the (32-bit) double word from a memory location specified by DS:ESI into EAX. After the load, ESI is automatically incremented by 4 if DF = 0 and decremented by 4 if DF = 1. No flags are affected. LODS can be preceded by the REP prefix. LODS is typically used within a loop structure because further processing of the data moved into EAX is normally required. MOVSD copies the (32-bit) double word at the memory location addressed by DS:ESI to the memory location at ES:EDI. DS is used as the segment register for the source and may be overridden. After the move, ESI and EDI are incremented by 4 if DF = 0 and are decremented by 4 if DF = 1. MOVS can be preceded by the REP prefix for block movement of ECX double words. No flags are affected.

String I/O Instructions   There are two new string I/O instructions in the 80386 beyond those of the 80286. These are INS mem32, DX (or INSD) and OUTS DX, mem32 (or OUTSD). INSD inputs 32-bit data from a port addressed by the contents of DX into a memory location specified by ES:EDI. ES cannot be overridden. After data transfer, EDI is automatically incremented by 4 if DF = 0 and decremented by 4 if DF = 1. INSD can be preceded by the REP prefix for block input of ECX double words. No flags are affected. OUTSD outputs 32-bit data from a memory location addressed by DS:ESI to a port addressed by the contents of DX. DS can be overridden. After data transfer, ESI is incremented by 4 if DF = 0 and decremented by 4 if DF = 1. OUTSD can be preceded by the REP prefix for block output of ECX double words.

Store and Scan String Instructions   There is a new 80386 STOS mem32 (or STOSD) instruction. STOS stores the contents of the EAX register to a double word addressed by ES and EDI. ES cannot be overridden. After storing, EDI is automatically incremented by 4 if DF = 0 and decremented by 4 if DF = 1. No flags are affected.

STOS can be preceded by the REP prefix for a block fill of ECX double words. There is also a new scan instruction, the SCAS mem32 (or SCASD) in the 80386. SCASD performs the 32-bit subtraction [EAX] − [memory addressed by ES and EDI]. The result of subtraction is not stored, and the flags are affected. SCASD can be preceded by the REPE or REPNE prefix for block search of ECX double words. All flags are affected.

Table Look-Up Translation Instruction

A modified version of the 80286 XLAT instruction is available in the 80386. XLAT mem8 (or XLATB) replaces the AL register from the table index to the table entry. AL should be the unsigned index into a table addressed by DS:BX for a 16-bit address (available in the 80286 and 80386) and DS:EBX for 32-bit address (available only in the 80386). DS can be overridden. No flags are affected.

High-Level Language Instructions

The three instructions ENTER, LEAVE, and BOUND (also available with the 80186/80286) in this category have been enhanced in the 80386.

The ENTER imm16, imm8 instruction creates a stack frame. The data imm8 defines the nesting depth of the subroutine and can be from 0 to 31. The value 0 specifies the first subroutine only. The data imm8 defines the number of stack frame pointers copied into the new stack frame from the preceding frame. After the instruction is executed, the 80386 uses EBP as the current frame pointer and ESP as the current stack pointer. The data imm16 specifies the number of bytes of local variables for which the stack space is to be allocated. If imm8 is zero, ENTER pushes the frame pointer EBP onto the stack; ENTER then subtracts the first operand imm16 from the ESP and sets EBP to the current ESP.

For example, a procedure with 28 bytes of local variables would have an ENTER 28, 0 instruction at its entry point and a LEAVE instruction before every RET. The 28 local bytes would be addressed as offset from EBP. Note that the LEAVE instruction sets ESP to EBP and then pops EBP. For the 80186 and 80286, the ENTER and LEAVE instructions use BP and SP instead of EBP and ESP. The 80386 uses BP (low 16 bits of EBP) and SP (low 16 bits of ESP) for 16-bit operands and uses EBP and ESP for 32-bit operands.

The BOUND instruction ensures that a signed array index is within the limits specified by a block of memory containing an upper and lower bound. The 80386 provides two forms of the BOUND instruction:

    BOUND   reg16,   mem32
    BOUND   reg32,   mem64

The first form is for 16-bit operands and is also available

with the 80186 and 80286. The second form is for 32-bit operands and is included in the 80386 instruction set. For example, consider BOUND EDI, ADDR. Suppose [ADDR] = 32-bit lower bound d_l and [ADDR + 4] = 32-bit upper bound d_u. If, after execution of this instruction, [EDI] < d_l or > d_u, the 80386 traps to interrupt 5; otherwise, the array is accessed.

The BOUND instruction is usually placed following the computation of an index value to ensure that the limits of the index value are not violated. This permits a check to determine whether or not an address of an array being accessed is within the array boundaries when the register indirect with index mode is used to access an array element.

Example 7–1*

Determine the effect of each of the following 80386 instructions:

- CDQ
- BTC CX, BX
- MOVSX ECX, E7H

Assume [EAX] = FFFFFFFFH, [ECX] = F1257124H, [EDX] = EEEEEEEEH, [BX] = 0004H, prior to execution of each of the given instructions.

Solution

- After CDQ,

$$[EAX] = FFFFFFFFH$$
$$[EDX] = FFFFFFFFH$$

- After BTC CX, BX, bit 4 of register CX is reflected in CF and then 1's complemented in CX, as is shown below.

Hence,

$$[CX] = 7134H$$
$$[BX] = 0004H$$

- MOVSX ECX, E7H copies the 8-bit data E7H into the low byte of ECX and then sign-extends to 32 bits. Therefore, after MOVSX ECX, E7H,

$$[ECX] = FFFFFFE7H$$

Example 7–2*

Write an 80386 assembly language program to multiply a signed 8-bit number in AL by a signed 32-bit number in ECX. Assume that the segment registers are already initialized.

Solution

CBW	;	Sign-extend byte to word
CWDE	;	Sign-extend word to 32-bit
IMUL EAX, ECX	;	Perform signed multiplication
HLT	;	Stop

Example 7–3*

Write an 80386 assembly language program to move two columns of 10,000 32-bit numbers from A (i) to B (i). In other words, move A (1) to B (1), A (2) to B (2), and so on.

Solution

MOV ECX, 10,000	;	Initialize counter
MOV BX, SOURCE SEG	;	Initialize DS
MOV DS, BX	;	register
MOV BX, DEST SEG	;	Initialize ES
MOV ES, BX	;	register
MOV ESI, SOURCE INDX	;	Initialize ESI
MOV EDI, DEST INDX	;	Initialize EDI
SED	;	Set DF to auto-increment
REP MOVSD	;	MOV A (i) to
HLT	;	B (i) until ECX = 0

7–2–4 80386 Memory

Since, upon hardware reset, the 80386 executes the first instruction at location FFFFFFF0H. The ROM can be programmed to initialize the system and take care of resets.

Memory on the 80386 is structured as 8-bit (byte), 16-bit (word), or 32-bit (double word) quantities. Words are stored in 2 consecutive bytes with the address of the low byte addressing the word. Double words are stored

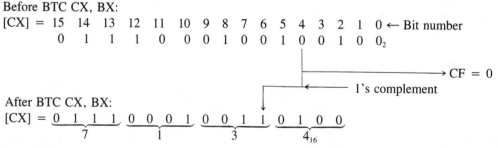

Before BTC CX, BX:
[CX] = 15 14 13 12 11 10 9 8 7 6 5 4 3 2 1 0 ← Bit number
         0   1   1   1   0   0 0 1 0 0 1 0 0 1 0 0_2

CF = 0
1's complement

After BTC CX, BX:
[CX] = 0 1 1 1 0 0 0 1 0 0 1 1 0 1 0 0
          7   1   3 4_{16}

*Reprinted with permission from Rafiquzzaman, M. *Microprocessors and Microcomputer-Based System Design,* copyright 1990, CRC Press, Inc., Boca Raton, FL.

in 4 consecutive bytes with byte 0 at the lowest address and byte 3 at the highest address. The lowest address containing byte 0 addresses the double word.

7-2-5   80386 I/O

The 80386 supports both standard and memory-mapped I/O. The I/O space contains 64K 8-bit ports, 16K 32-bit ports, or any combination of ports up to 64K bytes. I/O instructions do not go through paging or segment units. Therefore, the I/O space refers to physical memory. The M/$\overline{\text{IO}}$ pin distinguishes between memory and I/O. The 80386 includes IN and OUT instructions to support standard I/O with port addresses provided by the DL, DX, or EDX registers. All 8- or 16-bit port addresses are zero-extended on the upper address lines. The 80386 interrupts, and exceptions are similar to those of the 8086.

7-3   MOTOROLA MC68020

The MC68020 is Motorola's first 32-bit microprocessor. The design of the 68020 is based on that of the 68000. One of the major changes in the bus structure area is that, while the 68000 supports only asynchronous bus cycles, the 68020 performs data transfers using both synchronous and asynchronous bus cycles. Due to this enhancement, the 68020 can perform a normal read or write cycle in 3 clock cycles without wait states as compared to the 68000, which completes a read or write cycle in 4 clock cycles without wait states. As far as addressing mode is concerned, the 68020 includes several new modes beyond those of the 68000. Some of these modes include scaled indexing, larger displacements, and memory indirection. Furthermore, several new instructions are added to the 68020 instruction set. Some of these instructions include the following:

- Bit field instructions are provided for manipulating a string of consecutive bits with a variable length from 1 to 32 bits.
- Two new instructions perform conversion between packed BCD and ASCII or EBCDIC digits. Note that an example of packed BCD is a byte containing two BCD digits.
- Enhanced 68000 array-range checking (CHK2) and compare (CMP2) instructions are included. CHK2 includes lower and upper bound checking, while CMP2 compares a number with lower and upper values and affects flags accordingly.
- Two advanced instructions, namely, CALLM and RTM, are included to support modular programming.
- Two compare and swap instructions (CAS and CAS2) are provided to support multiprocessor systems.

A detailed comparison of the differences between the 68020 and 68000 will be provided later in this chapter.

The 68030 and 68040 are two enhanced versions of the 68020. The 68030 retains most of the 68020 features. The 68030 is a virtual memory microprocessor containing on-chip MMU (Memory Management Unit).

The 68030 includes one on-chip paged MMU (demand paging feature of the MC68851) for both instruction fetch and data access. This provides the 68030 with on-chip logical-to-physical address translation and on-chip virtual memory management hardware and allows eight different page sizes from 256 to 32K bytes. In addition to the 68020 instructions, four new 68030 instructions are included to perform memory management functions.

The 68040 expands the 68030 on-chip memory management logic to two units: one for instruction fetch and one for data access. This speeds up the 68040's execution time by performing logical-to-physical address translations in parallel.

The 68030 contains two on-chip caches (256-byte instruction cache and 256-byte data cache) compared to the 68020, which has an on-chip instruction cache of 256 bytes. The 68040, on the other hand, includes 4K bytes of on-chip instruction cache and 4K bytes of data cache. This large on-chip cache improves the cache hits. The 68040 also contains an on-chip floating-point unit capable of executing the basic floating-point instructions of the MC68881/MC68882 floating-point coprocessors. This on-chip floating-point capability of the 68040 provides it with both integer and floating-point arithmetic operations at high speed.

Although the 68020, 68030, and 68040 user programming models are unchanged from the 68000, the 68020 contains additional registers for cache access and control, the 68030 includes additional cache and MMU registers, and the 68040 contains additional cache, MMU, and floating-point registers.

All 68000 programs written in assembly language in user mode will run on the 68020/68030 or 68040. The 68030 and 68040 support all 68020 instructions except CALLM and RTM. This is due to the different memory protection technique used by the 68030 and 68040.

The 68040 provides the 18 addressing modes of the 68020/68030. All data formats offered by the 68000 family are also supported by the 68040. In addition, the 68040 supports a new 16-byte data format used by the new MOVE16 instruction used for the 16-byte block move. The 68040 includes all the 68030 instructions plus 20 new ones. Some 68040 instructions are 68030 enhancements. These primarily relate to MMU and cache control functions. The new 68040 instructions typically include floating-point arithmetic such as floating-point add, subtract, multiply, divide, and square root.

Let us now focus on the 68020 microprocessor in more detail.

7-3-1 MC68020 Functional Characteristics

The MC68020 is designed to execute all user object code written for previous members of the MC68000 family. It is manufactured using HCMOS (combining HMOS and CMOS on the same device) technology. The 68020 consumes a maximum of 1.75 W. It contains 200,000 transistors on a 3/8″ piece of silicon. The chip is packaged in a square (1.345″ × 1.345″) pin grid array (PGA) and contains 169 pins (114 pins used) arranged in a 13 × 13 matrix.

The processor speed of the 68020 can be 12.5, 16.67, 20, 25, or 33 MHz. The chip must be operated from a minimum frequency of 8 MHz. Like the 68000, it does not have any on-chip clock generation circuitry. The 68020 contains 18 addressing modes and 108 instructions. All addressing modes and instructions of the 68000 are included in the 68020. The 68020 supports coprocessors such as the MC68881/MC68882 floating-point and MC68851 MMU coprocessors.

These and other functional characteristics of the 68020 are compared with the 68000 in Table 7-2. Some of the 68020 characteristics in Table 7-2 will now be explained.

- The three independent ALUs are provided for data manipulation and address calculations.
- A 32-bit barrel shift register (occupies 7% of silicon) is included in the 68020 for very fast shift operations regardless of the shift count.
- The 68020 has three SPs. In the supervisor mode (when S = 1), two SPs can be accessed. These are MSP (when M = 1) and ISP (when M = 0). ISP can be used to simplify and speed up task switching for operating systems.
- The vector base register (VBR) is used in interrupt vector computation. For example, in the 68000, the interrupt address vector is obtained by multiplying an 8-bit vector by 4. In the 68020, on the other hand, the interrupt address vector is obtained by using VBR + 4 * 8-bit vector.
- The SFC (source function code) and DFC (destination function code) registers are 3 bits wide. These registers allow the supervisor to move data between address spaces. In supervisor mode, 3-bit addresses can be written into SFC or DFC using instructions such as MOVEC A2, SFC. The upper 29 bits of SFC are assumed to be zero. The MOVES.W(A0), D0 can then be used to move a word from a location within the address space specified by SFC and(A0) to D0. The 68020 outputs [SFC] to the FC2, FC1, and FC0 pins. By decoding these pins via an external decoder, the desired source memory location addressed by (A0) can be accessed.

- The new addressing modes in the 68020 include scaled indexing, 32-bit displacements, and memory indirection. In order to illustrate the concept of scaling, consider moving the contents of memory location 50_{10} to A1. Using the 68000, the following instruction sequence will accomplish this:

  MOVEA.W #10, A0
  MOVE.W #10, D0
  ASL #2, D0
  MOVEA.L 0 (A0, D0), A1

The scaled indexing can be used with the 68020 to perform the same as follows:

  MOVEA.W #10, A0
  MOVE.W #10, D0
  MOVEA.L (0, A0, D0 * 4), A1

Note that [D0] here is scaled by 4. Scaling by 1, 2, 4, or 8 can be obtained.

- The new 68020 instructions include bit field instructions to better support compilers and certain hardware applications such as graphics, 32-bit multiply and divide instructions, pack and unpack instructions for BCD, and coprocessor instructions. Bit field instructions can be used to input A/D converters and eliminate wasting main memory space when the A/D converter is not 32 bits wide. For example, if the A/D is 12 bits wide, then the following instruction, BFEXTU $22320000 {2:13}, D0, will input bits 2–13 of memory location $22320000 into D0. Note that $22320000 is the memory-mapped port, in this case, where the 12-bit A/D is connected at bits 2–13. The next A/D can be connected at bits 14–25, and so on.
- FC2, FC1, FC0 = 111 means CPU space cycle. The 68020 makes CPU space access for breakpoints, coprocessor operations, or interrupt acknowledge cycles. The CPU space classification is generated by the 68020 based upon execution of breakpoint instructions or coprocessor instructions or during an interrupt acknowledge cycle. The 68020 then decodes A16–A19 to determine the type of CPU space. For example, FC2, FC1, FC0 = 111 and A19, A18, A17, A16 = 0010 mean coprocessor instruction.
- For performing floating-point operations, the 68000 user must write subroutines using the 68000 instruction set. The floating-point capability in the 68020 can be obtained by connecting a floating-point coprocessor chip such as the Motorola 68881. The 68020 currently has two coprocessor chips: the 68881 (floating point) and the 68851 (memory management). The 68020 can have up to eight coprocessor chips. When a coprocessor is connected to the 68020, the coprocessor instructions are added to the 68020 instruction set automatically, and this is transparent

TABLE 7–2
Functional Characteristics, MC68000 vs. MC68020

Characteristic	68000	68020
Technology	HMOS	HCMOS
Number of pins	64, 68	169 (13 × 13 matrix; pins come out at bottom of chip; 114 pins currently used)
Control unit	Nanomemory (two-level memory)	Nanomemory (two-level memory)
Clock	6 MHz, 10 MHz, 12.5 MHz, 16.67 MHz, 20 MHz, 25 MHz, 33 MHz (no minimum requirement)	12.5 MHz, 16.67 MHz, 20 MHz, 25 MHz, 33 MHz (8-MHz minimum requirement)
ALU	1 16-bit ALU	3 32-bit ALUs
Address bus size	24 bits with A0 encoded from $\overline{UDS}$ and $\overline{LDS}$	32 bits with no encoding of A0 required
Data bus size	Uses D0–D7 for odd addresses and D8–D15 for even addresses during byte transfers; for word and long word, uses D0–D15	8, 16, and 32 bits (byte, word, and long word transfers occur, respectively, via D31–D24 lines, D31–D16 lines, and D31–D0 lines)
Instruction and data access	All word and long word accesses must be at even addresses for both instructions and data	Instructions must be accessed at even addresses; data accesses can be at any address
Instruction cache	None	128K 16-bit-word cache. At start of an instruction fetch, the 68020 always outputs LOW on $\overline{ECS}$ (early cycle start) pin and accesses the cache. If instruction is found in the cache, the 68020 inhibits outputting LOW on $\overline{AS}$ pin; otherwise, the 68020 sends LOW on $\overline{AS}$ pin and reads instruction from main memory.
Directly addressable memory	16 megabytes	4 gigabytes (4,294,964,296 bytes)
Registers	8 32-bit data registers 7 32-bit address registers 2 32-bit SPs 1 32-bit PC (24 bits used) 1 16-bit SR	8 32-bit data registers 7 32-bit address registers 3 32-bit SPs 1 32-bit PC (all bits used) 1 16-bit SR 1 32-bit VBR (vector base register) 2 3-bit function code registers (SFC and DFC) 1 32-bit CAAR (cache address register) 1 CACR (cache control register)
Addressing modes	14	18
Instruction set	56 instructions	108 instructions
Barrel shifter	No	Yes. For fast shift operations
Stack pointers	USP, SSP	USP, MSP (master SP), ISP (interrupt SP)
Status register	T, S, I0, I1, I2, X, N, Z, V, C	T0, T1, S, M, I0, I1, I2, X, N, Z, V, C
Coprocessor interface	Emulated in software; that is, by writing subroutines, coprocessor functions such as floating-point arithmetic can be obtained	Can be directly interfaced to coprocessor chips, and coprocessor functions such as floating-point arithmetic can be obtained via 68020 instructions
FC0, FC1, FC2 pins	FC0, FC, FC2 = 111 means interrupt acknowledge	FC0, FC1, FC2 = 111 means CPU space cycle; then by decoding A16–A19, one can obtain breakpoints, coprocessor functions, and interrupt acknowledge

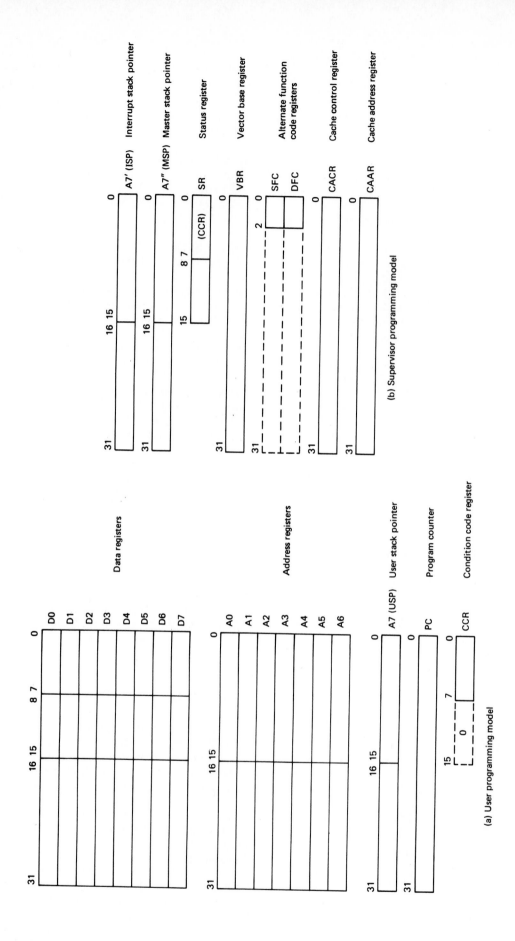

Figure 7–5 MC68020 programming model. (Reprinted with permission of Motorola)

to the user. For example, when the 68881 floating-point coprocessor is added to the 68020, instructions such as FADD (floating-point add) are available to the user. The programmer can then execute the instruction FADD FD0, FD1. Note that registers FD0 and FD1 are in the 68881. When the 68020 encounters the FADD instruction, it writes a command in the command register in the 68881, indicating that the 68881 has to perform this operation. The 68881 then responds to this by writing in the 68881 response register. Note that all coprocessor registers are memory-mapped. The 68020 thus can read the response register and obtain the result of the floating-point add from the appropriate location.

7–3–2 MC68020 Programmer's Model

The MC68020 programmer's model is based on sequential, nonconcurrent instruction execution. This implies that each instruction is completely executed before the next instruction is executed. Although instructions might operate concurrently in actual hardware, they do not operate concurrently in the programmer's model.

Figure 7–5 shows the MC68020 user and supervisor programming models. The user model has sixteen 32-bit general-purpose registers (D0–D7 and A0–A7), a 32-bit program counter (PC), and a condition code register (CCR) contained within the supervisor status register (SR). The supervisor model has two 32-bit supervisor stack pointers (ISP and MSP), a 16-bit status register (SR), a 32-bit vector base register (VBR), two 3-bit alternate function code registers (SFC and DFC), and two 32-bit cache-handling (address and control) registers

(CAAR and CACR). General-purpose registers A0–A6, user stack pointer (USP) A7, interrupt stack pointer (ISP) A_7', and master stack pointer (MSP) $A_7' A_7''$ are address registers that may be used as software stack pointers or base address registers.

The status register, as shown in Figure 7–6, consists of a user byte (condition code register, CCR) and a system byte. The system byte contains control bits to indicate that the processor is in the trace mode (T1, T0), supervisor/user state (S), and master/interrupt state (M). The user byte consists of the following condition codes: carry (C), overflow (V), zero (Z), negative (N), and extend (X). The conditional tests available to the 68020 are shown later in Table 7–6 (page 238).

The bits in the 68020 user byte are set or reset in the same way as those of the 68000 user byte. The bits I2, I1, I0, and S have the same meaning as those of the 68000. In the 68020, two trace bits (T1, T0) are included as opposed to one trace bit (T) in the 68000. These two bits allow the 68020 to trace on both normal instruction execution and jumps. The 68020 M bit is not included in the 68000 status register.

The vector base register (VBR) is used to locate the exception processing vector table in memory. VBR supports multiple vector tables so that each process can properly manage independent exceptions. The 68020 distinguishes address spaces as supervisor/user and program/data. To support full access privileges in the supervisor mode, the alternate function code registers (SFC and DFC) allow the supervisor to access any address space by preloading the SFC/DFC registers appropriately. The cache registers (CACR and CAAR) allow software manipulation of the instruction code. The CACR provides

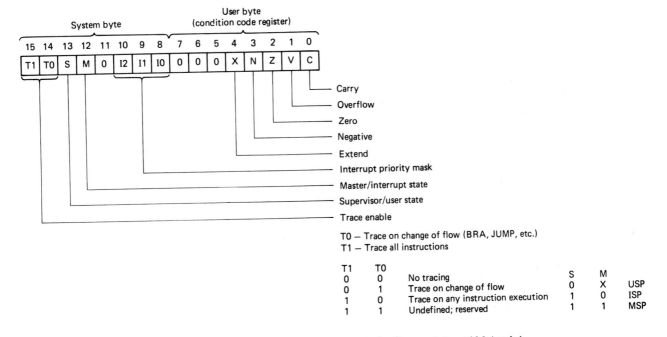

Figure 7–6 MC68020 status register. (Reprinted with permission of Motorola)

control and status accesses to the instruction cache, while the CAAR holds the address for those cache control functions that require an address.

7-3-3 MC68020 Addressing Modes

Table 7–3 lists the MC68020's 18 addressing modes. Table 7–4 compares the addressing modes of the MC68000 with those of the MC68020. Since 68000 addressing modes were covered in Chapter 6 in detail with examples, the 68020 modes not available in the 68000 will be covered in the following discussion.

ARI with Index (Scaled) and 8-Bit Displacement

- Assembler syntax: (d8, An, Xn.size * scale)
- EA = (An) + (Xn.size * scale) + d8
- Xn can be W or L.

If the index register (An or Dn) is 16 bits, then it is sign-extended to 32 bits and multiplied by 1, 2, 4, or 8 prior to being used in EA calculation; d8 is also sign-extended to 32 bits prior to EA calculation. An example is MOVE.W (0, A2, D2.W * 2), D1. Suppose that [A2] = \$50000000, [D2.W] = \$1000, and [\$50002000] = \$1571; then, after execution of this MOVE, [D1]$_{\text{low 16 bits}}$ = \$1571 since EA = \$50000000 + \$1000 * 2 + 0 = \$50002000.

ARI with Index and Base Displacement

- Assembler syntax: (bd, An, Xn.size * scale)
- EA = (An) + (Xn.size * scale) + bd
- Base displacement, bd, has value 0 when present or can be 16 or 32 bits.

The following figure shows the use of ARI with index, Xn, and base displacement, bd, for accessing tables or arrays:

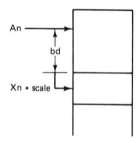

An example is MOVE.W (\$5000, A2, D1.W * 4), D5. If [A2] = \$30000000, [D1.W] = \$0200, and [\$30005800] = \$0174, then, after execution of this MOVE, [D5]$_{\text{low 16 bits}}$ = \$0174 since EA = \$5000 + \$30000000 + \$0200 * 4 = \$30005800.

TABLE 7–3
MC68020 Addressing Modes

Mode	Syntax
Register direct	
Data register direct	Dn
Address register direct	An
Register indirect	
Address register indirect (ARI)	(An)
Address register indirect with post-increment	(An)+
Address register indirect with predecrement	–(An)
Address register indirect with displacement	(d16, An)
Register indirect with index	
Address register indirect with index (8-bit displacement)	(d8, An, Xn)
Address register indirect with index (base displacement)	(bd, An, Xn)
Memory indirect	
Memory indirect, postindexed	([bd, An], Xn, od)
Memory indirect, preindexed	([bd, An, Xn], od)
Program counter indirect with displacement	(d16, PC)
Program counter indirect with index	
PC indirect with index (8-bit displacement)	(d8, PC, Xn)
PC indirect with index (base displacement)	(bd, PC, Xn)
Program counter memory indirect	
PC memory indirect, postindexed	([bd, PC], Xn, od)
PC memory indirect, preindexed	([bd, PC, Xn], od)
Absolute	
Absolute short	(xxx).W
Absolute long	(xxx).L
Immediate	#⟨data⟩

Reprinted with permission of Motorola.
Notes:
    Dn = data register, D0–D7
    An = address register, A0–A7
d8, d16 = 2's-complement or sign-extended displacement; added as part of effective address calculation; size is 8 (d8) or 16 (d16) bits; when omitted, assemblers use a value of 0
    Xn = address or data register used as an index register; form is Xn.size * scale, where size is .W or .L (indicates index register size) and scale is 1, 2, 4, or 8 (index register is multiplied by scale); use of size and/or scale is optional
    bd = 2's-complement base displacement; when present, size can be 16 or 32 bits
    od = outer displacement, added as part of effective address calculation after any memory indirection; use is optional with a size of 16 or 32 bits
    PC = program counter
⟨data⟩ = immediate value of 8, 16, or 32 bits
    ( ) = effective address
    [ ] = use as indirect address to long word address
    ARI = Address Register Indirect

Memory Indirect

Memory indirect is distinguished from address register indirect by use of square brackets in the assembler no-

TABLE 7–4
Addressing Modes, MC68000 vs. MC68020

Addressing Modes Available	Syntax	68000	68020
Data register direct	Dn	Yes	Yes
Address register direct	An	Yes	Yes
Address register indirect (ARI)	(An)	Yes	Yes
ARI with postincrement	(An)+	Yes	Yes
ARI with predecrement	−(An)	Yes	Yes
ARI with displacement (16-bit disp)	(d, An)	Yes	Yes
ARI with index (8-bit disp)	(d, An, Xn)	Yes*	Yes*
ARI with index (base disp: 0, 16, 32)	(bd, An, Xn)	No	Yes
Memory indirect (postindexed)	([bd, An], Xn, od)	No	Yes
Memory indirect (preindexed)	([bd, An, Xn], od)	No	Yes
PC indirect with disp. (16-bit)	(d, PC)	Yes	Yes
PC indirect with index (8-bit disp)	(d, PC, Xn)	Yes*	Yes*
PC indirect with index (base disp)	(bd, PC, Xn)	No	Yes
PC memory indirect (postindexed)	([bd, PC], Xn, od)	No	Yes
PC memory indirect (preindexed)	([bd, PC, Xn], od)	No	Yes
Absolute short	(xxx).W	Yes	Yes
Absolute long	(xxx).L	Yes	Yes
Immediate	#⟨data⟩	Yes	Yes

Reprinted with permission of Motorola.
*68000 has no scaling capability; 68020 can scale Xn by 1, 2, 4, or 8.

tation. The concept of memory indirect mode is depicted in the following figure:

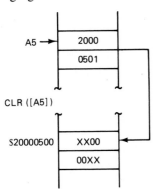

Here, register A5 points to the effective address $20000501. Since CLR ([A5]) is a 16-bit clear instruction, 2 bytes in locations $20000501 and $20000502 are cleared to 0.

Memory indirect mode can be indexed with scaling and displacements. There are two types of memory indirect mode with scaled indexing and displacements: postindexed memory indirect mode and preindexed memory indirect mode.

For postindexed memory indirect mode, an indirect memory address is first calculated using the base register

(An) and base displacement (bd). This address is used for an indirect memory access of a long word followed by adding a scaled indexed operand and an optional outer displacement (od) to generate the effective address. Note that bd and od can be zero, 16 bits, or 32 bits. In post-indexed memory indirect mode, indexing occurs after memory indirection.

- Assembler syntax: ([bd, An], Xn.size * scale, od)
- EA = ([bd + An]) + (Xn.size * scale + od)

An example is MOVE.W ([$0004, A1], D1.W * 2, 2), D2. If [A1] = $20000000, [$20000004] = $00003000, [D1.W] = $0002, and [$00003006] = $1A40, then, after execution of this MOVE, intermediate pointer = (4 + $20000000) = $20000004, [$20000004], which is $00003000 used as a pointer. Therefore, EA = $00003000 + $00000004 + 2 = $00003006. Hence, $[D2]_{\text{low 16 bits}}$ = $1A40.

For memory indirect preindexed mode, the scaled index operand is added to the base register (An) and base displacement (bd). This result is then used as an indirect address into the data space. The 32-bit value at this address is fetched and an optional outer displacement (od) is added to generate the effective address. The indexing, therefore, occurs before indirection.

- Assembler syntax: ([bd, An, Xn · size * scale], od)
  EA = (bd, An + Xn · size * scale) + od

As an example of the preindexed mode, consider several I/O devices in a system. The addresses of these devices can be held in a table pointed to by An, bd, and Xn. The actual programs for the devices can be stored in memory pointed to by the respective device addresses plus od.

The memory indirect preindexed mode will now be illustrated by a numerical example. Consider

MOVE.W ([$0002, A1, D0 · W * 2], 2), D1

If [A1] = $20000000, [D0 · W] = $0004, [$2000000A] = $00121502, [$00121504] = $F124, then after execution of this MOVE, intermediate pointer = $20000000 + $0002 + $0004*2 = $2000000A. Therefore, [$2000000A], which is $00121502, is used as the memory pointer.

$$EA = \$00121502 + 2$$
$$= \$00121504$$

Hence, $[D1]_{\text{low 16 bits}} = \$F124$.

7–3–4 MC68020 Instruction Set

The MC68020 instruction set includes all 68000 instructions plus some new ones. Some of the 68000 instructions are enhanced. Over 20 new instructions are added to provide new functionality. A list of these instructions is given in Table 7–5.

Succeeding sections will discuss the 68020 instructions listed next:

- 68020 new privileged move instructions
- RTD instruction
- CHK/CHK2 and CMP/CMP2 instructions
- TRAPcc instructions
- Bit field instructions
- PACK and UNPK instructions
- Multiplication and division instructions
- 68000 enhanced instructions

68020 New Privileged Move Instructions

The 68020 new privileged move instructions can be executed by the 68020 in the supervisor mode. They are listed below:

TABLE 7–5
68020 New Instructions

Instruction	Description
BFCHG	Bit field change
BFCLR	Bit field clear
BFEXTS	Bit field signed extract
BFEXTU	Bit field unsigned extract
BFFFO	Bit field find first one set
BFINS	Bit field insert
BFSET	Bit field set
BFTST	Bit field test
CALLM	Call module
CAS	Compare and swap
CAS2	Compare and swap (two operands)
CHK2	Check register against upper and lower bounds
CMP2	Compare register against upper and lower bounds
cpBcc	Coprocessor branch on coprocessor condition
cpDBcc	Coprocessor test condition, decrement, and branch
cpGEN	Coprocessor general function
cpRESTORE	Coprocessor restore internal state
cpSAVE	Coprocessor save internal state
cpSETcc	Coprocessor set according to coprocessor condition
cpTRAPcc	Coprocessor trap on coprocessor condition
PACK	Pack BCD
RTM	Return from module
UNPK	Unpack BCD

Reprinted with permission of Motorola.

Note that Rc includes VBR, SFC, DFC, MSP, ISP, USP, CACR, and CAAR. Rn can be either an address or a data register.

The operand size (.L) indicates that the MOVEC operations are always long word. Notice that only register to register operations are allowed. A control register (Rc) can be copied to an address or a data register (Rn) or vice versa. When the 3 bit SFC or DFC register is copied into Rn, all 32 bits of the register are overwritten and the upper 29 bits are "0."

The MOVES (move to alternate space) instruction allows the operating system to access any addressed space defined by the function codes. It is typically used when an operating system running in the supervisor mode must pass a pointer or value to a previously defined user program or data space.

Instruction	Operand Size	Operation	Notation
MOVE	16	SR → destination	MOVE SR, (EA)
MOVEC	32	Rc → Rn	MOVEC.L Rc, Rn
		Rn → Rc	MOVEC.L Rn, Rc
MOVES	8, 16, 32	Rn → destination using DFC	MOVES.S Rn, (EA)
		Source using SFC → Rn	MOVES.S (EA), Rn

The operand size (.S) indicates that the MOVES instruction can be byte (.B), word (.W), or long word (.L). The MOVES instruction allows register to memory or memory to register operations. When a memory to register move occurs, this instruction causes the contents of the source function code register to be placed on the external function hardware pins. For a register to memory move, the processor places the destination function code register on the external function code pins.

The MOVES instruction can be used to move information from one space to another, as shown by the following example.

Example 7–4

Find the contents of D5 and the function code pins FC2, FC1, and FC0 after execution of MOVES.B D5, (A5). Assume the following data prior to execution of this MOVES instruction:

$$[SFC] = 101_2, [DFC] = 100_2$$
$$[A5] = \$70000023, [D5] = \$718F2A05$$
$$[\$70000020] = \$01, [\$70000021] = \$F1$$
$$[\$70000022] = \$A2, [\$70000023] = \$2A$$

Solution

After execution of this MOVES instruction,
$$FC2\ FC1\ FC0\ = 100_2$$
$$[\$70000023] = \$05$$

Return and Delocate Instruction

The return and delocate (RTD) instruction is useful when a subroutine has the responsibility to remove parameters off the stack that were pushed onto the stack by the calling routine. Note that the calling routine's JSR (jump to subroutine) or BSR (branch to subroutine) instructions do not automatically push parameters onto the stack prior to the call as do the CALLM instructions. Rather, the pushed parameters must be placed there using the MOVE instruction.

The format of the RTD instruction is shown next:

Instruction	Operand Size	Operation	Notation
RTD	Unsized	(SP) → PC, SP + 4 + d → SP	RTD #⟨disp⟩

As an example, consider RTD #8, which, at the end of a subroutine, deallocates 8 bytes of unwanted parameters off the stack by adding 8 to the stack pointer and returns to the main program.

CHK/CHK2 and CMP/CMP2 Instructions

The 68020 check instruction (CHK) compares a 32-bit 2's complement integer value residing in a data register (Dn) against a lower bound (LB) value of zero and against

an upper bound (UB) value of the programmer's choice. These bounds are located beginning at the effective address (EA) specified in the instruction format. The CHK instruction has the following format:

$$CHK.S\ (EA),\ Dn$$

where the operand size (.S) designates word (.W) or long word (.L).

If the data register value is less than zero (Dn < 0) or if the data register is greater than the upper bound (Dn > UB), then the processor traps through exception vector 6 (offset $18) in the exception vector table. Of course, the operating system or the programmer must define a check service handler routine at this vector address. After completion of the CHK instruction, the negative (N) bit is the only condition code register (CCR) bit that is defined or affected. If the compared register (Dn) is less than zero, then the N bit is set to 1. If the data register exceeds the upper bound, then the N bit is cleared to 0. If the CHK instruction finds that the compared register value is within bounds (i.e., $0 \leq Dn \leq UB$ value), then all CCR bits except X (X is unaffected) are undefined (U), and program execution resumes with the next instruction in the instruction flow.

The CHK instruction can be used for maintaining array subscripts since all subscripts can be checked against an upper bound (i.e., UB = array size − 1). If the compared subscript is within the array bounds (i.e., $0 \leq$ subscript value $\leq$ UB value), then the subscript is valid, and the program continues normal instruction execution. If the subscript value is out of array limits (i.e., $0 >$ subscript value or subscript value $>$ UB value), then the processor traps through the CHK exception.

Example 7–5

Determine the effects of execution of CHK.L (A5), D3, where A5 represents a memory pointer to the array's upper bound value. Register D3 contains the subscript value to be checked against the array bounds. Assume the following data prior to execution of this CHK instruction:

$$[D3] = \$01507126$$
$$[A5] = \$00710004$$
$$[\$00710004] = \$01500000$$

Solution (see top of page 236.)

The long word array subscript value $01507126 contained in data register D3 is compared against the long word UB value $01500000 pointed to by address register A5. Since the value $01507126 contained in D3 exceeds the UB value $01500000 pointed to by A5, the N bit is cleared. (The remaining CCR bits are either undefined or not affected.) This out-of-bounds condition causes the program to trap to a check exception service routine.

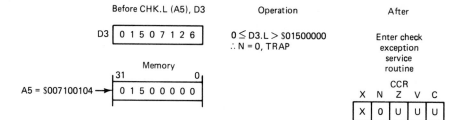

Before CHK.L (A5), D3

D3 | 0 1 5 0 7 1 2 6

Memory

A5 = $007100104 → [31] 0 1 5 0 0 0 0 0 [0]

Operation

$0 \leq D3.L > \$01500000$
$\therefore N = 0$, TRAP

After

Enter check
exception
service
routine

CCR

X	N	Z	V	C
X	0	U	U	U

The operation of the CHK instruction can be summarized as follows:

Instruction	Operand Size	Operation	Notation
CHK	16, 32	If Dn < 0 or Dn > source, then TRAP	CHK (EA), Dn

The 68020 CMP.S (EA), Dn instruction subtracts (EA) from Dn and affects the condition codes without any result. The operand size designator (.S) is either byte (.B) or word (.W) or long word (.L).

Both the CHK2 and the CMP2 instructions have similar formats:

$$CHK2.S \ (EA), Rn$$

and

$$CMP2.S \ (EA), Rn$$

They compare a value contained in a data or address register (designated by Rn ≥ against two (2) bounds chosen by the programmer. The size of the data to be compared (.S) may be specified as either byte (.B) or word (.W) or long word (.L). As shown in the following figure, the lower bound (LB) value must be located in memory at the effective address (EA) specified in the instruction, and the upper bound (UB) value must follow immediately at the next higher memory address. That is, UB addr = LB addr + size, where size = B (+1), W (+2), or L = (+4).

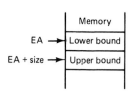

Memory

EA → Lower bound
EA + size → Upper bound

If the compared register is a data register (i.e., Rn = Dn) and the operand size (.S) is a byte or word, then only the appropriate low-order part of the data register is checked. If the compared register is an address register (i.e., Rn = An) and the operand size (.S) is a byte or word, then the bound operands are sign-extended to 32 bits and the extended operands are compared against the full 32 bits of the address register.

The CHK2 and CMP2 instructions both set the CCR carry bit (C) to 1 if the compared register's data is out of bounds. Likewise, the zero bit (Z) is set to 1 if the data is equal to either bound or otherwise cleared to 0. In the case where an upper bound equals the lower bound, the valid range for comparison becomes a single value. The only difference between the CHK2 and CMP2 instructions is that, for comparisons determined to be out of bounds, CHK2 causes exception processing utilizing the same exception vector as the CHK instructions, whereas the CMP2 instruction execution affects only the condition codes.

In both instructions, the compare is performed for either signed or unsigned bounds. The 68020 automatically evaluates the relationship between the two bounds to determine which kind of comparison to employ. If the programmer wishes to have the bounds evaluated as signed values, the arithmetically smaller value should be the lower bound. If the bounds are to be evaluated as unsigned values, the programmer should make the logically smaller value the lower bound.

The following CMP2 and CHK2 instruction examples are identical in that they both utilize the same registers, comparison data, and bound values. The difference is how the upper and lower bounds are arranged.

Example 7–6

Determine the effects of execution of CMP2.W (A2), D1. Assume the following data prior to execution of this CMP2 instruction:

$$[D1] = \$50000200, \ [A2] = \$00007000$$
$$[\$00007000] = \$B000, \ [\$00007002] = \$5000$$

Solution (see at top of page 237.)

In this example, the word value $B000 contained in memory (as pointed to by address register A2) is the lower bound and the word value immediately following $5000 is the upper bound. Since the lower bound is the arithmetically smaller value, the programmer is indicating to the 68020 to interpret the bounds as signed numbers. The 2's complement value $B000 is equivalent to an actual value of −$5000. Therefore, the instruction evaluates the word contained in data register D1 ($0200) to determine whether it is greater than or equal to the upper bound, +$5000, or less than or equal to the lower bound,

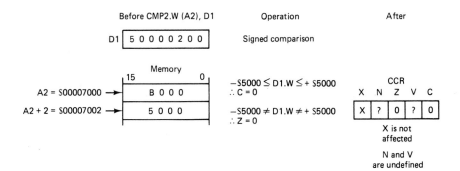

Before CMP2.W (A2), D1

D1 | 5 0 0 0 0 2 0 0

Memory
15   0

A2 = $00007000 → B 0 0 0

A2 + 2 = $00007002 → 5 0 0 0

Operation

Signed comparison

$-\$5000 \leq \text{D1.W} \leq +\$5000$
$\therefore C = 0$

$-\$5000 \neq \text{D1.W} \neq +\$5000$
$\therefore Z = 0$

After

CCR
X   N   Z   V   C

X | ? | 0 | ? | 0

X is not
affected

N and V
are undefined

$-\$5000$. Since the compared value $0200 is within bounds, the carry bit (C) is cleared to 0. Also, since $0200 is not equal to either bound, the zero bit (Z) is cleared. The following figure shows the range of valid values that D1 could contain:

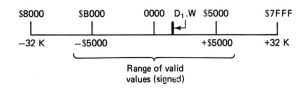

$8000 $B000   0000 D_1.W $5000 $7FFF

-32 K $-\$5000$ $+\$5000$ $+32$ K

Range of valid
values (signed)

A typical application for the CMP2 instruction would be to read in a number of user entries and verify that each entry is valid by comparing it against the valid range bounds. In the preceding CMP2 example, the user-entered value would be in register D1 and register A2 would point to a range for that value. The CMP2 instruction would verify whether the entry is in range by clearing the CCR carry bit if it is in bounds and setting the carry bit if it is out of bounds.

Example 7–7

Determine the effects of execution of CHK2.W (A2), D1. Assume the following data prior to execution of this CHK2 instruction:

$$[\text{D1}] = \$50000200, \quad [\text{A2}] = \$00007000$$
$$[\$00007000] = \$5000, \quad [\$00007002] = \$B000$$

Solution

This time, the value $5000 located in memory is the lower bound and the value $B000 is the upper bound.

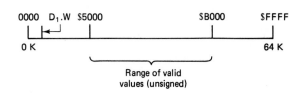

0000 D_1.W $5000 $B000 $FFFF

0 K   64 K

Range of valid
values (unsigned)

Now, since the lower bound contains the logically smaller value, the programmer is indicating to the 68020 to interpret the bounds as unsigned numbers, representing only a magnitude. Therefore, the instruction evaluates the word contained in register D1 ($0200) to determine whether it is greater than or equal to the lower bound, $5000, or less than or equal to the upper bound, $B000. Since the compared value $0200 is less than $5000, the carry bit is set to indicate an out-of-bounds condition and the program traps to the CHK/CHK2 exception vector service routine. Also, since $0200 is not equal to either bound, the zero bit (Z) is cleared. The figure above shows the range of valid values that D1 could contain.

A typical application for the CHK2 instruction would be to cause a trap exception to occur if a certain subscript value is not within the bounds of some defined array. Using the CHK2 example format just given, if we define an array of 100 elements with subscripts ranging from 50_{10}–40_{10}, and if the two words located at (A2) and (A2 + 2) contain 50 and 49, respectively, and register D1 contains 100_{10}, then execution of the CHK2 instruction would cause a trap through the CHK/CHK2 exception vector.

The operation of the CMP2 and CHK2 instructions can be summarized as follows:

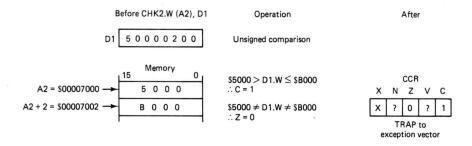

Before CHK2.W (A2), D1

D1 | 5 0 0 0 0 2 0 0

Memory
15   0

A2 = $00007000 → 5 0 0 0

A2 + 2 = $00007002 → B 0 0 0

Operation

Unsigned comparison

$\$5000 > \text{D1.W} \leq \$B000$
$\therefore C = 1$

$\$5000 \neq \text{D1.W} \neq \$B000$
$\therefore Z = 0$

After

CCR
X   N   Z   V   C

X | ? | 0 | ? | 1

TRAP to
exception vector

Instruction	Operand Size	Operation	Notation
CMP2	8, 16, 32	Compare Rn < source − lower bound or Rn > source − upper bound and set CCR	CMP2 ⟨EA⟩, Rn
CHK2	8, 16, 32	If Rn < source − lower bound or Rn > source − upper bound, then TRAP	CHK2 ⟨EA⟩, Rn

Trap-on-Condition Instructions The new trap-on-condition (TRAPcc) instruction allows a conditional trap exception on any of the condition codes shown in Table 7–6. These are the same conditions that are allowed for the set-on-condition (Scc) and the branch-on-condition (Bcc) instructions.

The TRAPcc instruction evaluates the selected test condition based on the state of the condition code flags, and, if the test is true, the 68020 initiates exception processing by trapping through the same exception vector as the TRAPV instruction (vector 7, offset \$1C, VBR = VBR + offset). The trap-on-condition instruction format is

$$\text{TRAPcc} \quad or \quad \text{TRAPcc.S} \ \#\langle\text{data}\rangle$$

where the operand size (.S) designates word (.W) or long word (.L).

If either a word or long word operand is specified, a 1- or 2-word immediate operand is placed following the instruction word. The immediate operand(s) consists

TABLE 7–6
Conditions for TRAPcc

Code	Description	Result
CC	Carry clear	$\overline{C}$
CS	Carry set	C
EQ	Equal	Z
F	Never true	0
GE	Greater or equal	$N . V + \overline{N} . \overline{V}$
GT	Greater than	$N . V . \overline{Z} + \overline{N} . \overline{V} . \overline{Z}$
HI	High	$\overline{C} . \overline{Z}$
LE	Less or equal	$Z + N . \overline{V} + \overline{N} . V$
LS	Low or same	$C + Z$
LT	Less than	$N . \overline{V} + \overline{N} . V$
MI	Minus	N
NE	Not equal	$\overline{Z}$
PL	Plus	N
T	Always true	1
VC	Overflow clear	$\overline{V}$
VS	Overflow set	V

Reprinted with permission of Motorola.

of argument parameters that are passed to the trap handler to further define requests or services it should perform. If cc is false, the 68020 does not interpret the immediate operand(s) but instead adjusts the program counter to the beginning of the following instruction. The exception handler can access this immediate data as an offset to the stacked PC. The stacked PC is the next instruction to be executed.

A summary of the TRAPcc instruction operation is shown next:

Instruction	Operand Size	Operation	Notation
TRAPcc	None	If cc, then TRAP	TRAPcc
	16		TRAPcc.W #⟨data⟩
	32		TRAPcc.L #⟨data⟩

Bit Field Instructions The bit field instructions, which allow an operation such as clear, set, 1's complement, input, insert, and test one or more bits in a string of bits (bit field), are listed next:

Instruction	Operand Size	Operation	Notation
BFTST	1–32	Field MSB → N, Z = 1 if all bits in field are zero; Z = 0 otherwise	BFTST (EA) {offset: width}
BFCLR	1–32	0's → field	BFCLR (EA) {offset: width}
BFSET	1–32	1's → field	BFSET (EA) {offset: width}
BFCHG	1–32	Field′ → field	BFCHG (EA) {offset: width}
BFEXTS	1–32	Field → Dn; sign-extended	BFEXTS (EA) {offset: width}, Dn
BFEXTU	1–32	Field → Dn; zero-extended	BFEXTU (EA) {offset: width}, Dn
BFINS	1–32	Dn → field	BFINS Dn, (EA) {offset: width}
BFFFO	1–32	Scan for first bit set in field	BFFFO (EA) {offset: width}, Dn

Note that the condition codes are affected according to the value in the field before execution of the instruction. All bit field instructions affect the N and Z bits as shown for BFTST. That is, for all instructions, Z = 1 if all bits in a field prior to execution of the instruction are zero; Z = 0 otherwise. N = 1 if the most significant bit of the field prior to execution of the instruction is one; N = 0 otherwise. C and V are always cleared. X is always unaffected.

Next, consider BFFFO. The offset of the first bit set in a bit field is placed in Dn; if no set bit is found, Dn contains the offset plus the field width.

EA = address of byte containing bit 0 of array
Offset = #(0–31) or Dn (-2^{31} to $2^{31} - 1$)
Width = #(1–32) or Dn (1–32, mod 32)

Immediate offset is from 0 to 31, while offset in Dn can be specified from -2^{31} to $2^{31} - 1$. All instructions are unsized. They are useful for memory conservation, graphics, and communications.

As an example, consider BFCLR $5002 {4:12}. Assume the following memory contents:

	7	6	5	4	3	2	1	0	← Bit number
$5001	1	0	1	0	0	0	0	1	
$5002 (Base address) →	1	0	0	1	1	1	0	0	
$5003	0	1	1	1	0	0	0	1	
$5004	0	0	0	1	0	0	1	0	

Bit 7 of the base address $5002 has the offset 0. Therefore, bit 3 of $5002 has the offset value of 4. Bit 0 of location $5001 has offset value − 1, bit 1 of $5001 has the offset value −2, and so on. The example BFCLR instruction just given clears 12 bits starting with bit 3 of $5002. Therefore, bits 0–3 of location $5002 and bits 0–7 of location $5003 are cleared to 0. Therefore, the memory contents change as follows:

	7	6	5	4	3	2	1	0	
$5001	1	0	1	0	0	0	0	1	Offset 4
$5002	1	0	0	1	0	0	0	0	Width 12
$5003	0	0	0	0	0	0	0	0	Offset 16
$5004	0	0	0	1	0	0	1	0	

The use of bit field instructions may result in memory savings. For example, assume that an input device such as a 12-bit A/D converter is interfaced via a 16-bit port of an MC68020-based microcomputer. Now, suppose that 1 million pieces of data are to be collected from this port. Each 12 bits can be transferred to a 16-bit memory location or bit field instructions can be used.

- Using a 16-bit location for each 12 bits:

  Memory bytes required = 2 * 1 million
  = 2 million bytes

- Using bit fields:

12 bits = 1.5 bytes
Memory requirements = 1.5 * 1 million
= 1.5 million bytes
Savings = 2 million bytes − 1.5 million bytes
= 500,000 bytes

Example 7–8

Determine the effect of each of the following bit field instructions:

- BFCHG $5004 {D5:D6}
- BFEXTU $5004 {2:4}, D5
- BFINS D4, (A0) {D5:D6}
- BFFFO $5004 {D6:4}, D5

Assume the data at the bottom of the page prior to execution of each of the given instructions.

Register contents are given in hex, CCR and memory contents in binary, and offset to the left of memory in decimal.

Solution

- BFCHG $5004 [D5:D6]

  Offset = − 1, Width = 4

AO 0000 5004

D5 FFFF FFFF

D6 0000 00004

CCR 01001

D4 7125 F214

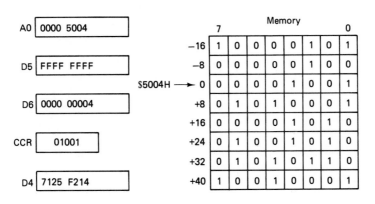

	7							0
−16	1	0	0	0	0	1	0	1
−8	0	0	0	0	0	1	0	0
$5004H → 0	0	0	0	0	1	0	0	1
+8	0	1	0	1	0	0	0	1
+16	0	0	0	0	1	0	1	0
+24	0	1	0	0	1	0	1	0
+32	0	1	0	1	0	1	1	0
+40	1	0	0	1	0	0	0	1

- BFEXTU $5004 [2:4], D5

  Offset = 2, Width = 4

  X N Z V C
  CCR | 0 0 0 0 0 |

  D5 | 0 0 0 0 0 0 0 2 |

- BFINS D4, (A0) {D5:D6}

  Offset = −1, Width = 4

  Memory

  | | 0 |

  $5004 | 1 | 0 | 0 | |

  X N Z V C
  CCR | 0 0 1 0 0 |

- BFFFO $5004 {D6:4}, D5

  Offset = 4, Width = 4

  X N Z V C
  CCR | 0 1 0 0 0 |

  D5 | 0 0 0 0 0 0 0 4 |
  (Hex)

Pack and Unpack Instructions The details of the PACK and UNPK instructions are listed next:

Instruction	Operand Size	Operation	Notation
PACK	16 → 8	Unpacked source + #data → packed destination	PACK −(An), −(An), #⟨data⟩
			PACK Dn, Dn, #⟨data⟩
UNPK	8 → 16	Packed source → unpacked source	UNPK −(An), −(An), #⟨data⟩
		unpacked source + #data → unpacked destination	UNPK Dn, Dn, #⟨data⟩

Both instructions have three operands and are unsized. They do not affect the condition codes. The PACK instruction converts two unpacked BCD digits to two packed BCD digits:

15   12 11   8 7   4 3   0
Unpacked BCD: | 0 0 0 0 | BCD0 | 0 0 0 0 | BCD1 |

7   4 3   0
Packed BCD: | BCD0 | BCD1 |

The UNPK instruction reverses the process and converts two packed BCD digits to two unpacked BCD digits. Immediate data can be added to convert numbers from one code to another. That is, these instructions can be used to translate codes such as ASCII or EBCDIC to BCD and vice versa.

The PACK and UNPK instructions are useful when an I/O device such as an ASCII keyboard is interfaced to an MC68020-based microcomputer. Data can be entered into the microcomputer via the keyboard in ASCII codes. The PACK instruction can be used with appropriate adjustments to convert these ASCII codes into BCD. Arithmetic operations can be performed inside the microcomputer, and the result will be in packed BCD. The UNPK instruction can similarly be used with appropriate adjustments to convert packed BCD to ASCII codes.

Example 7–9

Determine the effect of execution of each of the following PACK and UNPK instructions:

- PACK D0, D5, #$0000
- PACK − (A1), −(A4), #$0000
- UNPK D4, D6, #$3030
- UNPK −(A3), −(A2), #$3030

Assume the following data:

31   0
D0 | X X X X 32 37 |

31   0
D5 | X X X X X X 26 |

31   0
D4 | X X X X X X 35 |

31   0
D6 | X X X X X X 27 |

31   0
A2 | 3 0 0 5 0 0 A3 |

31   0
A3 | 5 0 7 1 2 4 B9 |

31   0
A1 | 5 0 7 1 2 4 B3 |

31   0
A4 | 3 0 0 5 0 0 A1 |

Memory
7   0

$507124B1	32
$507124B2	37
$507124B3	00
$507124B4	27
$507124B5	02
$507124B6	07
$507124B7	27
$507124B8	27

Solution

- PACK D0, D5, #$0000

$$[D0] = \quad 32 \quad 37$$
$$\text{low}$$
$$\text{word}$$
$$+ \quad 00 \quad 00$$
$$\overline{\quad 32 \quad 37}$$
$$\downarrow \quad \downarrow$$
$$[D5] = \quad 27$$

Note that ASCII code for 2 is 32 and for 7 is 37. Hence, this pack instruction converts ASCII code to packed BCD.

- PACK −(A1), −(A4), $0000

$$[\$5071\ 24B2] = 37 \qquad + 3237$$
$$[\$5071\ 24B1] = 32 \qquad + 0000$$
$$\overline{\qquad\qquad\qquad 3237}$$

$$\therefore [3005\ 00A0] = 27 \text{ packed BCD}$$

Hence, this pack instruction with the specified data converts two ASCII digits to their equivalent packed BCD form.

- UNPK D4, D6 #$3030

$$[D4] = XXXXXX\ 35$$
$$03 \quad 05$$
$$+ \ 30 \quad 30$$
$$\overline{\quad 33 \quad 35}$$

$$\therefore [D6] = XXXX\ 33\ 35$$
$$[D4] = XXXXXX\ 35$$

Therefore, this UNPK instruction with the assumed data converts from packed BCD to ASCII code.

- UNPK −(A3), −(A2), #$3030

$$[\$5071\ 24B8] = 27$$
$$\boxed{02 \quad 07}$$
$$30 \quad 30$$
$$\overline{\quad 32 \quad 37}$$

$$\therefore [\$300\ 500\ A2] = 37$$
$$[\$300\ 500\ A1] = 32$$

This UNPK instruction with the assumed data converts two packed BCD digits to their equivalent ASCII digits.

Multiplication and Division Instructions The 68020 includes the following signed and unsigned multiplication instructions:

Instruction	Operand Size	Operation
MULS.W (EA), Dn	16×16	(EA)16 * (Dn)16 →
or	→ 32	(Dn)32

Instruction	Operand Size	Operation
MULU		
MULS.L (EA), Dn	32×32	(EA) * Dn → Dn
or	→ 32	Dn holds low 32 bits of
MULU		result after multiplication. Upper 32 bits of the result are discarded.
MULS.L (EA), Dh:Dn	32×32	(EA) * Dn → Dh:Dn
or	→ 64	(EA) holds 32-bit multiplier before multiplication.
MULU		Dh holds high 32 bits of product after multiplication. Dn holds 32-bit multiplicand before multiplication and low 32 bits of product after multiplication.

(EA) can use all modes except An. The condition codes N, Z, and V are affected; C is always cleared to 0; and X is unaffected for both MULS and MULU. For signed multiplication, overflow (V = 1) can only occur for 32 × 32 multiplication producing a 32-bit result if the high-order 32 bits of 64-bit product are not the sign extension of the low-order 32 bits. In the case of unsigned multiplication, overflow (V = 1) can occur for 32 × 32 multiplication producing a 32-bit result if the high-order 32 bits of the 64-bit product are not zero.

Both MULS and MULU have a word form and a long word form. For the word form (16 × 16), the multiplier and multiplicand are both 16 bits and result is 32 bits. The result is saved in the destination data register. For the long word form (32 × 32), the multiplier and multiplicand are both 32 bits and the result is either 32 bits or 64 bits. When the result is 32 bits for a 32-bit × 32-bit operation, the low-order 32 bits of the 64-bit product are provided.

The signed and unsigned division instructions of the 68020 include the following, in which the source is the divisor, the destination is the dividend, and the result—remainder (r) and quotient (q)—is stored in the destination (Dn):

Instruction	Operation
DIVS.W (EA), Dn	32/16 → 16r:16q
or	
DIVU	
DIVS.L (EA), Dq	32/32 → 32q
or	No remainder is provided.
DIVU	
DIVS.L (EA), Dr:Dq	64/32 → 32r:32q
or	
DIVU	
DIVSL.L (EA), Dr:Dq	32/32 → 32r:32q
or	Dr contains 32-bit dividend.
DIVUL	

(EA) can use all modes except An. The condition codes for either signed or unsigned division are affected as follows: N = 1 if the quotient is negative; N = 0 otherwise. N is undefined for overflow or divide by zero. Z = 1 if the quotient is zero; Z = 0 otherwise. Z is undefined for overflow or divide by zero. V = 1 for division overflow; V = 0 otherwise. X is unaffected. Division by zero causes a trap. If overflow is detected before completion of the instruction, V is set to 1, but the operands are unaffected.

Both signed and unsigned division instructions have a word form and three long word forms. For the word form, the destination operand is 32 bits and the source operand is 16 bits. The 32-bit result in Dn contains the 16-bit quotient in the low word and the 16-bit remainder in the high word. The sign of the remainder is the same as the sign of the dividend.

For the instruction

DIVS.L   (EA),   Dq
or
DIVU

both destination and source operands are 32 bits. The result in Dq contains the 32-bit quotient and the remainder is discarded.

For the instruction

DIVS.L   (EA),   Dr:Dq
or
DIVU

the destination is 64 bits contained in any two data registers and the source is 32 bits. The 32-bit register Dr (D0–D7) contains the 32-bit remainder and the 32-bit register Dq (D0–D7) contains the 32-bit quotient.

For the instruction

DIVSL.L   (EA),   Dr:Dq
or
DIVUL

The 32-bit register Dr (D0–D7) contains the 32-bit dividend and the source is also 32 bits: After division, Dr contains the 32-bit remainder and Dq contains the 32-bit quotient.

Example 7-10

Determine the effect of execution of each of the following multiplication and division instructions:

- MULU.L #$2, D5 if [D5] = $FFFFFFFF
- MULS.L #$2, D5 if [D5] = $FFFFFFFF
- MULU.L #$2, D5:D2 if [D5] = $2ABC1800 and [D2] = $FFFFFFFF
- DIVS.L #$2, D5 if [D5] = $FFFFFFFC

- DIVS.L #$2, D2:D0 if [D2] = $FFFFFFFF and [D0] = $FFFFFFFC
- DIVSL.L #$2, D6:D1 if [D1] = $00041234 and [D6] = $FFFFFFFD

Solution

- MULU.L #$2, D5 if [D5] = $FFFFFFFF

$$
\begin{array}{r}
\$FFFFFFFF \\
* \quad \$00000002 \\
\hline
00000001 \quad FFFFFFFE
\end{array}
$$

$V = 1$ since this is nonzero   Low 32-bit result in D5

Therefore, [D5] = $FFFFFFFE, N = 0 since the most significant bit of the result is 0, Z = 0 since the result is nonzero, V = 1 since the high 32 bits of the 64-bit product are not zero, C = 0 (always), and X is not affected.

- MULS.L #$2, D5 if [D5] = $FFFFFFFF

$$
\begin{array}{r}
\$FFFFFFFF \quad (-1) \\
* \quad \$00000002 \quad (+2) \\
\hline
\$FFFFFFFF \quad \$FFFFFFFE \quad (-2)
\end{array}
$$

Result in D5

Therefore, [D5] = $FFFFFFFE, X is unaffected, C = 0, N = 1, V = 0, and Z = 0.

- MULU.L #$2, D5:D2 if [D5] = $2ABC1800 and [D2] = $FFFFFFFF

$$
\begin{array}{r}
\$FFFFFFFF \\
* \quad \$00000002 \\
\hline
00000001 \quad FFFFFFFE
\end{array}
$$

D5   D2

N = 0, Z = 0, V = 1 since the high 32 bits of the 64-bit product are not zero, C = 0, and X is not affected.

- DIVS.L #$2, D5 if [D5] = $FFFFFFFC

$$
\begin{array}{r}
-2 \\
\hline
\text{FFFF FFFE} \\
00000002 \overline{) \text{FFFF FFFC}} \\
\hline
+2 \qquad -4
\end{array}
$$

[D5] = $FFFFFFFE, X is unaffected, N = 1, Z = 0, V = 0, and C = 0 (always).

- DIVS.L #$2, D2:D0 if [D2] = $FFFFFFFF and [D0] = $FFFFFFFC

$$
\begin{array}{r}
\overbrace{-2}\overbrace{\ 0\ } \\
q = \text{FFFF FFFE},\ r = \text{0000 0000} \\
\underline{0000\ 0002\ \big|\ \text{FFFF FFFF FFFF FFFC}} \\
\underbrace{2}\underbrace{-4}
\end{array}
$$

[D2] = \$00000000 = remainder, [D0] = \$FFFFFFFE = quotient, X is unaffected, Z = 0, N = 1, V = 0, and C = 0 (always).

- DIVSL.L #\$2, D6:D1 if [D1] = \$00041234 and [D6] = \$FFFFFFFD

$$
\begin{array}{r}
\overbrace{-1} \\
q = \text{FFFFFFFF} \\
\underline{0000\ 0002\ \big|\ \text{FFFFFFFD}} \\
\underbrace{-3}
\end{array}
$$

[D6] = \$FFFFFFFF = remainder, [D1] = \$FFFFFFFF = quotient, X is unaffected, N = 1, Z = 0, V = 0, and C = 0 (always).

MC68000 Enhanced Instructions   The MC68020 includes the enhanced version of the 68000 instructions as listed next:

Instruction	Operand Size	Operation
BRA *label*	8, 16, 32	PC + d → PC
Bcc *label*	8, 16, 32	If cc is true, then PC + d → PC; else next instruction
BSR *label*	8, 16, 32	PC → −(SP); PC + d → PC
CMPI.S #data, (EA)	8, 16, 32	Destination − #data → CCR is affected
TST.S (EA)	8, 16, 32	Destination − 0 → CCR is affected
LINK.S An, −d	16, 32	An → −(SP); SP → An, SP + d → SP
EXTB.L Dn	32	Sign-extend byte to long word

Note that S can be B, W, or L. In addition to 8- and 16-bit signed displacements for BRA, Bcc, and BSR like the 68000, the 68020 also allows signed 32-bit displacements. LINK is unsized in the 68000. (EA) in CMPI and TST supports all MC68000 modes plus PC relative. Examples are CMPI.W #\$2000, (START, PC). In addition to EXT.W Dn and EXT.L Dn like the 68000, the 68020 also provides an EXTB.L instruction.

Example 7–11

Write a program in 68020 assembly language to multiply a 32-bit signed number in D2 by a 32-bit signed number in D3 by storing the multiplication result in the following manner:

(a) Store the 32-bit result in D2.

(b) Store the high 32 bits of the result in D3 and the low 32 bits of the result in D2.

Solution

(a)	MULS.L	D3, D2
	STOP JMP	STOP
(b)	MULS.L	D3, D3:D2
	STOP JMP	STOP

Example 7–12

Write a program in 68020 assembly language to convert 10 packed BCD digits stored at locations starting at \$2000 to their ASCII equivalent and store the result in a memory location starting at \$FFFFF8000. Assume the ASCII data bytes start at \$FFFF8000.

Solution

MOVEA.L #\$2000, A0	;	Load starting address of BCD array into A0
MOVEA.L #\$8000, A1	;	Load starting address of ASCII array into A1
MOVEQ.L #10, D0	;	Load data length into D0
START MOVE.B (A0)+, D1	;	Load BCD value
UNPK D1, D2, #\$3030	;	Convert to ASCII
MOVE.B D2, (A1)+	;	Store ASCII data to address pointed to by A1
DBF D0, START	;	Decrement and branch if false
JMP STOP	;	Otherwise Stop

7–3–5   MC68020 Hardware and I/O

MC68020 Hardware   The 68020 is arranged in a 13 × 13 matrix array (114 pins defined) and packaged in a pin grid array (PGA) or other package such as an RC suffix package. Unlike the 68000, which requires $\overline{\text{RESET}}$ and $\overline{\text{HALT}}$ to be simultaneously asserted for hardware reset, the 68020 needs to assert only the $\overline{\text{RESET}}$ pin for hardware reset.

Both the 32-bit address (A0–A31) and data (D0–D31) buses of the 68020 are nonmultiplexed. The 68020 transfers data with an 8-bit device via D31–D24, with a 16-bit device via D16–D31, and with a 32-bit device via D31–D0. Like the 68000, the three function code signals FC2, FC1, and FC0 identify the processor state (supervisor or user) and the address space of the bus cycle currently being executed as shown in Table 7–7.

Note that, in the 68000, FC2, FC1, FC0 = 111 indicates an interrupt acknowledge cycle. In the 68020,

TABLE 7–7
Function Code Lines

FC2	FC1	FC0	Cycle Type
0	0	0	(Undefined, reserved)*
0	0	1	User data space
0	1	0	User program space
0	1	1	(Undefined, reserved)*
1	0	0	(Undefined, reserved)*
1	0	1	Supervisor data space
1	1	0	Supervisor program space
1	1	1	CPU space

*Address space 3 is reserved for user definition, while 0 and 4 are reserved for future use by Motorola.

this means a CPU space cycle. In this cycle, by decoding address lines A19–A16, the 68020 can perform various types of functions such as coprocessor communication, breakpoint acknowledge, interrupt acknowledge, and module operations as follows:

A19	A18	A17	A16	Function Performed
0	0	0	0	Breakpoint acknowledge
0	0	0	1	Module operations
0	0	1	0	Coprocessor communication
1	1	1	1	Interrupt acknowledge

Note that A19, A18, A17, A16 = 0011_2 to 1110_2 is reserved by Motorola. In the coprocessor communication CPU space cycle, the 68020 determines the coprocessor type by decoding A15–A13 as follows:

A15	A14	A13	Coprocessor Type
0	0	0	MC68851 paged MMU
0	0	1	MC68881 floating-point coprocessor

The 68020 offers a feature called *dynamic bus sizing,* which enables designers to use 8- and 16-bit memory and I/O devices without sacrificing system performance. The SIZ0, SIZ1, $\overline{DSACK0}$, and $\overline{DSACK1}$ pins are used to implement this. These pins are defined as shown at bottom of this page.

During each bus cycle, the external device indicates its width via $\overline{DSACK1}$ and $\overline{DSACK0}$. The $\overline{DSACK1}$ and $\overline{DSACK0}$ pins are also used to indicate completion of a

bus cycle. At the start of a bus cycle, the 68020 always transfers data to D0–D31 lines, taking into consideration that the memory or I/O device may be 8, 16, or 32 bits wide. After the first bus cycle, the 68020 knows the device size by checking the $\overline{DSACK1}$ and $\overline{DSACK0}$ pins and generates additional bus cycles if needed to complete the transfer.

Unlike the 68000, the 68020 permits word and long word operands to start at an odd address (misaligned transfer). However, if the starting address is odd, additional bus cycles are required to complete the transfer. For example, for a 16-bit device, the 68020 requires 2 bus cycles for a write to an even address (aligned transfer) such as MOVE.L D1, $40002050 to complete the operation. On the other hand, the 68020 requires 3 bus cycles for MOVE.L D1, $40002051 for a 16-bit device to complete the transfer. Note that, like the 68000, instructions in the 68020 must start at even addresses.

Next, consider an example of dynamic bus sizing. The four bytes of a 32-bit data can be defined as follows:

31	23	15	7	0
OP0	OP1	OP2	OP3	

If this data is held in a data register Dn and is to be written to a memory or I/O location, then the address lines A1 and A0 define the byte position of data. For a 32-bit device, A1A0 = 00 (Addresses 0, 4, 8, . . .), A1A0 = 01 (address 1, 5, 9, . . .), A1A0 = 10 (addresses 2, 6, 10, . . .), and A1A0 = 11 (Addresses 3, 7, 11, . . .) will store OP0, OP1, OP2, and OP3, respectively. This data is written via the 68020 D31–D0 pins. However, if the device is 16-bit, data is always transferred as follows:

All even addressed bytes via D31–D24 pins

All odd addressed bytes via D23–D16 pins

Finally, for an 8-bit device, both even and odd addressed bytes are transferred via D31–D24 pins.

The 68020 always starts transferring data with the most significant byte first. As an example, consider MOVE.L D1,$20107420. Since the address is even, this is an aligned transfer. In the first bus cycle, the 68020

SIZ1	SIZ0	Number of Bytes Remaining to be Transferred
0	1	Byte
1	0	Word
1	1	3 bytes
0	0	Long words

DSACK1	DSACK0	Device Size
0	0	32-bit device
0	1	16-bit device
1	0	8-bit device
1	1	Data not ready; insert wait states

does not know the size of the device and, hence, outputs all combinations of data on D31–D0 pins, taking into consideration that the device may be 8-bit, 16-bit, or 32-bit wide. Assume that the content of D1 is $02A10512 (OP0 = $02, OP1 = $A1, OP2 = $05, and OP3 = $12). In the first bus cycle, the 68020 sends SIZ1 SIZ0 = 00, indicating a 32-bit transfer and then outputs data on its D31–D0 pins as follows:

D31:D24	D23:D16	D15:D8	D7:D0
$02	$A1	$05	$12

If the device is 8-bit, it will take data $02 from the D31–D24 pins in the first cycle and will then assert

DSACK1 and DSACK0 as 10, indicating an 8-bit device. The 68020 then transfers the remaining 24 bits ($A1 first, $05 next, and $12 last) via D31–D24 pins in three consecutive cycles with a total of four cycles to complete the transfer.

However, if the device is 16-bit, in the first cycle the device will take the 16-bit data $02A1 via D31–D16 pins and will then assert DSACK1 and DSACK0 as 01, indicating a 16-bit device. The 68020 then transfers the remaining 16 bits ($0512) via D31–D16 pins in the next cycle, requiring a total of two cycles for the transfer.

Finally, if the device is 32-bit, the device receives all 32-bit data $02A10512 via D31–D0 pins and asserts DSACK1 DSACK0 = 00 to indicate completion of transfer. Aligned data transfers for various devices are depicted below:

For 8-bit device:

	31 · · · · · · · · 0 ← Bit number							
Register D1	02	A1	05	12				
68020 pins D31 D24		SIZ1	SIZ0	A1	A0	DSACK1	DSACK0
First cycle	02	0	0	0	0	1	0
Second cycle	A1	1	1	0	1	1	0
Third cycle	05	1	0	1	0	1	0
Fourth cycle	12	0	1	1	1	1	0

For 16-bit device:

68020 pins D31 D24,	D23 D16	SIZ1	SIZ0	A1	A0	DSACK1	DSACK0
First cycle 02	A1	0	0	0	0	0	1
Second cycle 05	12	1	0	1	0	0	1

For 32-bit device:

68020 pins D31 D0	SIZ1	SIZ0	A1	A0	DSACK1	DSACK0
First cycle 02 A1 05 12	0	0	0	0	0	0

Next, consider a misaligned transfer such as MOVE.W D1, $20107421 with [D1] = $20F107A4. The 68020 outputs $0707A4XX on its D31–D0 pins in the first cycle where XX are don't cares. Data transfers to various devices are summarized below:

For 8-bit device:

	31 23 15 7 0 ← Bit number							
Register D1	20	F1	07	A4				
68020 pins D$_{31}$ D$_{24}$		SIZ1	SIZ0	A1	A0	DSACK1	DSACK0
First cycle	07	1	0	0	1	1	0
Second cycle	A4	0	1	0	0	1	0

For 16-bit device:

68020 pins	D$_{31}$ D$_{24}$, D$_{23}$ D$_{16}$		SIZ1	SIZ0	A1	A0	$\overline{DSACK1}$	$\overline{DSACK0}$
First cycle		07	1	0	0	1	0	1
Second cycle	A4·		0	1	0	0	0	1

For 32-bit device:

68020 pins	D$_{31}$ D$_{23}$	D$_{16}$, D$_{15}$ D$_8$, D$_7$	D$_0$	SIZ1	SIZ0	A1	A0	$\overline{DSACK1}$	$\overline{DSACK0}$
First cycle		07	A4		1	0	0	1	0	0

MC68020 I/O The 68020 I/O handling features are very similar to those of the 68000. For programmed I/O, the 68020 uses memory-mapped I/O. The external interrupts are handled via the 68020 $\overline{IPL2}$, $\overline{IPL1}$, and $\overline{IPL0}$ pins using autovectoring and nonautovectoring pins. However, the 68020 uses a new pin called $\overline{AVEC}$ rather than $\overline{VPA}$ (68000) for autovectoring. Nonautovectoring is handled using $\overline{DSACK}$ = 0 and $\overline{DSACK1}$ = 0 rather than $\overline{DTACK}$ = 0 (as with the 68000). Note that the 68020 does not have the $\overline{VPA}$ pin. Like the 68000, the 68020 uses the $\overline{BR}$, $\overline{BG}$, and $\overline{BGACK}$ pins for DMA transfer. The 68020 exceptions are similar to those of the 68000 with some variations such as coprocessor exceptions.

QUESTIONS AND PROBLEMS

7–1. (a) What is the basic difference between the 80386 and 80386SX?

(b) What is the basic difference between the 80386 and 80486?

7–2. What is the difference between the 80386 protected, real-address, and virtual 8086 modes?

7–3. Discuss the basic features of the 80486.

7–4. Assume the following 80386 register contents:

[EBX] = 00001000H
[ECX] = 04000002H
[EDX] = 20005000H

Prior to execution of each of the following 80386 instructions, determine the effective address after execution of each of the following instructions and identify the addressing modes:

(a) MOV [EBX * 4] [ECX], EDX

(b) MOV [EBX * 2] [ECX + 2020H], EDX

7–5. Determine the effect of each of the following 80386 instructions:

(a) MOVZX EAX, CH

Prior to execution of this MOVZX instruction, assume

[EAX] = 80001234H
[ECX] = 00008080H

(b) MOVSX EDX, BL

Prior to execution of this MOVSX instruction, assume

[EDX] = FFFFFFFFH
[EBX] = 05218888H

7–6. Write an 80386 assembly program to add a 64-bit number in [ECX] [EDX] with another 64-bit number in [EAX] [EBX]. Store the result in [EAX] [EBX].

7–7. Write an 80386 assembly program to divide a signed 32-bit number in DX:AX by an 8-bit signed number in BH. Store the 16-bit quotient and 16-bit remainder in AX and DX, respectively.

7–8. Write an 8086 assembly program to compute $\sum_{i=1}^{N} \times x_i^2$, where $N = 1000$ and the X_i's are signed 32-bit numbers. Assume that ΣX_i^2 can be stored as a 32-bit signed number.

7–9. Discuss 80386 I/O.

7–10. Discuss the main hardware differences between the 68000 and 68020.

7–11. Name three new 68020 instructions that are not provided with the 68000.

7–12. Discuss the basic difference between the 68020, 68030, and 68040.

7–13. Find the contents of affected registers and memory locations after execution of the 68020 instruction MOVE ($1000, A5, D3.W * 4), D1. Assume the following data prior to execution of this MOVE:

[A5] = $0000F210
[D3] = $00001002
[D1] = $F125012A

$$[\$00014218] = \$4567$$
$$[\$0001421A] = \$2345$$

7-14. Assume the following 68020 memory configuration:

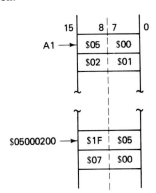

Draw the memory layout after execution of MOVE.W #$1234, ([A1]).

7-15. Find the 68020 compare instruction with the appropriate addressing mode to replace the following 68000 instruction sequence:

ASL.L #1, D5
CMP.L 0 (A0, D5.L), D0

7-16. Find the contents of D1, D2, A4, and CCR and the memory locations after execution of the following 68020 instructions:
(a) BFSET $5000 {D1:10}
(b) BFINS D2, (A4) {D1:D4}
Assume the following data prior to execution of each of these instructions:

$$[D1] = \$00000004, \quad [D4] = \$00000004$$
$$[D2] = \$12345678, \quad [A4] = \$00005000$$

	7			Memory				0
−16	0	1	1	0	1	1	1	1
−8	1	1	1	0	1	1	1	1
$5000 →	0	0	1	0	1	0	0	1
+8	0	1	0	1	1	1	0	0
+16	1	0	1	0	1	0	1	1

7-17. Identify the following 68020 instructions as valid or invalid. Justify your answers.
(a) DIVS A0, D1
(b) CHK.B D0, (A0)
(c) MOVE.L D0, (A0). Given [A0] = $1025671A prior to execution of the MOVE.

7-18. Determine the values of the Z and C flags after execution of each of the following 68020 instructions:
(a) CHK2 (A5), D3

(b) CMP2.L $2001, A5
Assume the following data prior to execution of each of these instructions:

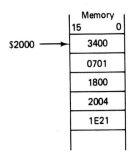

$$[D3] = \$02001740, \quad [A5] = \$00002004$$

7-19. Write a 68020 assembly program to add two 64-bit numbers in D1D0 with another 64-bit number in D2D3. Store the result in D1D0.

7-20. Write a 68020 assembly program to multiply a 32-bit signed number in D5 by another 16-bit signed number in D1. Store the 64-bit result in D5D1.

7-21. Write a subroutine in 68020 assembly language to compute

$$Y = \sum_{i=1}^{50} \frac{X_i^2}{50}$$

Assume the X_i's are signed 32-bit numbers and the array starts at $50000021. Neglect overflow.

7-22. What is meant by 68020 dynamic bus sizing?

7-23. Write a 68020 assembly language program that tests bits 10 through 16 of the 32-bit memory location (use bit 31 as offset 0), pointed to by the address in A0 to determine if they are all zero. If they are all zero, bits 2 through 8 of the 32-bit memory location pointed to by A1 are set to all ones; on the other hand, if there are nonzero, bit 2 through 8 are ones complemented.

7-24. Assume [D2] = $1A2FFFA1. Find the content of D2 after execution of the 68020 BFCHG D2{4:7}.

7-25. Consider the 68020 MOVE.B D1, $00000015. Find the 68020 data pins over which data will be transferred if $\overline{DSACK1}\ \overline{DSACK0}$ = 00. What are the 68020 data pins if $\overline{DSACK1}\ \overline{DSACK0}$ = 10?

7-26. If a 32-bit data transfer MOVE.L D0, $50607011 is performed to a 32-bit memory with [D0] = $81F27561, how many bus cycles are needed to perform the transfer? What are A1A0 equal to during each cycle? What is the SIZ1SIZ0 code during each cycle? What bytes of data are transferred during each bus cycle?

7-27. Discuss 68020 I/O.

8

Peripheral Interfacing

The purpose of the previous chapters was to provide an understanding of microcomputer hardware and software and, to some extent, interfacing with simple devices such as LEDs. The latter subject is of such importance that this chapter is devoted to interfacing typical microprocessors to common peripherals, such as the hexadecimal keyboard and display, cassette recorder, CRT (cathode ray tube) terminal, printer, and floppy disk. However, before describing these interfaces, we cover some of the basics of parallel and serial transmission.

8–1 PARALLEL VERSUS SERIAL TRANSMISSION

In various instances, it is desirable to transmit binary data from one system to another. In such situations, data can be transmitted using either parallel or serial transmission techniques:

- In *parallel transmission,* each bit of a data entity of the binary data is transmitted over a separate wire or line.
- In *serial transmission,* only one line is used to transmit the complete binary data bit by bit.

Data is usually sent starting with the least significant bit. In order to differentiate among various bits, a clock signal is used. Typical I/O devices that transmit and receive data serially are teletypes, cassette recorders, and so on. Serial I/O is more common than parallel I/O. Therefore, we will describe serial I/O transmission in more detail.

8–2 SYNCHRONOUS AND ASYNCHRONOUS SERIAL DATA TRANSMISSION

Serial data transmission can be divided into two types:

1. Synchronous
2. Asynchronous

8–2–1 Synchronous Serial Data Transmission

The basic feature of synchronous serial data transmission is that data is transmitted or received based on a clock signal. After deciding on a specific rate of data transmission, commonly known as *baud rate* (bits per second), the transmitting device sends a data bit at each clock pulse. In order to interpret data correctly, the receiving device must know the start and end of each data unit. Therefore, in synchronous data transmission, the receiver must know the number of data units to be transferred. Also, the receiver must be synchronized with data boundaries. Usually, one or two sync characters are used to indicate the start of each synchronous data stream:

SYNC
$$\overbrace{1101\ 0110}\quad 00111\ \ \dots\dots\dots$$
$$\uparrow$$
First bit of data

The data unit may contain a parity bit. In each data unit, data may consist of 5, 6, 7, or 8 bits. If fewer than 8 bits are used for data, then the rest of the bits are ignored. A 9-bit data unit with 8 bits of data and 1 parity bit is shown next:

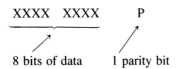

8 bits of data   1 parity bit

The parity can be either odd or even.

The synchronous receiver waits in a "hunt" mode while looking for data. As soon as it matches one or two SYNC characters based on the number of SYNC characters used, the receiver starts interpreting the data. In synchronous transmission, the transmitting device needs to send data continuously to the receiving device. However, if data is not ready to be transmitted, the transmitter will pad with SYNC characters until data is available.

As mentioned before, in synchronous transfer, the receiver must know the number of SYNC characters used and the number of data units and then goes into a "hunt" mode for matching the SYNC pattern for the next data.

8-2-2 Asynchronous Serial Data Transmission

In this type of data transfer, the transmitting device does not need to be synchronized to the receiving device. The transmitting device can send one or more data units when it has data ready to be sent. Each data unit must be formatted. In other words, each data unit must contain start and stop bits, indicating the beginning and the end of each data unit. An interface chip is required between the microcomputer and the serial I/O device. The interface chip performs the following two functions:

1. Converts an 8-bit parallel data unit from the microcomputer into serial data for transmitting it to the serial I/O device.

2. Converts serial data from the serial I/O device into 8-bit parallel data for transmitting to the microcomputer.

Next, we discuss the format of asynchronous serial data.

Asynchronous Serial Data Format   Each asynchronous serial data unit can be divided into equal time intervals, called *bit intervals*. A data bit can be either HIGH or LOW during each bit interval. An 8-bit data will have 8 bit intervals. Each data bit will correspond to one of the 8 bit intervals.

The format for asynchronous serial data contains the following information:

- A LOW start bit
- 5–8 data bits, denoting the actual data being transferred
- An optional parity bit for either odd or even parity
- 1, 1½, or 2 stop bits having HIGH levels (Note that 1½ stop bits means a HIGH level with a duration of 1.5 times the bit interval.)

Figure 8–1 shows an example of asynchronous serial data with a LOW start bit, 8-bit data, 1 odd-parity bit, and 1 stop bit.

Serial Data Rate   The serial data rate is known as the *baud rate*. The baud rate is defined as the number of bits of data transferred per second. Since each bit is transmitted over a duration of 1 bit interval,

$$\text{Baud rate} = \frac{1}{\text{bit interval}} = \text{bit/s}$$

8-2-3 Universal Synchronous/ Asynchronous Receivers/Transmitters (USARTs) and Universal Asynchronous Receivers/Transmitters (UARTs)

Microprocessor manufacturers typically provide the interfacing functions required by both synchronous and asynchronous serial transmission on a single chip, or USART. The Intel 8251 is an example of a typical USART. If the chip contains only the asynchronous capabilities, it is called a *universal asynchronous receiver/ transmitter* (UART) or an *asynchronous communications interface adapter* (ACIA). The Motorola 6850 is a typical example. For simplicity, we describe a typical UART in the following paragraphs.

Parallel/Serial Interface — The UART   A UART is a chip that provides all the interface functions when a microprocessor transmits or receives data to or from a serial I/O device. Figure 8–2 gives the basic structure of a typical UART. It consists of the following elements:

- A transmitter (Tx) that converts the parallel data unit from the transmitter data register (TxDR) into serial data for sending to the serial I/O device
- A receiver (Rx) that converts the serial data from the serial I/O device into parallel data and transfers this data to the receiver data register (RxDR) for sending it to the microprocessor
- A bidirectional data bus buffer for transferring parallel data from the microprocessor to the TxDR or from the RxDR to the microprocessor via the data bus

In order to send data to a serial device, the microprocessor outputs a data unit to the TxDR. Logic in the transmitter formats this data unit by including a start bit,

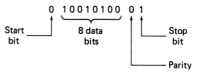

Figure 8–1 Asynchronous serial data using 8-bit data, odd parity, and 1 stop bit

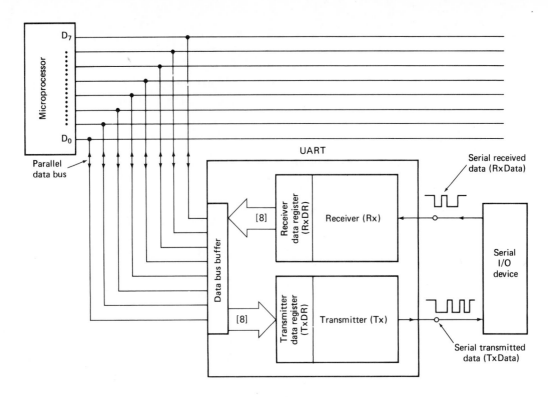

Figure 8-2 Basic structure for a UART (From *Microprocessors and Microcomputers: Hardware and Software,* by Tocci and Laskowski, © 1979, p. 194. Reprinted by permission of Prentice Hall, Inc., Englewood Cliffs, New Jersey)

a parity bit if required, and the appropriate number of stop bits. This data unit is then transferred to the transmit shift register. The transmit data clock provides the rate of this transfer.

This serial data (TxData) is then sent to the serial I/O device. The baud rate must be the same as the frequency of the transmit data clock.

In order to transmit data to the microprocessor, the serial I/O device sends a serial data unit to the UART's receiver via the UART's RxData line. The receiver interprets the first bit as a start bit as soon as the RxData line goes from HIGH to LOW. It then shifts the rest of the data unit into the receiver shift register. The receiver data clock provides the rate of this transfer. After shifting the complete data into the shift register, the data portion (D0–D7) is then transferred in parallel to the RxDR. The microprocessor, when ready, inputs this data into an internal register, such as the accumulator, via the data bus.

The UART typically has an internal register called the *control register*. The microprocessor can be programmed to write into this register with a control word. This word will tell the UART the format of the serial data, that is, the number of stop bits and data bits, the type of parity (even or odd), and so on.

Synchronization of Serial Data to the Receiver As soon as the start bit occurs, the receiver synchronizes to the serial data; that is, the receiver interprets the subsequent bits as data bits, parity bit (if any), and stop bits. In order to synchronize to the serial data properly, an external clock having a much higher frequency (usually 16 times) than the baud rate is applied to the UART's RxCLK input pin. Note that if RxCLK has a frequency 16 times the baud rate, then 1 period of RxCLK $= T_B16$.

After detecting the start bit (HIGH to LOW transition), the receiver samples the serial input after 8 RxCLK pulses to see if it is still LOW. This is to make sure that this is a start bit and not a glitch. After sensing the start bit at about the middle of the bit interval, the receiver samples the serial input after every 16 RxCLK pulses so that each bit is sampled in approximately the middle of the bit time. At the leading edge of the receiver data clock, these bits are then shifted into the receiver shift register. Note that the receiver data clock is obtained from RxCLK by passing RxCLK through a divide-by-16 counter, and therefore the receiver data clock has a frequency equal to the baud rate.

After data has been transferred to the receiver shift register, the UART verifies to determine whether data is received according to the format. This is done by using a status register, which is internal to the UART. Each bit in this register corresponds to a flag that is related to the format. For example, a framing error flag is set to 1 if the stop bits do not conform to the format. The parity flag is set to 1 if the parity used in the data unit does not match with the format.

The data bits are moved in parallel to the RxDR in order to be inputted by the microprocessor. The receiver then starts sampling the next serial data and transfers this into the receiver shift register. This data will not be transferred into the RxDR until the microprocessor inputs the first data unit. However, a third data unit may be transferred into the receiver shift register before the second data unit is shifted into the RxDR. This basically results in losing the second data unit. When this situation occurs, the UART will set an overrun flag in the status register HIGH. The overrun situation can be avoided by making sure that the microprocessor inputs data from the RxDR within the time it takes for the serial data to be completely moved into the receiver.

8–3 INTERFACING OF HEXADECIMAL KEYBOARD AND DISPLAY UNIT TO A MICROPROCESSOR

One of the most popular examples of a microcomputer I/O device is the keyboard display unit. The keyboard is used to enter programs and data. Typical examples of the keyboard include the inexpensive 4 × 4 hexadecimal keyboard or a typewriter-type ASCII keyboard. Popular displays with a microcomputer include inexpensive seven-segment displays.

8–3–1 Hexadecimal Keyboard

The hexadecimal keyboard contains all 16 hexadecimal keys from 0 through F arranged in a 4 × 4 matrix. In order to properly interface the keyboard to a microprocessor, three functions must be performed:

1. Identifying a key closure
2. Debouncing the key
3. Decoding the key to a meaningful code such as hexadecimal

Each one of these functions can be realized via hardware or software.

The hardware approach off-loads the microprocessor of the keyboard service functions. A keyboard controller chip such as the Intel 8279 performs most of these functions. Note that debouncing of each key is necessary because, in any contact involving electromechanical components, true contact closure occurs only after an oscillation period of several milliseconds. Usually, 10 to 20 ms elapse between the time the key is first pressed and the time the contact is stabilized. The same problem occurs when the key is released. These leading-edge and trailing-edge bounces are illustrated in Figure 8–3.

A simple hardware solution to the problem is the use of an RC filter. The software solution is accomplished by using a delay routine.

8–3–2 Hexadecimal Displays

Hexadecimal displays can be interfaced to a typical microcomputer using either the nonmultiplexed or multiplexed method. Using the nonmultiplexed technique, each hexadecimal digit can be interfaced to the microcomputer via a port. This means that in this system, a dedicated port for each hexadecimal digit is used. Figure 8–4 shows such an interface for a three-digit display. Assume 8-bit ports.

In Figure 8–4, BCD-to-seven-segment decoding is done in software. Using the multiplexing or scanning method, seven-segment information is sent to all displays

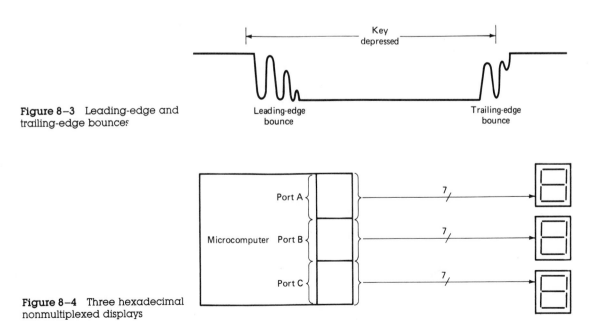

Figure 8–3 Leading-edge and trailing-edge bounces

Leading-edge bounce

Trailing-edge bounce

Key depressed

Figure 8–4 Three hexadecimal nonmultiplexed displays

Microcomputer Port A Port B Port C

7

7

7

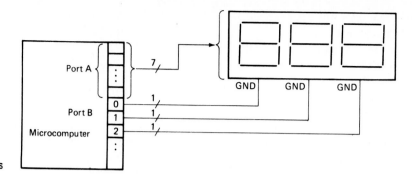

Figure 8–5 Multiplexed displays

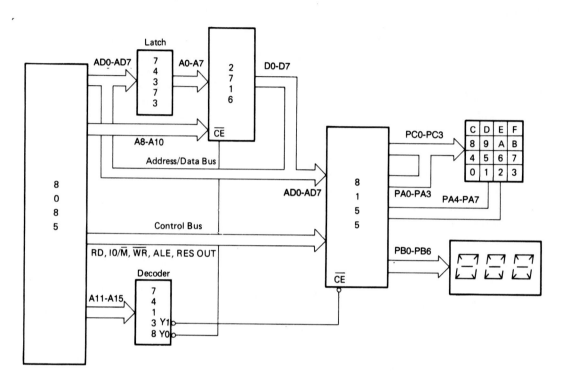

Figure 8–6 Block diagram of the keyboard/display interface

at the same time. However, the segment to be illuminated is grounded. This is shown in Figure 8–5.

8–3–3 Example of Hexadecimal Keyboard/Display Interface to the 8085

Keyboard/display interface chips such as the Intel 8279 provide automatic keyboard and display multiplexing and off-load the microcomputer of these functions. As an illustration of keyboard/display concepts, an example will be considered in the following.*

An 8085-based microcomputer will be designed that will scan a 4 × 4 hexadecimal keyboard and will drive three seven-segment displays. The microcomputer will take each key depressed and will scroll them in from the

right side of the display and keep scrolling as each key is pressed. The leftmost digit is just discarded, and the process continues indefinitely. This example is solved using keyboard interfacing via software and multiplexed displays as follows.

Hardware Refer to Figure 8–6 as we describe the operational functions and features of each block in the block diagram of the keyboard interface.

I/O ports of the 8155 are all used in this problem. Configured as an output port, port C of the 8155 is connected to the four rows of the keypad. Port A of the 8155 is configured as an input port with its low and high nibbles connected to columns and rows of the keypad. This wiring configuration gives all information of the keypad once port A is read.

The keyboard contains a 4 × 4 matrix keypad and eight 10 K resistors. These resistors connect all columns

*From *Microprocessors and Microcomputer Development Systems* by Rafiquzzaman, Problem 12–13. Copyright © 1984 by Harper and Row Publishers, Inc. Reprinted by permission.

and rows of the keypad to 5 V such that all port A bits will be high when no key closure occurs.

The address decoding logic ensures that the correct device is on the bus when that device is addressed by the microprocessor.

The memory includes both EPROM and RAM. The EPROM contains both the instructions and the lookup table. The instructions are used by the microprocessor to control the system operation. The lookup table contains the decimal numbers that are equivalent to the digital codes. The RAM is used for the stack.

The display consists of three hexadecimal displays (TIL311). This block is used to display the number each time a key is pushed. The detailed hardware schematic of the keyboard/display interface is shown in Figure 8–7.

Software The lookup table technique is utilized in this example to display the number corresponding to the key depressed. In the software, first the input port is read and checked to see whether the previous key has been released. This will eliminate inputting the wrong information when someone holds the key for a long time. When the key is released, it is debounced by waiting for 20 ms. The program will read the keyboard and check for key closure. If the key closure is found, it is debounced again by waiting for 20 ms, and the binary code corresponding to the key pressed is found by using the lookup table.

The matrix keyboard is interfaced using two ports: an output port and an input port. Rows are connected to the output port, and columns are connected to the input port. Scanning is used to read data from the keyboard. In matrix scan, rows are grounded by outputting zeros to all rows via port C and key closure is checked by reading the column data via input port A.

In order to display the key-in data, all the displays are cleared first. The least significant digit display will be the first key-in data and will be stored in memory at location 0AAAH. When the second key is depressed, the first data will be moved one position to the left and the second data will be stored in location 0BBBH. When the third key is depressed, the first data will be displayed on the leftmost display and the second data will be displayed on the next right of the display and the process will continue.

The flowchart and the assembly language listing are shown in Figures 8–8 and 8–9, respectively.

The data in TABLE (line 81) of Figure 8–9 is obtained by inspecting the keys of Figure 8–7. For example, the code for the F key is $0111\ 0111_2$. This is because when the F key is pressed, the top row and the rightmost column of Figure 8–7 become 0. This makes the port A data 77_{16}. Similarly, the codes for the other keys in TABLE can be obtained.

There are three subroutines in the program. These are DEBOUNCE, SETTIME, and HOLDTIME. DEBOUNCE is used to provide the 20-ms delay. SETTIME and HOLDTIME are used to display a digit by enabling the appropriate $\overline{\text{LATCH}}$ line of one of the displays.

In order to explain the program logic of Figure 8–9, let us display $FD9_{16}$ in the three-digit display of Figure 8–7. This display will take place in the following order: The F key will have to be pressed first and will be displayed on the rightmost display. The F key will then be saved in location $0AAA_{16}$ until the second key (D) is pressed. When the D key is actuated, the contents of $0AAA_{16}$ (F) will be outputted to the middle display, and this data is saved in location $0BBB_{16}$. The D key is then saved in location $0AAA_{16}$. When the third key (9) is pressed, it will be displayed in the rightmost display. $[0AAA_{16}]$ and $[0BBB_{16}]$ are displayed on the middle and leftmost displays, respectively.

As far as the software of Figure 8–9 is concerned, lines 1–15 initialize I/O ports and the stack pointer, output zeros to the three displays, and store zeros in locations $0AAA_{16}$ and $0BBB_{16}$. Note that, initially, zeros are outputted to all displays.

Lines 16–25 detect whether the previous key has been released. If it has been, then the key is debounced for 20 ms. This will avoid someone's holding a key for a long time. The program then detects a key actuation. If a key is pressed, it is debounced for 20 ms; otherwise, the program stays in the KEYCLOSE loop.

Lines 26–35 determine precisely which key is pressed. This is done by moving all 1's into the accumulator in line 26. The carry is cleared, and a 0 is moved from this carry to a particular bit position in the accumulator. This data is used to output 0 to each row in sequence. The rows and columns are read via port B. If a key is down in a particular row, the column connected to that row via the depressed key will also be 0. For example, in our case, the F key is first pressed; this means that the data 77_{16} for F (line 81) will appear at port B. Since the F key is pressed (in this example), the program branches from 35 to 40 and decodes the key. The program then branches to the label DONE; otherwise, the program loops through NEXTROW until the key is found.

Once the F key is found, the subroutine SETTIME is called in line 49. This subroutine in line 72 outputs the appropriate data for the key and disables all displays by sending 1's to all the $\overline{\text{LATCH}}$ lines of the displays via port B. SETTIME also provides some delay by using NOP for setting up time for DATA OUT and then returns to line 50 of the main program. In line 50, ANI 03FH sets up data in the accumulator for enabling the rightmost display by providing 0 in the most significant bit. CALL HOLDTIME in line 51 causes the program to branch to line 76 where the HOLDTIME subroutine outputs a LOW to the $\overline{\text{LATCH}}$ line of the rightmost display along with the data "F" (in this case) via the PB_0–PB_3 bits of port B.

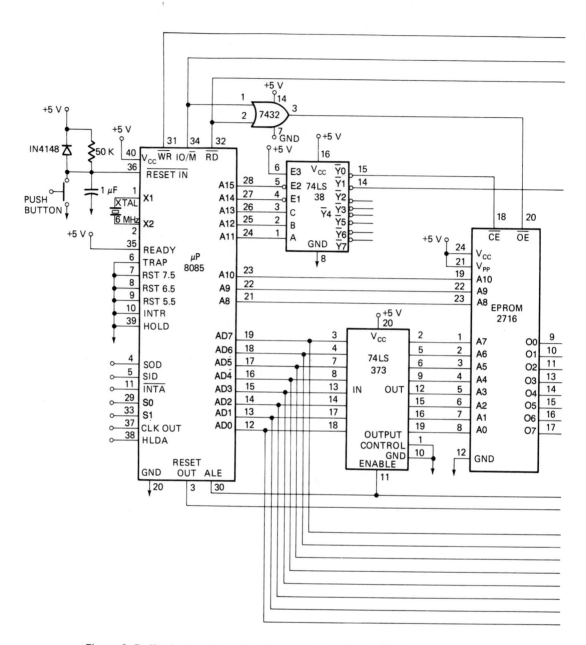

Figure 8–7 Hardware schematic of the keyboard/display interface

The LDA 0AAAH at line 52 loads 00H (stored in 0AAAH in line 14) into the accumulator. In line 53, this data is moved to register C, and then SETTIME is called in line 54. As before, SETTIME in line 72 first disables all latches, outputs 0 (in this case) to PB₀–PB₃, and then returns (with more delay for setting up DATA OUT) to line 55 of the main program. ANI 05FH in line 55 sets up data to enable the middle display. CALL HOLDTIME in line 56 outputs 0 to the middle display, enabling its LATCH line. It provides some hold time for DATA OUT

by using NOP, disables all latches, and then returns to line 57 of the main program.

LDA 0BBBH in line 57 loads 00H (stored in line 15) into the accumulator. As before, by using SETTIME and HOLDTIME subroutines, 0 is displayed on the leftmost display by enabling its LATCH line. STA 0AAAH in line 62 stores the rightmost digit, and STA 0BBBH in line 64 stores the middle digit in location 0BBBH.

JMP AGAIN in line 65 branches to line 16 where the activation of the D key is detected and displayed in

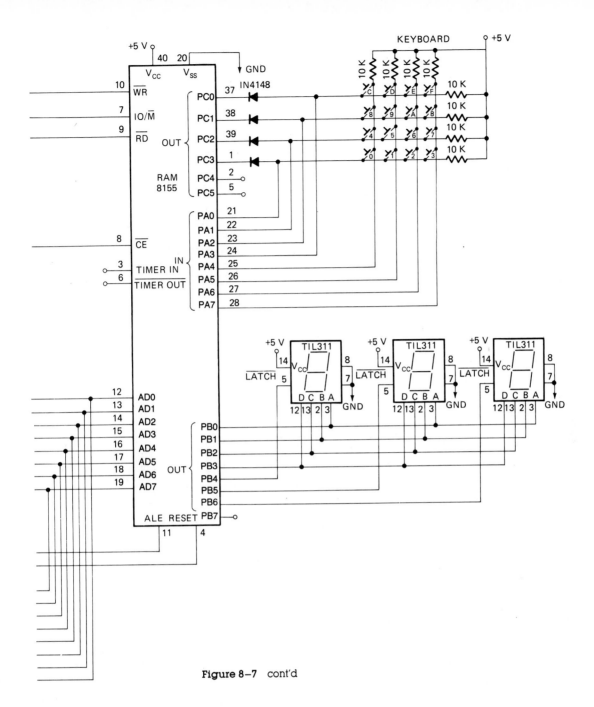

Figure 8–7 cont'd

the middle display and then the F key is moved to the leftmost display. Finally, the 9 key is outputted on the rightmost display.

The memory map is shown next:

Address Range	Device
0000H–07FFH	ROM
0900H–09FFH	RAM

Note that A8, A9, and A10 in RAM are don't cares.

Therefore, the other address ranges for RAM are available. Range 0900H–09FFH is shown as an example.

8–4 CASSETTE RECORDERS

Cassette recorders are sometimes used with microprocessors for storing information. This is because the cassette recorders are inexpensive, easy to handle, and faster compared to other mass storage devices such as teletypes.

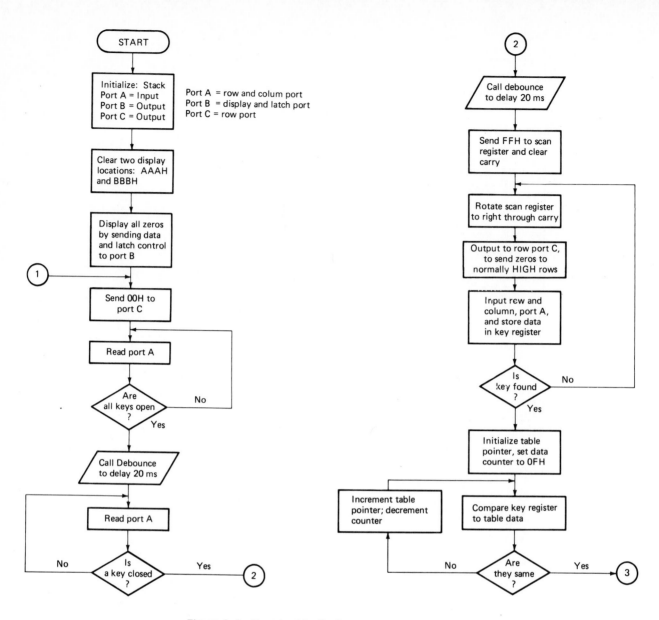

Figure 8–8 Flowchart for the keyboard/display interface

In this section, we describe the basics of one of the cassette interface standards known as the *Kansas City standard*. We then discuss the interfacing of a cassette recorder to the 8085 microprocessor. The hardware and software for this interface are developed by Intel.

8–4–1 Kansas City Standard

There are two main popular formats used by hobbyists: the Kansas City and the Tarbell standards. We describe the basics of the Kansas City standard.

The Kansas City standard uses the following frequencies to represent the logic levels:

Logic 0   4 cycles of a 1200-Hz tone
Logic 1   8 cycles of a 2400-Hz tone

In order to store information in a cassette from a microcomputer, an interface circuit is required to convert the voltage levels of the microcomputer into the proper audio frequencies to be recorded on the cassette. This interface circuit must also be able to convert the audio frequencies back to the voltage levels so that the microcomputer can read this data into its memory. This interface typically contains a UART to convert the microcomputer's parallel data into the cassette's serial format and vice versa.

Typically, a cassette can store 100,000 bytes of information. The amount of bytes used by a microcomputer at any one time is much less than this. Therefore, the information stored on a cassette is divided into blocks, called *records*. If multiple records are stored on a cassette, a gap is used to isolate one record from another. These records are required because the starting and stopping of a cassette between records requires certain times.

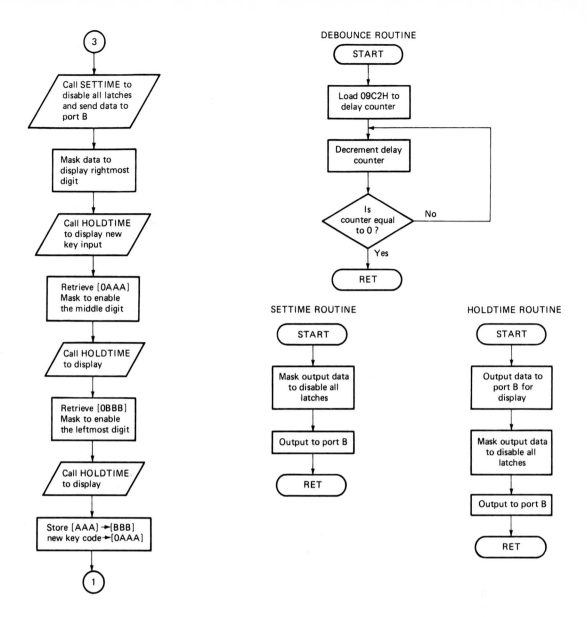

Figure 8-8 cont'd

Each record consists of four parts:

1. *Marking* — A standard amount of logic HIGH levels
2. *Record ID* — A code that identifies a record and the number of bytes in a specific record
3. *Stored data* — The data stored for ultimate use by the microcomputer
4. *Total* — A computed number used for determining errors

The record ID usually consists of 2 bytes, which provide a code for the record to identify it from other records. It also typically contains other information, such as the number of bytes contained in the record. The microcomputer uses this information to detect the end of recorded data.

The total is the number of bytes to be recorded on the cassette. This is calculated by the microcomputer as information is stored in the cassette. At the end of each stored data, the microcomputer stores the total. This data is used for detecting errors. For example, when the microcomputer reads a record, it calculates the number of bytes read. The microcomputer then compares this total number of bytes with the total, which is at the end of the stored data. If there is a discrepancy in the two values, an error occurs. The same record can be reread to check whether the error is due to incorrect recording.

Redundant Recording Errors may occur if a cassette tape has a worn surface or a bad spot. This can be eliminated by redundant recording. Each record is stored twice, one after the other, in the cassette tape. If a total error occurs in record 1, the microcomputer will read redundant record 1 with a good

```
                      1  "8085"
          (000B)      2  COMPORT   EQU      0BH
          (0009)      3  PORTA     EQU      09H
          (000A)      4  PORTB     EQU      0AH
          (000B)      5  PORTC     EQU      0BH
0000 3E0E             6  BEGIN     MVI      A,0EH        ;SET COMMAND REG. IN ORDER TO HAVE PORT A AS INPUT
0002 D30B             7            OUT      COMPORT      ; PORT B AS OUTPUT, AND PORT C AS OUTPUT
0004 310900           8            LXI      SP,0900H     ;INITIALIZE THE STACK POINTER AT ADDRESS 0900H
0007 3EF0             9            MVI      A,0F0H       ;INITIALIZE THE DISPLAY TO BE ALL ZEROS
0009 D30A            10            OUT      PORTB        ;SEND ZEROS TO OUT PORT B
000B 00              11  DELAY     NOP                   ;DELAY LATCH
000C 5600            12            ANI      00H          ;CLEAR ACCUMULATOR
000E D30A            13            OUT      PORTB        ;ENABLE ALL LATCHES TO HAVE ALL ZEROS DISPLAYED
0010 32AAAA          14            STA      0AAAH        ;INITIALIZE LOCATION 0AAAH IN RAM TO BE 0
0013 32BBBB          15            STA      0BBBH        ;INITIALIZE LOCATION 0BBBH IN RAM TO BE 0
0016 AF              16  AGAIN     XRA      A            ;CLEAR ACCUMULATOR
0017 D30B            17            OUT      PORTC        ;SEND ALL ZEROS TO PORT C
0019 DB09            18  KEYOPEN   IN       PORTA        ;GET DATA IN FROM PORT A
001B FEF0            19            CPI      0F0H         ;COMPARE DATA IN WITH F0H
001D C20019          20            JNZ      KEYOPEN      ;IF IT IS NOT ZERO ,THEN ALL KEYS ARE OPEN
0020 CD007D          21            CALL     DEBOUNCE
0023 DB09            22  KEYCLOSE  IN       PORTA        ;GET DATA IN FROM PORT A AGAIN
0025 FEF0            23            CPI      0F0H         ;COMPARE WITH F0H
0027 CA0023          24            JZ       KEYCLOSE     ;IF IT IS EQUAL TO ZERO, THEN KEY IS HOLD DOWN
002A CD007D          25            CALL     DEBOUNCE     ;DELAY 20MS
002D 3EFF            26            MVI      A,0FFH       ;SET ACC TO ALL ONE
002F B7              27            ORA      A            ;CLEAR CARRY
0030 17              28  NEXTROW   RAL                   ;ROTATE ZERO INTO FIRST ROW
0031 47              29            MOV      B,A          ;SAVE ROW MASK
0032 D30B            30            OUT      PORTC        ;OUTPUT TO ALL ROWS
0034 DB09            31            IN       PORTA        ;READ ROW AND COLUMN
0036 4F              32            MOV      C,A          ;SAVE ROW AND COLUMN CODE
0037 E6F0            33            ANI      0F0H         ;MASK ROW CODE
0039 FEF0            34            CPI      0F0H         ;CHECK COLUMN FOR A HIGH
003B C20043          35            JNZ      DECODE       ;IF HIGH, ROW FOUND AND REC, C HAS ROW AND COLUMN CODE
003E 37              36            STC                   ;SET CARRY
003F 78              37            MOV      A,B          ;IF KEY NOT FOUND IN THAT ROW, GO BACK TO NEXT ROW TO
                     38  *                               ;FIND THE NEXT KEY.
0040 C30030          39            JMP      NEXTROW      ;FIND THE KEY
0043 210095          40  DECODE    LXI      H,TABLE      ;LOAD STARTING ADDR, OF LOOK-UP TABLE
0046 060F            41            MVI      B,0FH        ;SET CHARACTER COUNTER
0048 79              42            MOV      A,C          ;GET ROW AND COLUMN CODE IN ACC
0049 BE              43  NEXT      CMP      M            ;COMPARE ROW AND COLUMN CODE WITH # IN LOOK-UP TABLE
004A CA0052          44            JZ       DONE         ;GO TO DONE IF # IS FOUND
004D 23              45            INX      H            ;IF NOT, INCREMENT HL REG. PAIR
004E 05              46            DCR      B            ;DECREMENT CHARACTER COUNTER
004F C20049          47            JNZ      NEXT         ;GO BACK TO NEXT TO FIND #
0052 78              48  DONE      MOV      A,B          ;GET CHARACTER ( 0 TO F )
0053 CD00B7          49            CALL     SETTIME      ;CREATE SET UP TIME FOR DATA OUT
0056 E63F            50            ANI      03FH         ;ENABLE ONE OF THREE LATCHES
0058 CD008D          51            CALL     HOLDTIME     ;CREATE HOLD TIME FOR DATA OUT
005B 3A0AAA          52            LDA      0AAAH        ;GET DATA STORED FROM MEMORY LOCATION # 0AAAH
```

Figure 8–9 Assembly language program listing

probability that this information is error-free. However, if record 1 is error-free, the microcomputer will not read the redundant record 1 and will proceed directly to record 2.

Interfacing the Cassette Recorder to a Typical Microprocessor

Figure 8–10 shows a typical schematic for interfacing a cassette recorder to a microprocessor. The main element of the interface is a UART, which is used to transform parallel data from the microprocessor to the serial form required by the cassette re-corder. The UART also formats each byte by adding 1 start bit and 2 stop bits before sending to the recorder. The parity error check is not usually used because of the total error. The TxCLK and RxCLK use a 4800-Hz clock. A clock divide ratio of 16 can be used with the UART to give a baud rate of $4800/16 = 300$. Each bit is $1/300 = 3.33$ ms. This is equal to the time required to store 8 cycles of a 2400-Hz tone or 4 cycles of a 1200-Hz tone.

The cassette interface in Figure 8–10 performs the following three functions:

```
005E 4F          53            MOV     C,A          ;SAVE IT IN REC. C
005F CD0087      54            CALL    SETTIME      ;CREATE SET UP TIME FOR DATA OUT
0062 E65F        55            ANI     05FH         ;ENABLE ONE OF THREE LATCHES
0064 CD008D      56            CALL    HOLDTIME     ;CREAT HOLD TIME FOR DATA OUT
0067 3A0BBB      57            LDA     0BBBH        ;

006A CD0087      58            CALL    SETTIME      ;CREATE SET-UP TIME FOR DATA OUT
006D E66F        59            ANI     06FH         ;ENABLE ONE OF THREE LATCHES
006F CD008D      60            CALL    HOLDTIME     ;CREATE HOLD TIME FOR DATA OUT
0072 78          61            MOV     A,B          ;STORE THE FIRST OLD DATA OUT IN LOCATION 0AAAH
0073 320AAA      62            STA     0AAAH        ;
0076 79          63            MOV     A,C          ;STORE THE SECOND OLD DATA OUT IN LOCATION 0BBBH
0077 320BBB      64            STA     0BBBH        ;
007A C30016      65            JMP     AGAIN        ;GO BACK TO GET ANOTHER KEY
007D 119C02      66 DEBOUNCE   LXI     D,069C2H     ;DELAY IN 20MS TO DEBOUNCE THE KEY
0080 1B          67 LOOP       DCX     D            ;
0081 7A          68            MOV     A,D          ;
0082 B3          69            ORA     E            ;
0083 C28080      70            JNZ     LOOP         ;
0086 C9          71            RET                  ;BACK TO MAIN PROGRAM
0087 F6F0        72 SETTIME    ORI     0F0H         ;DISABLE ALL LATCHES OF DISPLAYS
0089 D30A        73            OUT     PORTB        ;SEND CHARACTER OUT TOPORTB
008B 00          74            NOP                  ;DELAY TO GET SET UP TIME OF DATA OUT
008C C9          75            RET                  ;BACK TO MAIN PROGRAM
008D D30A        76 HOLDTIME   OUT     PORTB        ;DISPLAY THE RESULT
008F 00          77            NOP                  ;DELAY TO GET THE HOLD TIME OF DATA OUT
0090 F6F0        78            ORI     0F0H         ;DISABLE AGIAN ALL LATCHES
0092 D30A        79            OUT     PORTB        ;SEND CHARACTER OUT TO PORT B
0094 C9          80            RET                  ;BACK TO MAIN PROGRAM.
0095 77          81 TABLE      HEX     77           ;CHARACTER F
0096 B7          82            HEX     B7           ;   "      E
0097 D7          83            HEX     D7           ;   "      D
0098 E7          84            HEX     E7           ;   "      C
0099 7B          85            HEX     7B           ;   "      B
009A BB          86            HEX     BB           ;   "      A
009B DB          87            HEX     DB           ;NUMBER    9
009C EB          88            HEX     EB           ;   "      8
009D 7D          89            HEX     7D           ;   "      7
009E BD          90            HEX     BD           ;   "      6
009F DD          91            HEX     DD           ;   "      5
00A0 ED          92            HEX     ED           ;   "      4
00A1 7E          93            HEX     7E           ;   "      3
00A2 BE          94            HEX     BE           ;   "      2
00A3 DE          95            HEX     DE           ;   "      1
00A4 EE          96            HEX     EE           ;   "      0
                 97            END
```

Errors=   0

Figure 8–9 cont'd

1. Converts the UART's serial output from TTL logic levels to audio tones, as required by the Kansas City standard. The 2400-Hz and 1200-Hz tones are derived from a 4800-Hz clock. These signals are then recorded on the cassette recorder via its auxiliary input.

2. Converts the audio signals (earphone output) from the cassette recorder to serial logic levels for the UART's RxData input.

3. Turns the motor in the recorder ON and OFF. It uses the UART's RTS input and a relay to accomplish this. The microprocessor can write into the UART's control register to turn the motor ON and OFF.

8–4–2 Interfacing a Cassette Recorder to the Intel 8085*

The cassette recorder interface described in this section was developed by Intel. This interface makes use of the 8085 SID and SOD lines. It does not use any UART. Basically, data is transmitted with each bit composed of a tone burst followed by a pause. The first third of a bit period is always a tone burst, the middle third is either a tone burst continuous with the first or a pause corresponding to a 1 or 0, and the final third is always a pause,

*Courtesy of Intel Corporation.

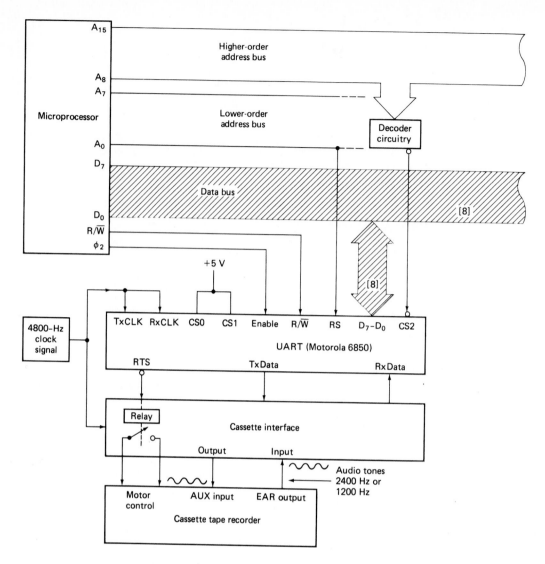

Figure 8–10 Typical cassette interface arrangement (From *Microprocessors and Micro-computers: Hardware and Software,* by Tocci and Laskowski, © 1979, p. 219. Reprinted by permission of Prentice-Hall, Inc., Englewood Cliffs, New Jersey)

as shown in Figure 8–11. Thus, data is distinguished by the burst/pause ratio.

We now describe the hardware and software in the following paragraphs.

Hardware The tone bursts are obtained from the 8085 SOD line, using analog signal conditioning to eliminate the dc component of the waveform. A suggested interface circuit is shown in Figure 8–11. In Figure 8–11, A2 buffers the incoming signal and A3 inverts it. The peaks of these two signals are transmitted through D1 or D2 and are filtered by an RC network. Comparator A4 then squares up the output and produces the logic signal read by the SID pin. Since the operational amplifiers are powered by the single 5-V supply, a 2-V reference level is obtained from a resistive voltage divider. The waveforms present at several points in the circuit are shown in Figure 8–12.

Software The algorithm for reading data off the tape is simple and straightforward. If the tone burst is longer than the pause, the bit is a 1; otherwise, it is a 0.

In the following discussion, we assume certain subroutines and then describe the basics of the program. Assume that TAPEO is a subroutine for outputting the contents of register C to a cassette recorder. TAPEIN reads 8 bits into register C. Let us now describe the output and input routines.

Output Routine TAPEO calls a subroutine named BURST three times for each bit. If bit 6 of the accumulator, A6 (SOD enable bit), is set when BURST is called, a square wave tone burst is transmitted. If A6 is not set, BURST simply delays for exactly the same amount of time before returning. The three calls are used to, respectively, output the initial burst, output the data burst/space, and create the space at the end of each bit.

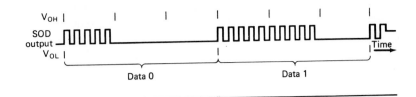

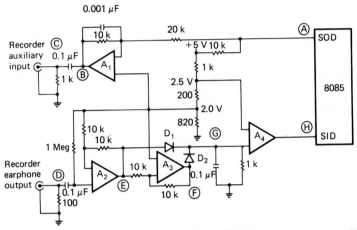

Figure 8–11 On-chip magnetic tape interface schematic (Courtesy of Intel Corp.)

NOTES: A_1–A_4: ¼LM324 Quad operational amplifiers
D_1–D_2: Any low current diode
All resistors ± 5%

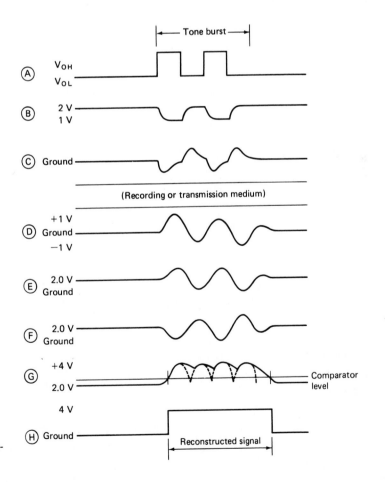

Figure 8–12 Analog signal waveforms (Courtesy of Intel Corp.)

Nine bits will be outputted: 8 data bits (LSB first) followed by a 0 bit. The start of the initial burst of the trailing 0 is needed to mark the end of the final space of the preceding data bit.

Start each bit by outputting a tone burst:

```
TAPEO:MVI B, 9
TO1:MVI A, C0
     CALL BURST
```

In these instructions, register B is initialized with 9 (8 data bits followed by the trailing 0 bit). MVI A, C0 will load 1100 0000 ($C0_{16}$) into the accumulator; that is, A7 (data bit) and A6 (SOD enable bit) are set to 1. When CALL BURST is executed, a tone burst is transmitted. Now, rotate register C through the carry:

```
MOV   A,  C
RAR
MOV   C,  A
```

MOV A, C transfers the contents of register C to the accumulator. The RAR instruction rotates the contents of the accumulator right 1 bit; that is, it shifts the LSB of the accumulator to the carry. MOV C, A saves the resultant data in register C. Next, move the carry to the SOD enable bit position A6. Simultaneously set A7 to 1 and clear all other bits. The output is a tone burst or space, depending on the previous contents of the carry:

```
MVI   A,  01
RAR
RAR
CALL  BURST
```

MVI A, 01 loads 01_{16} into the accumulator:

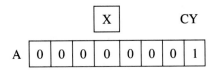

where X is the previous value of data.

After the first RAR,

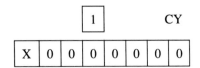

After the second RAR,

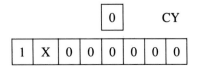

After execution of the CALL BURST, if X = 1, a tone burst will be sent via the SOD line. If X = 0, a pause will be sent.

Now, clear the accumulator and output a space:

```
XRA   A
CALL  BURST
```

XRA A EXCLUSIVE-ORs the accumulator with itself or, in other words, clears the accumulator. Now when CALL BURST is executed, a space or pause will be sent via the SOD line.

At this point, 1 bit composed of initial burst, burst/space, and final space is outputted via the SOD pin. Now, keep cycling until the full 9-bit sequence is finished:

```
DCR   B
MVI   D,   00
JNZ   TO1
RET
```

Input Routine TAPEIN uses a subroutine called BITIN to move the data in the SID pin into the carry. Initialize the bit counter and register D, which will keep track of the tone burst time. If a tone burst is being received when TAPEIN is called, wait until the burst is over:

```
TAPEIN:MVI  B,  8
       MVI  D,  00
TI1:CALL  BITIN
    JC   TI1
```

Now await the start of the next burst:

```
TI2:CALL  BITIN
    JNC   TI2
```

The next burst has now arrived. Keep reading the SID pin, decrementing register D (thus making it more negative) each cycle until the pause is detected:

```
TI3:DCR   D
    CALL  BITIN
    JC   TI3
```

Now continue reading the SID pin, incrementing the D register (back toward 0) each cycle until the next burst is received:

```
TI4:INR   D
    CALL  BITIN
    JNC   TI4
```

If the burst lasted longer than the space, D was not incremented all the way back to 0; it is still negative. If the space was longer, D was incremented up through 0; it is now positive. In other words, the sign bit of D will now correspond to the data bit that would lead to each of these results. Move the sign bit into the carry, and then rotate it into register C:

```
MOV   A,  D
RAL
MOV   A,  C
RAR
MOV   C,  A
MVI   D,  00
```

MOV A, D moves the contents of the D register (the sign bit of D corresponds to the data bit) into the accumulator. RAL shifts the MSB of the accumulator (data bit) into the carry. MOV A, C moves the contents of register C into the accumulator. RAR rotates the data bit from the carry into the MSB of the accumulator. MOV C, A saves the contents of the accumulator into the C register. MVI D, 00 initializes the D register to 00_{16}. Now, continue the same sequence until the last bit has been received:

```
DCR   B
JNZ   TI3
RET
```

The preceding description provides the basic concepts of a simple interface of the 8085 to a cassette recorder. A listing of the program is given in Figure 8–13. The program was developed by Intel using the ISIS-II 8080/8085 assembler.

8–5 CRT (CATHODE RAY TUBE) TERMINAL INTERFACING TO A MICROPROCESSOR

The CRT terminal is widely used as the most efficient input/output device for communicating between microcomputers and human beings. It is composed of a teletypewriter-type keyboard and a cathode ray tube (CRT). With the increasing popularity of CRT terminals, microprocessor manufacturers have designed a special LSI chip called the *CRT controller* to simplify and minimize the cost of interfacing the CRT terminals to microcomputers.

In this section, we will briefly discuss CRT basics, character generation techniques, and a typical CRT controller chip such as the Intel 8275.

8–5–1 CRT Basics

A cathode ray tube is an evacuated glass tube with a fluorescent coating on the inner surface of the screen. An electron gun placed at the end generates an electron beam. These electrons, when focused on the fluorescent inner coating, generate an illuminated phosphor dot. Figure 8–14 shows the basic diagram of a CRT.

The location of the dot on the screen can be controlled by deflecting the electron beam. Modern CRTs use the electromagnetic deflection technique. In this scheme, a display is created by moving the beam horizontally and vertically across the entire surface of the screen and si-

multaneously changing the intensity. The generation of the beam includes two types of scan on the screen. These are horizontal scan and vertical scan. In a *horizontal scan,* the beam starts in the upper left-hand corner and goes horizontally across the screen. The beam then goes off the screen and starts at the next lower left for another scan. After several horizontal scans, the beam reaches the bottom of the screen to complete one vertical scan. The beam then goes off the screen and starts another vertical scan from the top. This type of scanning is called *raster scan.* Most modern CRT terminals use this scanning for displaying alphanumeric characters. Note that the scanning is called raster because the picture is generated on the screen by continuously scanning an electron beam across the screen to create a regular pattern of closely spaced horizontal lines or raster, which covers the entire screen.

One of the most common examples of raster display is the home TV set. The typical bandwidth used in these TV sets is 4.5 MHz. The raster displays used with microcomputer systems cover a wider bandwidth from 10 to 20 MHz for displaying detailed information. In most microcomputer displays, each sweep field contains the entire picture or text to be displayed. However, in broadcast television, two successive sweep fields are used to create one complete picture. This is called the *interlaced scanning technique.* One of the problems with this method is that the refresh rate is reduced by 50%. For example, if the vertical sweep frequency is 60 Hz, then a particular line on the screen will be refreshed at 30 Hz. Since TV pictures contain large white areas, the low refresh rate provided by the interlaced scan is acceptable. However, for displaying alphanumeric characters on the CRT, small details in the picture will flicker on and off at the 30-MHz refresh rate. This problem can be avoided by using a long-persistence phosphor on the CRT screen.

In order to display characters, the screen is divided by horizontal and vertical lines into a dot matrix. A dot matrix of 5×7 or 7×9 is very common for representing a character. For example, a 5×7 dot matrix can be used to represent the character "A" as shown in Figure 8–15. To provide space around the character, one top line, one left, two right, and three bottom lines are left blank. Note that in the figure, the character is represented in a 5×7 dot matrix. This means that each character requires 35 dots, which can be either ON or OFF depending on the dots required by a character.

The pattern of dots for a particular character can be stored in a memory device. For example, the pattern for "A" can be stored as shown in Figure 8–16. Note that the dot pattern for each character is usually stored in a ROM. For one character, a 35-bit ROM is needed. In order to address this 7-row ROM, three address bits are needed. As each row is read from the ROM, the data can be transferred to a shift register and then shifted to the video input of the CRT. For a standard 64-character

```
                    149 ;      THE FOLLOWING CODE IS USED BY THE CASSETTE INTERFACE.
                    150 ;      SUBROUTINES TAPEO AND TAPEIN ARE USED RESPECTIVELY
                    151 ;      TO OUTPUT OR RECEIVE AN EIGHT BIT BYTE OF DATA.  REGISTER C
                    152 ;      HOLDS THE DATA IN EITHER CASE.  REGISTERS A,B,&C ARE ALL DESTROYED.
0010                153 CYCNO  EQU    16     ;TWICE THE NUMBER OF CYCLES PER TONE BURST
001E                154 HALFCYC EQU   20     ;DETERMINES TONE FREQUENCY
0016                155 CIRATE EQU    22     ;SETS SAMPLE RATE
00FA                156 LEADER EQU    250    ;NUMBER OF SUCCESIVE TONE BURSTS COMPRISING LEADER
00FA                157 LDRCHK EQU    250    ;USED IN PLAYBK TO VERIFY PRESENCE OF LEADER
                    158
                    159 ;BLKRCD        OUTPUTS A VERY LONG TONE BURST (<LEADER> TIMES
                    160 ;             THE NORMAL BURST DURATION) TO ALLOW RECORDER ELECTRONICS
                    161 ;             AND AGC TO STABILIZE.  THEN OUTPUTS THE REMAINDER OF THE
                    162 ;             256 BYTE PAGE POINTED TO BY <H>, STARTING AT BYTE <L>.
08B9 0EFA           163 BLKRCD MVI    C,LEADER;SET UP LEADER BURST LENGTH
08BB 3EC0           164        MVI    A,0C0H ;SET ACCUMULATOR TO RESULT IN TONE BURST
08BD CDF008         165 BR1    CALL   BURST  ;OUTPUT TONE
08C0 0D             166        DCR    C
08C1 C2BD08         167        JNZ    BR1    ;SUSTAIN LEADER TONE
08C4 AF             168        XRA    A      ;CLEAR ACCUMULATOR & OUTPUT SPACE, SO THAT
08C5 CDF008         169        CALL   BURST  ;\ START OF FIRST DATA BYTE CAN BE DETECTED
08C8 4E             170 BR2    MOV    C,M    ;GET DATA BYTE TO BE RECORDED
08C9 CDD108         171        CALL   TAPEO  ;OUTPUT REGISTER C TO RECORDER
08CC 2C             172        INR    L      ;POINT TO NEXT BYTE
08CD C2C808         173        JNZ    BR2
08D0 C9             174        RET           ;AFTER BLOCK IS COMPLETE
                    175
                    176
                    177 ;TAPEO         OUTPUTS THE BYTE IN REGISTER C TO THE RECORDER.
                    178 ;             REGISTERS A,B,C,D,&E ARE ALL USED.
08D1 F3             179 TAPEO: DI
08D2 D5             180        PUSH   D      ;D&E USED AS COUNTERS BY SUBROUTINE BURST
08D3 0609           181        MVI    B,9    ;WILL RESULT IN 8 DATA BITS AND ONE STOP BIT
08D5 AF             182 TO1    XRA    A      ;CLEAR ACCUMULATOR
08D6 3EC0           183        MVI    A,0C0H ;SET ACCUMULATOR TO CAUSE A TONE BURST
08D8 CDF008         184        CALL   BURST
08DB 79             185        MOV    A,C    ;MOVE NEXT DATA BIT INTO THE CARRY
08DC 1F             186        RAR
08DD 4F             187        MOV    C,A    ;CARRY WILL BECOME SOD ENABLE IN BURST ROUTINE
08DE 3E01           188        MVI    A,01H  ;SET BIT TO BE REPEATEDLY COMPLEMENTED IN BURST
08E0 1F             189        RAR
08E1 1F             190        RAR
08E2 CDF008         191        CALL   BURST  ;OUTPUT EITHER A TONE OR A PAUSE
08E5 AF             192        XRA    A      ;CLEAR ACCUMULATOR
08E6 CDF008         193        CALL   BURST  ;OUTPUT PAUSE
08E9 05             194        DCR    B
08EA C2D508         195        JNZ    TO1    ;REPEAT UNTIL BYTE FINISHED
08ED D1             196        POP    D      ;RESTORE STATUS AND RETURN
08EE FB             197        EI
08EF C9             198        RET
                    199
08F0 1610           200 BURST: MVI    D,CYCNO ;SET NUMBER OF CYCLES
08F2 30             201 BU1    SIM           ;COMPLEMENT SOD LINE IF SOD ENABLE BIT SET
08F3 1E1E           202        MVI    E,HALFCYC
08F5 1D             203 BU2    DCR    E      ;REGULATE TONE FREQUENCY
08F6 C2F508         204        JNZ    BU2
08F9 EE20           205        XRI    20H    ;COMPLEMENT SOD DATA BIT IN ACCUMULATOR
08FB 15             206        DCR    D
08FC C2F208         207        JNZ    BU1    ;CONTINUE UNTIL BURST (OR EQUIVILENT PAUSE) FINISHED
08FF C9             208        RET
                    209
```

Figure 8–13 Assembly language program listing

```
                   210 ;PLAYBK       WAITS FOR THE LONG LEADER BURST TO ARRIVE, THEN CONTINUES
                   211 ;             READING BYTES FROM THE RECORDER AND STORING THEM
                   212 ;             IN MEMORY STARTING AT LOCATION <HL>.
                   213 ;         CONTINUES UNTIL THE END OF THE CURRENT PAGE (<L>=0FFH) IS REACHED.
0900 0EFA          214 PLAYBK: MVI   C,LDRCHK      ;<LDRCHK> SUCCESSIVE HIGHS MUST BE READ
0902 CD3D09        215 PB1:    CALL  BITIN         ;\ TO VERIFY THAT THE LEADER IS PRESENT
0905 D20009        216         JNC   PLAYBK        ; \ AND ELECTRONICS HAS STABILIZED
0908 0D            217         DCR   C
0909 C20209        218         JNZ   PB1
090C CD1509        219 PB2:    CALL  TAPEIN        ;GET DATA BYTE FROM RECORDER
090F 71            220         MOV   M,C           ;STORE IN MEMORY
0910 2C            221         INR   L             ;INCREMENT POINTER
0911 C20C09        222         JNZ   PB2           ;REPEAT FOR REST OF CURRENT PAGE
0914 C9            223         RET
                   224
                   225 ;TAPEIN CASSETTE TAPE INPUT SUBROUTINE.  READS ONE BYTE OF DATA
                   226 ;         FROM THE RECORDER INTERFACE AND RETURNS WITH THE BYTE IN REGISTER C.
0915 0609          227 TAPEIN: MVI   B,9           ;READ EIGHT DATA BITS
0917 1600          228 TI1:    MVI   D,00H         ;CLEAR UP/DOWN COUNTER
0919 15            229 TI2:    DCR   D             ;DECREMENT COUNTER EACH TIME ONE LEVEL IS READ
091A CD3D09        230         CALL  BITIN
091D DA1909        231         JC    TI2           ;REPEAT IF STILL AT ONE LEVEL
0920 CD3D09        232         CALL  BITIN
0923 DA1909        233         JC    TI2
0926 14            234 TI3:    INR   D             ;INCREMENT COUNTER EACH TIME ZERO IS READ
0927 CD3D09        235         CALL  BITIN
092A D22609        236         JNC   TI3           ;REPEAT EACH TIME ZERO IS READ
092D CD3D09        237         CALL  BITIN
0930 D22609        238         JNC   TI3
0933 7A            239         MOV   A,D
0934 17            240         RAL                 ;MOVE COUNTER MOST SIGNIFICANT BIT INTO CARRY
0935 79            241         MOV   A,C
0936 1F            242         RAR                 ;MOVE DATA BIT RECIEVED <CY> INTO BYTE REGISTER
0937 4F            243         MOV   C,A
0938 05            244         DCR   B
0939 C21709        245         JNZ   TI1           ;REPEAT UNTIL FULL BYTE ASSEMBLED
093C C9            246         RET
                   247
093D 1E16          248 BITIN:  MVI   E,CKRATE
093F 1D            249 BI1:    DCR   E
0940 C23F09        250         JNZ   BI1           ;LIMIT INPUT SAMPLING RATE
0943 20            251         RIM                 ;SAMPLE SID LINE
0944 17            252         RAL                 ;MOVE DATA INTO CY BIT
0945 C9            253         RET
                   254
                   255         END
```

EXTERNAL SYMBOLS

USER SYMBOLS

BI1	A 092F	BITIN	A 093D	BITSI	A 0009	BITSO	A 000B	BITTIN	A 20C8	BLKRCD	A 0889	BR1 A 088D
BR2	A 08C8	BRI1	A 081F	BRI3	A 0827	BRI4	A 0829	BRID	A 081A	BU1	A 08F2	BU2 A 08F5
BURST	A 09F0	CI1	A 088E	CI2	A 0896	CI3	A 089E	CI4	A 08A1	CI5	A 08B6	CIN A 088A
CKRATE	A 0016	CO1	A 086F	CO2	A 0876	COUT	A 0869	CRT1	A 0803	CRTTST	A 0800	CYCNO A 0010
ECHO	A 080C	HALFBI	A 20CA	HALFCY	A 001E	LDRCHK	A 00FA	LEADER	A 00FA	PB1	A 0902	PB2 A 090C
PLAYBK	A 0900	S1	A 084A	SIGNON	A 0847	STRNG	A 0855	TAPEIN	A 0915	TAPEO	A 09D1	TI1 A 0917
TI2	A 0919	TI3	A 0926	TO1	A 08D5							

ASSEMBLY COMPLETE, NO ERROR(S)

Figure 8–13   cont'd

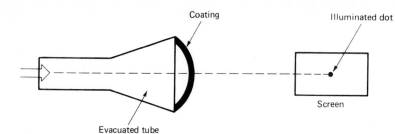

Figure 8–14 Basic diagram of a CRT (From *The CRT Controller Handbook* by Kane. Copyright © 1980 McGraw-Hill, Inc.)

Coating

Illuminated dot

Evacuated tube

Screen

	1	2	3	4	5	6	7	
0	0	0	0	0	0	0	0	0
1	0	0	0	●	0	0	0	0
2	0	0	●	0	●	0	0	0
3	0	●	0	0	0	●	0	0
4	0	●	0	0	0	●	0	0
5	0	●	●	●	●	●	0	0
6	0	●	0	0	0	●	0	0
7	0	●	0	0	0	●	0	0
8	0	0	0	0	0	0	0	0
9	0	0	0	0	0	0	0	0
10	0	0	0	0	0	0	0	0

Figure 8–15 Generation of "A" using 5 × 7 dot matrix

set, with each character represented by a 5 × 7 dot pattern, a 2240-bit (64 × 7 × 5) ROM is required. Also, each character can be addressed using six address lines for the 64- (2^6) character set, and then three row select or scan line address lines can be used to identify the dot row of that character. Note that ROM addressing can efficiently be accomplished by using a scan line counter. In Figure 8–16, the ROM, addressing logic, and parallel-to-serial shift register are referred to as a *character generator*. Also, memory is used in the CRT to store data to be displayed. This memory is called *screen memory*. The character generator obtains data from the screen memory and then sends the appropriate dot stream to the CRT.

8–5–2   The CRT Controller

In this section, we first describe the display functions associated with a typical CRT controller. We will then relate these functions to the Intel 8275 CRT controller.

A typical CRT controller provides all the logic functions for interfacing a microprocessor to a CRT. A simplified block diagram of a microprocessor-driven CRT logic is shown in Figure 8–17.

In Figure 8–17, the microprocessor and the CRT controller communicate via the shared RAM. The microprocessor writes the characters to be displayed in this

RAM. The CRT controller reads this memory using DMA and then generates the characters on the video display. A typical CRT controller chip provides the following main functions:

- Clocking and timing functions
- Cursor functions
- Scrolling

A CRT controller chip contains several registers and counters that can be programmed to generate timing signals and video interface signals required by a terminal. Also, the display functions are driven by various clocks generated from a master oscillator. Typical clocks include the dot clock and character clock. The basic timing is derived by a clock divider that generates signals with the correct period and in the current phase. Note that the counters in the CRT controller chip are used to store the current contents of the clock divider circuits.

The CRT controller chip usually can generate and display a special symbol such as a blinking signal or an underline on the CRT. This symbol is commonly called the *cursor*. It can be moved on the screen to a specific location where data needs to be modified.

The scrolling function usually implemented in the CRT controller moves currently displayed data to the top of the screen as new data is entered at the bottom.

Now let us briefly describe the display functions associated with a typical CRT controller such as the Intel 8275. The Intel 8275 programmable CRT controller is a single-chip 40-pin device to interface CRT raster scan displays with Intel microcomputer systems (using 8051, 8085, 8086, and 8088). Its primary function is to refresh the display by buffering the information from main memory and keeping track of the display position of the screen. The basic functions provided by the 8275 include raster timing, display row buffering, visual attribute decoding, cursor timing, and light pen detection.

The 8275 can be interfaced with the Intel 8257 DMA controller chip and character generator ROMs for dot matrix decoding. Dot level timing must be provided by external circuitry.

Display characters are read from memory and displayed on a row-by-row basis. The 8275 has two row buffers. While one row is being used for display, the other is being filled with the next row of characters to be displayed. The number of display characters per row

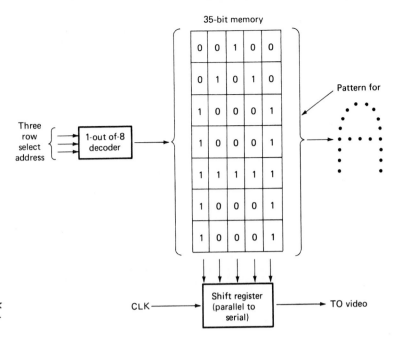

Figure 8–16 Generation of "A"
(From *The CRT Controller Handbook* by Kane. Copyright © 1980 McGraw-Hill, Inc.)

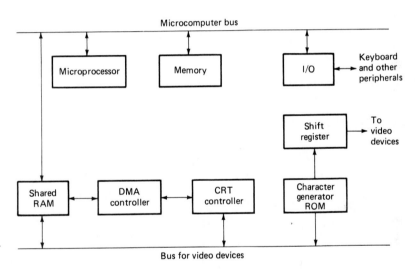

Figure 8–17 Microprocessor-driven CRT terminal-block diagram

and the number of character rows per frame are software programmable.

The 8275 uses the DMA technique to fill the row buffer that is not being used for display. It displays character rows one line at a time. The number of lines per character row, the underline position, and blanking of top and bottom lines are programmable.

The 8275 provides special control codes that can be used to minimize DMA overhead. It also provides visual attribute codes to cause special action or graphic symbols on the screen without the use of the character generator. The 8275 controls raster timing by generating horizontal retrace (HRTC) and vertical retrace (VRTC) signals. The timing of these signals is programmable.

The 8275 has a light pen input and several registers. The light pen consists of a microswitch and a tiny light sensor. When the light pen is pressed against the CRT screen, the microswitch enables the light sensor. When the raster sweep reaches the light sensor, it triggers the light pen output. If the output of the light pen is presented to the 8275 LPEN pin, the row and character position coordinates are stored in a pair of registers. These registers can be read on command. A bit in a status register located in the 8275 is set, indicating that the light pen signal was detected. The 8275 provides cursor functions. The cursor location is determined by a cursor row register and a character position register, which are loaded by command to the controller. The cursor can be programmed to appear on the display in many forms such as a blinking underline and a nonblinking underline. Finally, it should be pointed out that the 8275 does not provide any scrolling functions.

8–5 CRT (CATHODE RAY TUBE) TERMINAL INTERFACING TO A MICROPROCESSOR   **267**

8–6 PRINTER INTERFACE TO A MICROPROCESSOR

Typical microprocessors are interfaced to printers in order to produce hard copies. The two types of printers are the serial and the line printers:

- *Serial printers* print one character at a time.
- *Line printers* print several characters on a single line so fast that they appear to be printed at the same time.

Printers can also be classified as impact or nonimpact, depending on the techniques that are used to generate the characters:

- In *impact printers,* the printing element strikes the printing medium, such as paper, directly in order to print a character.
- In *nonimpact printers,* thermal or electrostatic methods are used to print a character rather than direct impact.

Another way to classify printers is by using character formation techniques:

- *Matrix printers* utilize dots or lines to form characters.
- *Character printers* use completely formed characters.

Microcomputers typically utilize inexpensive serial dot matrix–type impact printers. An example of this type of printer is the LRC 7040. The concepts associated with interfacing the 8085-based microcomputer system to the LRC 7040 matrix printer will be discussed next. There are two ways of interfacing the printer:

1. Direct microprocessor control
2. Indirect microprocessor control using a printer controller

The direct microprocessor control utilizes mostly software. The printer is interfaced directly to the microcomputer using I/O ports. On the other hand, using indirect microprocessor control, the printer can be interfaced to the microcomputer using a dot matrix printer controller chip such as the Intel 8295. The advantages of each system depend on the requirements of the system to which it is applied: The indirect control method is applied when the microprocessor has heavy task requirements, while the direct control method is valuable for systems that lightly load the microprocessor and where the cost constraints of additional hardware are significant.

8–6–1 LRC 7040 Printer

The LRC 7040, a dot matrix impact printer, is capable of printing up to 40 columns of alphanumeric informa-

tion. The printer is manufactured by LRC, Inc., of Riverton, Wyoming. The printer consists of four major sections: the frame, the print head, the main drive, and the paper controller. The LRC 7040 has eight inputs for the most basic configuration. One input controls the main drive motor ON or OFF, and seven inputs control the print solenoids using TTL drivers. In order to see how the solenoids generate the dots for each character, consider Figure 8–18.

The figure shows a 5×7 matrix of dots. Columns are labeled T1 through T5, and rows are labeled S1 through S7. Each row corresponds to one of the solenoid wires. The entire print head assembly is moved left to right across the paper so that at some time the print head is over the column T1, then it is over column T2, and so on. If the correct solenoids are energized at each one of the columns T1 through T5, then a character can be formed. Figure 8–18 shows how the number 4 is formed. At T1, solenoids S1 through S5 are active; at T2, solenoid S5 is active; at T3, all solenoids S1 through S7 are active; at both T4 and T5, solenoid S5 is active. Thus, the number 4 is formed.

A complete alphanumeric character is formed by choosing the correct pattern of active solenoids for each of five instants in line. The code for the number 4 consists of 5 bytes of data in the sequence $1F_{16}$, 10_{16}, $7F_{16}$, 10_{16}, 10_{16} as follows:

	S7	S6	S5	S4	S3	S2	S1	
Column T1	0	0	1	1	1	1	1	$= 1F_{16}$
Column T2	0	0	1	0	0	0	0	$= 10_{16}$
Column T3	1	1	1	1	1	1	1	$= 7F_{16}$
Column T4	0	0	1	0	0	0	0	$= 10_{16}$
Column T5	0	0	1	0	0	0	0	$= 10_{16}$

Note that S8 is assumed to be 0 here.

A printing sequence begins by turning the main motor drive ON and detecting when the print head has reached the left-hand margin of the print area. A microswitch (main drive switch) output from the printer indicates when the printer has reached the left-hand margin of the print

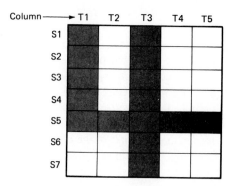

Figure 8–18 5×7 dot matrix pattern for generating the number 4

area. The microcomputer can then output a byte of data to energize the solenoids for 400 μs in order to print a particular column. The microcomputer can be programmed to determine which solenoids are to be turned on to print the next column. A delay of 900 μs between each column is needed to provide a space between dots. These steps must be repeated to print the complete alphanumeric character.

8–6–2 Interfacing the 8085 to the LRC 7040 Using Direct Microprocessor Control

Figure 8–19 shows a block diagram of interfacing the LRC 7040 printer to the 8085. Using this hardware, a program can be written to poll the home switch, and utilizing the time delays of 400 μs and 900 μs, the microcomputer can be programmed to print a hexadecimal digit (00–0F) stored in a buffer in the RAM. A table for storing each character with the bit patterns of 5 bytes of data for the dot matrix is necessary. A typical 8085 assembly language program for printing a character is shown in Figure 8–20.

The program assumes that a lookup table for storing the printer character code is available for each digit. The table starts at address 2000_{16} with the 5-byte code for digit 00_{16} stored from 2000_{16} through 2004_{16}; the code for 01_{16}, from 2005_{16} through 2009_{16}; and so on. Furthermore, the 400-μs and 900-μs delay routines are available. It is also assumed that the hexadecimal digit to be printed is available in address 3000_{16}. Finally, the program prints only one hexadecimal digit and then halts. This simple program is provided just as an illustration.

8–6–3 Printer Interface Using Printer Controller Chips

With direct microcomputer control, the microcomputer wastes time in a loop by checking the status of the HOME signal from the LRC 7040 printer. In order to minimize this problem, typical LSI printer controller chips such as the Intel 8295 can be used.

The Intel 8295 is packaged in a 40-pin DIP and provides serial or parallel transfer of data and commands from the 8085 to the printer controller. In parallel mode, data transfers are based on polling, interrupts, or DMA. Commands provide the formats of the printing characters and control all printer functions such as line feed and carriage return. The 8295 contains a 40-character buffer. When the buffer is full or a carriage return is received, a line is printed automatically. The 8295 provides buffering of up to 40 characters and contains a 7×7 character generator, accommodating 64 ASCII characters. Typical 8295 pins include the following:

$\overline{PFEED}$	Paper feed input switch
$\overline{CS}$	Chip select input
$\overline{RD}$	Read
$\overline{WR}$	Write
MOT	Main motor drive
STB	Solenoid strobe output
HOME	Home input switch; used by the 8295 to detect that print head is in home position
D0–D7	Data lines
IRQ/$\overline{SER}$	Bidirectional pin; is an interrupt request for the 8295 when high; when low, the 8295 operates in serial mode

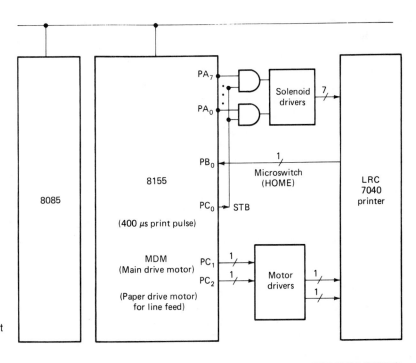

Figure 8–19 Interfacing the LRC 7040 printer to the 8085 using direct microcomputer control

```
TABLE    EQU    2000H      ; Point to character code table
DIGIT    EQU    3000H      ; Address of the hexadecimal digit
         ORG    1000H
START:   MVI    A,0DH      ; Configure ports A and C as outputs
         OUT    CSR        ; and Port B as input
STEP 1:  MVI    A,02H      ; Turn the MDM on
         OUT    PORT C
STEP 2:  IN     PORT B     ; Detect HOME
         RRC               ; switch
         JNC    STEP 2
STEP 3:  LDA    DIGIT      ; Get digit to be printed
         MOV    L,A        ; Extend the digit
         MVI    H,00H      ; to 16-bit
         LXI    B,2000H    ; Get starting address of table
         DAD    B
         MVI    D,05H      ; Character counter
STEP 4:  MOV    A,M        ; Turn on selected solenoids
         OUT    PORT A
         MVI    A,01H      ; STB = High
         OUT    PORT C
         CALL   D400       ; Generate 400-μs pulse
         INX    H          ; Get next byte
         CALL   D900       ; Delay 900 μs
         DCR    D
         JNZ    STEP 4
         MVI    A,04       ; Line feed for turning paper drive motor
         OUT    PORT C
         MVI    A,00H      ; Turn off
         OUT    PORT C     ; MDM
         HLT
```

Figure 8–20 8085 assembly language program for printing a character using the LRC 7040

$\overline{S1}-\overline{S7}$	Solenoid drive outputs
$\overline{PFM}$	Paper feed motor drive
DACK/SIN	In parallel mode, is used as DMA acknowledge pin; in serial model, is used as input for data
DRQ/$\overline{CTS}$	In parallel mode, is DMA request for the 8257; in serial mode, is used as clear to send pin

As mentioned, communication between the 8085 and the 8295 may take place in either a serial or a parallel mode. The selection of modes is inherent in the system hardware, and it is not programmable. For example, by connecting the IRQ/$\overline{SER}$ pin to logic 0, the serial mode is enabled immediately upon power-up. This is a bidirectional pin and can be used to connect to one of the 8085 interrupt lines to operate the 8295 in interrupt-driven and parallel modes. It should be pointed out that the two modes cannot be mixed in a single application.

We will next discuss the parallel system interface. The 8295 includes two internal registers that can be addressed by the 8085: one for input and one for output. These registers can be accessed by decoding the following lines:

$\overline{RD}$	$\overline{WR}$	$\overline{CS}$	
1	0	0	Input data register
0	1	0	Output status register

Data to the input data register is interpreted in one of two ways, depending on how the data is coded:

1. Data to the input data register can be a command data X_{16}, or $1Y_{16}$, where $X = 0$ through F, $Y = 1$ and 2. For example, command data $0D_{16}$ indicates carriage return. This data signifies the end of a line and enables the printer to start printing. Command 07_{16} indicates to the printer to print double-width characters. The command data 11_{16} indicates that the print head HOME is on the right. This command enables left to right printing for some printers whose print head is on the right.

2. Data to the input data register can be a character buffer for printing. The character codes to be stored in the 8295 are $2X_{16}$, $3X_{16}$, $4X_{16}$, or $5X_{16}$, where $X = 0$ through F. For example, the codes for 0 and % are 30_{16} and 25_{16}, respectively.

As far as the output status register is concerned, the 8295 status is available in this register at all times. For example, bit 1 of this 8-bit register is IBF (input buffer full); IBF = 1 whenever data is written to the input data register.

Figure 8–21 shows a flowchart of the 8085's communication with the 8295.

The IRQ output is available on the 8295 for interrupt-driven systems. This output is asserted true whenever the 8295 is ready to receive data (IBF = 0). A typical interface of the 8085 to the 8295 is shown in Figure 8–22. In Figure 8–22, the 8085 transfers data from the main memory to the 8295. In order to improve bus efficiency and the 8085's overhead, data may also be transferred from 8085 main memory to the 8295 via DMA cycles. Sending the enable DMA command (08_{16}) activates the DMA channel of the 8295. This command must be followed by 2 bytes specifying the length of the data string to be transferred (least significant byte first). The 8295 will then assert the required DMA requests to the 8257 DMA controller chip (which can be connected to the 8085 system bus) without any further 8085 intervention.

Data transferred in the DMA mode may be either commands or characters or a mixture of both. The procedure is as follows:

1. Set up the 8257 DMA channel by sending a starting address and a block length from the 8085.

2. Set up the 8295 by issuing the "Enable DMA" com-

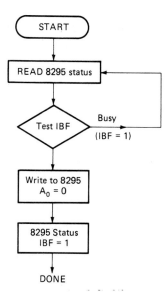

Figure 8–21 8085 to 8295 communication flowchart (Courtesy of Intel Corp.)

mand (08_{16}) followed by 2 bytes specifying the block length.

The DMA enabled flag (DE) in the 8295 status register will be true until the assigned data transfer is completed. Upon completion of the transfer, the flag is cleared and the IRQ is asserted. The 8295 then returns to the non-DMA mode of operation.

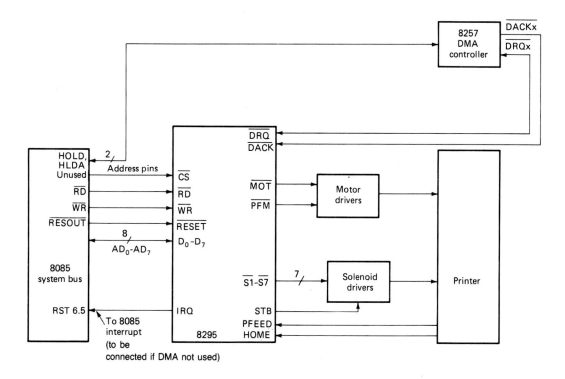

Figure 8–22 8085–8295 interface (Courtesy of Intel Corp.)

8-7 FLOPPY DISK INTERFACE TO A MICROPROCESSOR

A floppy disk is a magnetic mass storage device providing random access to stored data. Information is stored on the floppy disk in concentric circles called *tracks*. The outermost track is the one with the lowest track number, such as 00, and the innermost track is the one with the highest track number.

A read/write head is moved radially across the disk by a stepper motor in increments of the distance between tracks each time the stepper motor is stepped. In order to access a specific track (seek operation), the head is moved to track 00 and then moved to the desired track by pulsing the stepper motor an appropriate number of times. When the head is over the desired track, it is brought in contact with the floppy disk. Data is then read from or written to the disk. The head is then released from the disk in order to minimize wear on both the disk and the head.

A floppy disk controller such as the Intel 8271 interfaces a microprocessor such as the 8085 to the floppy disk drive. The 8271 receives commands and data from the 8085 and returns status and data to the 8085. On receipt of the commands, the floppy disk controller sends signals to the disk drive for reading or writing the data. The controller also performs formatting of the disk and an error check for any data errors.

The Intel 8271 is designed to interface one to four floppy disk drives to an 8085-based microcomputer. The 8271 is packaged in a 40-pin DIP. Typical pins include the following:

DB0–DB7	8-bit bidirectional data bus (input/output)
$\overline{WR}$	Write (input)
$\overline{RD}$	Read (input)
INT	Interrupt signal that the 8271 requires service
A1–A0	Microprocessor interface register select lines (input)
DRQ	DMA register signal for requesting a transfer of data between the 8257 and memory (output)
$\overline{DACK}$	DMA acknowledge signal for telling the 8271 that a DMA cycle has been granted (input)
Select 1, Select 0	Lines set by command byte from the 8085; used to specify the selected drive (output)
Write enable	Signal for enabling the drive write logic (output)
Seek/Step	Line used during drive seeks (output)
Direction	Line used to specify the seek direction (output)
Write protect	Signal for specifying floppy inserted is write protected (input)
$\overline{Index}$	Signal that gives indication of relative position of disk (input)

The 8085 utilizes the control interface circuit in the 8271 specify the 8271 commands. This interface is supported by several registers that are addressed by the 8085 via the A1, A0, $\overline{RD}$, and $\overline{WR}$ signals. Some of the registers include the command register, status register, and reset register as follows:

- The *command register* provides commands for Select 1 and Select 0 output signals.
- The *status register* provides the state of the 8271, such as whether the 8271 has requested interrupt or whether the command register is full.
- The *reset register* allows the 8271 to be reset by the program.

The INT line is used to signal the 8085 that an 8271 operation has been completed.

The 8271 can transfer data in either the DMA or the non-DMA mode. The DMA request (DRQ) signal is used to request a transfer of data between the 8271 and the 8085-based microcomputer's memory. The $\overline{DACK}$ signal tells the 8271 that a DMA cycle has been granted. The $\overline{RD}$ and $\overline{WR}$ signals are then used to specify the direction of the data transfer.

When configured to transfer data in the non-DMA mode, the 8085 must pass data to the 8271 in response to the non-DMA (interrupt or polled) data requests indicated by the data in the status register. The data is passed to and from the 8271 by asserting the $\overline{DACK}$ and the $\overline{RD}$ or $\overline{WR}$ signals. The 8271 operation is composed of three phases. These are the command phase, execution phase, and result phase. During the command phase, the 8085 executes an instruction to write the command into the 8271 command register. During the execution phase, the 8271 is on its own to carry out the commands. During the result phase, the 8271 signals the 8085 that the execution has finished. The 8085 must perform a read operation of one or more of the registers to determine the outcome of the operation.

8-8 DMA CONTROLLERS

As mentioned, direct memory access (DMA) is a type of data transfer between the microcomputer's main memory and an external device such as a disk without involving the microprocessor. The DMA controller is an LSI chip in a microcomputer system that supports DMA-type data transfer. The DMA controller can send commands to the memory in the same way as the microprocessor, and, therefore, the DMA controller can be considered as a second microprocessor in the system, except that its function is to perform I/O transfers.

DMA controllers perform data transfer at a very high rate because several functions for accomplishing the transfer are implemented in hardware. The DMA controller is provided with a number of I/O ports. A typical microcomputer system with a DMA controller is shown in Figure 8–23. The DMA controller in the figure connects one or more ports directly to memory so that data can be transferred between these ports and memory without going through the microprocessor. Therefore, the microprocessor is not involved in the data transfer.

The DMA controller shown in Figure 8–23 has two channels (channels 0 and 1). Each channel contains an *address register,* a *control register,* and a *counter* for block length. The purpose of the DMA controller is to move a string of data between the memory and an external device. In order to accomplish this, the microprocessor writes the starting address of memory where transfer is to take place in the address register and controls information such as the direction of transfer in the control register and the length of data to be transferred in the counter. The DMA controller then completes the transfer

independent of the microprocessor. However, in order to carry out the transfer, the DMA controller must not start the transfer until the microprocessor relinquishes the system bus and the external device is ready.

The interface between an I/O port and each channel typically has a number of control signals including DMAREQ, DMACK, and I/O read/write signals. When the I/O port is ready with an available buffer to receive data or has data ready to write into a memory location, it activates the DMAREQ line of the DMA controller. In order to accomplish the transfer, the DMA controller sends the DMACK signal to the port, telling the port that it can receive data from memory or send data to memory.

DMACK is similar to a chip select: When the DMACK signal on the port is activated by the DMA controller, the port is selected to transfer data between the I/O device and memory. The main difference between a normal and a DMA transfer is that the read or write operations have opposite meanings; that is, if the DMA controller activates the read line of the port, then data are read from a memory location to the port. However, this is a write operation to the port as far as the memory is concerned. This means that a read from a memory

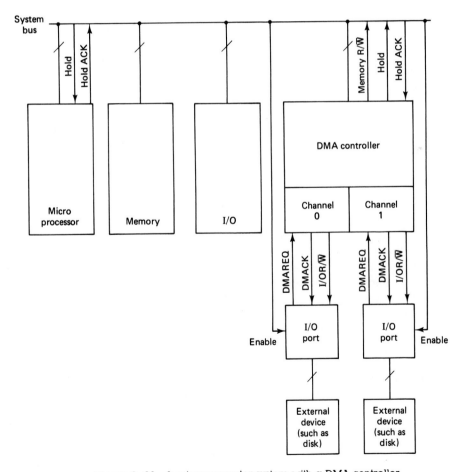

Figure 8–23 A microcomputer system with a DMA controller

location is a write to the port. Similarly, a write to a memory location is equivalent to a read from the port.

Figure 8–23 shows two types of R/$\overline{\text{W}}$ signals: the usual memory R/$\overline{\text{W}}$ and the I/OR/$\overline{\text{W}}$ for external devices. The DMA controller activates both of these lines at the same time in opposite directions; that is, for reading data from memory and writing into a port, the DMA controller activates the memory R/$\overline{\text{W}}$ HIGH and the I/OR/$\overline{\text{W}}$ LOW.

The I/O ports are available with two modes of operation: non-DMA and DMA. For non-DMA (microprocessor-controlled transfers), the ports operate in a normal mode. For DMA mode, the microprocessor first configures the port in the DMA mode and then signals the DMA controller to perform the transfer. The R/$\overline{\text{W}}$ line is complemented for providing proper direction of the data transfer during DMA transfer.

The DMA controller has a HOLD output signal and a HOLD ACK input signal. For each byte transfer, the microprocessor enables the I/O port for a DMA transfer. The port, when ready, generates the DMAREQ signal for the DMA controller. The DMA controller then activates the HOLD input signal of the microprocessor, requesting the microprocessor to relinquish the bus, and waits for a HOLD ACK back from the microprocessor.

After a few cycles, the microprocessor activates the HOLD ACK and tristates the output drivers to the system bus. The DMA controller then takes over the bus. The DMA controller

1. Outputs the starting address in the system bus.
2. Sends DMACK to the I/O port requesting DMA.
3. Outputs a normal R/$\overline{\text{W}}$ to memory and a complemented R/$\overline{\text{W}}$ to the I/O port.

The I/O port and memory then complete the transfer. After the transfer, the DMA controller disables all the signals, including the HOLD on the system bus, and tristates all its bus drivers. The microprocessor then takes over the bus and continues with its normal operation.

For efficient operation, the DMA controller is usually provided with a burst mode in which it has control over the bus until the entire block of data is transferred. In addition to the usual address, control, and counter registers, some DMA controllers are also provided with *data-chain registers,* which contain an address register, a control register, a counter, and a channel identification. These data-chain registers store the information for a specific channel for the next transfer. When the specified channel completes a DMA transfer, its registers are reloaded from the data-chain registers and the next transfer continues without any interruption from the microprocessor. In order to reload the data-chain registers for another transfer, the microprocessor can check the status register of the DMA controller to determine whether the DMA controller has already used the contents of the data-chain registers. In case it has, the microprocessor rein-

itializes the data-chain registers with appropriate information for the next block transfer, and the process continues.

In order to illustrate the functions of a typical DMA controller as just described, Motorola's MC68440 dual-channel DMA controller will be considered. The MC68440 is designed for the MC68000 family microprocessors to move blocks of data between memory and peripherals using DMA.

The 68440 includes two independent DMA channels with built-in priorities that are programmable. The 68440 can perform two types of DMA: cycle stealing and burst. In addition, it can provide noncontinuous block transfer (continue mode) and block transfer restart operation (reload mode).

Figure 8–24 shows a typical block diagram of the MC68000/68440/68230 interface to a disk. Data transfer between the disk and the memory takes place via port A of the 68230 using handshaking signals H1–H4.

The A8/D0 through A23/D15 lines are multiplexed. The 68440 multiplex control signals $\overline{\text{OWN}}$, $\overline{\text{UAS}}$, (upper address strobe), $\overline{\text{DBEN}}$ (data buffer enable), and $\overline{\text{DDIR}}$ (data direction) are used to control external demultiplexing devices such as the 74LS245 bidirectional buffer and the 74LS373 latch to separate address and data information on the A8/D0 through A23/D15 lines.

The 68440 has 17 registers plus a general control register for each of the two channels and is selected by the lower address lines (A1–A7) in the MPU mode. A1–A7 also provide the lower 7 address outputs in the DMA mode. The A1–A7 lines can select 128 (2^7) registers; however, with the A1–A7 lines, only 17 registers with addresses are defined in the range from 00_{16} through FF_{16} and some addresses are not used. As an example, the addresses of the channel status register and the channel priority register are, respectively, 00_{16} and $2D_{16}$.

The 68440 registers contain information about the data transfer such as the following:

- Source and destination addresses along with function codes
- Transfer count
- Operand size and device port size
- Channel priority
- Status and error information on channel activity

The processor service request register (PSRR) of the 68230 defines how the $\overline{\text{DMAREQ}}$ pin should be used and how the DMA transfer should take place, whether via handshaking or ports.

A data block contains a sequence of bytes or words starting at a particular address with the block length defined by the transfer count register. Figure 8–25 shows the data block format.

There are three phases of a DMA transfer: channel initialization, data transfer, and block termination. Dur-

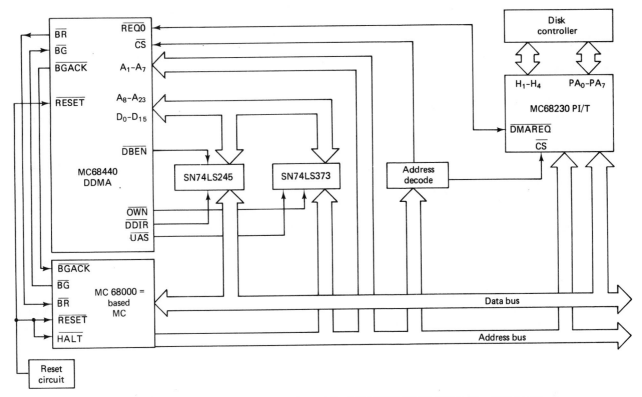

Figure 8–24 Typical system configuration of the MC68000/68440/68230. (Reprinted with permission of Motorola)

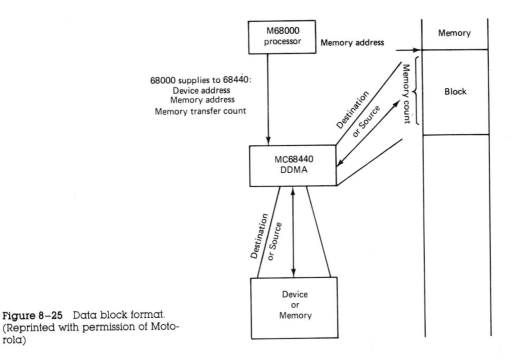

Figure 8–25 Data block format. (Reprinted with permission of Motorola)

ing *channel initialization*, the 68000 loads the 68440 registers with control information, address pointers, and transfer counts and then starts the channel. During *data transfer,* the 68440 acknowledges data transfer requests and performs addressing and bus controls for the transfer.

Finally, *block termination* takes place when the transfer is complete. During this phase, the 68440 informs the 68000 of the completion of data transfer via status register.

During the three phases of a data transfer operation,

the 68440 will be in one of three modes of operation: idle, MPU, and DMA. The 68440 goes into the *idle mode* when it is reset by an external device and waits for initialization by the 68000 or an operand transfer request from a peripheral. The *MPU mode* is assumed by the 68440 when its $\overline{CS}$ (chip select) is enabled by the 68000. In this mode, the 68440 internal registers can be read or written for controlling channel operation and for checking the status of a block transfer. The 68440 assumes the *DMA mode* when it takes over the bus to perform an operand transfer.

In Figure 8–24, upon reset, the 68440 goes into idle mode. In order to initialize the 68440 registers, the 68000 outputs appropriate register addresses on the bus. This will enable the 68440 $\overline{CS}$ line and place the 68440 in the MPU mode. The 68000 initializes the 68440 registers in this mode. The 68000 then executes the RESET instruction to place the 68440 back to the idle mode.

The 68000 now waits for a transfer request from the 68230. When the 68000 desires a DMA transfer between the disk and memory, it enables the $\overline{CS}$ line of the 68230.

The 68230, when ready, activates the $\overline{DMAREQ}$ line LOW, which in turn drives the $\overline{REQ0}$ line of the 68440 to LOW. The 68440 then outputs LOW on its $\overline{BR}$ line, requesting the 68000 to relieve the bus. The 68000, when ready, sends a LOW on its $\overline{BG}$ pin. This tells the 68440 to take over the bus. The 68440 then enters the DMA mode and sends a LOW on its $\overline{BGACK}$ pin to inform the 68000 of its taking over the bus. The 68440 transfers data between the disk and memory (inside the 68000-based microcomputer) via the 68230. Each time a byte is transferred, the 68440 decrements the transfer counter register and increments the address register. When the transfer is completed, the 68440 updates a bit in the status register to indicate this. It also asserts the $\overline{DTC}$ (data transfer complete) to indicate completion of the transfer.

The 68440 $\overline{DTC}$ pin can be connected to the 68230 PIRQ pin. The 68230 then outputs a HIGH on the 68440 $\overline{REQ0}$ pin, which in turn places a HIGH on the 68000 $\overline{BR}$, and the 68000 takes over the bus and goes back to normal operation.

QUESTIONS AND PROBLEMS

8–1. (a) What is the difference between synchronous and asynchronous serial data transmission?
(b) What is the difference between UART and USART?

8–2. Why is it desirable that the RxCLK in a UART have a much higher frequency than the baud rate?

8–3. Given a 2 × 2 keyboard connected to the 8085-based microcomputer via port 00 as shown in Figure P8–3. The 8085-based microcomputer is required to perform the following functions using a program in order to detect a key closed:
  • *Two-key rollover* — The 8085-based microcomputer outputs 0's via the 8355 (port 00) to rows 1 and 2 and inputs columns 1 and 2 to check for 0's. A 0 at a particular column indicates keys pressed. The program will loop until it finds all keys open before accepting a key closed. This is software realization of a two-key rollover.
  • *Debounce* — If a key is pressed, debounce it by inputting after 10 ms.
  • *Key detection* — In order to determine a particular key pressed, the 8085-based microcomputer outputs a 0 to one of the rows and a 1 to the other row and inputs the two columns to see whether one of the normally HIGH columns is pulled LOW. If it is, the 8085-based microcomputer will display DD in the data field of the display.

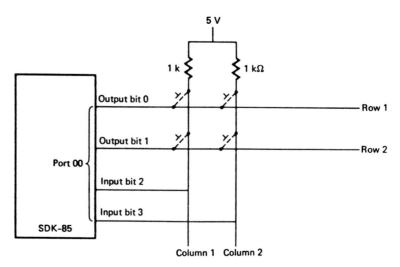

Figure P8–3

(a) Flowchart the problem.

(b) Convert the flowchart to an 8085 assembly language program.

8–4. What are the typical functions performed by a cassette interface connected between a microprocessor and a cassette recorder?

8–5. Using the concepts described in Section 8–4–2, write an 8085 assembly language program that will input 30 bytes of data and store them in a memory location starting at 2026_{16}.

8–6. Discuss the fundamental concepts associated with the CRT terminal.

8–7. Discuss the basic functions of the CRT controller chip.

8–8. Describe briefly the main characteristics to be considered while interfacing a typical microprocessor with (a) a printer and (b) a floppy disk.

8–9. Discuss the functions performed by a typical DMA controller chip.

8–10. Discuss the 68440/68000 configuration.

9

Interface Standards

When digital computers were first invented, there was no need for any type of hardware standardization. There were simply no other computers to interface to. However, over the past 20 years, computer systems and manufacturers have increased exponentially to the point where standardization is more than just a luxury. Standards are necessary to ensure that the line printer of one manufacturer will work with a computer of a different manufacturer, both of which have no formal association with each other.

Microprocessors have further increased the necessity of industry-wide standards because of their great numbers. Where mainframe computers used to handle most tasks, distributed microprocessor systems are taking over mainframe functions. Distributed processing relies heavily upon well-defined interface standards for inter-processor communication. Certainly, microprocessors used by engineers and scientists rely upon well-known interface standards. Floppy disk interfaces and printer/terminal interfaces are just a few of those found on microprocessor systems.

Digital hardware interfaces fall into the two general categories of parallel and serial:

- *Parallel interfaces* usually are characterized by short physical distances and high data rates.
- *Serial interfaces* are often characterized by longer physical distances and lower data transfer rates.

Some of the most common interfaces and their uses are listed in Table 9–1.

This chapter describes in some detail the IEEE 488 and the S-100 parallel interfaces along with the RS232C, RS422, RS423, and current loop serial interfaces. These interface standards are among the most common used today.

9–1 PARALLEL INTERFACE

9–1–1 IEEE 488 Interface Bus

The IEEE 488 standard was developed to reduce the amount of time and trouble it takes to establish a computer-controlled set of test equipment. Before the standard, each piece of test equipment had to have its own independent interface to the controlling computer. It is clear that interfacing more than two devices to a computer would get complicated if not expensive. With the IEEE 488 standard, computer-controlled test setups can be established in a matter of hours instead of days at no additional cost. These advantages make the IEEE 488 standard one of the most useful in industry today.

The IEEE 488 was first published in April of 1975, providing industry with a quick and easy way of connecting programmable measuring equipment. The standard was arrived at through many meetings in the early 1970s and is often referred to as the *Hewlett-Packard interface bus* (HPIB) because of Hewlett-Packard's con-

TABLE 9–1
Typical Interface Standards

	Interface	Applications
Parallel	IEEE Std 488 (GPIB)	Microcomputer to measurement equipment
	S-100	Internal microcomputer communication
Serial	RS232C	Microcomputer to terminal communication
	RS422, RS423	Microcomputer to peripheral, > 20 m
	Current loops	Microcomputer to teletype communication

tribution to the definition. The standard is also known as the *general-purpose interface bus* (GPIB).

The GPIB standard concerns itself with the interface between two basic categories of devices: system controllers and digital programmable instruments. Two approaches of standard interface are possible. One optimizes the interface for system controllers; the other, for digital programmable instruments. The IEEE standards committee chose an interface standard that is optimized for digital programmable instruments.

The two types of interface considered for the GPIB were a party-line bus structure and a star interconnect with a dedicated interface to each device. The party-line interface was chosen above the star interconnect approach because of hardware savings and other advantages.

In short, four other communication parameters were set for the standard:

1. The data transfer rate is not to exceed 1 megabyte per second.
2. The message length is variable over an 8-bit parallel byte serial bus.
3. The number of devices on the bus is not to exceed 15.
4. The maximum interconnecting length is set at 20 m or 2 m times the number of connected devices, whichever is less. Cable interconnection between any two devices must not exceed 4 m.

GPIB Signals This section describes the hardware implementation of the GPIB showing the function of each line. The GPIB connects *digital programmable instruments* (DPIs) to a system controller in the general form as shown in Figure 9–1.

The data bus is bidirectional and, as mentioned earlier, is 8-bit parallel. The data and the direction thereof are controlled by the control bus. Each device on the bus can be one of four types:

1. The controller
2. DPIs that talk only
3. DPIs that listen only
4. DPIs that talk or listen

The controller is the one device on the bus that is allowed to set the direction of data transfer as well as the devices that are to be used. There can be multiple controllers attached to the GPIB, but only one controller at a time may have command of the GPIB. If a second controller on the GPIB wishes to control the devices on the bus, then the first controller must relinquish its control over to the second controller. The controller, in most cases, is a computer with a GPIB hardware interface. Microprocessor-based computers have proven to be ideal controllers for the GPIB in addition to minicomputers.

A DPI that talks only is a device used to generate and place data onto the GPIB. An example of this kind of device would be a power meter that generates only power levels from a measurement source. The power meter has no ability for data to be sent to it; thus, it is only a talker.

A device that listens only is one that just receives data from the GPIB. A plotter would be an example of this kind of device. It requires only data for its pen operation and generates none of its own data.

There is also the third possibility of having a device that both talks and listens. A programmable sweep generator, for instance, must listen for its frequency setup parameters and then must talk back onto the GPIB to indicate where its present frequency is during the sweep.

GPIB control is maintained by the control bus, which is divided into interface management and transfer control groups. Figure 9–2 illustrates a GPIB with its discrete interface lines connected to an RF sweep generator, an RF power meter, and a graphic plotter. The HP9845 is the controller but can also be thought of as a DPI that talks or listens.

The interface management lines are generally considered to be used for communication setup and termination, while the transfer control lines handle the actual data exchange. This data exchange is commonly known as a *handshake*.

A handshake operation on the GPIB can be summarized in the following manner with the signals data valid (DAV), not ready for data (NRFD), and no data accepted (NDAC). Let us first assume that all operations on the GPIB bring us to the point of an actual handshake

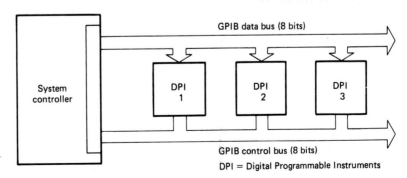

Figure 9–1 General GPIB system (From *PET and the IEEE 488 Bus (GPIB)* by Fisher and Jensen. Copyright © 1980 McGraw-Hill, Inc.)

DPI = Digital Programmable Instruments

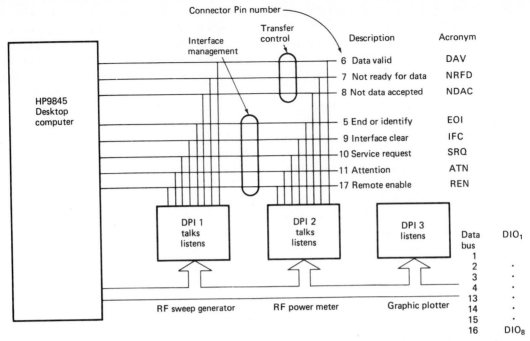

Figure 9–2 Expanded GPIB system (From *PET and the IEEE 488 Bus (GPIB)* by Fisher and Jensen. Copyright © 1980 McGraw-Hill, Inc.)

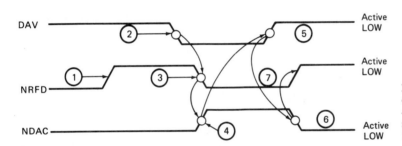

Figure 9–3 General handshake operation (From *PET and the IEEE 488 Bus (GPIB)* by Fisher and Jensen. Copyright © 1980 McGraw-Hill, Inc.)

between the power meter and the HP9845 desktop computer. The RF power meter will be transferring information to the HP9845.

The power meter (talker) waits for the HP9845 (listener) to raise its NRFD line (1) (Figure 9–3), saying, in effect, that it is ready to accept data that the talker will send down the bus. The power meter then places its data on the 8-bit data lines. After allowing for settling time, the power meter lowers its DAV line (2) to a true state (active LOW) to indicate that data is available for the HP9845. The HP9845 senses DAV going LOW and answers by lowering its NRFD line (3) when it is not ready to accept data. The HP9845 raises its NDAC line (4) after it has strobed the data into its internal registers, saying that it has accepted the data. The power meter then senses that the NDAC line has been pulled HIGH (false) and raises its DAV line (5) to indicate to the HP9845 that the data on the bus is no longer valid. The HP9845 detects the change in DAV and drops NDAC LOW (6), acknowledging the fact that data is being removed from the bus. The HP9845 raises

NRFD HIGH, indicating that it is ready for the next data byte.

This simple handshaking procedure is performed any time data or commands are sent over the bus. It should be noted here that the signals DAV, NRFD, and NDAC are implemented using open collector techniques to allow wire-OR operations from any of the devices on the bus.

Command and data bytes are distinguished on the bus by the attention (ATN) line. This active LOW line, when LOW, sends command and address information down the bus from the controller (HP9845). Only the controller can drive the ATN line. When ATN is HIGH, handshake operations consist only of data.

Identifying the difference between data and commands on the GPIB is important in understanding how transactions are accomplished. Commands are issued only by the controller. Four commonly used commands are: my talk address, my listen address, untalk, and unlisten. My talk address (we will use the simple equivalent TALK from now on) is a predefined code placed on the GPIB when ATN is LOW, which tells only a single device that it is going to talk. The difference between TALK commands for two different devices on the GPIB is a difference in address encoding within the TALK commands. Only one TALK command may be issued on the bus for a given transaction; two talkers are not allowed.

Once a device has been enabled to talk, it then places its data (ATN is HIGH) on the bus for any other devices to listen. The controller can then issue an UNTALK command, freeing the talker.

Unlike the TALK command, my listen address (LISTEN) may be sent to multiple devices for a single transaction. This implies that there can be more than one listener on the bus at any time. The bus can only operate as fast as the slowest device connected to the bus. LISTEN is similar to the TALK command in that the device address and the LISTEN command are encoded onto the GPIB when ATN is LOW. The UNLISTEN command simply frees all devices that were set to listen.

The GPIB interface clear (IFC) line provides system reset capability over the bus. When LOW, all DPIs on the bus are reset. IFC is driven only by the controller.

Most devices used on a GPIB can be used in a standalone mode. This implies that the device would have a manual mode and a bus mode. The GPIB remote enable (REN) line selects between the two modes. When LOW, all devices on the bus are put into remote mode, allowing the controller to handle the devices.

The last two lines included in the GPIB interface management group are service request (SRQ) and end or identify (EOI). SRQ is analogous to a common interrupt line on a microprocessor. Any device on the GPIB may bring SRQ LOW to request service from the controller. The EOI command, when ATN is LOW, causes up to eight different devices on the bus to place 1 bit of status information in assigned positions. This allows the controller quickly to poll eight devices to determine the origin of an SRQ. When ATN is HIGH (logic 0), EOI can be used by the controller and talker alike to indicate the end of a transmission to a listener. Table 9–2 summarizes the GPIB lines.

GPIB Operation The overall operation of the GPIB can best be described through an example using the block diagram of Figure 9–4. The RF sweep generator, power meter, and plotter are used automatically to plot the frequency response of an antenna as part of a test setup.

TABLE 9–2
GPIB Signals (From *PET and the IEEE 488 Bus (GPIB)* by Fisher and Jensen. Copyright © 1980 McGraw-Hill, Inc.)

Name of Line	Description
ATN	Attention: Issued only by controller to gain attention of bus devices before beginning handshake sequence and to denote address/control information on the data bus.
DAV	Data Valid: Issued by talker to notify listener that data has been placed on the DIO lines.
DIO1–DIO8	Data I/O: Eight data transfer lines; also called data bus.
EOI	End Or Identify: Issued by talker to notify listener that the data byte currently on the DIO lines is the last one. Issued by controller together with ATN to initiate a parallel poll sequence.
IFC	Interface Clear: Issued only by controller to bring all active bus devices to a known state.
NDAC	Not Data Accepted: Issued by listener while fetching data from the DIO lines.
NRFD	Not Ready For Data: Issued by all listeners. Released by each listener as it becomes ready to accept data.
REN	Remote Enable: Permanently grounded by the PET to maintain control over the system.
SRQ	Service Request: Issued by any device needing service from the controller. Not implemented in PET BASIC.

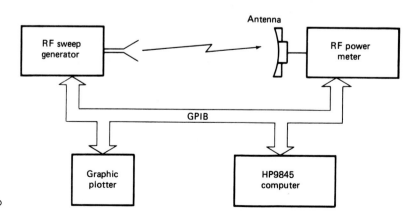

Figure 9–4 GPIB example setup

Before the details of the GPIB transactions are described, a flowchart is provided in Figure 9–5 to outline the sequence of events. We will take each logic block individually and describe the GPIB transactions. To aid in reducing the amount of timing diagrams, some equivalents are presented in Figure 9–6.

Now, in Figure 9–5, logic block (A) is simply executed by issuing an IFC command from the HP9845. Logic blocks (B)–(G) are programmed as follows:

Sweep generator

(B)

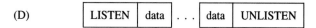

Software command to set sweep generator

Power meter

(C)

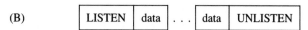

Software command to power meter

Sweep generator

(D)

Software command to start sweep generator

Sweep generator

(E)

Frequency data from generator

Power meter

(F)

Power reading data

Plotter

(G)

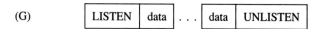

Plotting data from HP9845

The computer controller executes logic block (B) by first issuing a LISTEN command to the sweep generator. This alerts the sweep generator to be ready for the data that follows from the computer. The computer sends the sweep data to the sweep generator in the format necessary for the device to understand. The data sent to the sweep generator may actually be software commands that only it understands. Upon completion of the data transfer, the computer (controller) issues an UNLISTEN command to force all listeners off the GPIB.

Logic blocks (C) and (D) are essentially the same type of transaction. However, the format of the data being sent to the power meter may be different from that of the sweep generator and must be observed when programming the computer.

Logic block (E) is initiated by the computer with a TALK command to the sweep generator. This TALK command alerts the sweep generator to put its current value of frequency onto the GPIB so that the computer can read it. Once the computer has received all the data that is sent, it issues an UNTALK command to release the GPIB.

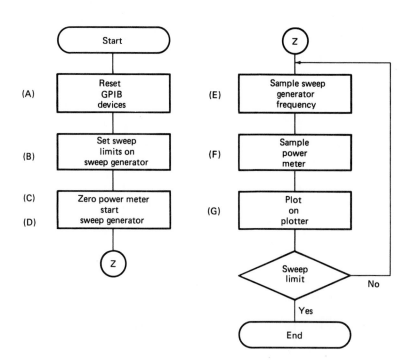

Figure 9–5 Flowchart showing the sequence of events for Figure 9–4

The power meter is sent a TALK command [block (F)] to allow it to place its power reading information on the GPIB so that the computer can read it. Similar to the sweep generator, an UNTALK command is issued to free the GPIB.

The last transaction of logic block (G) involves a LISTEN command to the plotter to ready it for the plot of data from the computer. The UNLISTEN command frees the plotter and readies the GPIB for the next transaction.

In most cases, data sent over the GPIB is in standard ASCII format. Very seldom will pure binary data be used in a transaction.

The HP9845 is not the only computer available as a GPIB controller. Any microprocessor can be made to interface to the GPIB by following IEEE Std 488. Intel currently manufactures an 8291 GPIB talker/listener chip, an 8292 GPIB controller chip, and an 8293 GPIB transceiver chip for use with the 8085, 8086, and 8048 microprocessors.

9–1–2 S-100 Bus Standard

The S-100 bus originally appeared in the ALTAIR 8800 computer, and ever since it has become a standard for small computing systems. The intent behind the S-100 bus was expandability, driven, to some extent, by the high cost of computer hardware. An S-100 owner could slowly build a system and avoid huge expenditures of money at one time. Today, there are so many S-100 compatible interfaces, memories, controllers, and peripherals that it would take at least a page to list them all.

As the name implies, the S-100 bus consists of 100 electrical buses used for interface. The standard circuit board size for S-100 systems is 5.3 inches by 10 inches. All S-100 boards have a 100-position card edge connector with 0.125-inch spacing at the bottom (50 connections on each side). The connector is offset with respect to the card center to prevent backward insertion. Cards are electrically connected together through a mother-board with 100 parallel buses on it. The S-100 bus operates on standard TTL voltage levels.

Electrically, the S-100 bus is divided into four categories:

1. Address bus
2. Data bus
3. Control bus
4. Power distribution

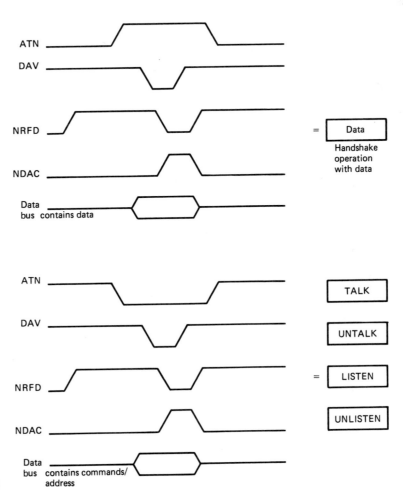

Figure 9–6 GPIB timing diagrams

It is beyond the scope of this section to describe fully the characteristics of each category in detail. Nonetheless, some of the features and attributes of each category are presented. Table 9–3 shows the 100 pin assignments for the S-100.

Three power supplies are available on the S-100: $+8$, $+18$, and -18 V. These supplies are unregulated and are used to feed separate on-card regulators for local regulation. The $+8$ V is regulated down to $+5$ V for TTL operation, and the 18-V supplies may be regulated to any other necessary voltage levels. Advantages to on-board regulation include higher noise isolation, greater thermal distribution, and easily selectable voltage levels.

The address bus consists of 16 address lines (A0–A15). The address lines are generated by either a microprocessor or a direct memory circuit so that only one memory location is addressed. The data bus consists of 16 lines: 8 lines for input (DI0–DI7) and 8 lines for output (DO0–DO7). These separated I/O lines are not necessary but cause no major disadvantages.

The remaining lines on the S-100 bus are control lines. They are used for timing, synchronization, data directional control, and computer status control. Clock signals 01 and 02, along with CLOCK, are generated by the microprocessor clock circuit, and these lines are the main system timing lines. Some lines on the S-100 bus have S and P prefixes, which indicate that they have direct correlation to the 8085 microprocessor control and status lines, respectively.

Some of the other control lines affect I/O on the S-100 bus. The availability of many new and unique I/O boards for the S-100 computer gives the owner a tremendous advantage in system configuration. Some of the products that simply plug into the S-100 include the following:

High-speed cassette interface
Complete floppy disk systems
Speech synthesizer
AC-power control units
Realtime clock, calendar, timing boards
Winchester disk interfaces
Multifunction system I/O boards
Analog I/O boards

Some of the drawbacks of the S-100 are crosstalk from clock lines to control lines on adjacent pins and potential short-circuiting between the adjacent $+8$-V and -16-V pins.

The S-100 is not a complete standard. There are differences in some control lines from a few manufacturers. Also, since the bus was originally defined for the 8085 microprocessor, the timing and control lines are more complicated than they need to be. However, new IEEE standards for a 16-bit S-100 bus have been adopted and will guarantee the existence of the S-100 for years to come.

TABLE 9–3
S-100 Parallel Bus Pin Definitions

Pin Number	Symbol	Name	Function
1	$+8$ V	$+8$ V	Unregulated voltage on bus, supplied to printed circuit boards and regulated to 5 V.
2	$+18$ V	$+18$ V	Positive preregulated voltage.
3	XRDY	External ready	External ready input to CPU board's ready circuitry.
4	V10	Vectored interrupt line 0	
5	V11	Vectored interrupt line 1	
6	V12	Vectored interrupt line 2	
7	V13	Vectored interrupt line 3	
8	V14	Vectored interrupt line 4	
9	V15	Vectored interrupt line 5	
10	V16	Vectored interrupt line 6	
11	V17	Vectored interrupt line 7	
12	XRDY2[a]	External ready 2	A second external ready line similar to XRDY.
13 to 17	To be defined		
18	STAT DSB	Status disable	Allows buffers for eight status lines to be three-stated.

Source: MITS-ALTAIR.
[a]New bus signal for 8800b.

TABLE 9–3
S-100 Parallel Bus Pin Definitions *(cont.)*

Pin Number	Symbol	Name	Function
19	C/C DSB	Command/control disable	Allows buffers for eight output command/control lines to be three-stated.
20	UNPROT	Unprotect	Input to memory protect flip flop on a given memory board.
21	SS	Single step	Indicates that machine is in the process of performing a single step (i.e., that SS flip flop on D/C is set).
22	ADD DSB	Address disable	Allows buffers for 16 address lines to be three-stated.
23	DO DSB	Data out disable	Allows buffers for eight data output lines to be three-stated.
24	02	Phase 2 clock	
25	01	Phase 1 clock	
26	PHLDA	Hold acknowledge	Processor command/control output signal which appears in response to HOLD signal; indicates that data and address bus will go to high-impedance state and processor will enter HOLD state after completion of current machine cycle.
27	PWAIT	Wait	Processor command/control signal which appears in response to READY signal going LOW; indicates that processor will enter a series of 0.5-µs WAIT states until READY again goes HIGH.
28	PINTE	Interrupt enable	Processor command/control output signal; indicates that interrupts are enabled, as determined by contents of CPU internal interrupt flip flop. When flip flop is set (enable interrupt instruction), interrupts are accepted by CPU; when it is reset (disable interrupt instruction), interrupts are inhibited.
29	A5	Address line 5	
30	A4	Address line 4	
31	A3	Address line 3	
32	A15	Address line 15	(MSB)
33	A12	Address line 12	
34	A9	Address line 9	
35	DO1	Data out line 1	
36	DO0	Data out line 0	(LSB)
37	A10	Address line 10	
38	DO4	Data out line 4	
39	DO5	Data out line 5	
40	DO6	Data out line 6	
41	DI2	Data in line 2	
42	DI3	Data in line 3	
43	DI7	Data in line 7	(MSB)
44	SM1	Machine cycle 1	Status output signal which indicates that processor is in fetch cycle for first byte of an instruction.
45	SOUT	Output	Status output signal which indicates that address bus contains address of an input device and data bus will contain output data when PWR is active.

Continued.

TABLE 9–3
S-100 Parallel Bus Pin Definitions (cont.)

Pin Number	Symbol	Name	Function
46	SINP	Input	Status output signal which indicates that address bus contains address of an input device and input data should be placed on data bus when PDBIN is active.
47	SMEMR	Memory read	Status output signal which indicates that data bus will be used to read memory data.
48	SHLTA	Halt	Status output signal which acknowledges a HALT instruction.
49	CLOCK	Clock	Inverted output of the phase 2 Clock.
50	GND	Ground	
51	+8 V	+8 V	Unregulated input to 5-V regulators.
52	−18 V	−18 V	Negative preregulated voltage.
53	SSWI	Sense switch input	Indicates that an input data transfer from the sense switches is to take place. This signal is used by the display/control logic to: 1. Enable sense switch drivers 2. Enable the display/control board driver's data input (FD10–FD17) 3. Disable the CPU board data input drivers (D10–D17).
54	EXT CLR	External clear	Clear signal for I/O devices (front-panel switch closure to ground).
55	RTC[a]	Real-time clock	60-Hz signal is used as timing reference by real-time clock/vectored interrupt board.
56	STSTB[a]	Status strobe	Output strobe signal supplied by 8224 clock generator. Primary purpose is to strobe 8212 status latch so that status is set up as soon in machine cycle as possible. This signal is also used by display/control logic.
57	DIG1[a]	Data input gate 1	Output signal from display/control logic which determines which set of data input drivers have control of CPU board's bidirectional data bus. If DIG1 is HIGH, CPU drivers have control; if it is LOW, display/control logic drivers have control.
58	FRDY[a]	Front panel ready	Output signal from display/control logic which allow front panel to control ready lines to CPU.
59 to 67	To be defined		
68	MWRITE	Memory write	Indicates that data present on data out bus are to be written into memory location currently on address bus.
69	PS	Protect status	Indicates status of memory protect flip flop on memory board currently addressed.
70	PROT	Protect	Input to memory protect flip flop on board currently addressed.
71	RUN	Run	Indicates that 64/RUN flip flop is reset; i.e., machine is in run mode.
72	PRDY	Processor ready	Memory and I/O wait.
73	PINT	Interrupt request	The processor recognizes an interrupt request on this line at the end of the current instruction or while halted. If the processor is in the hold state or the interrupt enable flip flop is reset, it will not honor the request.

TABLE 9–3
S-100 Parallel Bus Pin Definitions *(cont.)*

Pin Number	Symbol	Name	Function
74	PHOLD	Hold	Processor command/control input signal which requests that processor enter the hold state; allow an external device to gain control of address and data buses as soon as processor has completed its uses of these buses for current machine cycle.
75	PRESET	Reset	Processor command/control input; while activated, contents of program counter are cleared and instruction register is set to 0.
76	PSYNC	Sync	Processor command/control output; provides a signal to indicate beginning of each machine cycle.
77	PWR	Write	Processor command/control output; used for memory write or I/O output control. Data on data bus are stable, while PWR is active.
78	PDBIN	Data bus in	Processor command/control output; indicates to external circuits that data bus is in input mode.
79	A0	Address line 0	(LSB)
80	A1	Address line 1	
81	A2	Address line 2	
82	A6	Address line 6	
83	A7	Address line 7	
84	A8	Address line 8	
85	A13	Address line 13	
86	A14	Address line 14	
87	A11	Address line 11	
88	DO2	Data out line 2	
89	DO3	Data out line 3	
90	DO7	Data out line 7	
91	DI4	Data in line 4	
92	DI5	Data in line 5	
93	DI6	Data in line 6	
94	DI1	Data in line 1	
95	DI0	Data in line 0	(LSB)
96	SINTA	Interrupt acknowledge	Status output signal; acknowledges signal for interrupt request.
97	SWO	Write out	Status output signal; indicates that operation in current machine cycle will be a write memory or output function
98	SSTACK	Stack	Status output signal; indicates that address bus holds pushdown stack address from stack pointer.
99	POC	Power-on-clear	
100	GNd	Ground	

9–2   SERIAL INTERFACE

9–2–1   RS232C, RS422, and RS423 Serial Interfaces

Serial transmission of data has long been used as an efficient means for transmitting digital information across long distances. Other than the obvious savings in hardware, there is also an advantage in being able to use existing communications lines (telephone, Telex) to transfer information. The RS232C interface convention was developed to standardize the "interface between data terminal equipment and data communication equipment employing serial binary data exchange."

One of the most common uses for the RS232C is the connection of computer terminals to computers. This is done both directly and indirectly through modems. Other devices, such as PROM programmers and character printers, have also adopted RS232C standards in recent years.

The circuit interfaces of the RS232C can be categorized into three areas: data, timing, and control. Each interchange circuit must adhere to a well-defined design with limits on impedances and voltages. Figure 9–7 shows the interchange equivalent circuit model. This model is used to define the various parameters of the interface specification.

In the figure, V_O is the open-circuit voltage; R_O is the driver load dc resistance; C_O is the total effective capacitance associated with the driver, measured at the interface point and including any cable to the interface point; V_I is the voltage at the interface point; C_L is the total effective capacitance associated with the terminator, measured at the interface point and including any cable to the interface point; R_L is the terminator load dc resistance; and E_L is the open-circuit terminator voltage (bias).

It is not the purpose here to define totally all of the limits of the interchange parameters. However, some of the most useful specifications are listed next:

- $3000 \, \Omega < R_L + C_L < 7000 \, \Omega$ at direct current with an applied voltage between 3 and 25 V
- $C_L < 2500$ pF measured at the interface point
- Driver slew rate is less than 30 V/μs

- V_O and R_O are selected such that a short circuit between any two conductors in the cable does not cause a current greater than 0.5 A
- $5 \, V < V_I < 15 \, V$ when the driver is connected to the terminator with $E_L = 0$
- Data transfer rate is less than 20 kilobaud

The way in which data is interpreted on interchange circuits is different for data circuits and for timing and control circuits. Data circuits are characterized by the voltage diagram of Figure 9–8.

Timing and control circuit voltage levels are the same as for the data but can be interpreted as being on when the voltage is greater than $+3$ V. Timing and control circuits can also be thought of as being active LOW lines when using the data circuit convention.

Signals in the transition region are not defined, although they must conform to the RS232C standard while in the region. Because the transition region extends only to 3 V in either direction and the logic levels start at 5 V in either direction, there is an implied noise margin of 2 V.

All the interchange circuits defined in the RS232C standard are listed in Table 9–4. For most applications not involving modems (data communications equipment), the only circuits needed to establish an interface

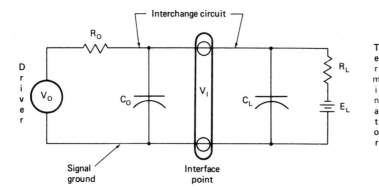

Figure 9–7 RS232C circuit model (Courtesy of Electronic Industries Association, 2001 Eye St., N.W., Washington, D.C. 20006)

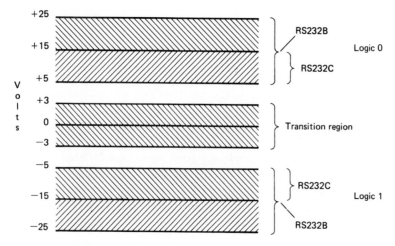

Figure 9–8 RS232B and C logic levels (From *Introduction to Microprocessor System Design* by Garland. Copyright © 1979 McGraw-Hill, Inc.)

TABLE 9–4
RS232C Interchange Circuits

Interchange Circuit	Pin Number	Description	Ground	Data		Control		Timing	
				From DCE	From DCE	From DCE	To DCE	To DCE	To DCE
AA	1	Protective ground	X						
AB	7	Signal ground/common return	X						
BA	2	Transmitted data			X				
BB	3	Received data		X					
CA	4	Request to send					X		
CB	5	Clear to send				X			
CC	6	Data set ready				X			
CD	20	Data terminal ready					X		
CE	22	Ring indicator				X			
CF	8	Received line signal detector				X			
CG	21	Signal quality detector				X			
CH	23	Data signal rate selector (DTE)					X		
CI	23	Data signal rate selector (DCE)				X			
DA	24	Transmitter signal element timing (DTE)							X
DB	15	Transmitter signal element timing (DCE)						X	
DD	17	Receiver signal element timing (DCE)						X	
SBA	14	Secondary transmitted data			X				
SBB	16	Secondary received data		X					
SCA	19	Secondary request to send					X		
SCB	13	Secondary clear to send				X			
SCF	12	Secondary received line signal detector				X			

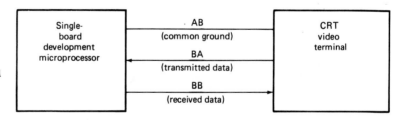

Figure 9–9 CRT terminal interfaced to a single-board development microprocessor (Courtesy of RCA Solid State)

are the signal ground (AB), transmitted data (BA), and received data (BB) circuits. One example of this would be the connection of a CRT terminal to a single-board development microprocessor, as shown in Figure 9–9.

Figure 9–10 illustrates a typical interface used for establishing an RS232C interface with a microprocessor. The UART takes parallel 8-bit data, converts them to serial data, and sends them to the RS232C interface through the RS232 converter. In addition, the UART also takes converted RS232 data, transforms it back into 8-bit parallel, and sends it to the microprocessor. The clock feeding the UART determines the rate at which serial data is being transmitted or received.

Transmitter register empty (TRE) is a signal for notifying the microprocessor that the UART is ready for another character to transmit. Transmitter register load (TRLD) causes a character on the data bus to be loaded

into the UART. Receive signals RDU and RDA are similarly used to coordinate the transfer of received data from the UART to the microprocessor. Read data available (RDA) alerts the microprocessor that there is a character available to be picked up. The microprocessor strobes the read data unload (RDU) line to force the UART to put its receive character on the data bus.

Practically all UARTs have separate input and output functions, which allows simultaneous operations in both directions. The RS232C interface blocks can easily be implemented using monolithic converters, such as the Motorola MC1488 and MC1489. If these blocks are implemented, the designer must observe the design requirements given for the RS232C model interchange circuit.

A more complicated RS232 interface can be established between *data terminal equipment* (DTE) and *data*

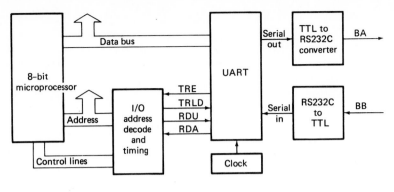

Figure 9-10   RS232C interface to an 8-Bit microprocessor (Courtesy RCA Solid State)

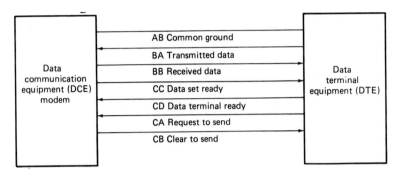

Figure 9-11   Modem terminal interface

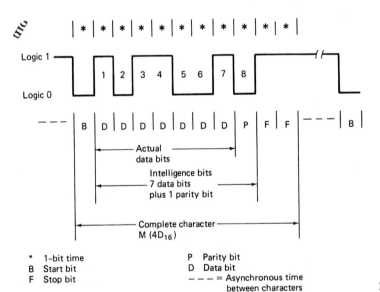

* 1-bit time
B Start bit
F Stop bit

P Parity bit
D Data bit
— — — = Asynchronous time between characters

Figure 9-12   Teletype ASCII format

communication equipment (DCE). The interface between a terminal and a modem is shown in Figure 9–11.

The signal data set ready (CC), when on (>3 V), indicates that the modem is connected to the communication lines and is ready to handle data. Data terminal ready (CD) indicates to the modem that it should connect to the communication lines in preparation for transmitting data from the DTE. Request to send (CA) is sent to the modem when both data terminal ready and data set ready are on. The request is acknowledged on the clear to send (CB) circuit. At this point, the DTE is permitted to transmit data onto the communication line through the modem.

The received line signal detector (CF), although not used in the example, is used to signal the DTE that a carrier is present. The ring indicator (CE) is used in conjunction with automatic answering equipment. The rest of the circuits are used for special applications and are not covered. However, it should be mentioned that high-speed synchronous communication is supported through element timing circuits DA, DB, and DD.

Table 9–4 also shows the pin assignments for the interchange circuits. Normally, a 25-pin DB25 connector is used but is not required. Careful attention must be paid when preparing cables for RS232 interfaces so as not to exceed the 2500-pF limit on the load. This presents a problem when running long lengths of cable and is one deficiency in the RS232C standard. Another detrimental restriction is the 20-kbit data rate limitation. More recent standards (RS422 balanced and RS423 unbalanced transmission lines) have been adopted to support transmission distances greater than 1000 m.

The data format of information sent over the RS232 interface is not specified by the standard. In most cases, standard 8-bit ASCII is used.

RS422 and RS423 are improvements in the RS232

standard. RS422 is used in balanced transmission lines, and RS423 is suitable for unbalanced transmission lines.

RS422 utilizes a low-impedance differential signal to increase the baud rate to 10 megabaud and the maximum line length to 4000 feet. The differential signal is generated by differential line drivers, such as the MC3487, and is sent on a twisted pair line. The differential signal is received and translated into standard logic levels by differential line receivers, such as the MC3486.

The RS423 uses a low-impedance single-ended driver instead of a differential driver to obtain longer

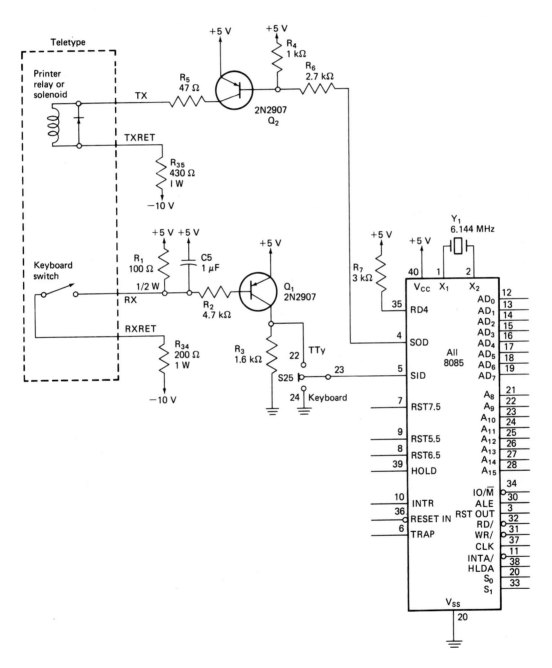

Figure 9-13 20-mA current loop teletype interface (Courtesy of Intel Corp.)

transmission distances and higher baud rates. Line drivers and receivers are required to interface to standard logic families.

9–2–2 Current Loops

A teletype has an input and an output loop. Information is transferred between a teletype and a computer (one character at a time) through the loops by interpreting a 20-mA current as a logic 1 and the absence of a current as a logic 0. A 60-mA current loop uses 60 mA to represent a logic 1.

Most teletypes operate at 110 baud, using a serialized ASCII format like the one shown in Figure 9–12. The start bit is required to tell the teletype to start its mechanical cycle so that it can interpret the incoming serial ASCII data. The format shown in Figure 9–12 can easily be generated in software using a microprocessor or by a UART.

Figure 9–13 shows a 20-mA teletype circuit. The 8085 SID and SOD lines are used for interfacing the teletype to the Intel SDK-85 microcomputer. The send–receive current loops of Figure 9–13 are separate and are called *full-duplex mode*.

A character is sent from the teletype keyboard to the SOD pin by opening or closing the keyboard switch. This switch is normally closed. This means that transistor Q1 is normally ON and the SID pin is normally HIGH. When the keyboard switch is opened, Q1 is turned OFF and the SID pin is driven to a LOW. Thus, the presence or absence of the current provides logic 1 or 0, respectively, and is used to represent the ASCII code of each character. In order to output data to the teletype, the 8085 sends a LOW to the SOD pin for turning transistor Q2 ON. This will send a 20-mA current to a relay in the teletype. On the other hand, when the 8085 sends a HIGH to the SOD pin, Q2 is turned OFF and, therefore, no current flows through the relay in the teletype. The presence or absence of this current in the relay provides the electromagnetic flux to print the desired character.

QUESTIONS AND PROBLEMS

9–1. What is meant by serial and parallel interface standards?

9–2. What type of data format is used in the IEEE 488 interface system?

9–3. What is the maximum length of interconnecting cables if it is desired to connect:
(a) 8 instruments via GPIB?
(b) 15 instruments via GPIB?

9–4. What is the maximum data transmission rate for an IEEE 488 interface?

9–5. Name the types of devices that can be connected to the IEEE 488.

9–6. What is the purpose of the ATN, SRQ, and IFC lines in the GPIB?

9–7. How many clock signals are available on the S-100 bus? Describe them.

9–8. What is the difference between the control signals that are prefixed with S and the control signals that are prefixed with P?

9–9. What is meant by the PSYNC, PDBIN, and SHLTA signals on the S-100 bus?

9–10. What voltage levels are used by the RS232C interface?

9–11. What is the difference between the BA and BB signals on the RS232C interface?

9–12. What is meant by the RS422 and RS423 standards?

9–13. What are the logic levels in the 20-mA and 60-mA current loops?

9–14. Why are current loops used with teletypes?

10

Typical Applications of Microprocessors

Typical applications of microprocessors are described in this chapter. These include a two-position controller, a root-mean-square (rms) meter using the 8085 microprocessor and keyboard/display interface with the 68000 microprocessor.

The two-position controller is illustrated in a simplified manner using both programmed I/O and interrupt I/O. This is presented to demonstrate the basic concepts of two different types of I/O to solve practically oriented problems. The rms meter and the keyboard/display interface are described in more detail.

10-1 SDK-85 AS A TWO-POSITION CONTROLLER

The control law of the two-position controller can be stated as follows:

$$\text{Valve output V} = 100\% \quad \text{for } E > 0$$
$$= \quad 0\% \quad \text{for } E < 0$$

where the error E is

$$E = PV - SP$$

PV denotes process variable; SP, the set point.

This relation shows that when the measured value exceeds the set point, full controller output results. When it is less than the set point, the controller output is zero. An example is a home furnace, which is either operating or not, depending on the state—open or closed—of a switch operated by the thermostat.

When the temperature at the thermostat falls, the switch is closed, the furnace operates, and the temperature rises. When a higher temperature is sensed at the thermostat, the switch is opened, shutting down the furnace. The up and down cycling continues indefinitely.

To prevent cycles from repeating too rapidly and becoming destructive to the equipment, a gap called the *differential, neutral,* or *dead zone* is built into the thermostat control so that nothing happens until the temperature overshoots the set point and passes the gap boundaries, going in either direction.

The following example provides insight into the basic concepts associated with the application of the SDK-85 as a two-position controller. Consider the cylindrical tank in Figure 10-1, which is emptied by a constant outflow of 1 m³/s.

The outflow of 1 m³/s will be maintained by a local flow controller, as shown in Figure 10-1, by controlling valve V2. Ths SDK-85 can be used as a two-position controller to open and close valve V1 with an open flow rate of 2 m³/s and a close flow rate of 0 m³/s. For level control, a neutral zone of 1 m and a set point of 12 m will be assumed. Hence, if the level is above 12.5 m, valve V1 will be closed by the SDK-85. If the level is below 11.5 m, valve V1 will be opened by the SDK-85. Therefore, in this application, an SDK-85–based two-position controller will be used to control the process shown in Figure 10-1. One can use either programmed I/O or interrupt I/O for the SDK-85.

In a typical process control application, the SDK-85 can be used to replace a number of conventional two-position controllers. For simplicity, one such controller is considered here as an example.

The level in Figure 10-1 is measured by a level sensor. An interface is required between the level sensor and the SDK-85. The interface may consist of either amplifiers and A/D converters or comparators. A typical interface using operational amplifiers as comparators is shown in Figure 10-2.

The interface shown in Figure 10-2 can be designed for using the SDK-85 with programmed I/O. When the

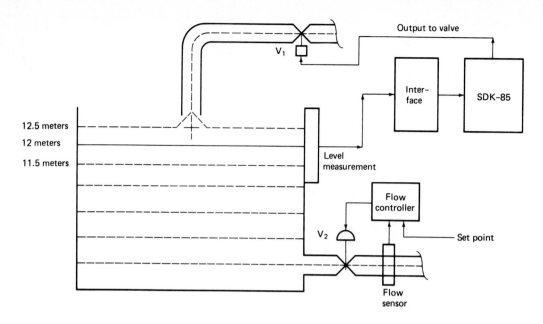

Figure 10-1 SDK-85 as a two-position controller

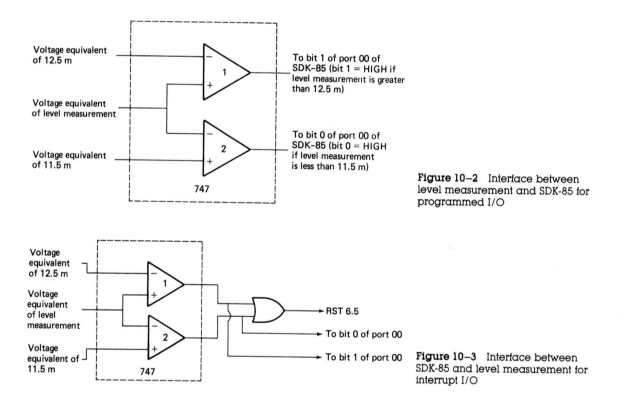

Figure 10-2 Interface between level measurement and SDK-85 for programmed I/O

Figure 10-3 Interface between SDK-85 and level measurement for interrupt I/O

level measurement exceeds 12.5 m, the output of operational amplifier 1 becomes 1 (HIGH), making bit 1 of port 00 HIGH. If the level measurement is below 11.5 m, the output of operational amplifier 2 becomes 1 (HIGH), making bit 0 of port 00 HIGH. Using programmed I/O, the SDK-85 can be programmed to input port 00. If bit 0 is HIGH, the SDK-85 will send a HIGH output through bit 2 of port 00 in order to open valve

V1. If bit 1 is HIGH, a LOW output is sent through bit 2 to close valve V1.

The interface between the level measurement and the SDK-85 will be different if interrupt I/O is used. A typical interface using interrupt I/O is shown in Figure 10-3. As mentioned before, based on the level measurement, one of the two operational amplifier outputs in Figure 10-3 will be HIGH, which in turn will make the output of the OR gate (RST6.5) HIGH and will interrupt the SDK-85. The SDK-85 will push the program counter onto the stack and will execute a service routine.

The program in the service routine will consist of reading port 00 and determining the source of the interrupt. The program will then send an output to open or close valve V1 in Figure 10–1 accordingly.

Figure 10–4 shows a typical configuration for the application of the SDK-85 as a two-position controller. A functional flowchart for this application is shown in Figure 10–5. Figures 10–6 and 10–7 give the detailed flowcharts using programmed and interrupt I/O, respectively. These flowcharts can then be translated into the respective assembly language programs.

In Figure 10–7, the flowcharts for the main program and the interrupt service routine are shown. The main program utilizes bits 0 and 1 of port 00 as inputs and bit 2 of port 00 as output. The program then enables the system interrupt and also executes a SIM to set the RST6.5 mask bit to 0. The 8085 is then halted for the RST6.5 interrupt. As soon as the RST6.5 interrupt occurs, the 8085 pushes the contents of the program counter

and jumps to the service routine. The RST6.5 service routine inputs port 00 and rotates bit 0 to carry to determine whether the valve is to be opened or closed (see Figure 10–3). The program then takes appropriate action by sending an output through bit 2 of port 00. A delay routine is executed to ensure that the proper action has taken place. A RETURN instruction pops the program counter from the stack, which contains a JUMP instruction. The main program branches to enable the interrupt and then to halt for the next RST6.5 interrupt.

10–2 8085-BASED RMS METER

The primary objective of this application is the complete development of a stand-alone microcomputer-based system that will measure, compute, and display the root-mean-square (rms) value of a sinusoidal voltage.

The completed system is required to

1. Sample a 60-Hz sinusoidal voltage 128 times.
2. Digitize the sample value through a microprocessor-controlled A/D converter.

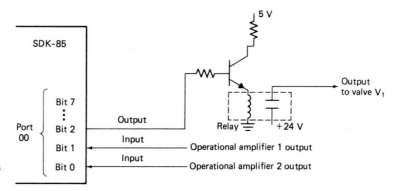

Figure 10–4 Interface between SDK-85 and valve V1

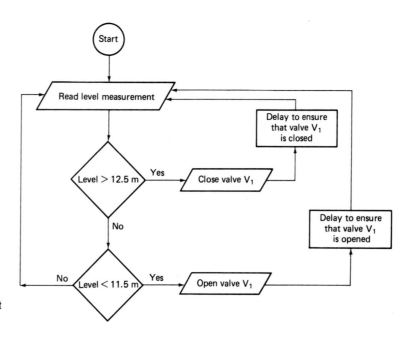

Figure 10–5 Functional flowchart of the two-position controller

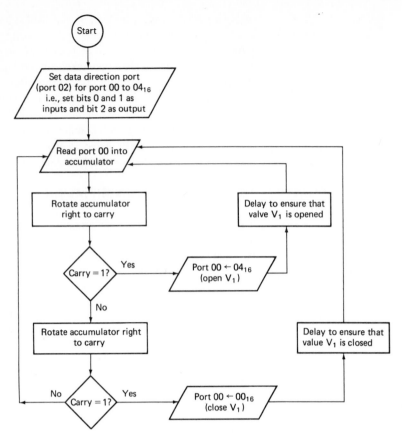

Figure 10–6 Detailed flowchart of the two-position controller, using programmed I/O

3. Input the digitized value to the 8085 microprocessor through the RST6.5 interrupt.

4. Compute the average and rms values of the waveform.

5. Display the rms value to the operator.

10–2–1 Introduction

The development project consists of the following steps:

1. System design—hardware and software

2. Software development—creation of software disk files; editing; assembly; debugging.

3. Hardware/software integration—creation of absolute file using linking editor; emulation using development system RAM, ROM; programming of target (user) system EPROM; emulation using target (user) system RAM, EPROM

4. System test using target (user) RAM, EPROM, and microprocessor

10–2–2 Technical Discussion

The microcomputer system may be considered in three sections: the microcomputer itself; the external circuitry used to sample, digitize, and display; and the software used to control I/O and process data. In addition, the microprocessor development system, while not a part of

the finished system, played an integral role in the development project. It will be discussed first.

10–2–3 Hewlett-Packard 64000 Development System

The Hewlet-Packard 64000 is a hard-disk–based, stand-alone microprocessor development system. Through it, a target system designer can create disk files of software routines (either in assembly language or in a high-level language such as Pascal), assemble or compile to create relocatable object files, and link several routines through the linkage editor to create absolute files. Moreover, the designer may use the system emulation option to exercise the target system while single stepping through the software, or the designer may execute it in real time with tracing and logic analyzer support.

The basic development system consists of one to six workstations and a common hard disk drive. The fully configured workstation includes hardware for target system hardware emulation, logic analysis, and PROM programming, as well as a software package to control these functions. Also included in the software package are assemblers and high-level compilers for a number of popular 8-bit microprocessors, a linkage editor, and an absolute loader.

To use the development system, the designer first creates a program source file with the system's text editor.

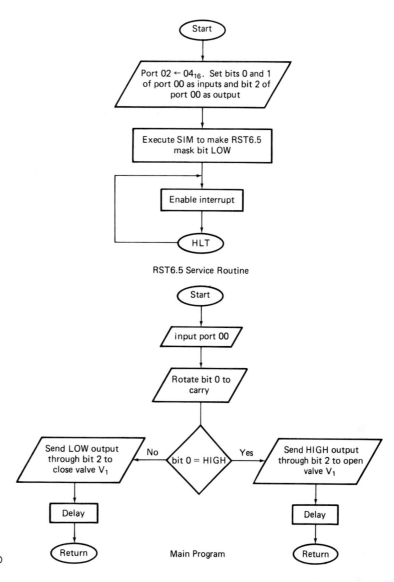

Start

Port 02 ← 04₁₆. Set bits 0 and 1 of port 00 as inputs and bit 2 of port 00 as output

Execute SIM to make RST6.5 mask bit LOW

Enable interrupt

HLT

RST6.5 Service Routine

Start

input port 00

Rotate bit 0 to carry

bit 0 = HIGH

Send LOW output through bit 2 to close valve V₁   No

Yes   Send HIGH output through bit 2 to open valve V₁

Delay

Delay

Return

Main Program

Return

Figure 10–7 Flowcharts of the two-position controller using interrupt I/O

This editor allows the correction of any character, word, or line. It also allows the insertion of lines into the source file or the deletion of lines from it. Next, the designer iteratively assembles (or compiles) the source file and edits it until an error-free, relocatable object file is created. These functions can, of course, be performed by a general-purpose computer whose software supports a text editor and appropriate cross assembler.

After the source program has been edited and assembled, the development system's unique features extend its usefulness beyond that of the general-purpose computer. First, the linkage editor collects the various object-code files to be used by the target system, reconciles references (labels), and creates an absolute (memory-image) file, which will then be used by the emulator. Next, the emulator, in conjunction with the target system hardware, executes the program and provides the designer with diagnostic information. Through emulation, the designer can single step through the program, read any register or memory location after any program step, and

trace the register contents through any portion of the program.

The HP 64000 emulation system uses a buffered master–slave architecture. Whereas the development system mainframe operates from a special 16-bit microprocessor, the actual emulation is performed within an emulation pod by a highspeed version of the target processor. Interfacing between mainframe bus and emulator processor is accomplished by the microprocessor emulator control board and the memory emulator control board, which are housed in the workstation chassis.

Hardware emulation attempts to duplicate as faithfully as possible the operation of the target microprocessor, while providing the designer with extra insights into the operation of the software and hardware system. Without access to the development system and its emulator, target system testing would require additional hardware and software (which would require testing themselves) to single step, load data, and display the contents of memory and registers. With the use of emulation, the designer possesses a powerful diagnostic tool with which the system can be developed.

Emulation may be performed on several levels. First, the emulation system can perform the function of the user's microprocessor and memory. In this case, the absolute file is loaded into a portion of emulation memory that has been designed as ROM. A separate portion of the emulation memory is allocated as RAM. Addresses in the emulation memory correspond to those in the target system memory. The designer can thus execute the program with neither the microprocessor nor the memory chips installed in the target system. As long as the appropriate interface chip (e.g., 8155 or 8755) is installed in the circuit and connected to the microcomputer data and control buses, the emulator processor will be able to exercise the target system in real time.

Alternatively, the designer may execute a program through the target system's RAM and ROM memory. In this case, all memory is designated as user memory. The emulator memory fetches instructions from user ROM and stores data in user RAM. However, the designer still has the capability of single stepping, tracing the registers, or running any portion of the program and displaying register contents at any predetermined breakpoint. This process represents the final step in emulation. When the hardware and software have been debugged, the emulator probe is removed and replaced by the target microprocessor, and the target system is ready for stand-alone operation.

10–2–4 8085-Based Microcomputer

The microcomputer used in this example incorporates the Intel 8085 microprocessor, 8156 RAM I/O, and 8755 EPROM I/O chips. These three devices constitute the core of a bus-oriented microcomputer. Figure 10–8 depicts the microcomputer circuit. The following tristated control lines are connected to all three devices:

ALE	Address latch enable; latches address lines
$\overline{RD}$	Used to read from device
$\overline{WR}$	Used to write a device
I/O/M	Used to designate either memory operation or I/O port operation
READY	Cycle delay; tied LOW to disable
CLK	Clock output of 8085
RESET	Generated by 8085 in response to external hardware; will reset all I/O ports to input

In addition, the following control signals of the 8085 are connected to fixed voltages or external hardware:

HOLD	Used to halt the processor for DMA; connected to ground to disable
INTR	RST0–RST7 interrupt; connected to ground to disable
RST5.5	Interrupt; connected to ground to disable
RST7.5	Interrupt; connected to ground to disable
$\overline{\text{RESET IN}}$	Will generate RESET signal and force program counter to 0000; connected to external hardware to initiate program
RST6.5	Vectored interrupt; connected to applications hardware, vector location = 0034H

The 8 address/data lines (AD0–AD7) are bused between the three devices. They are used to transmit the 8 data bits and the 8 lower-order address bits between the processor and the memory devices. Address lines A8–A10 are connected between the 8085 and the 8755. Since the 8156 RAM possesses only 256 bytes of memory (as opposed to the 8755), it does not require these additional address bits.

RAM (8156) and ROM (8755) are mapped by address bit A11. The 8755's ROM program resides in memory locations 0000_{16}–$07FF_{16}$ (the extent of its 2K-byte memory), and the chip is selected when A11 is LOW. Hence, the A11 line is connected to the $\overline{CE}$ pin of the 8755. In contrast, the 8156 RAM chip is selected when A11 is HIGH, thus giving it the memory range 0800_{16}–$08FF_{16}$ (256 bytes).

Output ports A and B of the 8156 interface to the external hardware. Port A is designated as an output from the 8085 and issues control bits to the conversion hardware. Port B is designated as an input and receives the 8-bit data word from the A/D converter.

I/O is performed by standard I/O. When executing an IN or OUT instruction, the 8085 deselects memory and selects I/O ports by bringing I/O$\overline{M}$ HIGH and transmitting the 8-bit port address on address lines AD0–AD7 and A8–A15. Since the 8156 is enabled when A11 is HIGH, the software designer must be certain to enable that bit in the port address.

On the 8156 chip, bits AD0–AD2 control the specific port accessed:

AD2	AD1	AD0	
0	0	0	Command/status register
0	0	1	Port A
0	1	0	Port B
0	1	1	Port C
1	0	0	Low-order timer
1	0	1	High-order timer

For this project, the command/status register and ports A and B are used. Therefore, AD2 will be LOW, and AD0 and AD1 will be either HIGH or LOW, depending on the port accessed.

Address bit A11 translates to address bit AD3 in the port address. Therefore, AD3 will be HIGH for all 8156 I/O port addresses:

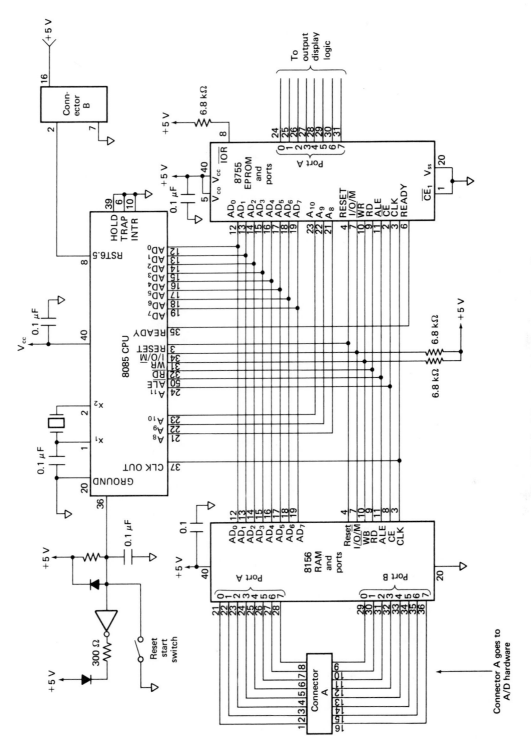

Figure 10–8 Microcomputer system schematic

299

Port Address	AD3	AD2	AD1	AD0	
08_{16}	1	0	0	0	Command/status register
09_{16}	1	0	0	1	Port A
$0A_{16}$	1	0	1	0	Port B

Data to the seven-segment LED displays is outputted from the 8085 processor through port A of the 8755 ROM I/O device. The output data word consists of a 4-bit hexadecimal number (lower 4 bits) and a 4-bit display address (upper 4 bits). A combination latch/hexadecimal seven-segment decoder (9356) latches data on a common data bus when its individual latch bit becomes HIGH. Each display/latch reads its data in turn.

Each bit of the 8755's port A must be defined as an output by a data direction register (DDRA). Also, writing into either port A or DDRA demands that the 8755 device be enabled. Therefore, A11 (corresponding to AD3 in an OUT operation) must be LOW. The resulting port addresses for the 8755 are as follows:

AD3	AD2	AD1	AD0	Port Address	
0	0	0	0	00_{16}	Port A
0	0	1	0	02_{16}	DDRA

Besides the three Intel devices, the microcomputer includes a 1-MHz crystal oscillator to provide a master clock, a RESET switch to reset the system, and latched LED displays to output the rms value to the operator.

10–2–5 A/D Conversion Hardware

This hardware is composed of three circuits: absolute value, sample and hold, and A/D converter.

The absolute value circuit used rectifies the input voltage within the feedback loop of an operational amplifier (see Figure 10–9). When the input voltage e_1 becomes negative, the output of operational amplifier 1 becomes positive by one diode drop and turns off the upper diode. No effective current flows from operational amplifier 1, and the output voltage of operational amplifier 2 is $-e_1 = abs(e_1)$. When e_1 becomes positive, the lower diode is turned off, and the output of operational amplifier 1 becomes $(-e_1 - 0.7$ V). The output of operational amplifier 2 then becomes $[-(-2e_1 + e_1)] = e_1$. In either case, the output voltage of operational amplifier 2 is the absolute value of the input sine wave, and no diode drop error is introduced.

After the input voltage is rectified, it is sampled by the sample and hold circuit. A SAMPLE signal of 650-μs duration is transmitted from I/O port A of the 8156 and inverted by a 4049 CMOS buffer. When SAMPLE is HIGH, the output of the buffer is LOW, and the 2N2222 transistor is turned off. Since it is not conducting, its collector voltage remains at 15 V, and the 4066 analog switch is closed. To open the switch, SAMPLE is set

LOW, the 2N2222 transistor saturates, and the gate voltage of the analog switch is effectively set to 0 V. When this analog switch is closed, a capacitor charges to sample voltage.

Finally, the sampled and rectified voltage is converted to an 8-bit digital word by the 8703 A/D converter. The 8703 is biased to provide a 9- to 10-V scale range (i.e., 00H is equivalent to 0 V; FFH, to 10 V). All signals to the I/O ports of the microcomputer are buffered to isolate the expensive CMOS A/D converters.

The 8 digital output bits are connected to port A of the 8156 and are read during the interrupt service routine. Conversion is begun by a programmed START CONVERSION pulse transmitted from the 8085 through port B of the 8156. After the A/D converter has completed conversion of the input voltage, the status line $\overline{BUSY}$ goes LOW. When enabled by the software-controlled ENABLE bit, the inverted signal $\overline{BUSY}$ triggers the RST6.5 interrupt, and the interrupt service routine reads the valid data.

Since the $\overline{BUSY}$ output from the 8703 remains LOW ($\overline{BUSY}$ remains HIGH) between conversions, a software latch must be used to prevent further interrupts. Therefore, $\overline{BUSY}$ is ANDed and ENABLE to provide an RST6.5 interrupt only when the microcomputer is ready to accept it. During the interrupt service routine, ENABLE is set LOW and remains in that state until the next sample is taken and the next A/D conversion is begun. Figure 10–10 depicts the timing of the control signals.

10–2–6 Software

The software used in this example exists as a single program, edited and assembled as an integral unit. It performs three primary functions: sampling of data, servicing interrupts, and computing the rms value. Each function may be considered separately.

When the system is reset by manually enabling the RESET line of the 8085, the program counter is automatically forced to 0000H. A JMP instruction at this address sends the processor to the beginning of the sampling and acquisition sequence (0037H). This portion of the program enables the RST6.5 interrupt, initializes the B register at 128 to count the samples, defines the 8156 I/O (port A = input, port B = output), and clears registers C, D, and E.

Next, the program turns on the sample bit (bit 1 of 8156's port B) for 650 μs by using a timing loop. It then disables SAMPLE and issues a START CONVERSION command (bit 2), after which it enables the software interrupt latch (bit 0). Finally, it reaches a HLT instruction and waits for the interrupt. Upon return from interrupt, the program will decrement the B register and branch back to the sampling sequence if 128 samples have not been taken. If the proper number of samples

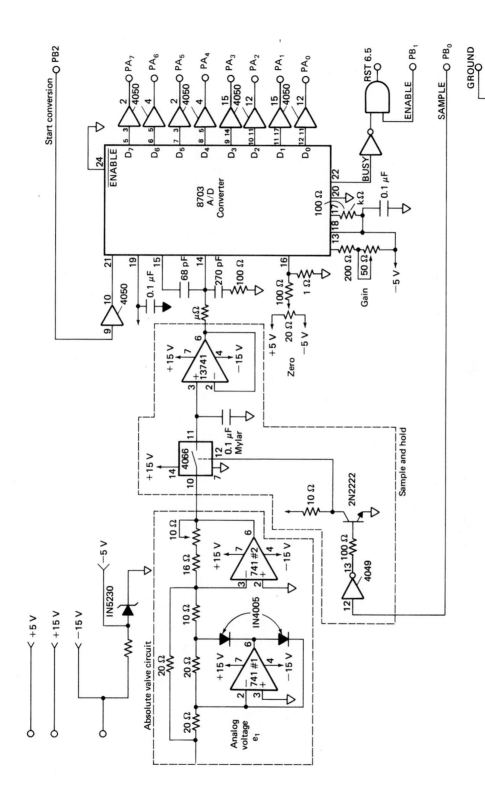

Figure 10–9 Absolute value, sample and hold, and A/D circuits

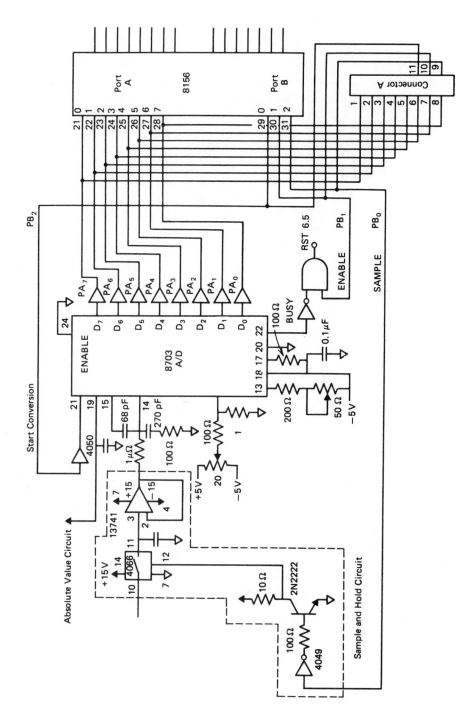

Figure 10–9 Absolute value, sample and hold, and A/D circuits (cont.)

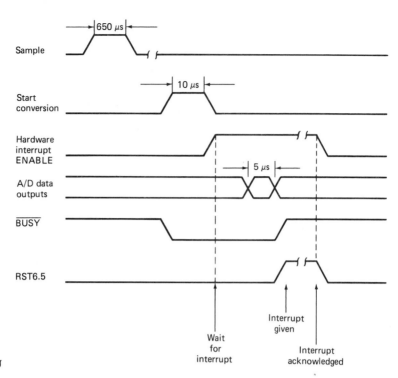

Figure 10–10 Hardward timing

has been taken, the processor falls through to the rms-calculation portion of the program.

The interrupt service routine (008E) first enables the output of the 8703 A/D converter. It then reads the 8-bit data word through port A of the 8156 (address 09) and adds it to a continuing sum in registers C, D, and E. Maintaining such a summing register avoids the problems of a 128-entry data table. Immediately after this step, the loop counter is decremented, and a jump is made back to the main program—the sample and hold routine. An interrupt instruction pushes a 2-byte address onto the stack. By jumping instead of returning, this address is not popped. To avoid a stack of 256 address locations, the contents of the stack are popped into unused registers H and L after the service routine. JMP was used in place of RET because of deficiencies in the emulator software.

Finally, the program computes the rms value of the sine wave by dividing the cumulative sum in C, D, and E by 128 for an average. The average is then multiplied by 142 with a short multiplication routine. This result is divided with the same divide-by-128 routine previously used. This yields the rms value:

$$\frac{142}{128} = 1.11 \quad \text{and} \quad 1.11 \times \text{average} = \text{rms}$$

Division of the sum in registers C, D, and E is accomplished by shifting the contents of this register group 7 times to the right. Multiplication is accomplished by rotating the sum of products and the multiplicand in steps. If the carry bit is set after rotation of the multi-

plicand left, the multiplier (142) is added to the shifted sum of products.

Once the rms value has been calculated, all that remains is to display the result to the operator. The display routine masks the hexadecimal data from register E in groups of 4 bits each. The masked data are sent out through port A of the 8755 so that the data will be present before display registers are clocked. Once the data is stable, the masked data is ORed with control bits to clock the display registers. Two 9356 latch/decoders are used for the display. The complete word is now outputted to the latch, and the display is latched to new data. The 4 upper bits of the register are then rotated into the 4 lower bits, and the same routine is followed.

The flowcharts are given in Figures 10–11 to 10–17. A listing of the programs appears on pages 306 and 307.

10–2–7 Methodology

The example is conducted in a straightforward manner. Hardware and software are designed as discussed in the technical discussion. Disk files of the software are created and debugged until error-free assemblies are achieved. The hardware is fabricated, and emulation is begun.

Among the many problems uncovered is a software deficiency in the HP 64000 emulation system. Apparently, the emulation processor cannot accept an interrupt if in a halt state. Once this problem is discovered, the applications program is modified to contain a self-jumping loop:

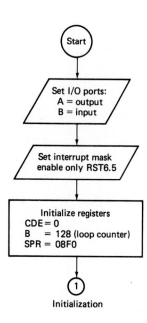

Figure 10-11 Initialization

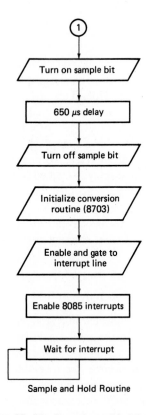

Figure 10-12 Sample and hold routine

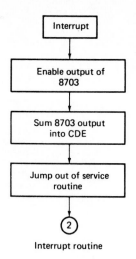

Figure 10-13 Interrupt routine

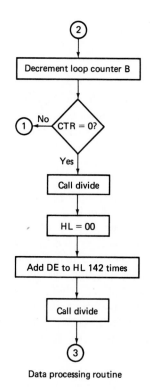

Figure 10-14 Data processing routine

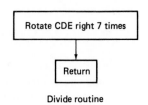

Figure 10-15 Divide routine

When the program reaches the JMP instruction, it falls into an infinite loop until interrupted. To return from the interrupt, the stack is popped and an unconditional branch to the next instruction after the WAIT loop is issued. No RET instruction is used as mentioned in the software discussion. This process is necessary since NEXT IN-STRUCTION ADDRESS placed onto the stack is actually the wait address. Thus, a RET instruction will throw the program into an infinite loop, and the program will never progress past this point.

After emulation from emulation memory is successful, the program is programmed into the 8755 EPROM, and emulation is executed from EPROM (user memory).

Finally, the emulation probe is replaced by the 8085 chip, and the target system is operated in stand-alone mode. Again, the system successfully sampled the waveform, computed the rms value, and displayed it to the operator. With this feat, the development phase of the project is complete.

10–2–8 Results

In stand-alone mode, the microcomputer system measured an input voltage and displayed the following results.

- *Case 1:* dc measurement*

    5.0 V dc   Displayed rms   8E
- *Case 2:* 7.5 V ac, unregulated*

    7.5 V ac   Displayed rms   A5–C0
- *Case 3:* 7.5 V ac, regulated line voltage*

    7.5 V ac   Displayed rms   BE–BD

*Measured with a Beckman 310 VOM.

The fluctuation in case 2 is attributable to wide variations over the sampling period of the line voltage. The accuracy of the 5.0-V dc test remains constant due to the efficiency of the constant voltage regulation. When the regulated 120-V line is used, calculated and measured values agree within 1 bit.

10–2–9 Conclusion

It is found that the developing and debugging of software and hardware components are greatly enhanced by the Hewlett-Packard 64000 development system. The excellent results obtained in this experiment (within 1-bit accuracy) are proof of the system's effectiveness.

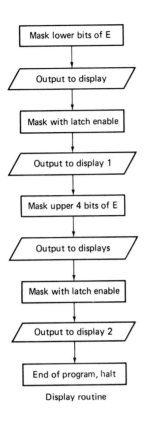

Figure 10–16   Display routine

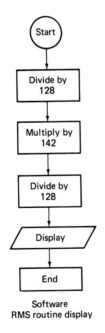

Figure 10–17   Software RMS routine display

FILE: ADCONV:GROUP9   HEWLETT-PACKARD: INTEL 8085 ASSEMBLER   PAGE 1

LINE LOC CODE ADDR   SOURCE STATEMENT

```
                        "8085"
        0000            ORG   0000H
 0000 C3  0034          JMP   START        PROGRAM COUNTER WILL BEGIN EXECUTION AT LOCATION 00H
                                           JUMP TO BEGINNING OF PROGRAM
        0034            ORG   034H         RST INTERRUPT VECTOR POINTS TO LOCATION 0034H
 0034 C3  008D          JMP   SVC
 0037 00       START    NOP
 0038 3E  0D            MVI   A,0DH        SET MASK ..  ENABLE ONLY RST 6.5 INTERRUPT
 003A 30                SIM
 003B 3E  02            MVI   A,02H        COMM. STATUS REG.; A=INPUT,B=OUTPUT
 003D D3                OUT   08H          B=LOOP COUNTER FOR 128 SAMPLES
      01  8000          LXI   B,3000H      C,D AND E WILL STORE CUMMULATIVE SUM OF SAMPLES
 0042 31  08F0          LXI   SP,08F0H     INITIALIZE STACK POINTER FOR RESTART
 0045 3E  01   SAMPLE   MVI   A,01H        TURN ON SAMPLE BIT
 004C 21  004F          LXI   H,004FH      BEGIN 650 MICROSECOND DELAY
      2B       LOOP1    DCX   H
      B4                MOV   A,L
      C2                ORA   H
                        JNZ   LOOP1
      D3  0A            OUT   0AH
                        NOP
 005A 3E  04   CONV     MVI   A,04H        INITIALIZE A/D CONVERSION ...PORT 0A-2=1 (LATCHED BIT)
      D3  0A            OUT   0AH
      3E  00            MVI   A,00H        TURN OFF INIT. CONV. PIN... PORT 0A-2
      D3  02            OUT   0AH          ENABLE 'AND' GATE PORT 0A-2
      D3  0A            OUT   0AH          ENABLE RST 6.5 INTERRUPT
      FB                EI
 0065          WAIT     JMP   WAIT         WAIT FOR INTERRUPT
                        NOP
      E1       BACK     POP   H
      05                DCR   B            DECREMENT LOOP COUNTER FOR 128 SAMPLES
      C2                JNZ   SAMPLE       IF COUNTER DOES NOT EQUAL 0, RETURN TO SAMPLE ROUTINE
                        NOP
      CD  007A          CALL  DIVIDE       CUMMULATIVE SUM OF SAMPLES (CDE) IS DIVIDED BY 128 = AVERAGE
      00                NOP
                        NOP
                        NOP
      C3  00A2          JMP   MULT         MOVE DE TO HL
      00                NOP                STORE HL IN MEMORY LOCATION 0800H FOR MULT. ROUTINE
                        NOP
 007A 06  07   DIVIDE   MVI   B,07H        B=COUNTER FOR SHIFTER...(DE) WILL BE SHIFTED RIGHT 7 TIMES
      AF       LOOP2    XRA   A            CLR CARRY BIT FOR SHIFTING
      1F                RAR
      4F                MOV   A,C
      7A                MOV   C,A
      1F                RAR
      57                MOV   A,D
      7B                MOV   D,A
      1F                RAR
      5F                MOV   A,E
                        MOV   E,A
 007C 05                DCR   B            DECREMENT LOOP COUNTER
      C2                JNZ   LOOP2        IF COUNTER DOES NOT = 0, JUMP BACK TO SHIFT
      C9                RET                RETURN FROM DIVIDE SUBROUTINE
      00                NOP
```

(continued)

FILE: ADCONV:GROUP9   HEWLETT-PACKARD: INTEL 8085 ASSEMBLER

```
LINE  LOC  CODE  ADDR         SOURCE STATEMENT

 58   008C  0C          SVC    NOP                    *SERVICE ROUTINE
 59   008D  3E    08           MVI    A,08H           ENABLE 8703 OUTPUT (8 BITS OF DATA) PORT 0A-3
 60   008F  D3    0A           OUT    0AH             CLEAR CARRY BIT
 61   0091  AF                 XRA    A
 62   0092  DB    09           IN     09H             INPUT DATA FROM A/D CONVERTER TO PORT 09
 63   0094  5F                 MOV    E,A             **********************************************
 64   0095  7A                 MOV    A,D             *
 65   0096  CE    00           ACI    00H             *    SUM OUTPUT FROM 8703 (INTO REGISTERS C,D AND E
 66   0098  57                 MOV    D,A             *             (E IS THE LOWEST ORDER BYTE)
 67   0099  79                 MOV    A,C             *
 68   009A  CE    00           ACI    00H             *
 69   009B  4F                 MOV    C,A
 70   009C  C3    009E         JMP    BACK
 71   009E              BACK   NOP
 72   00A1  00                 NOP                    **********************************************
 73   00A2  21    0000  MULT   LXI    H,00H           END OF SERVICE ROUTINE ***********************
 74   00A3                     MVI    B,08DH          *MULTIPLICATION SUBROUTINE
 75   00A6  12           LOOP4 DAD    B               *
 76   00A8  05                 DCR    B               *     ADD (D) (E) TO (H) (L) 141 TIMES
 77   00A9  C2    00A8         JNZ    LOOP4           *
 78   00AC  00                 NOP                    **********************************************
 79   00AD  54                 MOV    D,H
 80   00AE  5D                 MOV    E,L             MOV DATA IN REGISTERS H AND L TO D AND E FOR DIVIDE
 81   00AF  00                 NOP
 82   00B0  0E    00           MVI    C,00H
 83   00B1  CD    007A         CALL   DIVIDE          DIVIDE DATA IN C,D AND E BY 128
 84   00B3  00                 NOP
 85   00B6  CD    00BC         CALL   UPDAD
 86   00B7  00                 NOP
 87   00BA  00                 NOP
 88   00BB  76                 HLT                    END OF PROGRAM
 89   00BD  3E    FF    UPDAD  MVI    A,0FFH          DISPLAY ROUTINE
 90   00BF  D3    02           OUT    02H             SET DDR FOR PORT A
 91   00C1  AF                 XRA    A               CLEAR ACCUMULATOR
 92   00C2  7B                 MOV    A,E
 93   00C3  E6    0F           ANI    00H             MASK-0000 DDDD
 94   00C5  D3                 OUT    00H             SET DATA LINES D3-D0
 95   00C7  F6    0F           ORI    1FH             MASK-0011 DDDD
 96   00C9  D3    00           OUT    00H             LATCH DIGIT 0
 97   00CB  7B                 MOV    A,E
 98   00CD  AF                 XRA    A
 99   00CE  1F                 RAR                    ROTATE 4 MSB'S INTO 4 LSB LOCATION
100   00CF  1F                 RAR
101   00D0  1F                 RAR
102   00D1  1F                 RAR
103   00D1  E6    1F           ANI    1FH             MASK-0001 DDDD
104   00D3  F6    10           ORI    10H             MASK-0001 DDDD
105   00D5  D3                 OUT    30H             SET DATA D7-D4
106   00D7  D3    00           OUT    00H             MASK-0011 DDDD
107   00D9  AF                 XRA                    LATCH DIGIT 1
108   00DB  D3    30           OUT    30H             CLEAR ACC. bit CARRY
109   00DC  F6    00           ORI    00H             SET DATA D15-D8
110   00DE  F6    F0           ORI    0F0H            MASK-1111 0000
111   00E0  D3    00           OUT    00H             SET DIGIT 2 & 3
112   00E2  D3                 OUT                    END OF PROGRAM
113   00E4  76                 HLT
```

Errors=   0

10–3 68000-BASED SYSTEM DESIGN*

10–3–1 Problem Statement

A 68000-based system is designed to drive three seven-segment displays and monitor three key switches. The system starts by displaying 000. If the increment key is pressed, it will increment the display by 1. Similarly, if the decrement key is pressed, it will decrement the display by 1. The display goes from 00–FF in the hex mode and from 000–255 in the BCD mode. The system will count correctly in either mode. The change-mode key will cause the display to change from hex to decimal or vice versa, depending on its present mode. Figure 10–18 depicts the block diagram.

10–3–2 Solution Hardware

The simplest and the most straightforward system possible is built to obtain the required results. This means that there will be no RAM in the system; therefore, no subroutine will be used in the software and only programmed I/O (no interrupt) is used.

Figure 10–19 shows the detailed hardware schematic. The circuit is divided as follows.

Reset Circuit The reset circuit for the system is basically the same as the one used for the 8085. The circuit has a 0.1-μF capacitor and a 1-kΩ resistor to provide an RC time constant of 10^{-4} s for power on reset. (The reset switch should be held longer to provide power-on reset for at least 100 ms.) The $\overline{\text{RESET}}$ and $\overline{\text{HALT}}$ pins of the 68000 and the $\overline{\text{RESET}}$ pin of the 6821 are tied together for complete and total reset of the system.

Clock Signal An external pulse-generator is used to generate the clock signal for the system. The system is driven up to 3 MHz, the limit of the generator, without any problems. For higher frequencies, an on-chip crystal oscillator or user-designed oscillator can be used.

Buffering Because the 68000 is interfaced to other devices (a 6821 and two 2716's), the outputs of the 68000 that are used to drive these chips must be buffered in order to be certain that there is enough drive current. The buffering is done by a TTL open-collector inverter buffer

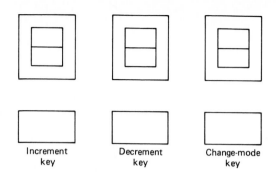

Figure 10–18 Block diagram for 68000-based system design

chip (7406). Since this chip is of the open-collective type, a 1-kΩ pull-up resistor is also needed.

Address Mapping The system has two 2K EPROM (2716's) and one 6800 peripheral I/O chip (6821). The 68000 address lines A1–A11 are needed to address the EPROM. So, A12 is used to select between the 2716's and the 6821 (0 for the 2716's and 1 for the 6821). Memory access for the EPROM is asynchronous, while the 6821 is synchronized with the E clock. A12 is inverted, through the buffer, so that the output of the inverter goes to $\overline{\text{CS2}}$ of the 6821 and also to $\overline{\text{VPA}}$ of the 68000 for synchronization. The 68000 $\overline{\text{VMA}}$ pin is also buffered and inverted, and it goes to CS0 of the 6821. The 6821 is chosen to be odd; thus, CS1 is activated by the inverted $\overline{\text{LDS}}$ line. Finally, address lines A1 and A2 are connected to RS0 and RS1, respectively.

The $\overline{\text{CE}}$ signals for the two 2716's come from two NAND gates. They are the results of the inverted A12 NANDed with the inverted $\overline{\text{LDS}}$ or the inverted $\overline{\text{UDS}}$, depending on whether the EPROM is odd or even. The $\overline{\text{DTACK}}$ pin of the 68000 and the $\overline{\text{OE}}$ pins of the 2716's are activated by the signal of R/$\overline{\text{W}}$ inverted. When the 68000 wants to read the EPROM, this signal will be high; thus, its inverted signal will provide a LOW to $\overline{\text{DTACK}}$. This does not cause any problem because when the 68000 accesses the 6821, $\overline{\text{VPA}}$ is activated and the 68000 will not look for $\overline{\text{DTACK}}$.

The configuration just described causes the memory map to be as follows:

	A23...A13	A12	A11	A10	A9	A8	A7	A6	A5	A4	A3	A2	A1	Hex
4K of	0 . . . 0	0	0	0	0	0	0	0	0	0	0	0	0	000000_{16}
EPROM						through								to
memory	0 . . . 0	0	1	1	1	1	1	1	1	1	1	1	1	$000FFF_{16}$
PA/	0 . . . 0	1	0	0	0	0	0	0	0	0	0	0	0	001001_{16} (A0 = 1)
DDRA														
CRA	0 . . . 0	1	0	0	0	0	0	0	0	0	0	1	1	001003_{16} (A0 = 1)
PB/DDRB	0 . . . 0	1	0	0	0	0	0	0	0	0	0	1	0	001005_{16} (A0 = 1)
CRB	0 . . . 0	1	0	0	0	0	0	0	0	0	0	1	1	001007_{16} (A0 = 1)

*Reprinted with permission from *Microprocessors and Microcomputer-Based System Design* by M. Rafiquzzaman, copyright 1990, CRC Press, Boca Raton, FL.

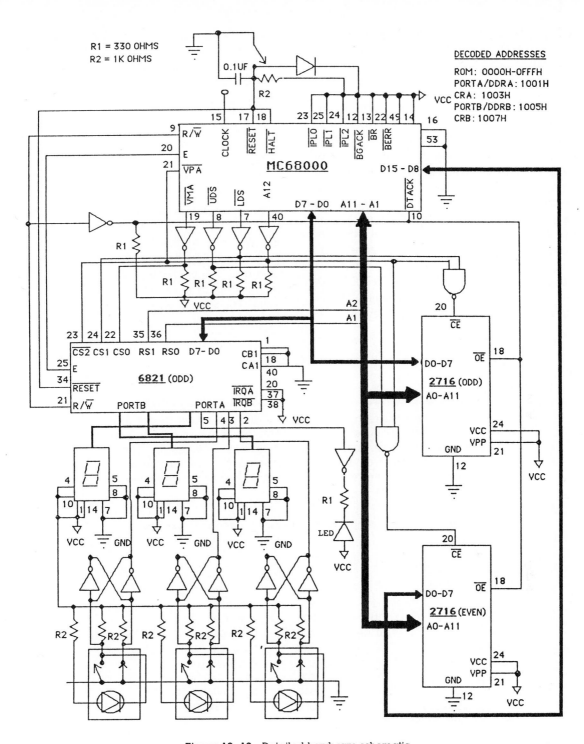

Figure 10-19 Detailed hardware schematic

I/O There are three seven-segment displays in the system (TIL311), an LED, and three switches. The three displays have internal latches and hex decoders; thus, the least significant displays are connected directly to port B of the 6821 chip, and the most significant line is connected to the upper 4 bits of port A. The latch will enable, for the displays are tied to ground so as to enable them at all times. The LED, when ON, will indicate that the display is in the BCD mode. Each of the three switches,

double-pole-single-throw–type, with an LED indicator, goes through two inverters (7404) for the hardware debounce, and the outputs of the inverters are connected to the lowest 3 bits of port A.

Unused-Pins Connection For the 68000, there are six unused, active-low, input pins, which must be disabled by connecting them to 5 V. These are $\overline{IPL0}$, $\overline{IPL1}$, $\overline{IPL2}$, $\overline{BERR}$, $\overline{BR}$, and $\overline{BGACK}$. Two of the 6821's unused pins ($\overline{\text{IRQA}}$ and $\overline{\text{IRQB}}$) are also disabled this way, while CA1 and CB1 are disabled by connecting them to ground.

10-3-3 Software

The Hewlett-Packard 64000 development system is used to design, develop, debug, and emulate the 68000-based system. The program consists of three major functions: initializing I/O ports and data registers; monitoring and debouncing key switches; and incrementing, decrementing, or changing mode.

The program configures port B of the 6821 as an output port to display the 2 lower significant nibbles of data. The higher 4 bits of port A are configured as output to display the most significant nibble of the data. Bit 3 is also an output bit; it turns the mode of the LEDs ON and OFF. The lowest 3 bits of port A are configured as inputs to detect the positions of the three key switches.

Register D3 is used to store the data in hex. Registers D4 and D7 are used to store the data in BCD mode, with the low-order byte in D4 and the high-order byte in D7. Bit 3 of D0 contains a logic 1 representing BCD mode and a logic 0 representing hex mode. Register D5 contains a 1, which will be used for incrementing BCD data since the 68000 ABCD does not have immediate mode. Register D6 contains 999, which is used for decrementing BCD.

The program monitors the three switches and stores the 3 input bits into register D0 if any one of the keys is pressed. The processor then waits until the depressed key is released and then checks the input data one by one. The processor then branches to the increment, decrement, or mode-change routine according to the depressed key. After execution, the processor will display the result on the three seven-segment displays. The assembly language program is listed next:

```
FILE: LAB2:KH0A22        HEWLETT-PACKARD: 68000 Assembler


1  "68000"
2  ****************************************************************
3  *THIS PROGRAM STARTS DISPLAYING 000 AND MONITORS THREE KEY  *
4  *SWITCHES THEN INCREMENT, DECREMENT, OR CONVERT HEX TO BCD  *
5  *OR VICE VERSA, DEPENDING ON WHICH KEY IS DEPRESSED, THE    *
6  *DISPLAY GOES FROM 00-FF IN HEX MODE OR 00-255 IN BCD MODE  *
7  ****************************************************************



FILE: LAB2:KH0A22   HEWLETT-PACKARD: 68000 Assembler
(continued)


LOCATION OBJECT
   CODE LINE                              SOURCE LINE
<1001>            8 PA      EQU    001001H
<1001>            9 DDRA    EQU    001001H
<1003>           10 CRA     EQU    001003H
<1005>           11 PB      EQU    001005H
<1005>           12 DDRB    EQU    001005H
<1007>           13 CRB     EQU    001007H
                 14         ORG    00000000H
000000 FFFF FFFF 15         DC.L   0FFFFFFFFH
000004 0000 0008 16         DC.L   START
                 17 *
                 18 * CONFIGURE THE INPUT AND OUTPUT PORTS,
                 19 * DISPLAY 000 ON THE 7-SEGMENT DISPLAYS,
                 20 * AND INITIALIZE ALL THE DATA REGISTERS.
                 21 * THE HEX MODE IS STORED IN D3 AND THE
                 22 * BCD MODE IS STORED IN D7 AND D4.
000008 4238 1003 23 START   CLR.B  CRA
00000C 11FC 00FB 24         MOVE.B #0F8H,DDRA  ;BIT 0-2 OF
                                               PORT A AS
                                               INPUT
000012 0BF8 0002 25         BSET.B #02H,CRA    ;BIT 3-7 OF
                                               PORT AS OUT-
                                               PUT
```

```
LOCATION OBJECT
   CODE LINE                        SOURCE LINE

000018 4238 1007   26          CLR.B    CRB
00001C 11FC 00FF   27          MOVE.B   #0FFH,DDRB    ;ALL 8 BITS OF
                                                       PORT B AS
                                                       OUTPUT
000022 08F8 0002   28          BSET.B   #02H,CRB
000028 4200        29          CLR.B    D0
00002A 11C0 1001   30          MOVE.B   D0,PA         ;DISPLAY 000
00002E 11C0 1005   31          MOVE.B   D0,PB
000032 4203        32          CLR.B    D3
000034 4244        33          CLR.W    D4
000036 7A01        34          MOVEQ.W  #01H,D5
000038 3C3C 0999   35          MOVE.W   #999H,D6
00003C 4207        36          CLR.B    D7
                   37  *
                   38 .* DEBOUNCE THE KEY SWITCHES
                   39  *
00003E 1238 1001   40 SCAN     MOVE.B   PA,D1         ;MONITOR THE
                                                      ;KEYS
000042 0201 0007   41          ANDI.B   #07H,D1       ;MASK OUT THE
                                                       OUTPUT PINS
000046 67F6        42          BEQ      SCAN          ;IF NO KEY IS
                                                       DEPRESSED GO TO
                                                       SCAN
000048 1438 1001   43          MOVE.B   PA,D2         ;READ THE DATA
                                                       AGAIN
00004C 0202 0007   44          ANDI.B   #07H,D2
000050 B401        45          CMP.B    D1,D2         ;CHECK TO SEE IF
                                                       THE DATA REMAIN
                                                       UNCHANGED
000052 66EA        46          BNE      SCAN          ;IF IT CHANGES GO
                                                       TO SCAN
                   47  *
                   48  * CHECK TO MAKE SURE THAT THE KEY IS
                   49  * RELEASED BEFORE THE NEXT KEY CAN BE
                   50  * ENTERED.
000054 1438 1001   51 KEYRL    MOVE.B   PA,D2
000058 0202 0007   52          ANDI.B   #07H,D2
00005C 66F6        53          BNE      KEYRL
                   54  * CHECK TO SEE WHICH KEY HAS BEEN EN-
                   55  * TERED. BITS 0,1, AND 2 OF D1 REPRESENT
                   56  * INCREMENT, DECREMENT, AND MODE EX-
                   57  * CHANGE RESPECTIVELY.
00005E 0801 0000   58          BTST.B   #0H,D1
000062 6600 003C   59          BNE      INCR          ;IF BIT-0 OF D1
                                                       IS 1 GOTO INCR
000066 0801 0001   60          BTST.B   #1H,D1
00006A 6700 0044   61          BEQ      MODE          ;IF BIT-1 IS 1
                                                       DECREMENT, OTHER-
                                                       WISE GOTO MODE
                   62  *
                   63  * DECREMENT BOTH HEX AND BCD AT THE SAME
                   64  * TIME.
00006E 0C03 0000   65          CMPI.B   #00H,D3
```

LOCATION OBJECT
  CODE LINE   SOURCE LINE

```
000072 67CA       66          BEQ     SCAN      ;IF THE NUMBER IS
                                                 0 NO DECREMENT,
                                                 GOTO SCAN
000074 5303       67          SUBQ.B  #1H,D3    ;DECREMENT HEX BY 1
000076 C603       68          AND.B   D3,D3     ;CLEAR THE CARRY
000078 C906       69          ABCD.B  D6,D4     ;DECREMENT BCD BY
                                                 1 BY ADDING IT
                                                 WITH 999
00007A CF06       70          ABCD.B  D6,D7
                  71 *
                  72 * DISPLAY THE NUMBER IN HEX IF BIT-3 OF
                  73 * D0 IS 0, OTHERWISE DISPLAY IN BCD.
                  74 *
00007C 0800 0003  75 DISPLAY  BTST.B  #3H,D0
000080 6700 0014  76          BEQ     HEX       ;IF BIT-3 OF D0
                                                 IS 0, GOTO HEX
000084 11C4 1005  77          MOVE.B  D4,PB     ;OUTPUT THE LSB
                                                 TO PORT B
000088 E94F       78          LSL.W   #4H,D7    ;SHIFT LEFT 4
                                                 TIMES
00008A 08C7 0003  79          BSET.B  #3H,D7    ;TURN OFF THE LED
00008E 11C7 1001  80          MOVE.B  D7,PA     ;OUTPUT THE MSB
                                                 TO UPPER 4 BITS
                                                 OF PORT A
000092 E84F       81          LSR.W   #4,D7
000094 60A8       82          BRA     SCAN
000096 11C0 1001  83 HEX      MOVE.B  D0,PA     ;OUTPUT 0 TO PORT A
00009A 11C3 1005  84          MOVE.B  D3,PB     ;OUTPUT THE HEX
                                                 NUMBER TO PORT B
00009E 609E       85          BRA     SCAN
                  86 *
                  87 * INCREMENT BOTH HEX AND BCD.
                  88 *
0000A0 0C03 00FF  89 INCR     CMPI.B  #0FFH,D3
0000A4 6798       90          BEQ     SCAN      ;IF THE NUMBER IS
                                                 FF NO INCREMENT
0000A6 5203       91          ADDQ.B  #1H,D3    ;INCREMENT HEX
                                                 NUMBER BY 1
0000A8 4202       92          CLR.B   D2
0000AA C905       93          ABCD.B  D5,D4     ;INCREMENT LSB OF
                                                 BCD BY 1
0000AC CF02       94          ABCD    D2,D7     ;INCREMENT MSB OF
                                                 BCD BY 1 IF CARRY
                                                 IS 1
0000AE 60CC       95          BRA     DISPLAY
                  96 *
                  97 * EXCHANGE THE MODE THEN DISPLAY THE
                  98 * NUMBER.
0000B0 0840 0003  99 MODE     BCHG    #3H,D0    ;EXCHANGE MODE BY
                                                 CHANGING BIT-3 OF
                                                 D0
0000B4 60C6       100         BRA     DISPLAY

Errors = 0
```

LINE#	SYMBOL	TYPE	REFERENCES
***	B	U	23,24,25,26,27,28,29,30,31, 32,36,40,41,43,44,45,51, 52,58,60,65,67,68,69,70, 75,77,79,80,83,84,89,91, 92
10	CRA	A	23,25
13	CRB	A	26,28
9	DDRA	A	24
12	DDRB	A	27
75	DISPLAY	A	95,100
83	HEX	A	76
89	INCR	A	59
51	KEYRL	A	53
***	L	U	15,16
99	MODE	A	61
8	PA	A	30,40,43,51,80,83
11	PB	A	31,77,84
40	SCAN	A	42,46,66,82,85,90
23	START	A	16
***	W	U	33,34,35,78,81

A

Detailed SDK-85 Schematic

Reproduced by permission of Intel Corp.

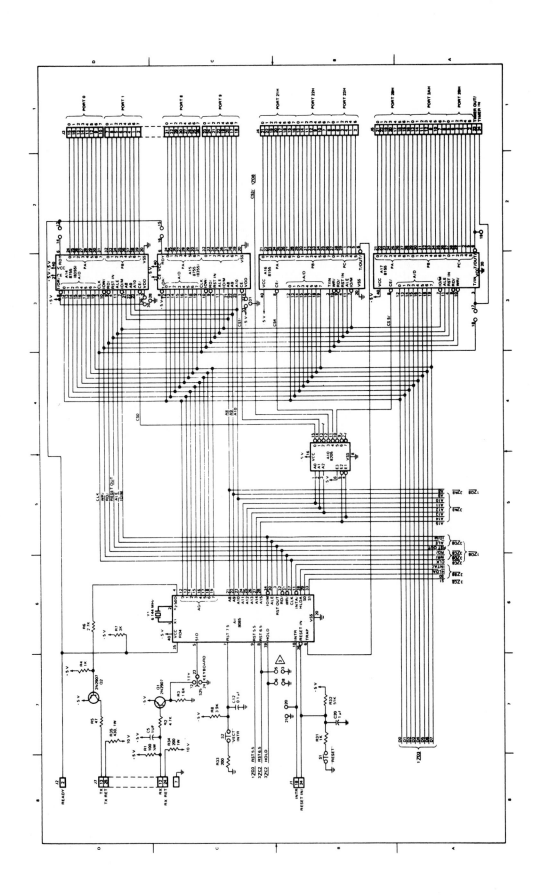

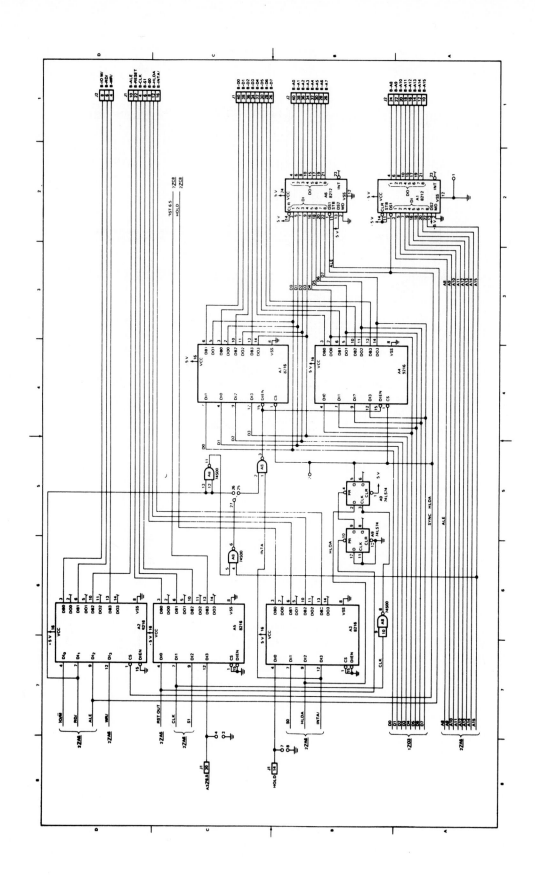

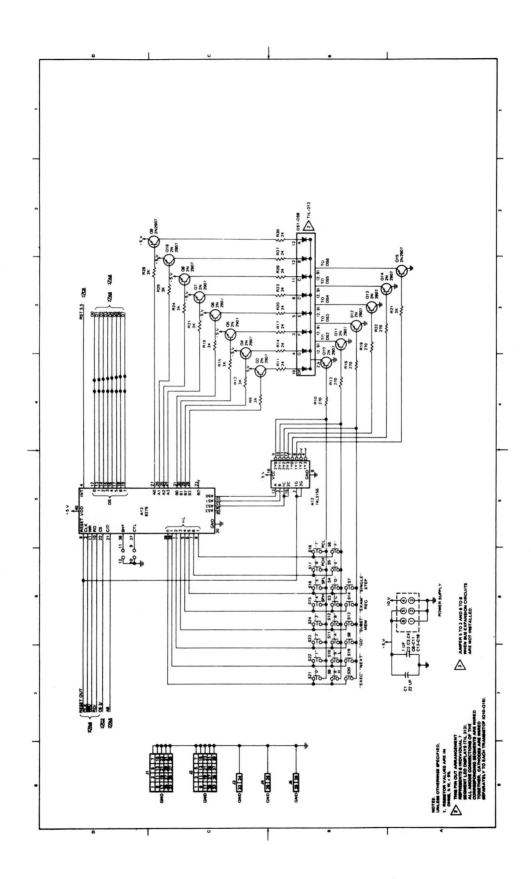

B

SDK-85 Monitor

```
LOC  OBJ        SEQ          SOURCE STATEMENT

                 1 ;****************************************************************
                 2 ;
                 3 ;                    PROGRAM: SDK-85 MONITOR    VER 2.1
                 4 ;
                 5 ;                    COPYRIGHT (C) 1977
                 6 ;                    INTEL CORPORATION
                 7 ;                    3065 BOWERS AVENUE
                 8 ;                    SANTA CLARA, CALIFORNIA  95051
                 9 ;
                10 ;****************************************************************
                11 ;
                12 ; ABSTRACT
                13 ; ========
                14 ;
                15 ; THIS PROGRAM IS A SMALL MONITOR FOR THE INTEL 8085 KIT AND
                16 ; PROVIDES A MINIMUM LEVEL OF UTILITY FUNCTIONS FOR THE USER EMPLOYING
                17 ; EITHER AN INTER-ACTIVE CONSOLE (I.E. TELETYPE) OR THE KIT'S
                18 ; KEYBOARD/LED DISPLAY. THE KEYBOARD MONITOR ALLOWS THE USER TO PERFORM
                19 ; SUCH FUNCTIONS AS MEMORY AND REGISTER MANIPULATION, PROGRAM LOADING,
                20 ; PROGRAM EXECUTION, INTERRUPTION OF AN EXECUTING PROGRAM, AND
                21 ; SYSTEM RESET.
                22 ;
                23 ; PROGRAM ORGANIZATION
                24 ; ======= ============
                25 ;
                26 ; THE PROGRAM IS ORGANIZED AS FOLLOWS :-
                27 ;        1) COLD START ROUTINE (RESET)
                28 ;        2) WARM START - REGISTER SAVE ROUTINE
                29 ;        3) INTERRUPT VECTORS
                30 ;        4) KEYBOARD MONITOR
                31 ;        5) TTY MONITOR
                32 ;        6) LAYOUT OF RAM USAGE
                33 ;
                34 ; THE KEYBOARD MONITOR BEGINS WITH THE COMMAND RECOGNIZER, FOLLOWED BY
                35 ; THE COMMAND ROUTINE SECTION, UTILITY ROUTINE SECTION AND MONITOR
                36 ; TABLES. THE COMMAND AND UTILITY ROUTINES ARE IN ALPHABETICAL ORDER
                37 ; WITHIN THEIR RESPECTIVE SECTIONS.
                38 ; THROUGHOUT THE KEYBOARD MONITOR, A COMMENT FIELD BEGINNING
                39 ; WITH "ARG - " INDICATES A STATEMENT WHICH LOADS A VALUE INTO
                40 ; A REGISTER AS AN ARGUMENT FOR A FUNCTION. WHEN THE DESIRED VALUE
                41 ; LIST OF KEYBOARD MONITOR ROUTINES
                42 ; ==== == ======== ======= ========
                43 ;
                44 ; CMMND
                45 ; -----
                46 ; EXAM
                47 ; GOCMD
                48 ; SSTEP
                49 ; SUBST
                50 ; -----
                51 ; CLEAR
                52 ; CLDIS
                53 ; CLDST
                54 ; DISPC
```

Reproduced by permission of Intel Corp.

```
LOC  OBJ         SEQ         SOURCE STATEMENT

                 55 ; ERR
                 56 ; GTHEX
                 57 ; HXDSP
                 58 ; ININT
                 59 ; INSDG
                 60 ; NXTRG
                 61 ; OUTPT
                 62 ; RDKBD
                 63 ; RETF
                 64 ; RETT
                 65 ; RGLOC
                 66 ; RSTOR
                 67 ; SETRG
                 68 ; UPDAD
                 69 ; UPDDT
                 70 ;
                 71          NAME    SDK85
                 72 ;
                 73 ;••••••••••••••••••••••••••••••••••••••••••••••••••••••••••••••••
                 74 ;
                 75 ;                      SET CONDITIONAL ASSEMBLY FLAG
                 76 ;
                 77 ;••••••••••••••••••••••••••••••••••••••••••••••••••••••••••••••••
                 78 ;
                 79 ;
0000             80 WAITS    SET     0         ;0=NO WAIT STATES
                 81                             ;1=A WAIT STATE IS GENERATED FOR EVERY M CYCLE
                 82                             ;THE APPROPRIATE DELAY TIME MUST BE USED FOR
                 83                             ;   ;TTY DELAY OR SET UP SINGLE
                 84                             ;   ;STEP TIMER FOR EACH CASE
                 85 ;
                 86 ;
                 87 ;••••••••••••••••••••••••••••••••••••••••••••••••••••••••••••••••
                 88 ;
                 89 ;                      MONITOR EQUATES
                 90 ;
                 91 ;••••••••••••••••••••••••••••••••••••••••••••••••••••••••••••••••
                 92 ;
2000             93 RAMST    EQU     2000H     ; START ADDRESS OF RAM - THIS PROGRAM ASSUMES
                 94 ; THAT 256 BYTES OF RANDOM ACCESS MEMORY BEGIN AT THIS ADDRESS.
                 95 ; THE PROGRAM USES STORAGE AT THE END OF THIS SPACE FOR VARIABLES,
                 96 ; SAVING REGISTERS AND THE PROGRAM STACK
                 97 ;
0017             98 RMUSE    EQU     23        ; RAM USAGE - CURRENTLY, 23 BYTES ARE USED FOR
                 99                             ; /SAVING REGISTERS AND VARIABLES
                100 ;
0018            101 SKLN     EQU     24        ; MONITOR STACK USAGE - MAX OF 12 LEVELS
                102 ;
000F            103 UBRLN    EQU     15        ; 5 USER BRANCHES - 3 BYTES EACH
                104 ;
0000            105 ADFLD    EQU     0         ; INDICATES USE OF ADDRESS FIELD OF DISPLAY
0090            106 ADISP    EQU     90H       ; CONTROL CHARACTER TO INDICATE OUTPUT TO
                107                             ; /ADDRESS FIELD OF DISPLAY
1900            108 CNTRL    EQU     1900H     ; ADDRESS FOR SENDING CONTROL CHARACTERS TO
                109                             ; /DISPLAY CHIP
0011            110 COMMA    EQU     11H       ; COMMA FROM KEYBOARD
0300            111 CSNIT    EQU     0         ; INITIAL VALUE FOR COMMAND STATUS REGISTER
0020            112 CSR      EQU     20H       ; OUTPUT PORT FOR COMMAND STATUS REGISTER
0094            113 DDISP    EQU     94H       ; CONTROL CHARACTER TO INDICATE OUTPUT TO
                114                             ; /DATA FIELD OF DISPLAY
0001            115 DOT      EQU     1         ; INDICATOR FOR DOT IN DISPLAY
1800            116 DSPLY    EQU     1800H     ; ADDRESS FOR SENDING CHARACTERS TO DISPLAY
0001            117 DTFLD    EQU     1         ; INDICATES USE OF DATA FIELD OF DISPLAY
0008            118 DTMSK    EQU     08H       ; MASK FOR TURNING ON DOT IN DISPLAY
0080            119 EMPTY    EQU     80H       ; HIGH ORDER 1 INDICATES EMPTY INPUT BUFFER
00CC            120 KBNIT    EQU     0CCH      ; CONTROL CHARACTER TO SET DISPLAY OUTPUT TO
                121                             ; /ALL ONES DURING BLANKING PERIOD
0000            122 KMODE    EQU     0         ; CONTROL CHAR. TO SET KEYBOARD/DISPLAY MODE
                123                             ; (2 KEY ROLLOVER, 8 CHARACTER LEFT ENTRY)
20E9            124 MNSTK    EQU     RAMST + 256 - RMUSE   ;START OF MONITOR STACK
0000            125 NODOT    EQU     0         ; INDICATOR FOR NO DOT IN DISPLAY
                126 ;NUMC - DEFINED LATER      ; NUMBER OF COMMANDS
                127 ;NUMRG - DEFINED LATER     ; NUMBER OF REGISTER SAVE LOCATIONS
0010            128 PERIO    EQU     10H       ; PERIOD FROM KEYBOARD
00FB            129 PRMPT    EQU     0FBH      ; PROMPT CHARACTER FOR DISPLAY (DASH)
0040            130 READ     EQU     40H       ; CONTROL CHARACTER TO INDICATE INPUT FROM
                131                             ; /KEYBOARD
0025            132 TIMHI    EQU     25H       ; OUTPUT PORT FOR HIGH ORDER BYTE OF TIMER VALUE
0024            133 TIMLO    EQU     24H       ; OUTPUT PORT FOR LOW ORDER BYTE OF TIMER VALUE
0040            134 TMODE    EQU     40H       ; TIMER MODE - SQUARE WAVE, AUTO RELOAD
00C0            135 TSTRT    EQU     0C0H      ; START TIMER
000E            136 UNMSK    EQU     0EH       ; UNMASK INPUT INTERRUPT
20C2            137 USRBR    EQU     RAMST + 256 - (RMUSE + SKLN + UBRLN)   ; START OF USER
                138                             ; /BRANCH LOCATIONS
                139          IF      1-WAITS ;TIMER VALUE FOR SINGLE STEP IF NO WAIT STATE
00C5            140 TIMER    EQU     197
                141          ENDIF
```

```
LOC  OBJ        SEQ         SOURCE STATEMENT

                142             IF      WAITS   ;TIMER VALUE FOR SINGLE STEP IF ONE WAIT STATE INSERTED
                143 TIMER       EQU     237
                144             ENDIF
                145 ;
                146 ;**************************************************************
                147 ;
                148 ;                           MONITOR MACROS
                149 ;
                150 ;**************************************************************
                151 ;
                152 TRUE        MACRO   WHERE   ; BRANCH IF FUNCTION RETURNS TRUE
                153             JC      WHERE
                154             ENDM
                155 ;
                156 FALSE       MACRO   WHERE   ; BRANCH IF FUNCTION RETURNS FALSE
                157             JNC     WHERE
                158             ENDM
                159 ;
                160 ;
                161 ;**************************************************************
                162 ;
                163 ; ***** "RESET" KEY ENTRY POINT - COLD START
                164 ; ***** RST 0 ENTRY POINT
                165 ;
0000 3E00       166             MVI     A,KMODE ; GET CONTROL CHARACTER
0002 320019     167             STA     CNTRL   ; SET KEYBOARD/DISPLAY MODE
0005 C3F101     168             JMP     CLDST   ; GO FINISH COLD START
                169 CLDBK:              ; THEN JUMP BACK HERE
                170 ;
                171 ; ***** RST 1 ENTRY POINT - WARM START
                172 ;
0008            173             ORG     8
                174 ;           SAVE REGISTERS
0008 22EF20     175             SHLD    LSAV    ; SAVE H & L REGISTERS
000B E1         176             POP     H       ; GET USER PROGRAM COUNTER FROM TOP OF STACK
000C 22F220     177             SHLD    PSAV    ; /AND SAVE IT
000F F5         178             PUSH    PSW
0010 E1         179             POP     H
0011 22ED20     180             SHLD    FSAV    ; SAVE FLIP/FLOPS & REGISTER A
0014 210000     181             LXI     H,0     ; CLEAR H & L
0017 39         182             DAD     SP      ; GET USER STACK POINTER
0018 22F420     183             SHLD    SSAV    ; /AND SAVE IT
001B 21ED20     184             LXI     H,BSAV+1 ; SET STACK POINTER FOR SAVING
001E F9         185             SPHL            ; /REMAINING REGISTERS
001F C5         186             PUSH    B       ; SAVE B & C
0020 D5         187             PUSH    D       ; SAVE D & E
0021 C33F00     188             JMP     RES10   ; LEAVE ROOM FOR VECTORED INTERRUPTS
                189 ;
                190 ; ***** TIMER INTERRUPT (TRAP) ENTRY POINT (RST 4.5)
0024            191             ORG     24H
0024 C35701     192             JMP     STP25   ; BACK TO SINGLE STEP ROUTINE
                193 ;
                194 ; ***** RST 5 ENTRY POINT
                195 ;
0028            196             ORG     28H
0028 C3C220     197             JMP     RSET5   ; BRANCH TO RST 5 LOCATION IN RAM
                198 ;
                199 ; ***** INPUT INTERRUPT ENTRY POINT (RST 5.5)
                200 ;
002C            201             ORG     2CH
002C C38E02     202             JMP     ININT   ; BRANCH TO INPUT INTERRUPT ROUTINE
                203 ;
                204 ; ***** RST 6 ENTRY POINT
                205 ;
0030            206             ORG     30H
0030 C3C520     207             JMP     RSET6   ; BRANCH TO RST 6 LOCATION IN RAM
                208 ;
                209 ; ***** HARD WIRED USER INTERRUPT ENTRY POINT (RST 6.5)
                210 ;
0034            211             ORG     34H
0034 C3C820     212             JMP     RST65   ; BRANCH TO RST 6.5 LOCATION IN RAM
                213 ;
                214 ; ***** RST 7 ENTRY POINT
                215 ;
0038            216             ORG     38H
0038 C3CB20     217             JMP     RSET7   ; BRANCH TO RST 7 LOCATION IN RAM
                218 ;
                219 ; ***** "VECTORED INTERRUPT" KEY ENTRY POINT (RST 7.5)
003C            220             ORG     3CH
003C C3CE20     221             JMP     USINT   ; BRANCH TO USER INTERRUPT LOCATION IN RAM
                222 ;
                223 RES10:      ; CONTINUE SAVING USER STATUS
003F 20         224             RIM             ; GET USER INTERRUPT STATUS AND INTERRUPT MASK
0040 E60F       225             ANI     0FH     ; KEEP STATUS & MASK BITS
0042 32F120     226             STA     ISAV    ; SAVE INTERRUPT STATUS & MASK
0045 3E0E       227             MVI     A,UNMSK ; UNMASK INTERRUPTS FOR MONITOR USE
0047 30         228             SIM
```

```
LOC  OBJ          SEQ         SOURCE STATEMENT

0048 F3           229         DI                      ; INTERRUPTS DISABLED WHILE MONITOR IS RUNNING
                  230                                 ; (EXCEPT WHEN WAITING FOR INPUT)
0049 20           231         RIM                     ; TTY OR KEYBOARD MONITOR ?
004A 07           232         RLC                     ; IS TTY CONNECTED ?
004B DAFA03       233         JC        GO            ; YES - BRANCH TO TTY MONITOR
                  234                                 ; NO - ENTER KEYBOARD MONITOR
                  235  ;
                  236  ;******************************************************************
                  237  ;
                  238  ;                           BEGINNING OF KEYBOARD MONITOR CODE
                  239  ;
                  240  ;******************************************************************
                  241  ;
                  242  ;           OUTPUT SIGN-ON MESSAGE
004E AF           243         XRA       A             ; ARG - USE ADDRESS FIELD OF DISPLAY
004F 0600         244         MVI       B,NODOT       ; ARG - NO DOT IN ADDRESS FIELD
0051 21A603       245         LXI       H,SGNAD       ; ARG - GET ADDRESS OF ADDRESS FIELD PORTION OF
                  246                                 ; /SIGN-ON MESSAGE
0054 CDB702       247         CALL      OUTPT         ; OUTPUT SIGN-ON MESSAGE TO ADDRESS FIELD
0057 3E01         248         MVI       A,DTFLD       ; ARG - USE DATA FIELD OF DISPLAY
0059 0600         249         MVI       B,NODOT       ; ARG - NO DOT IN DATA FIELD
005B 21AA03       250         LXI       H,SGNDT       ; ARG - GET ADDRESS OF DATA FIELD PORTION OF
                  251                                 ; /SIGN-ON MESSAGE
005E CDB702       252         CALL      OUTPT         ; OUTPUT SIGN-ON MESSAGE TO DATA FIELD
0061 3E80         253         MVI       A,EMPTY
0063 32FE20       254         STA       IBUFF         ; SET INPUT BUFFER EMPTY FLAG
                  255  ;
                  256  ;******************************************************************
                  257  ;
                  258  ; FUNCTION: CMMND - COMMAND RECOGNIZER
                  259  ; INPUTS: NONE
                  260  ; OUTPUTS: NONE
                  261  ; CALLS: RDKBD,ERR,SUBST,EXAM,GOCMD,SSTEP
                  262  ; DESTROYS: A,B,C,D,E,H,L,F/F'S
                  263  ;
                  264  CMMND:
0066 21E920       265         LXI       H,MNSTK       ; INITIALIZE MONITOR STACK POINTER
0069 F9           266         SPHL
                  267                                 ; OUTPUT PROMPT CHARACTER TO DISPLAY
006A 210019       268         LXI       H,CNTRL       ; GET ADDRESS FOR CONTROL CHARACTER
006D 3690         269         MVI       M,ADISP       ; OUTPUT CONTROL CHARACTER TO USE ADDRESS FIELD
006F 25           270         DCR       H             ; ADDRESS FOR OUTPUT CHARACTER
0070 36FB         271         MVI       M,PRMPT       ; OUTPUT PROMPT CHARACTER
0072 CDE702       272         CALL      RDKBD         ; READ KEYBOARD
0075 010400       273         LXI       B,NUMC        ; COUNTER FOR NUMBER OF COMMANDS IN C
0078 217803       274         LXI       H,CMDTB       ; GET ADDRESS OF COMMAND TABLE
                  275  CMD10:
007B BE           276         CMP       M             ; RECOGNIZE THE COMMAND ?
007C CA8700       277         JZ        CMD15         ; YES - GO PROCESS IT
007F 23           278         INX       H             ; NO - NEXT COMMAND TABLE ENTRY
0080 0D           279         DCR       C             ; END OF TABLE ?
0081 C27B00       280         JNZ       CMD10         ; NO - GO CHECK NEXT ENTRY
                  281                                 ; YES - COMMAND UNKNOWN
0084 C31502       282         JMP       ERR           ; DISPLAY ERROR MESSAGE AND GET ANOTHER COMMAND
                  283  CMD15:
0087 217C03       284         LXI       H,CMDAD       ; GET ADDRESS OF COMMAND ADDRESS TABLE
008A 0D           285         DCR       C             ; ADJUST COMMAND COUNTER
                  286                                 ; COUNTER ACTS AS POINTER TO COMMAND ADDRESS TABLE
008B 09           287         DAD       B             ; ADD POINTER TO TABLE ADDRESS TWICE BECAUSE
008C 09           288         DAD       B             ; TABLE HAS 2 BYTE ENTRIES
008D 7E           289         MOV       A,M           ; GET LOW ORDER BYTE OF COMMAND ADDRESS
008E 23           290         INX       H
008F 66           291         MOV       H,M           ; GET HIGH ORDER BYTE OF COMMAND ADDRESS IN H
0090 6F           292         MOV       L,A           ; PUT LOW ORDER BYTE IN L
                  293                                 ; COMMAND ROUTINE ADDRESS IS NOW IN H & L
0091 E9           294         PCHL                    ; BRANCH TO ADDRESS IN H & L
                  295  ;
                  296  ;******************************************************************
                  297  ;
                  298  ;                           COMMAND ROUTINES
                  299  ;
                  300  ;******************************************************************
                  301  ;
                  302  ; FUNCTION: EXAM - EXAMINE AND MODIFY REGISTERS
                  303  ; INPUTS: NONE
                  304  ; OUTPUTS: NONE
                  305  ; CALLS: CLEAR,SETRG,ERR,RGNAM,RGLOC,UPDDT,GTHEX,NXTRG
                  306  ; DESTROYS: A,B,C,D,E,H,L,F/F'S
                  307  ;
                  308  EXAM:
0092 0601         309         MVI       B,DOT         ; ARG - DOT IN ADDRESS FIELD OF DISPLAY
0094 CDD701       310         CALL      CLEAR         ; CLEAR DISPLAY
0097 CD4403       311         CALL      SETRG         ; GET REGISTER DESIGNATOR FROM KEYBOARD AND
                  312                                 ; /SET REGISTER POINTER ACCORDINGLY
                  313                                 ; WAS CHARACTER A REGISTER DESIGNATOR?
                  314         FALSE     ERR           ; NO - DISPLAY ERROR MSG. AND TERMINATE COMMAND
009A D21502       315+        JNC       ERR
```

```
                          316 EXM05:
009D CD0903               317          CALL     RGNAM    ; OUTPUT REGISTER NAME TO ADDRESS FIELD
00A0 CDFC02               318          CALL     RGLOC    ; GET REGISTER SAVE LOCATION IN H & L
00A3 7E                   319          MOV      A,M      ; GET REGISTER CONTENTS
00A4 32F820               320          STA      CURDT    ; STORE REGISTER CONTENTS AT CURRENT DATA
00A7 0601                 321          MVI      B,DOT    ; ARG - DOT IN DATA FIELD
00A9 CD6B03               322          CALL     UPDDT    ; UPDATE DATA FIELD OF DISPLAY
00AC 0601                 323          MVI      B,DTFLD  ; ARG - USE DATA FIELD OF DISPLAY
00AE CD2B02               324          CALL     GTHEX    ; GET HEX DIGITS - WERE ANY DIGITS RECEIVED?
                          325          FALSE    EXM10    ; NO - DO NOT UPDATE REGISTER CONTENTS
00B1 D2B800               326+         JNC      EXM10
00B4 CDFC02               327          CALL     RGLOC    ; YES - GET REGISTER SAVE LOCATION IN H & L
00B7 73                   328          MOV      M,E      ; UPDATE REGISTER CONTENTS
                          329 EXM10:
00B8 FE10                 330          CPI      PERIO    ; WAS LAST CHARACTER A PERIOD ?
00BA CAE901               331          JZ       CLDIS    ; YES - CLEAR DISPLAY AND TERMINATE COMMAND
00BD FE11                 332          CPI      COMMA    ; WAS LAST CHARACTER ',' ?
00BF C21502               333          JNZ      ERR      ; NO - DISPLAY ERROR MSG. AND TERMINATE COMMAND
00C2 CDA802               334          CALL     NXTRG    ; YES - ADVANCE REGISTER POINTER TO
                          335                            ;/NEXT REGISTER
                          336                            ; ANY MORE REGISTERS ?
                          337          TRUE     EXM05    ; YES - CONTINUE PROCESSING WITH NEXT REGISTER
00C5 DA9D00               338+         JC       EXM05
00C8 C3E901               339          JMP      CLDIS    ; NO - CLEAR DISPLAY AND TERMINATE COMMAND
                          340 ;
                          341 ;************************************************************
                          342 ;
                          343 ; FUNCTION: GOCMD - EXECUTE USER PROGRAM
                          344 ; INPUTS: NONE
                          345 ; OUTPUTS: NONE
                          346 ; CALLS: DISPC,RDKBD,CLEAR,GTHEX,ERR,OUTPT
                          347 ; DESTROYS: A,B,C,D,E,H,L,F/F'S
                          348 ;
                          349 GOCMD:
00CB CD0002               350          CALL     DISPC    ; DISPLAY USER PROGRAM COUNTER
00CE CDE702               351          CALL     RDKBD    ; READ FROM KEYBOARD
00D1 FE10                 352          CPI      PERIO    ; IS CHARACTER A PERIOD ?
00D3 CAEC00               353          JZ       G10      ; YES - GO EXECUTE THE COMMAND
                          354                            ; NO - ARG - CHARACTER IS STILL IN A
00D6 32FE20               355          STA      IBUFF    ; REPLACE CHARACTER IN INPUT BUFFER
00D9 0601                 356          MVI      B,DOT    ; ARG - DOT IN ADDRESS FIELD
00DB CDD701               357          CALL     CLEAR    ; CLEAR DISPLAY
00DE 0600                 358          MVI      B,ADFLD  ; ARG - USE ADDRESS FIELD
00E0 CD2B02               359          CALL     GTHEX    ; GET HEX DIGITS
00E3 FE10                 360          CPI      PERIO    ; WAS LAST CHARACTER A PERIOD ?
00E5 C21502               361          JNZ      ERR      ; NO - DISPLAY ERROR MSG. AND TERMINATE COMMAND
00E8 EB                   362          XCHG              ; PUT HEX VALUE FROM GTHEX TO H & L
00E9 22F220               363          SHLD     PSAV     ; HEX VALUE IS NEW USER PC
                          364 G10:
00EC 0600                 365          MVI      B,NODOT  ; YES - ARG - NO DOT IN ADDRESS FIELD
00EE CDD701               366          CALL     CLEAR    ; CLEAR DISPLAY
00F1 AF                   367          XRA      A        ; ARG - USE ADDRESS FIELD OF DISPLAY
00F2 0600                 368          MVI      B,NODOT  ; ARG - NO DOT IN ADDRESS FIELD
00F4 21A203               369          LXI      H,EXMSG  ; GET ADDRESS OF EXECUTION MESSAGE IN H & L
00F7 CDB702               370          CALL     OUTPT    ; DISPLAY EXECUTION MESSAGE
00FA C31B03               371          JMP      RSTOR    ; RESTORE USER REGISTERS INCL. PROGRAM COUNTER
                          372                            ;/I.E. BEGIN EXECUTION OF USER PROGRAM
                          373 ;
                          374 ;************************************************************
                          375 ;
                          376 ; FUNCTION: SSTEP - SINGLE STEP (EXECUTE ONE USER INSTRUCTION)
                          377 ; INPUTS: NONE
                          378 ; OUTPUTS: NONE
                          379 ; CALLS: DISPC,RDKBD,CLEAR,GTHEX,ERR
                          380 ; DESTROYS: A,B,C,D,E,H,L,F/F'S
                          381 ;
                          382 SSTEP:
00FD CD0002               383          CALL     DISPC    ; DISPLAY USER PROGRAM COUNTER
0100 CDE702               384          CALL     RDKBD    ; READ FROM KEYBOARD
0103 FE10                 385          CPI      PERIO    ; WAS CHARACTER A PERIOD ?
0105 CAE901               386          JZ       CLDIS    ; YES - CLEAR DISPLAY AND TERMINATE COMMAND
0108 FE11                 387          CPI      COMMA    ; WAS LAST CHARACTER ',' ?
010A CA2601               388          JZ       STP20    ; YES - GO SET TIMER
                          389                            ; NO - CHARACTER FROM KEYBOARD WAS NEITHER PERIOD NOR COMMA
010D 32FE20               390          STA      IBUFF    ; REPLACE THE CHARACTER IN THE INPUT BUFFER
0110 0601                 391          MVI      B,DOT    ; ARG - DOT IN ADDRESS FIELD
0112 CDD701               392          CALL     CLEAR    ; CLEAR DISPLAY
0115 0600                 393          MVI      B,ADFLD  ; ARG - USE ADDRESS FIELD OF DISPLAY
0117 CD2B02               394          CALL     GTHEX    ; GET HEX DIGITS - WERE ANY DIGITS RECEIVED ?
                          395          FALSE    ERR      ; NO - DISPLAY ERROR MSG. AND TERMINATE COMMAND
011A D21502               396+         JNC      ERR
011D EB                   397          XCHG              ; HEX VALUE FROM GTHEX TO H & L
011E 22F220               398          SHLD     PSAV     ; HEX VALUE IS NEW USER PC
0121 FE10                 399          CPI      PERIO    ; WAS LAST CHARACTER FROM GTHEX A PERIOD ?
0123 CAE901               400          JZ       CLDIS    ; YES - CLEAR DISPLAY AND TERMINATE COMMAND
                          401                            ; NO - MUST HAVE BEEN A COMMA
                          402 STP20:
```

```
LOC  OBJ        SEQ      SOURCE STATEMENT

0126 3AF120     403         LDA    ISAV     ; GET USER INTERRUPT MASK
0129 E608       404         ANI    08H      ; KEEP INTERRUPT STATUS
012B 32FD20     405         STA    TEMP     ; SAVE USER INTERRUPT STATUS
012E 2AF220     406         LHLD   PSAV     ; GET USER PC
0131 7E         407         MOV    A,M      ; GET USER INSTRUCTION
0132 FEF3       408         CPI    (DI)     ; DI INSTRUCTION ?
0134 C23B01     409         JNZ    STP21    ; NO
0137 AF         410         XRA    A     .  ; YES - RESET USER INTERRUPT STATUS
0138 C34201     411         JMP    STP22
                412 STP21:
013B FEFB       413         CPI    (EI)     ; EI INSTRUCTION ?
013D C24501     414         JNZ    STP23    ; NO
0140 3E08       415         MVI    A,08H    ; YES - SET USER INTERRUPT STATUS
                416 STP22:
0142 32FD20     417         STA    TEMP     ; SAVE NEW USER INTERRUPT STATUS
                418 STP23:
0145 3E40       419         MVI    A,(TIMER SHR 8) OR TMODE ; HIGH ORDER BITS OF TIMER VALUE
                420                                   ; /OR'ED WITH TIMER MODE
0147 D325       421         OUT    TIMHI
0149 3EC5       422         MVI    A,TIMER AND 0FFH ; LOW ORDER BITS OF TIMER VALUE
014B D324       423         OUT    TIMLO
014D 3AFF20     424         LDA    USCSR    ; GET USER IMAGE OF WHAT'S IN CSR
0150 F6C0       425         ORI    TSTRT    ; SET TIMER COMMAND BITS TO START TIMER
0152 D320       426         OUT    CSR      ; START TIMER
0154 C31B03     427         JMP    RSTOR    ; RESTORE USER REGISTERS
                428 ;
                429 STP25:                  ; BRANCH HERE WHEN TIMER INTERRUPTS AFTER
                430                          ;/ONE USER INSTRUCTION
0157 F5         431         PUSH   PSW      ; SAVE PSW
0158 3AFF20     432         LDA    USCSR    ; GET USER IMAGE OF WHAT'S IN CSR
015B E63F       433         ANI    3FH      ; CLEAR 2 HIGH ORDER BITS
015D F640       434         ORI    40H      ; SET TIMER STOP BIT
015F D320       435         OUT    CSR      ; STOP TIMER
0161 F1         436         POP    PSW      ; RETRIEVE PSW
0162 22EF20     437         SHLD   LSAV     ; SAVE H & L
0165 E1         438         POP    H        ; GET USER PROGRAM COUNTER FROM TOP OF STACK
0166 22F220     439         SHLD   PSAV     ; SAVE USER PC
0169 F5         440         PUSH   PSW
016A E1         441         POP    H
016B 22ED20     442         SHLD   FSAV     ; SAVE FLIP/FLOPS AND A REGISTER
016E 210000     443         LXI    H,0      ; CLEAR H & L
0171 39         444         DAD    SP       ; GET USER STACK POINTER
0172 22F420     445         SHLD   SSAV     ; SAVE USER STACK POINTER
0175 21ED20     446         LXI    H,BSAV+1          ; SET MONITOR STACK POINTER FOR
0178 F9         447         SPHL            ;/SAVING REMAINING USER REGISTERS
0179 C5         448         PUSH   B        ; SAVE B & C
017A D5         449         PUSH   D        ; SAVE D & E
017B 20         450         RIM             ; GET USER INTERRUPT MASK
017C E607       451         ANI    07H      ; KEEP MASK BITS
017E 21FD20     452         LXI    H,TEMP   ; GET USER INTERRUPT STATUS
0181 B6         453         ORA    M        ; OR IT INTO MASK
0182 32F120     454         STA    ISAV     ; SAVE INTERRUPT STATUS & MASK
0185 3E0E       455         MVI    A,UNMSK  ; UNMASK INTERRUPTS FOR MONITOR USE
0187 30         456         SIM
0188 C3FD00     457         JMP    SSTEP    ; GO GET READY FOR ANOTHER INSTRUCTION
                458 ;
                459 ;**********************************************************************
                460 ;
                461 ; FUNCTION: SUBST - SUBSTITUTE MEMORY
                462 ; INPUTS: NONE
                463 ; OUTPUTS: NONE
                464 ; CALLS: CLEAR,GTHEX,UPDAD,UPDDT,ERR
                465 ; DESTROYS: A,B,C,D,E,H,L,F/F'S
                466 ;
                467 SUBST:
018B 0601       468         MVI    B,DOT    ; ARG - DOT IN ADDRESS FIELD
018D CDD701     469         CALL   CLEAR    ; CLEAR THE DISPLAY
0190 0600       470         MVI    B,ADFLD  ; ARG - USE ADDRESS FIELD OF DISPLAY
0192 CD2B02     471         CALL   GTHEX    ; GET HEX DIGITS - WERE ANY DIGITS RECEIVED?
                472         FALSE  ERR      ; NO - DISPLAY ERROR MSG. AND TERMINATE COMMAND
0195 D21502     473+        JNC    ERR
0198 EB         474         XCHG            ; ASSIGN HEX VALUE RETURNED BY GTHEX TO
0199 22F620     475         SHLD   CURAD    ; / CURRENT ADDRESS
                476 SUB05:
019C FE11       477         CPI    COMMA    ; WAS ',' THE LAST CHARACTER FROM KEYBOARD?
019E C2CF01     478         JNZ    SUB15    ; NO - GO TERMINATE THE COMMAND
01A1 0600       479         MVI    B,NODOT  ; ARG - NO DOT IN ADDRESS FIELD
01A3 CD5F03     480         CALL   UPDAD    ; UPDATE ADDRESS FIELD OF DISPLAY
01A6 2AF620     481         LHLD   CURAD    ; GET CURRENT ADDRESS IN H & L
01A9 7E         482         MOV    A,M      ; GET DATA BYTE POINTED TO BY CURRENT ADDRESS
01AA 32F820     483         STA    CURDT    ; STORE DATA BYTE AT CURRENT DATA
01AD 0601       484         MVI    B,DOT    ; ARG - DOT IN DATA FIELD
01AF CD6B03     485         CALL   UPDDT    ; UPDATE DATA FIELD OF DISPLAY
01B2 0601       486         MVI    B,DTFLD  ; ARG - USE DATA FIELD
01B4 CD2B02     487         CALL   GTHEX    ; GET HEX DIGITS - WERE ANY HEX DIGITS RECEIVED?
01B7 F5         488         PUSH   PSW      ; (SAVE LAST CHARACTER)
                489         FALSE  SUB10    ; NO - LEAVE DATA UNCHANGED AT CURRENT ADDRESS
```

```
LOC  OBJ          SEQ         SOURCE STATEMENT

0188 D2C401       490+        JNC     SUB10
01BB 2AF620       491         LHLD    CURAD   ; YES - GET CURRENT ADDRESS IN H & L
01BE 73           492         MOV     M,E     ; STORE NEW DATA AT CURRENT ADDRESS
                  493                         ; MAKE SURE DATA WAS ACTUALLY STORED IN CASE
                  494                         ;/CURRENT ADDRESS IS IN ROM OR IS NON-EXISTANT
01BF 7B           495         MOV     A,E     ; DATA TO A FOR COMPARISON
01C0 BE           496         CMP     M       ; WAS DATA STORED CORRECTLY?
01C1 C21502       497         JNZ     ERR     ; NO - DISPLAY ERROR MSG. AND TERMINATE COMMAND
                  498 SUB10:
01C4 2AF620       499         LHLD    CURAD   ; INCREMENT CURRENT ADDRESS
01C7 23           500         INX     H
01C8 22F620       501         SHLD    CURAD
01CB F1           502         POP     PSW     ; RETRIEVE LAST CHARACTER
01CC C39C01       503         JMP     SUB05   ;
                  504 SUB15:
01CF FE10         505         CPI     PERIO   ; WAS LAST CHARACTER '.' ?
01D1 C21502       506         JNZ     ERR     ; NO - DISPLAY ERROR MSG. AND TERMINATE COMMAND
01D4 C3E901       507         JMP     CLDIS   ; YES - CLEAR DISPLAY AND TERMINATE COMMAND
                  508 ;
                  509 ;
                  510 ;********************************************************************
                  511 ;
                  512 ;                         UTILITY ROUTINES
                  513 ;
                  514 ;********************************************************************
                  515 ;
                  516 ; FUNCTION: CLEAR - CLEAR THE DISPLAY
                  517 ; INPUTS: B - DOT FLAG - 1 MEANS PUT DOT IN ADDRESS FIELD OF DISPLAY
                  518 ;                     - 0 MEANS NO DOT
                  519 ; OUTPUTS: NONE
                  520 ; CALLS: OUTPT
                  521 ; DESTROYS: A,B,C,D,E,H,L,F/F'S
                  522 ; DESCRIPTION:  CLEAR SENDS BLANK CHARACTERS TO BOTH THE ADDRESS FIELD
                  523 ;               AND THE DATA FIELD OF THE DISPLAY. IF THE DOT FLAG IS
                  524 ;               SET THEN A DOT WILL APPEAR AT THE RIGHT EDGE OF THE
                  525 ;               ADDRESS FIELD.
                  526 ;
                  527 CLEAR:
01D7 AF           528         XRA     A       ; ARG - USE ADDRESS FIELD OF DISPLAY
                  529                         ; ARG - FLAG FOR DOT IN ADDR. FIELD IS IN B
01D8 219A03       530         LXI     H,BLNKS ; ARG - ADDRESS OF BLANKS FOR DISPLAY
01DB CDB702       531         CALL    OUTPT   ; OUTPUT BLANKS TO ADDRESS FIELD
01DE 3E01         532         MVI     A,DTFLD ; ARG - USE DATA FIELD OF DISPLAY
01E0 0600         533         MVI     B,NODOT ; ARG - NO DOT IN DATA FIELD
01E2 219A03       534         LXI     H,BLNKS ; ARG - ADDRESS OF BLANKS FOR DISPLAY
01E5 CDB702       535         CALL    OUTPT   ; OUTPUT BLANKS TO DATA FIELD
01E8 C9           536         RET             ; RETURN
                  537 ;
                  538 ;********************************************************************
                  539 ;
                  540 ; FUNCTION: CLDIS - CLEAR DISPLAY AND TERMINATE COMMAND
                  541 ; INPUTS: NONE
                  542 ; OUTPUTS: NONE
                  543 ; CALLS: CLEAR
                  544 ; DESTROYS: A,B,C,D,E,H,L,F/F'S
                  545 ; DESCRIPTION: CLDIS IS JUMPED TO BY COMMAND ROUTINES WISHING TO
                  546 ;              TERMINATE NORMALLY. CLDIS CLEARS THE DISPLAY AND
                  547 ;              BRANCHES TO THE COMMAND RECOGNIZER.
                  548 ;
                  549 CLDIS:
01E9 0600         550         MVI     B,NODOT ; ARG - NO DOT IN ADDRESS FIELD
01EB CDD701       551         CALL    CLEAR   ; CLEAR THE DISPLAY
01EE C36600       552         JMP     CMMND   ; GO GET ANOTHER COMMAND
                  553 ;
                  554 ;********************************************************************
                  555 ;
                  556 ; FUNCTION: CLDST - COLD START
                  557 ; INPUTS: NONE
                  558 ; OUTPUTS: NONE
                  559 ; CALLS: NOTHING
                  560 ; DESTROYS: A
                  561 ; DESCRIPTION:  CLDST IS JUMPED TO BY THE MAIN COLD START PROCEDURE,
                  562 ;               COMPLETES COLD START INITIALIZATION, AND JUMPS BACK
                  563 ;               TO THE MAIN COLD START PROCEDURE.
                  564 ;
                  565 CLDST:
01F1 3ECC         566         MVI     A,KBNIT ; GET CONTROL CHARACTER
01F3 320019       567         STA     CNTRL   ; INITIALIZE KEYBOARD/DISPLAY BLANKING
01F6 3E00         568         MVI     A,CSNIT ; INITIAL VALUE OF COMMAND STATUS REGISTER
01F8 D320         569         OUT     CSR     ; INITIALIZE CSR
01FA 32FF20       570         STA     USCSR   ; INITIALIZE USER CSR VALUE
01FD C30800       571         JMP     CLDBK   ; BACK TO MAIN PROCEDURE
                  572 ;
                  573 ;********************************************************************
                  574 ;
                  575 ; FUNCTION: DISPC - DISPLAY PROGRAM COUNTER
                  576 ; INPUTS: NONE
```

```
                        577 ; OUTPUTS: NONE
                        578 ; CALLS: UPDAD,UPDDT
                        579 ; DESTROYS: A,B,C,D,E,H,L,F/F'S
                        580 ; DESCRIPTION: DISPC DISPLAYS THE USER PROGRAM COUNTER IN THE ADDRESS
                        581 ;              FIELD OF THE DISPLAY, WITH A DOT AT THE RIGHT EDGE
                        582 ;              OF THE FIELD. THE BYTE OF DATA ADDRESSED BY THE PROGRAM
                        583 ;              COUNTER IS DISPLAYED IN THE DATA FIELD OF THE DISPLAY.
                        584 ;
                        585 DISPC:
0200 2AF220            586        LHLD     PSAV      ; GET USER PROGRAM COUNTER
0203 22F620            587        SHLD     CURAD     ; MAKE IT THE CURRENT ADDRESS
0206 7E                588        MOV      A,M       ; GET THE INSTRUCTION AT THAT ADDRESS
0207 32F820            589        STA      CURDT     ; MAKE IT THE CURRENT DATA
020A 0601             590        MVI      B,DOT     ; ARG - DOT IN ADDRESS FIELD
020C CD5F03            591        CALL     UPDAD     ; UPDATE ADDRESS FIELD OF DISPLAY
020F 0600             592        MVI      B,NODOT   ; ARG - NO DOT IN DATA FIELD
0211 CD6B03            593        CALL     UPDDT     ; UPDATE DATA FIELD OF DISPLAY
0214 C9                594        RET
                        595 ;
                        596 ;**************************************************************
                        597 ;
                        598 ; FUNCTION: ERR - DISPLAY ERROR MESSAGE
                        599 ; INPUTS: NONE
                        600 ; OUTPUTS: NONE
                        601 ; CALLS: OUTPT
                        602 ; DESTROYS: A,B,C,D,E,H,L,F/F'S
                        603 ; DESCRIPTION: ERR IS JUMPED TO BY COMMAND ROUTINES WISHING TO
                        604 ;              TERMINATE BECAUSE OF AN ERROR.
                        605 ;              ERR OUTPUTS AN ERROR MESSAGE TO THE DISPLAY AND
                        606 ;              BRANCHES TO THE COMMAND RECOGNIZER.
                        607 ;
                        608 ERR:
0215 AF                609        XRA      A         ; ARG - USE ADDRESS FIELD
0216 0600             610        MVI      B,NODOT   ; ARG - NO DOT IN ADDRESS FIELD
0218 219E03            611        LXI      H,ERMSG   ; ARG - ADDRESS OF ERROR MESSAGE
021B CDB702            612        CALL     OUTPT     ; OUTPUT ERROR MESSAGE TO ADDRESS FIELD
021E 3E01             613        MVI      A,DTFLD   ; ARG - USE DATA FIELD
0220 0600             614        MVI      B,NODOT   ; ARG - NO DOT IN DATA FIELD
0222 219A03            615        LXI      H,BLNKS   ; ARG - ADDRESS OF BLANKS FOR DISPLAY
0225 CDB702            616        CALL     OUTPT     ; OUTPUT BLANKS TO DATA FIELD
0228 C36600            617        JMP      CMMND     ; GO GET A NEW COMMAND
                        618 ;
                        619 ;**************************************************************
                        620 ;
                        621 ; FUNCTION: GTHEX - GET HEX DIGITS
                        622 ; INPUTS: B - DISPLAY FLAG - 0 MEANS USE ADDRESS FIELD OF DISPLAY
                        623 ;                         - 1 MEANS USE DATA FIELD OF DISPLAY
                        624 ; OUTPUTS: A - LAST CHARACTER READ FROM KEYBOARD
                        625 ;          DE - HEX DIGITS FROM KEYBOARD EVALUATED MODULO 2**16
                        626 ;          CARRY - SET IF AT LEAST ONE VALID HEX DIGIT WAS READ
                        627 ;                - RESET OTHERWISE
                        628 ; CALLS: RDKBD,INSDG,HXDSP,OUTPT
                        629 ; DESTROYS: A,B,C,D,E,H,L,F/F'S
                        630 ; DESCRIPTION: GTHEX ACCEPTS A STRING OF HEX DIGITS FROM THE KEYBOARD,
                        631 ;              DISPLAYS THEM AS THEY ARE RECEIVED, AND RETURNS THEIR
                        632 ;              VALUE AS A 16 BIT INTEGER. IF MORE THAN 4 HEX DIGITS
                        633 ;              ARE RECEIVED, ONLY THE LAST 4 ARE USED. IF THE DISPLAY
                        634 ;              FLAG IS SET, THE LAST 2 HEX DIGITS ARE DISPLAYED IN THE
                        635 ;              DATA FIELD OF THE DISPLAY. OTHERWISE, THE LAST 4 HEX
                        636 ;              DIGITS ARE DISPLAYED IN THE ADDRESS FIELD OF THE
                        637 ;              DISPLAY. IN EITHER CASE, A DOT WILL BE DISPLAYED AT THE
                        638 ;              RIGHTMOST EDGE OF THE FIELD. A CHARACTER WHICH IS NOT
                        639 ;              A HEX DIGIT TERMINATES THE STRING AND IS RETURNED AS
                        640 ;              AN OUTPUT OF THE FUNCTION. IF THE TERMINATOR IS NOT
                        641 ;              A PERIOD OR A COMMA THEN ANY HEX DIGITS WHICH MAY HAVE
                        642 ;              BEEN RECEIVED ARE CONSIDERED TO BE INVALID. THE
                        643 ;              FUNCTION RETURNS A FLAG INDICATING WHETHER OR NOT ANY
                        644 ;              VALID HEX DIGITS WERE RECEIVED.
                        645 ;
                        646 GTHEX:
022B 0E00             647        MVI      C,0       ; RESET HEX DIGIT FLAG
022D C5                648        PUSH     B         ; SAVE DISPLAY AND HEX DIGIT FLAGS
022E 110000            649        LXI      D,0       ; SET HEX VALUE TO ZERO
0231 D5                650        PUSH     D         ; SAVE HEX VALUE
                        651 GTH05:
0232 CDE702            652        CALL     RDKBD     ; READ KEYBOARD
0235 FE10             653        CPI      10H       ; IS CHARACTER A HEX DIGIT?
0237 D25502            654        JNC      GTH20     ; NO - GO CHECK FOR TERMINATOR
                        655                          ; YES - ARG - NEW HEX DIGIT IS IN A
023A D1                656        POP      D         ; ARG - RETRIEVE HEX VALUE
023B CD9F02            657        CALL     INSDG     ; INSERT NEW DIGIT IN HEX VALUE
023E C1                658        POP      B         ; RETRIEVE DISPLAY FLAG
023F 0E01             659        MVI      C,1       ; SET HEX DIGIT FLAG
                        660                          ;/(I.E. A HEX DIGIT HAS BEEN READ)
0241 C5                661        PUSH     B         ; SAVE DISPLAY AND HEX DIGIT FLAGS
0242 D5                662        PUSH     D         ; SAVE HEX VALUE
0243 78                663        MOV      A,B       ; TEST DISPLAY FLAG
```

```
LOC  OBJ           SEQ         SOURCE STATEMENT

0244 0F            664         RRC               ; SHOULD ADDRESS FIELD OF DISPLAY BE USED ?
0245 D24902        665         JNC    GTH10       ; YES - USE HEX VALUE AS IS
                   666                            . NO - ONLY LOW ORDER BYTE OF HEX VALUE SHOULD
                   667                            ; /BE USED FOR DATA FIELD OF DISPLAY
0248 53            668         MOV    D,E         ; PUT LOW ORDER BYTE OF HEX VALUE IN D
                   669 GTH10:
                   670                            ; ARG - HEX VALUE TO BE EXPANDED IS IN D & E
0249 CD6C02        671         CALL   HXDSP       ; EXPAND HEX VALUE FOR DISPLAY
                   672                            ; ARG - ADDRESS OF EXPANDED HEX VALUE IN H & L
024C 78            673         MOV    A,B         ; ARG - PUT DISPLAY FLAG IN A
024D 0601          674         MVI    B,DOT       ; ARG - DOT IN APPROPRIATE FIELD
024F CDB702        675         CALL   OUTPT       ; OUTPUT HEX VALUE TO DISPLAY
0252 C33202        676         JMP    GTH05       ; GO GET NEXT CHARACTER
                   677 GTH20:                     ; LAST CHARACTER WAS NOT A HEX DIGIT
0255 D1            678         POP    D           ; RETRIEVE HEX VALUE
0256 C1            679         POP    B           ; RETRIEVE HEX DIGIT FLAG IN C
0257 FE11          680         CPI    COMMA       ; WAS LAST CHARACTER ',' ?
0259 CA6702        681         JZ     GTH25       ; YES - READY TO RETURN
025C FE10          682         CPI    PERIO       ; NO - WAS LAST CHARACTER '.' ?
025E CA6702        683         JZ     GTH25       ; YES - READY TO RETURN
                   684                            ; NO - INVALID TERMINATOR - IGNORE ANY HEX DIGITS READ
0261 110000        685         LXI    D,0         ; SET HEX VALUE TO ZERO
0264 C3F702        686         JMP    RETF        ; RETURN FALSE
                   687 GTH25:
0267 47            688         MOV    B,A         ; SAVE LAST CHARACTER
0268 79            689         MOV    A,C         ; SHIFT HEX DIGIT FLAG TO
0269 0F            690         RRC                ;/CARRY BIT
026A 78            691         MOV    A,B         ; RESTORE LAST CHARACTER
026B C9            692         RET                ; RETURN
                   693 ;
                   694 ;********************************************************************
                   695 ;
                   696 ; FUNCTION: HXDSP - EXPAND HEX DIGITS FOR DISPLAY
                   697 ; INPUTS: DE - 4 HEX DIGITS
                   698 ; OUTPUTS: HL - ADDRESS OF OUTPUT BUFFER
                   699 ; CALLS: NOTHING
                   700 ; DESTROYS: A,H,L,F/F'S
                   701 ; DESCRIPTION: HXDSP EXPANDS EACH INPUT BYTE TO 2 BYTES IN A FORM
                   702 ;              SUITABLE FOR DISPLAY BY THE OUTPUT ROUTINES. EACH INPUT
                   703 ;              BYTE IS DIVIDED INTO 2 HEX DIGITS. EACH HEX DIGIT IS
                   704 ;              PLACED IN THE LOW ORDER 4 BITS OF A BYTE WHOSE HIGH
                   705 ;              ORDER 4 BITS ARE SET TO ZERO. THE RESULTING BYTE IS
                   706 ;              STORED IN THE OUTPUT BUFFER. THE FUNCTION RETURNS THE
                   707 ;              ADDRESS OF THE OUTPUT BUFFER.
                   708 ;
                   709 HXDSP:
026C 7A            710         MOV    A,D         ; GET FIRST DATA BYTE
026D 0F            711         RRC                ; CONVERT 4 HIGH ORDER BITS
026E 0F            712         RRC                ; /TO A SINGLE CHARACTER
026F 0F            713         RRC
0270 0F            714         RRC
0271 E60F          715         ANI    0FH
0273 21F920        716         LXI    H,OBUFF     ; GET ADDRESS OF OUTPUT BUFFER
0276 77            717         MOV    M,A         ; STORE CHARACTER IN OUTPUT BUFFER
0277 7A            718         MOV    A,D         ; GET FIRST DATA BYTE AND CONVERT 4 LOW ORDER
0278 E60F          719         ANI    0FH         ; /BITS TO A SINGLE CHARACTER
027A 23            720         INX    H           ; NEXT BUFFER POSITION
027B 77            721         MOV    M,A         ; STORE CHARACTER IN BUFFER
027C 7B            722         MOV    A,E         ; GET SECOND DATA BYTE
027D 0F            723         RRC                ; CONVERT 4 HIGH ORDER BITS
027E 0F            724         RRC                ; /TO A SINGLE CHARACTER
027F 0F            725         RRC
0280 0F            726         RRC
0281 E60F          727         ANI    0FH
0283 23            728         INX    H           ; NEXT BUFFER POSITION
0284 77            729         MOV    M,A         ; STORE CHARACTER IN BUFFER
0285 7B            730         MOV    A,E         ; GET SECOND DATA BYTE AND CONVERT LOW ORDER
0286 E60F          731         ANI    0FH         ; /4 BITS TO A SINGLE CHARACTER
0288 23            732         INX    H           ; NEXT BUFFER POSITION
0289 77            733         MOV    M,A         ; STORE CHARACTER IN BUFFER
028A 21F920        734         LXI    H,OBUFF     ; RETURN ADDRESS OF OUTPUT BUFFER IN H & L
028D C9            735         RET
                   736 ;
                   737 ;********************************************************************
                   738 ;
                   739 ; FUNCTION: ININT - INPUT INTERRUPT PROCESSING
                   740 ; INPUTS: NONE
                   741 ; OUTPUTS: NONE
                   742 ; CALLS: NOTHING
                   743 ; DESTROYS: NOTHING
                   744 ; DESCRIPTION:  ININT IS ENTERED BY MEANS OF AN INTERRUPT VECTOR (IV2C)
                   745 ;              WHEN THE READ KEYBOARD ROUTINE IS WAITING FOR A
                   746 ;              CHARACTER AND THE USER HAS PRESSED A KEY ON THE
                   747 ;              KEYBOARD (EXCEPT "RESET" OR "VECTORED INTERRUPT").
                   748 ;              ININT STORES THE INPUT CHARACTER IN THE INPUT BUFFER AND
                   749 ;              RETURNS CONTROL TO THE READ KEYBOARD ROUTINE.
                   750 ;
```

```
LOC  OBJ        SEQ        SOURCE STATEMENT

                751 ININT:
028E E5         752            PUSH    H       ; SAVE H & L
028F F5         753            PUSH    PSW     ; SAVE F/F'S & REGISTER A
0290 210019     754            LXI     H,CNTRL ; ADDRESS FOR CONTROL CHARACTER OUTPUT
0293 3640       755            MVI     M,READ  ; OUTPUT CONTROL CHARACTER FOR READING
                756                            ; /FROM KEYBOARD
0295 25         757            DCR     H       ; ADDRESS FOR CHARACTER INPUT
0296 7E         758            MOV     A,M     ; READ A CHARACTER
0297 E63F       759            ANI     3FH     ; ZERO 2 HIGH ORDER BITS
0299 32FE20     760            STA     IBUFF   ; STORE CHARACTER IN INPUT BUFFER
029C F1         761            POP     PSW     ; RESTORE F/F'S & REGISTER A
029D E1         762            POP     H       ; RESTORE H & L
029E C9         763            RET
                764 ;
                765 ;********************************************************************
                766 ;
                767 ; FUNCTION: INSDG - INSERT HEX DIGIT
                768 ; INPUTS: A - HEX DIGIT TO BE INSERTED
                769 ;         DE - HEX VALUE
                770 ; OUTPUTS: DE - HEX VALUE WITH DIGIT INSERTED
                771 ; CALLS: NOTHING
                772 ; DESTROYS: A,F/F'S
                773 ; DESCRIPTION: INSDG SHIFTS THE CONTENTS OF D & E LEFT 4 BITS
                774 ;              (1 HEX DIGIT) AND INSERTS THE HEX DIGIT IN A IN THE LOW
                775 ;              ORDER DIGIT POSITION OF THE RESULT. A IS ASSUMED TO
                776 ;              CONTAIN A SINGLE HEX DIGIT IN THE LOW ORDER 4 BITS AND
                777 ;              ZEROS IN THE HIGH ORDER  4 BITS.
                778 ;
                779 INSDG:
029F EB         780            XCHG            ; PUT D & E IN H & L
02A0 29         781            DAD     H       ; SHIFT H & L LEFT 4 BITS
02A1 29         782            DAD     H
02A2 29         783            DAD     H
02A3 29         784            DAD     H
02A4 85         785            ADD     L       ; INSERT LOW ORDER DIGIT
02A5 6F         786            MOV     L,A
02A6 EB         787            XCHG            ; PUT H & L BACK IN D & E
02A7 C9         788            RET
                789 ;
                790 ;********************************************************************
                791 ;
                792 ; FUNCTION: NXTRG - ADVANCE REGISTER POINTER TO NEXT REGISTER
                793 ; INPUTS: NONE
                794 ; OUTPUTS: CARRY - 1 IF POINTER IS ADVANCED SUCCESSFULLY
                795 ;                - 0 OTHERWISE
                796 ; CALLS: NOTHING
                797 ; DESTROYS: A,F/F'S
                798 ; DESCRIPTION:  IF THE REGISTER POINTER POINTS TO THE LAST REGISTER IN
                799 ;               THE EXAMINE REGISTER SEQUENCE, THE POINTER IS NOT
                800 ;               CHANGED AND THE FUNCTION RETURNS FALSE. IF THE REGISTER
                801 ;               POINTER DOES NOT POINT TO THE LAST REGISTER THEN THE
                802 ;               POINTER IS ADVANCED TO THE NEXT REGISTER IN THE SEQUENCE
                803 ;               AND THE FUNCTION RETURNS TRUE.
                804 ;
                805 NXTRG:
02A8 3AFD20     806            LDA     RGPTR   ; GET REGISTER POINTER
02AB FE0C       807            CPI     NUMRG-1 ; DOES POINTER POINT TO LAST REGISTER?
02AD D2F702     808            JNC     RETF    ; YES - UNABLE TO ADVANCE POINTER - RETURN FALSE
02B0 3C         809            INR     A       ; NO - ADVANCE REGISTER POINTER
02B1 32FD20     810            STA     RGPTR   ; SAVE REGISTER POINTER
02B4 C3FA02     811            JMP     RETT    ; RETURN TRUE
                812 ;
                813 ;********************************************************************
                814 ;
                815 ; FUNCTION: OUTPT - OUTPUT CHARACTERS TO DISPLAY
                816 ; INPUTS: A - DISPLAY FLAG - 0 = USE ADDRESS FIELD
                817 ;                            1 = USE DATA FIELD
                818 ;         B - DOT FLAG - 1 = OUTPUT DOT AT RIGHT EDGE OF FIELD
                819 ;                        0 = NO DOT
                820 ;         HL - ADDRESS OF CHARACTERS TO BE OUTPUT
                821 ; CALLS: NOTHING
                822 ; DESTROYS: A,B,C,D,E,H,L,F/F'S
                823 ; DESCRIPTION:  OUTPT SENDS CHARACTERS TO THE DISPLAY. THE ADDRESS
                824 ;               OF THE CHARACTERS IS RECEIVED AS AN ARGUMENT. EITHER
                825 ;               2 CHARACTERS ARE SENT TO THE DATA FIELD, OR 4 CHARACTERS
                826 ;               ARE SENT TO THE ADDRESS FIELD, DEPENDING ON THE
                827 ;               DISPLAY FLAG ARGUMENT. THE DOT FLAG ARGUMENT DETERMINES
                828 ;               WHETHER OR NOT A DOT (DECIMAL POINT) WILL BE SENT
                829 ;               ALONG WITH THE LAST OUTPUT CHARACTER.
                830 ;
                831 OUTPT:
02B7 0F         832            RRC             ; USE DATA FIELD ?
02B8 DAC202     833            JC      OUT05   ; YES - GO SET UP TO USE DATA FIELD
02BB 0E04       834            MVI     C,4     ; NO - COUNT FOR ADDRESS FIELD
02BD 3E90       835            MVI     A,ADISP ; CONTROL CHARACTER FOR OUTPUT TO ADDRESS
                836                            ; /FIELD OF DISPLAY
02BF C3C602     837            JMP     OUT10
```

```
                          838 OUT05:
02C2 0E02                 839          MVI     C,2       ; COUNT FOR DATA FIELD
02C4 3E94                 840          MVI     A,DDISP   ; CONTROL CHARACTER FOR OUTPUT TO DATA FIELD
                          841                            ; /OF DISPLAY
                          842 OUT10:
02C6 320019               843          STA     CNTRL
                          844 OUT15:
02C9 7E                   845          MOV     A,M       ; GET OUTPUT CHARACTER
02CA EB                   846          XCHG              ; SAVE OUTPUT CHARACTER ADDRESS IN D & E
02CB 218403               847          LXI     H,DSPTB   ; GET DISPLAY FORMAT TABLE ADDRESS
02CE 85                   848          ADD     L         ; USE OUTPUT CHARACTER AS A POINTER TO
02CF 6F                   849          MOV     L,A       ; /DISPLAY FORMAT TABLE
02D0 7E                   850          MOV     A,M       ; GET DISPLAY FORMAT CHARACTER FROM TABLE
02D1 61                   851          MOV     H,C       ; TEST COUNTER WITHOUT CHANGING IT
02D2 25                   852          DCR     H         ; IS THIS THE LAST CHARACTER ?
02D3 C2DC02               853          JNZ     OUT20     ; NO - GO OUTPUT CHARACTER AS IS
02D6 05                   854          DCR     B         ; YES - IS DOT FLAG SET ?
02D7 C2DC02               855          JNZ     OUT20     ; NO - GO OUTPUT CHARACTER AS IS
02DA F608                 856          ORI     DTMSK     ; YES - OR IN MASK TO DISPLAY DOT WITH
                          857                            ; /LAST CHARACTER
                          858 OUT20:
02DC 2F                   859          CMA               ; COMPLEMENT OUTPUT CHARACTER
02DD 320018               860          STA     DSPLY     ; SEND CHARACTER TO DISPLAY
02E0 EB                   861          XCHG              ; RETRIEVE OUTPUT CHARACTER ADDRESS
02E1 23                   862          INX     H         ; NEXT OUTPUT CHARACTER
02E2 0D                   863          DCR     C         ; ANY MORE OUTPUT CHARACTERS ?
02E3 C2C902               864          JNZ     OUT15     ; YES - GO PROCESS ANOTHER CHARACTER
02E6 C9                   865          RET               ; NO - RETURN
                          866 ;
                          867 ;********************************************************************
                          868 ;
                          869 ; FUNCTION: RDKBD - READ KEYBOARD
                          870 ; INPUTS: NONE
                          871 ; OUTPUTS: A - CHARACTER READ FROM KEYBOARD
                          872 ; CALLS: NOTHING
                          873 ; DESTROYS: A,H,L,F/F'S
                          874 ; DESCRIPTION:   RDKBD DETERMINES WHETHER OR NOT THERE IS A CHARACTER IN
                          875 ;                THE INPUT BUFFER. IF NOT, THE FUNCTION ENABLES
                          876 ;                INTERRUPTS AND LOOPS UNTIL THE INPUT INTERRUPT
                          877 ;                ROUTINE STORES A CHARACTER IN THE BUFFER. WHEN
                          878 ;                THE BUFFER CONTAINS A CHARACTER, THE FUNCTION FLAGS
                          879 ;                THE BUFFER AS EMPTY AND RETURNS THE CHARACTER
                          880 ;                AS OUTPUT.
                          881 ;
                          882 RDKBD:
02E7 21FE20               883          LXI     H,IBUFF   ; GET INPUT BUFFER ADDRESS
02EA 7E                   884          MOV     A,M       ; GET BUFFER CONTENTS
                          885                            ; HIGH ORDER BIT = 1 MEANS BUFFER IS EMPTY
02EB B7                   886          ORA     A         ; IS A CHARACTER AVAILABLE ?
02EC F2F302               887          JP      RDK10     ; YES - EXIT FROM LOOP
02EF FB                   888          EI                ; NO - READY FOR CHARACTER FROM KEYBOARD
02F0 C3E702               889          JMP     RDKBD
                          890 RDK10:
02F3 3680                 891          MVI     M,EMPTY   ; SET BUFFER EMPTY FLAG
02F5 F3                   892          DI                ; RETURN WITH INTERRUPTS DISABLED
02F6 C9                   893          RET
                          894 ;
                          895 ;********************************************************************
                          896 ;
                          897 ; FUNCTION: RETF - RETURN FALSE
                          898 ; INPUTS: NONE
                          899 ; OUTPUTS: CARRY = 0 (FALSE)
                          900 ; CALLS: NOTHING
                          901 ; DESTROYS: CARRY
                          902 ; DESCRIPTION: RETF IS JUMPED TO BY FUNCTIONS WISHING TO RETURN FALSE.
                          903 ;              RETF RESETS CARRY TO 0 AND RETURNS TO THE CALLER OF
                          904 ;              THE ROUTINE INVOKING RETF.
                          905 ;
                          906 RETF:
02F7 37                   907          STC               ; SET CARRY TRUE
02F8 3F                   908          CMC               ; COMPLEMENT CARRY TO MAKE IT FALSE
02F9 C9                   909          RET
                          910 ;
                          911 ;********************************************************************
                          912 ;
                          913 ; FUNCTION: RETT - RETURN TRUE
                          914 ; INPUTS: NONE
                          915 ; OUTPUTS: CARRY = 1 (TRUE)
                          916 ; CALLS: NOTHING
                          917 ; DESTROYS: CARRY
                          918 ; DESCRIPTION: RETT IS JUMPED TO BY ROUTINES WISHING TO RETURN TRUE.
                          919 ;              RETT SETS CARRY TO 1 AND RETURNS TO THE CALLER OF
                          920 ;              THE ROUTINE INVOKING RETT.
                          921 ;
                          922 RETT:
02FA 37                   923          STC               ; SET CARRY TRUE
02FB C9                   924          RET
```

```
                   925 ;
                   926 ;••••••••••••••••••••••••••••••••••••••••••••••••••••••••••••
                   927 ;
                   928 ; FUNCTION: RGLOC - GET REGISTER SAVE LOCATION
                   929 ; INPUTS: NONE
                   930 ; OUTPUTS: HL - REGISTER SAVE LOCATION
                   931 ; CALLS: NOTHING
                   932 ; DESTROYS: B,C,H,L,F/F'S
                   933 ; DESCRIPTION:  RGLOC RETURNS THE SAVE LOCATION OF THE REGISTER
                   934 ;                 INDICATED BY THE CURRENT REGISTER POINTER VALUE.
                   935 ;
                   936 RGLOC:
02FC 2AFD20        937        LHLD     RGPTR    ; GET REGISTER POINTER
02FF 2600          938        MVI      H,0      ; /IN H & L
0301 01ED03        939        LXI      B,RGTBL  ; GET REGISTER SAVE LOCATION TABLE ADDRESS
0304 09            940        DAD      B        ; POINTER INDEXES TABLE
0305 6E            941        MOV      L,M      ; GET LOW ORDER BYTE OF REGISTER SAVE LOC.
0306 2620          942        MVI      H,(RAMST SHR 8) ; GET HIGH ORDER BYTE OF
                   943                             ; /REGISTER SAVE LOCATION
0308 C9            944        RET
                   945 ;
                   946 ;••••••••••••••••••••••••••••••••••••••••••••••••••••••••••••
                   947 ;
                   948 ; FUNCTION: RGNAM - DISPLAY REGISTER NAME
                   949 ; INPUTS: NONE
                   950 ; OUTPUTS: NONE
                   951 ; CALLS: OUTPT
                   952 ; DESTROYS: A,B,C,D,E,H,L,F/F'S
                   953 ; DESCRIPTION: RGNAM DISPLAYS, IN THE ADDRESS FIELD OF THE DISPLAY,
                   954 ;                 THE REGISTER NAME CORRESPONDING TO THE CURRENT
                   955 ;                 REGISTER POINTER VALUE.
                   956 ;
                   957 RGNAM:
0309 2AFD20        958        LHLD     RGPTR    ; GET REGISTER POINTER
030C 2600          959        MVI      H,0
030E 29            960        DAD      H        ; MULTIPLY POINTER VALUE BY 4
030F 29            961        DAD      H        ;/(REGISTER NAME TABLE HAS 4 BYTE ENTRIES)
0310 01B903        962        LXI      B,NMTBL  ; GET ADDRESS OF START OF REGISTER NAME TABLE
0313 09            963        DAD      B        ; ARG - ADD TABLE ADDRESS TO POINTER - RESULT IS
                   964                             ;/ADDRESS OF APPROPRIATE REGISTER NAME IN H & L
0314 AF            965        XRA      A        ; ARG - USE ADDRESS FIELD OF DISPLAY
0315 0600          966        MVI      B,NODOT  ; ARG - NO DOT IN ADDRESS FIELD
0317 CDB702        967        CALL     OUTPT    ; OUTPUT REGISTER NAME TO ADDRESS FIELD
031A C9            968        RET
                   969 ;
                   970 ;••••••••••••••••••••••••••••••••••••••••••••••••••••••••••••
                   971 ;
                   972 ; FUNCTION: RSTOR - RESTOR USER REGISTERS
                   973 ; INPUTS: NONE
                   974 ; OUTPUTS: NONE
                   975 ; CALLS: NOTHING
                   976 ; DESTROYS: A,B,C,D,E,H,L,F/F'S
                   977 ; DESCRIPTION:  RSTOR RESTORES ALL CPU REGISTERS, FLIP/FLOPS,
                   978 ;                 INTERRUPT STATUS, INTERRUPT MASK, STACK POINTER
                   979 ;                 AND PROGRAM COUNTER FROM THEIR RESPECTIVE
                   980 ;                 SAVE LOCATIONS IN MEMORY. BY RESTORING THE PROGRAM
                   981 ;                 COUNTER, THE ROUTINE EFFECTIVELY TRANSFERS CONTROL TO
                   982 ;                 THE ADDRESS IN THE PROGRAM COUNTER SAVE LOCATION.
                   983 ;
                   984 ;                 THE TIMING OF THIS ROUTINE IS CRITICAL TO THE
                   985 ;                 CORRECT OPERATION OF THE SINGLE STEP ROUTINE.
                   986 ;                 IF ANY MODIFICATION CHANGES THE NUMBER OF CPU
                   987 ;                 STATES NEEDED TO EXECUTE THIS ROUTINE THEN THE
                   988 ;                 TIMER VALUE MUST BE ADJUSTED BY THE SAME NUMBER.
                   989 ;
                   990 ; ***** THIS IS ALSO THE ENTRY POINT FOR THE TTY MONITOR
                   991 ;       TO RESTORE REGISTERS.
                   992 ;
                   993 RSTOR:
031B 3AF120        994        LDA      ISAV     ; GET USER INTERRUPT MASK
031E F618          995        ORI      18H      ; ENABLE SETTING OF INTERRUPT MASK AND
                   996                             ; /RESET RST7.5 FLIP FLOP
0320 30            997        SIM               ; RESTORE USER INTERRUPT MASK
                   998        RESTORE USER INTERRUPT STATUS
0321 3AF120        999        LDA      ISAV     ; GET USER INTERRUPT MASK
0324 E608         1000        ANI      08H      ; SHOULD USER INTERRUPTS BE ENABLED ?
0326 CA2D03       1001        JZ       RSR05    ; NO - LEAVE INTERRUPTS DISABLED
0329 FB           1002        EI                ; YES - ENABLE INTERRUPTS FOR USER PROGRAM
032A C33103       1003        JMP      RSR10
                  1004 RSR05:
032D 37           1005        STC               ; DUMMY INSTRUCTIONS - WHEN SINGLE STEP ROUTINE
032E D23103       1006        JNC      RSR10    ; /IS BEING USED, THE TIMER IS RUNNING AND
                  1007                             ; /EXECUTE TIME FOR THIS ROUTINE MUST NOT
                  1008                             ; /VARY.
                  1009 RSR10:
0331 21E920       1010        LXI      H,MNSTK  ; SET MONITOR STACK POINTER TO START OF STACK
0334 F9           1011        SPHL              ; /WHICH IS ALSO END OF REGISTER SAVE AREA
```

```
LOC  OBJ        SEQ       SOURCE STATEMENT

0335 D1        1012       POP      D       ; RESTORE REGISTERS
0336 C1        1013       POP      B
0337 F1        1014       POP      PSW
0338 2AF420    1015       LHLD     SSAV    ; RESTORE USER STACK POINTER
033B F9        1016       SPHL
033C 2AF220    1017       LHLD     PSAV
033F E5        1018       PUSH     H       ; PUT USER PROGRAM COUNTER ON STACK
0340 2AEF20    1019       LHLD     LSAV    ; RESTORE H & L REGISTERS
0343 C9        1020       RET              ; JUMP TO USER PROGRAM COUNTER
               1021 ;
               1022 ;****************************************************************
               1023 ;
               1024 ; FUNCTION: SETRG - SET REGISTER POINTER
               1025 ; INPUTS: NONE
               1026 ; OUTPUTS: CARRY - SET IF CHARACTER FROM KEYBOARD IS A REGISTER DESIGNATOR
               1027 ;                  RESET OTHERWISE
               1028 ; CALLS: RDKBD
               1029 ; DESTROYS: A,B,C,H,L,F/F'S
               1030 ; DESCRIPTION: SETRG READS A CHARACTER FROM THE KEYBOARD. IF THE
               1031 ;                  CHARACTER IS A REGISTER DESIGNATOR, IT IS CONVERTED TO
               1032 ;                  THE CORRESPONDING REGISTER POINTER VALUE, THE POINTER IS
               1033 ;                  SAVED, AND THE FUNCTION RETURNS 'TRUE'. OTHERWISE, THE
               1034 ;                  FUNCTION RETURNS 'FALSE'
               1035 ;
               1036 SETRG:
0344 CDE702    1037       CALL     RDKBD   ; READ FROM KEYBOARD
0347 FE10      1038       CPI      10H     ; IS CHARACTER A DIGIT?
0349 D2F702    1039       JNC      RETF    ; NO - RETURN FALSE - CHARACTER IS NOT A
               1040                        ; /REGISTER DESIGNATOR
034C D603      1041       SUI      3       ; YES - TRY TO CONVERT REGISTER DESIGNATOR TO
               1042                        ; / INDEX INTO REGISTER POINTER TABLE
               1043                        ; WAS CONVERSION SUCCESSFUL?
034E DAF702    1044       JC       RETF    ; NO - RETURN FALSE
0351 4F        1045       MOV      C,A     ; INDEX TO B & C
0352 0600      1046       MVI      B,0
0354 21AC03    1047       LXI      H,RGPTB ; GET ADDRESS OF REGISTER POINTER TABLE
0357 09        1048       DAD      B       ; INDEX POINTS INTO TABLE
0358 7E        1049       MOV      A,M     ; GET REGISTER POINTER FROM TABLE
0359 32FD20    1050       STA      RGPTR   ; SAVE REGISTER POINTER
035C C3FA02    1051       JMP      RETT    ; RETURN TRUE
               1052 ;
               1053 ;****************************************************************
               1054 ;
               1055 ; FUNCTION: UPDAD - UPDATE ADDRESS FIELD OF DISPLAY
               1056 ; INPUTS: B - DOT FLAG - 1 MEANS PUT DOT AT RIGHT EDGE OF FIELD
               1057 ;                        0 MEANS NO DOT
               1058 ; OUTPUTS: NONE
               1059 ; CALLS: HXDSP,OUTPT
               1060 ; DESTROYS: A,B,C,D,E,H,L,F/F'S
               1061 ; DESCRIPTION: UPDAD UPDATES THE ADDRESS FIELD OF THE DISPLAY USING
               1062 ;                  THE CURRENT ADDRESS.
               1063 ;
               1064 UPDAD:
035F 2AF620    1065       LHLD     CURAD   ; GET CURRENT ADDRESS
0362 EB        1066       XCHG             ; ARG - PUT CURRENT ADDRESS IN D & E
0363 CD6C02    1067       CALL     HXDSP   ; EXPAND CURRENT ADDRESS FOR DISPLAY
               1068                        ; ARG - ADDRESS OF EXPANDED ADDRESS IS IN H & L
0366 AF        1069       XRA      A       ; ARG - USE ADDRESS FIELD OF DISPLAY
               1070                        ; ARG - DOT FLAG IS IN B
0367 CDB702    1071       CALL     OUTPT   ; OUTPUT CURRENT ADDRESS TO ADDRESS FIELD
036A C9        1072       RET
               1073 ;
               1074 ;****************************************************************
               1075 ;
               1076 ; FUNCTION: UPDDT - UPDATE DATA FIELD OF DISPLAY
               1077 ; INPUTS: B - DOT FLAG - 1 MEANS PUT DOT AT RIGHT EDGE OF FIELD
               1078 ;                        0 MEANS NO DOT
               1079 ; OUTPUTS: NONE
               1080 ; CALLS: HXDSP,OUTDT
               1081 ; DESTROYS: A,B,C,D,E,H,L,F/F'S
               1082 ; DESCRIPTION: UPDDT UPDATES THE DATA FIELD OF THE DISPLAY USING
               1083 ;                  THE CURRENT DATA BYTE.
               1084 ;
               1085 UPDDT:
036B 3AF820    1086       LDA      CURDT   ; GET CURRENT DATA
036E 57        1087       MOV      D,A     ; ARG - PUT CURRENT DATA IN D
036F CD6C02    1088       CALL     HXDSP   ; EXPAND CURRENT DATA FOR DISPLAY
               1089                        ; ARG - ADDRESS OF EXPANDED DATA IS IN H & L
0372 3E01      1090       MVI      A,DTFLD ; ARG - USE DATA FIELD OF DISPLAY
               1091                        ; ARG - DOT FLAG IS IN B
0374 CDB702    1092       CALL     OUTPT   ; OUTPUT CURRENT DATA TO DATA FIELD
0377 C9        1093       RET
               1094 ;
               1095 ;****************************************************************
               1096 ;
               1097 ;                        MONITOR TABLES
               1098 ;
```

```
                      1099 ;****************************************************************
                      1100 ;
                      1101 ; COMMAND TABLE
                      1102 ;    COMMAND CHARACTERS AS RECEIVED FROM KEYBOARD
                      1103 CMDTB:
0378 12               1104          DB     12H     ; GO COMMAND
0379 13               1105          DB     13H     ; SUBSTITUTE MEMORY COMMAND
037A 14               1106          DB     14H     ; EXAMINE REGISTERS COMMAND
037B 15               1107          DB     15H     ; SINGLE STEP COMMAND
0004                  1108 NUMC     EQU    $-CMDTB ; NUMBER OF COMMANDS
                      1109 ;
                      1110 ;****************************************************************
                      1111 ;
                      1112 ; COMMAND ROUTINE ADDRESS TABLE
                      1113 ; (MUST BE IN REVERSE ORDER OF COMMAND TABLE)
                      1114 CMDAD:
037C FD00             1115          DW     SSTEP   ; ADDRESS OF SINGLE STEP ROUTINE
037E 9200             1116          DW     EXAM    ; ADDRESS OF EXAMINE REGISTERS ROUTINE
0380 8B01             1117          DW     SUBST   ; ADDRESS OF SUBSTITUTE MEMORY ROUTINE
0382 CB00             1118          DW     GOCMD   ; ADDRESS OF GO ROUTINE
                      1119 ;
                      1120 ;****************************************************************
                      1121 ;
                      1122 DSPTB:   ; TABLE FOR TRANSLATING CHARACTERS FOR OUTPUT
                      1123 ;
                      1124 ;                     DISPLAY
                      1125 ;                     FORMAT   CHARACTER
                      1126 ;                     =======  =========
                      1127 ;
0000                  1128 ZERO     EQU    $ - DSPTB
0384 F3               1129          DB     0F3H     ; 0
0385 60               1130          DB     60H      ; 1
0386 B5               1131          DB     0B5H     ; 2
0387 F4               1132          DB     0F4H     ; 3
0388 66               1133          DB     66H      ; 4
0005                  1134 FIVE     EQU    $ - DSPTB
0005                  1135 LETRS    EQU    $ - DSPTB
0389 D6               1136          DB     0D6H     ; 5 AND S
038A D7               1137          DB     0D7H     ; 6
038B 70               1138          DB     70H      ; 7
0008                  1139 EIGHT    EQU    $ - DSPTB
038C F7               1140          DB     0F7H     ; 8
038D 76               1141          DB     76H      ; 9
000A                  1142 LETRA    EQU    $ - DSPTB
038E 77               1143          DB     77H      ; A
000B                  1144 LETRB    EQU    $ - DSPTB
038F C7               1145          DB     0C7H     ; B (LOWER CASE)
000C                  1146 LETRC    EQU    $ - DSPTB
0390 93               1147          DB     93H      ; C
000D                  1148 LETRD    EQU    $ - DSPTB
0391 E5               1149          DB     0E5H     ; D (LOWER CASE)
000E                  1150 LETRE    EQU    $ - DSPTB
0392 97               1151          DB     97H      ; E
000F                  1152 LETRF    EQU    $ - DSPTB
0393 17               1153          DB     17H      ; F
0010                  1154 LETRH    EQU    $ - DSPTB
0394 67               1155          DB     67H      ; H
0011                  1156 LETRL    EQU    $ - DSPTB
0395 83               1157          DB     83H      ; L
0012                  1158 LETRP    EQU    $ - DSPTB
0396 37               1159          DB     37H      ; P
0013                  1160 LETRI    EQU    $ - DSPTB
0397 60               1161          DB     60H      ; I
0014                  1162 LETRR    EQU    $ - DSPTB
0398 05               1163          DB     05H      ; R (LOWER CASE)
0015                  1164 BLANK    EQU    $ - DSPTB
0399 00               1165          DB     00H      ; BLANK
                      1166 ;
                      1167 ;****************************************************************
                      1168 ;
                      1169 ; MESSAGES FOR OUTPUT TO DISPLAY
                      1170 ;
039A 15               1171 BLNKS:   DB     BLANK,BLANK,BLANK,BLANK ; FOR ADDRESS OR DATA FIELD
039B 15
039C 15
039D 15
039E 15               1172 ERMSG:   DB     BLANK,LETRE,LETRR,LETRR ; ERROR MESSAGE FOR ADDR. FIELD
039F 0E
03A0 14
03A1 14
03A2 0E               1173 EXMSG:   DB     LETRE,BLANK,BLANK,BLANK ; EXECUTION MESSAGE
03A3 15
03A4 15
03A5 15
                      1174                                         ; /FOR ADDRESS FIELD
03A6 15               1175 SGNAD:   DB     BLANK,BLANK,EIGHT,ZERO ; SIGN ON MESSAGE (ADDR. FIELD)
03A7 15
```

```
LOC  OBJ       SEQ        SOURCE STATEMENT

03A8 08
03A9 00
03AA 08    1176 SGNDT:  DB      EIGHT,FIVE              ; SIGN ON MESSAGE (DATA FIELD)
03AB 05
           1177 ;
           1178 ;**************************************************************************
           1179 ;
           1180 RGPTB:   ; REGISTER POINTER TABLE
           1181               ; THE ENTRIES IN THIS TABLE ARE IN THE SAME ORDER
           1182               ; AS THE REGISTER DESIGNATOR KEYS ON THE KEYBOARD.
           1183               ; EACH ENTRY CONTAINS THE REGISTER POINTER VALUE WHICH
           1184               ; CORRESPONDS TO THE REGISTER DESIGNATOR. REGISTER
           1185               ; POINTER VALUES ARE USED TO POINT INTO THE REGISTER
           1186               ; NAME TABLE (NMTBL) AND REGISTER SAVE LOCATION
           1187               ; TABLE (RGTBL).
           1188 ;
03AC 06    1189      DB      6       ; INTERRUPT MASK
03AD 09    1190      DB      9       ; SPH
03AE 0A    1191      DB      10      ; SPL
03AF 0B    1192      DB      11      ; PCH
03B0 0C    1193      DB      12      ; PCL
03B1 07    1194      DB      7       ; H
03B2 08    1195      DB      8       ; L
03B3 00    1196      DB      0       ; A
03B4 01    1197      DB      1       ; B
03B5 02    1198      DB      2       ; C
03B6 03    1199      DB      3       ; D
03B7 04    1200      DB      4       ; E
03B8 05    1201      D3      5       ; FLAGS
           1202 ;
           1203 ;**************************************************************************
           1204 ;
           1205 NMTBL:           ; REGISTER NAME TABLE
           1206               ; NAMES OF REGISTERS IN DISPLAY FORMAT
03B9 15    1207      DB      BLANK,BLANK,BLANK,LETRA  ; A REGISTER
03BA 15
03BB 15
03BC 0A
03BD 15    1208      DB      BLANK,BLANK,BLANK,LETRB  ; B REGISTER
03BE 15
03BF 15
03C0 0B
03C1 15    1209      DB      BLANK,BLANK,BLANK,LETRC  ; C REGISTER
03C2 15
03C3 15
03C4 0C
03C5 15    1210      DB      BLANK,BLANK,BLANK,LETRD  ; D REGISTER
03C6 15
03C7 15
03C8 0D
03C9 15    1211      DB      BLANK,BLANK,BLANK,LETRE  ; E REGISTER
03CA 15
03CB 15
03CC 0E
03CD 15    1212      DB      BLANK,BLANK,BLANK,LETRF  ; FLAGS
03CE 15
03CF 15
03D0 0F
03D1 15    1213      DB      BLANK,BLANK,BLANK,LETRI  ; INTERRUPT MASK
03D2 15
03D3 15
03D4 13
03D5 15    1214      DB      BLANK,BLANK,BLANK,LETRH  ; H REGISTER
03D6 15
03D7 15
03D8 10
03D9 15    1215      DB      BLANK,BLANK,BLANK,LETRL  ; L REGISTER
03DA 15
03DB 15
03DC 11
03DD 15    1216      DB      BLANK,LETRS,LETRP,LETRH  ; STACK POINTER HIGH ORDER BYTE
03DE 05
03DF 12
03E0 10
03E1 15    1217      DB      BLANK,LETRS,LETRP,LETRL  ; STACK POINTER LOW ORDER BYTE
03E2 05
03E3 12
03E4 11
03E5 15    1218      DB      BLANK,LETRP,LETRC,LETRH  ; PROGRAM COUNTER HIGH BYTE
03E6 12
03E7 0C
03E8 10
03E9 15    1219      DB      BLANK,LETRP,LETRC,LETRL  ; PROGRAM COUNTER LOW BYTE
03EA 12
03EB 0C
03EC 11
           1220 ;
```

```
LOC  OBJ       SEQ       SOURCE STATEMENT
              1221 ;**********************************************************************
              1222 ;
              1223 ; REGISTER SAVE LOCATION TABLE
              1224 ; ADDRESSES OF SAVE LOCATIONS OF REGISTERS IN THE ORDER IN WHICH
              1225 ; THE REGISTERS ARE DISPLAYED BY THE EXAMINE COMMAND
              1226 ;
              1227 RGTBL:
03ED EE       1228          DB        ASAV AND 0FFH   ; A REGISTER
03EE EC       1229          DB        BSAV AND 0FFH   ; B REGISTER
03EF EB       1230          DB        CSAV AND 0FFH   ; C REGISTER
03F0 EA       1231          DB        DSAV AND 0FFH   ; D REGISTER
03F1 E9       1232          DB        ESAV AND 0FFH   ; E REGISTER
03F2 ED       1233          DB        FSAV AND 0FFH   ; FLAGS
03F3 F1       1234          DB        ISAV AND 0FFH   ; INTERRUPT MASK
03F4 F0       1235          DB        HSAV AND 0FFH   ; H REGISTER
03F5 EF       1236          DB        LSAV AND 0FFH   ; L REGISTER
03F6 F5       1237          DB        SPHSV AND 0FFH  ; STACK POINTER HIGH ORDER BYTE
03F7 F4       1238          DB        SPLSV AND 0FFH  ; STACK POINTER LOW ORDER BYTE
03F8 F3       1239          DB        PCHSV AND 0FFH  ; PROGRAM COUNTER HIGH ORDER BYTE
03F9 F2       1240          DB        PCLSV AND 0FFH  ; PROGRAM COUNTER LOW ORDER BYTE
000D          1241 NUMRG    EQU       ($ - RGTBL)     ; NUMBER OF ENTRIES IN
              1242                               ; /REGISTER SAVE LOCATION TABLE
              1243 ;
              1244 ;**********************************************************************
              1245 ;**********************************************************************
              1246 ;
              1247 ;                         SDK-85 TTY MONITOR
              1248 ;
              1249 ;**********************************************************************
              1250 ;**********************************************************************
              1251 ;
              1252 ;
              1253 ; ABSTRACT
              1254 ; ========
              1255 ;
              1256 ; THIS PROGRAM WAS ADAPTED, WITH FEW CHANGES, FROM THE SDK-80 MONITOR.
              1257 ; THIS PROGRAM RUNS ON THE 8085 BOARD AND IS DESIGNED TO PROVIDE
              1258 ; THE USER WITH A MINIMAL MONITOR.  BY USING THIS PROGRAM,
              1259 ; THE USER CAN EXAMINE AND CHANGE MEMORY OR CPU REGISTERS, LOAD
              1260 ; A PROGRAM (IN ABSOLUTE HEX) INTO RAM, AND EXECUTE INSTRUCTIONS
              1261 ; ALREADY IN MEMORY.  THE MONITOR ALSO PROVIDES THE USER WITH
              1262 ; ROUTINES FOR PERFORMING CONSOLE I/O.
              1263 ;
              1264 ;
              1265 ; PROGRAM ORGANIZATION
              1266 ; ======= ============
              1267 ;
              1268 ; THE LISTING IS ORGANIZED IN THE FOLLOWING WAY.  FIRST THE COMMAND
              1269 ; RECOGNIZER, WHICH IS THE HIGHEST LEVEL ROUTINE IN THE PROGRAM.
              1270 ; NEXT THE ROUTINES TO IMPLEMENT THE VARIOUS COMMANDS.  FINALLY,
              1271 ; THE UTILITY ROUTINES WHICH ACTUALLY DO THE DIRTY WORK.  WITHIN
              1272 ; EACH SECTION, THE ROUTINES ARE ORGANIZED IN ALPHABETICAL
              1273 ; ORDER, BY ENTRY POINT OF THE ROUTINE.
              1274 ;
              1275 ; MACROS USED IN THE TTY MONITOR ARE DEFINED IN THE KEYBOARD MONITOR.
              1276 ;
              1277 ; LIST OF FUNCTIONS
              1278 ; ==== == =========
              1279 ;
              1280 ;      GETCM
              1281 ;      -----
              1282 ;
              1283 ;      DCMD
              1284 ;      GCMD
              1285 ;      ICMD
              1286 ;      MCMD
              1287 ;      SCMD
              1288 ;      XCMD
              1289 ;      -----
              1290 ;
              1291 ;      CI
              1292 ;      CNVBN
              1293 ;      CO
              1294 ;      CROUT
              1295 ;      DELAY
              1296 ;      ECHO
              1297 ;      ERROR
              1298 ;      FRET
              1299 ;      GETCH
              1300 ;      GETHX
              1301 ;      GETNM
              1302 ;      HILO
              1303 ;      NMOUT
              1304 ;      PRVAL
              1305 ;      REGDS
              1306 ;      RGADR
              1307 ;      SRET
```

```
LOC  OBJ          SEQ          SOURCE STATEMENT

                  1308 ;      STHF0
                  1309 ;      STHLF
                  1310 ;      VALDG
                  1311 ;      VALDL
                  1312 ;      -----
                  1313 ;
                  1314 ;
                  1315 ;****************************************************************
                  1316 ;
                  1317 ;
                  1318 ;                        MONITOR EQUATES
                  1319 ;
                  1320 ;
                  1321 ;****************************************************************
                  1322 ;
                  1323 ;
001B              1324 BRCHR  EQU     1BH       ; CODE FOR BREAK CHARACTER (ESCAPE)
07FA              1325 BRTAB  EQU     07FAH     ; LOCATION OF START OF BRANCH TABLE IN ROM
000D              1326 CR     EQU     0DH       ; CODE FOR CARRIAGE RETURN
001B              1327 ESC    EQU     1BH       ; CODE FOR ESCAPE CHARACTER
000F              1328 HCHAR  EQU     0FH       ; MASK TO SELECT LOWER HEX CHAR FROM BYTE
00FF              1329 INVRT  EQU     0FFH      ; MASK TO INVERT HALF BYTE FLAG
000A              1330 LF     EQU     0AH       ; CODE FOR LINE FEED
0000              1331 LOWER  EQU     0         ; DENOTES LOWER HALF OF BYTE IN ICMD
                  1332 ;LSGNON EQU    ---       ; LENGTH OF SIGNON MESSAGE - DEFINED LATER
                  1333 ;MNSTK  EQU     ---       ; START OF MONITOR STACK - DEFINED IN
                  1334                           ; /KEYBOARD MONITOR
                  1335 ;NCMDS  EQU     ---       ; NUMBER OF VALID COMMANDS - DEFINED LATER
000F              1336 NEWLN  EQU     0FH       ; MASK FOR CHECKING MEMORY ADDR DISPLAY
007F              1337 PRTY0  EQU     07FH      ; MASK TO CLEAR PARITY BIT FROM CONSOLE CHAR
                  1338 ;RAMST  EQU     ---       ; START ADDRESS OF RAM - DEFINED IN
                  1339                           ; KEYBOARD MONITOR
                  1340 ;RTABS  EQU     ---       ; SIZE OF ENTRY IN RTAB TABLE
0080              1341 SSTRT  EQU     80H       ; SHIFTED START BIT
0040              1342 STOPB  EQU     40H       ; STOP BIT
00C0              1343 STRT   EQU     0C0H      ; UNSHIFTED START BIT
001B              1344 TERM   EQU     1BH       ; CODE FOR ICMD TERMINATING CHARACTER (ESCAPE)
00FF              1345 UPPER  EQU     0FFH      ; DENOTES UPPER HALF OF BYTE IN ICMD
                  1346
                  1347 ;DELAY VALUES IF NO WAIT STATE
                  1348 ;
                  1349         IF      1-WAITS
048C              1350 IBTIM  EQU     1164      ;INTER-BIT TIME DELAY
048C              1351 OBTIM  EQU     1164      ;OUTPUT INTER-BIT TIME DELAY
1230              1352 TIM4   EQU     4656      ;4 BIT TIME DELAY
0246              1353 WAIT   EQU     582       ;DELAY UNTIL READY TO SAMPLE BITS
                  1354         ENDIF
                  1355 ;
                  1356 ;DELAY VALUES IF ONE WAIT STATE
                  1357 ;
                  1358         IF      WAITS
                  1359 IBTIM  EQU     930       ;INTER-BIT DELAY
                  1360 OBTIM  EQU     930       ;OUTPUT INTER-BIT TIME DELAY
                  1361 TIM4   EQU     3720      ;4 BIT TIME DELAY
                  1362 WAIT   EQU     465       ;DELAY UNTIL READY TO SAMPLE BITS
                  1363         ENDIF
                  1364 ;
                  1365 ;
                  1366 ;****************************************************************
                  1367 ;
                  1368 ;
                  1369 ;                        RESTART ENTRY POINT
                  1370 ;
                  1371 ;
                  1372 ;****************************************************************
                  1373 ;
                  1374 ;
                  1375 ;
                  1376 ;****************************************************************
                  1377 ;
                  1378 ;
                  1379 ;                        PRINT SIGNON MESSAGE
                  1380 ;
                  1381 ;
                  1382 ;****************************************************************
                  1383 ;
                  1384 ;
                  1385 GO:
03FA 218C07       1386         LXI     H,SGNON ; GET ADDRESS OF SIGNON MESSAGE
03FD 0614         1387         MVI     B,LSGNON        ; COUNTER FOR CHARACTERS IN MESSAGE
                  1388 MSGL:
03FF 4E           1389         MOV     C,M     ; FETCH NEXT CHAR TO C REG
0400 CDC405       1390         CALL    CO      ; SEND IT TO THE CONSOLE
0403 23           1391         INX     H       ; POINT TO NEXT CHARACTER
0404 05           1392         DCR     B       ; DECREMENT BYTE COUNTER
0405 C2FF03       1393         JNZ     MSGL    ; RETURN FOR NEXT CHARACTER
                  1394
```

```
LOC  OBJ          SEQ      SOURCE STATEMENT

                  1395 ;
                  1396 ;**************************************************************
                  1397 ;
                  1398 ;
                  1399 ;                   COMMAND RECOGNIZING ROUTINE
                  1400 ;
                  1401 ;
                  1402 ;**************************************************************
                  1403 ;
                  1404 ; FUNCTION: GETCM
                  1405 ; INPUTS: NONE
                  1406 ; OUTPUTS: NONE
                  1407 ; CALLS: GETCH,ECHO,ERROR
                  1408 ; DESTROYS: A,B,C,H,L,F/F'S
                  1409 ; DESCRIPTION: GETCM RECEIVES AN INPUT CHARACTER FROM THE USER
                  1410 ;                  AND ATTEMPTS TO LOCATE THIS CHARACTER IN ITS COMMAND
                  1411 ;                  CHARACTER TABLE.  IF SUCCESSFUL, THE ROUTINE
                  1412 ;                  CORRESPONDING TO THIS CHARACTER IS SELECTED FROM
                  1413 ;                  A TABLE OF COMMAND ROUTINE ADDRESSES, AND CONTROL
                  1414 ;                  IS TRANSFERRED TO THIS ROUTINE.  IF THE CHARACTER
                  1415 ;                  DOES NOT MATCH ANY ENTRIES, CONTROL IS PASSED TO
                  1416 ;                  THE ERROR HANDLER.
                  1417 ;
                  1418 GETCM:
0408 21E920        1419        LXI     H,MNSTK ; ALWAYS WANT TO RESET STACK PTR TO MONITOR
040B F9           1420        SPHL            ; /STARTING VALUE SO ROUTINES NEEDN'T CLEAN UP
040C 0E2E         1421        MVI     C,'.'   ; PROMPT CHARACTER TO C
040E CDF805       1422        CALL    ECHO    ; SEND PROMPT CHARACTER TO USER TERMINAL
0411 C31404       1423        JMP     GTC03   ; WANT TO LEAVE ROOM FOR RST BRANCH
                  1424 GTC03:
0414 CD1F06       1425        CALL    GETCH   ; GET COMMAND CHARACTER TO A
0417 CDF805       1426        CALL    ECHO    ; ECHO CHARACTER TO USER
041A 79           1427        MOV     A,C     ; PUT COMMAND CHARACTER INTO ACCUMULATOR
041B 010600       1428        LXI     B,NCMDS ; C CONTAINS LOOP AND INDEX COUNT
041E 21AE07       1429        LXI     H,CTAB  ; HL POINTS INTO COMMAND TABLE
                  1430 GTC05:
0421 BE           1431        CMP     M       ; COMPARE TABLE ENTRY AND CHARACTER
0422 CA2D04       1432        JZ      GTC10   ; BRANCH IF EQUAL - COMMAND RECOGNIZED
0425 23           1433        INX     H       ; ELSE, INCREMENT TABLE POINTER
0426 0D           1434        DCR     C       ; DECREMENT LOOP COUNT
0427 C22104       1435        JNZ     GTC05   ; BRANCH IF NOT AT TABLE END
042A C31106       1436        JMP     ERROR   ; ELSE, COMMAND CHARACTER IS ILLEGAL
                  1437 GTC10:
042D 21A007       1438        LXI     H,CADR  ; IF GOOD COMMAND, LOAD ADDRESS OF TABLE
                  1439                        ; /OF COMMAND ROUTINE ADDRESSES
0430 09           1440        DAD     B       ; ADD WHAT IS LEFT OF LOOP COUNT
0431 09           1441        DAD     B       ; ADD AGAIN - EACH ENTRY IN CADR IS 2 BYTES LONG
0432 7E           1442        MOV     A,M     ; GET LSP OF ADDRESS OF TABLE ENTRY TO A
0433 23           1443        INX     H       ; POINT TO NEXT BYTE IN TABLE
0434 66           1444        MOV     H,M     ; GET MSP OF ADDRESS OF TABLE ENTRY TO H
0435 6F           1445        MOV     L,A     ; PUT LSP OF ADDRESS OF TABLE ENTRY INTO L
0436 E9           1446        PCHL            ; NEXT INSTRUCTION COMES FROM COMMAND ROUTINE
                  1447 ;
                  1448 ;
                  1449 ;**************************************************************
                  1450 ;
                  1451 ;
                  1452 ;                   COMMAND IMPLEMENTING ROUTINES
                  1453 ;
                  1454 ;
                  1455 ;**************************************************************
                  1456 ;
                  1457 ;
                  1458 ; FUNCTION: DCMD
                  1459 ; INPUTS: NONE
                  1460 ; OUTPUTS: NONE
                  1461 ; CALLS: ECHO,NMOUT,HILO,GETCM,CROUT,GETNM
                  1462 ; DESTROYS: A,B,C,D,E,H,L,F/F'S
                  1463 ; DESCRIPTION: DCMD IMPLEMENTS THE DISPLAY MEMORY (D) COMMAND
                  1464 ;
                  1465 DCMD:
0437 0E02         1466        MVI     C,2     ; GET 2 NUMBERS FROM INPUT STREAM
0439 CD5B06       1467        CALL    GETNM
043C D1           1468        POP     D       ; ENDING ADDRESS TO DE
043D E1           1469        POP     H       ; STARTING ADDRESS TO HL
                  1470 DCM05:
043E CDEB05       1471        CALL    CROUT   ; ECHO CARRIAGE RETURN/LINE FEED
0441 7C           1472        MOV     A,H     ; DISPLAY ADDRESS OF FIRST LOCATION IN LINE
0442 CDC706       1473        CALL    NMOUT
0445 7D           1474        MOV     A,L     ; ADDRESS IS 2 BYTES LONG
0446 CDC706       1475        CALL    NMOUT
                  1476 DCM10:
0449 0E20         1477        MVI     C,' '
044B CDF805       1478        CALL    ECHO    ; USE BLANK AS SEPARATOR
044E 7E           1479        MOV     A,M     ; GET CONTENTS OF NEXT MEMORY LOCATION
044F CDC706       1480        CALL    NMOUT   ; DISPLAY CONTENTS
0452 CDA006       1481        CALL    HILO    ; SEE IF ADDRESS OF DISPLAYED LOCATION IS
```

```
LOC  OBJ         SEQ          SOURCE STATEMENT

                 1482                        ; /GREATER THAN OR EQUAL TO ENDING ADDRESS
                 1483         FALSE  DCM15   ; IF NOT, MORE TO DISPLAY
0455 D25E04      1484+        JNC    DCM15
0458 CDEB05      1485         CALL   CROUT   ; CARRIAGE RETURN/LINE FEED TO END LINE
045B C30804      1486         JMP    GETCM   ; ALL DONE
                 1487 DCM15:
045E 23          1488         INX    H       ; IF MORE TO GO, POINT TO NEXT LOC TO DISPLAY
045F 7D          1489         MOV    A,L     ; GET LOW ORDER BITS OF NEW ADDRESS
0460 E60F        1490         ANI    NEWLN   ; SEE IF LAST HEX DIGIT OF ADDRESS DENOTES
                 1491                        ; /START OF NEW LINE
0462 C24904      1492         JNZ    DCM10   ; NO - NOT AT END OF LINE
0465 C33E04      1493         JMP    DCM05   ; YES - START NEW LINE WITH ADDRESS
                 1494 ;
                 1495 ;
                 1496 ;****************************************************************
                 1497 ;
                 1498 ;
                 1499 ; FUNCTION: GCMD
                 1500 ; INPUTS: NONE
                 1501 ; OUTPUTS: NONE
                 1502 ; CALLS: ERROR,GETHX,RSTTF
                 1503 ; DESTROYS: A,B,C,D,E,H,L,F/F'S
                 1504 ; DESCRIPTION: GCMD IMPLEMENTS THE BEGIN EXECUTION (G) COMMAND.
                 1505 ;
                 1506 GCMD:
0468 CD2606      1507         CALL   GETHX   ; GET ADDRESS (IF PRESENT) FROM INPUT STREAM
                 1508         FALSE  GCM05   ; BRANCH IF NO NUMBER PRESENT
046B D27D04      1509+        JNC    GCM05
046E 7A          1510         MOV    A,D     ; ELSE, GET TERMINATOR
046F FE0D        1511         CPI    CR      ; SEE IF CARRIAGE RETURN
0471 C21106      1512         JNZ    ERROR   ; ERROR IF NOT PROPERLY TERMINATED
0474 21F220      1513         LXI    H,PSAV  ; WANT NUMBER TO REPLACE SAVE PGM COUNTER
0477 71          1514         MOV    M,C
0478 23          1515         INX    H
0479 70          1516         MOV    M,B
047A C38304      1517         JMP    GCM10
                 1518 GCM05:
047D 7A          1519         MOV    A,D     ; IF NO STARTING ADDRESS, MAKE SURE THAT
047E FE0D        1520         CPI    CR      ; /CARRIAGE RETURN TERMINATED COMMAND
0480 C21106      1521         JNZ    ERROR   ; ERROR IF NOT
                 1522 GCM10:
0483 C31B03      1523         JMP    RSTOR   ; RESTORE REGISTERS AND BEGIN EXECUTION
                 1524                        ; (RSTOR IS IN KEYBOARD MONITOR)
                 1525 ;
                 1526 ;
                 1527 ;****************************************************************
                 1528 ;
                 1529 ;
                 1530 ; FUNCTION: ICMD
                 1531 ; INPUTS: NONE
                 1532 ; OUTPUTS: NONE
                 1533 ; CALLS: ERROR,ECHO,GETCH,VALDL,VALDG,CNVBN,STHLF,GETNM,CROUT
                 1534 ; DESTROYS: A,B,C,D,E,H,L,F/F'S
                 1535 ; DESCRIPTION: ICMD IMPLEMENTS THE INSERT CODE INTO MEMORY (I) COMMAND.
                 1536 ;
                 1537 ICMD:
0486 0E01        1538         MVI    C,1
0488 CD5B06      1539         CALL   GETNM   ; GET SINGLE NUMBER FROM INPUT STREAM
048B 3EFF        1540         MVI    A,UPPER
048D 32FD20      1541         STA    TEMP    ; TEMP WILL HOLD THE UPPER/LOWER HALF BYTE FLAG
0490 D1          1542         POP    D       ; ADDRESS OF START TO DE
                 1543 ICM05:
0491 CD1F06      1544         CALL   GETCH   ; GET A CHARACTER FROM INPUT STREAM
0494 4F          1545         MOV    C,A
0495 CDF805      1546         CALL   ECHO    ; ECHO IT
0498 79          1547         MOV    A,C     ; PUT CHARACTER BACK INTO A
0499 FE1B        1548         CPI    TERM    ; SEE IF CHARACTER IS A TERMINATING CHARACTER
049B CAC704      1549         JZ     ICM25   ; IF SO, ALL DONE ENTERING CHARACTERS
049E CD7907      1550         CALL   VALDL   ; ELSE, SEE IF VALID DELIMITER
                 1551         TRUE   ICM05   ; IF SO SIMPLY IGNORE THIS CHARACTER
04A1 DA9104      1552+        JC     ICM05
04A4 CD5E07      1553         CALL   VALDG   ; ELSE, CHECK TO SEE IF VALID HEX DIGIT
                 1554         FALSE  ICM20   ; IF NOT, BRANCH TO HANDLE ERROR CONDITION
04A7 D2C104      1555+        JNC    ICM20
04AA CDBB05      1556         CALL   CNVBN   ; CONVERT DIGIT TO BINARY
04AD 4F          1557         MOV    C,A     ; MOVE RESULT TO C
04AE CD3F07      1558         CALL   STHLF   ; STORE IN APPROPRIATE HALF WORD
04B1 3AFD20      1559         LDA    TEMP    ; GET HALF BYTE FLAG
04B4 B7          1560         ORA    A       ; SET F/F'S
04B5 C2B904      1561         JNZ    ICM10   ; BRANCH IF FLAG SET FOR UPPER
04B8 13          1562         INX    D       ; IF LOWER, INC ADDRESS OF BYTE TO STORE IN
                 1563 ICM10:
04B9 EEFF        1564         XRI    INVRT   ; TOGGLE STATE OF FLAG
04BB 32FD20      1565         STA    TEMP    ; PUT NEW VALUE OF FLAG BACK
04BE C39104      1566         JMP    ICM05   ; PROCESS NEXT DIGIT
                 1567 ICM20:
04C1 CD3407      1568         CALL   STHF0   ; ILLEGAL CHARACTER
```

```
04C4 C31106      1569              JMP    ERROR    ; MAKE SURE ENTIRE BYTE FILLED THEN ERROR
                 1570 ICM25:
04C7 CD3407      1571              CALL   STHF0    ; HERE FOR ESCAPE CHARACTER - INPUT IS DONE
04CA CDEB05      1572              CALL   CROUT    ; ADD CARRIAGE RETURN
04CD C30804      1573              JMP    GETCM
                 1574 ;
                 1575 ;
                 1576 ;*********************************************************************
                 1577 ;
                 1578 ;
                 1579 ; FUNCTION: MCMD
                 1580 ; INPUTS: NONE
                 1581 ; OUTPUTS: NONE
                 1582 ; CALLS: GETCH,HILO,GETNM
                 1583 ; DESTROYS: A,B,C,D,E,H,L,F/F'S
                 1584 ; DESCRIPTION: MCMD IMPLEMENTS THE MOVE DATA IN MEMORY (M) COMMAND.
                 1585 ;
                 1586 MCMD:
04D0 0E03        1587              MVI    C,3
04D2 CD5B06      1588              CALL   GETNM    ; GET 3 NUMBERS FROM INPUT STREAM
04D5 C1          1589              POP    B        ; DESTINATION ADDRESS TO BC
04D6 E1          1590              POP    H        ; ENDING ADDRESS TO HL
04D7 D1          1591              POP    D        ; STARTING ADDRESS TO DE
                 1592 MCM05:
04D8 E5          1593              PUSH   H        ; SAVE ENDING ADDRESS
04D9 62          1594              MOV    H,D
04DA 6B          1595              MOV    L,E      ; SOURCE ADDRESS TO HL
04DB 7E          1596              MOV    A,M      ; GET SOURCE BYTE
04DC 60          1597              MOV    H,B
04DD 69          1598              MOV    L,C      ; DESTINATION ADDRESS TO HL
04DE 77          1599              MOV    M,A      ; MOVE BYTE TO DESTINATION
04DF 03          1600              INX    B        ; INCREMENT DESTINATION ADDRESS
04E0 78          1601              MOV    A,B
04E1 B1          1602              ORA    C        ; TEST FOR DESTINATION ADDRESS OVERFLOW
04E2 CA0804      1603              JZ     GETCM    ; IF SO, CAN TERMINATE COMMAND
04E5 13          1604              INX    D        ; INCREMENT SOURCE ADDRESS
04E6 E1          1605              POP    H        ; ELSE, GET BACK ENDING ADDRESS
04E7 CDAA06      1606              CALL   HILO     ; SEE IF ENDING ADDR>=SOURCE ADDR
                 1607              FALSE  GETCM    ; IF NOT, COMMAND IS DONE
04EA D20804      1608+             JNC    GETCM
04ED C3D804      1609              JMP    MCM05    ; MOVE ANOTHER BYTE
                 1610 ;
                 1611 ;
                 1612 ;*********************************************************************
                 1613 ;
                 1614 ;
                 1615 ; FUNCTION: SCMD
                 1616 ; INPUTS: NONE
                 1617 ; OUTPUTS: NONE
                 1618 ; CALLS: GETHX,GETCM,NMOUT,ECHO
                 1619 ; DESTROYS: A,B,C,D,E,H,L,F/F'S
                 1620 ; DESCRIPTION: SCMD IMPLEMENTS THE SUBSTITUTE INTO MEMORY (S) COMMAND.
                 1621 ;
                 1622 SCMD:
04F0 CD2606      1623              CALL   GETHX    ; GET A NUMBER, IF PRESENT, FROM INPUT
04F3 C5          1624              PUSH   B
04F4 E1          1625              POP    H        ; GET NUMBER TO HL - DENOTES MEMORY LOCATION
                 1626 SCM05:
04F5 7A          1627              MOV    A,D      ; GET TERMINATOR
04F6 FE20        1628              CPI    ' '      ; SEE IF SPACE
04F8 CA0005      1629              JZ     SCM10    ; YES - CONTINUE PROCESSING
04FB FE2C        1630              CPI    ','      ; ELSE, SEE IF COMMA
04FD C20804      1631              JNZ    GETCM    ; NO - TERMINATE COMMAND
                 1632 SCM10:
0500 7E          1633              MOV    A,M      ; GET CONTENTS OF SPECIFIED LOCATION TO A
0501 CDC706      1634              CALL   NMOUT    ; DISPLAY CONTENTS ON CONSOLE
0504 0E2D        1635              MVI    C,'-'
0506 CDF805      1636              CALL   ECHO     ; USE DASH FOR SEPARATOR
0509 CD2606      1637              CALL   GETHX    ; GET NEW VALUE FOR MEMORY LOCATION, IF ANY
                 1638              FALSE  SCM15    ; IF NO VALUE PRESENT, BRANCH
050C D21005      1639+             JNC    SCM15
050F 71          1640              MOV    M,C      ; ELSE, STORE LOWER 8 BITS OF NUMBER ENTERED
                 1641 SCM15:
0510 23          1642              INX    H        ; INCREMENT ADDRESS OF MEMORY LOCATION TO VIEW
0511 C3F504      1643              JMP    SCM05
                 1644 ;
                 1645 ;
                 1646 ;*********************************************************************
                 1647 ;
                 1648 ;
                 1649 ; FUNCTION: XCMD
                 1650 ; INPUTS: NONE
                 1651 ; OUTPUTS: NONE
                 1652 ; CALLS: GETCH,ECHO,REGDS,GETCM,ERROR,RGADR,NMOUT,CROUT,GETHX
                 1653 ; DESTROYS: A,B,C,D,E,H,L,F/F'S
                 1654 ; DESCRIPTION: XCMD IMPLEMENTS THE REGISTER EXAMINE AND CHANGE (X)
                 1655 ;                     COMMAND.
```

```
                    1656 ;
                    1657 XCMD:
0514 CD1F06         1658          CALL    GETCH    ; GET REGISTER IDENTIFIER
0517 4F             1659          MOV     C,A
0518 CDF805         1660          CALL    ECHO     ; ECHO IT
051B 79             1661          MOV     A,C
051C FE0D           1662          CPI     CR
051E C22705         1663          JNZ     XCM05    ; BRANCH IF NOT CARRIAGE RETURN
0521 CDEA06         1664          CALL    REGDS    ; ELSE, DISPLAY REGISTER CONTENTS
0524 C30804         1665          JMP     GETCM    ; THEN TERMINATE COMMAND
                    1666 XCM05:
0527 4F             1667          MOV     C,A      ; GET REGISTER IDENTIFIER TO C
0528 CD1B07         1668          CALL    RGADR    ; CONVERT IDENTIFIER INTO RTAB TABLE ADDR
052B C5             1669          PUSH    B
052C E1             1670          POP     H        ; PUT POINTER TO REGISTER ENTRY INTO HL
052D 0E20           1671          MVI     C,' '
052F CDF805         1672          CALL    ECHO     ; ECHO SPACE TO USER
0532 79             1673          MOV     A,C
0533 32FD20         1674          STA     TEMP     ; PUT SPACE INTO TEMP AS DELIMITER
                    1675 XCM10:
0536 3AFD20         1676          LDA     TEMP     ; GET TERMINATOR
0539 FE20           1677          CPI     ' '      ; SEE IF A BLANK
053B CA4305         1678          JZ      XCM15    ; YES - GO CHECK POINTER INTO TABLE
053E FE2C           1679          CPI     ','      ; NO - SEE IF COMMA
0540 C20804         1680          JNZ     GETCM    ; NO - MUST BE CARRIAGE RETURN TO END COMMAND
                    1681 XCM15:
0543 7E             1682          MOV     A,M
0544 B7             1683          ORA     A        ; SET F/F'S
0545 C24E05         1684          JNZ     XCM18    ; BRANCH IF NOT AT END OF TABLE
0548 CDEB05         1685          CALL    CROUT    ; ELSE, OUTPUT CARRIAGE RETURN LINE FEED
054B C30804         1686          JMP     GETCM    ; AND EXIT
                    1687 XCM18:
054E E5             1688          PUSH    H        ; PUT POINTER ON STACK
054F 5E             1689          MOV     E,M
0550 1620           1690          MVI     D,RAMST SHR 8    ; ADDRESS OF SAVE LOCATION FROM TABLE
0552 23             1691          INX     H
0553 46             1692          MOV     B,M      ; FETCH LENGTH FLAG FROM TABLE
0554 D5             1693          PUSH    D        ; SAVE ADDRESS OF SAVE LOCATION
0555 D5             1694          PUSH    D
0556 E1             1695          POP     H        ; MOVE ADDRESS TO HL
0557 C5             1696          PUSH    B        ; SAVE LENGTH FLAG
0558 7E             1697          MOV     A,M      ; GET 8 BITS OF REGISTER FROM SAVE LOCATION
0559 CDC706         1698          CALL    NMOUT    ; DISPLAY IT
055C F1             1699          POP     PSW      ; GET BACK LENGTH FLAG
055D F5             1700          PUSH    PSW      ; SAVE IT AGAIN
055E B7             1701          ORA     A        ; SET F/F'S
055F CA6705         1702          JZ      XCM20    ; IF 8 BIT REGISTER, NOTHING MORE TO DISPLAY
0562 2B             1703          DCX     H        ; ELSE, FOR 16 BIT REGISTER, GET LOWER 8 BITS
0563 7E             1704          MOV     A,M
0564 CDC706         1705          CALL    NMOUT    ; DISPLAY THEM
                    1706 XCM20:
0567 0E2D           1707          MVI     C,'-'
0569 CDF805         1708          CALL    ECHO     ; USE DASH AS SEPARATOR
056C CD2606         1709          CALL    GETHX    ; SEE IF THERE IS A VALUE TO PUT INTO REGISTER
                    1710          FALSE   XCM30    ; NO - GO CHECK FOR NEXT REGISTER
056F D28705         1711+         JNC     XCM30
0572 7A             1712          MOV     A,D
0573 32FD20         1713          STA     TEMP     ; ELSE, SAVE THE TERMINATOR FOR NOW
0576 F1             1714          POP     PSW      ; GET BACK LENGTH FLAG
0577 E1             1715          POP     H        ; PUT ADDRESS OF SAVE LOCATION INTO HL
0578 B7             1716          ORA     A        ; SET F/F'S
0579 CA7E05         1717          JZ      XCM25    ; IF 8 BIT REGISTER, BRANCH
057C 70             1718          MOV     M,B      ; SAVE UPPER 8 BITS
057D 2B             1719          DCX     H        ; POINT TO SAVE LOCATION FOR LOWER 8 BITS
                    1720 XCM25:
057E 71             1721          MOV     M,C      ; STORE ALL OF 8 BIT OR LOWER 1/2 OF 16 BIT REG
                    1722 XCM27:
057F 110300         1723          LXI     D,RTABS  ; SIZE OF ENTRY IN RTAB TABLE
0582 E1             1724          POP     H        ; POINTER INTO REGISTER TABLE RTAB
0583 19             1725          DAD     D        ; ADD ENTRY SIZE TO POINTER
0584 C33605         1726          JMP     XCM10    ; DO NEXT REGISTER
                    1727 XCM30:
0587 7A             1728          MOV     A,D      ; GET TERMINATOR
0588 32FD20         1729          STA     TEMP     ; SAVE IN MEMORY
058B D1             1730          POP     D        ; CLEAR STACK OF LENGTH FLAG AND ADDRESS
058C D1             1731          POP     D        ; /OF SAVE LOCATION
058D C37F05         1732          JMP     XCM27    ; GO INCREMENT REGISTER TABLE POINTER
                    1733 ;
                    1734 ;
                    1735 ;**********************************************************************
                    1736 ;
                    1737 ;
                    1738 ;                    UTILITY ROUTINES
                    1739 ;
                    1740 ;
                    1741 ;**********************************************************************
                    1742 ;
```

```
                      1743 ;
                      1744 ; FUNCTION: CI
                      1745 ; INPUTS: NONE
                      1746 ; OUTPUTS: A - CHARACTER FROM TTY
                      1747 ; CALLS: DELAY
                      1748 ; DESTROYS: A,F/F'S
                      1749 ; DESCRIPTION: CI WAITS UNTIL A CHARACTER HAS BEEN ENTERED AT THE
                      1750 ;                 TTY AND THEN RETURNS THE CHARACTER, VIA THE A
                      1751 ;                 REGISTER, TO THE CALLING ROUTINE.  THIS ROUTINE
                      1752 ;                 IS CALLED BY THE USER VIA A JUMP TABLE IN RAM.
                      1753 ;
                      1754 CI:
0590 F3              1755          DI
0591 D5              1756          PUSH     D       ; SAVE DE
                      1757 CI05:
0592 20              1758          RIM              ; GET INPUT BIT
0593 17              1759          RAL              ; INTO CARRY WITH IT
0594 DA9205          1760          JC       CI05    ; BRANCH IF NO START BIT
0597 114602          1761          LXI      D,WAIT  ; WAIT UNTIL MIDDLE OF BIT
059A CDF105          1762          CALL     DELAY
059D C5              1763          PUSH     B       ; SAVE BC
059E 010800          1764          LXI      B,8     ; B<--0, C<--8 BITS TO RECEIVE
                      1765 CI10:
05A1 118C04          1766          LXI      D,IBTIM
05A4 CDF105          1767          CALL     DELAY   ; WAIT UNTIL MIDDLE OF NEXT BIT
05A7 20              1768          RIM              ; GET THE BIT
05A8 17              1769          RAL              ; INTO CARRY
05A9 78              1770          MOV      A,B     ; GET PARTIAL RESULT
05AA 1F              1771          RAR              ; SHIFT IN NEXT DATA BIT
05AB 47              1772          MOV      B,A     ; REPLACE RESULT
05AC 0D              1773          DCR      C       ; DEC COUNT OF BITS TO GO
05AD C2A105          1774          JNZ      CI10    ; BRANCH IF MORE LEFT
05B0 118C04          1775          LXI      D,IBTIM ; ELSE, WANT TO WAIT OUT STOP BIT
05B3 CDF105          1776          CALL     DELAY
05B6 78              1777          MOV      A,B     ; GET RESULT
05B7 C1              1778          POP      B
05B8 D1              1779          POP      D       ; RESTORE SAVED REGISTERS
05B9 FB              1780          EI
05BA C9              1781          RET              ; THAT'S IT
                      1782 ;
                      1783 ;
                      1784 ;**********************************************************************
                      1785 ;
                      1786 ;
                      1787 ; FUNCTION: CNVBN
                      1788 ; INPUTS: C - ASCII CHARACTER '0'-'9' OR 'A'-'F'
                      1789 ; OUTPUTS: A - 0 TO F HEX
                      1790 ; CALLS: NOTHING
                      1791 ; DESTROYS: A,F/F'S
                      1792 ; DESCRIPTION: CNVBN CONVERTS THE ASCII REPRESENTATION OF A HEX
                      1793 ;                 CNVBN INTO ITS CORRESPONDING BINARY VALUE.  CNVBN
                      1794 ;                 DOES NOT CHECK THE VALIDITY OF ITS INPUT.
                      1795 ;
                      1796 CNVBN:
05BB 79              1797          MOV      A,C
05BC D630            1798          SUI      '0'     ; SUBTRACT CODE FOR '0' FROM ARGUMENT
05BE FE0A            1799          CPI      10      ; WANT TO TEST FOR RESULT OF 0 TO 9
05C0 F8              1800          RM               ; IF SO, THEN ALL DONE
05C1 D607            1801          SUI      7       ; ELSE, RESULT BETWEEN 17 AND 23 DECIMAL
05C3 C9              1802          RET              ; SO RETURN AFTER SUBTRACTING BIAS OF 7
                      1803 ;
                      1804 ;
                      1805 ;**********************************************************************
                      1806 ;
                      1807 ;
                      1808 ; FUNCTION: CO
                      1809 ; INPUTS: C - CHARACTER TO OUTPUT TO TTY
                      1810 ; OUTPUTS: C - CHARACTER OUTPUT TO TTY
                      1811 ; CALLS: DELAY
                      1812 ; DESTROYS: A,F/F'S
                      1813 ; DESCRIPTION: CO SENDS ITS INPUT ARGUMENT TO THE TTY.
                      1814 ;
                      1815 CO:
05C4 F3              1816          DI
05C5 C5              1817          PUSH     B       ; SAVE BC
05C6 D5              1818          PUSH     D       ; SAVE DE
05C7 3EC0            1819          MVI      A,STRT  ; START BIT MASK
05C9 0607            1820          MVI      B,7     ; B WILL COUNT BITS TO SEND
                      1821 CO05:
05CB 30              1822          SIM              ; SEND A BIT
05CC 118C04          1823          LXI      D,OBTIM ; WAIT FOR TTY TO HANDLE IT
05CF CDF105          1824          CALL     DELAY
05D2 79              1825          MOV      A,C     ; PICK UP BITS LEFT TO SEND
05D3 1F              1826          RAR              ; LOW ORDER BIT TO CARRY
05D4 4F              1827          MOV      C,A     ; PUT REST BACK
05D5 3E80            1828          MVI      A,SSTRT ; SHIFTED ENABLE BIT
05D7 1F              1829          RAR              ; SHIFT IN DATA BIT
```

```
LOC  OBJ         SEQ        SOURCE STATEMENT

05D8 EE80        1830          XRI    80H      ; COMPLEMENT DATA BIT
05DA 05          1831          DCR    B        ; DEC COUNT
05DB F2CB05      1832          JP     CO05     ; SEND IF MORE BITS NEED TO BE SENT
05DE 3E40        1833          MVI    A,STOPB  ; ELSE, SEND STOP BITS
05E0 30          1834          SIM
05E1 113012      1835          LXI    D,TIM4   ; WAIT 4 BIT TIME (FAKE PARITY + 3 STOP BITS)
05E4 CDF105      1836          CALL   DELAY
05E7 D1          1837          POP    D
05E8 C1          1838          POP    B        ; RESTORE SAVED REGISTERS
05E9 FB          1839          EI
05EA C9          1840          RET             ; ALL DONE
                 1841 ;
                 1842 ;
                 1843 ;************************************************************
                 1844 ;
                 1845 ;
                 1846 ; FUNCTION CROUT
                 1847 ; INPUTS: NONE
                 1848 ; OUTPUTS: NONE
                 1849 ; CALLS: ECHO
                 1850 ; DESTROYS: A,B,C,F/F'S
                 1851 ; DESCRIPTION: CROUT SENDS A CARRIAGE RETURN (AND HENCE A LINE
                 1852 ;              FEED) TO THE CONSOLE.
                 1853 ;
                 1854 CROUT:
05EB 0E0D        1855          MVI    C,CR
05ED CDF805      1856          CALL   ECHO
05F0 C9          1857          RET
                 1858 ;
                 1859 ;
                 1860 ;************************************************•••••••••••••
                 1861 ;
                 1862 ;
                 1863 ; FUNCTION: DELAY
                 1864 ; INPUTS: DE - 16 BIT INTEGER DENOTING NUMBER OF TIMES TO LOOP
                 1865 ; OUTPUTS: NONE
                 1866 ; CALLS: NOTHING
                 1867 ; DESTROYS: A,D,E,F/F'S
                 1868 ; DESCRIPTION: DELAY DOES NOT RETURN TO CALLER UNTIL INPUT ARGUMENT
                 1869 ;              IS COUNTED DOWN TO 0.
                 1870 ;
                 1871 DELAY:
05F1 1B          1872          DCX    D        ; DECREMENT INPUT ARGUMENT
05F2 7A          1873          MOV    A,D
05F3 B3          1874          ORA    E
05F4 C2F105      1875          JNZ    DELAY    ; IF ARGUMENT NOT 0, KEEP GOING
05F7 C9          1876          RET
                 1877 ;
                 1878 ;
                 1879 ;************************************************************
                 1880 ;
                 1881 ;
                 1882 ; FUNCTION: ECHO
                 1883 ; INPUTS: C - CHARACTER TO ECHO TO TERMINAL
                 1884 ; OUTPUTS: C - CHARACTER ECHOED TO TERMINAL
                 1885 ; CALLS: CO
                 1886 ; DESTROYS: A,B,F/F'S
                 1887 ; DESCRIPTION: ECHO TAKES A SINGLE CHARACTER AS INPUT AND, VIA
                 1888 ;              THE MONITOR, SENDS THAT CHARACTER TO THE USER
                 1889 ;              TERMINAL.  A CARRIAGE RETURN IS ECHOED AS A CARRIAGE
                 1890 ;              RETURN LINE FEED, AND AN ESCAPE CHARACTER IS ECHOED AS $.
                 1891 ;
                 1892 ECHO:
05F8 41          1893          MOV    B,C      ; SAVE ARGUMENT
05F9 3E1B        1894          MVI    A,ESC
05FB B8          1895          CMP    B        ; SEE IF ECHOING AN ESCAPE CHARACTER
05FC C20106      1896          JNZ    ECH05    ; NO - BRANCH
05FF 0E24        1897          MVI    C,'$'    ; YES - ECHO AS $
                 1898 ECH05:
0601 CDC405      1899          CALL   CO       ; DO OUTPUT THROUGH MONITOR
0604 3E0D        1900          MVI    A,CR
0606 B8          1901          CMP    B        ; SEE IF CHARACTER ECHOED WAS A CARRIAGE RETURN
0607 C20F06      1902          JNZ    ECH10    ; NO - NO NEED TO TAKE SPECIAL ACTION
060A 0E0A        1903          MVI    C,LF     ; YES - WANT TO ECHO LINE FEED, TOO
060C CDC405      1904          CALL   CO
                 1905 ECH10:
060F 48          1906          MOV    C,B      ; RESTORE ARGUMENT
0610 C9          1907          RET
                 1908 ;
                 1909 ;
                 1910 ;************************************************************
                 1911 ;
                 1912 ;
                 1913 ; FUNCTION: ERROR
                 1914 ; INPUTS: NONE
                 1915 ; OUTPUTS: NONE
                 1916 ; CALLS: ECHO,CROUT,GETCM
```

```
                   1917 ; DESTROYS: A,B,C,F/F'S
                   1918 ; DESCRIPTION: ERROR PRINTS THE ERROR CHARACTER (CURRENTLY AN ASTERISK)
                   1919 ;               ON THE CONSOLE, FOLLOWED BY A CARRIAGE RETURN-LINE FEED,
                   1920 ;               AND THEN RETURNS CONTROL TO THE COMMAND RECOGNIZER.
                   1921 ;
                   1922 ERROR:
0611 0E2A          1923        MVI     C,'*'
0613 CDF805        1924        CALL    ECHO      ; SEND * TO CONSOLE
0616 CDEB05        1925        CALL    CROUT     ; SKIP TO BEGINNING OF NEXT LINE
0619 C30804        1926        JMP     GETCM     ; TRY AGAIN FOR ANOTHER COMMAND
                   1927 ;
                   1928 ;
                   1929 ;****************************************************************
                   1930 ;
                   1931 ;
                   1932 ; FUNCTION: FRET
                   1933 ; INPUTS: NONE
                   1934 ; OUTPUTS: CARRY - ALWAYS 0
                   1935 ; CALLS: NOTHING
                   1936 ; DESTROYS: CARRY
                   1937 ; DESCRIPTION: FRET IS JUMPED TO BY ANY ROUTINE THAT WISHES TO
                   1938 ;               INDICATE FAILURE ON RETURN.  FRET SETS THE CARRY
                   1939 ;               FALSE, DENOTING FAILURE, AND THEN RETURNS TO THE
                   1940 ;               CALLER OF THE ROUTINE INVOKING FRET.
                   1941 ;
                   1942 FRET:
061C 37            1943        STC               ; FIRST SET CARRY TRUE
061D 3F            1944        CMC               ; THEN COMPLEMENT IT TO MAKE IT FALSE
061E C9            1945        RET               ; RETURN APPROPRIATELY
                   1946 ;
                   1947 ;
                   1948 ;****************************************************************
                   1949 ;
                   1950 ;
                   1951 ; FUNCTION: GETCH
                   1952 ; INPUTS: NONE
                   1953 ; OUTPUTS: C - NEXT CHARACTER IN INPUT STREAM
                   1954 ; CALLS: CI
                   1955 ; DESTROYS: A,C,F/F'S
                   1956 ; DESCRIPTION: GETCH RETURNS THE NEXT CHARACTER IN THE INPUT STREAM
                   1957 ;               TO THE CALLING PROGRAM.
                   1958 ;
                   1959 GETCH:
061F CD9005        1960        CALL    CI        ; GET CHARACTER FROM TERMINAL
0622 E67F          1961        ANI     PRTY0     ; TURN OFF PARITY BIT IN CASE SET BY CONSOLE
0624 4F            1962        MOV     C,A       ; PUT VALUE IN C REGISTER FOR RETURN
0625 C9            1963        RET
                   1964 ;
                   1965 ;
                   1966 ;****************************************************************
                   1967 ;
                   1968 ;
                   1969 ; FUNCTION: GETHX
                   1970 ; INPUTS: NONE
                   1971 ; OUTPUTS: BC - 16 BIT INTEGER
                   1972 ;          D - CHARACTER WHICH TERMINATED THE INTEGER
                   1973 ;          CARRY - 1 IF FIRST CHARACTER NOT DELIMITER
                   1974 ;                - 0 IF FIRST CHARACTER IS DELIMITER
                   1975 ; CALLS: GETCH,ECHO,VALDL,VALDG,CNVBN,ERROR
                   1976 ; DESTROYS: A,B,C,D,E,F/F'S
                   1977 ; DESCRIPTION: GETHX ACCEPTS A STRING OF HEX DIGITS FROM THE INPUT
                   1978 ;               STREAM AND RETURNS THEIR VALUE AS A 16 BIT BINARY
                   1979 ;               INTEGER.  IF MORE THAN 4 HEX DIGITS ARE ENTERED,
                   1980 ;               ONLY THE LAST 4 ARE USED.  THE NUMBER TERMINATES WHEN
                   1981 ;               A VALID DELIMITER IS ENCOUNTERED.  THE DELIMITER IS
                   1982 ;               ALSO RETURNED AS AN OUTPUT OF THE FUNCTION.  ILLEGAL
                   1983 ;               CHARACTERS (NOT HEX DIGITS OR DELIMITERS) CAUSE AN
                   1984 ;               ERROR INDICATION.  IF THE FIRST (VALID) CHARACTER
                   1985 ;               ENCOUNTERED IN THE INPUT STREAM IS NOT A DELIMITER,
                   1986 ;               GETHX WILL RETURN WITH THE CARRY BIT SET TO 1;
                   1987 ;               OTHERWISE, THE CARRY BIT IS SET TO 0 AND THE CONTENTS
                   1988 ;               OF BC ARE UNDEFINED.
                   1989 ;
                   1990 GETHX:
0626 E5            1991        PUSH    H         ; SAVE HL
0627 210000        1992        LXI     H,0       ; INITIALIZE RESULT
062A 1E00          1993        MVI     E,0       ; INITIALIZE DIGIT FLAG TO FALSE
                   1994 GHX05:
062C CD1F06        1995        CALL    GETCH     ; GET A CHARACTER
062F 4F            1996        MOV     C,A
0630 CDF805        1997        CALL    ECHO      ; ECHO THE CHARACTER
0633 CD7907        1998        CALL    VALDL     ; SEE IF DELIMITER
                   1999        FALSE   GHX10     ; NO - BRANCH
0636 D24506        2000+       JNC     GHX10
0639 51            2001        MOV     D,C       ; YES - ALL DONE, BUT WANT TO RETURN DELIMITER
063A E5            2002        PUSH    H
063B C1            2003        POP     B         ; MOVE RESULT TO BC
```

```
LOC  OBJ          SEQ        SOURCE STATEMENT

063C E1          2004           POP    H        ; RESTORE HL
063D 7B          2005           MOV    A,E      ; GET FLAG
063E B7          2006           ORA    A        ; SET F/F'S
063F C23207      2007           JNZ    SRET     ; IF FLAG NON-0, A NUMBER HAS BEEN FOUND
0642 CA1C06      2008           JZ     FRET     ; ELSE, DELIMITER WAS FIRST CHARACTER
                 2009 GHX10:
0645 CD5E07      2010           CALL   VALDG    ; IF NOT DELIMITER, SEE IF DIGIT
                 2011           FALSE  ERROR    ; ERROR IF NOT A VALID DIGIT, EITHER
0648 D21106      2012+          JNC    ERROR
064B CDBB05      2013           CALL   CNVBN    ; CONVERT DIGIT TO ITS BINARY VALUE
064E 1EFF        2014           MVI    E,0FFH   ; SET DIGIT FLAG NON-0
0650 29          2015           DAD    H        ; *2
0651 29          2016           DAD    H        ; *4
0652 29          2017           DAD    H        ; *8
0653 29          2018           DAD    H        ; *16
0654 0600        2019           MVI    B,0      ; CLEAR UPPER 8 BITS OF BC PAIR
0656 4F          2020           MOV    C,A      ; BINARY VALUE OF CHARACTER INTO C
0657 09          2021           DAD    B        ; ADD THIS VALUE TO PARTIAL RESULT
0658 C32C06      2022           JMP    GHX05    ; GET NEXT CHARACTER
                 2023 ;
                 2024 ;
                 2025 ;********************************************************************
                 2026 ;
                 2027 ;
                 2028 ; FUNCTION: GETNM
                 2029 ; INPUTS: C - COUNT OF NUMBERS TO FIND IN INPUT STREAM
                 2030 ; OUTPUTS: TOP OF STACK - NUMBERS FOUND IN REVERSE ORDER (LAST ON TOP
                 2031 ;                                 OF STACK)
                 2032 ; CALLS: GETHX,HILO,ERROR
                 2033 ; DESTROYS: A,B,C,D,E,H,L,F/F'S
                 2034 ; DESCRIPTION: GETNM FINDS A SPECIFIED COUNT OF NUMBERS, BETWEEN 1
                 2035 ;                  AND 3, INCLUSIVE,  IN THE INPUT
                 2036 ;                  STREAM AND RETURNS THEIR VALUES ON THE STACK.  IF 2
                 2037 ;                  OR MORE NUMBERS ARE REQUESTED, THEN THE FIRST MUST BE
                 2038 ;                  LESS THAN OR EQUAL TO THE SECOND, OR THE FIRST AND
                 2039 ;                  SECOND NUMBERS WILL BE SET EQUAL.  THE LAST NUMBER
                 2040 ;                  REQUESTED MUST BE TERMINATED BY A CARRIAGE RETURN
                 2041 ;                  OR AN ERROR INDICATION WILL RESULT.
                 2042 ;
                 2043 GETNM:
065B 2E03        2044           MVI    L,3      ; PUT MAXIMUM ARGUMENT COUNT INTO L
065D 79          2045           MOV    A,C      ; GET THE ACTUAL ARGUMENT COUNT
065E E603        2046           ANI    3        ; FORCE TO MAXIMUM OF 3
0660 C8          2047           RZ              ; IF 0, DON'T BOTHER TO DO ANYTHIING
0661 67          2048           MOV    H,A      ; ELSE, PUT ACTUAL COUNT INTO H
                 2049 GNM05:
0662 CD2606      2050           CALL   GETHX    ; GET A NUMBER FROM INPUT STREAM
                 2051           FALSE  ERROR    ; ERROR IF NOT THERE - TOO FEW NUMBERS
0665 D21106      2052+          JNC    ERROR
0668 C5          2053           PUSH   B        ; ELSE, SAVE NUMBER ON STACK
0669 2D          2054           DCR    L        ; DECREMENT MAXIMUM ARGUMENT COUNT
066A 25          2055           DCR    H        ; DECREMENT ACTUAL ARGUMENT COUNT
066B CA7706      2056           JZ     GNM10    ; BRANCH IF NO MORE NUMBERS WANTED
066E 7A          2057           MOV    A,D      ; ELSE, GET NUMBER TERMINATOR TO A
066F FE0D        2058           CPI    CR       ; SEE IF CARRIAGE RETURN
0671 CA1106      2059           JZ     ERROR    ; ERROR IF SO - TOO FEW NUMBERS
0674 C36206      2060           JMP    GNM05    ; ELSE, PROCESS NEXT NUMBER
                 2061 GNM10:
0677 7A          2062           MOV    A,D      ; WHEN COUNT 0, CHECK LAST TERMINATOR
0678 FE0D        2063           CPI    CR
067A C21106      2064           JNZ    ERROR    ; ERROR IF NOT CARRIAGE RETURN
067D 01FFFF      2065           LXI    B,0FFFFH       ; HL GETS LARGEST NUMBER
0680 7D          2066           MOV    A,L      ; GET WHAT'S LEFT OF MAXIMUM ARG COUNT
0681 B7          2067           ORA    A        ; CHECK FOR 0
0682 CA8A06      2068           JZ     GNM20    ; IF YES, 3 NUMBERS WERE INPUT
                 2069 GNM15:
0685 C5          2070           PUSH   B        ; IF NOT, FILL REMAINING ARGUMENTS WITH 0FFFFH
0686 2D          2071           DCR    L
0687 C28506      2072           JNZ    GNM15
                 2073 GNM20:
068A C1          2074           POP    B        ; GET THE 3 ARGUMENTS OUT
068B D1          2075           POP    D
068C E1          2076           POP    H
068D CDA006      2077           CALL   HILO     ; SEE IF FIRST >= SECOND
                 2078           FALSE  GNM25    ; NO - BRANCH
0690 D29506      2079+          JNC    GNM25
0693 54          2080           MOV    D,H      ; YES - MAKE SECOND EQUAL TO THE FIRST
0694 5D          2081           MOV    E,L
                 2082 GNM25:
0695 E3          2083           XTHL            ; PUT FIRST ON STACK - GET RETURN ADDR
0696 D5          2084           PUSH   D        ; PUT SECOND ON STACK
0697 C5          2085           PUSH   B        ; PUT THIRD ON STACK
0698 E5          2086           PUSH   H        ; PUT RETURN ADDRESS ON STACK
                 2087 GNM30:
0699 3D          2088           DCR    A        ; DECREMENT RESIDUAL COUNT
069A F8          2089           RM              ; IF NEGATIVE, PROPER RESULTS ON STACK
069B E1          2090           POP    H        ; ELSE, GET RETURN ADDR
```

```
LOC  OBJ          SEQ        SOURCE STATEMENT

069C E3           2091          XTHL              ; REPLACE TOP RESULT WITH RETURN ADDR
069D C39906       2092          JMP     GNM30     ; TRY AGAIN
                  2093 ;
                  2094 ;
                  2095 ;••••••••••••••••••••••••••••••••••••••••••••••••••••••••••••••
                  2096 ;
                  2097 ;
                  2098 ; FUNCTION: HILO
                  2099 ; INPUTS: DE - 16 BIT INTEGER
                  2100 ;         HL - 16 BIT INTEGER
                  2101 ; OUTPUTS: CARRY - 0 IF HL<DE
                  2102 ;                - 1 IF HL>=DE
                  2103 ; CALLS: NOTHING
                  2104 ; DESTROYS: F/F'S
                  2105 ; DESCRIPTION: HILO COMPARES THE 2 16 BIT INTEGERS IN HL AND DE.  THE
                  2106 ;              INTEGERS ARE TREATED AS UNSIGNED NUMBERS.  THE CARRY
                  2107 ;              BIT IS SET ACCORDING TO THE RESULT OF THE COMPARISON.
                  2108 ;
                  2109 HILO:
06A0 C5           2110          PUSH    B         ; SAVE BC
06A1 47           2111          MOV     B,A       ; SAVE A IN B REGISTER
06A2 E5           2112          PUSH    H         ; SAVE HL PAIR
06A3 7A           2113          MOV     A,D       ; CHECK FOR DE = 0000H
06A4 B3           2114          ORA     E
06A5 CAC106       2115          JZ      HIL05     ; WE'RE AUTOMATICALLY DONE IF IT IS
06A8 23           2116          INX     H         ; INCREMENT HL BY 1
06A9 7C           2117          MOV     A,H       ; WANT TO TEST FOR 0 RESULT AFTER
06AA B5           2118          ORA     L         ; /INCREMENTING
06AB CAC106       2119          JZ      HIL05     ; IF SO, HL MUST HAVE CONTAINED 0FFFFH
06AE E1           2120          POP     H         ; IF NOT, RESTORE ORIGINAL HL
06AF D5           2121          PUSH    D         ; SAVE DE
06B0 3EFF         2122          MVI     A,0FFH    ; WANT TO TAKE 2'S COMPLEMENT OF DE CONTENTS
06B2 AA           2123          XRA     D
06B3 57           2124          MOV     D,A
06B4 3EFF         2125          MVI     A,0FFH
06B6 AB           2126          XRA     E
06B7 5F           2127          MOV     E,A
06B8 13           2128          INX     D         ; 2'S COMPLEMENT OF DE TO DE
06B9 7D           2129          MOV     A,L
06BA 83           2130          ADD     E         ; ADD HL AND DE
06BB 7C           2131          MOV     A,H
06BC 8A           2132          ADC     D         ; THIS OPERATION SETS CARRY PROPERLY
06BD D1           2133          POP     D         ; RESTORE ORIGINAL DE CONTENTS
06BE 78           2134          MOV     A,B       ; RESTORE ORIGINAL CONTENTS OF A
06BF C1           2135          POP     B         ; RESTORE ORIGINAL CONTENTS OF BC
06C0 C9           2136          RET               ; RETURN WITH CARRY SET AS REQUIRED
                  2137 HIL05:
06C1 E1           2138          POP     H         ; IF HL CONTAINS 0FFFFH, THEN CARRY CAN
06C2 78           2139          MOV     A,B       ; /ONLY BE SET TO 1
06C3 C1           2140          POP     B         ; RESTORE ORIGINAL CONTENTS OF REGISTERS
06C4 C33207       2141          JMP     SRET      ; SET CARRY AND RETURN
                  2142 ;
                  2143 ;
                  2144 ;••••••••••••••••••••••••••••••••••••••••••••••••••••••••••••••••••
                  2145 ;
                  2146 ;
                  2147 ; FUNCTION: NMOUT
                  2148 ; INPUTS: A - 8 BIT INTEGER
                  2149 ; OUTPUTS: NONE
                  2150 ; CALLS: ECHO,PRVAL
                  2151 ; DESTROYS: A,B,C,F/F'S
                  2152 ; DESCRIPTION: NMMOUT CONVERTS THE 8 BIT, UNSIGNED INTEGER IN THE
                  2153 ;              A REGISTER INTO 2 ASCII CHARACTERS.  THE ASCII CHARACTERS
                  2154 ;              ARE THE ONES REPRESENTING THE 8 BITS.  THESE TWO
                  2155 ;              CHARACTERS ARE SENT TO THE CONSOLE AT THE CURRENT PRINT
                  2156 ;              POSITION OF THE CONSOLE.
                  2157 ;
                  2158 NMOUT:
06C7 E5           2159          PUSH    H         ; SAVE HL - DESTROYED BY PRVAL
06C8 F5           2160          PUSH    PSW       ; SAVE ARGUMENT
06C9 0F           2161          RRC
06CA 0F           2162          RRC
06CB 0F           2163          RRC
06CC 0F           2164          RRC               ; GET UPPER 4 BITS TO LOW 4 BIT POSITIONS
06CD E60F         2165          ANI     HCHAR     ; MASK OUT UPPER 4 BITS - WANT 1 HEX CHAR
06CF 4F           2166          MOV     C,A
06D0 CDE206       2167          CALL    PRVAL     ; CONVERT LOWER 4 BITS TO ASCII
06D3 CDF805       2168          CALL    ECHO      ; SEND TO TERMINAL
06D6 F1           2169          POP     PSW       ; GET BACK ARGUMENT
06D7 E60F         2170          ANI     HCHAR     ; MASK OUT UPPER 4 BITS - WANT 1 HEX CHAR
06D9 4F           2171          MOV     C,A
06DA CDE206       2172          CALL    PRVAL
06DD CDF805       2173          CALL    ECHO
06E0 E1           2174          POP     H         ; RESTORE SAVED VALUE OF HL
06E1 C9           2175          RET
                  2176 ;
                  2177 ;
                  2178 ;••••••••••••••••••••••••••••••••••••••••••••••••••••••••••••••••••
```

```
                     2179 ;
                     2180 ;
                     2181 ; FUNCTION;  PRVAL
                     2182 ; INPUTS: C - INTEGER, RANGE 0 TO F
                     2183 ; OUTPUTS: C - ASCII CHARACTER
                     2184 ; CALLS: NOTHING
                     2185 ; DESTROYS: B,C,H,L,F/F'S
                     2186 ; DESCRIPTION: PRVAL CONVERTS A NUMBER IN THE RANGE 0 TO F HEX TO
                     2187 ;                   THE CORRESPONDING ASCII CHARACTER, 0-9,A-F.  PRVAL
                     2188 ;                   DOES NOT CHECK THE VALIDITY OF ITS INPUT ARGUMENT.
                     2189 ;
                     2190 PRVAL:
06E2 21B407          2191          LXI     H,DIGTB ; ADDRESS OF TABLE
06E5 0600            2192          MVI     B,0     ; CLEAR HIGH ORDER BITS OF BC
06E7 09              2193          DAD     B       ; ADD DIGIT VALUE TO HL ADDRESS
06E8 4E              2194          MOV     C,M     ; FETCH CHARACTER FROM MEMORY
06E9 C9              2195          RET
                     2196 ;
                     2197
                     2198 ;**************************************************************
                     2199 ;
                     2200 ;
                     2201 ; FUNCTION: REGDS
                     2202 ; INPUTS: NONE
                     2203 ; OUTPUTS: NONE
                     2204 ; CALLS: ECHO,NMOUT,ERROR,CROUT
                     2205 ; DESTROYS: A,B,C,D,E,H,L,F/F'S
                     2206 ; DESCRIPTION: REGDS DISPLAYS THE CONTENTS OF THE REGISTER SAVE
                     2207 ;                   LOCATIONS, IN FORMATTED FORM, ON THE CONSOLE.  THE
                     2208 ;                   DISPLAY IIS DRIVEN FROM A TABLE, RTAB, WHICH CONTAINS
                     2209 ;                   THE REGISTER'S PRINT SYMBOL, SAVE LOCATION ADDRESS,
                     2210 ;                   AND LENGTH (8 OR 16 BITS).
                     2211 ;
                     2212 REGDS:
06EA 21C407          2213          LXI     H,RTAB  ; LOAD HL WITH ADDRESS OF START OF TABLE
                     2214 REG05:
06ED 4E              2215          MOV     C,M     ; GET PRINT SYMBOL OF REGISTER
06EE 79              2216          MOV     A,C
06EF B7              2217          ORA     A       ; TEST FOR 0 - END OF TABLE
06F0 C2F706          2218          JNZ     REG10   ; IF NOT END, BRANCH
06F3 CDEB05          2219          CALL    CROUT   ; ELSE, CARRIAGE RETURN/LINE FEED TO END
06F6 C9              2220          RET             ; /DISPLAY
                     2221 REG10:
06F7 CDF805          2222          CALL    ECHO    ; ECHO CHARACTER
06FA 0E3D            2223          MVI     C,'='
06FC CDF805          2224          CALL    ECHO    ; OUTPUT EQUALS SIGN, I.E. A=
06FF 23              2225          INX     H       ; POINT TO START OF SAVE LOCATION ADDRESS
0700 5E              2226          MOV     E,M     ; GET LSP OF SAVE LOCATION ADDRESS TO E
0701 1620            2227          MVI     D,RAMST SHR 8   ; PUT MSP OF SAVE LOC ADDRESS INTO D
0703 23              2228          INX     H       ; POINT TO LENGTH FLAG
0704 1A              2229          LDAX    D       ; GET CONTENTS OF SAVE ADDRESS
0705 CDC706          2230          CALL    NMOUT   ; DISPLAY ON CONSOLE
0708 7E              2231          MOV     A,M     ; GET LENGTH FLAG
0709 B7              2232          ORA     A       ; SET SIGN F/F
070A CA1207          2233          JZ      REG15   ; IF 0, REGISTER IS 8 BITS
070D 1B              2234          DCX     D       ; ELSE, 16 BIT REGISTER SO MORE TO DISPLAY
070E 1A              2235          LDAX    D       ; GET LOWER 8 BITS
070F CDC706          2236          CALL    NMOUT   ; DISPLAY THEM
                     2237 REG15:
0712 0E20            2238          MVI     C,' '
0714 CDF805          2239          CALL    ECHO
0717 23              2240          INX     H       ; POINT TO START OF NEXT TABLE ENTRY
0718 C3ED06          2241          JMP     REG05   ; DO NEXT REGISTER
                     2242 ;
                     2243 ;
                     2244 ;**************************************************************
                     2245 ;
                     2246 ;
                     2247 ; FUNCTION: RGADR
                     2248 ; INPUTS: C - CHARACTER DENOTING REGISTER
                     2249 ; OUTPUTS: BC - ADDRESS OF ENTRY IN RTAB CORRESPONDING TO REGISTER
                     2250 ; CALLS: ERROR
                     2251 ; DESTROYS: A,B,C,D,E,H,L,F/F'S
                     2252 ; DESCRIPTION: RGADR TAKES A SINGLE CHARACTER AS INPUT.  THIS CHARACTER
                     2253 ;                   DENOTES A REGISTER.  RGADR SEARCHES THE TABLE RTAB
                     2254 ;                   FOR A MATCH ON THE INPUT ARGUMENT.  IF ONE OCCURS,
                     2255 ;                   RGADR RETURNS THE ADDRESS OF THE ADDRESS OF THE
                     2256 ;                   SAVE LOCATION CORRESPONDING TO THE REGISTER.  THIS
                     2257 ;                   ADDRESS POINTS INTO RTAB.  IF NO MATCH OCCURS, THEN
                     2258 ;                   THE REGISTER IDENTIFIER IS ILLEGAL AND CONTROL IS
                     2259 ;                   PASSED TO THE ERROR ROUTINE.
                     2260 ;
                     2261 RGADR:
071B 21C407          2262          LXI     H,RTAB  ; HL GETS ADDRESS OF TABLE START
071E 110300          2263          LXI     D,RTABS ; DE GET SIZE OF A TABLE ENTRY
                     2264 RGA05:
0721 7E              2265          MOV     A,M     ; GET REGISTER IDENTIFIER
0722 B7              2266          ORA     A       ; CHECK FOR TABLE END (IDENTIFIER IS 0)
```

```
LOC  OBJ        SEQ      SOURCE STATEMENT

0723 CA1106     2267         JZ      ERROR     ; IF AT END OF TABLE, ARGUMENT IS ILLEGAL
0726 B9         2268         CMP     C         ; ELSE, COMPARE TABLE ENTRY AND ARGUMENT
0727 CA2E07     2269         JZ      RGA10     ; IF EQUAL, WE'VE FOUND WHAT WE'RE LOOKING FOR
072A 19         2270         DAD     D         ; ELSE, INCREMENT TABLE POINTER TO NEXT ENTRY
072B C32107     2271         JMP     RGA05     ; TRY AGAIN
                2272 RGA10:
072E 23         2273         INX     H         ; IF A MATCH, INCREMENT TABLE POINTER TO
072F 44         2274         MOV     B,H       ; /SAVE LOCATION ADDRESS
0730 4D         2275         MOV     C,L       ; RETURN THIS VALUE
0731 C9         2276         RET
                2277 ;
                2278 ;
                2279 ;****************************************************************
                2280 ;
                2281 ;
                2282 ; FUNCTION: SRET
                2283 ; INPUTS: NONE
                2284 ; OUTPUTS: CARRY = 1
                2285 ; CALLS: NOTHING
                2286 ; DESTROYS: CARRY
                2287 ; DESCRIPTION: SRET IS JUMPED TO BY ROUTINES WISHING TO RETURN SUCCESS.
                2288 ;                SRET SETS THE CARRY TRUE AND THEN RETURNS TO THE
                2289 ;                CALLER OF THE ROUTINE INVOKING SRET.
                2290 ;
                2291 SRET:
0732 37         2292         STC               ; SET CARRY TRUE
0733 C9         2293         RET               ; RETURN APPROPRIATELY
                2294 ;
                2295 ;
                2296 ;****************************************************************
                2297 ;
                2298 ;
                2299 ; FUNCTION: STHF0
                2300 ; INPUTS: DE - 16 BIT ADDRESS OF BYTE TO BE STORED INTO
                2301 ; OUTPUTS: NONE
                2302 ; CALLS: STHLF
                2303 ; DESTROYS: A,B,C,H,L,F/F'S
                2304 ; DESCRIPTION: STHF0 CHECKS THE HALF BYTE FLAG IN TEMP TO SEE IF
                2305 ;                IT IS SET TO LOWER.  IF SO, STHF0 STORES A 0 TO
                2306 ;                PAD OUT THE LOWER HALF OF THE ADDRESSED BYTE;
                2307 ;                OTHERWISE, THE ROUTINE TAKES NO ACTION.
                2308 ;
                2309 STHF0:
0734 3AFD20     2310         LDA     TEMP      ; GET HALF BYTE FLAG
0737 B7         2311         ORA     A         ; SET F/F'S
0738 C0         2312         RNZ               ; IF SET TO UPPER, DON'T DO ANYTHING
0739 0E00       2313         MVI     C,0       ; ELSE, WANT TO STORE THE VALUE 0
073B CD3F07     2314         CALL    STHLF     ; DO IT
073E C9         2315         RET
                2316 ;
                2317 ;
                2318 ;****************************************************************
                2319 ;
                2320 ;
                2321 ; FUNCTION: STHLF
                2322 ; INPUTS: C - 4 BIT VALUE TO BE STORED IN HALF BYTE
                2323 ;         DE - 16 BIT ADDRESS OF BYTE TO BE STORED INTO
                2324 ; OUTPUTS: NONE
                2325 ; CALLS: NOTHING
                2326 ; DESTROYS: A,B,C,H,L,F/F'S
                2327 ; DESCRIPTION: STHLF TAKES THE 4 BIT VALUE IN C AND STORES IT IN
                2328 ;                HALF OF THE BYTE ADDRESSED BY REGISTERS DE.  THE
                2329 ;                HALF BYTE USED (EITHER UPPER OR LOWER) IS DENOTED
                2330 ;                BY THE VALUE OF THE FLAG IN TEMP.  STHLF ASSUMES
                2331 ;                THAT THIS FLAG HAS BEEN PREVIOUSLY SET
                2332 ;                (NOMINALLY BY ICMD).
                2333 ;
                2334 STHLF:
073F D5         2335         PUSH    D
0740 E1         2336         POP     H         ; MOVE ADDRESS OF BYTE INTO HL
0741 79         2337         MOV     A,C       ; GET VALUE
0742 E60F       2338         ANI     0FH       ; FORCE TO 4 BIT LENGTH
0744 4F         2339         MOV     C,A       ; PUT VALUE BACK
0745 3AFD20     2340         LDA     TEMP      ; GET HALF BYTE FLAG
0748 B7         2341         ORA     A         ; CHECK FOR LOWER HALF
0749 C25207     2342         JNZ     STH05     ; BRANCH IF NOT
074C 7E         2343         MOV     A,M       ; ELSE, GET BYTE
074D E6F0       2344         ANI     0F0H      ; CLEAR LOWER 4 BITS
074F B1         2345         ORA     C         ; OR IN VALUE
0750 77         2346         MOV     M,A       ; PUT BYTE BACK
0751 C9         2347         RET
                2348 STH05:
0752 7E         2349         MOV     A,M       ; IF UPPER HALF, GET BYTE
0753 E60F       2350         ANI     0FH       ; CLEAR UPPER 4 BITS
0755 47         2351         MOV     B,A       ; SAVE BYTE IN B
0756 79         2352         MOV     A,C       ; GET VALUE
0757 0F         2353         RRC
```

```
LOC  OBJ            SEQ         SOURCE STATEMENT

0758 0F            2354        RRC
0759 0F            2355        RRC
075A 0F            2356        RRC                    ; ALIGN TO UPPER 4 BITS
075B B0            2357        ORA     B              ; OR IN ORIGINAL LOWER 4 BITS
075C 77            2358        MOV     M,A            ; PUT NEW CONFIGURATION BACK
075D C9            2359        RET
                   2360 ;
                   2361 ;
                   2362 ;**************************************************************
                   2363 ;
                   2364 ;
                   2365 ; FUNCTION: VALDG
                   2366 ; INPUTS: C - ASCII CHARACTER
                   2367 ; OUTPUTS: CARRY - 1 IF CHARACTER REPRESENTS VALID HEX DIGIT
                   2368 ;                - 0 OTHERWISE
                   2369 ; CALLS: NOTHING
                   2370 ; DESTROYS: A,F/F'S
                   2371 ; DESCRIPTION: VALDG RETURNS SUCCESS IF ITS INPUT ARGUMENT IS
                   2372 ;                AN ASCII CHARACTER REPRESENTING A VALID HEX DIGIT
                   2373 ;                (0-9,A-F), AND FAILURE OTHERWISE.
                   2374 ;
                   2375 VALDG:
075E 79            2376        MOV     A,C
075F FE30          2377        CPI     '0'            ; TEST CHARACTER AGAINST '0'
0761 FA1C06        2378        JM      FRET           ; IF ASCII CODE LESS, CANNOT BE VALID DIGIT
0764 FE39          2379        CPI     '9'            ; ELSE, SEE IF IN RANGE '0'-'9'
0766 FA3207        2380        JM      SRET           ; CODE BETWEEN '0' AND '9'
0769 CA3207        2381        JZ      SRET           ; CODE EQUAL '9'
076C FE41          2382        CPI     'A'            ; NOT A DIGIT - TRY FOR A LETTER
076E FA1C06        2383        JM      FRET           ; NO - CODE BETWEEN '9' AND 'A'
0771 FE47          2384        CPI     'G'
0773 F21C06        2385        JP      FRET           ; NO - CODE GREATER THAN 'F'
0776 C33207        2386        JMP     SRET           ; OKAY - CODE IS 'A' TO 'F', INCLUSIVE
                   2387 ;
                   2388 ;
                   2389 ;**************************************************************
                   2390 ;
                   2391 ;
                   2392 ; FUNCTION: VALDL
                   2393 ; INPUTS: C - CHARACTER
                   2394 ; OUTPUTS: CARRY - 1 IF INPUT ARGUMENT VALID DELIMITER
                   2395 ;                - 0 OTHERWISE
                   2396 ; CALLS: NOTHING
                   2397 ; DESTROYS: A,F/F'S
                   2398 ; DESCRIPTION: VALDL RETURNS SUCCESS IF ITS INPUT ARGUMENT IS A VALID
                   2399 ;                DELIMITER CHARACTER (SPACE, COMMA, CARRIAGE RETURN) AND
                   2400 ;                FAILURE OTHERWISE.
                   2401 ;
                   2402 VALDL:
0779 79            2403        MOV     A,C
077A FE2C          2404        CPI     ','            ; CHECK FOR COMMA
077C CA3207        2405        JZ      SRET
077F FE0D          2406        CPI     CR             ; CHECK FOR CARRIAGE RETURN
0781 CA3207        2407        JZ      SRET
0784 FE20          2408        CPI     ' '            ; CHECK FOR SPACE
0786 CA3207        2409        JZ      SRET
0789 C31C06        2410        JMP     FRET           ; ERROR IF NONE OF THE ABOVE
                   2411 ;
                   2412 ;
                   2413 ;**************************************************************
                   2414 ;
                   2415 ;
                   2416 ;                          MONITOR TABLES
                   2417 ;
                   2418 ;
                   2419 ;**************************************************************
                   2420 ;
                   2421 ;
                   2422 SGNON:                         ; SIGNON MESSAGE
078C 0D            2423        DB      CR,LF,'SDK-85   VER 2.1',CR,LF
078D 0A
078E 53444B2D
0792 38352020
0796 20564552
079A 20322E31
079E 0D
079F 0A
0014              2424 LSGNON  EQU     $-SGNON ; LENGTH OF SIGNON MESSAGE
                  2425 ;
                  2426 CADR:                          ; TABLE OF ADDRESSES OF COMMAND ROUTINES
07A0 0000         2427        DW      0              ; DUMMY
07A2 1405         2428        DW      XCMD
07A4 F004         2429        DW      SCMD
07A6 D004         2430        DW      MCMD
07A8 8604         2431        DW      ICMD
07AA 6804         2432        DW      GCMD
07AC 3704         2433        DW      DCMD
```

```
LOC   OBJ        SEQ        SOURCE STATEMENT

                 2434 ;
                 2435 CTAB:                      ; TABLE OF VALID COMMAND CHARACTERS
07AE 44          2436        DB       'D'
07AF 47          2437        DB       'G'
07B0 49          2438        DB       'I'
07B1 4D          2439        DB       'M'
07B2 53          2440        DB       'S'
07B3 58          2441        D3       'X'
0006             2442 NCMDS  EQU      $-CTAB      ; NUMBER OF VALID COMMANDS
                 2443 ;
                 2444 DIGTB:                      ; TABLE OF PRINT VALUES OF HEX DIGITS
07B4 30          2445        DB       '0'
07B5 31          2446        DB       '1'
07B6 32          2447        DB       '2'
07B7 33          2448        DB       '3'
07B8 34          2449        DB       '4'
07B9 35          2450        DB       '5'
07BA 36          2451        DB       '6'
07BB 37          2452        DB       '7'
07BC 38          2453        DB       '8'
07BD 39          2454        DB       '9'
07BE 41          2455        DB       'A'
07BF 42          2456        DB       'B'
07C0 43          2457        DB       'C'
07C1 44          2458        DB       'D'
07C2 45          2459        DB       'E'
07C3 46          2460        DB       'F'
                 2461 ;
                 2462 RTAB:                       ; TABLE OF REGISTER INFORMATION
07C4 41          2463        DB       'A'         ; REGISTER IDENTIFIER
07C5 EE          2464        DB       ASAV AND 0FFH  ; ADDRESS OF REGISTER SAVE LOCATION
07C6 00          2465        DB       0           ; LENGTH FLAG - 0=8 BITS, 1=16 BITS
0003             2466 RTABS  EQU      $-RTAB      ; SIZE OF AN ENTRY IN THIS TABLE
07C7 42          2467        DB       'B'
07C8 EC          2468        D3       BSAV AND 0FFH
07C9 00          2469        DB       0
07CA 43          2470        DB       'C'
07CB EB          2471        DB       CSAV AND 0FFH
07CC 00          2472        DB       0
07CD 44          2473        DB       'D'
07CE EA          2474        DB       DSAV AND 0FFH
07CF 00          2475        DB       0
07D0 45          2476        DB       'E'
07D1 E9          2477        DB       ESAV AND 0FFH
07D2 00          2478        DB       0
07D3 46          2479        DB       'F'
07D4 ED          2480        DB       FSAV AND 0FFH
07D5 00          2481        DB       0
07D6 49          2482        DB       'I'
07D7 F1          2483        DB       ISAV AND 0FFH
07D8 00          2484        D3       0
07D9 48          2485        DB       'H'
07DA F0          2486        DB       HSAV AND 0FFH
07DB 00          2487        DB       0
07DC 4C          2488        DB       'L'
07DD EF          2489        DB       LSAV AND 0FFH
07DE 00          2490        DB       0
07DF 4D          2491        DB       'M'
07E0 F0          2492        DB       HSAV AND 0FFH
07E1 01          2493        DB       1
07E2 53          2494        DB       'S'
07E3 F5          2495        DB       SSAV+1 AND 0FFH
07E4 01          2496        DB       1
07E5 50          2497        DB       'P'
07E6 F3          2498        DB       PSAV+1 AND 0FFH
07E7 01          2499        DB       1
07E8 00          2500        DB       0           ; END OF TABLE MARKERS
07E9 00          2501        DB       0
                 2502 ;
07FA             2503        ORG      BRTAB       ; BRANCH TABLE FOR USER ACCESSIBLE ROUTINES
                 2504 ;
07FA C3C405      2505        JMP      CO          ; TTY CONSOLE OUTPUT
07FD C39005      2506        JMP      CI          ; TTY CONSOLE  INPUT
                 2507 ;
                 2508 ;****************************************************************************
                 2509 ;
                 2510 ; IN THE FOLLOWING LOCATIONS, THE USER MAY PLACE JUMP INSTRUCTIONS TO
                 2511 ; ROUTINE3 FOR HANDLING THE FOLLOWING:-
                 2512 ;      A) RST 5,6 & 7 INSTRUCTIONS
                 2513 ;      B) HARDWIRED USER INTERRUPT (RST 6.5)
                 2514 ;      C) KEYBOARD "VECTORED INTERRUPT" KEY (RST 7.5)
                 2515 ;
20C2             2516        ORG      USRBR       ; START OF USER BRANCH LOCATIONS
                 2517 ;
20C2 00          2518 RSET5: DB       0,0,0       ; JUMP TO RST 5 ROUTINE
20C3 00
20C4 00
20C5 00          2519 RSET6: DB       0,0,0       ; JUMP TO RST 6 ROUTINE
```

```
LOC  OBJ        SEQ        SOURCE STATEMENT

 20C6 00
 20C7 00
 20C8 00        2520 RST65:  DB      0,0,0    ; JUMP TO RST 6.5 (HARDWIRED USER INTERRUPT)
 20C9 00
 20CA 00
 20CB 00        2521 RSET7:  DB      0,0,0    ; JUMP TO RST 7 ROUTINE
 20CC 00
 20CD 00
 20CE 00        2522 USINT:  DB      0,0,0    ; JUMP TO "VECTORED INTERRUPT" KEY ROUTINE
 20CF 00
 20D0 00
                2523 ;
                2524 ;*****************************************************************
                2525 ;
                2526 ; SPACE IS RESERVED HERE FOR THE MONITOR STACK
                2527 ;
                2528 ;*****************************************************************
                2529 ;
 20E9           2530        ORG     MNSTK    ; START OF MONITOR STACK
                2531 ;
                2532 ;    SAVE LOCATIONS FOR USER REGISTERS
                2533 ;
 20E9 00        2534 ESAV:   DB      0        ; E REGISTER
 20EA 00        2535 DSAV:   DB      0        ; D REGISTER
 20EB 00        2536 CSAV:   DB      0        ; C REGISTER
 20EC 00        2537 BSAV:   DB      0        ; B REGISTER
 20ED 00        2538 FSAV:   DB      0        ; FLAGS
 20EE 00        2539 ASAV:   DB      0        ; A REGISTER
 20EF 00        2540 LSAV:   DB      0        ; L REGISTER
 20F0 00        2541 HSAV:   DB      0        ; H REGISTER
 20F1 00        2542 ISAV:   DB      0        ; INTERRUPT MASK
                2543 PSAV:                    ; PROGRAM COUNTER
 20F2 00        2544 PCLSV:  DB      0        ;   LOW ORDER BYTE
 20F3 00        2545 PCHSV:  DB      0        ;   HIGH ORDER BYTE
                2546 SSAV:                    ; STACK POINTER
 20F4 00        2547 SPLSV:  DB      0        ;   LOW ORDER BYTE
 20F5 00        2548 SPHSV:  DB      0        ;   HIGH ORDER BYTE
                2549 ;
                2550 ;*****************************************************************
                2551 ;
                2552 ; MONITOR STORAGE LOCATIONS
                2553 ;
 20F6 0000      2554 CURAD:  DW      0        ; CURRENT ADDRESS
 20F8 00        2555 CURDT:  DB      0        ; CURRENT DATA
 0004           2556 OBUFF:  DS      4        ; OUTPUT BUFFER
                2557 TEMP:                    ; TEMPORARY LOCATION FOR TTY MONITOR
                2558                          ; TEMPORARY LOCATION FOR SINGLE STEP ROUTINE
 20FD 00        2559 RGPTR:  DB      0        ; REGISTER POINTER
 20FE 00        2560 IBUFF:  DB      0        ; INPUT BUFFER
 20FF 00        2561 USCSR:  DB      0        ; USER SHOULD STORE IMAGE OF CSR HERE EACH TIME
                2562                          ; /CSR IS CHANGED. OTHERWISE, SINGLE STEP
                2563                          ; /ROUTINE WILL DESTROY CSR CONTENTS.
                2564        END
```

PUBLIC SYMBOLS

EXTERNAL SYMBOLS

USER SYMBOLS

ADFLD A 0000	ADISP A 0090	ASAV A 20EE	BLANK A 0015	BLNKS A 039A	BRCHR A 001B	BRTAB A 07FA
BSAV A 20EC	CADR A 07A0	CI A 0590	CI05 A 0592	CI10 A 05A1	CLDBK A 0008	CLDIS A 01E9
CLDST A 01F1	CLEAR A 01D7	CMD10 A 007B	CMD15 A 0087	CMDAD A 037C	CMDTB A 0378	CMMND A 0066
CNTRL A 1900	CNVBN A 05BB	CO A 05C4	CO05 A 05CB	COMMA A 0011	CR A 000D	CROUT A 05EB
CSAV A 20EB	CSNIT A 0000	CSR A 0020	CTAB A 07AE	CURAD A 20F6	CURDT A 20F8	DCM05 A 043E
DCM10 A 0449	DCM15 A 045E	DCMD A 0437	DDISP A 0094	DELAY A 05F1	DIGTB A 07B4	DISPC A 0200
DOT A 0001	DSAV A 20EA	DSPLY A 1800	DSPTB A 0384	DTFLD A 0001	DTMSK A 0008	ECH05 A 0601
ECH10 A 060F	ECHO A 05F8	EIGHT A 0008	EMPTY A 0080	ERMSG A 039E	ERR A 0215	ERROR A 0611
ESAV A 20E9	ESC A 001B	EXAM A 0092	EXM05 A 009D	EXM10 A 00B8	EXMSG A 03A2	FALSE + 0001
FIVE A 0005	FRET A 061C	FSAV A 20ED	G10 A 00EC	GCM05 A 047D	GCM10 A 0483	GCMD A 0468
GETCH A 061F	GETCM A 0408	GETHX A 0626	GETNM A 065B	GHX05 A 062C	GHX10 A 0645	GNM05 A 0662
GNM10 A 0677	GNM15 A 0685	GNM20 A 068A	GNM25 A 0695	GNM30 A 0699	GO A 03FA	GOCMD A 00CB
GTC03 A 0414	GTC05 A 0421	GTC10 A 042D	GTH05 A 0232	GTH10 A 0249	GTH20 A 0255	GTH25 A 0267
GTHEX A 022B	HCHAR A 00FF	HIL05 A 06C1	HILO A 06A0	HSAV A 20F0	HXDSP A 026C	IBTIM A 048C
IBUFF A 20FE	ICM05 A 0491	ICM10 A 04B9	ICM20 A 04C1	ICM25 A 04C7	ICMD A 0486	ININT A 028E
INSDG A 029F	INVRT A 00FF	ISAV A 20F1	KBNIT A 00CC	KMODE A 0000	LETRA A 000A	LETRB A 000B
LETRC A 000C	LETRD A 000D	LETRE A 000E	LETRF A 000F	LETRH A 0010	LETRI A 0013	LETRL A 0011
LETRP A 0012	LETRR A 0014	LETRS A 0005	LF A 000A	LOWER A 0000	LSAV A 20EF	LSGNON A 0014
MCM05 A 04D8	MCMD A 04D0	MNSTK A 20E9	MSGL A 03FF	NCMDS A 0006	NEWLN A 000F	NMOUT A 06C7
NMTBL A 03B9	NODOT A 0000	NUMC A 0004	NUMRG A 000D	NXTRG A 02A8	OBTIM A 048C	OBUFF A 20F9
OUT05 A 02C2	OUT10 A 02C6	OUT15 A 02C9	OUT20 A 02DC	OUTPT A 02B7	PCHSV A 20F3	PCLSV A 20F2
PERIO A 0010	PRMPT A 00FB	PRTY0 A 007F	PRVAL A 06E2	PSAV A 20F2	RAMST A 2000	RDK10 A 02F3
RDKBD A 02E7	READ A 0040	REG05 A 06ED	REG10 A 06F7	REG15 A 0712	REGDS A 06EA	RES10 A 003F
RETF A 02F7	RETT A 02FA	RGA05 A 0721	RGA10 A 072E	RGADR A 071B	RGLOC A 02FC	RGNAM A 0309
RGPTB A 03AC	RGPTR A 20FD	RGTBL A 03ED	RMUSE A 0017	RSET5 A 20C2	RSET6 A 20C5	RSET7 A 20CB

348 APPENDIX B / SDK-85 MONITOR

```
RSR05   A 032D    RSR10   A 0331    RST65   A 20C8    RSTOR   A 031B    RTAB    A 07C4    RTABS   A 0003    SCM05   A 04F5
SCM10   A 0500    SCM15   A 0510    SCMD    A 04F0    SETRG   A 0344    SGNAD   A 03A6    SGNDT   A 03AA    SGNON   A 078C
SKLN    A 0018    SPHSV   A 20F5    SPLSV   A 20F4    SRET    A 0732    SSAV    A 20F4    SSTEP   A 00FD    SSTRT   A 0080
STH05   A 0752    STHF0   A 0734    STHLF   A 073F    STOPB   A 0040    STP20   A 0126    STP21   A 013B    STP22   A 0142
STP23   A 0145    STP25   A 0157    STRT    A 00C0    TIM4    A 1230    TIMER   A 00C5    TIMHI   A 0025    TMODE   A 0040
TEMP    A 20FD    TERM    A 001B    TIM4    A 1230    TIMER   A 00C5    TIMHI   A 0025    TIMLO   A 0024    TMODE   A 0040
TRUE    + 0000    TSTRT   A 00C0    UBRLN   A 000F    UNMSK   A 000E    UPDAD   A 035F    UPDDT   A 036B    UPPER   A 00FF
USCSR   A 20FF    USINT   A 20CE    USRBR   A 20C2    VALDG   A 075E    VALDL   A 0779    WAIT    A 0246    WAITS   A 0000
XCM05   A 0527    XCM10   A 0536    XCM15   A 0543    XCM18   A 054E    XCM20   A 0567    XCM25   A 057E    XCM27   A 057F
XCM30   A 0587    XCMD    A 0514    ZERO    A 0000
```

ASSEMBLY COMPLETE, NO ERRORS

```
ADFLD   105#   358    393    470
ADISP   106#   269    835
ASAV    1228   2464   2539#
BLANK   1164#  1171   1171   1171   1171   1172   1173   1173   1173   1175   1175   1207   1207   1207   1208   120d
        1208   1209   1209   1210   1210   1210   1211   1211   1211   1212   1212   1212   1212   1213   1213   1213
        1214   1214   1214   1215   1215   1215   1216   1217   1218   1219
BLNKS   530    534    615    1171#
BRCHR   1324#
BRTAB   1325#  2503
BSAV    184    446    1229   2468   2537#
CADR    1438   2426#
CI      1754#  1960   2506
CI05    1757#  1760
CI10    1765#  1774
CLDBK   169#   571
CLDIS   331    339    386    400    507    549#
CLDST   168    565#
CLEAR   310    357    366    392    469    527#   551
CMD10   275#   280
CMD15   277    283#
CMDAD   284    1114#
CMDTB   274    1103#  1108
CMMND   264#   552    617
CNTRL   108#   167    268    567    754    843
CNVBN   1556   1796#  2013
CO      1390   1815#  1899   1904   2505
CO05    1821#  1832
COMMA   110#   332    387    477    680
CR      1326#  1511   1520   1662   1855   1900   2058   2063   2406   2423   2423
CROUT   1471   1485   1572   1685   1854#  1925   2219
CSAV    1230   2471   2536#
CSNIT   111#   568
CSR     112#   426    435    569
CTAB    1429   2435#  2442
CURAD   475    481    491    499    501    587    1065   2554#
CURDT   320    483    589    1086   2555#
DCM05   1470#  1493
DCM10   1476#  1492
DCM15   1484   1487#
DCMD    1465#  2433
DDISP   113#   840
DELAY   1762   1767   1776   1824   1836   1871#  1875
DIGTB   2191   2444#
DISPC   350    383    585#
DOT     115#   309    321    356    391    468    484    590    674
DSAV    1231   2474   2535#
DSPLY   116#   860
DSPTB   847    1122#  1128   1134   1135   1139   1142   1144   1146   1148   1150   1152   1154   1156   1158   1160
        1162   1164
DTFLD   117#   248    323    486    532    613    1090
DTMSK   118#   856
ECH05   1896   1898#
ECH10   1902   1905#
ECHO    1422   1426   1478   1546   1636   1660   1672   1708   1856   1892#  1924   1997   2168   2173   2222   2224
        2239
EIGHT   1139#  1175   1176
EMPTY   119#   253    891
ERMSG   611    1172#
ERR     282    315    333    361    396    473    497    506    608#
ERROR   1436   1512   1521   1569   1922#  2012   2052   2059   2064   2267
ESAV    1232   2477   2534#
ESC     1327#  1894
EXAM    308#   1116
EXM05   316#   338
EXM10   326    329#
EXMSG   369    1173#
FALSE   156#   314    325    395    472    489    1483   1508   1554   1607   1638   1710   1999   2011   2051   2078
FIVE    1134#  1176
FRET    1942#  2008   2378   2383   2385   2410
FSAV    180    442    1233   2480   2538#
G10     353    364#
GCM05   1509   1518#
GCM10   1517   1522#
GCMD    1506#  2432
GETCH   1425   1544   1658   1959#  1995
```

GETCM	1410♦	1406	1573	1603	1608	1631	1665	1680	1686	1926
GETHX	1507	1623	1637	1709	1990♦	2050				
GETNM	1467	1539	1588	2043♦						
GHX05	1994♦	2022								
GHX10	2000	2009♦								
GNM05	2049♦	2060								
GNM10	2056	2061♦								
GNM15	2069♦	2072								
GNM20	2068	2073♦								
GNM25	2079	2082♦								
GNM30	2087♦	2092								
GO	233	1385♦								
GOCMD	349♦	1118								
GTC03	1423	1424♦								
GTC05	1430♦	1435								
GTC10	1432	1437♦								
GTH05	651♦	676								
GTH10	665	669♦								
GTH20	654	677♦								
GTH25	681	683	687♦							
GTHEX	324	359	394	471	487	646♦				
HCHAR	1328♦	2165	2170							
HIL05	2115	2119	2137♦							
HILO	1481	1606	2077	2109♦						
HSAV	1235	2486	2492	2541♦						
HXDSP	671	709♦	1067	1088						
IBTIM	1350♦	1766	1775							
IBUFF	254	355	390	760	883	2560♦				
ICM05	1543♦	1552	1566							
ICM10	1561	1563♦								
ICM20	1555	1567♦								
ICM25	1549	1570♦								
ICMD	1537♦	2431								
ININT	202	751♦								
INSDG	657	779♦								
INVRT	1329♦	1564								
ISAV	226	403	454	994	999	1234	2483	2542♦		
KBNIT	120♦	566								
KMODE	122♦	166								
LETRA	1142♦	1207								
LETRB	1144♦	1208								
LETRC	1146♦	1209	1218	1219						
LETRD	1148♦	1210								
LETRE	1150♦	1172	1173	1211						
LETRF	1152♦	1212								
LETRH	1154♦	1214	1216	1218						
LETRI	1160♦	1213								
LETRL	1156♦	1215	1217	1219						
LETRP	1158♦	1216	1217	1218	1219					
LETRR	1162♦	1172	1172							
LETRS	1135♦	1216	1217							
LF	1330♦	1903	2423	2423						
LOWER	1331♦									
LSAV	175	437	1019	1236	2489	2540♦				
LSGNON	1387	2424♦								
MCM05	1592♦	1609								
MCMD	1586♦	2430								
MNSTK	124♦	265	1010	1419	2530					
MSGL	1388♦	1393								
NCMDS	1428	2442♦								
NEWLN	1336♦	1490								
NMOUT	1473	1475	1480	1634	1698	1705	2158♦	2230	2236	
NMTBL	962	1205♦								
NODOT	125♦	244	249	365	368	479	533	550	592	610	614	966
NUMC	273	1108♦								
NUMRG	807	1241♦								
NXTRG	334	805♦								
OBTIM	1351♦	1823								
OBUFF	716	734	2556♦							
OUT05	833	838♦								
OUT10	837	842♦								
OUT15	844♦	864								
OUT20	853	855	858♦							
OUTPT	247	252	370	531	535	612	616	675	831♦	967	1071	1092
PCHSV	1239	2545♦								
PCLSV	1240	2544♦								
PERIO	128♦	330	352	360	385	399	505	682		
PRMPT	129♦	271								
PRTY0	1337♦	1961								
PRVAL	2167	2172	2190♦							
PSAV	177	363	398	406	439	586	1017	1513	2498	2543♦
RAMST	93♦	124	137	942	1690	2227				
RDK10	887	890♦								
RDKBD	272	351	384	652	882♦	889	1037			
READ	130♦	755								
REG05	2214♦	2241								
REG10	2218	2221♦								
REG15	2233	2237♦								
REGDS	1664	2212♦								
RES10	188	223♦								

```
RETF    686    808    906#   1039   1044
RETT    811    922#   1051
RGA05   2264#  2271
RGA10   2269   2272#
RGADR   1668   2261#
RGLOC   318    327    936#
RGNAM   317    957#
RGPTB   1047   1180#
RGPTR   806    810    937    958    1050   2559#
RGTBL   939    1227#  1241
RMUSE   98#    124    137
RSET5   197    2518#
RSET6   207    2519#
RSET7   217    2521#
RSR05   1001   1004#
RSR10   1003   1006   1009#
RST65   212    2520#
RSTOR   371    427    993#   1523
RTAB    2213   2262   2462#  2466
RTABS   1723   2263   2466#
SCM05   1626#  1643
SCM10   1629   1632#
SCM15   1639   1641#
SCMD    1622#  2429
SDK85   71
SETRG   311    1036#
SGNAD   245    1175#
SGNDT   250    1176#
SGNON   1386   2422#  2424
SKLN    101#   137
SPHSV   1237   2548#
SPLSV   1238   2547#
SRET    2007   2141   2291#  2380   2381   2386   2405   2407   2409
SSAV    183    445    1015   2495   2546#
SSTEP   382#   457    1115
SSTRT   1341#  1828
STH05   2342   2348#
STHF0   1568   1571   2309#
STHLF   1558   2314   2334#
STOPB   1342#  1833
STP20   388    402#
STP21   409    412#
STP22   411    416#
STP23   414    418#
STP25   192    429#
STRT    1343#  1819
SUB05   476#   503
SUB10   490    498#
SUB15   478    504#
SUBST   467#   1117
TEMP    405    417    452    1541   1559   1565   1674   1676   1713   1729   2310   2340   2557#
TERM    1344#  1548
TIM4    1352#  1835
TIMER   140#   419    422
TIMHI   132#   421
TIMLO   133#   423
TMODE   134#   419
TRUE    152#   337    1551
TSTRT   135#   425
UBRLN   103#   137
UNMSK   136#   227    455
UPDAD   480    591    1064#
UPDDT   322    485    593    1085#
UPPER   1345#  1540
USCSR   424    432    570    2561#
USINT   221    2522#
USRBR   137#   2516
VALDG   1553   2010   2375#
VALDL   1550   1998   2402#
WAIT    1353#  1761
WAITS   80#    139    1349
XCM05   1663   1666#
XCM10   1675#  1726
XCM15   1678   1681#
XCM18   1684   1687#
XCM20   1702   1706#
XCM25   1717   1720#
XCM27   1722#  1732
XCM30   1711   1727#
XCMD    1657#  2428
ZERO    1128#  1175
```

CROSS REFERENCE COMPLETE

```
RGNAM   317    957#
RGPTB   1047   1180#
RGPTR   806    810    937    958    1050   2559#
RGTBL   939    1227#  1241
RMUSE   98#    124    137
RSET5   197    2518#
RSET6   207    2519#
RSET7   217    2521#
RSR05   1001   1004#
RSR10   1003   1006   1009#
RST65   212    2520#
RSTOR   371    427    993#   1523
RTAB    2213   2262   2462#  2466
RTABS   1723   2263   2466#
SCM05   1626#  1643
SCM10   1629   1632#
SCM15   1639   1641#
SCMD    1622#  2429
SDK85   71
SETRG   311    1036#
SGNAD   245    1175#
SGNDT   250    1176#
SGNON   1386   2422#  2424
SKLN    101#   137
SPHSV   1237   2548#
SPLSV   1238   2547#
SRET    2007   2141   2291#  2380   2381   2386   2405   2407   2409
SSAV    183    445    1015   2495   2546#
SSTEP   382#   457    1115
SSTRT   1341#  1828
STH05   2342   2348#
STHFO   1568   1571   2309#
STHLF   1558   2314   2334#
STCPB   1342#  1833
STP20   388    402#
STP21   409    412#
STP22   411    416#
STP23   414    418#
STP25   192    429#
STRT    1343#  1819
SUB05   476#   503
SUB10   490    498#
SUB15   478    504#
SUBST   467#   1117
TEMP    405    417    452    1541   1559   1565   1674   1676   1713   1729   231;   2340   2557#
TERM    1344#  1548
TIM2    1352#  1835
TIMER   140#   419    422
TIMHI   132#   421
TIMLO   133#   423
TMODE   134#   419
TRUE    152#   337    1551
TSTRT   135#   425
UBRLN   103#   137
UNMSK   136#   227    455
UPDAD   480    591    1064#
UPDDT   322    485    593    1085#
UPPER   1345#  1540
USCSR   424    432    570    2561#
USINT   221    2522#
USRBR   137#   2516
VALDG   1553   2010   2375#
VALDL   1550   1998   2402#
WAIT    1353#  1761
WAITS   80#    139    1349
XCM05   1663   1666#
XCM10   1675#  1726
XCM15   1678   1681#
XCM18   1684   1687#
XCM20   1702   1706#
XCM25   1717   1720#
XCM27   1722#  1732
XCM30   1711   1727#
XCMD    1657#  2428
ZERO    1128#  1175
```

CROSS REFERENCE COMPLETE

C

SDK-85 Teletype Operation

C–1 CONSOLE COMMANDS

This portion of the SDK-85 monitor communicates via a teletypewriter (console). Operation consists of dialogue between the operator and the monitor in the monitor's command language. After you press the [RESET] button on the SDK-85 keypad, the monitor begins the dialogue by typing a sign-on message on the console (MCS-85 kit) and then requests a command by typing a prompt character (.). Commands are in the form of a single alphabetic character specifying the command, followed by a list of numeric or alphabetic parameters. Numeric parameters are entered as hexadecimal numbers. The monitor recognizes the characters 0 through 9 and A through F as legal hexadecimal digits. Longer numbers may be entered, but only the last 4 digits will be retained. The only command requiring an alphabetic parameter is the X command. The nature of such parameters will be discussed in the section explaining the command.

C–2 USE OF THE MONITOR FOR PROGRAMMING AND CHECKOUT

The monitor allows you to enter, check out, and execute small programs. It contains facilities for memory display and modification, 8085 CPU register display and modification, program loading from the console device, and program initiation with a breakpoint facility. In addition, the [VECT INTR] key on the keyboard may be used to initiate your own keyboard interrupt routine.

Reproduced by permission of Intel Corp.

C–3 COMMAND STRUCTURE

In the following paragraphs, the monitor command language is discussed. Each command is described, and examples of its use are included for clarity. Error conditions that may be encountered while operating the monitor are also described.

The monitor requires each command to be terminated by a carriage return. With the exception of the S and X commands, the command is not acted upon until the carriage return is sensed. Therefore, you may abort any command, before entering the carriage return, by typing any illegal character (such as RUBOUT).

Except where indicated otherwise, a single space is synonymous with the comma for use as a delimiter. Consecutive spaces or commas, or a space or a comma immediately following the command letter, are illegal in all commands except the X command (see below). Items enclosed in parentheses () are optional.

C–3–1 Display Memory Command, D

D⟨low address⟩,⟨high address⟩

Selected areas of addressable memory may be accessed and displayed by the D command. The D command produces a formatted listing, on the console, of the memory contents between ⟨low address⟩ and ⟨high address⟩ inclusive. Each line of the listing begins with the address of the first memory location displayed on that line, represented as 4 hexadecimal digits, followed by up to 16 memory locations, each one represented by 2 hexadecimal digits.

G(⟨entry point⟩)

```
D COMMAND EXAMPLE

D9, 26
0009   EF   20   E1   22   F2   20   F5
0010   E1   22   ED   20   21   00   00   39   22   F4   20   21   ED   20   F9   C5
0020   D5   C3   3F   00   C3   57   01
```

C-3-2 Program Execute Command, G

Control of the CPU is transferred from the monitor to the user program by means of the program execute command G. The entry point should be an address in RAM that contains an instruction in the program. If no entry is specified, the monitor uses, as an address, the value on top of the stack when the monitor was entered.

```
G COMMAND EXAMPLE

G2000
Control is passed to location 2000.
```

C-3-3 Insert Instructions into RAM, I

I⟨address⟩

⟨data⟩

Single instructions, or an entire user program, are entered into RAM with the I command. After sensing the carriage return terminating the command line, the monitor waits for the user to enter a string of hexadecimal digits (0–9, A–F). Each digit in the string is converted into its binary value and then loaded into memory, beginning at the starting address specified and continuing into sequential memory locations. Two hexadecimal digits are loaded into each byte of memory.

Separators between digits (spaces, commas, carriage returns) are ignored; illegal characters, however, will terminate the command with an error message. The character ESC or ALTMODE (which is echoed to the console as $) terminates the digit string.

```
I COMMAND EXAMPLE 1

I2010
112233445566778899$
This command puts the following pattern into
RAM:
2010   11   22   33   44   55   66   77   88   99
```

```
I COMMAND EXAMPLE 2

I2040
123456789$
This command puts the following pattern into
RAM:
2040   12   34   56   78   90
Note that since an odd number of hexadecimal
digits was entered initially, a zero was appended to
the digit string.
```

C-3-4 Move Memory Command, M

M⟨low address⟩,⟨high address⟩,⟨destination⟩

The M command moves the contents of memory between ⟨low address⟩ and ⟨high address⟩ inclusive to the area of RAM beginning at ⟨destination⟩. The contents of the source field remain undisturbed, unless the receiving field overlaps the source field.

The move operation is performed on a byte-to-byte basis, beginning at ⟨low address⟩. Care should be taken if ⟨destination⟩ is between ⟨low address⟩ and ⟨high address⟩. For example, if location 2010 contains 1A, the command M2010, 201F 2011 will result in locations 2010 to 2020 containing 1A1A1A . . . , and the original contents of memory will be lost.

The monitor will continue to move data until the source field is exhausted or until it reaches address FFFF. If the monitor reaches FFFF without exhausting the source field, it will move data into this location and then stop.

```
M COMMAND EXAMPLE

M2010, 204F, 2050
64 bytes of memory are moved from 2010–204F to
2050–208F by this command.
```

C-3-5 Substitute Memory Command, S

S⟨address⟩(⟨data⟩)

The S command allows you to examine and optionally modify memory locations individually. The command functions as follows:

1. Type an S, followed by the hexadecimal address of the first memory location you wish to examine, followed by a space or a comma.

2. The contents of the location are displayed, followed by a dash (-).

3. To modify the contents of the location displayed, type in the new data, followed by a space, comma, or carriage return. If you do not wish to modify the location, type only the space, comma, or carriage return. The next higher memory location will automatically be displayed as in step 2.

4. Type a carriage return. The S command will be terminated.

S COMMAND EXAMPLE

S2050 AA– BB–CC 01–13 23–24
Location 2050, which contains AA, is unchanged, but location 2051 (which used to contain BB) now contains CC, 2052 (which used to contain 01) now contains 13, and 2053 (which used to contain 23) now contains 24.

C–3–6 Examine/Modify CPU Registers Command, X

X(⟨register identifier⟩)

Display and modification of the CPU registers are accomplished via the X command. The X command uses ⟨register identifier⟩ to select the particular register to be displayed. A register identifier is a single alphabetic character denoting a register, as defined in Table C–1. The command operates as follows:

1. Type an X, followed by a register identifier or a carriage return.

TABLE C–1
X Command Register Identifiers

Identifier Code	Register
A	Register A
B	Register B
C	Register C
D	Register D
E	Register E
F	Flags byte
I	Interrupt mask
H	Register H
L	Register L
M	Registers H and L combined
S	Stack pointer
P	Program counter

2. The contents of the register are displayed (2 hexadecimal digits for A, B, C, D, E, F, I, H, and L are 4 hexadecimal digits for M, S, and P), followed by a dash (-).

3. The register may be modified at this time by typing the new value, followed by a space, comma, or carriage return. If no modification is desired, type only the space, comma, or carriage return.

4. If a space or comma is typed in step 3, the next register in sequence will be displayed as in step 2 (unless P was just displayed, in which case the command is terminated). If a carriage return is entered in step 3, the X command is terminated.

5. If a carriage return is typed in step 1, an annotated list of all registers and their contents is displayed.

Note: The bits in the flag byte F and interrupt mask I are encoded as follows:

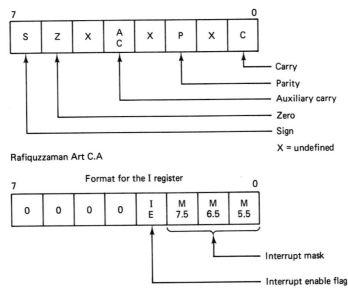

Rafiquzzaman Art C.A

For more information on the 8085's interrupt masks, consult the MCS-85 user's manual.

C-4 PROGRAM DEBUGGING — BREAKPOINT FACILITY

The monitor treats the RST1 instruction (CF) as a special sequence initiator. Upon execution of an RST1 instruction, the monitor will automatically save the complete CPU status and output the sign-on message "MCS-85 kit" to the console. You may at that time display the contents of the CPU status register by initiating an X command. After examining the machine status and making any necessary changes, you can resume execution of the program by inputting G and carriage return on the console. You can step through large portions of your program by inserting RST1 instructions at key locations.

C-5 ERROR CONDITIONS — INVALID CHARACTERS

Each character is checked as it is entered from the console. As soon as the monitor determines that the last character entered is illegal in its context, it aborts the command and issues an * to indicate the error.

INVALID CHARACTER EXAMPLE

D2000, 205G*
The character G was encountered in a parameter list where only hexadecimal digits and delimiters are valid.

C-6 ADDRESS VALUE ERRORS

Some commands require an address pair of the form ⟨low address⟩, ⟨high address⟩. If, on these commands, the value of ⟨low address⟩ is greater than or equal to the value of ⟨high address⟩, the action indicated by the command will be performed on the data at low address only. Addresses are evaluated modulo 2^{16}. Thus, if a hexadecimal address greater than FFFF is entered, only the last 4 hexadecimal digits will be used. Another type of address error may occur when you specify a part of memory in a command that does not exist in the hardware configuration you are using.

In general, if a nonexistent portion of memory is specified as the source field for an instruction, the data fetched will be unpredictable. If a nonexistent portion of memory is given as the destination field in a command, the command has no effect.

D

Intel 8080/8085 Assembly Language Reference Card

Reproduced by permission of Intel Corp.

ARITHMETIC AND LOGICAL GROUP

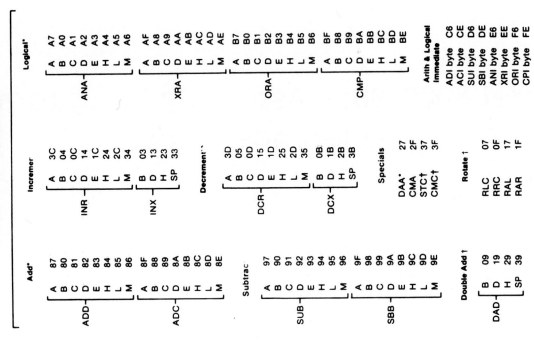

Add*

ADD
A	87
B	80
C	81
D	82
E	83
H	84
L	85
M	86

ADC
A	8F
B	88
C	89
D	8A
E	8B
H	8C
L	8D
M	8E

Subtrac

SUB
A	97
B	90
C	91
D	92
E	93
H	94
L	95
M	96

SBB
A	9F
B	98
C	99
D	9A
E	9B
H	9C
L	9D
M	9E

Double Add †

DAD
B	09
D	19
H	29
SP	39

Incremer

INR
A	3C
B	04
C	0C
D	14
E	1C
H	24
L	2C
M	34

INX
B	03
D	13
H	23
SP	33

Decrement''

DCR
A	3D
B	05
C	0D
D	15
E	1D
H	25
L	2D
M	35

DCX
B	0B
D	1B
H	2B
SP	3B

Specials
DAA*	27
CMA	2F
STC†	37
CMC†	3F

Rotate †
RLC	07
RRC	0F
RAL	17
RAR	1F

Logical*

ANA
A	A7
B	A0
C	A1
D	A2
E	A3
H	A4
L	A5
M	A6

XRA
A	AF
B	A8
C	A9
D	AA
E	AB
H	AC
L	AD
M	AE

ORA
A	B7
B	B0
C	B1
D	B2
E	B3
H	B4
L	B5
M	B6

CMP
A	BF
B	B8
C	B9
D	BA
E	BB
H	BC
L	BD
M	BE

Arith & Logical Immediate
ADI byte	C6
ACI byte	CE
SUI byte	D6
SBI byte	DE
ANI byte	E6
XRI byte	EE
ORI byte	F6
CPI byte	FE

DATA TRANSFER GROUP

Move

MOV
A,A	7F
A,B	78
A,C	79
A,D	7A
A,E	7B
A,H	7C
A,L	7D
A,M	7E

MOV
B,A	47
B,B	40
B,C	41
B,D	42
B,E	43
B,H	44
B,L	45
B,M	46

MOV
C,A	4F
C,B	48
C,C	49
C,D	4A
C,E	4B
C,H	4C
C,L	4D
C,M	4E

MOV
D,A	57
D,B	50
D,C	51
D,D	52
D,E	53
D,H	54
D,L	55
D,M	56

Move (cont)

MOV
E,A	5F
E,B	58
E,C	59
E,D	5A
E,E	5B
E,H	5C
E,L	5D
E,M	5E

MOV
H,A	67
H,B	60
H,C	61
H,D	62
H,E	63
H,H	64
H,L	65
H,M	66

MOV
L,A	6F
L,B	68
L,C	69
L,D	6A
L,E	6B
L,H	6C
L,L	6D
L,M	6E

MOV
M,A	77
M,B	70
M,C	71
M,D	72
M,E	73
M,H	74
M,L	75

XCHG   EB

Move Immediate

MVI
A, byte	3E
B, byte	06
C, byte	0E
D, byte	16
E, byte	1E
H, byte	26
L, byte	2E
M, byte	36

Load Immediate

LXI
B, dble	01
D, dble	11
H, dble	21
SP, dble	31

Load/Store
LDAX B	0A
LDAX D	1A
LHLD adr	2A
LDA adr	3A
STAX B	02
STAX D	12
SHLD adr	22
STA adr	32

byte = constant, or logical/arithmetic expression that evaluates to an 8-bit data quantity. (Second byte of 2-byte instructions).

dble = constant, or logical/arithmetic expression that evaluates to a 16-bit data quantity. (Second and Third bytes of 3-byte instructions).

adr = 16-bit address (Second and Third bytes of 3-byte instructions).

* = all flags (C, Z, S, P, AC) affected.

** = all flags except CARRY affected; (exception: INX and DCX affect no flags).

† = only CARRY affected.

All mnemonics copyright ©Intel Corporation 1976.

RESTART TABLE

Name	Code	Restart Address
RST 0	C7	0000_{16}
RST 1	CF	0008_{16}
RST 2	D7	0010_{16}
RST 3	DF	0018_{16}
RST 4	E7	0020_{16}
TRAP	Hardware* Function	0024_{16}
RST 5	EF	0028_{16}
RST 5 5	Hardware* Function	$002C_{16}$
RST 6	F7	0030_{16}
RST 6 5	Hardware* Function	0034_{16}
RST 7	FF	0038_{16}
RST 7 5	Hardware* Function	$003C_{16}$

*NOTE The hardware functions refer to the on-chip interrupt feature of the 8085 only

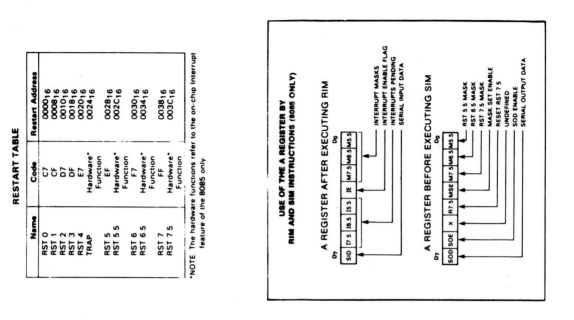

USE OF THE A REGISTER BY RIM AND SIM INSTRUCTIONS (8085 ONLY)

A REGISTER AFTER EXECUTING RIM

D_7							D_0
SID	I7.5	I6.5	I5.5	IE	M7.5	M6.5	M5.5

- INTERRUPT MASKS
- INTERRUPT ENABLE FLAG
- INTERRUPTS PENDING
- SERIAL INPUT DATA

A REGISTER BEFORE EXECUTING SIM

D_7							D_0
SOD	SOE	X	R7.5	MSE	M7.5	M6.5	M5.5

- RST 5.5 MASK
- RST 6.5 MASK
- RST 7.5 MASK
- MASK SET ENABLE
- RESET RST 7.5
- UNDEFINED
- SOD ENABLE
- SERIAL OUTPUT DATA

BRANCH CONTROL GROUP

Jump

JMP adr	C3
JNZ adr	C2
JZ adr	CA
JNC adr	D2
JC adr	DA
JPO adr	E2
JPE adr	EA
JP adr	F2
JM adr	FA
PCHL	E9

Call

CALL adr	CD
CNZ adr	C4
CZ adr	CC
CNC adr	D4
CC adr	DC
CPO adr	E4
CPE adr	EC
CP adr	F4
CM adr	FC

Return

RET	C9
RNZ	C0
RZ	C8
RNC	D0
RC	D8
RPO	E0
RPE	E8
RP	F0
RM	F8

Restart

	0	C7
	1	CF
	2	D7
RST	3	DF
	4	E7
	5	EF
	6	F7
	7	FF

I/O AND MACHINE CONTROL

Stack Ops

PUSH	B	C5
	D	D5
	H	E5
	PSW	F5
POP	B	C1
	D	D1
	H	E1
	PSW*	F1
XTHL		E3
SPHL		F9

Input/Output

OUT byte	D3
IN byte	DB

Control

DI	F3
EI	FB
NOP	00
HLT	76

New Instructions (8085 Only)

RIM	20
SIM	30

INTEL® 8080/8085
INSTRUCTION SET REFERENCE TABLES

BRANCH CONTROL INSTRUCTIONS

Flag Condition	Jump		Call		Return	
Zero=True	JZ	CA	CZ	CC	RZ	C8
Zero=False	JNZ	C2	CNZ	C4	RNZ	C0
Carry=True	JC	DA	CC	DC	RC	D8
Carry=False	JNC	D2	CNC	D4	RNC	D0
Sign=Positive	JP	F2	CP	F4	RP	F0
Sign=Negative	JM	FA	CM	FC	RM	F8
Parity=Even	JPE	EA	CPE	EC	RPE	E8
Parity=Odd	JPO	E2	CPO	E4	RPO	E0
Unconditional	JMP	C3	CALL	CD	RET	C9

ACCUMULATOR OPERATIONS

	Code	Function
XRA A	AF	Clear A and Clear Carry
ORA A	B7	Clear Carry
CMC	3F	Complement Carry
CMA	2F	Complement Accumulator
STC	37	Set Carry
RLC	07	Rotate Left
RRC	0F	Rotate Right
RAL	17	Rotate Left Thru Carry
RAR	1F	Rotate Right Thru Carry
DAA	27	Decimal Adjust Accum.

INTERNAL REGISTER ORGANIZATION

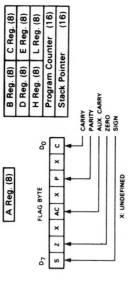

A Reg. (8)

B Reg. (8)	C Reg. (8)
D Reg. (8)	E Reg. (8)
H Reg. (8)	L Reg. (8)
Program Counter (16)	
Stack Pointer (16)	

FLAG BYTE

D7 [S | Z | X | AC | X | P | X | C] D0

- CARRY
- PARITY
- AUX CARRY
- ZERO
- SIGN

X: UNDEFINED

REGISTER-PAIR ORGANIZATION

PSW

A (8)	FLAGS (8)

B	(B/C) (16)
D	(D/E) (16)
H	(H/L) (16)
Prog. Ctr.	(16)
Stack Ptr.	(16)

NOTE: Leftmost Byte is high-order byte for arithmetic operations and addressing. Left byte is pushed on stack first. Right byte is popped first.

REGISTER PAIR AND STACK OPERATIONS

	Register Pair						Function
	PSW (A/F)	B (B/C)	D (D/E)	H (H/L)	SP	PC	
INX		03	13	23	33		Increment Register Pair
DCX		0B	1B	2B	3B		Decrement Register Pair
LDAX		0A	1A	7E(1)			Load A Indirect (Reg. Pair holds Adrs)
STAX		02	12	77(2)			Store A Indirect (Reg. Pair holds Adrs)
LHLD				2A			Load H/L Direct (Bytes 2 and 3 hold Adrs)
SHLD				22			Store H/L Direct (Bytes 2 and 3 hold Adrs)
LXI		01	11	21	31		Load Reg. Pair Immediate (Bytes 2 and 3 hold immediate data)
PCHL						C3(3) / E9	Load PC with H/L (Branch to Adrs in H/L)
XCHG			EB				Exchange Reg. Pairs D/E and H/L
DAD		09	19	29	39		Add Reg. Pair to H/L
PUSH	F5	C5	D5	E5			Push Reg. Pair on Stack
POP	F1	C1	D1	E1			Pop Reg. Pair off Stack
XTHL				E3			Exchange H/L with Top of Stack
SPHL						F9	Load SP with H/L

Notes: 1. This is MOV A,M.   2. This is MOV M,A.   3. This is JMP.

Opcode		Opcode		Opcode		Opcode	
00	NOP	2B	DCX H	81	ADD C	AC	XRA H
01	LXI B,dble	2C	INR L	82	ADD D	AD	XRA L
02	STAX B	2D	DCR L	83	ADD E	AE	XRA M
03	INX B	2E	MVI L,byte	84	ADD H	AF	XRA A
04	INR B	2F	CMA	85	ADD L	B0	ORA B
05	DCR B	30	SIM*	86	ADD M	B1	ORA C
06	MVI B,byte	31	LXI SP,dble	87	ADD A	B2	ORA D
07	RLC	32	STA adr	88	ADC B	B3	ORA E
08	---	33	INX SP	89	ADC C	B4	ORA H
09	DAD B	34	INR M	8A	ADC D	B5	ORA L
0A	LDAX B	35	DCR M	8B	ADC E	B6	ORA M
0B	DCX B	36	MVI M,byte	8C	ADC H	B7	ORA A
0C	INR C	37	STC	8D	ADC L	B8	CMP B
0D	DCR C	38	---	8E	ADC M	B9	CMP C
0E	MVI C,byte	39	DAD SP	8F	ADC A	BA	CMP D
0F	RRC	3A	LDA adr	90	SUB B	BB	CMP E
10	---	3B	DCX SP	91	SUB C	BC	CMP H
11	LXI D,dble	3C	INR A	92	SUB D	BD	CMP L
12	STAX D	3D	DCR A	93	SUB E	BE	CMP M
13	INX D	3E	MVI A,byte	94	SUB H	BF	CMP A
14	INR D	3F	CMC	95	SUB L	C0	RNZ
15	DCR D	40	MOV B,B	96	SUB M	C1	POP B
16	MVI D,byte	41	MOV B,C	97	SUB A	C2	JNZ adr
17	RAL	42	MOV B,D	98	SBB B	C3	JMP adr
18	---	43	MOV B,E	99	SBB C	C4	CNZ adr
19	DAD D	44	MOV B,H	9A	SBB D	C5	PUSH B
1A	LDAX D	45	MOV B,L	9B	SBB E	C6	ADI byte
1B	DCX D	46	MOV B,M	9C	SBB H	C7	RST 0
1C	INR E	47	MOV B,A	9D	SBB L	C8	RZ
1D	DCR E	48	MOV C,B	9E	SBB M	C9	RET
1E	MVI E,byte	49	MOV C,C	9F	SBB A	CA	JZ adr
1F	RAR	4A	MOV C,D	A0	ANA B	CB	---
20	RIM*	4B	MOV C,E	A1	ANA C	CC	CZ adr
21	LXI H,dble	4C	MOV C,H	A2	ANA D	CD	CALL adr
22	SHLD adr	4D	MOV C,L	A3	ANA E	CE	ACI byte
23	INX H	4E	MOV C,M	A4	ANA H	CF	RST 1
24	INR H	4F	MOV C,A	A5	ANA L	D0	RNC
25	DCR H	50	MOV D,B	A6	ANA M	D1	POP D
26	MVI H,byte	51	MOV D,C	A7	ANA A	D2	JNC adr
27	DAA	52	MOV D,D	A8	XRA B	D3	OUT byte
28	---	53	MOV D,E	A9	XRA C	D4	CNC adr
29	DAD H	54	MOV D,H	AA	XRA D	D5	PUSH D
2A	LHLD adr	55	MOV D,L	AB	XRA E	D6	SUI byte
		56	MOV D,M			D7	RST 2
		57	MOV D,A			D8	RC
		58	MOV E,B			D9	---
		59	MOV E,C			DA	JC adr
		5A	MOV E,D			DB	IN byte
		5B	MOV E,E			DC	CC adr
		5C	MOV E,H			DD	---
		5D	MOV E,L			DE	SBI byte
		5E	MOV E,M			DF	RST 3
		5F	MOV E,A			E0	RPO
		60	MOV H,B			E1	POP H
		61	MOV H,C			E2	JPO adr
		62	MOV H,D			E3	XTHL
		63	MOV H,E			E4	CPO adr
		64	MOV H,H			E5	PUSH H
		65	MOV H,L			E6	ANI byte
		66	MOV H,M			E7	RST 4
		67	MOV H,A			E8	RPE
		68	MOV L,B			E9	PCHL
		69	MOV L,C			EA	JPE adr
		6A	MOV L,D			EB	XCHG
		6B	MOV L,E			EC	CPE adr
		6C	MOV L,H			ED	---
		6D	MOV L,L			EE	XRI byte
		6E	MOV L,M			EF	RST 5
		6F	MOV L,A			F0	RP
		70	MOV M,B			F1	POP PSW
		71	MOV M,C			F2	JP adr
		72	MOV M,D			F3	DI
		73	MOV M,E			F4	CP adr
		74	MOV M,H			F5	PUSH PSW
		75	MOV M,L			F6	ORI byte
		76	HLT			F7	RST 6
		77	MOV M,A			F8	RM
		78	MOV A,B			F9	SPHL
		79	MOV A,C			FA	JM adr
		7A	MOV A,D			FB	EI
		7B	MOV A,E			FC	CM adr
		7C	MOV A,H			FD	---
		7D	MOV A,L			FE	CPI byte
		7E	MOV A,M			FF	RST 7
		7F	MOV A,A				
		80	ADD B				

*8085 Only.

All mnemonics copyright ©Intel Corporation 1976.

HEX-ASCII TABLE

00	NUL			21	!	42	B	63	c
01	SOH			22	"	43	C	64	d
02	STX			23	#	44	D	65	e
03	ETX			24	$	45	E	66	f
04	EOT			25	%	46	F	67	g
05	ENQ			26	&	47	G	68	h
06	ACK			27	'	48	H	69	i
07	BEL			28	(	49	I	6A	j
08	BS			29	)	4A	J	6B	k
09	HT			2A	*	4B	K	6C	l
0A	LF			2B	+	4C	L	6D	m
0B	VT			2C	,	4D	M	6E	n
0C	FF			2D	–	4E	N	6F	o
0D	CR			2E	.	4F	O	70	p
0E	SO			2F	/	50	P	71	q
0F	SI			30	0	51	Q	72	r
10	DLE			31	1	52	R	73	s
11	DC1	(X-ON)		32	2	53	S	74	t
12	DC2	(TAPE)		33	3	54	T	75	u
13	DC3	(X-OFF)		34	4	55	U	76	v
14	DC4	~~(TAPE)~~		35	5	56	V	77	w
15	NAK			36	6	57	W	78	x
16	SYN			37	7	58	X	79	y
17	ETB			38	8	59	Y	7A	z
18	CAN			39	9	5A	Z	7B	{
19	EM			3A	:	5B	[	7C		
1A	SUB			3B	;	5C	\	7D	}
1B	ESC			3C	<	5D	]		(ALT MODE)
1C	FS			3D	=	5E	^ (↑)	7E	
1D	GS			3E	>	5F	— (←)	7F	DEL
1E	RS			3F	?	60	`		(RUB OUT)
1F	US			40	@	61	a		
20	SP			41	A	62	b		

E

Number Systems, Codes, and Digital Logic

This appendix describes some of the fundamental concepts needed to implement and use a microcomputer effectively. Thus, the basics of number systems, codes, and digital logic are presented.

E-1 NUMBER SYSTEMS

A microcomputer, like almost all digital machines, utilizes two states to represent information. These two states are given the symbols 1 and 0. It is important to remember that these 1's and 0's are symbols for the two states and have no inherent numerical meanings of their own. These two digits are called *binary digits* (bits) and can be used to represent numbers of any magnitude.

E-1-1 General Number Representation

Decimal Number System In the decimal number system (base 10), which is most familiar to us, the integer number 125_{10} can be expressed as

$$125_{10} = 1 \times 10^2 + 2 \times 10^1 + 5 \times 10^0$$

Now, consider the fractional decimal number 0.532_{10}. This number can be expressed as

$$0.532_{10} = 5 \times 10^{-1} + 3 \times 10^{-2} + 2 \times 10^{-3}$$

Finally, consider the mixed number 125.532_{10}:

$$125.532_{10} = 1 \times 10^2 + 2 \times 10^1 + 5 \times 10^0$$
$$+ 5 \times 10^{-1} + 3 \times 10^{-2}$$
$$+ 2 \times 10^{-3}$$

Binary Number System The binary number system has a base or radix of 2 and has two allowable digits, 0 and 1. It is interesting to note that the value of the least significant bit of a binary number determines whether the number is odd or even. For example, if the least significant bit is 1, then the number is odd; otherwise, the number is even.

The binary number 101.01_2 can be interpreted as

$$101.01_2 = 1 \times 2^2 + 0 \times 2^1 + 1 \times 2^0 + 0 \times 2^{-1} + 1 \times 2^{-2}$$

Octal Number System The radix or base of the octal number system is 8. There are eight digits, 0 through 7, allowed in this number system.

Consider the octal number 25.32_8, which can be interpreted as

$$25.32_8 = 2 \times 8^1 + 5 \times 8^0 + 3 \times 8^{-1} + 2 \times 8^{-2}$$

The decimal value of this number is found by completing the summation as follows:

$$16 + 5 + 3 \times \tfrac{1}{8} + 2 \times \tfrac{1}{64} = 16 + 5 + 0.375 + 0.03125 = 21.40625_{10}$$

One converts a number from binary to octal representation easily and mechanically by taking the binary digits in groups of 3 bits to an octal digit. Suppose that it is desired to convert 1001.11_2 into octal form. First, take groups of 3 bits starting at the radix point. Where there are not enough leading or trailing bits to complete the triplet, 0's are appended. Now each group of 3 bits is converted to its corresponding octal digit:

$$\underbrace{001}_{1}\ \underbrace{001}_{1}\ .\ \underbrace{110}_{6}{}_2 = 11.6_8$$

The conversion back to binary from octal is simply the reverse of the binary-to-octal process. For example, conversion from 11.6_8 to binary is accomplished by expanding each octal digit to its equivalent binary values as follows:

$$1 \quad 1 \; . \; 6_8$$
$$\underbrace{} \quad \underbrace{} \quad \underbrace{} = 1001.11_2$$
$$001 \quad 001 \; . \; 110$$

Hexadecimal Number System   The hexadecimal or base-16 number system has 16 individual digits. Each of these digits, as in all number systems, must be represented by a single symbol unique from the other symbols in the number system. The digits in the hexadecimal number system are 0 through 9 and the letters A through F. Letters were chosen to represent the hexadecimal digits greater than 9 since a single symbol is required for each digit. Table E–1 lists the 16 digits of the hexadecimal number system and their corresponding decimal and binary values.

E–1–2   Converting Numbers from One Base to Another

Binary-to-Decimal Conversion and Vice Versa   Consider converting 1100.01_2 to its decimal equivalent:

$$1100.01_2 = 1 \times 2^3 + 1 \times 2^2 + 0 \times 2^1 + 0 \times 2^0 + 0 \times 2^{-1} + 1 \times 2^{-2}$$
$$= 8 + 4 + 0 + 0 + 0 + 0.25$$
$$= 12.25_{10}$$

Continuous division by 2, keeping track of the remainders, provides a simple method of converting a decimal number to its binary equivalent. As an example, to convert decimal 12_{10} to its binary equivalent, proceed as follows:

TABLE E–1
Number Systems

Hexadecimal	Decimal	Binary
0	0	0000
1	1	0001
2	2	0010
3	3	0011
4	4	0100
5	5	0101
6	6	0110
7	7	0111
8	8	1000
9	9	1001
A	10	1010
B	11	1011
C	12	1100
D	13	1101
E	14	1110
F	15	1111

Quotient	+	Remainder
$\dfrac{12}{2} = 6$	+	0
$\dfrac{6}{2} = 3$	+	0
$\dfrac{3}{2} = 1$	+	1
$\dfrac{1}{2} = 0$	+	1

$$1\;1\;0\;0_2$$

Thus, $12_{10} = 1100_2$.

Finally, convert 13.25_{10} to its binary equivalent. It is convenient to carry out separate conversions for the integer and fractional parts. Consider first the integer number 13:

Quotient	+	Remainder
$\dfrac{13}{2} = 6$	+	1
$\dfrac{6}{2} = 3$	+	0
$\dfrac{3}{2} = 1$	+	1
$\dfrac{1}{2} = 0$	+	1

$$13_{10} = 1\;1\;0\;1_2$$

Now convert the fractional part 0.25_{10} as follows:

$$\begin{array}{cc} 0.25 & 0.50 \\ \underline{\times 2} & \underline{\times 2} \\ \textcircled{0}50 & \textcircled{1}00 \\ \downarrow & \downarrow \\ 0 & 1 \end{array}$$

Thus, $0.25_{10} = 0.01_2$. Therefore, $13.25_{10} = 1101.01_2$.

Binary-to-Hexadecimal Conversion and Vice Versa   The conversions between hexadecimal and binary numbers are done in the same manner as the conversions between octal and binary, except that groups of 4 are used. The following example illustrates this:

$$1011011_2 = \underbrace{0101}_{5} \;\; \underbrace{1011}_{B} = 5B_{16}$$

Note that the binary integer number is grouped in 4, starting from the least significant bit. Zeros are added with the most significant 4 bits if necessary. As with octal numbers, for fractional numbers this grouping into 4 bits is started from the radix point.

Now, consider converting $2AB_{16}$ into its binary equivalent as follows:

$$2AB_{16} = \begin{array}{ccc} 2 & A & B \\ \downarrow & \downarrow & \downarrow \\ 0010 & 1010 & 1011 \end{array}$$
$$= 001010101011_2$$

Hexadecimal-to-Decimal Conversion and Vice Versa Consider converting the hexadecimal number $23A_{16}$ into its decimal equivalent and vice versa. This can be accomplished as follows:

$$23A_{16} = 2 \times 16^2 + 3 \times 16^1 + 10 \times 16^0$$
$$= 512 + 48 + 10 = 570_{10}$$

Note here that the value 10 is substituted for A.

Now, to convert 570_{10} back to $23A_{16}$,

	Quotient	+	Remainder
$\dfrac{570}{16} =$	35	+	A
$\dfrac{35}{16} =$	2	+	3
$\dfrac{2}{16} =$	0	+	2

$$2\ 3\ A_{16}$$

Thus, $570_{10} = 23A_{16}$.

E–2 CODES

Codes are extensively used with microprocessors to define alphanumeric characters and other information. Some of the popular types of codes used with microprocessors are described in the following sections.

E–2–1 Binary-Coded Decimal Code (8421 Code)

The 10 decimal digits 0 through 9 can be represented by their corresponding 4-bit binary numbers. The digits coded in this fashion are called *Binary-Coded Decimal digits in 8421 code,* or BCD digits. Two BCD numbers are usually packed into a byte to form "packed BCD." Table E–2 lists the BCD representation of the 10 decimal digits. The six possible remaining 4-bit codes as shown in Table E–2 are not used and represent illegal BCD codes if they occur.

A complete and adequate set of necessary characters includes the following:

- 26 lowercase letters
- 26 uppercase letters
- 10 numeric digits (0–9)
- About 25 special characters, including +, /, #, %, and so on

This totals up to 87 characters. To represent 87 characters

TABLE E–2
BCD Representation of the 10 Decimal Digits

Decimal Digits		BCD Representation
0		0000
1		0001
2		0010
3		0011
4		0100
5		0101
6		0110
7		0111
8		1000
9		1001
10		1010
11		1011
12	← Illegal →	1100
13	BCD code	1101
14		1110
15		1111

with some type of binary code would require at least 7 bits. With 7 bits, there are $2^7 = 128$ possible binary numbers; 87 of these combinations of 0 and 1 bits serve as the code groups representing the 87 different characters.

The 8-bit byte has been universally accepted as the data unit for representing character codes. The two most common alphanumeric codes are known as the *American Standard Code for Information Interchange* (ASCII) and the *Extended Binary-Coded Decimal Interchange Code* (EBCDIC). ASCII is typically used with microprocessors.

Eight bits are used to represent characters when 7 bits suffice because the eighth bit is frequently used to test for errors and is referred to as a *parity bit*. It can be set to 1 or 0 so that the number of 1 bits in the byte is either always odd or always even.

E–3 ARITHMETIC OPERATIONS

Normally in a microcomputer, the ALU, which is the heart of the microprocessor chip and performs the arithmetic and logic functions, operates in either an integer binary or a BCD mode. In both cases, the numbers are usually treated internally as integers, and any fractional arithmetic must be implemented by the programmer in the program. The ALUs perform functions such as addition, subtraction, magnitude comparison, ANDing, and ORing of two binary or packed BCD numbers.

E–3–1 Binary Arithmetic

Addition There are only four possible combinations that can occur when adding two binary digits (bits):

Augend	+	Addend	=	Result	+	Carry
0	+	0	=	0		
1	+	0	=	1		
0	+	1	=	1		
1	+	1	=	0	+	1

The following are some examples of binary addition. The corresponding decimal additions are also included.

$$
\begin{array}{lll}
 & 111 \leftarrow & \text{Carry} \\
010 \quad (2) & 101.11 & (5.75) \\
\underline{+011} \quad (3) & \underline{+011.10} & (3.50) \\
101 \quad (5) & 1\ 001.01 & (9.25)
\end{array}
$$

Final carry

Addition is the most important arithmetic operation in microprocessors because the operations of subtraction, multiplication, and division as they are performed in microprocessors and in most modern digital computers use only addition as their basic operation.

Subtraction Microprocessors can usually only add binary digits; they cannot subtract. Therefore, the operation of subtraction in microprocessors is performed using the operation of addition.

Let us, first of all, describe the procedure of subtracting decimal numbers using addition. This process requires the use of the 10's complement form. The 10's complement of a number can be obtained by subtracting the number from 10.

Consider the decimal subtraction $7 - 4 = 3$. The 10's complement of 4 is $10 - 4 = 6$. The decimal subtraction can be performed using the 10's complement addition:

$$
\begin{array}{lr}
\text{Minuend} & 7 \\
\text{10's complement of subtrahend} & \underline{6} \\
 & 13
\end{array}
$$

Ignore final carry

When a larger number is subtracted from a smaller number, there is no carry to be discarded. Consider the decimal subtraction of $4 - 7 = -3$. The 10's complement of 7 is $10 - 7 = 3$. Therefore,

$$
\begin{array}{lr}
\text{Minuend} & 4 \\
\text{10's complement of subtrahend} & \underline{3} \\
 & 7
\end{array}
$$

No final carry

When there is no final carry, the final answer is the negative of the 10's complement of 7. Therefore, the correct result of subtraction is $-(10 - 7) = -3$.

The same procedures can be applied for performing

binary subtraction. In the case of binary subtraction, the 2's complement of the subtrahend is used.

The 2's complement of a binary number is obtained by replacing each 0 with a 1 and each 1 with a 0 and adding 1 to the resulting number. The first step generates a 1's complement or simply the complement of a binary number. For example, the 1's complement of 10010101 is 01101010.

The 2's complement of a binary number is formed by adding 1 to the 1's complement of the number. For example, the 2's complement of 10010101 is found as follows:

$$
\begin{array}{lr}
\text{Binary number} & 10010101 \\
\text{1's complement} & 01101010 \\
\text{Add 1} & \underline{+1} \\
\text{2's complement} & 01101011
\end{array}
$$

Now, using the 2's complement, binary subtraction can be carried out.

Consider the following subtraction using the normal procedure:

$$
\begin{array}{lrr}
\text{Minuend} & 0101 & (5) \\
\text{Subtrahend} & \underline{-0011} & (-3) \\
\text{Result} & 0010 & (2)
\end{array}
$$

Using the 2's complement subtraction,

$$
\begin{array}{lr}
\text{Minuend} & 0101 \\
\text{2's complement of subtrahend} & \underline{1101} \\
 & 1\ 0010
\end{array}
$$

Discard final carry

The final answer is 0010 (decimal 2).

Consider another example:

$$
\begin{array}{lrr}
\text{Minuend} & 0101 & (5) \\
\text{Subtrahend} & \underline{-1001} & (-9) \\
 & -0100 & (-4)
\end{array}
$$

Using the 2's complement,

$$
\begin{array}{lr}
\text{Minuend} & 0101 \\
\text{2's complement of subtrahend} & \underline{0111} \\
 & 1100
\end{array}
$$

No final carry

Therefore, the final answer is $-(\text{2's complement of } 1100) = -0100$, which is -4 in decimal.

Microprocessors typically handle signed numbers by using the most significant bit of a number as the sign bit. If this bit is 0, then the number is positive; otherwise, the number is negative. For example, the number -22_{10} is represented as follows:

```
  1        1 1 0 1 0 1 0
  ↑        ‾‾‾‾‾‾‾‾‾‾‾‾‾
Sign bit          2's complement of
(negative)        001 0110 (7-bit
                  since most signifi-
                  cant bit is used as
                  sign bit)
```

Multiplication

Multiplication Binary multiplication can be carried out in the same way as is done with the decimal numbers using pencil and paper.

Consider the following example:

```
    0110    Multiplicand  =  6_10
    0101    Multiplier    =  5_10
   ‾‾‾‾‾‾
    0110  ⎫
    0000  ⎪
    0110  ⎬  Partial products
    0000  ⎭
  ‾‾‾‾‾‾‾‾
  0011110   Final product  =  30_10
```

As can be seen here, the process of binary multiplication is very simple. It only involves multiplying by 1's and 0's. Basically, the binary multiplication process involves adding and shifting operations. A number of binary multiplication algorithms are available with microprocessors.

Division Binary division can be carried out in the same way as the division of decimal numbers.

As an example, consider the following:

```
              0011    Quotient
Divisor  10 | 0110    Dividend
              010     6 ÷ 2 = 3
             ‾‾‾‾
             0010
             0010
            ‾‾‾‾‾
                0    Remainder
```

There are numerous binary division algorithms available with microprocessors.

E-3-2 Hexadecimal Arithmetic

Addition Consider the following example of hexadecimal addition:

```
    36B
  + 1A2
  ‾‾‾‾‾
    50D
```

Here, B + 2 = D; A + 6 = 16 (decimal), which is 0 in hexadecimal with a carry.

Subtraction Consider subtracting $15A_{16}$ from $3F2_{16}$:

Subtrahend, $15A_{16}$	0001	0101	1010
2's complement of sub- trahend	1110	1010	0110
Convert to hexadecimal	E	A	6
Add minuend	3	F	2
1	2	9	8

Ignore final carry

The final answer is 298_{16}.

E-3-3 Multiword Binary Addition and Subtraction

In many cases, the word length of a particular microprocessor may not be large enough to represent the desired magnitude of a number. Suppose, for example, that numbers in the range from 0 to 65,535 are to be used in an 8-bit microprocessor in binary addition and subtraction operations using the 2's complement number representation. This can be accomplished by storing the 16-bit addends and augends each in two 8-bit memory locations. Addition or subtraction of the two 16-bit numbers is implemented by adding or subtracting the lower 8 bits of each number, storing the result in an 8-bit memory location or register, and then adding the two high-order parts of the addend and augend with any carry generated from the first addition. The latter partial sum will be the high-order portion of the sum. Therefore, the two 8-bit sums together comprise the 16-bit result.

16-Bit Addition Consider the following example of 16-bit addition:

	Upper half of the 16-bit number	Lower half of the 16-bit number
	0 1 0 0 1 0 1 1	0 1 1 1 1 0 1 0
	+0 0 1 0 1 1 1 0	0 0 1 0 1 1 0 1
Intermediate carries	1 1 1	1 1 1 1
	0 1 1 1 1 0 0 1	1 0 1 0 0 1 1 1
	High byte of the answer	Low byte of the answer

16-Bit Subtraction Consider $23A6_{16} - 124A_{16} = 115C_{16}$:

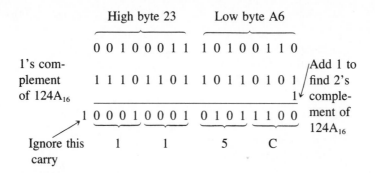

High byte 23   Low byte A6

0 0 1 0 0 0 1 1   1 0 1 0 0 1 1 0

1's com-
plement   1 1 1 0 1 1 0 1   1 0 1 1 0 1 0 1   Add 1 to
of $124A_{16}$ find 2's
                                          1   comple-
ment of
$124A_{16}$

1 0 0 0 1 0 0 0 1   0 1 0 1 1 1 0 0

Ignore this   1   1   5   C
carry

E-3-4 Fixed-Point and Floating-Point Representation

Up to this point, the numbers used in the arithmetic operations had their radix or decimal point fixed in a particular location. It was assumed that the numbers used were integers or that the radix points were aligned in addition and subtraction operations. A number representation assuming a fixed location of the radix point is called *fixed-point representation*. The range of numbers that can be represented in fixed-point notation is severely limited. The following numbers are examples of fixed-point numbers:

$$0110.1100_2, \quad 51.12_{10}, \quad DE.2A_{16}$$

An alternate approach to number representation is to adopt the equivalent of scientific notation in the microprocessor. A number would then be represented as $N \times r^p$, where N is the mantissa, r is the base or radix of the number system, and p is the exponent or power to which r is raised. Some examples of numbers in *floating-point notation* and their fixed-point decimal equivalents are as follows:

Fixed-Point Decimal Number	Floating-Point Representation
258_{10}	0.258×10^3
0.0167_{10}	0.167×10^{-1}
1101.101_2	0.1101101×2^4
$BE.2A9_{16}$	$0.BE2A9 \times 16^2$

In converting from fixed-point to floating-point number representation, we normalize the resulting mantissas; that is, the digits of the fixed-point numbers are shifted so that the highest-order nonzero digit appears to the right of the decimal point and consequently a 0 always appears to the left of the decimal point. This convention is normally adopted in floating-point number representation. Since all numbers will be assumed to be in normalized form, the binary point is not required to be represented in the microcomputer registers.

E-4 BOOLEAN ALGEBRA AND DIGITAL LOGIC

Boolean algebra is very important in microprocessor applications because it provides the basis for logic operations, decision making, and condition testing.

Boolean algebra uses the three basic operators OR, AND, and EXCLUSIVE-OR (XOR), which generate a single-digit result with two binary digits as inputs. A fourth Boolean operator, NOT, complements a binary digit.

E-4-1 OR Operation

Most microprocessors have an OR instruction to perform the OR operation between two binary numbers. Consider ORing 31_{16} with 21_{16}. This can be accomplished by expressing the numbers in binary and performing the OR operation bit by bit:

$$
\begin{array}{ccc}
 & 3A_{16} & 0011 \quad 1010 \\
\text{OR} & 21_{16} & 0010 \quad 0001 \\
\hline
 & & 0011 \quad 1011 \\
 & 3 & B_{16}
\end{array}
$$

E-4-2 AND Operation

Most microprocessors have an instruction to perform the AND operation between two numbers. As an example, consider ANDing 31_{16} with $A1_{16}$:

$$
\begin{array}{ccc}
 & 31_{16} & 0011 \quad 0001 \\
\text{AND} & A1_{16} & 1010 \quad 0001 \\
\hline
 & & 0010 \quad 0001 \\
 & 2 & 1_{16}
\end{array}
$$

E-4-3 EXCLUSIVE-OR Operation

Most microprocessors have an instruction to perform the XOR operation. Consider XORing $3A_{16}$ with 21_{16}:

$$
\begin{array}{lcc}
3A_{16} & 0011 & 1010 \\
21_{16} & 0010 & 0001 \\
\hline
& 0001 & 1011 \\
\end{array}
$$

$$1 \quad B_{16}$$

It is interesting to note that XORing any number with another number of the same length, but with all 1's, will generate the 1's complement of the original number. For example, consider XORing 31_{16} with FF_{16}:

$$
\begin{array}{lcc}
31_{16} & 0011 & 0001 \\
\text{1's complement of } 31_{16} & 1100 & 1110 \\
\end{array}
$$

$$C \quad E_{16}$$

$$
\begin{array}{lcc}
31_{16} \oplus FF_{16} & 0011 & 0001 \\
& 1111 & 1111 \\
\hline
& 1100 & 1110 \\
\end{array}
$$

$$C \quad E_{16}$$

E-4-4 NOT Operation

The NOT operation inverts or provides the 1's complement of one or more binary digits. This operation takes a single input and generates one output. The NOT operation of a binary digit provides the following result:

$$NOT1 = 0$$
$$NOT0 = 1$$

The output of an OR operation can be operated by a NOT to provide NOR. Similarly, the output of an AND operated by a NOT generates a NAND operation. Microprocessors can use the XOR instruction to obtain the 1's complement or NOT of a number. This can be accomplished by XORing a number with all 1's (FF_{16} for an 8-bit microprocessor).

F

SDK-85 — Details*

Figures F–1 and F–2 show a photograph and a simplified block diagram of the SDK-85, respectively. The SDK-85 kit consists of four main chips:

1. One Intel 8205 decoder
2. One Intel 8155 static RAM with I/O ports and timer

3. One Intel 8355 ROM with I/O or 8755 EPROM with I/O
4. One Intel 8279 programmable keyboard/display controller

The complete SDK-85 schematic is included in Appendix A for reference. The modules in the dashed boxes of Figure F–2 are provided on the SDK-85 board for future expansion.

*Modified from Intel Manuals. Courtesy of Intel Corp.

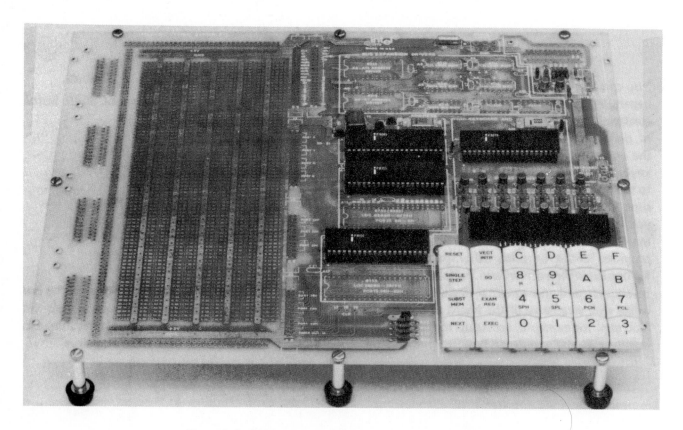

Figure F–1 SDK-85 microcomputer kit (Courtesy of Intel Corp.)

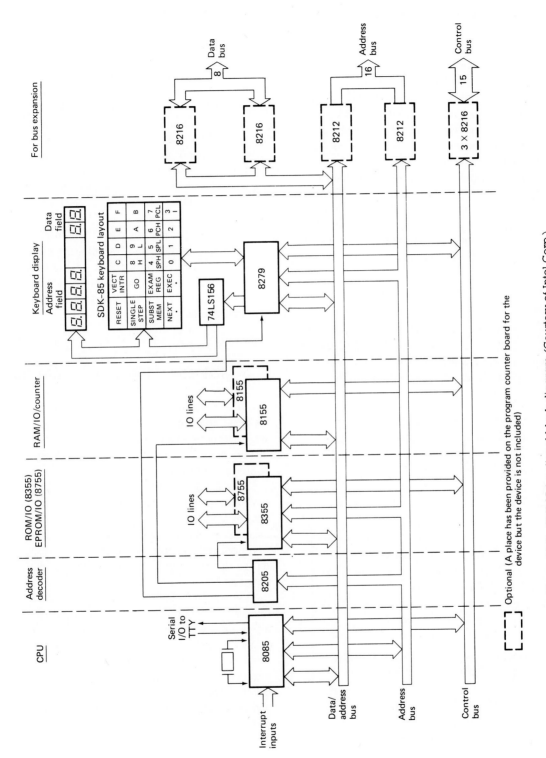

Figure F–2 SDK-85 functional block diagram (Courtesy of Intel Corp.)

The Intel 8085, the CPU of the SDK-85, was covered earlier. This appendix describes the memory, I/O, and other elements in the SDK-85 system.

F–1 PROGRAMMING THE SDK-85

The Intel SDK-85 (System Design Kit-85) is a single-board microcomputer kit containing an 8085 microprocessor, an Intel 8155 RAM and I/O, and Intel 8355 or 8755 preprogrammed monitor ROM or PROM, an Intel 8279 keyboard/display interface IC (integrated circuit), and the 8205 decoders. The board also contains a 24-key hexadecimal keyboard and six-digit seven-segment displays for the hexadecimal displays of the address and data. A monitor program provided by Intel in the SDK-85 ROM or PROM permits programming the SDK-85 via the keyboard or a teletype and displaying the answers after program execution on the seven-segment displays or as a teletype printout. The hardware aspects of the CPU (8085) of the SDK-85 were described earlier.

F–2 SDK-85 MEMORY MAP

Figure F–3 shows the memory map of the SDK-85. The basic SDK-85 with one 8155 and one 8355/8755 provides for the memory blocks marked "Monitor ROM" and "Basic RAM." The SDK-85 monitor requires all 2K ROM

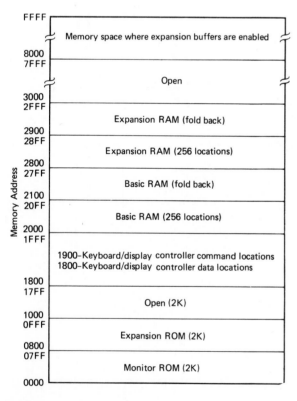

Figure F–3 SDK-85 memory map (Courtesy of Intel Corp.)

locations of the 8355. Some of the basic RAM locations are used by the SDK-85 monitor. Table F–1 gives the basic RAM locations used by the monitor. Note that RAM locations 20C2–20D0 are used for jumping to service routines during various interrupts. If these locations are not utilized during interrupts, one may use them for writing other programs. This means that with the basic SDK-85, the user has RAM locations 2000–20D0 for writing the programs if there are no interrupts. However, if locations 20C2–20D0 are used for interrupt servicing, then the available user RAM locations are 2000–20C1.

An expansion 8155 can be plugged into the SDK-85 space provided for the RAM expansion. Since the monitor does not use any of these expansion RAM locations, all 256 locations are available to the user. An expansion 8355 or 8755, when added to the appropriate space on the SDK-85 boards, provides for the expansion ROM.

The sections indicated by "fold back" in Figure F–3 provide for the exact mapping of basic RAM or expansion RAM, as shown. The sections indicated by "open" can be used for expansion by adding additional memory chips in the wire-wrap area of the SDK-85 or on other boards.

F–3 SDK-85 OPERATIONAL FEATURES

The user can program the SDK-85 and display or print the result using either a keyboard/display or a teletypewriter. Programming the SDK-85 using the keyboard/display is covered in the following. Teletypewriter operation is described in Appendix C.

The keyboard/display of the SDK-85 consists of a keyboard (having 16 hexadecimal keys and a number of control keys) and 6 seven-segment LED displays. The user enters the programs by pressing the keys on the keyboard and can observe the address, data, or message on the display. Figure F–4 illustrates the SDK-85 keyboard and display.

As shown in Figure F–4, the keyboard has 24 buttons, 16 of which are hexadecimal digits (0–F) for entering address or data and 8 of which are function buttons. Some of the hexadecimal buttons, such as 3, 4, 5, 6, 7, 8, and 9, have dual purposes. Each one of these buttons has an 8085 register name on it in addition to its hexadecimal value. This is done to reduce the number of buttons on the keyboard. These buttons can be used to display the contents of the 8085 registers. For example, pressing first $\boxed{\begin{array}{c}\text{EXAM}\\\text{REG}\end{array}}$ and then $\boxed{\begin{array}{c}8\\\text{H}\end{array}}$ will display H in the address field and its contents in the data field of the display. The display unit has 6 hexadecimal positions. The first 4 display positions usually represent 4 hexadecimal digits to indicate a 16-bit address, and the next

TABLE F–1
RAM Locations Used by Monitor (Courtesy of Intel Corporation)

Locations	
20C2	User may place a JMP instruction to an RST5 routine in locations 20C2–20C4
20C5	JMP to RST6 routine
20C8	JMP to RST6.5 routine (hardwired user interrupt)
20CB	JMP to RST7 routine
20CE	JMP to VECT INTR key routine
20D1–20E8	Monitor stack (temporary storage used by monitor)
20E9	E register
20EA	D register
20EB	C register
20EC	B register
20ED	Flags
20EE	A register
20EF	L register
20F0	H register
20F1	Interrupt mask
20F2	Program counter, low byte
20F3	Program counter, high byte
20F4	Stack pointer, low byte
20F5	Stack pointer, high byte
20F5	Current address
20F8	Current data
20F9–20FC	Output buffer and temporary locations
20FD	Register pointer
20FE	Input buffer
20FF	8155 Command/status register image

Loaded by user (20C2–20E8)

Storage for user register images (20E9–20F3)

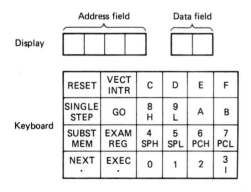

Figure F–4 SDK-85 keyboard and display

2 hexadecimal digits serve to display the 8-bit data contained in the 16-bit address.

RESET Key

The RESET key is used for controlling the SDK-85 under a monitor program stored in the 8355/8755 ROM/EPROM. If this key is pressed, the message "-8085" will be displayed across the address and data fields, indicating that the SDK-85 is under control of the ROM monitor program and is waiting for commands from the keyboard. The user can enter programs into the RAM, modify and execute them, and do other operations.

SUBST MEM , NEXT . , and EXEC . Keys

The substitute memory key can be used to display the contents of a ROM location or to display and change the contents of a RAM location. One would use the SUBST MEM , NEXT . , and EXEC . keys to display or modify the contents of a memory location in the following ways:

1. Press the SUBST MEM key.

2. Enter the address (4 hexadecimal digits or 16-bit address) whose contents are to be displayed or modified. This address will then be displayed in the SDK-85 address field.

3. Press the NEXT . key. The contents of a memory location whose address is in the address field will be displayed in the data field with a decimal point at the extreme right.

4. New data can be displayed in the data field by entering 2 hexadecimal digits via the keyboard. However, the location shown in the address field of the display will not contain this data until the NEXT .

or the [EXEC .] key is pressed. If one presses the [NEXT .] key, then the contents of a memory location shown in the address field will be modified with the data displayed in the data field. However, the display will show the next memory location with its contents. On the other hand, if one presses the [EXEC .] key, the contents of a memory location will be changed with data displayed in the data field, and the command will be terminated. Note that only the RAM locations can be modified. If the contents of a memory location cannot be changed (i.e., if this is a ROM location or it does not exist), then an error message will occur.

The following example illustrates the use of the [SUBST MEM], [NEXT .], and [EXEC .] keys. Suppose that it is desired to enter the following instruction sequence:

Address	Data	8085 Assembly Language Instructions
2005	21	LXI H, 2009
2006	09	
2007	20	
2008	CF	RST1

The instruction LXI H, 2009 will load registers H,L with 2009. The execution of RST1 takes the SDK-85 under control of the monitor. To enter the program, first press the [RESET] key and "-8085" will be displayed. Then proceed as shown below.

[EXAM REG] **Key**

One can use the [EXAM REG] key to display and change the contents of the 8085 register. This key can be used in the following ways:

	To Be Observed		
Keys To Be Pressed	Address Field	Data Field	Comments
[SUBST MEM]			
[2]	0002.		
[0]	0020.		
[0]	0200.		
[5]	2005.		
[NEXT]	2005	**.	Data stored in 2005 at this point
[2]	2005	02.	
[1]	2005	21.	
[NEXT]	2006	**.	Data stored in 2006 at this point
[9 L]	2006	09.	
[NEXT]	2007	**.	Data stored in 2007 at this point
[2]	2007	02.	
[0]	2007	20.	
[NEXT]	2008	**.	Data stored in 2008 at this point
[C]	2008	0C.	
[F]	2008	CF.	
[EXEC]	—		

1. Press the $\boxed{\begin{array}{c}\text{EXAM}\\\text{REG}\end{array}}$ key. The address and data field displays will be blanked out. A decimal point will be displayed at the extreme right of the address field.

2. Enter a register name by pressing register key $\boxed{\text{A}}$, $\boxed{\text{B}}$, $\boxed{\text{C}}$, $\boxed{\text{D}}$, $\boxed{\text{E}}$, $\boxed{\text{F}}$, $\boxed{\begin{array}{c}3\\\text{I}\end{array}}$, $\boxed{\begin{array}{c}4\\\text{SPH}\end{array}}$, $\boxed{\begin{array}{c}5\\\text{SPL}\end{array}}$, $\boxed{\begin{array}{c}6\\\text{PCH}\end{array}}$, $\boxed{\begin{array}{c}7\\\text{PCL}\end{array}}$, $\boxed{\begin{array}{c}8\\\text{H}\end{array}}$, or $\boxed{\begin{array}{c}9\\\text{L}\end{array}}$. The register name will be displayed in the address field, and its contents along with a decimal point on the extreme right will appear in the data field.

3. New data can be displayed in the data field by entering 2 hexadecimal digits via the keyboard. However, the register shown in the address field of the display will not contain the data until the $\boxed{\text{NEXT}}$ or the $\boxed{\text{EXEC}}$ key is pressed. If one presses the $\boxed{\text{NEXT}}$ key, then the contents of a register shown in the address field will be modified with the data displayed in the data field. However, the display will show the next register in sequence (Table F–2) along with its contents. If one presses the $\boxed{\text{EXEC}}$ key, then the contents of a register displayed in the address field will be modified with data in the data field, and the command will be terminated.

As can be seen from Table F–2, the meanings of all the registers, except registers I (interrupt mask register) and F (processor status word register), are obvious. The contents of registers I and F can be examined using the $\boxed{\begin{array}{c}\text{EXAM}\\\text{REG}\end{array}}$ key. The formats are shown in Figures F–5 and F–6.

TABLE F–2
Register Display Sequence (Courtesy of Intel Corporation)

Key/Display Code	Register
A	CPU register A
B	CPU register B
C	CPU register C
D	CPU register D
E	CPU register E
F	CPU flags byte
I	Interrupt mask
H	CPU register H
L	CPU register L
SPH	Stack pointer, high byte
SPL	Stack pointer, low byte
PCH	Program counter, high byte
PCL	Program counter, low byte

The following example demonstrates the use of the $\boxed{\begin{array}{c}\text{EXAM}\\\text{REG}\end{array}}$ key. Consider modifying the program counter contents with 2002. Press $\boxed{\text{RESET}}$ and then proceed as follows:

Keys To Be Pressed	Address Field	Data Field
$\boxed{\text{EXAM REG}}$		
$\boxed{\begin{array}{c}6\\\text{PCH}\end{array}}$	PCH	**.
$\boxed{2}$	PCH	02.
$\boxed{0}$	PCH	20.
$\boxed{\text{NEXT}}$	PCL	**.
$\boxed{0}$	PCL	00.
$\boxed{2}$	PCL	02.
$\boxed{\text{EXEC}}$	—	

Note that ** represents the contents of the register whose name is in the address field of the display.

In order to display the current contents of a register, do not press $\boxed{\text{RESET}}$. This initializes all the 8085 registers to contain 00_{16}. To get out of the current command mode, press the $\boxed{\text{EXEC}}$ key.

$\boxed{\text{GO}}$ Key

The $\boxed{\text{GO}}$ key can be used to display the contents of the program counter (PCH and PCL) in the address field along with a decimal point at the extreme right. The contents of the program counter can then be modified by entering new numbers via the keyboard.

The $\boxed{\text{EXEC}}$ key can be pressed to transfer control of the 8085 to the program counter contents shown in the address field. Prior to this transfer, the address and data fields are blanked out and E is displayed at the extreme left of the address field.

If another key besides the $\boxed{\text{EXEC}}$ key is pressed, an error message occurs. The $\boxed{\text{RESET}}$ key can be pressed in order to transfer control to the monitor.

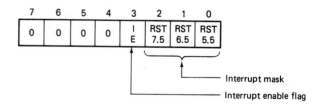

Figure F–5 Format of interrupt mask (I) register (Courtesy of Intel Corporation)

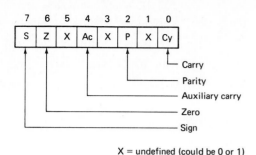

X = undefined (could be 0 or 1)

Figure F-5 Format of interrupt mask (I) register (Courtesy of Intel Corp.)

SINGLE STEP Key

The SINGLE STEP key can be used to display the program counter contents (PCH and PCL) in the address field along with a decimal point at the extreme right of the field. The contents of a memory location addressed by the program counter are displayed in the data field. The NEXT key can be pressed to execute the instruction displayed in the data field, which is addressed by the program counter. After execution of this instruction, the control is transferred to the monitor. The address field will show the next program counter contents. The data field will display the next instruction to be executed (the contents of a memory location addressed by the program counter).

The EXEC key can be pressed to place the address shown in the address field into the program counter. This terminates the single-step command and does not execute any instruction. At this point, one can display or change the contents of a register or memory location and examine the program logic. One can then proceed through a program executing each instruction by pressing first the SINGLE STEP key and then the NEXT key.

VECT INTR Key

Pressing the VECT INTR key causes the 8085 to branch to location $003C_{16}$ in the monitor for servicing the RST7.5 interrupt. An instruction for unconditional jump to location $20CE_{16}$ (user RAM) is placed at $003C_{16}$ in the monitor. The user can write a program to jump to a keyboard interrupt routine. Locations $20CE_{16}$–$20D0_{16}$ can be used for this purpose. The RESET command or instructions such as RST0 or RST1 or JMP 00_{16} can be used to transfer control to the monitor. Note that in order for the VECT INTR key to work, one must make sure of the following:

1. The 8085 interrupts are enabled.
2. RST7.5 is unmasked using the SIM instruction or by loading the I register with an appropriate code.

F-3-1 Program Execution

In order to execute a program in the SDK-85, first press the RESET key, then press the GO key, enter the 4-digit hexadecimal address (the starting address of the program whose execution is desired), and finally press the EXEC key. The answer will appear in the display.

F-3-2 Program Debugging by the SDK-85

The SDK-85 has the following debugging features:

1. A single-step feature causes the 8085 to execute one instruction at a time. The user can examine, verify, and change the contents of registers or memory locations by going through the program logic. The user can thus locate any errors in the program. The SDK-85 monitor has the single-stepping feature.
2. A breakpoint feature causes the 8085 to stop executing a program at a particular location. This feature can be used to detect any errors in a section of a program.

The breakpoint complements single stepping. One can use breakpoints to detect any errors in a program segment. Each instruction in this segment can be single stepped in order to precisely locate the error.

A breakpoint can be placed at a particular location in a program by inserting the RST1 instruction (CF_{16}) at that location. After execution of this instruction, the current contents of memory locations and registers are saved. The control is then transferred to the monitor. The user can examine and verify these memory locations and register contents to detect any errors. Pressing the GO and the EXEC keys will cause the 8085 to continue program execution at the instruction after the RST1. While inserting a breakpoint, one must place RST1 at the first byte of an instruction. One may use NOP for any other bytes left from this instruction. As an example, consider the following segment of a large program:

```
.    .
.    .
.    .
200A   3A   LDA 2005
200B   05
200C   20
.    .
.    .
```

Now, if it is desired to place a breakpoint in this program segment, one must place it at 200A (the first word of the instruction) rather than at 200B or 200C. NOPs may be used for these locations:

```
           .
           .
           .
    200A  CF  RST1
    200B  00  NOP
    200C  00  NOP
           .
           .
           .
```

F–3–3 SDK-85 Monitor

The SDK-85 monitor is a program that is contained in 2K bytes of ROM or EPROM occupying memory addresses from 0000_{16} to $07FF_{16}$. This monitor provides the capability of communicating with the SDK-85 via a keyboard/display unit or a teletypewriter. One may choose either one by modifying the strapping connections.

One can use the various routines provided in the SDK-85 monitor for displaying the results or providing time delays. Table F–3 gives the calling addresses and descriptions of the various useful monitor routines. A listing of the SDK-85 monitor is given in Appendix B.

If one wants to display 6 digits of data (24 bits) in the address and data fields of the display at the same time, both UPDAD and UPDDT display routines in the SDK-85 monitor must be in sequence. Note that the UPDAD routine when called destroys [A] and some other registers. On the other hand, the UPDDT routine when called destroys [D,E] and some other registers. There-

fore, if the UPDAD is called before UPDDT, at least [A] must be saved in the memory so that the UPDDT can then be called after reloading this data into the accumulator from memory. As an example, consider $[D,E] = 0603_{16}$ and $[A] = 05_{16}$. In order to display this data at the same time in both address and data fields, the following instruction sequence can be used:

```
    2002  31  LXI SP, 20C2
    2003  C2
    2004  20
    2005  32  STA 2000
    2006  00
    2007  20
    2008  CD  CALL UPDAD
    2009  63
    200A  03
    200B  3A  LDA 2000
    200C  00
    200D  20
    200E  CD  CALL UPDDT
    200F  6E
    2010  03
    2011  76  HLT
```

After executing this instruction sequence, the display will be as follows:

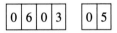

Now, if the UPDDT is called before UPDAD, at least the contents of the D,E register pair must be saved (pushed) onto the stack. This data can be popped from

TABLE F–3
Monitor Routine Calling Addresses (Courtesy of Intel Corporation)

Calling Address	Mnemonic	Description
0363	UPDAD	*Update Address* Update address field of the display. The contents of the D,E register pair are displayed in the address field of the display. The contents of all the CPU registers and flags are affected.
036E	UPDDT	*Update Data* Update data field of the display. The contents of the A register are displayed in hexadecimal notation in the data field of the display. The contents of all CPU registers and flags are affected.
02E7	RDKBD	*Read Keyboard* This routine waits until a character is entered in the hexadecimal keyboard and upon return places the value of the character in the A register. The A, H, and L registers and the flag flip-flops are affected. *Note:* For RDKBD to work correctly, one must first unmask RST5.5 using the SIM instruction.
05F1	DELAY	*Time Delay* This routine takes the 16-bit contents of register pair D,E and counts down to zero, then returns to the calling program. The A, D, and E registers and the flags are affected.

the stack into the D,E pair after calling the UPDDT. Finally, the UPDAD can be called to display the contents of D,E. As an example, consider $[D,E] = 0158_{16}$ and $[A] = 09_{16}$. In order to display this data at the same time in both address and data fields, the following instruction sequence can be used:

2000	31	LXI SP, 20C2
2001	C2	
2002	20	
2003	11	LXI D, 0158
2004	58	
2005	01	
2006	3E	MVI A, 09
2007	09	
2008	D5	PUSH D
2009	CD	CALL UPDDT
200A	6E	
200B	03	
200C	D1	POP D
200D	CD	CALL UPDAD
200E	63	
200F	03	
2010	76	HLT

After executing this instruction sequence, the display will be as follows:

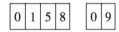

F-3-4 Guidelines for Writing the Source or Assembly Language Programs*

1. Even though there is no assembler in the SDK-85, typical 8085 assembler rules are followed for writing assembly language programs.

2. An assembler indicates the beginning and ending of each field by means of special symbols or delimiters. In writing the assembly language programs in this book, we use the standard Intel 8085 assembler delimiters as follows:

:	After a label
Space	Between OP code and address
,	Between operands in address field
;	Before a comment

3. We use hexadecimal notation for addresses and data.

Example F-1

Write a program in 8085 assembly language and then hexadecimal language to add two 8-bit numbers stored in locations 2000_{16} and 2001_{16}. Display the result in the data field of the SDK-85 display.

*From *8080A/8085 Assembly Language Programming* by Leventhal. Copyright © 1978 McGraw-Hill, Inc.

Solution

The assembly language program can be written as follows:

Label	Mnemonic	Operand	Comments
	LXI	H, 2000H	; Load 2000_{16} into H, L pair
	MOV	A, M	; Load [2000] into [A]
	INX	H	; Increment H,L to 2001
	ADD	M	; Add [2000] with [2001]
	CALL	UPDDT	; Display result
	HLT		

Note that this program uses stack because of the CALL UPDDT instruction. Therefore, the stack pointer should have been initialized to 20C2. However, if the stack pointer is not initialized, then the SDK-85 arbitrarily assumes a value for the stack pointer. Hence, in most of the SDK-85 examples in this book, the stack pointer is not initialized at the beginning of the programs.

The assembly language program can be translated into a hexadecimal machine language program as follows:

2000	DATA1	
2001	DATA2	
2002	21	LXI H, 2000H
2003	00	
2004	20	
2005	7E	MOV A, M
2006	23	INX H
2007	86	ADD M
2008	CD	CALL UPDDT
2009	6E	
200A	03	
200B	76	HLT

Locations 2000_{16} and 2001_{16} contain the two 8-bit data to be added.

The instruction 21_{16} in location 2002_{16} loads 2000_{16} into the H,L register pair. The instruction $7E_{16}$ in 2005_{16} moves DATA1 into the accumulator. Location 2006_{16} contains 23_{16}, which increments the H,L pair to 2001_{16}. The instruction 86_{16} adds DATA2 to DATA1 and leaves the result of addition in the accumulator. Finally, the instruction sequence

$$
\begin{array}{c}
\text{CD} \\
\text{6E} \\
\text{03}
\end{array}
$$

displays the result (contents of the accumulator) in the data field of the SDK-85.

Assume that DATA1 = 05_{16} and DATA2 = 02_{16}. To enter the program, first press the ⬚RESET key to start the monitor. The message "-8085" will be displayed. Then proceed as follows:

Press Keys	See on Display in Address Field	See on Display in Data Field
SUBST MEM		
2	0002.	
0	0020.	
0	0200.	
0	2000.	
NEXT	2000	**.
5 SPL	2000	05.
NEXT	2001	**.
2	2001	02.
NEXT	2002	**.
2	2002	02.
1	2002	21.
NEXT	2003	**.
0	2003	00.
NEXT	2004	**.
2	2004	02.
0	2004	20.
NEXT	2005	**.
7 PCL	2005	07.
E	2005	7E.
NEXT	2006	**.
2	2006	02.
3	2006	23.
NEXT	2007	**.
8 H	2007	08.
6 PCH	2007	86.
NEXT	2008	**.
C	2008	0C.
D	2008	CD.
NEXT	2009	**.
6	2009	06.
E	2009	6E.
NEXT	200A	**.
0	200A	00.
3 1	200A	03.
NEXT	200B	**.
7 PCL	200B	07.
6 PCH	200B	76.
NEXT	200C	**.

Note that, in this program, ** indicates unpredictable hexadecimal digits. Note also that the [NEXT] key must be pressed at the end of the program to enter 76_{16} into location $200B_{16}$. Always press the [NEXT] key after entering a program. This will store the last instruction of the program in the specified memory location displayed in the address field of the display.

To execute the example program, proceed as follows:

1. Press the [RESET] key.
2. Press the [GO] key.
3. Enter the starting address of the program. The starting address in this program is 2002_{16}, and not 2000_{16}, since the first address of a program must contain an instruction. Locations 2000 and 2001 contain the two 8-bit data to be added. Hence, enter 2002 by pressing [2], [0], [0], [2].
4. Press the [EXEC] key.

The program is now executed, and the result of addition, 07, will be displayed as follows:

Address field   Data field

| * | * | * | * | | 0 | 7 |

Unpredictable address

Example F-2

Suppose that, in entering the program for Example F-1, the programmer makes an error and loads the contents of location 2003_{16} as 01_{16} rather than 00_{06}. The program that results is as follows:

2000	05	DATA1
2001	02	DATA2
2002	21	LXI H, 2001
2003	01	
2004	20	
2005	7E	MOV A, M
2006	23	INX H
2007	86	ADD M
2008	CD	CALL UPDDT
2009	6E	
200A	03	
200B	76	HLT

The intent of this program is to add the contents of 2000_{16}

and 2001_{16}, that is, to add 05_{16} with 02_{16}, and display 07_{16} in the data field of the SDK-85 display. Instead, because of the error, the contents of 2001_{16} are added with the contents of 2002_{16}. In other words, 02_{16} is added with 21_{16}, and the result, 23_{16}, is displayed in the data field of the SDK-85 display. This can be explained as follows.

The instruction 21_{16} in location 2002_{16} loads 2001_{16} into the H,L register pair. The instruction $7E_{16}$ in 2005_{16} moves 02_{16} into the accumulator. Location 2006_{16} contains 23_{16}, which increments the H,L pair to 2002_{16}. The instruction 86_{16} adds the contents of 2002_{16}, that is, 21_{16}, with 02_{16} and leaves the result, 23_{16}, in the accumulator. Finally, the instruction sequence

$$CD$$
$$6E$$
$$03$$

displays 23_{16} in the data field of the SDK-85 display. Because of the programmer's error in entering 01_{16} rather than 00_{16} into location 2003_{16}, a result of 23_{16}, rather than 07_{16}, is displayed. Debug the program using breakpoints and single stepping to rectify the error.

Solution

First, let us place a breakpoint arbitrarily in location 2006_{16}; that is, replace 23_{16} with the instruction CF_{16} (RST1). The results at this point should be as follows:

Contents of accumulator $= 05_{16}$
Contents of H $= 20$, L $= 00$

Now, execute the program with the breakpoint in location 2006_{16} by pressing $\boxed{\text{RESET}}$ and then $\boxed{\text{GO}}$, enter 2002, and finally press $\boxed{\text{EXEC}}$; "-8085" will be displayed. Press $\boxed{\text{EXAM REG}}$ and the appropriate register each time you display the contents of a register, and obtain the following results:

Contents of accumulator $= 02$
Contents of H $= 20$, L $= 01$

Obviously, the program is wrong. Now, let us try to single step the program. We do the following steps:

1. Press the $\boxed{\text{RESET}}$ key.
2. Press the $\boxed{\begin{matrix}\text{SINGLE}\\\text{STEP}\end{matrix}}$ key.

3. Press $\boxed{2}$, $\boxed{0}$, $\boxed{0}$, $\boxed{2}$.
4. Press the $\boxed{\text{NEXT}}$ key.

The CPU has now executed the first instruction 21_{16}. To examine the registers, press $\boxed{\text{EXEC}}$ before $\boxed{\text{EXAM REG}}$. (Otherwise, you get an error and have to press $\boxed{\text{EXAM REG}}$ again.) The register contents should have been

Contents of H $= 20$, L $= 00$

Instead, they are

Contents of H $= 20$, L $= 01$

Obviously, we have incorrect data in location 2003_{16} or 2004_{16}. We find that the contents of the L register are loaded with incorrect data, and location 2003_{16} contains data to be loaded into the L register, which is 01_{16} rather than 00_{16}. We correct the error by entering 00_{16} into location 2003_{16} and also remove CF_{16} from location 2006_{16} and replace it with 23_{16}. We execute the program again and find the result of 07_{16} in the data field of the display.

Example F–3

Given the following instruction sequence,

2000	3E	MVI A, 01
2001	01	
2002	C6	ADI 04
2003	04	
2004	32	STA 2009
2005	09	
2006	20	

enter the program into the SDK-85, single step it, and display the following:

1. Display register A after executing 3E at location 2000.

2. Display register A after executing C6 at location 2002.

3. Display the contents of location 2009 after executing 32 at location 2004.

Solution

Enter the program into the SDK-85 and single step it in the following way:

Keys To Be Pressed	Comments
$\boxed{\text{RESET}}$	
$\boxed{\text{SINGLE STEP}}$	Puts SDK-85 in single-step mode
$\boxed{2}$	
$\boxed{0}$	

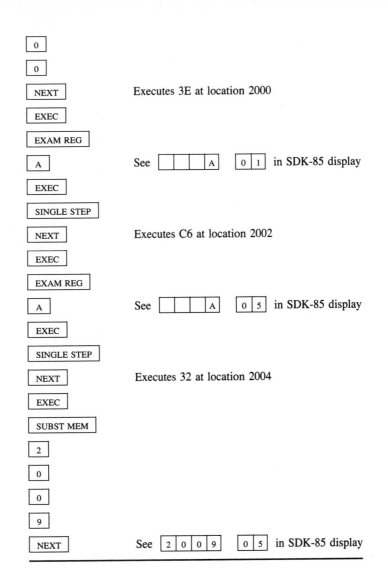

0	
0	
NEXT	Executes 3E at location 2000
EXEC	
EXAM REG	
A	See ⬚⬚ A 0 1 in SDK-85 display
EXEC	
SINGLE STEP	
NEXT	Executes C6 at location 2002
EXEC	
EXAM REG	
A	See ⬚⬚ A 0 5 in SDK-85 display
EXEC	
SINGLE STEP	
NEXT	Executes 32 at location 2004
EXEC	
SUBST MEM	
2	
0	
0	
9	
NEXT	See 2 0 0 9 0 5 in SDK-85 display

Example F–4

Find the status flags (S, Z, Ac, P, and Cy) for the operation of $3D_{16} + E8_{16}$ (a) analytically and (b) by single stepping a program on the SDK-85.

Solution

(a)

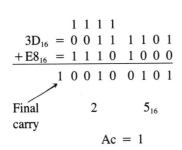

$$
\begin{array}{r}
1\ 1\ 1\ 1 \\
3D_{16} = 0\ 0\ 1\ 1\ \ 1\ 1\ 0\ 1 \\
+E8_{16} = 1\ 1\ 1\ 0\ \ 1\ 0\ 0\ 0 \\
\hline
1\ 0\ 0\ 1\ 0\ \ 0\ 1\ 0\ 1
\end{array}
$$

Final   2 5_{16}
carry

$Ac = 1$

The result of addition is

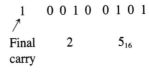

1   0 0 1 0 0 1 0 1

Final   2 5_{16}
carry

Analytically,

$S = 0$ because most significant bit of 25_{16} is 0.

$Z = 0$ because result 25_{16} is nonzero.

$Ac = 1$ because intermediate carry out of third to fourth bit is 1.

$P = 0$ because of three 1's (odd) in 25_{16}.

$Cy = 1$ because final carry is 1.

(b) Using the 8085 instruction set, the following instruction sequence can be obtained for $3D_{16} + E8_{16}$:

```
2000   3E   MVI A, 3D
2001   3D
2002   C6   ADI E8
2003   E8
```

In order to obtain the status flags, enter this instruction sequence into the SDK-85, single step the program, and obtain and interpret the contents of the F register. In other words, press the following keys on the SDK-85:

Keys To Be Pressed	Comments
RESET	
SINGLE STEP	Puts SDK-85 in single-step mode
2	
0	
0	
0	
NEXT	Executes $3E_{16}$ in location 2000_{16}
NEXT	Executes $C6_{16}$ in location 2002_{16}

Now the execution of the program for $3D_{16} + E8_{16}$ is complete, and the result 25_{16} is in the accumulator. Remember that, in the single-step mode, only the instructions to be executed are displayed along with their addresses. The operands or data $3D_{16}$ and $E8_{16}$ do not appear on the display. Therefore, after execution of the instruction $3E_{16}$ in 2000_{16}, the SDK-85 display will show

$$\boxed{2}\,\boxed{0}\,\boxed{0}\,\boxed{2}\quad\boxed{C}\,\boxed{6}$$

After the $\boxed{\overset{NEXT}{.}}$ key is pressed, $C6_{16}$ is executed and the display shows location 2004 with its contents:

$$\boxed{2}\,\boxed{0}\,\boxed{0}\,\boxed{4}\quad\boxed{X}\,\boxed{X}\quad\text{Unpredictable data}$$

Now, to examine the processor status word (PSW) register, press the $\boxed{\text{EXEC}}$, $\boxed{\text{EXAM REG}}$, and $\boxed{\text{F}}$ keys.

The display will show

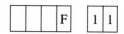

The results can be interpreted as follows. From Figure F–6, we know the format of the status flag byte to be

S	Z	X	Ac	X	P	X	Cy

X = undefined

We convert 11_{16} into binary and obtain

$$0\ 0\ 0\ 1\ 0\ 0\ 0\ 1_2$$

We compare this with the status flag byte and see that

$$S = 0, Z = 0, Ac = 1, P = 0, Cy = 1$$

which agrees with the results obtained analytically. Remember that the display 11_{16} is not the result of adding 3E and E8. It is the content of the processor status word. The result of the addition can be obtained by displaying the accumulator contents and can be seen to be 25_{16}.

Example F–5

The SDK-85 is required to perform a parity check on an 8-bit word and display EE in the data field if the parity is even or DD if the parity is odd. For this example, (a) flowchart the problem, (b) convert the flowchart to 8085 assembly and machine (hexadecimal) language programs, and (c) execute the program on the SDK-85.

Solution

(a) In the flowchart of Figure F–7, data to be checked for parity, if loaded directly into the accumulator by MVI A, DATA or by LDA ADDR, will not affect any of the status flags since, in the 8085, execution of the MVI and LDA instructions does not affect any flags. Therefore, flags must be affected by using some other operation. One way is to add 00_{16} with data, and the result in the

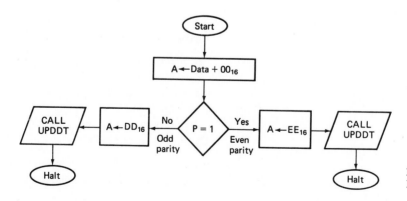

Figure F–7 Flowchart for Example F–5

accumulator will be the data that sets the parity bit to 1 if the data has an even number of 1's. Then loading the accumulator with EE_{16} and calling the SDK-85 display routine UPDDT, EE can be displayed in the data field. However, if the parity bit is set to 0 (number of 1's in the data is odd), then loading DD_{16} into the accumulator and calling the display routine UPDDT, DD can be displayed in the data field.

(b) The flowchart can be translated into an 8085 assembly language program as follows:

```
          MVI   A, 00    ;  Initialize accumulator with
                            00
          ADI   DATA     ;  Add [A] with data whose
                            parity is to be checked
          JPE   EVEN     ;  Check for parity
          MVI   A, DD
          CALL  UPDDT    ;  If parity odd, display DD
          HLT
EVEN:     MVI   A, EE    ;  If parity even, display EE
          CALL  UPDDT
          HLT
```

The assembly language program can be translated into an 8085 hexadecimal program as follows:

```
2000    3E      MVI A, 00
2001    00
2002    C6      ADI DATA
2003    DATA
2004    EA      JPE 200D
2005    0D
2006    20
2007    3E      MVI A, DD
2008    DD
2009    CD      CALL UPDDT
200A    6E
200B    03
200C    76      HLT
200D    3E      MVI A, EE
200E    EE
200F    CD      CALL UPDDT
2010    6E
2011    03
2012    76      HLT
```

(c) Now enter this program into the SDK-85 and then execute it as follows:

1. Press the [RESET] key.
2. Press the [GO] key.
3. Press [2], [0], [0], [0], the starting address of the program.
4. Finally, press the [EXEC] key.

The result EE or DD will be displayed in the data field based on whether the parity of data is even or odd.

Note that the HLT (76_{16}) instruction should be the last instruction in some SDK-85 programs. If HLT (76_{16}) appears in the middle of a program, then, after the program is executed once, the contents of the memory lo-

cation following HLT (76_{16}) are changed to 00_{16}. This is how some systems have been designed by Intel. Therefore, after executing such a program once, one must reload the location following HLT (76_{16}) with proper instructions. In Example F-5, after the program is executed once, the contents 3E of location 200D (following the 76 at 200C) are changed to 00_{16}. Therefore, in order to reexecute the program again, the user must reload location 200D with 3E.

F-4 SDK-85 INPUT/OUTPUT AND INTERFACING

The three basic types of I/O transfer described earlier are now discussed in relation to the Intel SDK-85 microcomputer. Note that the SDK-85 does not have any DMA controller chip. Therefore, data transfer using DMA cannot be performed with the SDK-85.

F-4-1 SDK-85 Programmed I/O

The SDK-85 programmed I/O is based upon the 8085 I/O instructions and the 8085 support chips.

F-4-2 SDK-85 I/O Ports

The SDK-85 ports are obtained by using the 8355/8755 and 8155/8156 chips. As mentioned before, the 8355 in the SDK-85 provides two 8-bit I/O ports: ports A and B. In the SDK-85, these ports are configured as port 00 and port 01. Associated with each of these ports is a data direction register. Ports 02_{16} and 03_{16} are the data direction registers for ports 00_{16} and 01_{16}, respectively. The two data direction registers (ports 02_{16} and 03_{16}) control the direction of the data flow into and out of the data registers (00_{16} and 01_{16}). A 1 at a specific bit in the data direction register sets up the corresponding bit in the data register as an output. A 0 at a specific bit in the data direction register configures the corresponding bit in the data register as an input. For example, consider the following instruction sequence:

```
          MVI   A,  09
          OUT   02
```

This instruction sequence will set the bits of port 00_{16} as shown in Figure F-8: bits 0 and 3 as outputs and the other bits (bits 1, 2, and 4–7) as inputs.

Inputting port 00 by the IN 00 instruction will load the accumulator with bits 1, 2, 4, 5, 6, 7 from port 00 and bits 0 and 3 as don't care data since they are configured as outputs. Outputting port 00 by the OUT 00 instruction will send bits 0 and 3 of the accumulator as outputs.

The 8355/8755 I/O ports of the SDK-85 are shown in Table F-4. Note that if the SDK-85 has the 8755 chip

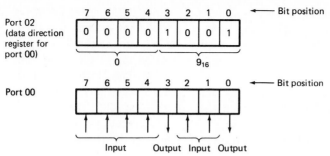

Port 02
(data direction
register for
port 00)

7	6	5	4	3	2	1	0	← Bit position
0	0	0	0	1	0	0	1	

0   9_{16}

Port 00

7	6	5	4	3	2	1	0	← Bit position

Input   Output Input Output

Figure F–8 Configuring port 00

TABLE F–4
SDK-85 Commonly Used I/O Ports

Port	Function
00	8355 port A
01	8355 port B
02	8355 port A Data Direction Register
03	8355 port B Data Direction Register
08	8755 port A
09	8755 port B
20	8155 command/status register
21	8155 port A
22	8155 port B
23	8155 port C
24	8155 low-order byte of timer count
25	8155 high-order byte of timer count

instead of the 8355, then ports A and B of the 8755 are numbered as 08_{16} and 09_{16}, respectively.

The 8155 provides three I/O ports, namely, two 8-bit ports (ports A and B) and one 6-bit I/O port (port C). In the SDK-85, ports A, B, and C are numbered as ports 21, 22, and 23, respectively. The command/status register in the 8155 is numbered as port 20. At this point, we are interested only in bits 0, 1, 2, and 3 of the command/status register (port 20). Bits 0 and 1 of port 20 configure all bits of ports 21 and 22 as either all inputs or all outputs (0 for input, 1 for output). Bits 2 and 3 set up all bits of port 23 as either inputs or outputs (00 for input, or ALT1; 11 for output, or ALT2). Unlike the 8355/8755, the individual bits of the 8155 I/O ports cannot be programmed as inputs or outputs. All bits of ports A, B, and C of the 8155 can be set up as either all inputs or all outputs by writing an appropriate code in the command/status register (port 20). Note that inputting port 20 into the accumulator will provide the contents of the status register, whereas outputting into this port will send the accumulator contents into the command register. Also note that a HIGH at RESET makes all the bits of the command register 0. This will configure all the I/O ports in the 8155 as inputs.

Finally, the SDK-85 uses the basic 8155 timer in the single-step command. Since the contents of the 8155 command register cannot be read, an image of this register should be maintained. If single stepping is used in de-

bugging a program with the SDK-85, the contents of the 8155 command register are changed, and this is undesirable. However, the SDK-85 monitor is written in such a way that after each single stepping, the monitor updates the contents of the command register with the contents of the command register image (location 20FF) in memory. The monitor will thus store the proper code in the command register. A few examples are shown next:

• 8155 ports all configured as inputs

```
MVI   A, 00
STA   20FF
OUT   20
```

• 8155 ports A and B configured as outputs

```
MVI   A, 03
STA   20FF
OUT   20
```

The most commonly used I/O ports of the SDK-85 are summarized in Table F–4. Tables F–5 through F–8 give the pin assignments of the SDK-85 connectors J1, J2, J3, and J4. Note that the SDK-85 monitor initializes memory location 20FF to 00_{16} during RESET. One can reenter its content with the SUBST MEM key if necessary.

F–4–3 Light-Emitting Diodes and Seven-Segment Displays

LEDs are extensively used as status indicators and various other types of displays. An LED is typically driven by low voltage and low current. This makes the LED a very attractive device for use with microprocessors. We will use the LEDs as typical output devices with the SDK-85 to demonstrate the concepts of programmed I/O. Table F–9 provides the current and voltage requirements of red, yellow, and green LEDs.

Interfacing an LED to a microcomputer was described earlier. Basically, an LED will light when its cathode is sufficiently negative with respect to its anode. The microcomputer can therefore light the LED either by grounding the cathode (if the anode is tied to +5 V) or by applying +5 V to the anode (if the cathode is grounded) through an appropriate resistor value. The SDK-85 output ports (like most TTL or MOS devices)

TABLE F–5
Bus Expansion Connector J1 Pin Assignments (Courtesy of Intel Corporation)

Assignment	Pin	Pin	Marking	Assignment	I/O
Ground	1	2	—	OPEN	—
Ground	3	4	CLK	Buffered CLK	O
Ground	5	6	S1	Buffered S1	O
Ground	7	8	S0	Buffered S0	O
Ground	9	10	ALE	Buffered ALE	O
Ground	11	12	HLDA	Buffered HLDA	O
Ground	13	14	HOLD	Buffered $\overline{\text{HOLD}}$	I
Ground	15	16	INTA/	Buffered $\overline{\text{INTA}}$	O
Ground	17	18	INTR	INTR	I
Ground	19	20	RST6.5	Buffered RST6.5	I
Ground	21	22	RST	Buffered $\overline{\text{RESET OUT}}$	O
Ground	23	24	RST IN/	$\overline{\text{RESET INPUT}}$	I
Ground	25	26	D7	Buffered D7	I/O
Ground	27	28		Buffered D6	I/O
Ground	29	30		Buffered D5	I/O
Ground	31	32	Data bus	Buffered D4	I/O
Ground	33	34		Buffered D3	I/O
Ground	35	36		Buffered D2	I/O
Ground	37	38		Buffered D1	I/O
Ground	39	40	D0	Buffered D0	I/O

TABLE F–6
Bus Expansion Connector J2 Pin Assignments (Courtesy of Intel Corporation)

Assignment	Pin	Pin	Marking	Assignment	I/O
Ground	1	2	RDY	READY	I
Ground	3	4	WR/	Buffered $\overline{\text{WR}}$	O
Ground	5	6	RD/	Buffered $\overline{\text{RD}}$	O
Ground	7	8	IO/$\overline{\text{M}}$	Buffered IO/$\overline{\text{M}}$	O
Ground	9	10	A15	Buffered A15	O
Ground	11	12		Buffered A14	O
Ground	13	14		Buffered A13	O
Ground	15	16		Buffered A12	O
Ground	17	18		Buffered A11	O
Ground	19	20		Buffered A10	O
Ground	21	22		Buffered A9	O
Ground	23	24	Address bus	Buffered A8	O
Ground	25	26		Buffered A7	O
Ground	27	28		Buffered A6	O
Ground	29	30		Buffered A5	O
Ground	31	32		Buffered A4	O
Ground	33	34		Buffered A3	O
Ground	35	36		Buffered A2	O
Ground	37	38		Buffered A1	O
Ground	39	40	A0	Buffered A0	O

TABLE F–7
I/O Port Connector J3 Pin Assignments (Courtesy of Intel Corporation)

Assignment[a]	Pin	Pin	Marking[b]	Assignment
P1-6	1	2		P1-7
P1-4	3	4		P1-5
P1-2	5	6	Port 1	P1-3
P1-0	7	8		P1-1
P0-6	9	10		P0-7
P0-4	11	12		P0-5
P0-2	13	14	Port 0	P0-3
P0-0	15	16		P0-1
P9-6	17	18		P9-7
P9-4	19	20		P9-5
P9-2	21	22	Port 9	P9-3
P9-0	23	24		P9-1
P8-6	25	26		P8-7
P8-4	27	28		P8-5
P8-2	29	30	Port 8	P8-3
P8-0	31	32		P8-1
Ground	33	34		Ground

[a]Pn-m stands for Port n, bit m (e.g., P9-6 means Port 9, bit 6).
[b]Ports 0 and 1 are ports A and B of 8355 (A14) ports 8 and 9 are ports A and B of 8755 (A15).

TABLE F–8
I/O Port Connector J4 Pin Assignments (Courtesy of Intel Corporation)

Assignment	Pin	Pin	Marking[a]	Assignment
P23H-4	1	2		P23H-5
P23H-2	3	4	Port 23H	P23H-3
P23H-0	5	6		P23H-1
P22H-6	7	8		P22H-7
P22H-4	9	10		P22H-5
P22H-2	11	12	Port 22H	P22H-3
P22H-0	13	14		P22H-1
P21H-6	15	16		P21H-7
P21H-4	17	18		P21H-5
P21H-2	19	20	Port 21H	P21H-3
P21H-0	21	22		P21H-1
Open	23	24		Open
Ground	25	26		Ground

[a]Port 21H is port A, port 22H is port B, and port 23H is port C of 8155 (A16).

TABLE F–9
Current and Voltage Requirements of LEDs

	Red	Yellow	Green
Current	10 mA	10 mA	20 mA
Voltage	1.7 V	2.2 V	2.4 V

can drive the cathodes of LEDs better than the anodes; a typical configuration is given in Figure F–9.

Note that a logic 0 from the microcomputer lights the LED; that is, the LED uses active-low, or negative logic. The 7407 is a hexadecimal noninverting open-collector buffer/driver. We could have used any npn transistor in place of the 7407.

F–4–4 SDK-85 On-Board Seven-Segment Displays

As an example of driving the seven-segment displays by the SDK-85, we first describe the SDK-85 on-board display. Figure F–10 illustrates a typical seven-segment display, and Figure F–11 shows a common cathode and a common anode display configuration. In a common cath-

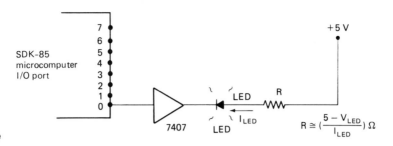

Figure F–9 SDK-85 LED interface

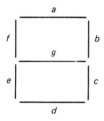

Figure F–10 A seven-segment display (Courtesy of Intel Corp.)

ode arrangement, the microprocessor sends a HIGH to light a segment and a LOW to turn it off. In a common anode configuration, the microprocessor sends a LOW to light a segment and a HIGH to turn it off.

Figure F–12 shows the segment connections for the display. The numbering of the displays with respect to their locations on the SDK-85 is shown in Figure F–13, and Table F–10 gives the RAM display locations and numbers.

The seven-segment displays on the SDK-85 board are interfaced to the SDK-85 via the 8279 keyboard/display controller chip. The 8279 is mapped into the SDK-85 memory. The instruction sequence given next will output data to one of the displays:

LXI H, 1900
MVI A, NUMBER $+ 80_{16}$
MOV M, A
LXI H, 1800
MVI A, CODE
MOV M, A
START: JMP START

Note that the appropriate display can be enabled by writing a control code. NUMBER + 80, into location 1900. This automatically writes a command word into the 8279 command register. Also, writing a display code into location 1800 will output this code to the display.

Finally, in Figure F–13, a logic 0 lights a segment and a logic 1 turns it off. Table F–11 contains the hexadecimal codes to light the segments and decimal point (dp) individually. For example, the instruction sequence given next will light the decimal point in the data digit 1 of the data field:

LXI H, 1900
MVI A, 84
MOV M, A
LXI H, 1800
MVI A, F7
MOV M, A
START: JMP START

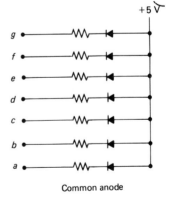

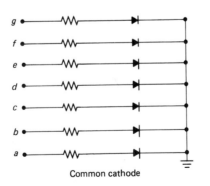

Figure F–11 Display configurations (From *Microcomputer Experimentation with the Intel SDK-85,* by Leventhal and Walsh © 1980, p. 73. Reprinted by permission of Prentice-Hall, Inc., Englewood Cliffs, New Jersey)

Common cathode   Common anode

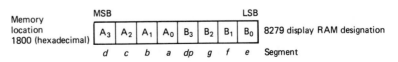

Memory location 1800 (hexadecimal)	MSB							LSB	8279 display RAM designation
	A_3	A_2	A_1	A_0	B_3	B_2	B_1	B_0	
	d	c	b	a	dp	g	f	e	Segment

Figure F–12 Data format (Courtesy of Intel Corp.)

Address field   Data field

| 1 | 2 | 3 | 4 |

| 1 | 2 |

Figure F–13 Display configuration (Courtesy of Intel Corp.)

TABLE F–10
8279 Display RAM Locations and the Corresponding Numbers (Courtesy of Intel Corporation)

Purpose	*8279 Display RAM Location Number*
Address digit 1	0
Address digit 2	1
Address digit 3	2
Address digit 4	3
Data digit 1	4
Data digit 2	5
Unused	6
Unused	7

TABLE F–11
Codes for Lighting Segments (Memory Location 1800_{16}) (From *Microcomputer Experimentation with the Intel SDK-85,* by Leventhal and Walsh, © 1980, p. 75. Reprinted by permission of Prentice-Hall, Inc., Englewood Cliffs, New Jersey)

Segment	*Pattern (Hexadecimal)*
a	EF
b	DF
c	BF
d	7F
e	FE
f	FD
g	FB
dp	F7

F–4–5 External Seven-Segment Displays

We can drive an external seven-segment display by the SDK-85 to display any hexadecimal digit from 0 to F. The SDK-85 will be used as a decoder in this case; that is, the SDK-85 will convert a hexadecimal digit into a seven-segment code.

A simple approach is to form a decode table that contains the seven-segment code for each hexadecimal digit (0 to F). This table can be stored in the SDK-85 memory and can be used as a lookup table. A program can then be written to find the appropriate code from the lookup table and output it to the desired segments.

Example F–6 illustrates the concept of driving an external seven-segment display by the SDK-85.

Example F–6

The SDK-85 is required to drive the LEDs connected to bit 0 of ports 0 and 1 based on the input conditions set by switches on bit 1 of ports 0 and 1, as shown in Figure F–14. The I/O conditions are as follows:

1. If the input to bit 1 of port 0 is HIGH and the input to bit 1 of port 1 is LOW, then the LED connected to port 0 will be on and the LED connected to port 1 will be off.
2. If the input to bit 1 of port 0 is LOW and that of port 1 is HIGH, then the LED of port 0 will be off and that of port 1 will be on.
3. If the bit 1 inputs of both ports 0 and 1 are the same (either both HIGH or both LOW), then both LEDs of ports 0 and 1 will be on

For this example, (a) design the hardware interface; (b) flowchart the problem; (c) convert the flowchart to an 8085 hexadecimal program; and (d) implement the hardware, enter the program into the SDK-85, and execute it.

Solution

(a) The hardware interface can be designed as shown in Figure F–14. All grounds must be connected together.

Note that, from Table F–7, pins 15 and 16 of the J3 connector are bits 0 and 1 of port 00, and pins 7 and 8 of the J3 connector are bits 0 and 1 of port 01.

The 8355 can source up to 400 μA of current at a minimum output high of 2.4 V. In practice, the true sourcing capability into a transistor base as shown in Figure F–14 is almost never specified and has to be estimated (guessed). A conservative estimate is 1.5 mA. Assume that the LED is red with a current of 10 mA at 1.7 V (Table F–9).

The basic design problem now is to determine the β for the transistors (Q1 and Q2) and the values of R1 and R2. Assume that $V_{CE(sat)} \simeq 0$.

$$R1 = \frac{(2.4 - 0.7)\ \text{V}}{400\ \mu\text{A}} = 4.25\ \text{k}\Omega$$

$$R2 = \frac{5\ \text{V} - 1.7\ \text{V} - V_{CE(sat)}}{10\ \text{mA}} = \frac{(5 - 1.7)\ \text{V}}{10\ \text{mA}}$$
$$= 330\ \Omega$$

We know that $I_C = \beta I_B$.

$$I_B = I_{source} = 400\ \mu\text{A} = 400 \times 10^{-6}$$
$$I_C = I_{LED} = 10\ \text{mA} = 10 \times 10^{-3}$$

Thus,

$$\beta = \frac{I_C}{I_B} = \frac{10 \times 10^{-3}}{400 \times 10^{-6}} = 25$$

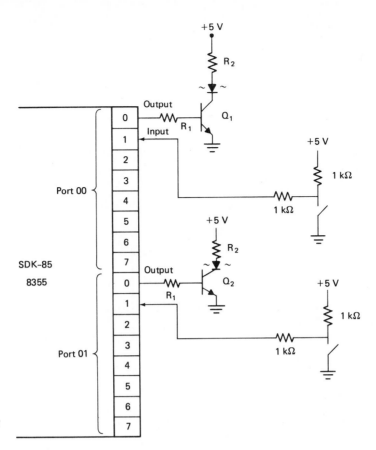

Figure F–14 Circuit for Example F–6

Therefore, use R1 = 4.25 kΩ and R2 = 330 Ω and select a transistor with a minimum saturation β of 25.

As far as the input switches are concerned, a HIGH is inputted when the switch is open, and a LOW is inputted when the switch is closed (active-low). The hardware interface design is now complete.

(b) The problem is intentionally solved in a long way in order to demonstrate the concept of masking and also that the program logic is easy to follow. The flowchart can be drawn as shown in Figure F–15, and the logic described as follows.

At (A) The data direction registers (ports 02 and 03) are initialized. Since ports 00 and 01 have bit 0 as output and bit 1 as input, the data direction registers are located with 01_{16} as follows:

7	6	5	4	3	2	1	0	← Bit position
0	0	0	0	0	0	0	1	

We fill unused bits with 0's

Notice that, in this example, we are using only 2 bits (bits 0 and 1) in each port.

At (B) We use registers B and C as counters. B is loaded with 00_{16}, and it will contain the difference in the number of 1's of bit positions 1 between ports 00 and 01. C is loaded with 02_{16} to count the number of 1's in bit positions 1 of each port. C is used to count the number of bit positions of the input bit containing the switch signal.

At (C) The contents of port 00 are inputted into the accumulator.

At (D) Notice that the least significant bits of both ports in this example are configured as outputs, and we are interested in the status of the switch at bit position 1. Therefore, to check the status of the switch at bit position 1 of each port, we must do one of the following:

1. Shift each I/O port (ports 00 and 01) twice to the right through the carry flag—the first shift is to get rid of the least significant bit, which is configured as an output, and the second shift is to check the status of the switch input at bit position 1. In this case, counter C is not required since only 1 bit (switch position) is of concern.
2. Force the bit at bit position 0 of each port to 0 by masking (ANDing) and count both bits at positions 0 and 1. In this case, counter C must be set to 02_{16}. As an example, if port 00 contains

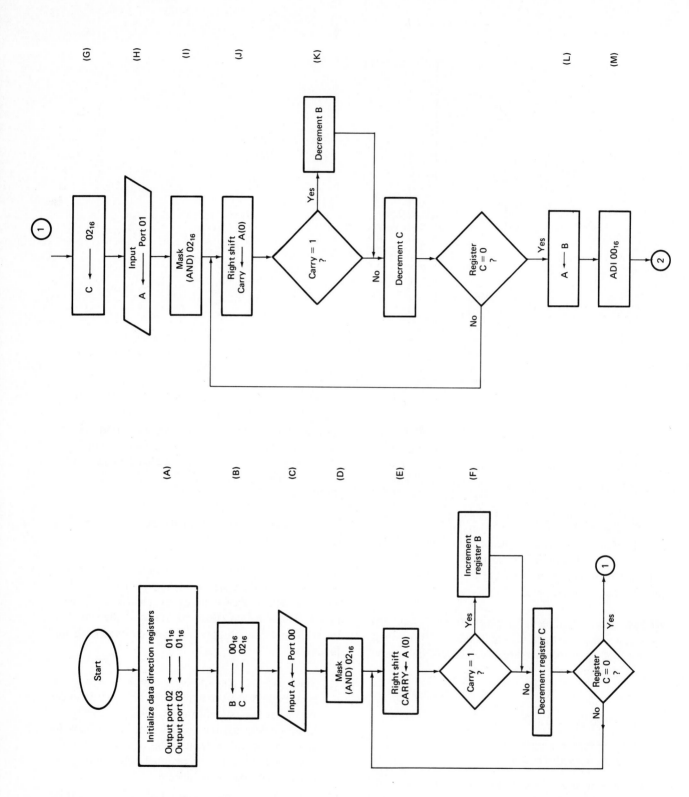

(A) (B) (C) (D) (E) (F)

(G) (H) (I) (J) (K) (L) (M)

Figure F–15   Flowchart for Example F–6

390

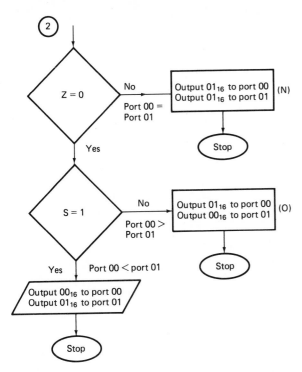

(2)

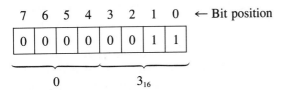

Figure F-15 Flowchart for Example F-6 (cont.)

```
7  6  5  4  3  2  1  0   ← Bit position
┌──┬──┬──┬──┬──┬──┬──┬──┐
│0 │0 │0 │0 │0 │0 │1 │1 │
└──┴──┴──┴──┴──┴──┴──┴──┘
    0              3₁₆
```

then, in order to force the bit (1 in this case) at bit position 0 to 0 and to retain the bit (1 in this case) at bit position 1, we must mask or AND the data 03_{16} with 02_{16} as follows:

$$
\begin{array}{lr}
 & 03_{16} = 0\ 0\ 0\ 0 \quad 0\ 0\ 1\ 1 \\
\text{AND} & 02_{16} = 0\ 0\ 0\ 0 \quad 0\ 0\ 1\ 0 \\
\hline
 & \phantom{02_{16} =} 0\ 0\ 0\ 0 \quad 0\ 0\ 1\ 0
\end{array}
$$

Value   LSB forced to 0
retained

3. Mask and test the accumulator for 0 (input LOW). This eliminates counter C and simplifies the program.

In the flowchart, scheme 2 is used.

At (E)   The accumulator is shifted 1 bit right to carry.

At (F)   The carry bit is checked. If the carry bit is 1, register B is incremented, and then register C is decremented. Register C is used to make sure that two shifts are made. If the carry bit is 0, register C is decremented. Register C is then checked for zero. If it is not zero, the program branches back to (E). If register C is zero,

counter B contains the number of HIGH (1) switch positions of port 00, and (G) is executed.

At (G)   Counter C is reinitialized to 02_{16} for checking the number of 1's for the switch of port 01.

At (H)   Port 01 is inputted into the accumulator.

At (I)   Port 01 is masked with 02_{16} to force the least significant bit to 0 and to retain the status of the switch.

At (J)   Port 01 is shifted right through carry.

At (K)   The carry flag is then checked. If it is 1, register B is decremented (i.e., subtract number of 1's of port 01 switch from number of 1's of port 00 switch). Register C is then checked for zero. If it is not zero, the program loops back to (J). If the contents of C are zero, the program goes to (L).

At (L)   The contents of B, which contain our result, are moved to the accumulator.

At (M)   Since the MOVE instruction in the 8085 does not affect the status flags, 00_{16} is added to the contents of the accumulator to accomplish that.

At (N)   The Z flag is checked to see whether register B contains a zero result (i.e., if the number of HIGH switch positions in port 00 is equal to the number of HIGH switch positions in port 01). If Z = 1, both LEDs at ports 00 and 01 are turned on by outputting 01_{16} through them. If Z = 0, the program goes to (O).

At (O)   The sign status S is checked. If S = 1, the contents of B are negative (i.e., the port 00 HIGH switch positions are smaller than those of port 01), the LED on port 00 is turned off by outputting 00_{16}, and the LED on port 01 is turned on by outputting 01_{16}. Finally, if S = 0, the contents of register B are positive (i.e., the port 00 HIGH switch positions are greater than those of port 01), the LED on port 00 is turned on by outputting 01_{16}, and the LED on port 01 is turned off by outputting 00_{16}.

(c) The flowchart can be translated into a hexadecimal program. The program is written intentionally in a long way so that the program logic is easy to follow:

2000	3E	MVI A, 01
2001	01	
2002	D3	OUT 02
2003	02	
2004	D3	OUT 03
2005	03	
2006	06	MVI B, 00
2007	00	
2008	0E	MVI C, 02
2009	02	
200A	DB	IN 00
200B	00	
200C	E6	ANI 02
200D	02	

200E	1F	RAR
200F	D2	JNC 2013
2010	13	
2011	20	
2012	04	INR B
2013	0D	DCR C
2014	C2	JNZ 200E
2015	0E	
2016	20	
2017	0E	MVI C, 02
2018	02	
2019	DB	IN 01
201A	01	
201B	E6	ANI 02
201C	02	
201D	1F	RAR
201E	D2	JNC 2022
201F	22	
2020	20	
2021	05	DCR B
2022	0D	DCR C
2023	C2	JNZ 201D
2024	1D	
2025	20	
2026	78	MOV A, B
2027	C6	ADI 00
2028	00	
2029	CA	JZ 2038
202A	38	
202B	20	
202C	FA	JM 203F
202D	3F	
202E	20	
202F	3E	MVI A, 01
2030	01	
2031	D3	OUT 00
2032	00	
2033	3E	MVI A, 00
2034	00	
2035	D3	OUT 01
2036	01	
2037	76	HLT
2038	3E	MVI A, 01

2039	01	
203A	D3	OUT 00
203B	00	
203C	D3	OUT 01
203D	01	
203E	76	HLT
203F	3E	MVI A, 00
2040	00	
2041	D3	OUT 00
2042	00	
2043	3E	MVI A, 01
2044	01	
2045	D3	OUT 01
2046	01	
2047	76	HLT

(d) Now enter the program into the SDK-85 and execute it. Verify the LEDs for various conditions of the input switches.

F–4–6 SDK-85 Interrupts

The 8085 interrupt I/O described earlier is utilized in designing the SDK-85 interrupts. However, the SDK-85 uses some of the 8085 interrupts internally, and hence the rest of them are available to the user. Table F–12 provides a listing of how the various 8085 interrupts are utilized in the SDK-85 along with their vector addresses. Note that the SDK-85 monitor maps the 8085 vector addresses into new memory locations. Also note that there are two different versions of the SDK-85 monitor: the newer one (June 1978) and the older one (December 1977). These two versions have different vector addresses, as shown in Table F–12. The various SDK-85 interrupts are described in more detail next.

RST7.5 The | VECT INTR | key on the SDK-85 keyboard uses the RST7.5 interrupt. When this key is pressed, the SDK-85 monitor causes the program to branch to 20CE (for new SDK-85 monitor) or 20D4 (for old SDK-85 monitor). There are only enough locations

TABLE F–12
SDK-85 Interrupts and Vector Addresses (From *Microcomputer Experimentation with the Intel SDK-85,* by Leventhal and Walsh, © 1980, p. 225. Reprinted by permission of Prentice-Hall, Inc., Englewood Cliffs, New Jersey)

Interrupt	Description	Vector Address	
		Newer Version	Older Version
TRAP	8155 timer interrupt	Monitor ROM	Monitor ROM
RST7.5	Vectored interrupt key	20CE	20D4
RST6.5	User interrupt	20C8	20CE
RST5.5	Keyboard interrupt	Monitor ROM	Monitor ROM
INTR	User interrupt	20C2 (RST5)	20C8 (RST5)
		20C5 (RST6)	20CB (RST6)
		20CB (RST7)	20D1 (RST7)

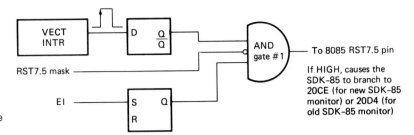

Figure F–16 RST7.5 interrupt on the SDK-85

at 20CE or 20D4 to place a JUMP instruction to branch to the actual service routine.

Note that, in order to understand how the RST7.5 can be activated using the ┌─────────┐ VECT INTR └─────────┘ key, AND gate 1 and its associated circuitry are redrawn as shown in Figure F–16. In Figure F–16, if the output of AND gate 1 is HIGH, the SDK-85 will be interrupted. The SDK-85 will branch to either 20CE or 20D4. However, in order to make this output of the AND gate HIGH, the user must do the following:

1. Execute the EI instruction in order to set the RS flip-flop to HIGH. This will make one of the AND gate inputs HIGH.

2. Execute the SIM instruction with proper data in order to make the RST7.5 mask LOW. This is inverted (shown by the small circle) at the input of the AND gate. Therefore, this signal will be HIGH at the input of the AND gate. The instruction sequence

    MVI A, 0B
    SIM

    will reset the RST7.5 mask bit to a LOW.

3. After the two AND gate inputs have been set to HIGH in steps 1 and 2, the third input can be set to HIGH by pressing the ┌─────────┐ VECT INTR └─────────┘ key. When this key is pressed by the user, a pulse is generated. The leading edge of this pulse sets a D flip-flop to HIGH. Therefore, this AND gate input will be HIGH, making the output of AND gate 1 HIGH. Thus, the SDK-85 will be interrupted and will cause the processor to branch to 003C (RST7.5 vector address on the 8085). The SDK-85 monitor places a 3-byte JUMP instruction at this location to go either to 20CE or to 20D4. Another JUMP can be placed at one of these locations to go to the actual service routine.

RST6.5 The RST6.5 interrupt is available to the user. The vector address for this interrupt is either 20C8 (for new SDK-85 monitor) or 20CE (for old SDK-85 monitor). An interrupt service routine can be written at one of these locations depending on the SDK-85 monitor.

RST5.5 The RST5.5 interrupt is used by the SDK-85 keyboard. Its service routine is provided by the SDK-85 monitor. The routines ININT (located at 028E) and RDKBD (located at 02E7) are used for this purpose.

When the user presses a key (except the ┌─────────┐ RESET └─────────┘ and ┌─────────┐ VECT INTR └─────────┘ keys) on the SDK-85 keyboard, the SDK-85 is interrupted via RST5.5. The processor branches to location 002C (RST5.5 address vector on the 8085). The SDK-85 monitor places a 3-byte JUMP instruction at this location to branch to 028E for the ININT routine. This program inputs a character from the keyboard and stores it in 20FE. The user can then call the RDKBD routine to display the SDK-85 keyboard codes shown in Table F–13. The RDKBD waits for a keyboard code to be stored in 20FE by the ININT routine. If there is a code stored in 20FE by the ININT, the RDKBD routine moves this code into the accumulator. The user can execute CALL UPDDT to display the character code in the SDK-85 data field.

TABLE F–13
SDK-85 Keyboard Codes (From *Microcomputer Experimentation with the Intel SDK-85*, by Leventhal and Walsh, © 1980, pp. 227–228. Reprinted by permission of Prentice-Hall, Inc., Englewood Cliffs, New Jersey)

Key	Code (Hexadecimal)
0	00
1	01
2	02
3	03
4	04
5	05
6	06
7	07
8	08
9	09
A	0A
B	0B
C	0C
D	0D
E	0E
F	0F
EXEC	10
NEXT	11
GO	12
SUBST MEM	13
EXAM REG	14
SINGLE STEP	15

Note that, in order to understand how the RST5.5 is used by the ININT routine, AND gate 3 and its associated circuitry are redrawn as shown in Figure F–17. In Figure F–17, in order to activate the RST5.5 (i.e., branch to ININT routine and then be able to use the RDKBD routine), the user must do the following:

1. Execute the EI instruction in order to set the RS flip-flop to HIGH. This will make one of the inputs to AND gate 3 HIGH.

2. Execute the SIM instruction with proper data in order to make the RST5.5 mask LOW. This is inverted (shown by the circle) at the input of the AND gate. Therefore, this signal will appear as HIGH at the AND gate input.

3. Finally, when a key is pressed on the SDK-85 keyboard, the input of AND gate 3 connected to the keyboard will be HIGH. This will make the output of AND gate 3 HIGH, thus interrupting the SDK-85. The program will branch to 002C, where a 3-byte JUMP instruction is placed by the SDK-85 monitor to branch to the ININT routine.

INTR Among the eight RST instructions, the following are available with the SDK-85: RST5 (20C2 or 20C8), RST6 (20C5 or 20CB), and RST7 (20CB or 20D1). The other five RST instructions are used by the monitor. Note that in response to a HIGH at the $\overline{\text{INTR}}$, the SDK-85 generates an $\overline{\text{INTA}}$ LOW. This $\overline{\text{INTA}}$ can then be used to enable external hardware (a tristate buffer) in order to provide one of the three available RST instructions with the SDK-85 such as the RST5, RST6, or RST7. The SDK-85 then executes this instruction and goes to the appropriate vector address, where a JUMP instruction can be placed to branch to the actual service routine.

Example F–7*

Write a program in 8085 hexadecimal language to use the SDK-85 as a continuous decimal counter. The program will be capable of (a) displaying the count in the data field of the display, (b) varying the speed of the count by changing the contents of location 2010_{16}, and (c) stopping the count by using the [VECT INTR] key.

*Courtesy of Intel Corporation.

Solution

The program can be written as follows:

2000	31	LXI SP, 2080
2001	80	
2002	20	
2003	3E	MVI A, 08
2004	08	
2005	30	SIM
2006	FB	EI
2007	78	MOV A, B
2008	3C	INR A
2009	27	DAA
200A	47	MOV B, A
200B	C5	PUSH B
200C	CD	CALL UPDDT
200D	6E	
200E	03	
200F	16	MVI D, 18
2010	18	
2011	CD	CALL DELAY
2012	F1	
2013	05	
2014	C1	POP B
2015	C3	JMP 2006
2016	06	
2017	20	
—		
20CE	FB	EI
20CF	76	HLT
20D0	C9	RET

Press [RESET] and enter this program into the SDK-85 and execute it by pressing [GO] , typing in 2000, and pressing [EXEC] . Then stop the count, pressing the [VECT INTR] key. Note that [RESET] initializes all registers to 00_{16}. You can vary the speed of the count by using [SUBST MEM] to change the contents of location 2010.

Let us now elaborate on the logic of the example program. LXI SP, 2080 at location 2000 initializes the stack pointer at 2080. MVI A, 08 at 2003 loads the accumulator with 08_{16}, and then, using the SIM instruction at 2005, the [VECT INTR] button is enabled. EI at 2006 enables the interrupt system. MOV A, B moves the contents of B into the accumulator. Remember that the B register contains 00_{16} because [RESET] is pressed at the beginning. The accumulator is then incremented by INR A at 2008. DAA at 2009 converts the contents

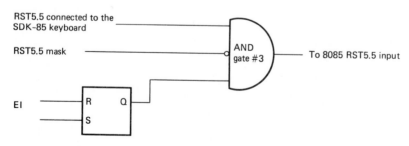

Figure F–17 RST5.5 interrupt on the SDK-85

of the accumulator to decimal. The 'A' contents are then moved to B by MOV B, A at 200A. The B and C contents are saved onto the stack by PUSH B at 200B; [C] is arbitrary. CALL UPDDT at 200C displays the count in the data field of the display.

MVI D, 18 at 200F loads D with 18_{16}, and register E contains arbitrary data. The contents of D determine the speed of the count. This data is arbitrarily selected initially. CALL DELAY at 2011 provides a delay period between each display of the count. This delay routine is in the monitor, takes the 16-bit contents of register pair D,E and counts down to 0, and then returns to the calling program. Registers A, D, and E and the flags are affected.

POP B at 2014 pops the values of the B,C pair from the stack into the accumulator. JMP 2006 at 2015 takes the program back to the beginning of the program.

The instructions at 20CE, 20CF, and 20D0 provide an interrupt service routine for the | VECT INTR | key. For example, EI at 20CE enables the interrupt, HLT at 20CF allows the program to wait for a key depression, and RET at 20D0 resumes the count. Remember that when | VECT INTR | is pressed, the control of the program branches to location 20CE.

Example F–8

The SDK-85 is required to read the output of a tristate A/D converter, such as the Teledyne 8703, through port 21. It uses bit 0 of port 00 to send an output to start the conversion. The SDK-85 is then interrupted by the BUSY or DATA VALID signal. The microcomputer reads the output of the A/D through I/O port 21 by enabling the tristate output through bit 1 of port 00.

Design the interface hardware, using a simplified block diagram, between the SDK-85 and the A/D converter. Use the RST6.5 interrupt first and then repeat the example using the INTR (say, RST6) interrupt.

Solution

The A/D converter used is the Teledyne 8703 8-bit with tristate outputs. The timing diagrams of the Teledyne

8703 A/D converter can be drawn from the manufacturer's specification as shown in Figure F–18.

The relevant control lines are as follows:

- INITIATE CONVERSION—Active-high with a minimum pulse width of 500 ns.
- BUSY—A logic '1' on the BUSY pin indicates a conversion cycle is in process. A logic '1' to logic '0' indicates that the conversion is complete and the result has been latched at the DIGITS OUT pins. A logic '0' to logic '1' transition indicates that a new conversion cycle has been initiated.
- DATA VALID—A logic '1' at the DATA VALID pin indicates that the DIGITS OUT pins are latched with the result of the last conversion cycle. The DATA VALID output goes to logic '0' approximately 5 μs before completion of the conversion cycle. During this 5-μs interval, new data is transferred to the DIGITS OUT pins and data at the DIGITS OUT is not valid.
- $\overline{\text{OUTPUT ENABLE}}$—Active-low. The SDK-85 can be programmed to send an INITIATE CONVERSION pulse to the 8703 for at least 500 ns. This can be accomplished by sending a HIGH and then a LOW to the INITIATE CONVERSION pin of the 8703. Either the DATA VALID or the BUSY signal can be connected to the interrupt pin (RST6.5 or INTR in this example) of the SDK-85 to interrupt the processor after conversion is complete.

If the BUSY signal is used, then the BUSY pin of the 8703 will be connected to the SDK-85 interrupt pin through an inverter. The SDK-85 can be programmed to send an INITIATE CONVERSION pulse to the 8703. After about 300 ns, the BUSY signal goes to HIGH, which is inverted for the SDK-85 interrupt signal and thus provides a LOW at the interrupt pin. This will not interrupt the processor. As can be seen from the 8703 timing diagrams, the BUSY signal goes to LOW after the conversion is complete. This LOW at the BUSY pin is inverted for the processor interrupt signal and will interrupt the processor. The interrupt service routine can be written to input the 8703 output into the

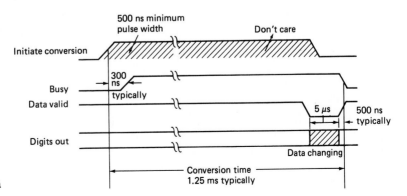

Figure F–18 8703 timing diagram

SDK-85. Note that since the acceptance of any maskable interrupt (RST6.5 or INTR in this example) disables all the interrupts, the LOW BUSY signal after conversion is complete will not be able to interrupt the processor again.

However, if desired, the interrupt pin can be reset utilizing external hardware to prevent the LOW BUSY signal from interrupting the processor a second time after returning from the service routine and after the reenabling of the interrupt system. The circuit that results is given in Figure F–19.

The SDK-85 can be programmed to send a HIGH and then a LOW through bit 0 of port 00 to provide the INITIATE CONVERSION pulse for at least 500 ns. The SDK-85 can also be programmed to send a HIGH output through bit 2 of port 00 to provide a HIGH at the input of the AND gate. Note that the I/O port output of the SDK-85 is latched, thus ensuring that the HIGH input will remain at the input of the AND gate. The SDK-85 then waits for the BUSY signal to go to LOW. This waiting can be accomplished by using the HLT instruction. The following instruction sequence will perform this function:

MVI	A, 07	Set data direction port to configure bits 0–
OUT	02	2 as outputs
MVI	A, 03	Send a HIGH INITIATE CONVERSION
		pulse and a HIGH OUTPUT ENABLE
OUT	00	
MVI	A, 06	Send a HIGH to input of AND gate and reset
OUT	00	INITIATE CONVERSION pulse
HLT		Wait for interrupt

As soon as the BUSY signal goes to LOW, the interrupt line becomes HIGH, and if the interrupt is enabled, the SDK-85 will be interrupted. The SDK-85 will complete the current instruction and will branch to the appropriate address vector for the particular interrupt used where a 3-byte JUMP instruction can be placed to branch to the interrupt service routine. The first few instructions of the service routine will be to send a LOW output through bit 1 of port 00 to enable the output of the 8703. Then the SDK-85 can be programmed to input the A/D converter output through port 21. Finally, the interrupt can be disabled by sending a LOW through bit 2 of port 00, thus providing a LOW to the input of the AND gate.

We now describe the use of the DATA VALID signal

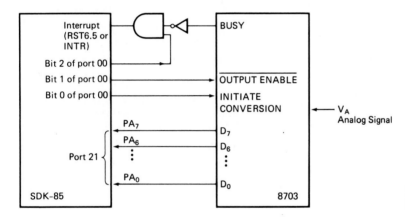

Figure F–19 Interfacing 8703 to SDK-85 using BUSY signal

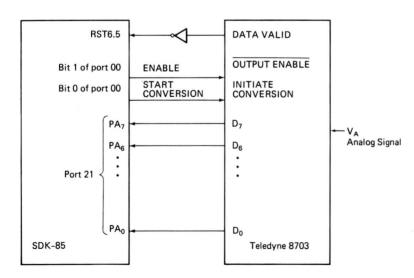

Figure F–20 Interfacing 8703 to SDK-85 using DATA VALID signal

in the following. Using the RST6.5 and the DATA VALID lines, the hardware interface can be designed as shown in Figure F–20.

In the interface circuit of Figure F–20, the SDK-85 can be programmed to send a HIGH output through bit 0 of port 00 and a LOW output through bit 0 of port 00 to provide the INITIATE CONVERSION pulse for at least 500 ns. The SDK-85 then waits for the DATA VALID signal to go to LOW, indicating that conversion is complete. This waiting can be accomplished using the HLT instruction in the program. When the DATA VALID signal goes to LOW and if the RST6.5 is unmasked and enabled, the SDK-85 will be interrupted. The SDK-85 will complete the current instruction and will branch to location $20C8_{16}$ where a 3-byte JUMP instruction can be placed to branch to the interrupt service routine. The first few instructions of the service routine will be to send a LOW output through bit 1 of port 00 to enable the output of the A/D converter. Then the SDK-85 can be programmed to input the A/D converter output through port 21. Note that the 8703 latches the data when the DATA VALID signal goes to HIGH after 5 μs. Therefore, the

data must be inputted into the SDK-85 5 μs after the occurrence of the interrupt. Note that the duration between the occurrence of the interrupt and the outputting of the A/D converter output into the SDK-85 is much more than 5 μs.

Next, we consider using the 8085 INTR (RST6) interrupt and the DATA VALID signals. The hardware interface can be designed as shown in Figure F–21. Here, as before, the SDK-85 can be programmed to send a HIGH output through bit 0 of port 00 and a LOW output through bit 0 of port 00 to provide the INITIATE CONVERSION pulse. The HLT instruction can then be used in the program for the SDK-85 to wait until the conversion is complete. As soon as the DATA VALID signal goes to LOW, indicating that the conversion is complete, the INTR is set to HIGH. Now, if the interrupt is enabled, the SDK-85 will be interrupted. The processor will complete the current instruction and will output the $\overline{\text{INTA}}$ LOW, which will enable the 74LS244 tristate buffer, where the OP code for RST6 ($F7_{16}$) can be placed by means of DIP switches. Thus, upon enabling the 74LS244 by the $\overline{\text{INTA}}$ signal, the RST6 instruction will be strobed

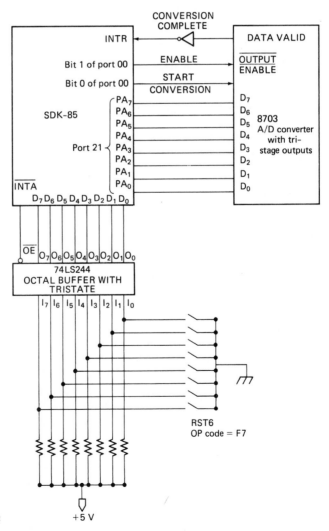

Figure F–21 SDK-85 8703 schematic

onto the data lines. This will cause the processor to jump to location 20C5, where a 3-byte CALL instruction can be executed to branch to the interrupt service routine. The interrupt service routine can be written to send a LOW output through bit 1 of port 00 to enable the OUTPUT ENABLE and then input the 8-bit A/D converter output through I/O port 21.

Note that, as in RST6.5, the duration between the occurrence of INTR and the inputting of the A/D converter output into the SDK-85 is much more than 5 μs. This means that the A/D converter output is inputted into the SDK-85 after the 8703 latches the data.

F–4–7   DMA with the SDK-85

The SDK-85 is not provided with any DMA controller chip such as the 8257. Therefore, laboratory experiments involving DMA transfer cannot be performed with the SDK-85.

F–4–8   SDK-85 SID and SOD Lines

The SDK-85 SID and SOD lines are not available to the user. These lines are used by the teletype.

SDK-85 PROGRAMMING AND I/O PROBLEMS

F–1. Write an 8085 assembly language program to add two 24-bit numbers and display the result in the SDK-85.

F–2. Using the 8085 programming language, write the assembly and machine (hexadecimal) language programs for the following and then enter and execute the programs on the SDK-85.

(a) Add the 16-bit number in memory locations 2000_{16} and 2001_{16} to the 16-bit number in memory locations 2002_{16} and 2003_{16}. The most significant 8 bits of the two numbers to be added are in memory locations 2001_{16} and 2003_{16}. Display the result in the address field of the SDK-85.

(b) Display the larger of the contents of memory locations 2000_{16} and 2001_{16} in the data field of the SDK-85. Assume that the memory locations 2000_{16} and 2001_{16} contain unsigned binary numbers.

(c) Display in the data field of the SDK-85 the square of the contents of memory location 2000_{16} from a lookup table containing the squares of the numbers from 0 to 9. Assume that the memory location 2000_{16} contains a number between 0 and 9 inclusive.

F–3. Write a program to display in the data field of the SDK-85 the number of negative elements (most significant bit 1) in a data set. The length of the set is 10_{10} ($0A_{16}$), and it is stored in memory location 2000_{16}. The data starts in memory location 2001_{16}. Execute the program in the SDK-85. Assume the data sequence as 01_{16}, $F2_{16}$, 09_{16}, 10_{16}, $E9_{16}$, 11_{16}, 00_{16}, AA_{16}, 49_{16}, BD_{16}.

F–4. (a) Draw a flowchart to find the maximum data in a data set. The size of the data set is 10_{10} ($0A_{16}$) and is stored in memory location 2000_{16}. The first data is contained in memory location 2001_{16}. Assume that the numbers in the data set are all 8-bit unsigned binary numbers.

(b) Convert the flowchart to 8085 assembly and machine (hexadecimal) language programs to display the result in the data field of the SDK-85. Enter and execute the program on the SDK-85. Use the same data sequence as in Problem F–3.

F–5. Write a program in the 8085 assembly and machine languages to add the two BCD numbers 56 and 28 stored in locations 2000_{16} and 2001_{16}. Enter the program into the SDK-85. Execute the program and have the answer appear in the data field of the SDK-85 display.

F–6. For the following program, run single step and list the contents of the program counter, the H and L registers, the accumulator, and the processor status word after executing the instruction in location 2007_{16}, and verify the answer analytically by going through the program logic. The, modify the program and execute it on the SDK-85 to display the answer in the data field.

2000	03	Data
2001	04	Data
2002	21	LXI H, 2000
2003	00	
2004	20	
2005	7E	MOV A, M
2006	23	INX H
2007	96	SUB M
2008	C3	JMP 2008
2009	08	
200A	20	

F–7. Find analytically the status flags (S, Z, Ac, P, and Cy) for the following operations:
(a) $3D_{16} - E8_{16}$
(b) $3D \oplus 3D$
Then verify the answer by writing a program and single stepping it on the SDK-85.

F–8. Repeat Example F–5 without using the instructions involving the parity flag.

F–9. It is desired to add a 16-bit number contained in the B, C register pair with another 16-bit number in the H, L pair. If the result of addition is even, display EE in the SDK-85 data field. If the result of addition is odd, display DD in the data field.

(a) Flowchart the problem.

(b) Convert the flowchart to an 8085 machine language program showing the assembly language mnemonics with the machine OP codes.

(c) Enter and execute the program.

F–10. Write and execute a program on the 8085 to divide a number at location 2000_{16} by 128_{10} at location 2001_{16}. Display the final answer in the SDK-85 data field. Neglect the remainder.

F–11. The SDK-85 is required to perform the following functions:

1. Ports 00 and 01 have two switch inputs (connected to bits 1 and 2) and one LED output (connected to bit 0) each.

2. The LED at port 00 is to be turned on and the LED at port 01 is to be turned off if port 00 has more HIGH inputs than port 01.

3. The port 00 LED is to be off and the port 01 LED on if port 01 has more HIGH inputs than port 00.

4. If the number of HIGH inputs for each port are equal, both LEDs are to be turned on.

(a) Flowchart the problem.

(b) Convert the flowchart to the 8085 assembly and hexadecimal language programs.

(c) Interface the switches and the LEDs to the SDK-85 and then run and execute the program.

F–12. Using the SDK-85, the following functions are to be performed:

1. Port 00 has three input switches (bits 1, 2, and 3), and one output LED is connected to bit 0.

2. Port 01 has one output LED connected to bit 2.

3. The port 00 LED is to be on and the port 01 LED is to be off if port 00 has an even number of HIGH inputs.

4. The port 01 LED is to be on and the port 00 LED is to be off if port 00 has an odd number of HIGH inputs.

(a) Flowchart the problem.

(b) Convert the flowchart to 8085 assembly language and then machine language programs.

(c) Run and execute the program after interfacing the switches and LEDs to the SDK-85.

F–13. Flowchart and write a program for using the SDK-85 as an integrated circuit tester. Figure F–22 shows the I/O hardware needed to test a NAND gate. The SDK-85 is to be programmed to generate the various logic conditions for the NAND inputs, monitor the NAND output, and activate the LED connected to bit 3 of port 00 if the chip is found to be faulty. Otherwise, turn on the LED connected to bit 4 of port 00. The test sequence will consist of all four different combinations of the inputs.

(a) Implement the hardware.

(b) Run and execute the programs.

F–14. Write and execute a program on the SDK-85 that will light the decimal point on the rightmost digit of the on-board display and leave the display on for 10 s.

F–15. Write and execute a program on the SDK-85 that continuously examines the keyboard, displaying the last two keys pressed, and saves only those key numbers that represent hexadecimal digits starting at location 2040_{16}.

F–16. Write and execute a program on the SDK-85 that loads eight switch inputs from port 01 and

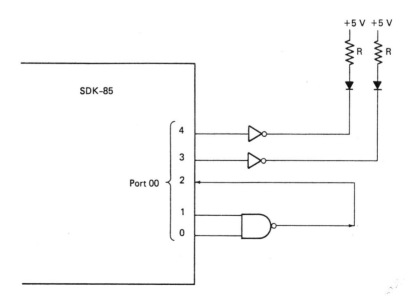

Figure F–22 Hardware schematic for Problem F-13

displays them when requested to do so by the VECT INTR key.

F-17. Repeat Example F-8 for both INTR and RST6.5 interrupts using an A/D converter of your choice and do the following:

(a) Design and implement the necessary hardware interface.

(b) Write a program in 8085 assembly language to read and display the output of the (A/D) for an analog voltage signal applied to the (A/D) input.

(c) Convert the flowchart to an 8085 hexadecimal language program.

(d) Run and execute the program to display the A/D output in the data field of the SDK-85 display.

(e) Convert the answer in the SDK-85 data display into analog voltage and compare it with the A/D analog input.

Intel 8085, 8086, and Support Chips — Data Sheets

Reproduced by permission of Intel Corp.

intel® 8085

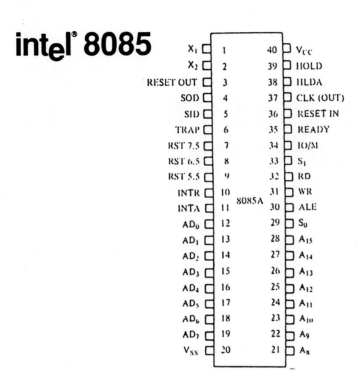

X₁	1	40 Vᴄᴄ
X₂	2	39 HOLD
RESET OUT	3	38 HLDA
SOD	4	37 CLK (OUT)
SID	5	36 RESET IN
TRAP	6	35 READY
RST 7.5	7	34 IO/M
RST 6.5	8	33 S₁
RST 5.5	9	32 RD
INTR	10	31 WR
INTA	11 8085A	30 ALE
AD₀	12	29 S₀
AD₁	13	28 A₁₅
AD₂	14	27 A₁₄
AD₃	15	26 A₁₃
AD₄	16	25 A₁₂
AD₅	17	24 A₁₁
AD₆	18	23 A₁₀
AD₇	19	22 A₉
Vₛₛ	20	21 A₈

Figure G–1 8085 Pinout

Figure G–1 shows the 8085 pins and signals. The following table describes the function of each pin:

Symbol	Function
$A_8 - A_{15}$ (Output, three-state)	Address bus: The most significant 8 bits of the memory address or the 8 bits of the I/O address.
AD_{0-7} (Input/output, three-state)	Multiplexed address/data bus: Lower 8-bits of the memory address (or I/O address) appear on the bus during the first clock cycle (T state) of a machine cycle. It then becomes the data bus during the second and third clock cycles.
ALE (Output)	Address Latch Enable: It occurs during the first clock state of a machine cycle and enables the address to get latched into the on-chip latch.
$S_0, S_1,$ and $IO/\overline{M}$ (Output)	Machine cycle status:

$IO/\overline{M}$	S_1	S_0	Status
0	0	1	Memory write
0	1	0	Memory read
1	0	1	I/O write

SYMBOL.	FUNCTION			
	IO/$\overline{\text{M}}$	S_1	S_0	STATUS
	1	1	0	I/O read
	0	1	1	Op code fetch
	1	1	1	Interrupt acknowledge
	*	0	0	Halt
	*	X	X	Hold
	*	X	X	Reset

* – 3-state (high impedance)

X – unspecified

S_1 can be used as an advanced R/$\overline{\text{W}}$ status. IO/$\overline{\text{M}}$, S_0, and S_1 become valid at the beginning of a machine cycle and remain stable throughout the cycle. The falling edge of ALE may be used to latch the state of these lines.

$\overline{\text{RD}}$ (Output, three-state)	READ control: A low level on $\overline{\text{RD}}$ indicates the selected memory or I/O device is to be read.
$\overline{\text{WR}}$ (Output, three-state)	WRITE control: A low level on $\overline{\text{WR}}$ indicates the data on the data bus is to be written into the selected memory or I/O location.
READY (Input)	If READY is high during a read or write cycle, it indicates that the memory or peripheral is ready to send or receive data. If READY is low, the CPU will wait an integral number of clock cycles for READY to go high before completing the read or write cycle.
HOLD (Input)	HOLD indicates that another master is requesting the use of the address and data buses. The CPU, upon receiving the hold request, will relinquish the use of the bus as soon as the completion of the current bus transfer. Internal processing can continue. The processor can regain the bus only after the HOLD is removed. When the HOLD is acknowledged, the address, data, $\overline{\text{RD}}$, $\overline{\text{WR}}$, and IO/$\overline{\text{M}}$ lines are three-stated.
HLDA (Output)	HOLD ACKNOWLEDGE: Indicates that the CPU has received the HOLD request and that it will relinquish the bus in the next clock cycle. HLDA goes low after the HOLD request is removed. The CPU takes the bus one-half clock cycle after HLDA goes low.
INTR (Input)	INTERRUPT REQUEST: Is used as a general-purpose interrupt. It is sampled only during the next to the last clock cycle of an instruction and during HOLD and HALT states. If it is active, the PC will be inhibited from incrementing and an $\overline{\text{INTA}}$ will be issued. During this cycle a RESTART or CALL instruction can be inserted to jump to the interrupt service routine. The INTR is enabled and disabled by software. It is disabled by RESET and immediately after an interrupt is accepted.
$\overline{\text{INTA}}$ (Output)	INTERRUPT ACKNOWLEDGE: Is used instead of (and has the same timing as) $\overline{\text{RD}}$ during the instruction cycle after an INTR is accepted. It can be used to activate the 8259 interrupt chip or some other interrupt port.
RST5.5 RST6.5 RST7.5 (Inputs)	RESTART INTERRUPTS: These three inputs have the same timing as INTR except they cause an internal RESTART to be automatically inserted.
TRAP (Input)	Trap interrupt is a nonmaskable RESTART interrupt. It is recognized at the same time as INTR or RST5.5–7.5. It is unaffected by any mask or interrupt enable. It has the highest priority of any interrupt.
$\overline{\text{RESET IN}}$ (Input)	Sets the program counter to zero and resets the interrupt enable and HLDA flip-flops.
RESET OUT (Output)	Indicates CPU is being reset. Can be used as a system reset.

Symbol	Function
X_1, X_2 (Input)	X_1 and X_2 are connected to a crystal, LC, or RC network to drive the internal clock generator. X_1 can also be an external clock input from a logic gate. The input frequency is divided by 2 to give the processor's internal operating frequency.
CLK (Output)	Clock output for use as a system clock. The period of CLK is twice the X_1, X_2 input period.
SID (Input)	Serial Input Data line. The data on this line is loaded into accumulator bit 7 whenever a RIM instruction is executed.
SOD (Output)	Serial Output Data line. The output SOD is set or reset as specified by the SIM instruction.
V_{cc}	+5 V supply.
V_{ss}	*Ground reference.

intel®

8086/8086-2/8086-4
16-BIT HMOS MICROPROCESSOR

- **Direct Addressing Capability to 1 MByte of Memory**

- **Assembly Language Compatible with 8080/8085**

- **14 Word, By 16-Bit Register Set with Symmetrical Operations**

- **24 Operand Addressing Modes**

- **Bit, Byte, Word, and Block Operations**

- **8-and 16-Bit Signed and Unsigned Arithmetic in Binary or Decimal Including Multiply and Divide**

- **5 MHz Clock Rate (8 MHz for 8086-2) (4 MHz for 8086-4)**

- **MULTIBUS™ System Compatible Interface**

The Intel® 8086 is a new generation, high performance microprocessor implemented in N-channel, depletion load, silicon gate technology (HMOS), and packaged in a 40-pin CerDIP package. The processor has attributes of both 8- and 16-bit microprocessors. It addresses memory as a sequence of 8-bit bytes, but has a 16-bit wide physical path to memory for high performance.

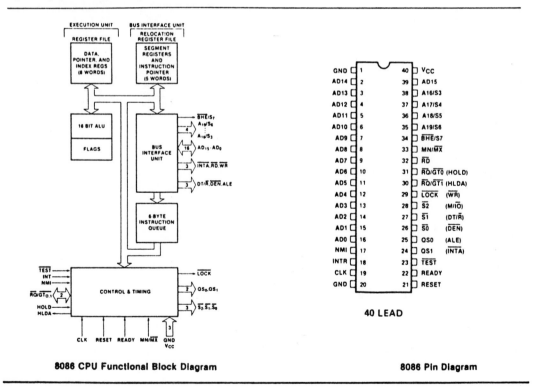

8086 CPU Functional Block Diagram

8086 Pin Diagram

I8284

CLOCK GENERATOR AND DRIVER
FOR 8086, 8088, 8089 PROCESSORS

- **Generates the System Clock for the 8086, 8088 and 8089**

- **Uses a Crystal or a TTL Signal for Frequency Source**

- **Single +5V Power Supply**

- **18-Pin Package**

- **Generates System Reset Output from Schmitt Trigger Input**

- **Provides Local Ready and MULTIBUS™ Ready Synchronization**

- **Capable of Clock Synchronization with other 8284's**

- **Industrial Temperature Range −40° to +85°C**

The I8284 is a bipolar clock generator/driver designed to provide clock signals for the 8086, 8088 & 8089 and peripherals. It also contains READY logic for operation with two MULTIBUS™ systems and provides the processors required READY synchronization and timing. Reset logic with hysteresis and synchronization is also provided.

I8284 PIN CONFIGURATION

CYSNC	1	18	Vcc
PCLK	2	17	X1
$\overline{AEN1}$	3	16	X2
RDY1	4	15	TNK
READY	5	14	EFI
RDY2	6	13	F/$\overline{C}$
$\overline{AEN2}$	7	12	OSC
CLK	8	11	$\overline{RES}$
GND	9	10	RESET

I8284 BLOCK DIAGRAM

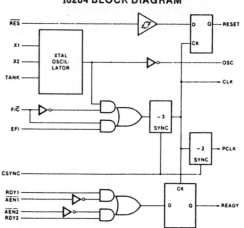

I8284 PIN NAMES

X1 ı X2 ı	CONNECTIONS FOR CRYSTAL
TANK	USED WITH OVERTONE CRYSTAL
F/C	CLOCK SOURCE SELECT
EFI	EXTERNAL CLOCK INPUT
CSYNC	CLOCK SYNCHRONIZATION INPUT
RDY1 ı RDY2 ı	READY SIGNAL FROM TWO MULTIBUS™ SYSTEMS
$\overline{AEN1}$ ı $\overline{AEN2}$ ı	ADDRESS ENABLED QUALIFIERS FOR RDY1,2
$\overline{RES}$	RESET INPUT
RESET	SYNCHRONIZED RESET OUTPUT
OSC	OSCILLATOR OUTPUT
CLK	MOS CLOCK FOR THE PROCESSOR
PCLK	TTL CLOCK FOR PERIPHERALS
READY	SYNCHRONIZED READY OUTPUT
Vcc	+5 VOLTS
GND	0 VOLTS

8288
BUS CONTROLLER
FOR 8086, 8088, 8089 PROCESSORS

- **Bipolar Drive Capability**

- **Provides Advanced Commands**

- **Provides Wide Flexibility in System Configurations**

- **3-State Command Output Drivers**

- **Configurable for Use with an I/O Bus**

- **Facilitates Interface to One or Two Multi-Master Busses**

The Intel® 8288 Bus Controller is a 20-pin bipolar component for use with medium-to-large 8086 processing systems. The bus controller provides command and control timing generation as well as bipolar bus drive capability while optimizing system performance.

A strapping option on the bus controller configures it for use with a multi-master system bus and separate I/O bus.

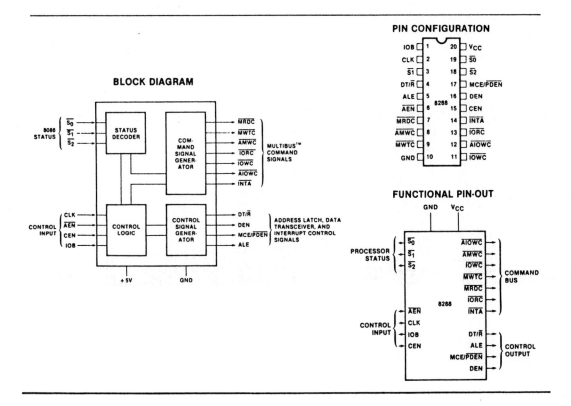

®

2142
1024 X 4 BIT STATIC RAM

	2142-2	2142-3	2142	2142L2	2142L3	2142L
Max. Access Time (ns)	200	300	450	200	300	450
Max. Power Dissipation (mw)	525	525	525	370	370	370

- **High Density 20 Pin Package**
- **Access Time Selections From 200-450ns**
- **Identical Cycle and Access Times**
- **Low Operating Power Dissipation .1mW/Bit Typical**
- **Single +5V Supply**

- **No Clock or Timing Strobe Required**
- **Completely Static Memory**
- **Directly TTL Compatible: All Inputs and Outputs**
- **Common Data Input and Output Using Three-State Outputs**

The Intel® 2142 is a 4096-bit static Random Access Memory organized as 1024 words by 4-bits using N-channel Silicon-Gate MOS technology. It uses fully DC stable (static) circuitry throughout — in both the array and the decoding — and therefore requires no clocks or refreshing to operate. Data access is particularly simple since address setup times are not required. The data is read out nondestructively and has the same polarity as the input data. Common input/output pins are provided.

The 2142 is designed for memory applications where high performance, low cost, large bit storage, and simple interfacing are important design objectives. It is directly TTL compatible in all respects: inputs, outputs, and a single +5V supply.

The 2142 is placed in a 20-pin package. Two Chip Selects ($\overline{CS}_1$ and CS_2) are provided for easy and flexible selection of individual packages when outputs are OR-tied. An Output Disable is included for direct control of the output buffers.

The 2142 is fabricated with Intel's N-channel Silicon-Gate technology — a technology providing excellent protection against contamination permitting the use of low cost plastic packaging.

PIN CONFIGURATION   LOGIC SYMBOL   BLOCK DIAGRAM

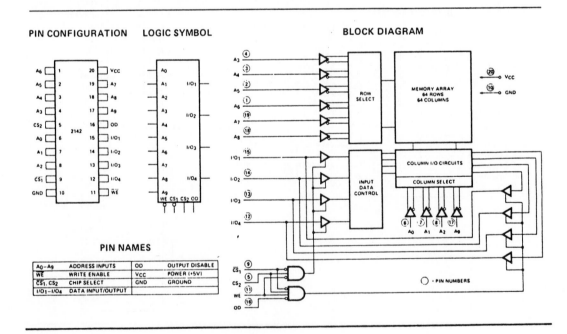

PIN NAMES

A_0–A_9	ADDRESS INPUTS	OD	OUTPUT DISABLE
$\overline{WE}$	WRITE ENABLE	Vcc	POWER (+5V)
$\overline{CS}_1$, CS_2	CHIP SELECT	GND	GROUND
I/O_1–I/O_4	DATA INPUT/OUTPUT		

intel®

2716
16K (2K × 8) UV ERASABLE PROM

- ■ **Fast Access Time**
  - — 350 ns Max. 2716-1
  - — 390 ns Max. 2716-2
  - — 450 ns Max. 2716
  - — 650 ns Max. 2716-6

- ■ **Single +5V Power Supply**

- ■ **Low Power Dissipation**
  - — 525 mW Max. Active Power
  - — 132 mW Max. Standby Power

- ■ **Pin Compatible to Intel® 2732 EPROM**

- ■ **Simple Programming Requirements**
  - — **Single Location Programming**
  - — **Programs with One 50 ms Pulse**

- ■ **Inputs and Outputs TTL Compatible during Read and Program**

- ■ **Completely Static**

The Intel® 2716 is a 16,384-bit ultraviolet erasable and electrically programmable read-only memory (EPROM). The 2716 operates from a single 5-volt power supply, has a static standby mode, and features fast single address location programming. It makes designing with EPROMs faster, easier and more economical.

The 2716, with its single 5-volt supply and with an access time up to 350 ns, is ideal for use with the newer high performance +5V microprocessors such as Intel's 8085 and 8086. The 2716 is also the first EPROM with a static standby mode which reduces the power dissipation without increasing access time. The maximum active power dissipation is 525 mW while the maximum standby power dissipation is only 132 mW, a 75% savings.

The 2716 has the simplest and fastest method yet devised for programming EPROMs — single pulse TTL level programming. No need for high voltage pulsing because all programming controls are handled by TTL signals. Program any location at any time—either individually, sequentially or at random, with the 2716's single address location programming. Total programming time for all 16,384 bits is only 100 seconds.

PIN CONFIGURATION

2716

A7	1	24	VCC
A6	2	23	A8
A5	3	22	A9
A4	4	21	VPP
A3	5	20	OE
A2	6	19	A10
A1	7	18	CE
A0	8	17	O7
O0	9	16	O6
O1	10	15	O5
O2	11	14	O4
GND	12	13	O3

(16K)

2732†

A7	1	24	VCC
A6	2	23	A8
A5	3	22	A9
A4	4	21	A11
A3	5	20	OE/VPP
A2	6	19	A10
A1	7	18	CE
A0	8	17	O7
O0	9	16	O6
O1	10	15	O5
O2	11	14	O4
GND	12	13	O3

(32K)

†Refer to 2732 data sheet for specifications

PIN NAMES

A0– A10	ADDRESSES
CE/PGM	CHIP ENABLE/PROGRAM
OE	OUTPUT ENABLE
O0–O7	OUTPUTS

MODE SELECTION

PINS \ MODE	CE/PGM (18)	OE (20)	VPP (21)	VCC (24)	OUTPUTS (9-11, 13-17)
Read	V_{IL}	V_{IL}	+5	+5	D_{OUT}
Standby	V_{IH}	Don't Care	+5	+5	High Z
Program	Pulsed V_{IL} to V_{IH}	V_{IH}	+25	+5	D_{IN}
Program Verify	V_{IL}	V_{IL}	+25	+5	D_{OUT}
Program Inhibit	V_{IL}	V_{IH}	+25	+5	High Z

BLOCK DIAGRAM

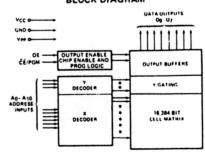

2732
32K (4K x 8) UV ERASABLE PROM

- **Fast Access Time:**
  - — 450 ns Max. 2732
  - — 550 ns Max. 2732-6

- **Single +5V ± 5% Power Supply**

- **Output Enable for MCS-85™ and MCS-86™ Compatibility**

- **Low Power Dissipation:**
  150mA Max. Active Current
  30mA Max. Standby Current

- **Pin Compatible to Intel® 2716 EPROM**

- **Completely Static**

- **Simple Programming Requirements**
  - — Single Location Programming
  - — Programs with One 50ms Pulse

- **Three-State Output for Direct Bus Interface**

The Intel® 2732 is a 32,768-bit ultraviolet erasable and electrically programmable read-only memory (EPROM). The 2732 operates from a single 5-volt power supply, has a standby mode, and features an output enable control. The total programming time for all bits is three and a half minutes. All these features make designing with the 2732 in microcomputer systems faster, easier, and more economical.

An important 2732 feature is the separate output control, Output Enable ($\overline{OE}$), from the Chip Enable control ($\overline{CE}$). The $\overline{OE}$ control eliminates bus contention in multiple bus microprocessor systems. Intel's Application Note AP-30 describes the microprocessor system implementation of the $\overline{OE}$ and $\overline{CE}$ controls on Intel's 2716 and 2732 EPROMs. AP-30 is available from Intel's Literature Department.

The 2732 has a standby mode which reduces the power dissipation without increasing access time. The maximum active current is 150mA, while the maximum standby current is only 30mA, an 80% savings. The standby mode is achieved by applying a TTL-high signal to the $\overline{CE}$ input.

PIN CONFIGURATION

A_7	1	24	V_{CC}
A_6	2	23	A_8
A_5	3	22	A_9
A_4	4	21	A_{11}
A_3	5	20	$\overline{OE}/V_{PP}$
A_2	6	19	A_{10}
A_1	7	18	$\overline{CE}$
A_0	8	17	O_7
O_0	9	16	O_6
O_1	10	15	O_5
O_2	11	14	O_4
GND	12	13	O_3

PIN NAMES

A_0-A_{11}	ADDRESSES
$\overline{CE}$	CHIP ENABLE
$\overline{OE}$	OUTPUT ENABLE
O_0-O_7	OUTPUTS

MODE SELECTION

PINS \ MODE	$\overline{CE}$ (18)	$\overline{OE}/V_{PP}$ (20)	V_{CC} (24)	OUTPUTS (9-11,13-17)
Read	V_{IL}	V_{IL}	+5	D_{OUT}
Standby	V_{IH}	Don't Care	+5	High Z
Program	V_{IL}	V_{PP}	+5	D_{IN}
Program Verify	V_{IL}	V_{IL}	+5	D_{OUT}
Program Inhibit	V_{IH}	V_{PP}	+5	High Z

BLOCK DIAGRAM

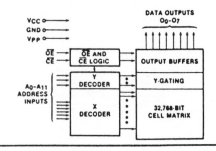

8355/8355-2
16,384-BIT ROM WITH I/O

- 2048 Words × 8 Bits

- Single +5V Power Supply

- Directly compatible with 8085A and 8088 Microprocessors

- 2 General Purpose 8-Bit I/O Ports

- Each I/O Port Line Individually Programmable as Input or Output

- Multiplexed Address and Data Bus

- Internal Address Latch

- 40-Pin DIP

The Intel® 8355 is a ROM and I/O chip to be used in the 8085A and 8088 microprocessor systems. The ROM portion is organized as 2048 words by 8 bits. It has a maximum acess time of 400 ns to permit use with no wait states in the 8085A CPU.

The I/O portion consists of 2 general purpose I/O ports. Each I/O port has 8 port lines and each I/O port line is individually programmable as input or output.

The 8355-2 has a 300ns access time for compatibility with the 8085A-2 and full speed 5 MHz 8088 microprocessors.

PIN CONFIGURATION

BLOCK DIAGRAM

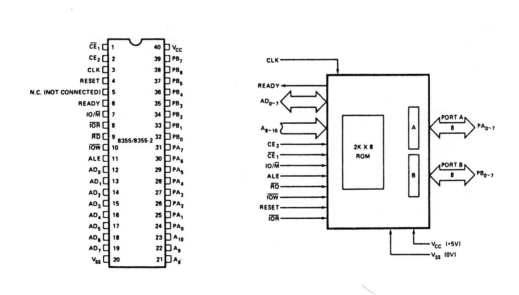

Symbol	Function	Symbol	Function
ALE (Input)	When ALE (Address Latch Enable is high, AD_{0-7}, $IO/\overline{M}$, A_{8-10}, CE, and $\overline{CE}$ enter address latched. The signals (AD, $IO/\overline{M}$, A_{8-10}, CE, $\overline{CE}$) are latched in at the trailing edge of ALE.	CLK (Input)	The CLK is used to force the READY into its high impedance state after it has been forced low by $\overline{CE}$ low, CE high and ALE high.
AD_{0-7} (Input)	Bidirectional Address/Data bus. The lower 8-bits of the ROM or I/O address are applied to the bus lines when ALE is high.	READY (Output)	Ready is a 3-state output controlled by $\overline{CE_1}$, CE_2, ALE and CLK. READY is forced low when the Chip Enables are active during the time ALE is high, and remains low until the rising edge of the next CLK (see Figure 6).
	During an I/O cycle, Port A or B are selected based on the latched value of AD_0. If $\overline{RD}$ or $\overline{IOR}$ is low when the latched chip enables are active, the output buffers present data on the bus.		
A_{8-10} (Input)	These are the high order bits of the ROM address. They do not affect I/O operations.	PA_{0-7} (Input/ Output)	These are general purpose I/O pins. Their input/output direction is determined by the contents of Data Direction Register (DDR). Port A is selected for write operations when the Chip Enables are active and $\overline{IOW}$ is low and a 0 was previously latched from AD_0.
$\overline{CE_1}$ CE_2 (Input)	Chip Enable Inputs: $\overline{CE_1}$ is active low and CE_2 is active high. The 8355 can be accessed only when BOTH Chip Enables are active at the time the ALE signal latches them up. If either Chip Enable input is not active, the AD_{0-7} and READY outputs will be in a high impedance state.		Read operation is selected by either $\overline{IOR}$ low and active Chip Enables and AD_0 low, or $IO/\overline{M}$ high, $\overline{RD}$ low, active chip enables, and AD_0 low.
		PB_{0-7} (Input/ Output)	This general purpose I/O port is identical to Port A except that it is selected by a 1 latched from AD_0.
		RESET (Input)	An input high on RESET causes all pins in Port A and B to assume input mode.
$IO/\overline{M}$ (Input)	If the latched $IO/\overline{M}$ is high when $\overline{RD}$ is low, the output data comes from an I/O port. If it is low the output data comes from the ROM.	$\overline{IOR}$ (Input)	When the Chip Enables are active, a low on $\overline{IOR}$ will output the selected I/O port onto the AD bus. $\overline{IOR}$ low performs the same function as the combination $IO/\overline{M}$ high and $\overline{RD}$ low. When $\overline{IOR}$ is not used in a system, $\overline{IOR}$ should be tied to V_{CC} ("1").
$\overline{RD}$ (Input)	If the latched Chip Enables are active when $\overline{RD}$ goes low, the AD_{0-7} output buffers are enabled and output either the selected ROM location or I/O port. When both $\overline{RD}$ and $\overline{IOR}$ are high, the AD_{0-7} output buffers are 3-state.		
		V_{CC}	+5 volt supply.
		V_{SS}	Ground Reference.
$\overline{IOW}$ (Input)	If the latched Chip Enables are active, a low on $\overline{IOW}$ causes the output port pointed to by the latched value of AD_0 to be written with the data on AD_{0-7}. The state of $IO/\overline{M}$ is ignored.		

intel®

8755A/8755A-2
16,384-BIT EPROM WITH I/O

- **2048 Words × 8 Bits**

- **Single +5V Power Supply (V_CC)**

- **Directly Compatible with 8085A and 8088 Microprocessors**

- **U.V. Erasable and Electrically Reprogrammable**

- **Internal Address Latch**

- **2 General Purpose 8-Bit I/O Ports**

- **Each I/O Port Line Individually Programmable as Input or Output**

- **Multiplexed Address and Data Bus**

- **40-Pin DIP**

The Intel® 8755A is an erasable and electrically reprogrammable ROM (EPROM) and I/O chip to be used in the 8085A and 8088 microprocessor systems. The EPROM portion is organized as 2048 words by 8 bits. It has a maximum access time of 450 ns to permit use with no wait states in an 8085A CPU.

The I/O portion consists of 2 general purpose I/O ports. Each I/O port has 8 port lines, and each I/O port line is individually programmable as input or output.

The 8755A-2 is a high speed selected version of the 8755A compatible with the 5 MHz 8085A-2 and the full speed 5 MHz 8088.

PIN CONFIGURATION

BLOCK DIAGRAM

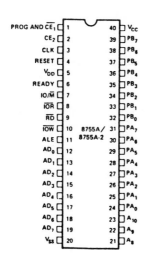

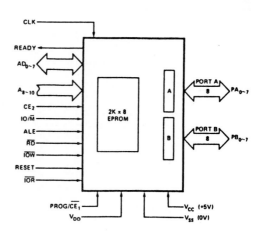

8755A FUNCTIONAL PIN DEFINITION

Symbol	Function
ALE (input)	When Address Latch Enable goes high, AD_{0-7}, IO/M, A_{8-10}, CE_2, and $\overline{CE_1}$ enter the address latches. The signals (AD, IO/M, A_{8-10}, CE) are latched in at the trailing edge of ALE.
AD_{0-7} (input/output)	Bidirectional Address/Data bus. The lower 8-bits of the PROM or I/O address are applied to the bus lines when ALE is high.
	During an I/O cycle, Port A or B are selected based on the latched value of AD_0. If $\overline{RD}$ or $\overline{IOR}$ is low when the latched Chip Enables are active, the output buffers present data on the bus.
A_{8-10} (input)	These are the high order bits of the PROM address. They do not affect I/O operations.
PROG/$\overline{CE_1}$ CE_2 (input)	Chip Enable Inputs: $\overline{CE_1}$ is active low and CE_2 is active high. The 8755A can be accessed only when *BOTH* Chip Enables are active at the time the ALE signal latches them up. If either Chip Enable input is not active, the AD_{0-7} and READY outputs will be in a high impedance state. $\overline{CE_1}$ is also used as a programming pin. (See section on programming.)
IO/$\overline{M}$ (input)	If the latched IO/$\overline{M}$ is high when $\overline{RD}$ is low, the output data comes from an I/O port. If it is low the output data comes from the PROM.
$\overline{RD}$ (input)	If the latched Chip Enables are active when $\overline{RD}$ goes low, the AD_{0-7} output buffers are enabled and output either the selected PROM location or I/O port. When both $\overline{RD}$ and $\overline{IOR}$ are high, the AD_{0-7} output buffers are 3-stated.
$\overline{IOW}$ (input)	If the latched Chip Enables are active, a low on $\overline{IOW}$ causes the output port pointed to by the latched value of AD_0 to be written with the data on AD_{0-7}. The state of IO/$\overline{M}$ is ignored.
CLK (input)	The CLK is used to force the READY into its high impedance state after it has been forced low by $\overline{CE_1}$ low, CE_2 high, and ALE high.

Symbol	Function
READY (output)	READY is a 3-state output controlled by CE_2, $\overline{CE_1}$, ALE and CLK. READY is forced low when the Chip Enables are active during the time ALE is high, and remains low until the rising edge of the next CLK. (See Figure 6.)
PA_{0-7} (input/output)	These are general purpose I/O pins. Their input/output direction is determined by the contents of Data Direction Register (DDR). Port A is selected for write operations when the Chip Enables are active and $\overline{IOW}$ is low and a 0 was previously latched from AD_0, AD_1.
	Read operation is selected by either $\overline{IOR}$ low and active Chip Enables and AD_0 and AD_1 low, *or* IO/$\overline{M}$ high, $\overline{RD}$ low, active Chip Enables, and AD_0 and AD_1 low.
PB_{0-7} (input/output)	This general purpose I/O port is identical to Port A except that it is selected by a 1 latched from AD_0 and a 0 from AD_1.
RESET (input)	In normal operation, an input high on RESET causes all pins in Ports A and B to assume input mode (clear DDR register).
$\overline{IOR}$ (input)	When the Chip Enables are active, a low on $\overline{IOR}$ will output the selected I/O port onto the AD bus. $\overline{IOR}$ low performs the same function as the combination of IO/$\overline{M}$ high and $\overline{RD}$ low. When $\overline{IOR}$ is not used in a system, $\overline{IOR}$ should be tied to V_{CC} ("1").
V_{CC}	+5 volt supply.
V_{SS}	Ground Reference.
V_{DD}	V_{DD} is a programming voltage, and must be tied to +5V when the 8755A is being read.
	For programming, a high voltage is supplied with $V_{DD} = 25V$, typical. (See section on programming.)

intel®

8155/8156/8155-2/8156-2
2048 BIT STATIC MOS RAM WITH I/O PORTS AND TIMER

- ■ **256 Word x 8 Bits**
- ■ **Single +5V Power Supply**
- ■ **Completely Static Operation**
- ■ **Internal Address Latch**
- ■ **2 Programmable 8 Bit I/O Ports**

- ■ **1 Programmable 6-Bit I/O Port**
- ■ **Programmable 14-Bit Binary Counter/ Timer**
- ■ **Compatible with 8085A and 8088 CPU**
- ■ **Multiplexed Address and Data Bus**
- ■ **40 Pin DIP**

The 8155 and 89156 are RAM and I/O chips to be used in the 8085A and 8088 microprocessor systems. The RAM portion is designed with 2048 static cells organized as 256 x 8. They have a maximum access time of 400 ns to permit use with no wait states in 8085A CPU. The 8155-2 and 8156-2 have maximum access times of 330 ns for use with the 8085A-2 and the full speed 5 MHz 8088 CPU.

The I/O portion consists of three general purpose I/O ports. One of the three ports can be programmed to be status pins, thus allowing the other two ports to operate in handshake mode.

A 14-bit programmable counter/timer is jalso included on chip to provide either a square wave or terminal count pulse for the CPU system depending on timer mode.

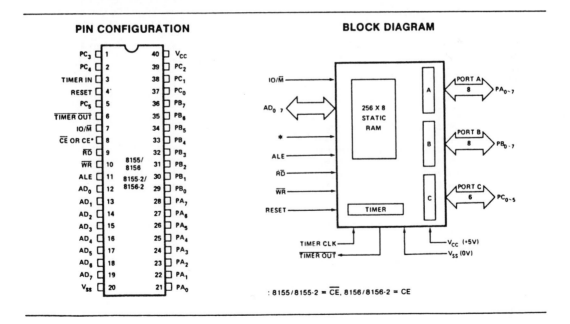

PIN CONFIGURATION

8155/8156
8155-2/8156-2

Pin	Signal	Pin	Signal
1	PC_3	40	V_{CC}
2	PC_4	39	PC_2
3	TIMER IN	38	PC_1
4	RESET	37	PC_0
5	PC_5	36	PB_7
6	$\overline{TIMER\ OUT}$	35	PB_6
7	$IO/\overline{M}$	34	PB_5
8	$\overline{CE}$ OR CE*	33	PB_4
9	$\overline{RD}$	32	PB_3
10	$\overline{WR}$	31	PB_2
11	ALE	30	PB_1
12	AD_0	29	PB_0
13	AD_1	28	PA_7
14	AD_2	27	PA_6
15	AD_3	26	PA_5
16	AD_4	25	PA_4
17	AD_5	24	PA_3
18	AD_6	23	PA_2
19	AD_7	22	PA_1
20	V_{SS}	21	PA_0

BLOCK DIAGRAM

: 8155/8155-2 = $\overline{CE}$, 8156/8156-2 = CE

8155/8156 PIN FUNCTIONS

Symbol	Function
RESET (input)	Pulse provided by the 8085A to initialize the system (connect to 8085A RESET OUT). Input high on this line resets the chip and initializes the three I/O ports to input mode. The width of RESET pulse should typically be two 8085A clock cycle times.
AD_{0-7} (input)	3-state Address/Data lines that interface with the CPU lower 8-bit Address/Data Bus. The 8-bit address is latched into the address latch inside the 8155/56 on the falling edge of ALE. The address can be either for the memory section or the I/O section depending on the $IO/\overline{M}$ input. The 8-bit data is either written into the chip or read from the chip, depending on the $\overline{WR}$ or $\overline{RD}$ input signal.
CE or $\overline{CE}$ (input)	Chip Enable: On the 8155, this pin is $\overline{CE}$ and is ACTIVE LOW. On the 8156, this pin is CE and is ACTIVE HIGH.
$\overline{RD}$ (input)	Read control: Input low on this line with the Chip Enable active enables and AD_{0-7} buffers. If $IO/\overline{M}$ pin is low, the RAM content will be read out to the AD bus. Otherwise the content of the selected I/O port or command/status registers will be read to the AD bus.
$\overline{WR}$ (input)	Write control: Input low on this line with the Chip Enable active causes the data on the Address/Data bus to be written to the RAM or I/O ports and command/status register depending on $IO/\overline{M}$.

Symbol	Function
ALE (input)	Address Latch Enable: This control signal latches both the address on the AD_{0-7} lines and the state of the Chip Enable and $IO/\overline{M}$ into the chip at the falling edge of ALE.
$IO/\overline{M}$ (input)	Selects memory if low and I/O and command/status registers if high.
$PA_{0-7}(8)$ (input/output)	These 8 pins are general purpose I/O pins. The in/out direction is selected by programming the command register.
$PB_{0-7}(8)$ (input/output)	These 8 pins are general purpose I/O pins. The in/out direction is selected by programming the command register.
$PC_{0-5}(6)$ (input/output)	These 6 pins can function as either input port, output port, or as control signals for PA and PB. Programming is done through the command register. When PC_{0-5} are used as control signals, they will provide the following: PC_0 — A INTR (Port A Interrupt) PC_1 — ABF (Port A Buffer Full) PC_2 — $\overline{A\ STB}$ (Port A Strobe) PC_3 — B INTR (Port B Interrupt) PC_4 — $\overline{B\ BF}$ (Port B Buffer Full) PC_5 — B STB (Port B Strobe)
TIMER IN (input)	Input to the counter-timer.
$\overline{TIMER\ OUT}$ (output)	Timer output. This output can be either a square wave or a pulse depending on the timer mode.
V_{CC}	+5 volt supply.
V_{SS}	Ground Reference.

intel®

8255A/8255A-5
PROGRAMMABLE PERIPHERAL INTERFACE

- ■ MCS-85™ Compatible 8255A-5
- ■ 24 Programmable I/O Pins
- ■ Completely TTL Compatible
- ■ Fully Compatible with Intel® Micro-processor Families
- ■ Improved Timing Characteristics

- ■ Direct Bit Set/Reset Capability Easing Control Application Interface
- ■ 40-Pin Dual In-Line Package
- ■ Reduces System Package Count
- ■ Improved DC Driving Capability

The Intel® 8255A is a general purpose programmable I/O device designed for use with Intel® microprocessors. It has 24 I/O pins which may be individually programmed in 2 groups of 12 and used in 3 major modes of operation. In the first mode (MODE 0), each group of 12 I/O pins may be programmed in sets of 4 to be input or output. In MODE 1, the second mode, each group may be programmed to have 8 lines of input or output. Of the remaining 4 pins, 3 are used for hand-shaking and interrupt control signals. The third mode of operation (MODE 2) is a bidirectional bus mode which uses 8 lines for a bidirectional bus, and 5 lines, borrowing one from the other group, for handshaking.

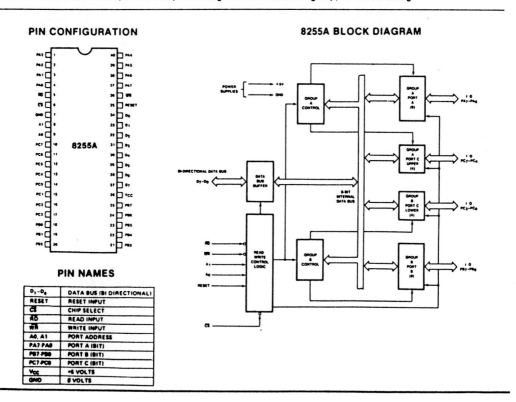

PIN CONFIGURATION

8255A

PIN NAMES

D₇-D₀	DATA BUS (BI DIRECTIONAL)
RESET	RESET INPUT
CS	CHIP SELECT
RD	READ INPUT
WR	WRITE INPUT
A0, A1	PORT ADDRESS
PA7-PA0	PORT A (BIT)
PB7-PB0	PORT B (BIT)
PC7-PC0	PORT C (BIT)
Vcc	+5 VOLTS
GND	0 VOLTS

8255A BLOCK DIAGRAM

intel

8279/8279-5
PROGRAMMABLE KEYBOARD/DISPLAY INTERFACE

- Simultaneous Keyboard Display Operations
- Scanned Keyboard Mode
- Scanned Sensor Mode
- Strobed Input Entry Mode
- 8-Character Keyboard FIFO
- 2-Key Lockout or N-Key Rollover with Contact Debounce
- Dual 8- or 16-Numerical Display

- Single 16-Character Display
- Right or Left Entry 16-Byte Display RAM
- Mode Programmable from CPU
- Programmable Scan Timing
- Interrupt Output on Key Entry
- Available in EXPRESS
  — Standard Temperature Range
  — Extended Temperature Range

The Intel® 8279 is a general purpose programmable keyboard and display I/O interface device designed for use with Intel® microprocessors. The keyboard portion can provide a scanned interface to a 64-contact key matrix. The keyboard portion will also interface to an array of sensors or a strobed interface keyboard, such as the hall effect and ferrite variety. Key depressions can be 2-key lockout or N-key rollover. Keyboard entries are debounced and strobed in an 8-character FIFO. If more than 8 characters are entered, overrun status is set. Key entries set the interrupt output line to the CPU.

The display portion provides a scanned display interface for LED, incandescent, and other popular display technologies. Both numeric and alphanumeric segment displays may be used as well as simple indicators. The 8279 has 16x8 display RAM which can be organized into dual 16x4. The RAM can be loaded or interrogated by the CPU. Both right entry, calculator and left entry typewriter display formats are possible. Both read and write of the display RAM can be done with auto-increment of the display RAM address.

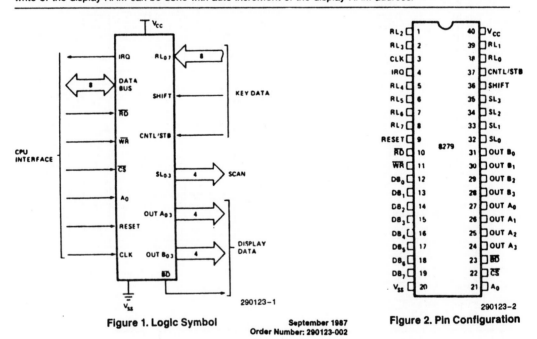

Figure 1. Logic Symbol

September 1987
Order Number: 290123-002

290123-1

290123-2

Figure 2. Pin Configuration

8279/8279-5

HARDWARE DESCRIPTION

The 8279 is packaged in a 40 pin DIP. The following is a functional description of each pin.

Table 1. Pin Description

Symbol	Pin No.	Name and Function
DB_0–DB_7	19–12	**BI-DIRECTIONAL DATA BUS:** All data and commands between the CPU and the 8279 are transmitted on these lines.
CLK	3	**CLOCK:** Clock from system used to generate internal timing.
RESET	9	**RESET:** A high signal on this pin resets the 8279. After being reset the 8279 is placed in the following mode: 1) 16 8-bit character display—left entry. 2) Encoded scan keyboard—2 key lockout. Along with this the program clock prescaler is set to 31.
CS	22	**CHIP SELECT:** A low on this pin enables the interface functions to receive or transmit.
A_0	21	**BUFFER ADDRESS:** A high on this line indicates the signals in or out are interpreted as a command or status. A low indicates that they are data.
$\overline{RD}$, $\overline{WR}$	10–11	**INPUT/OUTPUT READ AND WRITE:** These signals enable the data buffers to either send data to the external bus or receive it from the external bus.
IRQ	4	**INTERRUPT REQUEST:** In a keyboard mode, the interrupt line is high when there is data in the FIFO/Sensor RAM. The interrupt line goes low with each FIFO/Sensor RAM read and returns high if there is still information in the RAM. In a sensor mode, the interrupt line goes high whenever a change in a sensor is detected.
V_{SS}, V_{CC}	20, 40	**GROUND AND POWER SUPPLY PINS.**
SL_0–SL_3	32–35	**SCAN LINES:** Scan lines which are used to scan the key switch or sensor matrix and the display digits. These lines can be either encoded (1 of 16) or decoded (1 of 4).
RL_0–RL_7	38, 39, 1, 2, 5–8	**RETURN LINE:** Return line inputs which are connected to the scan lines through the keys or sensor switches. They have active internal pullups to keep them high until a switch closure pulls one low. They also serve as an 8-bit input in the Strobed Input mode.
SHIFT	36	**SHIFT:** The shift input status is stored along with the key position on key closure in the Scanned Keyboard modes. It has an active internal pullup to keep it high until a switch closure pulls it low.
CNTL/STB	37	**CONTROL/STROBED INPUT MODE:** For keyboard modes this line is used as a control input and stored like status on a key closure. The line is also the strobe line that enters the data into the FIFO in the Strobed Input mode. (Rising Edge). It has an active internal pullup to keep it high until a switch closure pulls it low.
OUT A_0–OUT A_3 OUT B_0–OUT B_3	27-24 31–28	**OUTPUTS:** These two ports are the outputs for the 16 x 4 display refresh registers. The data from these outputs is synchronized to the scan lines (SL_0–SL_3) for multiplexed digit displays. The two 4 bit ports may be blanked independently. These two ports may also be considered as one 8-bit port.
$\overline{BD}$	23	**BLANK DISPLAY:** This output is used to blank the display during digit switching or by a display blanking command.

H

Motorola MC68000 and Support Chips — Data Sheets

Reprinted with permission of Motorola.

 **MOTOROLA**

Advance Information

16-BIT MICROPROCESSING UNIT

Advances in semiconductor technology have provided the capability to place on a single silicon chip a microprocessor at least an order of magnitude higher in performance and circuit complexity than has been previously available. The MC68000 is the first of a family of such VLSI microprocessors from Motorola. It combines state-of-the-art technology and advanced circuit design techniques with computer sciences to achieve an architecturally advanced 16-bit microprocessor.

The resources available to the MC68000 user consist of the following:

- 32-Bit Data and Address Registers
- 16 Megabyte Direct Addressing Range
- 56 Powerful Instruction Types
- Operations on Five Main Data Types
- Memory Mapped I/O
- 14 Addressing Modes

As shown in the programming model, the MC68000 offers seventeen 32-bit registers in addition to the 32-bit program counter and a 16-bit status register. The first eight registers (D0-D7) are used as data registers for byte (8-bit), word (16-bit), and long word (32-bit) data operations. The second set of seven registers (A0-A6) and the system stack pointer may be used as software stack pointers and base address registers. In addition, these registers may be used for word and long word address operations. All seventeen registers may be used as index registers.

MC68000L4
(4 MHz)
MC68000L6
(6 MHz)
MC68000L8
(8 MHz)
MC68000L10
(10 MHz)

HMOS
(HIGH-DENSITY, N-CHANNEL,
SILICON-GATE DEPLETION LOAD)

**16-BIT
MICROPROCESSOR**

L SUFFIX
CERAMIC PACKAGE
CASE 746

64-pin dual in-line package

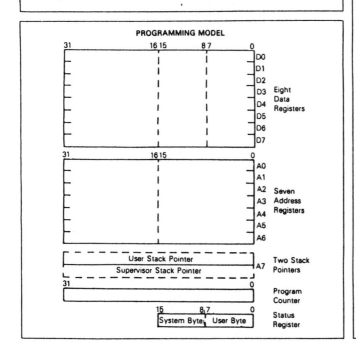

PROGRAMMING MODEL

68-Terminal Chip Carrier

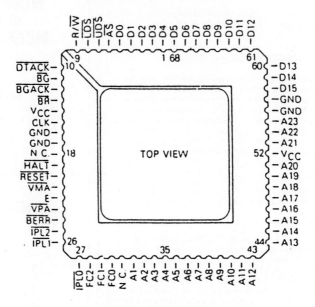

68-Pin Quad Pack

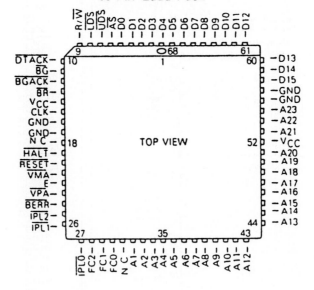

 **MOTOROLA**

MC68230L8
MC68230L10

Advance Information

HMOS
(HIGH-DENSITY N-CHANNEL SILICON-GATE)

PARALLEL INTERFACE/TIMER

MC68230 PARALLEL INTERFACE/TIMER

The MC68230 Parallel Interface/Timer provides versatile double buffered parallel interfaces and an operating system oriented timer to MC68000 systems. The parallel interfaces operate in unidirectional or bidirectional modes, either 8 or 16 bits wide. In the unidirectional modes, an associated data direction register determines whether the port pins are inputs or outputs. In the bidirectional modes the data direction registers are ignored and the direction is determined dynamically by the state of four handshake pins. These programmable handshake pins provide an interface flexible enough for connection to a wide variety of low, medium, or high speed peripherals or other computer systems. The PI/T ports allow use of vectored or autovectored interrupts, and also provide a DMA Request pin for connection to the MC68450 Direct Memory Access Controller or a similar circuit. The PI/T timer contains a 24-bit wide counter and a 5-bit prescaler. The timer may be clocked by the system clock (PI/T CLK pin) or by an external clock (TIN pin), and a 5-bit prescaler can be used. It can generate periodic interrupts, a square wave, or a single interrupt after a programmed time period. Also it can be used for elapsed time measurement or as a device watchdog.

- MC68000 Bus Compatible
- Port Modes Include:
  Bit I/O
  Unidirectional 8-Bit and 16-Bit
  Bidirectional 8-Bit and 16-Bit
- Selectable Handshaking Options
- 24-Bit Programmable Timer
- Software Programmable Timer Modes
- Contains Interrupt Vector Generation Logic
- Separate Port and Timer Interrupt Service Requests
- Registers are Read/Write and Directly Addressable
- Registers are Addressed for MOVEP (Move Peripheral) and DMAC Compatibility

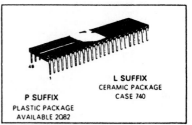

L SUFFIX
CERAMIC PACKAGE
CASE 740

P SUFFIX
PLASTIC PACKAGE
AVAILABLE 2Q82

PIN ASSIGNMENT

D5	1	48	D4
D6	2	47	D3
D7	3	46	D2
PA0	4	45	D1
PA1	5	44	D0
PA2	6	43	R/$\overline{W}$
PA3	7	42	$\overline{DTACK}$
PA4	8	41	$\overline{CS}$
PA5	9	40	CLK
PA6	10	39	$\overline{RESET}$
PA7	11	38	VSS
VCC	12	37	PC7/$\overline{TIACK}$
H1	13	36	PC6/$\overline{PIACK}$
H2	14	35	PC5/$\overline{PIRQ}$
H3	15	34	PC4/$\overline{DMAREQ}$
H4	16	33	PC3/TOUT
PB0	17	32	PC2/TIN
PB1	18	31	PC1
PB2	19	30	PC0
PB3	20	29	RS1
PB4	21	28	RS2
PB5	22	27	RS3
PB6	23	26	RS4
PB7	24	25	RS5

 **MOTOROLA**

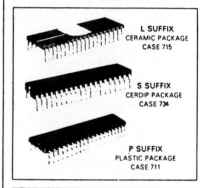

┌─────────────────────┐
│ **MC6821**   │
│ (1.0 MHz)   │
│ **MC68A21**   │
│ (1.5 MHz)   │
│ **MC68B21**   │
│ (2.0 MHz)   │
└─────────────────────┘

PERIPHERAL INTERFACE ADAPTER (PIA)

The MC6821 Peripheral Interface Adapter provides the universal means of interfacing peripheral equipment to the M6800 family of microprocessors. This device is capable of interfacing the MPU to peripherals through two 8-bit bidirectional peripheral data buses and four control lines. No external logic is required for interfacing to most peripheral devices

The functional configuration of the PIA is programmed by the MPU during system initialization. Each of the peripheral data lines can be programmed to act as an input or output, and each of the four control/interrupt lines may be programmed for one of several control modes. This allows a high degree of flexibility in the overall operation of the interface.

- 8-Bit Bidirectional Data Bus for Communication with the MPU
- Two Bidirectional 8-Bit Buses for Interface to Peripherals
- Two Programmable Control Registers
- Two Programmable Data Direction Registers
- Four Individually-Controlled Interrupt Input Lines; Two Usable as Peripheral Control Outputs
- Handshake Control Logic for Input and Output Peripheral Operation
- High-Impedance Three-State and Direct Transistor Drive Peripheral Lines
- Program Controlled Interrupt and Interrupt Disable Capability
- CMOS Drive Capability on Side A Peripheral Lines
- Two TTL Drive Capability on All A and B Side Buffers
- TTL-Compatible
- Static Operation

MOS

(N-CHANNEL, SILICON-GATE, DEPLETION LOAD)

PERIPHERAL INTERFACE ADAPTER

L SUFFIX
CERAMIC PACKAGE
CASE 715

S SUFFIX
CERDIP PACKAGE
CASE 734

P SUFFIX
PLASTIC PACKAGE
CASE 711

MAXIMUM RATINGS

Characteristics	Symbol	Value	Unit
Supply Voltage	V_{CC}	-0.3 to $+7.0$	V
Input Voltage	V_{in}	-0.3 to $+7.0$	V
Operating Temperature Range MC6821, MC68A21, MC68B21 MC6821C, MC68A21C, MC68B21C	T_A	T_L to T_H 0 to 70 -40 to $+85$	°C
Storage Temperature Range	T_{stg}	-55 to $+150$	°C

THERMAL CHARACTERISTICS

Characteristic	Symbol	Value	Unit
Thermal Resistance Ceramic Plastic Cerdip	θ_{JA}	50 100 60	°C/W

This device contains circuitry to protect the inputs against damage due to high static voltages or electric fields; however, it is advised that normal precautions be taken to avoid application of any voltage higher than maximum-rated voltages to this high-impedance circuit. Reliability of operation is enhanced if unused inputs are tied to an appropriate logic voltage (i.e., either V_{SS} or V_{CC})

PIN ASSIGNMENT

V_{SS}	1 ●	40	CA1
PA0	2	39	CA2
PA1	3	38	$\overline{IRQA}$
PA2	4	37	$\overline{IRQB}$
PA3	5	36	RS0
PA4	6	35	RS1
PA5	7	34	$\overline{RESET}$
PA6	8	33	D0
PA7	9	32	D1
PB0	10	31	D2
PB1	11	30	D3
PB2	12	29	D4
PB3	13	28	D5
PB4	14	27	D6
PB5	15	26	D7
PB6	16	25	E
PB7	17	24	CS1
CB1	18	23	$\overline{CS2}$
CB2	19	22	CS0
V_{CC}	20	21	$R/\overline{W}$

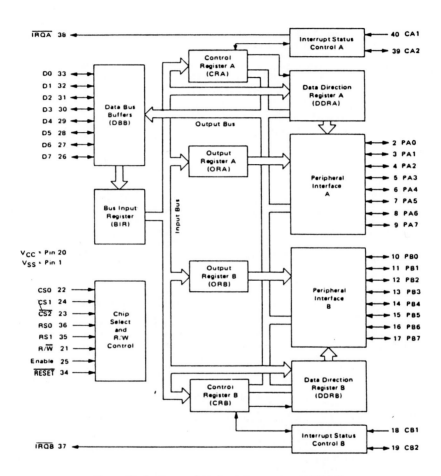

Figure H-1 Expanded Block Diagram of MC6821

PIA INTERFACE SIGNALS FOR MPU

The PIA interfaces to the M6800 bus with an 8-bit bidirectional data bus, three chip select lines, two register select lines, two interrupt request lines, a read/write line, an enable line and a reset line. To ensure proper operation with the MC6800, MC6802, or MC6808 microprocessors, VMA should be used as an active part of the address decoding.

Bidirectional Data (D0-D7) — The bidirectional data lines (D0-D7) allow the transfer of data between the MPU and the PIA. The data bus output drivers are three-state devices that remain in the high-impedance (off) state except when the MPU performs a PIA read operation. The read/write line is in the read (high) state when the PIA is selected for a read operation.

Enable (E) — The enable pulse, E, is the only timing signal that is supplied to the PIA. Timing of all other signals is referenced to the leading and trailing edges of the E pulse.

Read/Write (R/$\overline{W}$) — This signal is generated by the MPU to control the direction of data transfers on the data bus. A low state on the PIA read/write line enables the input buffers and data is transferred from the MPU to the PIA on the E signal if the device has been selected. A high on the read/write line sets up the PIA for a transfer of data to the bus. The PIA output buffers are enabled when the proper address and the enable pulse E are present.

$\overline{RESET}$ — The active low $\overline{RESET}$ line is used to reset all register bits in the PIA to a logical zero (low). This line can be used as a power-on reset and as a master reset during system operation.

Chip Selects (CS0, CS1, and $\overline{CS2}$) — These three input signals are used to select the PIA. CS0 and CS1 must be high and $\overline{CS2}$ must be low for selection of the device. Data transfers are then performed under the control of the enable and read/write signals. The chip select lines must be stable for the duration of the E pulse. The device is deselected when any of the chip selects are in the inactive state.

Register Selects (RS0 and RS1) — The two register select lines are used to select the various registers inside the PIA. These two lines are used in conjunction with internal Control Registers to select a particular register that is to be written or read.

The register and chip select lines should be stable for the duration of the E pulse while in the read or write cycle.

Interrupt Request ($\overline{IRQA}$ and $\overline{IRQB}$) — The active low Interrupt Request lines ($\overline{IRQA}$ and $\overline{IRQB}$) act to interrupt the MPU either directly or through interrupt priority circuitry. These lines are "open drain" (no load device on the chip). This permits all interrupt request lines to be tied together in a wire-OR configuration.

Each Interrupt Request line has two internal interrupt flag bits that can cause the Interrupt Request line to go low. Each flag bit is associated with a particular peripheral interrupt line. Also, four interrupt enable bits are provided in the PIA which may be used to inhibit a particular interrupt from a peripheral device.

Servicing an interrupt by the MPU may be accomplished by a software routine that, on a prioritized basis, sequentially reads and tests the two control registers in each PIA for interrupt flag bits that are set.

The interrupt flags are cleared (zeroed) as a result of an MPU Read Peripheral Data Operation of the corresponding data register. After being cleared, the interrupt flag bit cannot be enabled to be set until the PIA is deselected during an E pulse. The E pulse is used to condition the interrupt control lines (CA1, CA2, CB1, CB2). When these lines are used as interrupt inputs, at least one E pulse must occur from the inactive edge to the active edge of the interrupt input signal to condition the edge sense network. If the interrupt flag has been enabled and the edge sense circuit has been properly conditioned, the interrupt flag will be set on the next active transition of the interrupt input pin.

PIA PERIPHERAL INTERFACE LINES

The PIA provides two 8-bit bidirectional data buses and four interrupt/control lines for interfacing to peripheral devices.

Section A Peripheral Data (PA0-PA7) — Each of the peripheral data lines can be programmed to act as an input or output. This is accomplished by setting a "1" in the corresponding Data Direction Register bit for those lines which are to be outputs. A "0" in a bit of the Data Direction Register causes the corresponding peripheral data line to act as an input. During an MPU Read Peripheral Data Operation, the data on peripheral lines programmed to act as inputs appears directly on the corresponding MPU Data Bus lines. In the input mode, the internal pullup resistor on these lines represents a maximum of 1.5 standard TTL loads.

The data in Output Register A will appear on the data lines that are programmed to be outputs. A logical "1" written into the register will cause a "high" on the corresponding data line while a "0" results in a "low." Data in Output Register A may be read by an MPU "Read Peripheral Data A" operation when the corresponding lines are programmed as outputs. This data will be read property if the voltage on the peripheral data lines is greater than 2.0 volts for a logic "1" output and less than 0.8 volt for a logic "0" output. Loading the output lines such that the voltage on these lines does not reach full voltage causes the data transferred into the MPU on a Read operation to differ from that contained in the respective bit of Output Register A.

Section B Peripheral Data (PB0-PB7) — The peripheral data lines in the B Section of the PIA can be programmed to act as either inputs or outputs in a similar manner to PA0-PA7. They have three-state capability, allowing them to enter a high-impedance state when the peripheral data line is used as an input. In addition, data on the peripheral data lines

PB0-PB7 will be read properly from those lines programmed as outputs even if the voltages are below 2.0 volts for a "high" or above 0.8 V for a "low". As outputs, these lines are compatible with standard TTL and may also be used as a source of up to 1 milliampere at 1.5 volts to directly drive the base of a transistor switch.

Interrupt Input (CA1 and CB1) — Peripheral input lines CA1 and CB1 are input only lines that set the interrupt flags of the control registers. The active transition for these signals is also programmed by the two control registers.

Peripheral Control (CA2) — The peripheral control line CA2 can be programmed to act as an interrupt input or as a peripheral control output. As an output, this line is compatible with standard TTL; as an input the internal pullup resistor on this line represents 1.5 standard TTL loads. The function of this signal line is programmed with Control Register A.

Peripheral Control (CB2) — Peripheral Control line CB2 may also be programmed to act as an interrupt input or peripheral control output. As an input, this line has high input impedance and is compatible with standard TTL. As an output it is compatible with standard TTL and may also be used as a source of up to 1 milliampere at 1.5 volts to directly drive the base of a transistor switch. This line is programmed by Control Register B.

INTERNAL CONTROLS

INITIALIZATION

A $\overline{RESET}$ has the effect of zeroing all PIA registers. This will set PA0-PA7, PB0-PB7, CA2 and CB2 as inputs, and all interrupts disabled. The PIA must be configured during the restart program which follows the reset.

There are six locations within the PIA accessible to the MPU data bus: two Peripheral Registers, two Data Direction Registers, and two Control Registers. Selection of these locations is controlled by the RS0 and RS1 inputs together with bit 2 in the Control Register, as shown in Table H-1.

Details of possible configurations of the Data Direction and Control Register are as follows:

Table H-1 Internal Addressing

RS1	RS0	Control Register Bit CRA-2	Control Register Bit CRB-2	Location Selected
0	0	1	X	Peripheral Register A
0	0	0	X	Data Direction Register A
0	1	X	X	Control Register A
1	0	X	1	Peripheral Register B
1	0	X	0	Data Direction Register B
1	1	X	X	Control Register B

X = Don't Care

PORT A-B HARDWARE CHARACTERISTICS

As shown in Figure H-2, the MC6821 has a pair of I/O ports whose characteristics differ greatly. The A side is designed to drive CMOS logic to normal 30% to 70% levels, and incorporates an internal pullup device that remains connected even in the input mode. Because of this, the A side requires more drive current in the input mode than Port B. In contrast, the B side uses a normal three-state NMOS buffer which cannot pullup to CMOS levels without external resistors. The B side can drive extra loads such as Darlingtons without problem. When the PIA comes out of reset, the A port represents inputs with pullup resistors, whereas the B side (input mode also) will float high or low, depending upon the load connected to it.

Notice the differences between a Port A and Port B read operation when in the output mode. When reading Port A, the actual pin is read, whereas the B side read comes from an output latch, ahead of the actual pin.

CONTROL REGISTERS (CRA and CRB)

The two Control registers (CRA and CRB) allow the MPU to control the operation of the four peripheral control lines CA1, CA2, CB1, and CB2. In addition they allow the MPU to enable the interrupt lines and monitor the status of the interrupt flags. Bits 0 through 5 of the two registers may be written or read by the MPU when the proper chip select and register select signals are applied. Bits 6 and 7 of the two registers are read only and are modified by external interrupts occurring on control lines CA1, CA2, CB1, or CB2. The format of the control words is shown in Figure H-3.

DATA DIRECTION ACCESS CONTROL BIT (CRA-2 and CRB-2)

Bit 2, in each Control Register (CRA and CRB), determines selection of either a Peripheral Output Register or the corresponding Data Direction E Register when the proper register select signals are applied to RS0 and RS1. A "1" in bit 2 allows access of the Peripheral Interface Register, while a "0" causes the Data Direction Register to be addressed.

Interrupt Flags (CRA-6, CRA-7, CRB-6, and CRB-7) — The four interrupt flag bits are set by active transitions of signals on the four Interrupt and Peripheral Control lines when those lines are programmed to be inputs. These bits cannot be set directly from the MPU Data Bus and are reset indirectly by a Read Peripheral Data Operation on the appropriate section.

Control of CA2 and CB2 Peripheral Control Lines (CRA-3, CRA-4, CRA-5, CRB-3, CRB-4, and CRB-5) — Bits 3, 4, and 5 of the two control registers are used to control the CA2 and CB2 Peripheral Control lines. These bits determine if the control lines will be an interrupt input or an output control signal. If bit CRA-5 (CRB-5) is low, CA2 (CB2) is an interrupt input line similar to CA1 (CB1). When CRA-5 (CRB-5) is high, CA2 (CB2) becomes an output signal that may be used to control peripheral data transfers. When in the output mode, CA2 and CB2 have slightly different loading characteristics.

Control of CA1 and CB1 Interrupt Input Lines (CRA-0, CRB-1, CRA-1, and CRB-1) — The two lowest-order bits of the control registers are used to control the interrupt input lines CA1 and CB1. Bits CRA-0 and CRB-0 are used to enable the MPU interrupt signals $\overline{IRQA}$ and $\overline{IRQB}$, respectively. Bits CRA-1 and CRB-1 determine the active transition of the interrupt input signals CA1 and CB1.

Figure H–2   Port A and Port B Equivalent Circuits

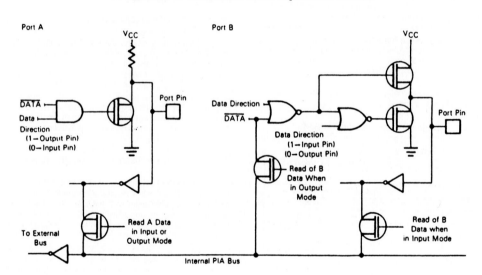

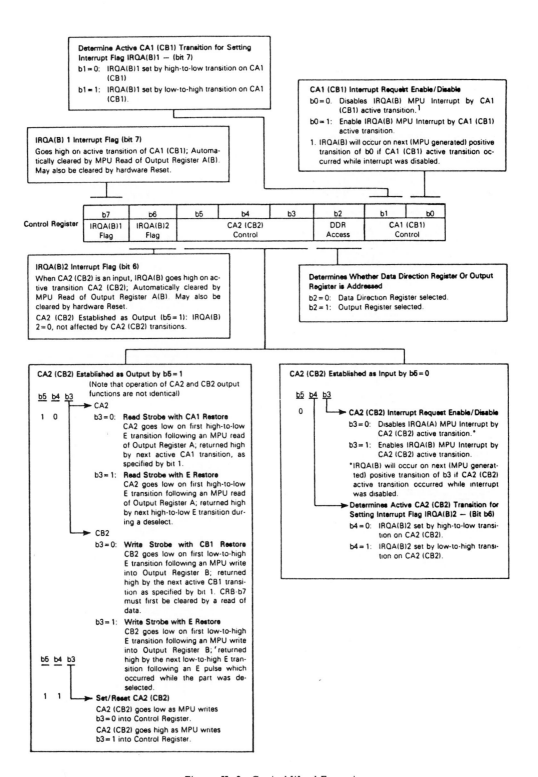

Figure H-3 Control Word Format

 **MOTOROLA**

16K BIT STATIC RANDOM ACCESS MEMORY

The MCM6116 is a 16,384-bit Static Random Access Memory organized as 2048 words by 8 bits, fabricated using Motorola's high-performance silicon-gate CMOS (HCMOS) technology. It uses a design approach which provides the simple timing features associated with fully static memories and the reduced power associated with CMOS memories. This means low standby power without the need for clocks, nor reduced data rates due to cycle times that exceed access time.

Chip Enable ($\overline{E}$) controls the power-down feature. It is not a clock but rather a chip control that affects power consumption. In less than a cycle time after Chip Enable ($\overline{E}$) goes high, the part automatically reduces its power requirements and remains in this low-power standby as long as the Chip Enable ($\overline{E}$) remains high. The automatic power-down feature causes no performance degradation.

The MCM6116 is in a 24-pin dual-in-line package with the industry standard JEDEC approved pinout and is pinout compatible with the industry standard 16K EPROM/ROM.

● Single +5 V Supply
● 2048 Words by 8-Bit Operation
● HCMOS Technology
● Fully Static: No Clock or Timing Strobe Required
● Maximum Access Time: MCM6116-12 — 120 ns
                           MCM6116-15 — 150 ns
                           MCM6116-20 — 200 ns
● Power Dissipation: 70 mA Maximum (Active)
                      15 mA Maximum (Standby-TTL Levels)
                      2 mA Maximum (Standby)
● Low Power Version Also Available — MCM61L16
● Low Voltage Data Retention (MCM61L16 Only):
  50 μA Maximum

HCMOS
(COMPLEMENTARY MOS)

**2,048×8 BIT
STATIC RANDOM
ACCESS MEMORY**

P SUFFIX
PLASTIC PACKAGE
CASE 709

PIN ASSIGNMENTS

```
        A7 [ 1  •      24 ] VCC
        A6 [ 2         23 ] A8
        A5 [ 3         22 ] A9
        A4 [ 4         21 ] W̄
        A3 [ 5         20 ] Ḡ
        A2 [ 6         19 ] A10
        A1 [ 7         18 ] Ē
        A0 [ 8         17 ] DQ7
       DQ0 [ 9         16 ] DQ6
       DQ1 [ 10        15 ] DQ5
       DQ2 [ 11        14 ] DQ4
       VSS [ 12        13 ] DQ3
```

PIN NAMES	
A0-A10	Address Input
DQ0-DQ7	Data Input/Output
$\overline{W}$	Write Enable
$\overline{G}$	Output Enable
$\overline{E}$	Chip Enable
VCC	Power (+5 V)
VSS	Ground

BLOCK DIAGRAM

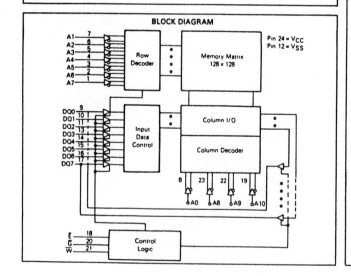

ABSOLUTE MAXIMUM RATINGS (See Note)

Rating	Value	Unit
Temperature Under Bias	− 10 to + 80	°C
Voltage on Any Pin With Respect to V_{SS}	− 1.0 to + 7.0	V
DC Output Current	20	mA
Power Dissipation	1.2	Watt
Operating Temperature Range	0 to + 70	°C
Storage Temperature Range	− 65 to + 150	°C

> This device contains circuitry to protect the inputs against damage due to high static voltages or electric fields; however, it is advised that normal precautions be taken to avoid application of any voltage higher than maximum rated voltages to this high-impedance circuit.

NOTE: Permanent device damage may occur if ABSOLUTE MAXIMUM RATINGS are exceeded. Functional operation should be restricted to RECOMMENDED OPERATING CONDITIONS. Exposure to higher than recommended voltages for extended periods of time could affect device reliability.

DC OPERATING CONDITIONS AND CHARACTERISTICS
(Full operating voltage and temperature ranges unless otherwise noted.)

RECOMMENDED OPERATING CONDITIONS

Parameter	Symbol	Min	Typ	Max	Unit
Supply Voltage	V_{CC}	4.5	5.0	5.5	V
	V_{SS}	0	0	0	V
Input Voltage	V_{IH}	2.2	3.5	6.0	V
	V_{IL}	− 1.0*	−	0.8	V

*The device will withstand undershoots to the − 1.0 volt level with a maximum pulse width of 50 ns at the − 0.3 volt level. This is periodically sampled rather than 100% tested.

RECOMMENDED OPERATING CHARACTERISTICS

Parameter	Symbol	MCM6116 Min	MCM6116 Typ*	MCM6116 Max	MCM61L16 Min	MCM61L16 Typ*	MCM61L16 Max	Unit
Input Leakage Current (V_{CC} = 5.5 V, V_{in} = GND to V_{CC})	$|I_{LI}|$	−	−	1	−	−	1	µA
Output Leakage Current (Ē = V_{IH} or Ḡ = V_{IH} $V_{I/O}$ = GND to V_{CC})	$|I_{LO}|$	−	−	1	−	−	1	µA
Operating Power Supply Current (Ē = V_{IL}, $I_{I/O}$ = 0 mA)	I_{CC}	−	35	70	−	35	55	mA
Average Operating Current Minimum cycle, duty = 100%	I_{CC2}	−	35	70	−	35	55	mA
Standby Power (Ē = V_{IH})	I_{SB}	−	5	15	−	5	12	µA
Supply Current (Ē ≥ V_{CC} − 0.2 V, V_{in} ≥ V_{CC} − 0.2 V or V_{in} ≤ 0.2 V)	I_{SB1}	−	20	2000	−	4	100	µA
Output Low Voltage (I_{OL} = 2.1 mA)	V_{OL}	−	−	0.4	−	−	0.4	V
Output High Voltage (I_{OH} = − 1.0 mA)**	V_{OH}	2.4	−	−	2.4	−	−	V

*V_{CC} = 5 V, T_A = 25°C
**Also, output voltages are compatible with Motorola's new high-speed CMOS logic family if the same power supply voltage is used.

CAPACITANCE (f = 1.0 MHz, T_A = 25°C, periodically sampled rather than 100% tested.)

Characteristic	Symbol	Typ	Max	Unit
Input Capacitance except Ē	C_{in}	3	5	pF
Input/Output Capacitance and Ē Input Capacitance	$C_{I/O}$	5	7	pF

MODE SELECTION

Mode	Ē	Ḡ	W̄	V_{CC} Current	DQ
Standby	H	X	X	I_{SB}, I_{SB1}	High Z
Read	L	L	H	I_{CC}	Q
Write Cycle (1)	L	H	L	I_{CC}	D
Write Cycle (2)	L	L	L	I_{CC}	D

AC OPERATING CONDITIONS AND CHARACTERISTICS
(Full operating voltage and temperature unless otherwise noted.)

Input Pulse Levels .... 0 Volt to 3.5 Volts   Input and Output Timing Reference Levels .... 1.5 Volts

Input Rise and Fall Times .... 10 ns   Output Load .... 1 TTL Gate and $C_L = 100$ pF

READ CYCLE

Parameter	Symbol	MCM6116-12 MCM61L16-12		MCM6116-15 MCM61L16-15		MCM6116-20 MCM61L16-20		Unit
		Min	Max	Min	Max	Min	Max	
Address Valid to Address Don't Care (Cycle Time when Chip Enable is Held Active)	t_{AVAX}	120	—	150	—	200	—	ns
Chip Enable Low to Chip Enable High	t_{ELEH}	120	—	150	—	200	—	ns
Address Valid to Output Valid (Access)	t_{AVQV}	—	120	—	150	—	200	ns
Chip Enable Low to Output Valid (Access)	t_{ELQV}	—	120	—	150	—	200	ns
Address Valid to Output Invalid	t_{AVQX}	10	—	15	—	15	—	ns
Chip Enable Low to Output Invalid	t_{ELQX}	10	—	15	—	15	—	ns
Chip Enable High to Output High Z	t_{EHQZ}	0	40	0	50	0	60	ns
Output Enable to Output Valid	t_{GLQV}	—	80	—	100	—	120	ns
Output Enable to Output Invalid	t_{GLQX}	10	—	15	—	15	—	ns
Output Enable to Output High Z	t_{GLQZ}	0	40	0	50	0	60	ns
Address Invalid to Output Invalid	t_{AXQX}	10	—	15	—	15	—	ns
Address Valid to Chip Enable Low (Address Setup)	t_{AVEL}	0	—	0	—	0	—	ns
Chip Enable to Power-Up Time	t_{PU}	0	—	0	—	0	—	ns
Chip Disable to Power-Down Time	t_{PD}	—	30	—	30	—	30	ns

WRITE CYCLE

Parameter	Symbol	MCM6116-12 MCM61L16-12		MCM6116-15 MCM61L16-15		MCM6116-20 MCM61L16-20		Unit
		Min	Max	Min	Max	Min	Max	
Chip Enable Low to Write High	t_{ELWH}	70	—	90	—	120	—	ns
Address Valid to Write High	t_{AVWH}	105	—	120	—	140	—	ns
Address Valid to Write Low (Address Setup)	t_{AVWL}	20	—	20	—	20	—	ns
Write Low to Write High (Write Pulse Width)	t_{WLWH}	70	—	90	—	120	—	ns
Write High to Address Don't Care	t_{WHAX}	5	—	10	—	10	—	ns
Data Valid to Write High	t_{DVWH}	35	—	40	—	60	—	ns
Write High to Data Don't Care (Data Hold)	t_{WHDX}	5	—	10	—	10	—	ns
Write Low to Output High Z	t_{WLQZ}	0	50	0	60	0	60	ns
Write High to Output Valid	t_{WHQV}	5	—	10	—	10	—	ns
Output Disable to Output High Z	t_{GHQZ}	0	40	0	50	0	60	ns

TIMING PARAMETER ABBREVIATIONS

```
                            t X X X X
signal name from which interval is defined ┘ │ │ │
        transition direction for first signal ┘ │ │
    signal name to which interval is defined ────┘ │
        transition direction for second signal ────┘
```

The transition definitions used in this data sheet are:

H = transition to high
L = transition to low
V = transition to valid
X = transition to invalid or don't care
Z = transition to off (high impedance)

TIMING LIMITS

The table of timing values shows either a minimum or a maximum limit for each parameter. Input requirements are specified from the external system point of view. Thus, address setup time is shown as a minimum since the system must supply at least that much time (even though most devices do not require it). On the other hand, responses from the memory are specified from the device point of view. Thus, the access time is shown as a maximum since the device never provides data later than that time.

8086 Instruction Set — Details

TABLE I–1
8086 Data Transfer Instructions

			Addressing Mode		Illustration	
Operation	Instructions	Interpretation	Source	Destination	Example	Comments
Move	MOV mem/reg 2, mem/reg 1	[mem/reg 2] ← [mem/reg 1]	Memory or Register	Memory or Register	MOV BX, CX	Mem uses DS as segment register; no memory-to-memory operation allowed; i.e., MOV mem, mem not permitted; segment register cannot be specified as reg 1 or reg 2; no flags affected
	MOV mem, data	[mem] ← data	Immediate	Memory	MOV [D1], 3476H	Mem uses DS as segment register; 8- or 16-bit data specify whether memory location is 8- or 16-bit; no flags affected
	MOV reg, data	[reg] ← data	Immediate	Register	MOV S1, 0F125H	Segment register cannot be specified as reg; data can be 8- or 16-bit; no flags affected
	MOV segreg, mem/reg	[segreg] ← [mem/reg]	Memory or Register	Register	MOV DS, CX	Mem uses DS as segment register; used for initializing CS, DS, ES, SS; no flags affected
	MOV mem/reg, segreg	[mem/reg] ← [segreg]	Register	Memory or Register	MOV CX, DS	Mem uses DS as segment register; no flags affected
Push	PUSH mem	[SP] ← [SP] − 2 [[SP]] ← [mem]	Memory	—	PUSH [BX]	Mem uses DS as segment register; no flags affected; PUSH as 16-bit memory contents
	PUSH reg	[SP] ← [SP] − 2 [SP] ← [reg]	Register	—	PUSH DX	Reg must be a 16-bit register; cannot be used to PUSH segment register or flag register
	PUSH segreg	[SP] ← [SP] − 2 [[SP]] ← [segreg]	Register	—	PUSH ES	PUSH CS is illegal
Pop	POP mem	[mem] ← [[SP]] [SP] ← [SP] + 2	Memory	—	POP [DI]	Mem uses DS as segment register; no flags affected
	POP reg	[reg] ← [[SP]] [SP] ← [SP] + 2	Register	—	POP CX	Cannot be used to POP segment registers or flag register

Reprinted by permission of Intel Corp.

Continued.

TABLE I–1
8086 Data Transfer Instructions *(cont.)*

| Operation | Instructions | Interpretation | Addressing Mode | | Illustration | |
			Source	Destination	Example	Comments
	POP segreg	[segreg] ← [[SP]] [SP] ← [SP] + 2	Register	—	POP DS	POP CS is illegal
Escape	ESC		—	—	ESC	When 8086 encounters an ESC, it usually treats this as an NOP; coprocessor decodes instruction and carries out operation using 6-bit OP code independent of the 8086; for ESC OP code, memory, 8086 accesses data in memory for coprocessor; for ESC data, register, coprocessor operates on 8086 register
Lock	LOCK	Lock bus during next instruction	—	—	LOCK	1-byte prefix causes 8086 (in maximum mode) to assert its bus LOCK signal while following instruction is executed; signal is used in multiprocessing; LOCK pin of 8086 can be used to lock other processors off system bus during execution of an instruction; thus 8086 can be assured of uninterrupted access to common system resources such as shared RAM
Exchange	XCHG mem, reg	[mem] ↔ [reg]	Register	Memory	XCHG [BX], DX	Reg and mem can be both 8- or 16-bit; mem uses DS as segment register; reg cannot be segment register; no flags affected
	XCHG reg, reg	[reg] ↔ [reg]	Register	Register	XCHG CL, DL	Reg can be 8- or 16-bit; reg cannot be segment register; no flags affected
Translate table	XLAT	[AL] ← [[AL] + BX]]	—	—	XLAT	Instruction is useful for translating characters from one code such as ASCII to another such as EBCDIC; a no-operand instruction; called an instruction with implied addressing mode; loads AL with contents of a 20-bit physical address computed from DS, BX, and AL; can be used to read elements in a table where BX can be loaded with a 16-bit value to point to starting address (offset from DS) and AL can be loaded with element number (0 being first element number); no flags affected; XLAT is equivalent to MOV AL, [AL] [BX]

TABLE I–2
8086 I/O Instructions

Operation	Instructions	Interpretation	Addressing Mode		Illustration	
			Source	Destination	Example	Comments
I/O	IN AL, DX	[AL] ← [PORT DX]	Register indirect (port)	Register (AL only)	IN AL, DX	Input AL with 8-bit contents of port addressed by DX; 1-byte instruction
	IN AX, DX	[AX] ← [PORT DX]	Register indirect (port)	Register (AX only)	IN AX, DX	Input AX with 16-bit contents of port addressed by DX and DX + 1; 1-byte instruction
	IN AL, PORT	[AL] ← [PORT]	Register (port)	Register (AL only)	IN AL, PORT A	Input AL with 8-bit contents of port addressed by second byte of instruction
	IN AX, PORT	[AX] ← [PORT]	Register (port)	Register (AX only)	IN AX, PORT	Input AX with 16-bit contents of port addressed by 8-bit address in second byte of instruction
	OUT DX, AL	[PORT DX] ← [AL]	Register (AL only)	Register indirect (port)	OUT DX, AL	Output 8-bit contents of AL into an I/O port addressed by contents of DX
	OUT DX, AX	[PORT DX] ← [AX]	Register (AX only)	Register indirect (port)	OUT DX, AX	Output 16-bit contents of AX into an I/O port addressed by DX
	OUT PORT, AL	[PORT] ← [AL]	Register (AL only)	Register indirect (port)	OUT PORT, AL	Output 8-bit contents of AL into port specified in second byte of instruction
	OUT PORT, AX	[PORT] ← [AX]	Register (AX only)	Register (port)	OUT PORT, AX	Output 16-bit contents of AX into port specified in second byte of instruction

TABLE I–3
8086 Address Object Transfers*

Operation	Instructions	Interpretation	Addressing Mode		Illustration	
			Source	Destination	Example	Comments
Load EA	LEA reg, offset	[reg] ← offset portion of address in DS	Memory	Register	LEA SI, ADDR (value ADDR is loaded into SI, which can then be used as offset for memory in DS) LEA DI, ADDR + 5 (loads value ADDR + 5 into DI)	LEA (load effective address) loads value in source operand rather than its contents to register (such as SI, DI, BX), which is allowed to contain offset for accessing memory; no flags affected; useful if address computation is required during program execution
Load pointer using DS	LDS reg, mem	[reg] ← [mem] [DS] ← [mem + 2]	Memory	Register	LDS BX, BEGIN	Load a 16-bit register (such as BX, BP, SI, DI) with contents of specified memory and load DS with

*Address object transfers provide programmer with some control over the addressing mechanism.

Continued.

TABLE I-3
8086 Address Object Transfers* *(cont.)*

Operation	Instructions	Interpretation	Addressing Mode		Illustration	
			Source	Destination	Example	Comments
						contents of location that follows; no flags affected; DS used as segment register for mem
Load pointer using ES	LES reg, mem	[reg] ← [mem] [ES] ← [mem + 2]	Memory	Register	LES SI, [BX]	DS used as segment register for mem; in the example, SI is loaded with 16-bit value from memory location addressed by 20-bit physical address computed from DS and BX; 16-bit contents of next memory are loaded into ES; no flags affected

TABLE I-4
8086 Flag Register Instructions

Operation	Instructions	Interpretation	Addressing Mode		Illustration	
			Source	Destination	Example	Comments
Load AH from flags	LAHF	[AH] ← [flags, low byte]	—	—	LAHF	Instruction has implied addressing mode; loads AH with low byte of flag register; no flags affected
Store AH in flags	SAHF	[flags, low byte] ← [AH]	—	—	SAHF	Instruction has implied addressing mode; contents of AH are stored into low byte of flag register; all flags affected (low byte of SR)
Push flags into stack	PUSHF	[SP] ← [SP] − 2 [[SP]] ← [flags]	—	—	PUSHF	Instruction pushes 16-bit flag register onto stack; no flags affected
Pop flags off stack	POPF	[flags] ← [[SP]] [SP] ← [SP] + 2	—	—	POPF	Instruction pops top two stack bytes in 16-bit flag register; all flags affected (low byte of SR)

TABLE I–5
8086 Arithmetic Instructions

Operation	Instructions	Interpretation	Addressing Mode		Illustration	
			Source	Destination	Example	Comments
Add	ADD mem/reg 2, mem/reg 1	[mem/reg 2] ← [mem/reg 2] + [mem/reg 1]	Memory *or* Register	Memory *or* Register	ADD BL, [SI]	Add two 8- or 16-bit data; no memory-to-memory ADD permitted; all flags affected; mem uses DS as segment register; reg 1 or reg 2 cannot be segment register
	ADD mem, data	[mem] ← [mem] + data	Immediate	Memory	ADD START, 02H	Mem uses DS as segment register; data can be 8- or 16-bit; all flags affected
	ADD reg, data	[reg] ← [reg] + data	Immediate	Register	ADD BX, 0354H	Data can be 8- or 16-bit; no segment registers allowed; all flags affected
Add with carry	ADC mem/reg 2, [mem/reg 1]	[mem/reg 2] ← [mem/reg 2] + [mem/reg 1] + CY	Memory *or* Register	Memory *or* Register	ADC [SI], BL	Mem or reg can be 8- or 16-bit; all flags affected; no segment registers allowed; no memory-to-memory ADC permitted
	ADC mem, data	[mem] ← [mem] + data + CY	Immediate	Memory	ADC [BX], 05H	Data can be 8- or 16-bit; mem uses DS as segment register; all flags affected
	ADC reg, data	[reg] ← [reg] + data + CY	Immediate	Register	ADC SI, 05FIH	Data can be 8- or 16-bit; reg cannot be segment register; all flags affected
Increment	INC reg16	[reg16] ← [reg16] + 1	—	Register	INC BX	1-byte instruction used to increment a 16-bit register except segment register; does not affect carry flag
	INC mem/ reg8	[mem] ← [mem] + 1 *or* [reg8] ← [reg8] + 1	Memory *or* Register	— —	INC BYTE PTR ADDR (BYTE PTR is an assembler directive to indicate that ADDR is a byte address)	2-byte instruction used to increment a byte or word in memory *or* an 8-bit register content; segment register cannot be incremented; does not affect carry flag
ASCII adjust after addition	AAA	ASCII adjust [AL] after addition	—	—	AAA	Instruction has implied addressing mode; is used to adjust [AL] after addition of two ASCII characters; adjust means convert re-

Continued.

TABLE I-5
8086 Arithmetic Instructions *(cont.)*

| Operation | Instructions | Interpretation | Addressing Mode | | Illustration | |
			Source	Destination	Example	Comments
						sults to correct binary number
Decimal adjust after addition	DAA	Decimal adjust [AL] after addition	—	—	DAA	Instruction uses implied addressing mode; converts [AL] into BCD; should be used after BCD addition
Subtraction	SUB mem/reg 1, mem/reg 2	[mem/reg 1] ← [mem/reg 1] − [mem/reg 2]	Memory *or* Register	Memory *or* Register	SUB CX, DX *or* SUB BH, BH	No memory-to-memory SUB permitted; all flags affected; mem uses DS as segment register
	SUB mem, data	[mem] ← [mem] − data	Immediate	Memory	SUB ADDR, 02H	Data can be 8- or 16-bit; mem used DS as segment register; all flags affected
	SUB reg, data	[reg] ← [reg] − data	Immediate	Memory	SUB CL, 03H	Data can be 8- or 16-bit; all flags affected
Subtraction with borrow	SBB mem/reg 1, mem/reg 2	[mem/reg 1] ← [mem/reg 1] − [mem/reg 2] − CY	Memory *or* Register	Memory *or* Register	SBB BX, CX	Same as SUB mem/reg 1, mem/reg 2 except this is a subtraction with borrow
	SBB mem, data	[mem] ← [mem] − data − CY	Immediate	Memory	SBB ADDR, 05H	Same as SUB mem, data except this is a subtraction with borrow
	SBB reg, data	[reg] ← [reg] − data − CY	Immediate	Register	SBB BX, 0302H	Same as SUB reg, data except this is a subtraction with borrow
Decrement	DEC reg16	[reg16] ← [reg16] − 1	—	Register	DEC CX	1-byte instruction used to decrement a 16-bit register except segment register; does not affect carry flag
	DEC mem/ reg8	[mem] ← [mem] − 1 *or* [reg8] ← [reg8] − 1	—	Memory *or* Register	DEC BYTE PTR ADDR *or* DEC BL	Used to decrement a byte or word in memory *or* an 8-bit register content; segment register cannot be decremented; does not affect carry flag
ASCII adjust after subtraction	AAS	ASCII adjust [AL] after subtraction	—	—	AAS	Instruction has implied addressing mode; is used to adjust [AL] after subtraction of two ASCII characters

TABLE I–5
8086 Arithmetic Instructions (cont.)

| Operation | Instructions | Interpretation | Addressing Mode | | Illustration | |
			Source	Destination	Example	Comments
Decimal adjust after subtraction	DAS	Decimal adjust [AL] after subtraction	—	—	DAS	Instruction uses implied addressing mode; converts [AL] into BCD; should be used after BCD subtraction
Negation	NEG mem/reg	[mem/reg] ← [mem/reg]' + 1	—	Memory or Register	NEG BL or NEG BYTE PTR ADDR	Mem/reg can be 8- or 16-bit; performs 2's complement subtraction of specified operand from zero; i.e., 2's complement of a number is formed; all flags affected except CF = 0 if [mem/reg] is zero; otherwise CF = 1
Compare	CMP mem/reg 1, mem/reg 2	[mem/reg 1] − [mem/reg 2] → flags affected, no result	Memory or Register	Memory or Register	CMP BH, CL	Mem/reg can be 8- or 16-bit; no memory comparison allowed; result of subtraction not provided; all flags affected
	CMP mem/reg, data	[mem/reg] − data → flags affected, no result	Immediate	Memory or Register	CMP ADDR, 0561H or CMP BL, 02H	Subtract 8- or 16-bit data from [mem/reg] and affect flags; no result provided
Multiplication (unsigned)	MUL mem/reg	8 × 8: [AX] ← [AL]* [mem8/reg8] 16 × 16: [DX] [AX] ← [AX]* [mem16/reg16]	Memory or Register	—	MUL BH or MUL WORD PTR [BX]	Mem/reg can be 8- or 16-bit; only CF and OF affected; unsigned multiplication
Multiplication (signed)	IMUL mem/reg	8 × 8: [AX] ← [AL]* [mem8/reg8] 16 × 16: [DX] [AX] ← [AX]* [mem16/reg16]	Memory or Register	—	IMUL CL or IMUL BYTE PTR START	Mem/reg can be 8- or 16-bit; only CF and OF affected; signed multiplication
ASCII adjust after multiplication	AAM	ASCII adjust after multiplication	—	—	AAM	Instruction has implied addressing mode; after multiplying two unpacked BCD numbers, adjust product in AX to become an unpacked BCD result; ZF, SF, and PF affected

Continued.

TABLE I–5
8086 Arithmetic Instructions *(cont.)*

Operation	Instructions	Interpretation	Addressing Mode		Illustration	
			Source	Destination	Example	Comments
Division (unsigned)	DIV mem/reg	$16 \div 8$: $$\frac{[AX]}{[mem8/reg8]} \rightarrow$$ [AH] ← remainder [AL] ← quotient $32 \div 16$: $$\frac{[DX] \quad [AX]}{[mem16/reg16]} \rightarrow$$ [DX] ← remainder [AX] ← quotient	Memory *or* Register	—	DIV BL *or* DIV WORD PTR ADDR	Mem/reg is 8-bit for 16-bit by 8-bit division and 16-bit for 32-bit by 16-bit division; unsigned division; no flags affected; division by zero automatically generates internal interrupt
Division (signed)	IDIV mem/reg	Same as DIV mem/reg	Memory *or* Register	—	IDIV BL *or* IDIV WORD PTR ADDR	Same as DIV mem/reg except signed division
ASCII adjust for division	AAD	ASCII adjust for division	—	—	AAD	Instruction has implied addressing mode; converts two unpacked BCD digits in AX into equivalent binary number in AL; must be used before dividing two unpacked BCD digits by an unpacked BCD byte
Sign extension	CBW	Convert a byte to a word	—	—	CBW	Extend sign bit (bit 7) of AL into AH
	CWD	Convert a word to a double word (32-bit)	—	—	CWD	Extend sign bit (bit 15) of AX into DX

TABLE I–6
8086 Logical Instructions

Operation	Instructions	Interpretation	Addressing Mode		Illustration	
			Source	Destination	Example	Comments
AND	AND mem/reg 1, mem/reg 2	[mem/reg 1] ← [mem/reg 1] ∧ [mem/reg 2]	Memory *or* Register	Memory *or* Register	AND BL, CH	Instruction logically ANDs 8- or 16-bit data in [mem/reg 1] with 8- or 16-bit in [mem/reg 2]; all flags affected; OF and CF cleared to zero; no segment registers allowed; no memory-to-memory operation allowed; mem uses DS as segment register

TABLE I–6
8086 Logical Instructions *(cont.)*

Operation	Instructions	Interpretation	Addressing Mode		Illustration	
			Source	*Destination*	*Example*	*Comments*
	AND mem, data	[mem] ← [mem] ∧ data	Immediate	Memory	AND START, 02H	Data can be 8- or 16-bit; mem uses DS as segment register; all flags affected with OF and CF cleared to zero
	AND reg, data	[reg] ← [reg] ∧ data	Immediate	Register	AND CX, 027IH	Data can be 8- or 16-bit; reg cannot be segment register; all flags affected with OF and CF cleared to zero
NOT (1's complement)	NOT reg	[reg] ← [reg]′	—	Register	NOT BX	Finds 1's complement of a register; mem and reg can be 8- or 16-bit; segment registers not allowed; no flags affected
	NOT mem	[mem] ← [mem]′	—	Memory	NOT [SI]	Mem uses DS as segment register; no flags affected
OR	OR mem/reg 1, mem/reg 2	[mem/reg 1] ← [mem/reg 1] [mem/reg 2] ∨	Memory *or* Register	Memory *or* Register	OR BX, CX	No memory-to-memory operation allowed; [mem] or [reg 1] or [reg 2] can be 8- or 16-bit; all flags affected with OF and CF cleared to zero; no segment registers allowed; mem uses DS as segment register
	OR mem, data	[mem] ← [mem] ∨ data	Immediate	Memory	OR [DI], 02H	Mem and data can be 8- or 16-bit; mem uses DS as segment register; all flags affected with OF and CF cleared to zero
	OR reg, data	[reg] ← [reg] ∨ data	Immediate	Register	OR BL, 03H	Reg and data can be 8- or 16-bit; no segment registers allowed; all flags affected with OF and CF cleared to zero
Test	TEST mem/reg 1, mem/reg 2	[mem/reg 1] ∧ [mem/reg 2] → no result, flags affected	Memory *or* Register	Memory *or* Register	TEST CL, BL	No memory-to-memory TEST allowed; no result provided; all flags affected with CF and OF cleared to

Continued.

TABLE I–6
8086 Logical Instructions *(cont.)*

| Operation | Instructions | Interpretation | Addressing Mode | | Illustration | |
			Source	Destination	Example	Comments
						zero; [mem], [reg 1] or [reg 2] can be 8- or 16-bit; no segment registers allowed; mem uses DS as segment register
	TEST mem, data	[mem] ∧ data → no result, flags affected	Immediate	Memory	TEST START, 02H	Mem and data can be 8- or 16-bit; no result provided; all flags affected with CF and OF cleared to zero; mem uses DS as segment register
	TEST reg, data	[reg] ∧ data → no result, flags affected	Immediate	Register	TEST CL, 02H	Reg and data can be 8- or 16-bit; no result provided; all flags affected with CF and OF cleared to zero; reg cannot be segment register
XOR	XOR mem/reg 1, mem/reg 2	[mem/reg 1] ← [mem/reg 1] ⊕ [mem/reg 2]	Memory or Register	Memory or Register	XOR BL, CL	No memory-to-memory operation allowed; [mem] or [reg 1] or [reg 2] can be 8- or 16-bit; all flags affected with CF and OF cleared to zero; mem uses DS as segment register
	XOR mem, data	[mem] ← [mem] ⊕ data	Immediate	Memory	XOR [BX], 2	Data and mem can be 8- or 16-bit; mem uses DS as segment register; mem cannot be segment register; all flags affected with CF and OF cleared to zero
	XOR reg, data	[reg] ← [reg] ⊕ data	Immediate	Register	XOR BL, 03H	Reg or mem can be 8- or 16-bit; mem uses DS as segment register; all flags affected with CF and OF cleared to zero
Shift and Rotate	SAL mem/ reg, 1	Shift arithmetic left once byte or word in mem/reg	Immediate	Memory or Register	SAL BYTE PTR START, 1 or SAL BL, 1	FOR BYTE:

TABLE I–6
8086 Logical Instructions (cont.)

Operation	Instructions	Interpretation	Addressing Mode		Illustration	
			Source	Destination	Example	Comments
					FOR WORD:	Mem uses DS as segment register; reg cannot be segment register; OF and CF affected; if sign bit is changed during or after shifting, OF is set to 1
	SAL mem/ reg, CL	Shift arithmetic left byte or word by shift count on CL	Register	Memory or Register	SAL BYTE PTR [SI], CL or SAL BX, CL	Operation same as SAL mem/reg, 1; CL contains shift count up to 255; zero and negative shifts illegal; [CL] used as shift count when shift is greater than 1; OF and SF affected; if sign bit of [mem] is changed during or after shifting, OF is set to 1; mem uses DS as segment register
	SHL mem/ reg, 1	Shift logical left once byte or word in mem/reg	Immediate	Memory or Register	SHL BL, 1	Same as SAL mem/reg, 1
	SHL mem/ reg, CL	Shift logical left byte or word in mem/reg by shift count in CL	Register	Memory or Register	SHL BYTE PTR [SI], CL	Same as SAL mem/reg, CL except OF is cleared to zero
	SAR mem/ reg, 1	Shift arithmetic right once byte or word in mem/reg	Immediate	Memory or Register	SAR AX, 1	FOR BYTE FOR WORD
	SAR mem/ reg, CL	Shift arithmetic right byte or word in mem/reg by [CL]	Register	Memory or Register	SAR DX, CL	Operation same as SAR mem/reg, 1; but shift count is specified in CL for shifts up to 255_{10}; zero and negative shifts illegal

Continued.

TABLE I–6
8086 Logical Instructions *(cont.)*

Operation	Instructions	Interpretation	Addressing Mode		Illustration	
			Source	*Destination*	*Example*	*Comments*
	SHR mem/reg, 1	Shift logical right once byte or word in mem/reg	Immediate	Memory *or* Register	SHR BX, 1	FOR BYTE / FOR WORD
	SHR mem/reg, CL	Shift logical right byte or word in mem/reg by [CL]	Register	Memory *or* Register	SHR BX, CL	Operation same as SHR mem/reg, 1; but shift count is specified in CL for shifts up to 255_{10}; zero and negative shifts illegal
	ROL mem/reg, 1	Rotate left once byte or word in mem/reg	Immediate	Memory *or* Register	ROL BX, 1	FOR BYTE / FOR WORD
	ROL mem/reg, CL	Rotate left byte or word by contents of CL	Register	Memory *or* Register	ROL DX, CL	[CL] contains rotate count up to 255_{10}; zero and negative shifts illegal; CL used as rotate count when rotate is greater than 1; mem uses DS as segment register
	ROR mem/reg, 1	Rotate right once byte or word in mem/reg	Immediate	Memory *or* Register	ROR AX, 1	FOR BYTE / FOR WORD
	ROR mem/reg, CL	Rotate right byte or word in mem/reg by [CL]	Register	Memory *or* Register	ROR AX, CL	Operation same as ROR mem/reg, 1; [CL] specifies number of rotates up to 255_{10}; zero and negative rotates illegal; mem uses DS as segment register

TABLE I–6
8086 Logical Instructions (cont.)

Operation	Instructions	Interpretation	Addressing Mode		Illustration	
			Source	Destination	Example	Comments
	RCL mem/reg, 1	Rotate through carry left once byte or word in mem/reg	Immediate	Register	RCL BX, 1	FOR BYTE FOR WORD
	RCL mem/reg, CL	Rotate through carry left byte or word in mem/reg by [CL]	Register	Memory or Register	RCL DX, CL	Operation same as RCL mem/reg, 1 except number of rotates is specified in CL for rotates up to 255_{10}; zero and negative rotates illegal
	RCR mem/reg, 1	Rotate through carry right once byte or word in mem/reg	Immediate	Memory or Register	RCR AX, 1	FOR BYTE FOR WORD
	RCR mem/reg, CL	Rotate through carry right byte or word in mem/reg by [CL]	Register	Memory or Register	RCR DX, CL	Operation same as RCR mem/reg, 1 except number of rotates is specified in CL for rotates up to 255_{10}; zero and negative rotates illegal

TABLE I–7
8086 String Instructions

Operation	Instructions	Interpretation	Addressing Mode		Illustration	
			Source	Destination	Example	Comments
Load string	LODS BYTE or LODSB	For byte [AL] ← [[SI]] [SI ← [SI] ± 1	Byte or Word	—	LODS BYTE or LODSB	Load 8-bit data into AL or 16-bit data into AX from memory location addressed by SI in segment DS; if DF = 0, then SI is incremented by 1 for byte or 2 for word after the load; if DF = 1, then SI is
	LODS WORD or LODSW	FOR WORD [AX] ← [[SI]] [SI] ← [SI] ± 2			LODS WORD or LODSW	

Continued.

TABLE I–7
8086 String Instructions *(cont.)*

Operation	Instructions	Interpretation	Addressing Mode		Illustration	
			Source	Destination	Example	Comments
						decremented by 1 for byte or 2 for word; no flags affected
Move string	MOVS BYTE *or* MOVSB	For byte [[DI]] ← [[SI]] [SI ← [SI] ± 1 [DI] ← [DI] ± 1	Byte *or* Word	—	MOVS BYTE *or* MOVSB	Move 8- or 16-bit data from memory location addressed by SI in segment DS location addressed by DI in ES; segment DS can be overridden by a prefix but destination segment must be ES and cannot be overridden; if DF = 0, then SI and DI are incremented by 1 for byte or 2 for word; if DF = 1, then SI and DI are decremented by 1 for byte or 2 for word
	MOVS WORD *or* MOVSW	For word [[DI]] ← [[SI]] [SI] ← [SI] ± 2 [DI] ← [DI] ± 2			MOVS WORD *or* MOVSW	
Store string	STOS BYTE *or* STOSB	For byte [[DI]] ← [AL] [DI] ← [DI] ± 1	Byte *or* Word	—	STOS BYTE *or* STOSB	Store 8-bit data from AL or 16-bit data from AX into memory location addressed by DI in segment ES; segment ES cannot be overridden; if DF = 0, then DI is incremented by 1 for byte or 2 for word after the store; if DF = 1, then DI is decremented by 1 for byte or 2 for word; no flags affected
	STOS WORD *or* STOSW	For word [[DI]] ← [AX] [DI] ← [DI] ± 2			STOS WORD *or* STOSW	
Compare string	CMPS BYTE *or* CMPSB	For byte [[SI]] − [[DI]] → flags affected [SI] ← [SI] ± 1 [DI] ← [DI] ± 1	Byte *or* Word	—	CMPS BYTE *or* CMPSB	8- or 16-bit data addressed by [DI] in ES is subtracted from 8- or 16-bit data addressed by SI in DS; flags affected without providing any result; if DF = 0, then SI and DI are incremented by 1 for byte or 2 for word after the compare; if DF = 1, then SI and DI are decremented by 1 for byte or 2 for word; segment ES in destination cannot be overridden
	CMPS WORD *or* CMPSW	For word [[SI]] − [[DI]] → flags affected [SI] ← [SI] ± 2 [DI] ← [DI] ← ± 2			CMPS WORD *or* CMPSW	
Compare memory with AL or AX	SCAS BYTE *or* SCASB	For byte [AL] − [[DI]] → flags affected [DI] ← [DI] ± 1	Byte *or* Word	—	SCAS BYTE *or* SCASB	8- or 16-bit data addressed by [DI] in ES is subtracted from 8- or 16-bit data in AL or

TABLE I-7
8086 String Instructions (cont.)

| Operation | Instructions | Interpretation | Addressing Mode | | Illustration | |
			Source	Destination	Example	Comments
	SCAS WORD *or* SCASW	For word $[AX] - [[DI]]$ → flags affected $[DI] \leftarrow [DI] \pm 2$			SCAS WORD *or* SCASW	AX; flags affected without affecting [AL] or [AX] or string data; ES cannot be overridden; if DF = 0, then DI is incremented by 1 for byte or 2 for word; if DF = 1, then DI is decremented by 1 for byte or 2 for word

TABLE I-8
8086 Unconditional Transfers

| Operation | Instructions | Interpretation | Addressing Mode | | Illustration | |
			Source	Destination	Example	Comments
Call subroutine (intrasegment direct)	CALL PROC (NEAR)	Call a subroutine in same segment with signed 16-bit displacement (to call a subroutine in ±32K)	Relative	—	A subroutine can be declared as NEAR by using an assembler directive; subroutine can then be called in same segment by using CALL	NEAR in statement BEGIN PROC NEAR indicates subroutine "BEGIN" is in same segment and BEGIN is 16-bit signed; CALL BEGIN instruction decrements SP by 2, pushes IP onto stack, then adds signed 16-bit value of BEGIN to IP; CS is unchanged; thus a subroutine is called in same segment (intrasegment direct)
Call subroutine (intrasegment indirect)	CALL reg16	Call a subroutine in same segment addressed by contents of a 16-bit general register	Register	—	CALL BX	8086 decrements SP by 2 and pushes IP onto stack; then specified 16-bit register contents (such as BX, SI, DI) provide new value for IP; CS is unchanged (intrasegment indirect)
Call subroutine (intrasegment indirect)	CALL mem16	Call a subroutine addressed by contents of a memory location pointed to by 8086 16-bit register such as BX, SI, DI	Memory indirect	—	CALL [BX]	8086 decrements SP by 2 and pushes IP onto stack; 8086 then loads contents of a memory location addressed by contents of a 16-bit register such as BX, SI, DI into IP; [CS] is unchanged (intrasegment indirect)
Call subroutine (intersegment direct)	CALL PROC (FAR)	Call a subroutine in another segment	Memory	—	A subroutine can be declared as FAR by using	FAR in statement BEGIN PROC FAR indicates subroutine "BE-

Continued.

TABLE I–8
8086 Unconditional Transfers *(cont.)*

Operation	Instructions	Interpretation	Addressing Mode		Illustration	
			Source	Destination	Example	Comments
					statement BE-GIN PROC FAR; subroutine BEGIN can be called from another segment by using CALL BEGIN	GIN" is in another segment and value of BEGIN is 32 bits wide; 8086 decrements SP by 2, pushes CS onto stack, and moves low 16-bit value of specified 32-bit number such as "BEGIN" in CALL BEGIN into CS; SP is again decremented by 2; IP is pushed onto stack; IP is then loaded with high 16-bit value of BEGIN; thus subroutine is called in another code segment (intersegment direct)
Call a subroutine in another segment (intersegment indirect)	CALL DWORD PTR [reg16]	Call a subroutine in another segment	Memory indirect	—	Call DWORD PTR [BX] loads into IP contents of memory locations addressed by [BX] and [BX + 1] in DS; it then loads into CS contents of memory locations addressed by [BX + 2] and [BX + 3] in DS	Instruction decrements SP by 2 and pushes CS onto stack; CS is then loaded with contents of memory locations addressed by [reg16 + 2] and [reg16 + 3] in DS; SP is again decremented by 2; IP is pushed onto stack; IP is then loaded with contents of memory locations addressed by [reg16] and [reg16 + 1] in DS; typical 8086 registers used for reg16 are BX, SI, DI (intrersegment indirect)
Return	RET	• POPs IP for intrasegment CALLs • POPs IP and CS for intersegment CALLs	—	—	RET	Assembler generates intrasegment return if programmer has defined subroutine as NEAR; for intrasegment return, following operations take place: [IP] ← [[SP]], [SP] ← [SP] + 2; on the other hand, assembler generates intersegment return if subroutine has been defined as FAR; in this case, following operations take place:

TABLE I–8
8086 Unconditional Transfers (cont.)

Operation	Instructions	Interpretation	Addressing Mode		Illustration	
			Source	Destination	Example	Comments
Unconditional jump (intrasegment direct)	JMP label	Unconditional jump with a signed 8-bit (SHORT) or signed 16-bit (NEAR) displacement in same segment	Relative	—	JMP START	[IP] ← [[SP]], [SP] ← [SP] + 2, [CS] ← [[SP]], [SP] ← [SP] + 2; an optional 16-bit displacement "START" can be specified with intersegment return such as RET START; in this case, 16-bit displacement is added to SP value; this feature may be used to discard parameter pushed onto stack before execution of CALL instruction Label START can be signed 8-bit (called SHORT jump) or signed 16-bit (called NEAR jump) displacement; assembler usually determines displacement value; if assembler finds displacement value to be signed 8-bit (-128 to $+127$, 0 being positive), then it uses 2 bytes for instruction, 1 byte for OP code followed by a byte for displacement; assembler sign-extends 8-bit displacement and then adds it to IP; [CS] is unchanged; on the other hand, if assembler finds displacement to be signed 16-bit (±32K), then it uses 3 bytes for instruction, 1 byte for OP code followed by 2 bytes for displacement; assembler adds signed 16-bit displacement to IP; [CS] is unchanged; thus JMP provides jump in same segment (intrasegment direct jump)

Continued.

TABLE I–8
8086 Unconditional Transfers (cont.)

Operation	Instructions	Interpretation	Addressing Mode		Illustration	
			Source	Destination	Example	Comments
Unconditional jump (intra-segment register indirect)	JMP reg16	[IP] ← [reg16], [CS] is unchanged	Register indirect	—	JMP BX	Jump to address specified by contents of a 16-bit register such as BX, SI, DI in same code segment; in JMP BX, [BX] is loaded into IP and [CS] is unchanged (intrasegment register indirect jump)
Unconditional jump (intra-segment memory indirect)	JMP mem16	[IP] ← [mem], [CS] is unchanged	Memory indirect	—	JMP [BX]	Jump to address specified by contents of a 16-bit memory location addressed by 16-bit register such as BX, SI, DI; in JMP [BX], it copies contents of a memory location addressed by BX in DS into IP; CS is unchanged (intrasegment memory indirect jump)
Unconditional jump (inter-segment direct)	JMP label (FAR)	Unconditionally jump to another segment	Memory	—	A jump can be declared as FAR by using statement START PROC FAR; instruction JMP START can be used after this to jump to label START in another segment	5-byte instruction; first byte is OP code followed by 4 bytes of 32-bit immediate data; bytes 2 and 3 are loaded into IP; bytes 4 and 5 are loaded into CS to jump unconditionally to another segment (intersegment direct)
Unconditional jump to another segment (intersegment indirect)	JMP DWORD PTR [reg16]	Unconditionally jump to another segment	Memory	—	JMP DWORD PTR [BX] loads into IP contents of memory locations addressed by [BX] and [BX + 1] in DS; it then loads into CS contents of memory locations addressed by [BX + 2] and [BX + 3] in DS	Instruction loads contents of memory locations addressed by [reg16] and [reg16 + 1] in DS into IP; then loads contents of memory locations addressed by [reg16 + 2] and [reg16 + 3] in DS into CS; typical 8086 registers used for reg16 are BX, SI, DI (intersegment indirect)

TABLE I–9
8086 Conditional Branch Instructions

Operation	Instructions	Interpretation	Addressing Mode		Illustration	
			Source	Destination	Example	Comments
Conditional branch	JA/JNBE disp8	Jump if above/jump if not below original	Relative	—	JA/JNBE START	Jump if above/jump if not below or equal with 8-bit signed displacement; i.e., displacement can be from -128_{10} to $+127_{10}$, 0 being positive; JA and JNBE are mnemonics representing same instruction; jump if both CF and ZF = 0; used for unsigned comparison
	JAE/JNB/JNC disp8	Jump if above or equal/jump if not below/jump if no carry	Relative	—	JAE/JNB/ JNC START	Same as JA/JNBE except that 8086 jumps if CF = 0; used for unsigned comparison
	JB/JC/JNAE disp8	Jump if below/jump if carry/jump if not above or equal	Relative	—	JB/JC/JNAE START	Same as JA/JNBE except that jump is taken if CF = 1; used for unsigned comparison
	JBE/JNA disp8	Jump if below or equal/jump if not above	Relative	—	JBE/JNA START	Same as JA/JNBE except that jump is taken if CF = 1 or Z = 1; used for unsigned comparison
	JE/JZ disp8	Jump if equal/jump if zero	Relative	—	JE/JZ START	Same as JA/JNBE except that jump is taken if ZF = 1; used for both signed and unsigned comparison
	JG/JNLE disp8	Jump if greater/jump if not less or equal	Relative	—	JG/JNLE START	Same as JA/JNBE except that jump is taken if $((SF \oplus OF) \text{ or } ZF) = 0$; used for signed comparison
	JGE/JNL disp8	Jump if greater or equal/jump if not less	Relative	—	JGE/JNL START	Same as JA/JNBE except that jump is taken if $(SF \oplus OF) = 0$; used for signed comparison
	JL/JNGE disp8	Jump if less/jump if not greater or equal	Relative	—	JL/JNGE START	Same as JA/JNBE except that jump is taken if $(SF \oplus OF) = 1$; used for signed comparison
	JLE/JNG disp8	Jump if less or equal/jump if not greater	Relative	—	JLE/JNG START	Same as JA/JNBE except that jump is taken if $((SF \oplus OF) \text{ or } ZF) = 1$; used for signed comparison

TABLE I–10
8086 Loop Instructions

| Operation | Instructions | Interpretation | Addressing Mode | | Illustration | |
			Source	Destination	Example	Comments
Loop	LOOP disp8	Loop if CX not equal to zero	Relative	—	LOOP START	Decrement CX by 1 without affecting flags and loop with signed 8-bit displacement (from -128_{10} to $+127_{10}$, 0 being positive) if $CX \neq 0$
	LOOPE/ LOOPZ disp8	Loop while equal/loop while zero	Relative	—	LOOPE/ LOOPZ START	Decrement CX by 1 without affecting flags and loop with signed 8-bit displacement if $CX \neq 0$ and $ZF = 1$, which results from execution of previous instruction
	LOOPNE/ LOOPNZ disp8	Loop while not equal/loop while not zero	Relative	—	LOOPNE/ LOOPNZ START	Decrement CX by 1 without affecting flags and loop with signed 8-bit displacement if $CX \neq 0$ and $ZF = 0$, which results from execution of previous instruction
	JCXZ disp8	Jump if CX equal to zero	Relative	—	JCXZ START	Jump if $CX = 0$; useful at beginning of a loop to bypass loop if $CX = 0$

TABLE I–11
8086 Interrupt Instructions

| Operation | Instructions | Interpretation | Addressing Mode | | Illustration | |
			Source	Destination	Example	Comments
Interrupt	INTn (n can be 0–255_{10})	$[SP] \leftarrow [SP] - 2$ $[[SP]] \leftarrow$ flags $IF \leftarrow 0$ $TF \leftarrow 0$ $[SP] \leftarrow [SP] - 2$ $[[SP]] \leftarrow [CS]$ $[CS] \leftarrow 4n + 2$ $[SP] \leftarrow [SP] - 2$ $[[SP]] \leftarrow [IP]$ $[IP] \leftarrow 4n$	Immediate	—	INT 50	Software interrupts can be used as supervisor calls, i.e., request for service from an operating system; different interrupt type can be used for each type of service that operating system could supply for an application program; software interrupts can also be used for checking interrupt service routines written for hardware-initiated interrupts
	INTO	Interrupt on overflow	—	—	INTO	Generates internal interrupt if $OF = 1$; executes INT4; can be used after arithmetic operation to activate service routine if $OF = 1$; when INTO is executed and if $OF = 1$,

TABLE I–11
8086 Interrupt Instructions *(cont.)*

Operation	Instructions	Interpretation	Addressing Mode		Illustration	
			Source	*Destination*	*Example*	*Comments*
	IRET	Interrupt return	—	—	IRET	operations similar to INTn take place POPs IP, CS, and flags from stack; used as return instruction at end of service routine for both hardware and software interrupts

TABLE I–12
8086 Processor Control Instructions

Operation	Instructions	Interpretation	Addressing Mode		Illustration	
			Source	*Destination*	*Example*	*Comments*
Flag operations, external synchronization, and no operation	STC	$CF \leftarrow 1$	—	—	STC	Set carry flag to 1
	CLC	$CF \leftarrow 0$	—	—	CLC	Clear carry flag to zero
	CMC	$CF \leftarrow CF'$	—	—	CMC	1's complement carry
	STD	$DF \leftarrow 1$	—	—	STD	Set direction flag to 1
	CLD	$DF \leftarrow 0$	—	—	CLD	Clear direction flag to zero
	STI	$IF \leftarrow 1$	—	—	STI	Set interrupt enable flag to 1 to enable maskable interrupts
	CLI	$IF \leftarrow 0$	—	—	CLI	Clear interrupt enable flag to zero to disable maskable interrupts
	NOP	No operation	—	—	NOP	8086 does nothing
	HLT	Halt	—	—	HLT	Halt
	WAIT	8086 enters wait state	—	—	WAIT	Causes CPU to enter wait state if 8086 TEST pin is high; while in wait state, 8086 continues to check TEST pin for low; if TEST pin goes back to zero, 8086 executes next instruction; this feature can be used to synchronize operation of 8086 to an event in external hardware
	ESC external OP code, source	Escape to external processes	Immediate	Register *or* Memory	ESC data, register or memory	Instruction used to pass instructions to coprocessor such as 8087 floating-point coprocessor, which simulatneously monitors system bus with 8086; coprocessor OP codes are 6 bits wide; coprocessor treats normal 8086 instructions as NOPs; 8086 fetches all instructions from memory; when the 8086 encounters an ESC instruction, it usually treats this as a NOP; the coprocessor decodes this operation using the 6-bit OP code independent of the 8086; for ESC OP code, memory, the 8086 accesses data in memory for the

Continued.

TABLE I–12
8086 Processor Control Instructions — cont'd

Operation	Instructions	Interpretation	Addressing Mode		Illustration	
			Source	Destination	Example	Comments
						coprocessor; for ESC data, register the coprocessor operates on 8086 register, the 8086 treats this as a NOP
	LOCK	Lock bus during next instruction				LOCK is a one-byte prefix that causes the 8086 (configured in maximum mode) to assert its bus LOCK signal while the following instruction is executed; this signal is used in multiprocessing; the LOCK pin of the 8086 can be used to lock other processors off the system bus during execution of an instruction; in this way, the 8086 can be assured of uninterrupted access to common system resources such as shared RAM.

Glossary

Absolute Addressing   Also called *direct addressing*. For 8-bit microprocessors, it consists of 3 bytes: The first byte is the OP code, and the next 2 bytes contain the 16-bit operand address. The effective address is specified as part of the instruction.

Accumulator   Used for storing the result after most ALU operations; 8 bits long for 8-bit microprocessors.

Address   Pattern of 0's and 1's that represents a specific location in memory or a particular input/output device.

Addressing Mode   The manner in which a microprocessor determines the operand and destination addresses in an instruction cycle.

American Standard Code for Information Interchange (ASCII)   An 8-bit code commonly used with microprocessors for representing alphanumeric codes.

Analog-to-Digital (A/D) Converter   Transforms an analog voltage into its digital equivalent.

Arithmetic and Logic Unit (ALU)   A digital circuit that performs arithmetic and logic operations on two *n*-bit digital words.

Assembler   A program that translates an assembly language program into a machine language program.

Assembly Language   A type of microprocessor programming language that uses a semi-English-language statement.

Asynchronous Serial Data Transmission   The transmitting device does not need to be synchronized with the receiving device.

Auto-Decrement Addressing Mode   The contents of a specified microprocessor register are first decremented by *K* (1 for byte, 2 for 16-bit, and 4 for 32-bit) and then the resulting value is used as the address of the operand.

Auto-Increment Addressing Mode   The contents of a specified microprocessor register are first used as the address of the operand and then the register contents are automatically incremented by *K* (1 for byte, 2 for 16-bit, and 4 for 32-bit).

Base-Page Addressing   This instruction uses 2 bytes: The first byte is the OP code, and the second byte is the low-order address byte. The high-order address byte is assumed to be the base-page number.

Baud Rate   Rate of data transmission in bits per second.

Binary-Coded Decimal (BCD)   The representation of 10 decimal digits, 0 through 9, by their corresponding 4-bit binary numbers.

Bit   The abbreviation for the term *binary digit*. A binary digit can have only two values: 0 or 1.

Bit-Slice Microprocessor   Divides the elements of a central processing unit (ALU, registers, and control unit) among several ICs. The registers and ALU are usually contained in a single chip. These microprocessors can be cascaded to produce microprocessors of variable word lengths such as 8, 12, 16, 32. The control unit of a bit-slice microprocessor is typically microprogrammed.

Block Transfer DMA   A peripheral device requests the DMA transfer via the DMA request line, which is connected directly or through a DMA controller chip to the microprocessor. The DMA controller chip completes the DMA transfer and transfers the control of the bus to the microprocessor.

Breakpoint   Allows the user to execute the section of a program until one of the breakpoint conditions is met. It is then halted. The designer may then single step or examine memory and registers. Typical breakpoint conditions are program counter address or data references.

Buffer   A circuit used to isolate one or more signal sources from the portion or portions of the microprocessor system using the signal. It is a current amplifier.

Bus   A number of conductors organized to provide a means of communication among different elements in a microcomputer system.

Byte   An 8-bit binary number.

Cathode Ray Tube (CRT)   Evacuated glass tube with a fluorescent coating on the inner side of the screen.

Central Processing Unit (CPU)   The portion of a computer containing the ALU, register section, and control unit.

Clock   Timing signals providing synchronization among the various components in a microcomputer system.

Codes   Extensively used with microprocessors to define alphanumeric characters and other information.

Compiler   A program that converts a high-level language program into a machine language program.

Complementary Metal-Oxide Semiconductor (CMOS)   Provides low power density and high noise immunity.

Conditional Branching   Conditional branch instructions are used to change the order of execution of a program based on the conditions set by the status flags.

Control Unit   Part of the microprocessor. Its purpose is to read and decode instructions from the memory.

Coprocessor Fabricated in a single chip for performing scientific computations at high speed. The coprocessor is regarded as a companion to the host microprocessor.

CRT Controller Provides all logic functions for interfacing the microprocessor to a CRT.

Cycle Stealing DMA The DMA controller transfers a byte of data between the microprocessor and a peripheral device by stealing a clock cycle of the microprocessor.

Daisy Chain Interrupt Priorities of interrupting devices are defined by connecting them in a daisy chain.

Data Counter (DC) Also known as *memory address register* (MAR). Stores the address of data; typically, 16 bits long for 8-bit microprocessors.

Debugger A program that executes and debugs the object program generated by the assembler or compiler. The debugger provides single stepping, breakpoints, and program tracing.

Direct Addressing See *Absolute Addressing*.

Direct Memory Access (DMA) A type of input/output technique in which data can be transferred between the microcomputer memory and external devices without the microprocessor's involvement.

Dynamic RAM Stores data in capacitors and, therefore, must be refreshed; uses refresh circuitry.

EAROM (Electrically Alterable Read-Only Memory) Can be programmed without removing the memory from its sockets. This memory is also called *read-mostly memory* since it has much slower write times than read times.

ECL (Emitter-Coupled Logic) Offers ultra-high speed and high power dissipation; nonsaturated bipolar logic.

Editor A program that produces an error-free source program written in assembly or high-level languages.

EPROM (Erasable Programmable Read-Only Memory) Can be programmed and erased using ultraviolet light. The chip must be removed from the microcomputer system for programming.

Extended Binary-Coded Decimal Interchange Code (EBCDIC) An 8-bit code commonly used with microprocessors for representing character codes.

Flowchart Representation of a program in a schematic form. It is convenient to flowchart a problem before writing the actual programs.

Handshaking Exchange of control signals between the microprocessor and an external device.

High-Level Language A type of programming language that uses a more understandable human-oriented language.

Hardware Electronic circuitry making a computer.

Hexadecimal Number System Base-16 number system.

HMOS High-performance MOS reduces the channel length of the NMOS transistor and provides increased density and speed in LSI and VLSI circuits.

IEEE Std 488 A parallel interface designed by Hewlett-Packard providing an industry standard for connecting programmable measuring equipment. Also known as *Hewlett-Packard interface bus* (HPIB) or *general-purpose interface bus* (GPIB).

I²L (Integrated Injection Logic) Saturated bipolar logic derived from the old Direct Coupled Transistor Logic (DCTL); combines the density of MOS with the speed of bipolar.

Immediate Addressing Data is specified as part of the instruction. For 8-bit data, it uses 2 bytes: The first byte is the OP code, and the second byte contains data.

Implied Addressing Contains a single byte, and no operand address is required with the instruction.

In-Circuit Emulation The most powerful hardware debugging technique. It is especially valuable when hardware and software are being debugged simultaneously.

Index Register Typically used as a counter, in address modification, or for general storage functions.

Indexed Addressing Typically uses 3 bytes: The first byte is for the OP code, and the next 2 bytes are for the 16-bit address. The effective address of the instruction is determined by the sum of the 16-bit address and the contents of the index register.

Indirect Addressing The address part of the instruction is not the effective address, but it contains the address of a memory location whose contents defines the effective address.

Input/Output Processor (IOP) Performs most of the I/O functions for the 16- and 32-bit microprocessors and unburdens the microprocessors of these I/O functions.

Instruction Cycle The sequence of operations that a microprocessor has to carry out while executing an instruction.

Instruction Register (IR) A register storing instructions; typically, 8 bits long for 8-bit microprocessors.

Instruction Set List of instructions that a microprocessor is designed to execute.

Interleaved DMA Using this technique, the DMA controller takes over the system bus when the microprocessor is not using it.

Internal Interrupt Activated internally by exceptional conditions such as overflow and division by zero.

Interpreter A program that executes a set of machine language instructions in response to each high-level statement in order to carry out the function.

Interrupt I/O An external device can force the microcomputer system to stop executing the current program temporarily so that it can execute another program known as the *interrupt service routine*.

Keyboard Has a number of pushbutton-type switches configured in a matrix form (rows × columns).

Keybounce When a mechanical switch opens or closes, it bounces (vibrates) for a small period of time (about 10 to 20 ms) before settling down.

Large-Scale Integration (LSI) An LSI chip contains more than 100 gates.

Linkage Editors Connect the individual programs together that are assembled or compiled independently.

Logic Analyzer A hardware development aid for microprocessor-based design. It gathers data on the fly and displays it.

Machine Language A type of microprocessor programming language that uses binary or hexadecimal numbers.

Macroinstruction Commonly known as an instruction; initiates execution of a complete microprogram.

Macroprogram The assembly language program

Mask ROM Programmed by a masking operation performed on the chip during the manufacturing process. Its contents cannot be changed by the user.

Maskable Interrupt Can be enabled or disabled by executing typically the instructions EI and DI, respectively. If the microprocessor's interrupt is disabled, the microprocessor ignores this interrupt.

Memory Access Time Average time taken to read a unit of information from the memory.

Memory Address Register (MAR) Also known as the *data counter* (DC). Stores the address of data; typically, 16 bits long for 8-bit microprocessors.

Memory Cycle Time Average time lapse between two successive read operations.

Memory-Mapped I/O The microprocessor does not differentiate between input/output and memory; it uses RAM addresses to represent input/output ports.

Microcomputer Consists of a microprocessor, a memory unit, and an input/output unit.

Microinstruction Most microprocessors have an internal memory called *control memory*. This memory is used to store a number of codes, or microinstructions. These microinstructions are combined together to design the instruction set of the microprocessor.

Microprocessor The Central Processing Unit (CPU) of a microcomputer.

Microprocessor Development System A tool for designing and debugging both hardware and software for microcomputer-based systems.

Microprocessor-Halt DMA Data transfer is performed between the microprocessor and a peripheral device either by completely stopping the microprocessor or by the technique of cycle stealing.

Microprogramming The microprocessor can use microprogramming to design the instruction set. Each instruction in the instruction register initiates execution of a microprogram in the control unit to perform the operation required by the instruction.

Monitor Consists of a number of subroutines grouped together to provide "intelligence" to a microcomputer system. This intelligence gives the microcomputer system the capabilities for debugging a user program, system design, and displays.

Nibble A 4-bit binary number.

NMOS Is denser and faster in comparison to PMOS. Most 8-bit microprocessors are fabricated using this technology.

Nonmaskable Interrupt Occurrence of this type of interrupt cannot be ignored by the microprocessor, even though the microprocessor's interrupt capability is disabled. Its effect cannot be disabled by instruction.

Octal Number System Base-8 number system.

One-Pass Assembler This assembler goes through the assembly language program once and translates the assembly language program into a machine language program. This assembler has the problem of defining forward references.

OP Code (Operation Code) The instruction represented in binary form.

Operating System Consists of a number of program modules to provide resource management. Typical resources include microprocessors, disks, and printers.

Page Some microprocessors, such as the Motorola 6800 and the MOS 6502, divide the 65,536 memory locations into 256 blocks. Each of these blocks is called a *page* and contains 256 addresses.

Parallel Transmission Each bit of binary data is transmitted over a separate wire.

Parity The number of 1's in a word is odd for odd parity and even for even parity.

Personal Computer Low-cost affordable computer used by an individual or a small group for video games, daily schedules, and industrial applications.

Pipelining Technique in which instruction fetch and execute cycles are overlapped.

PMOS Original MOS technology; offers high density but low speed. Used in fabricating earlier microprocessors.

Polled Interrupt A software approach for determining the source of interrupt in a multiple interrupt system.

POP Operation Reading from the top or bottom of the stack.

Primary Memory Storage in which all programs are executed. The microprocessor can directly access only those items that are stored in primary memory.

Processor Memory A set of microprocessor registers for holding temporary results when a computation is in progress.

Program Counter (PC) Stores the address of an instruction; typically, 16 bits long for 8-bit microprocessors.

Programmed I/O The microprocessor executes a program to perform all data transfers between the microcomputer system and external devices.

PROM (Programmable Read-Only Memory) Can be programmed by the user by using proper equipment. Once programmed, its contents cannot be altered.

Pseudostatic RAM Dynamic RAM with internal refresh circuitry.

PUSH Operation Writing to the top or bottom of the stack.

Random-Access Memory (RAM) Type of memory whose contents can be both read and altered; volatile, that is, its contents are lost in case of power failure.

Read-Only Memory (ROM) Type of memory whose contents can only be read; nonvolatile, that is, its contents are retained in case of power failure.

Register Volatile storage within the microprocessor used for storing one or more words.

Register Indirect Uses a register pair that contains the address of data.

Rollover Occurs when more than one key is pushed simultaneously.

RS232 The RS232 interface convention is developed to standardize the interface between data terminal equipment and data communication equipment employing serial binary data exchange.

RS422 An improved version of the RS232 standard. It is used in balanced transmission and utilizes a low-impedance differential signal to increase the baud rate to 10 Mbaud and the maximum line length to 4000 feet.

RS423 An improvement of the RS232 standard. It is used in unbalanced transmission lines. It uses a low-impedance single-ended driver instead of a differential driver to obtain longer distances and higher baud rates.

S-100 A parallel interface standard designed by ALTAIR for internal computer communication.

Sample and Hold Circuit When connected to the input of an A/D converter, it keeps a rapidly varying signal fixed during the A/D conversion process by storing it in a capacitor.

Schottky TTL Provides high speed, reasonable density, and compatibility with standard TTL; nonsaturated logic.

Secondary Memory Storage medium composed of slow devices such as cassette recorders and floppy disks. It is used to store programs in excess of main memory.

Serial Transmission Only one line is used to transmit the complete binary data bit by bit.

Single-Chip Microcomputer Microcomputer (CPU, memory, and input/output) on a chip.

Single-Chip Microprocessor Microcomputer CPU (microprocessor) on a chip.

Single Step Allows the user to execute a program one instruction at a time and examine memory and registers.

Software Programs in a computer.

SOS Particularly amenable to CMOS designs; can make CMOS as fast as TTL and as dense as PMOS.

Stack A number of RAM locations set aside for reading data from or writing data into these locations. It is automatically used by subroutines and interrupts.

Stack Pointer Register Stores the address of the stack; typically, 16 bits long.

Standard I/O Utilizes a control pin, the IO/$\overline{M}$ pin, on the microprocessor chip in order to distinguish between input/output and memory. Typically, IN and OUT instructions are used for performing input/output operations.

Static RAM Stores data in flip-flops; does not need to be refreshed.

Status Register Also referred to as the *processor status word* or *condition code register* for storing status flags such as carry, zero, sign, and parity.

Subroutine A program that carries out a particular function and that can be called by another program known as the *main program*. A subroutine needs to be placed only once in memory and can be called by the main program as many times as the programmer wants.

Synchronous Serial Data Transmission Data is transmitted or received based on a clock signal.

Tristate Buffer Has three output states: logic 0, 1, and a high-impedance state. It is typically enabled by a control signal to provide logic 0 or 1 outputs. This type of buffer can also be disabled by the control signal to place it in a high-impedance state.

2's Complement The 2's complement of a binary number is obtained by replacing each 0 with a 1 and each 1 with a 0 and adding 1 to the resulting number.

Two-Pass Assembler This assembler goes through the assembly language program twice. In the first pass, the assembler defines the labels with the addresses. In the second pass, the assembler translates the assembly language program to the machine language.

UART (Universal Asynchronous Receiver/Transmitter) A chip that provides all the interface functions when a microprocessor transmits or receives data to or from a serial device.

Vectored Interrupt A hardware approach for determining the source of interrupt in a multiple interrupt system.

Very Large-Scale Integration (VLSI) A VLSI chip contains more than 1000 gates.

Word The bit size of a microprocessor refers to the number of bits that can be processed simultaneously by the basic arithmetic circuits of the microprocessor. A number of bits taken as a group in this manner is called a *word*.

Bibliography

Artwick, B. A., *Microcomputer Interfacing*, Prentice-Hall, 1980.

Boyce, J. C., *Microprocessor and Microcomputer Basics*, Prentice-Hall, 1979.

Chi, C. S., "Advances in Mass Storage Technology," *IEEE Computer*, Vol. 15., no. 5, pp. 60–74, May 1982.

Chow, C. K., "On Optimization of Storage Hierarchies," *IBM Journal of Research and Development*, pp. 194–203, May 1974.

Cohn, D. L., and Melsa, J. L., *A Step by Step Introduction to 8080 Microprocessor Systems*, Dilithium Press, 1977.

Danhof, K. J., and Smith, C. L., *Computing System Fundamentals: An Approach Based on Microcomputers*, Addison-Wesley, 1981.

Denning, P. J., "Virtual Memory," *ACM Computing Surveys*, Vol. 2, no. 3, pp. 153–159, September 1970.

Electronic Industries Association, Washington, D.C., *EIA Standard, RS-232-C Interface*, Electronic Industries Association, 1969.

Fisher, E., and Jensen, C. W., *Pet and the IEEE 488 Bus (GPIB)*, Osborne/McGraw-Hill, 1979.

Garland, H. *Introduction to Microprocessor System Design*, McGraw-Hill, 1979.

Gibson, G. A., and Liu, Y., *Microcomputers for Engineers and Scientists*, Prentice-Hall, 1980.

Gill, Arthur, *Machine and Assembly Language Programming of the PDP-11*, 2nd ed., Prentice-Hall, 1983.

Gladstone, B. E., "Comparing Microcomputer Development System Capabilities," *Computer Design*, pp. 83–90, February 1979.

Gorsline, G., *16-Bit Modern Microcomputers – The Intel I8086 Family*, Prentice-Hall, 1985.

Greenfield, J. D., *Practical Digital Design Using IC's*, John Wiley and Sons, 1977.

Greenfield, J. D., and Wray, W. C., *Using Microprocessors and Microcomputers: The 6800 Family*, John Wiley and Sons, 1981.

Grinich, V. H., and Jackson, H. G., *Introduction to Integrated Circuits*, McGraw-Hill, 1975.

Hall, D. V., *Microprocessors and Digital Systems*, McGraw-Hill, 1980.

Hamacher, V. C., Vranesic, Z. G., and Zaky, S. G., *Computer Organization*, McGraw-Hill, 1984.

Harman, T. L., and Lawson, B., *The Motorola MC68000 Microprocessor Family*, Prentice-Hall, 1984.

Hartman, B., "16-Bit 68000 Microprocessor Concepts on 32-Bit Frontier," MC68000 Article Reprints, Motorola, pp. 50–57, March 1981.

Hayes, J. P., *Computer Architecture and Organization*, McGraw-Hill, 1978.

Hayes, J. P., *Digital System Design and Microprocessors*, McGraw-Hill, 1984.

Haynes, John L., "Circuit Design With Lotus 1-2-3," *BYTE*, Vol. 10, no. 11, pp. 143–156, 1985.

Hewlett-Packard, "HP 64000," *Hewlett-Packard Journal*, 1980.

Hnatek, E. R., *A User's Handbook of Semiconductor Memories*, John Wiley and Sons, 1977.

Holt, C. A., *Electronic Circuits – Digital and Analog*, John Wiley and Sons, 1978.

Horden, Ira, "Microcontrollers Offer Realtime Robotics Control," *Computer Design*, pp. 98–101, October 15, 1985.

Intel, *8080/8085 Assembly Language Programming Manual*, Intel Corporation, 1978.

Intel, *The 8086 Family User's Family*, Intel Corporation, 1979.

Intel, *Intel Component Data Catalog*, Intel Corporation, 1979.

Intel, *MCS-85 User's Manual*, Intel Corporation, 1978.

Intel, *MCS-86 User's Manual*, Intel Corporation, 1982.

Intel, *Memory Components Handbook*, Intel Corporation, 1983.

Intel, *Microprocessor Peripheral Handbook*, Intel Corporation, 1982.

Intel, *SDK-85 User's Manual*, Intel Corporation, 1978.

Intel Marketing Communications, *The Semiconductor Memory Book*, John Wiley and Sons, 1978.

Isaacson, R., et al., "The Oregon Report – Personal Computing," selected reprints from *IEEE Computer*, pp. 226–237.

Johnson, C. D., *Process Control Instrumentation Technology*, John Wiley and Sons, 1977.

Johnson, R. C., "Microsystems Exploit Mainframe Methods," *Electronics, 1981*.

Kane, G., *CRT Controller Handbook*, Osborne/McGraw-Hill, 1980.

Kane, G., Hawkins, D., and Leventhal, L., *68000 Assembly Language Programming*, Osborne/McGraw-Hill, 1981.

King, T., and Knight, B., *Programming the MC68000*, Addison-Wesley, 1983.

Krutz, R. L., *Microprocessors and Logic Design,* John Wiley and Sons, 1980.

Lesea, A., and Zaks, R., *Microprocessor Interfacing Techniques,* Sybex, 1978.

Leventhal, L. A., *8080A/8085 Assembly Language Programming,* Osborne/McGraw-Hill, 1978.

Leventhal, L. A., *Introduction to Microprocessors: Software, Hardware, Programming,* Prentice-Hall, 1978.

Leventhal, L., and Walsh, C., *Microcomputer Experimentation with the Intel SDK-85,* Prentice-Hall, 1980.

Lewin, M., *Logic Design and Computer Organization,* Addison-Wesley, 1983.

Mano, M., *Computer System Architecture,* Prentice-Hall, 1983.

MITS-ALTAIR, *S-100 Bus,* MITS, Inc., Albuquerque, NM.

Morse, S., *The 8086/8088 Primer,* 2nd ed., Hayden, 1982.

Motorola, *6809 Applications Notes,* Motorola Corporation, 1978.

Motorola, *MC68000 User's Manual,* Motorola Corporation, 1979.

Motorola, *16-Bit Microprocessor — MC68000 User's Manual,* 4th ed., Prentice-Hall, 1984.

Motorola, *MC68000 16-Bit Microprocessor User's Manual,* Motorola Corporation, 1982.

Motorola, *MC68000 Supplement Material (Technical Training),* Motorola Corporation, 1982.

Motorola, *Microprocessor Data Material,* Motorola Corporation, 1981.

Motorola, *MC68020 User's Manual,* Motorola Corporation, 1985.

Osborne, A., *An Introduction to Microcomputers: Vol. I, Basic Concepts,* rev. ed. Osborne/McGraw-Hill, 1980, 2nd ed., 1982.

Osborne, A., and Kane, G., *The Osborne Four- and Eight-Bit Microprocessor Handbook,* Osborne/McGraw-Hill, 1980.

Osborne, A., and Kane, G., *The Osborne 16-Bit Microprocessor Handbook,* Osborne/McGraw-Hill, 1981.

Rafiquzzaman, M., *Microprocessors and Microcomputer Development Systems — Designing Microprocessor-Based Systems,* Harper and Row, 1984.

Rafiquzzaman, M., *Microprocessors and Microcomputer-Based System Design,* CRC Press, 1990.

RCA, *Evaluation Kit Manual for the RCA CDP1802 COSMAC Microprocessor,* RCA Solid State Division, Somerville, NJ.

Rector, R., and Alexy, G., *The 8086 Book,* Osborne/McGraw-Hill, 1980.

Rockwell International, *Microelectronic Devices Data Catalog,* 1979.

Rosenblatt, A., "PCs and Workstations," *IEEE Spectrum,* January 1991.

Short, K. L., *Microprocessors and Programmed Logic,* Prentice-Hall, 1981.

Sloan, M. E., *Introduction to Minicomputers and Microcomputers,* Addison-Wesley, 1980.

Sowell, E. F., *Programming in Assembly Language: MACRO II,* Addison-Wesley, 1984.

Starnes, T. W., "Compact Instruction Set Gives the MC68000 Power While Simplifying its Operation," MC68000 Article Reprints, Motorola, pp. 43–47, March 1981.

Streitmatter, G. A., and Fiore, V., *Microprocessors, Theory and Applications,* Reston Publishing Co., 1979.

Stone, H. S., *Introduction to Computer Architecture,* SRA, 1980.

Stone, H. S., *Microcomputer Interfacing,* Addison-Wesley, 1982.

Stritter, E., and Gunter, T., "A Microprocessor Architecture for a Changing World: The Motorola 68000," *IEEE Computers,* Vol. 12, no. 2, pp. 43–52, February 1970.

Tanenbaum, A. S., *Structured Computer Organization,* Prentice-Hall, 1984.

Teledyne, *Teledyne Semiconductor Catalog,* 1977.

Texas Instruments, *The TTL Data Book,* Vol. 1, 1984.

Texas Instruments, *The TTL Data Book for Design Engineers,* 2nd ed., 1976.

Tocci, R. J., and Laskowski, L. P., *Microprocessors and Microcomputers: Hardware and Software,* Prentice-Hall, 1979.

Wakerly, J.F., *Microcomputer Architecture and Programming,* John Wiley and Sons, 1981.

Zilog, *Z8000 Advance Specification,* Zilog, Inc., 1978.

Zorpette, Glenn, "Microprocessors — The Beauty of 32-Bits," *IEEE Spectrum,* Vol. 22, no. 9, pp. 65–71, September 1985.

Index

Absolute addressing, 50, 115, 120, 165, 456
Access mode, 26
Access rate, 26
Access time, 26
Accumulator (A), 11-12, 456. *See also* Registers
Acquisition time, 34
Address 2, 456
Address decoding, 30
Address field, 49
Address formats, 49
Address mapping, HP68000, 308-309
Addressing modes, 456
  absolute, 50, 165
  address modification, 51
  address register indirect, 163-165
  alterable, 166
  ARI with index (scaled) and 8-bit displacement, 232
  ARI with index and base displacement, 232
  base register, 51, 219, 220
  based addressing, 116
  based index mode with displacement, 220
  based index, 116, 220
  based scaled index mode with displacement, 220
  based scaled index, 220
  control, 166
  data, 166
  direct, 115, 220
  displacement, 219
  immediate, 64, 219, 457
  immediate data, 166
  implied, 116, 166, 457
  index, 51, 116, 219, 457
  inherent, 50, 64
  memory indirect, 50, 233-234
  memory, 166, 219
  port, 116
  program counter relative, 165
  register direct, 163
  register indirect, 51, 64, 115, 220
  register, 64, 219
  relative, 51-53, 116
  scale, 219
  scaled index, 220
  string, 116
  usefulness of, 53-54
Address register, *see* Registers
Altair 8800, 283
American Standard Code for Information Interchange
    (ASCII), 5
AM9511, 54
Analog-to-Digital (A/D) conversion, 7, 33-34, 456
Aperture time, 34
Apple Macintosh, 7, 8
Applications, 293-313
Argument passing convention, 57
Arithmetic and logic unit (ALU), 1, 22, 456
Arithmetic instructions, *see* Instructions
Arithmetic operations, 365-368
Assemblers, 4, 5, 456
  cross, 58
  macro-, 57-58
  meta-, 58
  one-pass, 57
  resident, 58
  two-pass, 57
Assembly language, 4-5, 57-59, 456
Asynchronous communications interface adapter (ACIA),
    249
Asynchronous serial data transmission, 249, 456
Auxiliary carry flag, *see* Flags
Auxiliary storage, *see* Memory, secondary

Backup storage, *see* Memory, secondary
Barrel shifter, *see* Registers
Base pointer register, *see* Registers
Base register, *see* Registers
BASIC, 6
Baud rate, 248, 456
Bidirectional, 10
Binary arithmetic, 365-366

Binary coded decimal (BCD), *see* Instructions
Binary digits, 1, 363
Binary operation (OP) codes, 3
Bipolar ROM, 26
Bipolar technologies, 1, 9
Bits, 1, 2, 456
Block termination, 275
Block transfer DMA, 44, 456
Boolean algebra, 368-369
Buffers, 33, 456
Bus Interface Unit (BIU), 111-113
Bus, 2, 9, 456
   address, 2, 10, 148-150
   bidirectional, 2, 10
   control, 2, 10
   data, 2, 10, 148-150
   unidirectional, 10
Byte, 1, 23

C, 6
C + +, 6
Cache memory, 3, 25, 214
Cassette recorders:
   interfacing to a typical microprocessor, 258-259
   interfacing to the Intel 8085, 259-263
   Kansas City standard, 256-258
   Tarbell standard, 256
Cathode ray tube (CRT), 457
   basics, 263, 266
   controller, 263, 266-267
Central Processing Unit (CPU), 1, 9, 456
Channel initialization, 274-275
Circuits:
   buffering, 308
   clock signal, 308
   clock, 2, 456
   input, 37
   output, 37-39
   parallel-resonant LC, 84
   reset, 308
Clock circuits, 2, 456
Clock signals, 10-11
COBOL, 6
Codes, 3, 4, 5, 12, 213, 365, 456
Code segment (CS) register, *see* Registers
Command registers, *see* Registers
COMPAQ, 8
Compilers, 4, 456
Condition code register, *see* Registers
Conditional I/O, *see* Input/Output (I/O)
Conditionals, 5
Control bus, 2, 21-22
Control registers, *see* Registers
Control unit, 21-22, 456
Coprocessor interface, 46
Coprocessors, 45-46
Counter register, *see* Registers
Current/pneumatic (I/P), 7
Cursor, 266
Cycle stealing DMA, 44-45, 457
Cycle time, 26

Daisy chain interrupts, *see* Interrupts
Data bus, 2
Data channel, 32
Data communication equipment (DCE), 290
Data Counter (DC), *see* Registers
Data direction registers, *see* Registers
Data registers, *see* Registers
Data terminal equipment (DTE), 289-290
Data transfer, 275
Dead zone, 293
DEC VAX 11/750, 3, 213
DEC VAX 11/780, 3, 213
Decimal digit, 1
Decoding, 30
Destination address, 49
Destination index (DI) register, *see* Registers
Differential zone, 293
Digital Equipment Corporation, *see* DEC
Digital programmable instruments (DPIs), 279
Digital-to-Analog (D/A) converter, 7
Direct addressing, *see* Absolute addressing
Direct Digital Control (DDC), 7
Direction flag, *see* Flags
Direct-access memory, 26
Direct memory access (DMA), 26, 43-44, 276, 457
   block transfer, 44
   controller chips, 32
   controllers, 273-276
   cycle stealing, 44-45
   Intel 8085, 101-102
   Intel 8086, 142
   Intel SDK-85, 398
   interleaved, 45
   I/O, *see* Input/Output (I/O)
   microprocessor-halt, 44
   Motorola 68000, 204-205
Displacement, *see* Modifier (M)
Distributed processing, 8

Effective address (EA), 50, 115
Electrically alterable ROM (EAROM), 26-27, 457
Erasable PROM (EPROM), 26, 150-151, 457
Erasable ROM (EROM), 26-27
Exception handling, 205, 207
Execution Unit (EU), 111, 113-115
External interrupt, *see* Interrupts
Extra segment (ES) register, *see* Registers

Fields:
   comment, 58
   label, 58
   OP-code, 49, 58
   operand, 58
First-In-First-Out (FIFO), 111
Fixed-point representation, 368
Flags, 18
   auxiliary carry, 19, 62, 114
   carry, 19, 115
   direction (DF), 115
   Intel 8085, 62
   Intel 80386, 219

Flags (*Contd.*)
  interrupt (IF), 115
  overflow, 19, 115
  parity, 19, 62, 115
  sign, 19, 115
  sign status, 62
  trap (TF), 115
  zero, 19, 62, 115
Floating Gate Avalanche Injection MOS (FAMOS), 27
Floating-point arithmetic, 213-214, 368
Floating-point hardware, 214
Floppy disk, 25
  interface to a microprocessor, 272
  tracks, 272
FORTRAN, 6
Full-duplex, 292

General Electric, 3
General-purpose interface bus (GPIB), 278-283
General-purpose registers, *see* Registers

Handshake ports, 35
Handshaking, 33, 279, 457
Hardware, 1, 456
Hardwired control, 21
HCMOS, 3
Hewlett-Packard 64000, 296-298, 310
Hewlett-Packard 64000 , system design, 308-310
Hewlett-Packard interface bus (HPIB), 278
Hexadecimal arithmetic, 367
Hexadecimal displays, 251-255
Hexadecimal keyboard, 251-255
Hexadecimal operation (OP) codes, 3
Hexadecimal programs, 4
High-level language, 5-6, 457
Hit rate, 214
HMOS , 3, 457
Honeywell, 7
Horizontal scan, 263

IBM PC, 7, 8, 110, 111
IBM PDP-11/70, 25, 54
IBM 360/85, 25
IBM 386PC, 111
IBM 486PC, 111
Idle mode, 276
IEEE 488 interface bus, 278-283
IEEE 488 standard, 278, 457
Immediate addressing, *see* Addressing
Implied addressing, *see* Addressing
Index registers, *see* Registers
Indexed addressing, *see* Addressing
Indirect addressing, *see* Addressing
Input/Output (I/O), 1, 9, 31
  conditional, 36
  direct memory access, 32, 43-46
  instructions, 57
  Intel 8085, 87-94
  Intel 8086, 138-139
  Intel 80386, 227
  Intel SDK-85, 383

  interrupt, 32, 39-43
  memory-mapped, 35-36
  Motorola 68020, 246
  ports, 31, 34, 87-93, 151-152, 383-384
  programmed, 31-32, 34-39, 81-94, 138-139
  standard, 35-36, 459
  summary of methods, 45-46
  terms used in, 33-34
  unconditional, 36
Input/Output Processor (IOP), 139-140, 457
Instruction fetch, 28, 86
Instruction pointer (IP), 12, 112
Instruction register (IR), *see* Registers
Instruction sets, 2, 4, 457
Instructions:
  address field, 49
  arithmetic, 54, 126-128, 175-178, 221
  binary-coded decimal, 180
  bit manipulation, 128-129, 180, 221
  byte-set-on-condition, 222
  CHK/CHK2 and CMP/CMP2, 235-237
  conditional branch, 55, 130-132
  conditional jumps and loops, 223
  data movement, 172-175
  data transfer, 54, 125, 223-224
  flag control, 224
  formats, 49
  high-level language, 225-226
  I/O, 57
  immediate mode, 50
  instruction cycle, 50
  interrupt, 132
  iteration control, 132
  logical, 54, 178, 224
  MC68000 enhanced, 243
  Motorola 68000, 161-162, 166-184
  multiplication and division, 241-243
  new privilege move, 234
  operation-code field, 49
  privileged, 159
  processor control, 132
  program control, 54-57, 181-183
  pseudo-, 58-59, 78, 132-137
  register modes, 50
  return and delocate, 235
  shift and rotate, 178, 180
  string, 129-130, 224-225
  subroutine call, 55
  system control, 183-184
  table look-up translation instruction, 225
  trap-on-condition, 238-240
  unconditional branch, 54
  unconditional transfer, 130
Integrated Circuit (IC), 8
Intel 386, 111
Intel 386SX, 8
Intel 432, 3
Intel 2142, 402
Intel 2716, 403
Intel 4004, 1, 3
Intel 8008, 3

Intel 8048, 9
Intel 8051, 8
Intel 8080, 4, 11, 38, 39
Intel 8080/8085, assembly language reference card, 358-362
Intel 8085, 3, 4, 10, 11, 12, 21, 22-23, 39, 45, 50, 54,
    55, 58
  addressing modes
    direct addressing, 63-64
    immediate addressing, 64
    implied (or inherent) addressing, 64
    register adressing, 64
    register indirect addressing, 64
  cassette recorder interface to, 259-263
  CPU pins and signals, 82-85
  data sheets, 402-419
  DMA, 101-102
  instruction fetch timing diagram, 86
  instruction set, 64-81
  instruction timing and execution, 85
    memory READ timing diagram, 86-87
    memory WRITE timing diagram, 86-87
  interrupt system, 94-101
  memory addressing, 62-63
  programmed I/O, 87-94
  register structure, 61-62
  and RMS meters, 295-305
  serial input data (SID) and serial output data (SOD), 102
  status flags, 62
  system design, 102-104
  timing methods, 81-85
Intel 8085A, 3
Intel 8085AH, 3, 61
Intel 8085AH-1, 62
Intel 8085AH-2, 61
Intel 8086, 3, 11, 21, 23, 32
  architecture
    Bus Interface Unit (BIU), 111-113
    Execution Unit (EU), 111, 113-115
  assembler-dependent instructions, 132
  assembler pseudo-instructions, 132-137
  basic features, 110-111
  data sheets, 402-419
  family, 110
  input/output
    DMA, 142
    8089 Input/Output Processor (IOP), 139-140
    external maskable interrupts, 140-141
    internal interrupts, 140
    interrupt pointer tables, 142
    interrupt priorities, 142
    interrupt procedures, 141-142
    predefined interrupts, 140
    programmed I/O, 138-139
  instruction set, 433-453
    arithmetic instructions, 126-128
    bit manipulation instructions, 128-130
    conditional branch instructions, 130-132
    data transfer instructions, 125-126
    unconditional transfers, 130
  memory addressing modes
    based, 116

    based indexed, 116
    implied, 116
    indexed, 116
    memory direct, 115
    port, 116
    register indirect, 115-116
    relative, 116
    string, 116
  memory, 110
  system design
    address and data bus concepts, 148-150
    bus cycle, 147-148
    dynamic RAMs, 151
    8086-based microcomputer, 152, 156
    I/O ports, 151-152
    pins and signals, 142, 145-147
    ROMs and EPROMs, 150-151
    static RAMs, 151
  versions of, 110
Intel 8087, 214
Intel 8088, 21, 110
Intel 8096, 8
Intel 8155, 91-93
Intel 8156, 91-93, 298
Intel 8205, 30
Intel 8271, 272
Intel 8279, 252
Intel 8295, 269-271
Intel 8355, 88-91
Intel 8755, 88-91, 298
Intel 80186, 3, 11, 111
Intel 80188, 111
Intel 80286, 3, 11, 111, 214
Intel 80386, 3, 12, 18, 25, 46, 111
  addressing modes
    memory addressing, 219-220
    register/immediate, 219
  basic programming model
    data types, 217
    memory organization and segmentation, 217
    registers, 217, 219
  functional characteristics, 214-215
  I/O, 227
  instruction set, 220-221
    arithmetic instructions, 221
    bit instructions, 221-222
    byte-set-on-condition instructions, 222-223
    conditional jumps and loops, 223
    data transfer instructions, 223-224
    flag control instructions, 224
    high-level language instructions, 225-226
    logical instructions, 224
    string instructions, 224-225
    table look-up translation instruction, 225
  internal architecture, 215
  memory, 226-227
  processing modes, 216-217
  system block diagram, 215-216
Intel 80387, 46
Intel 80486, 3, 18, 25, 213, 214
Intel 80960, 3

Intel I8087, 54
Intel MCS-51, 8
Intel MCS-96, 8
Intel SDK-85, 4, 10, 293-295
   DMA and, 398
   external seven-segment displays, 388-392
   I/O ports, SDK-85, 383-384
   interrupts, 392-398
   light-emitting diodes (LEDs), 384
   memory map, 372
   monitor, 318-352
   on-board seven-segment displays, 386-388
   operational features, 372-376
     monitor, 377-378
     program debugging by the, 376-377
   programmed I/O, 383
   programming the, 372
   schematic, 315-317
   seven-segment displays, 384, 386
   SID and SOD lines, 398
   teletype operation, 353-356
   writing assembly language programs, 378-383
Intel support chips, data sheets, 402-419
Interface standards:
   parallel interface
     IEEE 488 interface bus, 278-283
     S-100 bus standard, 283-284
   serial interface
     current loops, 292
     RS232C, RS422, and RS423, 287-292
Interfacing:
   asynchronous serial data transmission, 249
   cassette recorders, 255-256
   CRT terminal to a microprocessor, 263-267
   DMA controllers, 272-276
   floppy disk to a microprocessor, 272
   hexadecimal keyboard and display unit to a microprocessor, 251-255
   parallel vs. serial transmission, 248
   parallel/serial interface--UART, 249-250
   printer to a microprocessor, 268-271
   synchronization of serial data to the receiver, 250-251
   synchronous and asynchronous serial data transmission, 248
   synchronous serial data transmission, 248-249
Interlaced scanning technique, 263
Internal interrupts, see Interrupts
Interrupt address vector, 41
Interrupt I/O, see Input/Output (I/O)
Interrupt flags, see Flags
Interrupt pin, 39
Interrupt Request (INT or IRQ), 22
Interrupt service routine, 22, 32, 39-40
Interrupts:
   autovector, 201-202, 203-204
   daisy chain, 42-43, 457
   external, 40
   Intel 8085, 94-101
   Intel 8086, 140-142
   internal, 41, 140, 457
   maskable, 40, 94, 140, 458

   nonautovector, 202, 203-204
   nonmaskable, 41, 94
   polled, 41-42
   spurious, 202

Keyboards, 457. See also Hexadecimal keyboards

Languages, see Programming languages, 3
Large-scale integration (LSI) chips, 2, 457
Last-In-First-Out (LIFO), 19-20, 56
Light-emitting diodes (LEDs), 384
Linkage, 56, 457
Linkers, 5
Locality of reference, 25, 214
Logical segment, 133
LOTUS, 7
LRC, Inc., 268

Machine language, 3-4, 457
Macros, 5, 57, 457
Mainframe on a chip, 213
Maskable interrupt, see Interrupts
Mask ROM, 26, 457
MCS-4, 3
Memory, 1, 23, 25-26, 458
   access modes, 26
   addressing, 166, 219
   array design and interfacing, 29-31
   byte, 1, 23
   cache, 3, 25, 214
   cost, 26
   direct access, 26
   foldback, 30
   Intel 80386, 217, 226-227
   Intel 8085, 62-63
   Intel 8086, 110, 115-116
   Intel SDK-85, 372
   Motorola 68000, 160
   nonvolatile, 23
   primary, 23
   processor, 23
   random-access (RAM), 26,
   READ and WRITE operations, 27-29, 86-87
   read-only (ROM), 26-27, 150-151
   secondary, 23
   serial access, 26
   speed, 26
   unit, 9
   volatile, 23
   words, 23
Memory Address Register (MAR), see Registers
Memory Management Unit (MMU), 25
Memory-mapped I/O, see Input/Output (I/O)
Metal-Nitride-Oxide Semiconductor (MNOS), 27
Metal-Oxide Semiconductor (MOS), 1
Microcomputers, 1, 459
   applications of, 6-8
   architecture, 9-10
   elements of, 9
   evolution of, 3
   I/O, 31-46

Microcomputers (*Contd.*)
  Intel 8086-based, 152-156
  memory, 23-31
  programming languages, 3
  single-chip processor, 11-23
  single-chip, 1
  software concepts, 49-58
  vs. microprocessor, 2
Microcontrollers, 8
Micromainframe, 213
Microprocessors, 1, 3, 459. *See also* individual types
  applications of, 293-310
  functional block diagram of, 22-23
  input circuits, 37
  output circuits, 37-39
  single-chip, 1, 11-23
  vs. microcomputer, 2
Microprocessor-halt DMA, 44, 458
Microprogramming, 21, 458
Modifier (M), 51
MOS, 1
MOS ROM, 26
MOS 6502, 22, 23
Motorola 2716, 207-208
Motorola 6116, 207-208
Motorola 6800, 3, 4, 11, 12, 23
Motorola 6809, 3, 11, 57
Motorola 6821, 196, 207
Motorola 6839, 54
Motorola 6850, 249
Motorola 68000, 1, 3, 11, 21, 36, 50, 54, 55
  addressing modes
    absolute addressing, 165
    address register indirect addressing, 163-165
    alterable, 166
    control, 166
    immediate data addressing, 166
    implied addressing, 166
    memory, 166
    program counter relative addressing, 165
    register direct addressing, 162
  basic features, 159-160
  data sheets, 421-432
  DMA, 204-205
  effective address, 162
  exception handling, 205, 207
  instruction format, 161-162
  instruction set, 166-187
    arithmetic instructions, 175-178
    bit manipulation instructions, 180-181
    data movement instructions, 172-175
    logical instructions, 178
    program control instructions, 181-183
    shift and rotate instructions, 178, 180
    system control instructions, 183-184
  interrupt system
    autovector and nonautovector interrupts, 203-204
    external interrupts, 201-202
    internal interrupts, 202
    interrupt address vector, 203
    interrupt map, 202-203

memory addressing, 161
memory interface, 193, 196
multiprocessing using TAS instruction and $\overline{\text{AS}}$ signal, 209
pins and signals, 187-192
  DMA control lines, 192
  interrupt control lines, 192
  status lines, 192
  synchronous and asynchronous control lines, 188-189
  system control lines, 189-192
programmed I/O, 196-201
read and write cycle timing diagrams, 193
registers, 160
68000/2716/6116/6821-based microcomputer, 207, 209
stack, 184-186
support chips, data sheets, 421-432
system diagram, 196-207
Motorola 68008, 1-2, 159
Motorola 68010, 3, 11, 159
Motorola 68012, 159
Motorola 68020, 3, 11, 18, 21, 20, 22, 36, 46, 54
  addressing modes, 232-234
    ARI with index (scaled) and 8-bit displacement, 232
    ARI with index and base displacement, 232
    memory indirect, 233-234
  basic features, 227
  functional characteristics, 228-229, 231
  hardware, 243-245
  I/O, 246
  instruction set, 234
    CHK/CHK2 and CMP/CMP2 instrutions, 235-238
    MC68000 enhanced instructions, 243
    multiplication and division instructions, 241-243
    new privileged move instruction, 234-235
    pack and unpack instructions, 240-241
    return and delocate instruction, 235
    trap-on-condition instructions, 238-240
  programmers model, 231-232
Motorola 68030, 3, 18, 21, 25, 196, 213, 227
Motorola 68040, 3, 18, 21, 25, 213, 227
Motorola 68230, 198-201, 274
Motorola 68440, 274
Motorola 68881, 46, 54
Motorola 88100, 3
MPU mode, 276
Multiphase clock, 2
Multiword binary addition and subtraction, 367

Nanoprogramming, 21
National Semiconductor IMP-16, 3
n-bit digital word, 1
Negative flag, *see* Flags, sign
Nesting, 55
Neutral zone, 293
Nibble, 1, 458
NMOS, 3
Nonautovector interrupt, *see* Interrupts
Nonmaskable interrupt, *see* Interrupts
Number systems
  binary, 363

Number systems (*Contd.*)
  converting from one base to another, 364-365
  decimal, 363
  hexadecimal, 364
  octal, 363-364

Object codes, 4, 5
Offset, *see* Modifier (M)
One-address format, 49-50
Operating system mode, 159, 458
Operation (OP) code field, 49, 58
Operation (OP) codes, 3, 458
Operation word, 161
OS/2, 8
Overflow flag, *see* Flags

Page, 23, 458
Paging, 213
Parallel interface
  IEEE 488 interface bus, 278-283
  S-100 bus standard, 283-284
Parallel transmission, 248, 458
Parallel-resonant LC circuit, 84
Parameter passing convention, 57
Parity flags, *see* Flags
Pascal, 6
Peripheral devices, 2
Peripheral interfacing, *see* Interfacing
Personal computer (PC), 7, 458
Pins:
  Intel 8085, 82-85
  Intel 8086, 142, 145-147
  Motorola 68000, 187-192
Pipelined processing, 215
Pipelining, 111, 213, 458
PMOS, 3
Polled interrupts, *see* Interrupts
Ports:
  handshake, 35
  I/O, 31, 34, 87-93, 151-152, 383-384
Position dependent, 53
Printers:
  character, 268
  impact, 268
  interface using printer controller chips, 269
  interfacing the Intel 8085 to the LRC 7040, 269
  line, 268
  LRC 7040, 268-269
  matrix, 268
  nonimpact, 268
  serial, 268
Privileged instructions, 159-160
Processor status word register, *see* Registers
Program Counter (PC), 62, 458. *See also* Registers
Programmable ROM (PROM), 26-27
Programmed I/O, *see* Input/Output (I/O)
Programming languages
  assembly, 3, 4-5, 57-59
  high-level, 3, 5-6
  machine, 3-4
  modular, 55

PROM programmer, 26, 458
Proportional-Integral-Derivative (PID), 7
Pseudo-instructions, 58-59, 78, 132-137

Random-Access Memory (RAM), 2, 9, 26, 151, 458
Raster scan, 263
RCA, 3
READ and WRITE, 27-29
Read-Mostly Memory (RMM), 27
Read-Only Memory (ROM), 2, 9, 26-27, 458
Read/Write (R/$\overline{\text{W}}$), 22
$\overline{\text{Ready}}$, 22
Records, 256-257
Recursive, 56
Reduced Instruction Set Computer (RISC), 3, 7-8
Redundant recording, 257-258
Reference address (RA), 51
Registers, 2, 458
  Accumulator (A), 12, 113
  address, 272
  barrel shifter, 18
  base, 51, 114
  base pointer (BP), 114
  code segment (CS), 112
  command (control), 35
  command, 272
  control, 250, 273
  counter, 114, 273
  data, 34, 114
  Data Counter (DC), 12
  data chain, 274
  data direction, 34
  data segment (DS), 112
  destination index (DI), 114
  extra segment (ES), 112
  flag, 114
  general-purpose, 16, 18
  index, 18, 51, 114, 457
  Instruction (IR), 12, 457
  Intel 8085, 61-62
  Intel 8086, 113-115
  Intel 80386, 217, 219
  linkage, 56
  Memory Address Register (MAR), 12
  Motorola 68000, 160
  Program Counter (PC), 12
  reset, 272
  source index (SI), 114
  stack pointer (SP), 19-20, 114
  stack segment (SS), 112
  status, 18-19, 272, 459
  use of, 12-16
Reset, 22, 272
RMS meters, 295-296
  8085-based microcomputer, 298, 303
  Hewlett-Packard 64000 development system, 296-298
  methodology, 303, 305
  results, 305
Robotics, 8
Rockwell International PPS-4, 3

S-100 bus standard, 283-284
Sample and hold, 34
Scans, 263
Schematics, Intel SDK-85, 315-317
Segment, 217
Segmentation, 213
Semirandom memory, *see* Direct access memory
Serial input data (SID), 102, 398
Serial interface:
   current loops, 292
    RS232C, RS422, and RS423, 287-292
Serial output data (SOD),102, 398
Serial transmission, 248, 458
Seven-segment displays, 384, 386-392
Side-effect, 57
Signals:
   Intel 8085, 82-85
   Intel 8086, 142, 145-147
   Motorola 68000, 187-192
Sign flags, *see* Flags
Sign status flags, *see* Flags
Silicon Graphics, Inc., 8
Single-chip microprocessor, *see* Microprocessors, single-chip
Single-phase clock, 2
Source codes, 4
Source index (SI) register, *see* Registers
Spurious interrupt, *see* Interrupts
Stack operations, 20-21, 184-186
Stack pointer register, *see* Registers
Stack pointers, 20, 62
Stack segment register, *see* Registers
Standard I/O, *see* Input/Output (I/O)
Status register, *see* Registers
Storage:
   media, 2
   nonvolatile, 2, 9, 23
   volatile, 2, 9, 23
Subroutines, 55, 458
   difference from macroprograms, 57-58
   linkage convention, 56

Sun Microsystems, Inc., 7, 214
Supervisor mode, 159-160
Symbol table, 57
Synchronous serial data transmission, 248-249, 458

T states, 147
Tarbell standard, 256
Teletypes, 292
Temperature control, 6-7
32 bit microprocessors, 212-214. *See also* Intel 80386,
    Motorola 68020
Three-address format, 49
Timing, 81-85
Toshiba, 7
Transistor-transistor logic (TTL), 3
Trap flag, *see* Flags
Traps, 41, 204
Two-address format, 49
Two-position controller, 293-295

Unconditional I/O, *see* Input/Output (I/O)
Unidirectional, 10
Universal asynchronous receiver/transmitter (UARTs), 249-
    251, 458
Universal synchronous/asynchronous receivers/transmitters
    (USARTs), 249
UNIX, 8

Vectored interrupt, *see* Interrupts
Vertical scan, 263
Very Large-Scale Integration (VLSI), 2
Viatron, 3

Words, 1, 2, 458
Workstation, 7

Zero-address format, 49, 50
Zero flag, *see* Flags
Zilog Z80, 3, 4, 45, 50, 51, 52, 57
Zilog Z8000, 21